THE TRANSPORT PHENOMENA PROBLEM SOLVER®

REGISTERED TRADEMARK

MOMENTUM • ENERGY • MASS

Staff of Research and Education Association,
Dr. M. Fogiel, Director

Research and Education Association
505 Eighth Avenue
New York, N. Y. 10018

THE TRANSPORT PHENOMENA PROBLEM SOLVER®

Printed in the United States of America

Library of Congress Catalog Card Number 84-61816

International Standard Book Number 0-87891-562-1

Revised Printing, 1986

WHAT THIS BOOK IS FOR

Students have generally found transport phenomena a difficult subject to understand and learn. Despite the publication of hundreds of textbooks in this field, each one intended to provide an improvement over previous textbooks, students continue to remain perplexed as a result of the numerous conditions that must often be remembered and correlated in solving a problem. Various possible interpretations of terms used in transport phenomena have also contributed to much of the difficulties experienced by students.

In a study of the problem, REA found the following basic reasons underlying students' difficulties with transport phenomena taught in schools:

(a) No systematic rules of analysis have been developed which students may follow in a step-by-step manner to solve the usual problems encountered. This results from the fact that the numerous different conditions and principles which may be involved in a problem, lead to many possible different methods of solution. To prescribe a set of rules to be followed for each of the possible variations, would involve an enormous number of rules and steps to be searched through by students, and this task would perhaps be more burdensome than solving the problem directly with some accompanying trial and error to find the correct solution route.

(b) Textbooks currently available will usually explain a given principle in a few pages written by a professional who has an insight in the subject matter that is not shared by students. The explanations are often written in an abstract manner which leaves the students confused as to the application of the principle. The explanations given are not sufficiently detailed and extensive to make the student aware of the wide range of applications and different aspects of the principle being studied. The numerous possible variations of principles and their applications are usually not discussed, and it is left for the students to discover these for themselves while doing exercises. Accordingly, the average student is expected to rediscover that which has been long known and practiced, but not published or explained extensively.

(c) The examples usually following the explanation of a topic are too few in number and too simple to enable the student to obtain a thorough grasp of the principles involved. The explanations do not provide sufficient basis to enable a student to solve problems that may be subsequently assigned for homework or given on examinations.

The examples are presented in abbreviated form which leaves out much material between steps, and requires that students derive the omitted material themselves. As a result, students find the examples difficult to understand--contrary to the purpose of the examples.

Examples are, furthermore, often worded in a confusing manner. They do not state the problem and then present the solution. Instead, they pass through a general discussion, never revealing what is to be solved for.

Examples, also, do not always include diagrams/graphs, wherever appropriate, and students do not obtain the training to draw diagrams or graphs to simplify and organize their thinking.

(d) Students can learn the subject only by doing the exercises themselves and reviewing them in class, to obtain experience in applying the principles with their different ramifications.

In doing the exercises by themselves, students find that they are required to devote considerably more time to transport phenomena than to other subjects of comparable credits, because they are uncertain with regard to the selection and application of the theorems and principles involved. It is also often necessary for students to discover those "tricks" not revealed in their texts (or review books), that make it possible to solve problems easily. Students must usually resort to methods of trial-and-error to discover these "tricks", and as a result they find that they may sometimes spend several hours in solving a single problem.

(e) When reviewing the exercises in classrooms, instructors usually request students to take turns in writing solutions on the boards and explaining them to the class. Students often find it difficult to explain in a manner that holds the interest of the class, and enables the remaining students to follow the material written on the boards. The remaining students seated in the class are, furthermore, too occupied with copying the material from the boards, to listen to the oral explanations and concentrate on the methods of solution.

This book is intented to aid students in transport phenomena in overcoming the difficulties described, by supplying detailed illustrations of the solution methods which are usually not apparent to students. The solution methods are illustrated by problems selected from those that are most often assigned for class work and given on examinations. The problems are arranged in order of complexity to enable students to learn and understand a particular topic by reviewing the problems in sequence. The problems are illustrated with detailed step-by-step explanations, to save students the large amount of time that is often needed to fill in the gaps that are usually found between steps of illustrations in textbooks or reviw/outline books.

The staff of REA considers transport phenomena a subject that is best learned by allowing students to view the methods of analysis and solution techniques themselves. This approach to learning the subject matter is similar to that practiced in various scientific laboratories, particularly in the medical fields.

In using this book, students may review and study the illustrated problems at their own pace; they are not limited to the time allowed for explaining problems on the board in class.

When students want to look up a particular type of problem and solution, they can readily locate it in the book by referring to the index which has been extensively prepared. It is also possible to locate a particular type of problem by glancing at just the material within the boxed portions. To facilitate rapid scanning of the problems, each problem has a heavy border around it. Furthermore, each problem is identified with a number immediately above the problem at the right-hand margin.

To obtain maximum benefit from the book, students should familiarize themselves with the section, "How To Use This Book," located in the front pages.

To meet the objectives of this book, staff members of REA have selected problems usually encountered in assignments and examinations, and have solved each problem meticulously to illustrate the steps which are difficult for students to comprehend. Special gratitude is expressed to them for their efforts in this area, as well as to the numerous contributors who devoted brief periods of time to this work.

Gratitude is also expressed to the many persons involved in the difficult task of typing the manuscript with its endless changes, and to the REA art staff who prepared the numerous detailed illustrations together with the layout and physical features of the book.

The difficult task of coordinating the efforts of all persons was carried out by Carl Fuchs. His conscientious work deserves much appreciation. He also trained and supervised art and production personnel in the preparation of the book for printing.

Finally, special thanks are due to Helen Kaufmann for her unique talents to render those difficult border-line decisions and constructive suggestions related to the design and organization of the book.

Max Fogiel, Ph.D.
Program Director

HOW TO USE THIS BOOK

This book can be an invaluable aid to students in transport phenomena as a supplement to their textbooks. The book is subdivided into 18 chapters, each dealing with a separate topic. The subject matter is developed beginning with fluid mechanics, laminar and turbulent flow, dimensional analysis, energy balance and extending through conduction, forced convection, boundary layer analysis, steady and unsteady state heat transfer, diffusion in gases and liquids and chemical reactions. An extensive number of applications have been included, since these appear to be more troublesome to students.

TO LEARN AND UNDERSTAND A TOPIC THOROUGHLY

1. Refer to your class text and read the section pertaining to the topic. You should become acquainted with the principles discussed there. These principles, however, may not be clear to you at that time.

2. Then locate the topic you are looking for by referring to the "Table of Contents" in front of this book, "The Transport Phenomena Problem Solver."

3. Turn to the page where the topic begins and review the problems under each topic, in the order given. For each topic, the problems are arranged in order of complexity, from the simplest to the more difficult. Some problems may appear similar to others, but each problem has been selected to illustrate a different point or solution method.

To learn and understand a topic thoroughly and retain its contents, it will generally be necessary for students to review the problems several times. Repeated review is essential in order to gain experience in recognizing the principles that should be applied, and in selecting the best solution technique.

TO FIND A PARTICULAR PROBLEM

To locate one or more problems related to a particular subject matter, refer to the index. In using the index, be certain to note that the numbers given there refer to problem numbers, not page numbers. This arrangement of the index is intended to facilitate finding a problem more rapidily, since two or more problems may appear on a page.

If a particular type of problem cannot be found readily, it is recommended that the student refer to the "Table of Contents" in the front pages, and then turn to the chapter which is applicable to the problem being sought. By scanning or glancing at the material that is boxed, it will generally be possible to find problems related to the one being sought, without consumming considerable time. After the problems have been located, the solutions can be reviewed and studied in detail. For this purpose of locating problems rapidly, students should acquaint themselves with the organization of the book as found in the "Table of Contents".

In preparing for an exam, locate the topics to be covered on the exam in the "Table of Contents," and then review the problems under those topics several times. This should equip the student with what might be needed for the exam.

CONTENTS

CHAPTER 1

FLUID STATICS AND VISCOSITY

FLUID STATICS

• PROBLEM 1-1

Find the absolute and gage pressure at the bottom of a large open container (see fig.) having oil at the top, and water at the bottom. The height of the vessel is 3.66 m (12.0 ft). The water level is 0.61 m (2.0 ft) measured from the bottom. The remaining portion is filled with the oil having a density of 917 kg/m^3 (0.917 g/m^3). Also calculate the pressure at a distance of 3.05 m from the top. Make any relevant assumptions.

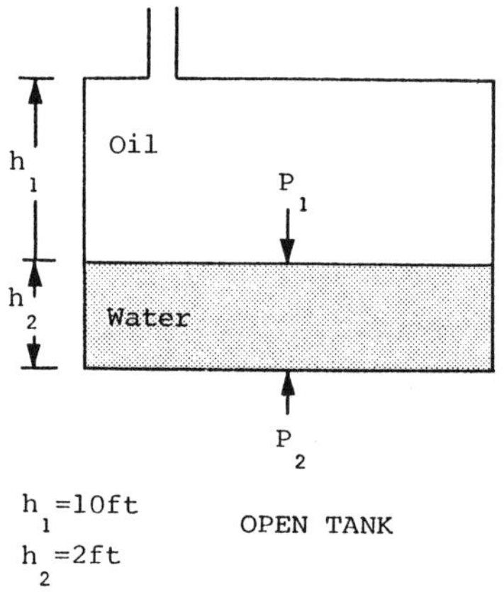

OPEN TANK

Solution: Assume the atmospheric pressure as

$$P_0 = 14.696 \text{ psia}$$

$$= 1.01325 \times 10^5 \text{ Pa}$$

Density of water is given by

$$\rho_{water} = 62.43 \text{ lbf/ft}^3$$

$$= 1000 \text{ kg/m}^3$$

and that of oil is

$$\rho_{oil} = 0.917 \times 62.43$$

$$= 57.248 \text{ lbf/ft}^3$$

Acceleration due to gravity is,

$$g = 32.2 \text{ ft/sec}^2$$

$$= 9.8066 \text{ m/sec}^2$$

Let the pressure at a depth of 10 ft be P_1.

Therefore, P_1 is given by,

$$P_1 = P_0 + \rho \frac{g}{g_c} h_1 \qquad (1)$$

where g_c = gravitational conversion factor

$$= 32.2 \frac{\text{lbm}\cdot\text{ft}}{\text{lbf}\cdot\text{sec}^2}$$

$$= 1.0 \frac{\text{kg}\cdot\text{m}}{\text{N}\cdot\text{sec}^2}$$

Substituting all the values in equation (1) we get

$$P_1 = 14.696 + (57.248)\left(\frac{32.2}{32.2}\right)(10)\left(\frac{1}{144}\right)$$

$$= 18.67 \text{ psia}$$

and in SI units,

$$P_1 = 1.0132 \times 10^5 + (1000)\left(\frac{9.8066}{1.0}\right)(3.05)$$

$$= 1.312 \times 10^5 \text{ Pa.}$$

Similarly, let P_2 be the pressure at the bottom

i.e. $P_2 = P_1 + \rho_{water} \frac{g}{g_c} h_2$

Again, substituting all the values, we get

$$P_2 = 18.67 + (62.43)\left(\frac{32.2}{32.2}\right)(2.0)\left(\frac{1}{144}\right)$$

$$= 19.55 \text{ psia}$$

and in SI units,

$$P_2 = 1.312 \times 10^5 + (1000)\left(\frac{9.8066}{1.0}\right)(0.61)$$

$$= 1.372 \times 10^5 \text{ Pa.}$$

Finally, the gage pressure is given by

$$P_g = P_{ab} - P_{atm}.$$

$$= 19.55 - 14.696$$

$$= 4.85 \text{ psig.}$$

• PROBLEM 1-2

A large open tank contains oil 3 ft (0.91 m) deep from the top and the rest is filled with water. The tank is 10 ft (3.05 m) deep and the specific gravity of the oil is 0.8. Calculate the pressure exerted by the oil and the water at the bottom of the tank.

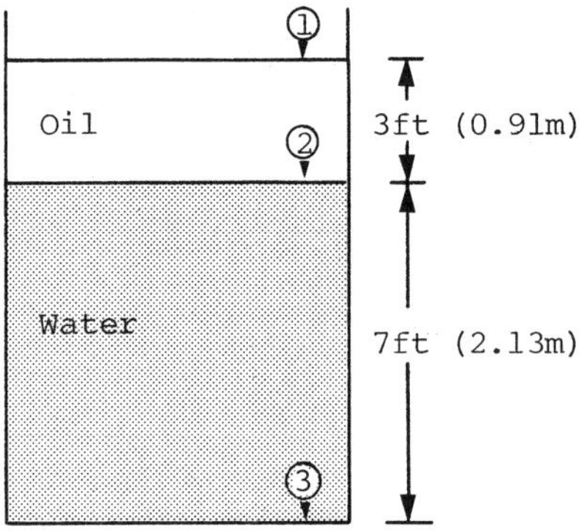

Solution: Applying the Bernoulli's equation between (1) and (2) (see fig)

$$\frac{P_1}{\gamma} + z_1 = \frac{P_2}{\gamma} + z_2$$

Here

$$P_1 = 0 \text{ psfg}$$

$$z_1 = 10 \text{ ft.}$$

$$z_2 = 7 \text{ ft.}$$

and the specific weight of oil

$$\gamma = 0.8 \times 62.4 \text{ lbf/ft}^3$$

Therefore,

$$P_2 = (10 - 7) \times 0.80 \times 62.4$$

$$= 150 \text{ psfg}$$

Next, applying the Bernoulli's equation between (2) and (3) (see fig.)

$$\frac{P_2}{\gamma} + z_2 = \frac{P_3}{\gamma} + z_3$$

Note "γ" is the specific weight of water,

i.e. $\gamma = 62.4 \text{ lbf/ft}^3$

and $z_3 = 0$ ft.

Therefore, $P_3 = 62.4 \dfrac{150}{62.4} + 7$

$$= 587 \text{ psfg.}$$

• PROBLEM 1-3

Obtain a relationship for the pressure in a tank open to the atmosphere and filled with an isothermal, ideal gas, as a function of the height.

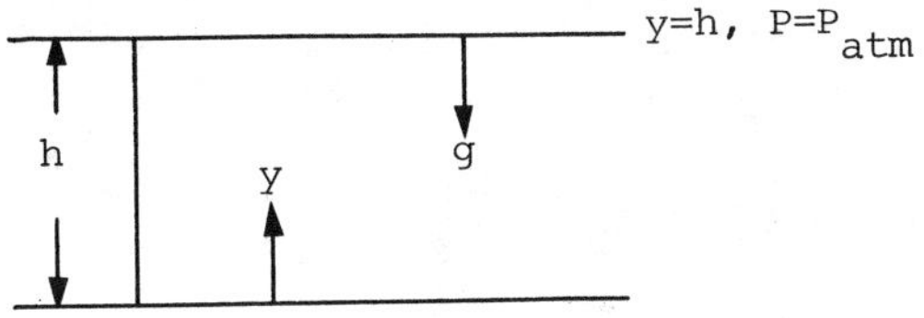

Solution: In the fluid statics of gases, a relation between the pressure and density is integrated, i.e., the equation $\nabla P = \rho g$. (1)

The simplest case is that of the isothermal ideal gas, where $P = \rho RT/M$. Selecting the y axis parallel to g, eq. (1) becomes

$$\frac{dP}{dy} = -\rho g = -\frac{PMg}{RT}$$

Separating variables, the above differential equation becomes

$$\int_{P_{atm}}^{P} \frac{dP}{P} = -\int_{o}^{y} \frac{Mg}{RT}\, dy$$

or

$$\frac{P}{P_{atm}} = \exp\left\{-\frac{Mgy}{RT}\right\}$$

• PROBLEM 1-4

Find the volumetric flow rate in the pipe shown in the figure. The differential manometer reads 1 ft. Assume one dimensional ideal flow.

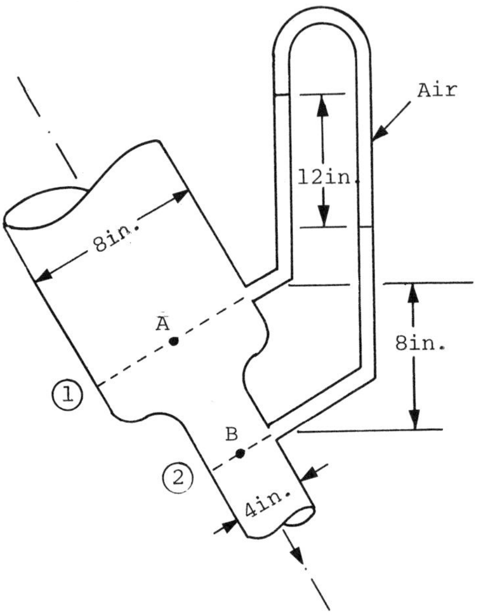

PIPE CONTRACTION

Solution: Since the flow is frictionless (ideal), the following relation is obtained by the Bernoulli's equation

$$h_A + \frac{v_A^2}{2g} = h_B + \frac{v_B^2}{2g} \tag{1}$$

But

$$h_A - h_B = 1 \text{ ft. (given)}$$

Applying the continuity equation,

$$\rho_A v_A A_A = \rho_B v_B A_B$$

Assuming constant density, i.e., $\rho_A = \rho_B$ we have

$$v_A \frac{\pi}{4}\left(\frac{8}{12}\right)^2 = v_B \frac{\pi}{4}\left(\frac{4}{12}\right)^2$$

or

$$4v_A = v_B \tag{2}$$

From (1) and (2) we have

$$v_B = 2.07 \text{ ft/sec}$$

Therefore, the flow rate is

$$= A_A \, v_A$$

$$= \frac{\pi}{4}\left(\frac{8}{12}\right)^2 2.07$$

$$= 0.723 \text{ cfs}$$

• PROBLEM 1-5

One end of the manometer B is open to atmosphere and the other end is connected to another manometer A by means of an inverted U-tube. The left end of the manometer A is connected to a pipe line having a pressure of 1.7 psi below atmospheric pressure. The manometric heights in A and B are 1.5 ft. and 1.25 ft. respectively. If the specific gravity of the liquid in A is 1.6, what is the specific gravity of the liquid in B? Neglect the densities of the gas in the pipe and the air trapped in the tubes.

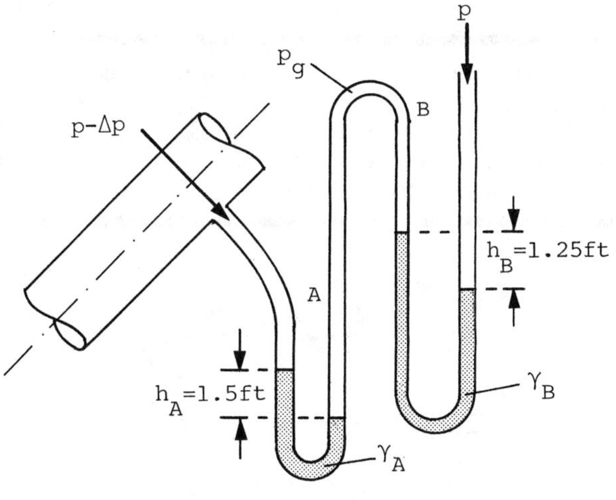

Solution: Let p_g be the pressure in the connecting tube and p be the atmospheric pressure.

Applying Bernoulli's equation to the tubes A and B, yields

$$\frac{p - \Delta p}{\gamma_A} + h_A = \frac{p_g}{\gamma_A} \tag{1}$$

and for the tube B

$$\frac{p_g}{\gamma_B} + h_B = \frac{p}{\gamma_B} \tag{2}$$

Eliminating p_g from eq. 1 and 2, we get

$$p - h_B\gamma_B = p - \Delta p + h_A\gamma_A$$

i.e.
$$\gamma_B = \frac{\Delta p - h_A\gamma_A}{h_B}$$

Thus,
$$\gamma_B = \frac{(1.7)(144) - (1.5)(1.6)(62.4)}{1.25}$$

$$= 76 \text{ lb.wt/ft}^3$$

Now the specific gravity of the liquid in tube B,

$$= \frac{\text{density of the liquid}}{\text{density of water}}$$

$$= \frac{76.0}{62.4}$$

$$= 1.22$$

• PROBLEM 1-6

Two ducts A and B containing water are connected to an inclined manometer as shown in the fig. Duct B is at a constant pressure of 6 psi. Calculate the new manometer reading along the inclined tube if the pressure in duct A is increased by 10 psi.

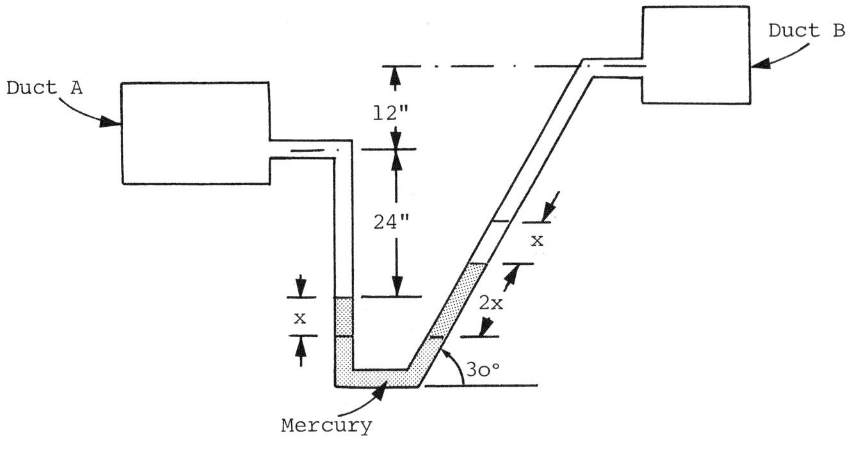

MERCURY MANOMETER

Solution: Initially,

$$p_A + 2\left(\frac{62.4}{144}\right) = 6 + 3\left(\frac{62.4}{144}\right) \qquad (1)$$

when the pressure in duct A is increased by 10 psi the above equation becomes,

$$(p_A + 10) + \left(\frac{62.4}{144}\right)(2 + x) = 6 + 13.6\left(\frac{62.4}{144}\right)(x + \frac{x}{2}) + \left(\frac{62.4}{144}\right)\left(3 - \frac{x}{2}\right) \qquad (2)$$

Eliminating p_A from equations 1 and 2, yields

$$\frac{62.4}{144}\left(\frac{x}{2}\right) + \frac{62.4}{144}(x) + 10 - 13.6\left(\frac{62.4}{144}\right)\frac{3x}{2} = 0$$

Solving, $x = 1.22$ ft.

Therefore, the new reading along the inclined tube is

$= 1.22 + 2\ (1.22)$

$= 3.67$ ft.

• PROBLEM 1-7

Oil is flowing at the rate of 3.14 cfs in a pipe of varying cross section. At section A, the diameter is 6 in and the pressure is 12 psig. At another section B, the diameter is 16 in. Assume the heat loss between sections A and B to be 6 ft of oil. Calculate the pressure at B. Specific gravity of oil may be taken as 0.85.

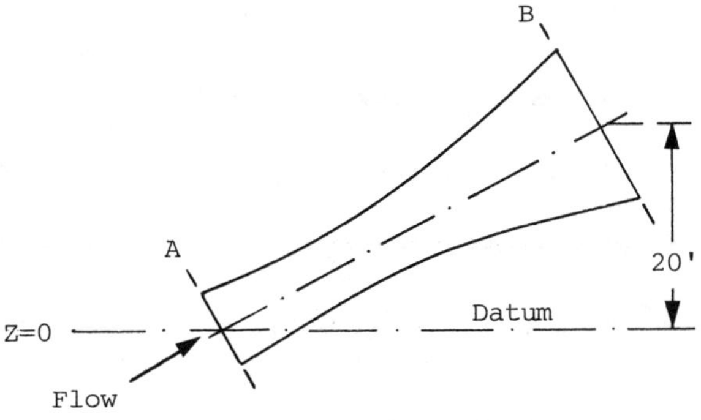

Solution: Applying Bernoulli's equation between A and B,

$$\frac{p_A}{\gamma} + \frac{v_A^2}{2g_c} + z_A = \frac{p_B}{\gamma} + \frac{v_B^2}{2g_c} + z_B + h_L$$

where, $z_B - z_A = 20$ ft.

h_L = head loss between sections A and B = 6.0 ft.

$$\gamma = 0.85 \times \gamma_{water}$$

$$= 0.85 \times 62.4 \text{ lbf/ft}^3$$

$$p_A = 12 \times 144 \text{ psf}$$

p_B in psi

To find v_A and v_B apply continuity equation,

$$Q = A \times v$$

i.e. $$v_A = \frac{3.14}{\pi/4 \left(\frac{6}{12}\right)^2} = 16 \text{ ft/sec.}$$

Similarly,

$$v_B = \frac{3.14}{\pi/4 \left(\frac{16}{12}\right)^2} = 2.25 \text{ ft/sec.}$$

Substituting the values of v_A and v_B in the Bernoulli's equation gives

$$\frac{12 \times 144}{(0.85)(62.4)} + \frac{16^2}{(2)(32.2)} = \frac{p_B \times 144}{(0.85)(62.4)} + \frac{(2.25)^2}{(2)(32.2)} + 20.0 + 6.0.$$

Solving,

$$p_B = 3.86 \text{ psig}$$

• PROBLEM 1-8

Find the specific gravity of the liquid in the double U-tube water manometer in terms of the various column heights as shown in the fig.

Solution: In the figure the liquid is shown above the water because its density is less than that of water.

Since there is not much difference in atmospheric pressure between points "a" and "d",

$$p_a - p_d \simeq 0$$

Also, $p_a - p_d$ is equal to the sum of the pressure differences across each fluid column.

i.e. $$p_a - p_d = 0 = (p_a - p_b) + (p_b - p_c) + (p_c - p_d)$$

Applying $p = \rho gh$ to each of the above terms,

$$p_a - p_b = p_a - p_{b'} = \rho_{H_2O}\, g(h_1 - h_2)$$

$$p_b - p_c = p_b - p_{c'} = \rho g(h_2 - h_3)$$

and $$p_c - p_d = p_{c''} - p_d = \rho_{H_2O}\, g(h_3 - h_4)$$

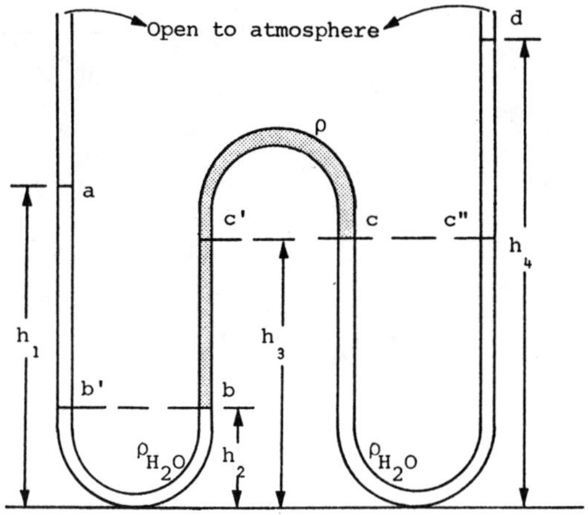

WATER MANOMETER

Substituting and omitting "g"

$$0 = \rho_{H_2O}\,(h_1 - h_2) + \rho(h_2 - h_3) + \rho_{H_2O}\,(h_3 - h_4)$$

or $$0 = \rho_{H_2O}\left[(h_1 - h_2) + (h_3 - h_4)\right] + \rho(h_2 - h_3)$$

i.e.

$$\frac{\rho}{\rho_{H_2O}} = \gamma = \frac{(h_1 - h_2) + (h_3 - h_4)}{(h_3 - h_2)}$$

SHEAR STRESS AND VISCOSITY

• PROBLEM 1-9

Determine the force required to move a thin plate of 30 x 60 cm^2 size through a liquid of viscosity μ = 0.05 kg/ms at a velocity of 0.40 m/sec. The liquid is filled between two long parallel plates as shown in Fig. 1.

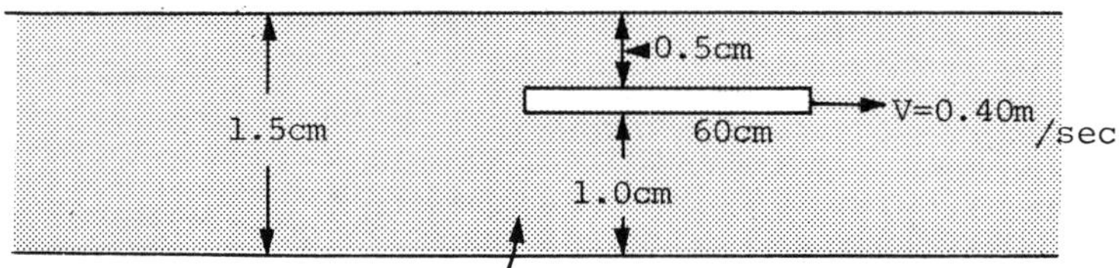

fig. 1

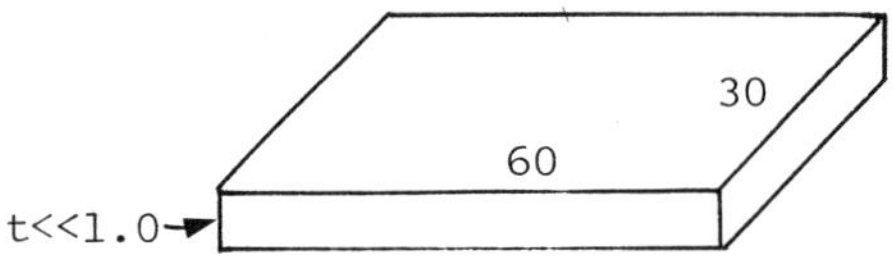

fig. 2

Solution: Total force,

$$F_T = F_{TOP} + F_{BOTTOM}$$

where

$$F_{TOP} = \text{(shear stress) (area)}$$

$$= \mu(V/h_{upper})(A)$$

$$= (0.05)(0.4/0.005)(0.3)(0.6)$$

$$= 0.72 \text{ N}$$

Similarly,

$$F_{BOTTOM} = (0.05)(0.4/0.01)(0.3)(0.6)$$

$$= 0.36 \text{ N}$$

Therefore,

$$F_{TOTAL} = 0.72 + 0.36$$

$$= 1.08 \text{ N}$$

• PROBLEM 1-10

The space between two parallel plates 0.001 ft. apart is filled with oil of viscosity μ = 0.7 cp. Calculate the steady-state momentum flux τ_{yx} in lb_f/ft^2 when the lower plate velocity is 1 ft/sec in the x-direction as shown in the fig.

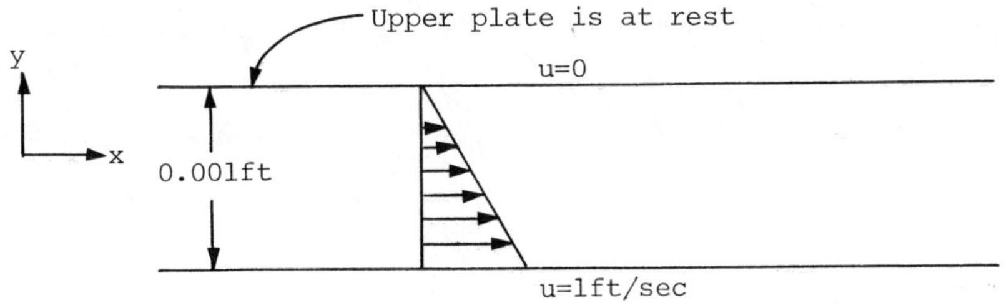

FULLY DEVELOPED LAMINAR FLOW

Solution: Since the velocity profile is a linear function of only y, then

$$\frac{\partial u}{\partial y} = \frac{du}{dy} = \frac{\Delta u}{\Delta y}$$

$$\frac{\Delta u}{\Delta y} = \frac{(1.0 - 0)}{(0 - 0.001)}$$

$$= -1000 \text{ sec}^{-1}$$

$$\tau_{yx} = -\mu \frac{du}{dy}$$

where $\mu = 0.7$ cp

$$= (0.7 \text{ cp})(2.0886 \times 10^{-5} \text{ lb}_f \text{ sec/ft}^2\text{cp})$$

$$= 1.46 \times 10^{-5} \text{ lb}_f \text{ sec/ft}^2$$

Substituting,

$$\tau_{yx} = -(1.46 \times 10^{-5})(-1000)$$

$$= 1.46 \times 10^{-2} \text{ lb}_f/\text{ft}^2$$

• PROBLEM 1-11

Referring to the fig., compute the stress on each plate when the lower plate velocity is 10 ft/min. in the positive x-direction and the upper plate velocity is 35 ft/min. in the negative x-direction. The plates are placed 2 in. apart and the fluid viscosity between the plates remains constant at 150 cp. Also calculate the fluid velocity at every 0.5 in. interval.

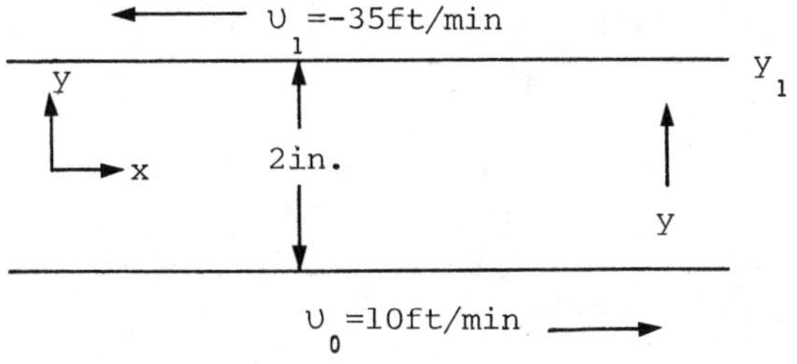

Solution: Writing the general equation for the shear stress,

$$\tau_y(A) \int_0^{y_1} \frac{dy}{A} = - \int_{v_0}^{v_1} \mu \, dv$$

where μ and A are constants.

Therefore, $\tau_y (y_1 - 0) = - \mu(v_1 - v_0)$

which gives $\tau_y = -\mu \frac{(v_1 - v_0)}{(y_1 - 0)}$ (1)

Substituting,

$$v_0 = 10 \text{ ft/min} = \frac{1}{6} \text{ ft/sec.}$$

$$v_1 = - 35 \text{ ft/min} = - \frac{35}{60} \text{ ft/sec}$$

$$y_1 = \frac{2}{12} \text{ ft}$$

$$= 150 \times 2.0886 \times 10^{-5} \text{ lb}_f \text{ sec/ft}^2$$

Substituting in eq. (1) gives

$$\tau_y = \frac{- (150)(2.0886 \times 10^{-5})(-\frac{35}{60} - \frac{10}{60})}{2/12}$$

$$= 0.0141 \text{ lb}_f/\text{ft}^2$$

Velocity at ½ in., 1 in. and 1½ in. distance from the lower plate can be calculated as follows.

Rewriting the equation (1)

$$\tau_y = -\mu \frac{(v_1 - v_0)}{(y_1 - 0)}$$

or

$$\frac{\tau_y}{\mu} = - \frac{(v_1 - v_0)}{y_1}$$

$$= \frac{(v_0 - v_1)}{y_1} \qquad (2)$$

For any value of y ($0 \leq y \leq 2.0$), the equation (2) becomes,

$$\frac{\tau_y}{\mu} = \frac{(v_0 - v)}{y} \qquad (3)$$

From (2) and (3),

$$\frac{(v_0 - v)}{y} = \frac{(v_0 - v_1)}{y_1}$$

or $$(v_0 - v) = (v_0 - v_1)(\frac{y}{y_1})$$

or $$v_0 - (v_0 - v_1)(\frac{y}{y_1}) = v$$

or $$v = v_0 - (v_0 - v_1)(\frac{y}{y_1})$$

or $$v = 10 - \left(10 - (-35)\right)(\frac{y}{2})$$

or $$v = 10 - 45(\frac{y}{2})$$

at $x = \frac{1}{2}$ in

$$v = 10 - 45(\frac{\frac{1}{2}}{2})$$

$$= -1.25 \text{ ft/min}$$

at $x = 1$ in

$$v = - 12.5 \text{ ft/min}$$

at $x = 1\frac{1}{2}$ in

$$v = -23.75 \text{ ft/min}$$

• PROBLEM 1-12

Two parallel flat plates are spaced 0.3 mm apart. The upper plate having a shear area 1.0 m^2 is moving at a velocity of 1.0 m/sec. If the viscosity of the lubricating oil between the plates is 9.6 x 10^{-2}N·s/m^2, find the surface resistance of the upper plate. Assume a linear velocity profile as shown in the fig.

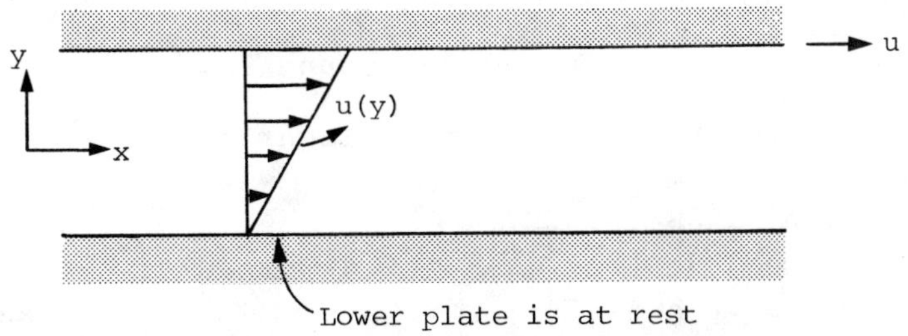

Solution: The surface resistance,

$$F = \tau(\text{area})$$

where $\tau = \mu\frac{\Delta u}{\Delta y}$

$$= (9.6 \times 10^{-2})\left(\frac{1.0 - 0}{\left(\frac{0.3}{1000} - 0\right)}\right)$$

$$= 320 \text{ N/m}^2$$

Substituting the value of τ in the relation for surface resistance

$$F = 320 \ (1)$$

$$= 320 \text{ N}$$

• PROBLEM 1-13

Two parallel flat plates, area 1 ft^2, are spaced 0.1 ft. apart. The lower plate is moving with a velocity of 0.1 ft/sec while the top plate is at rest. If the force required to move the plate is 0.002 poundals, find the viscosity of fluid between the plates.

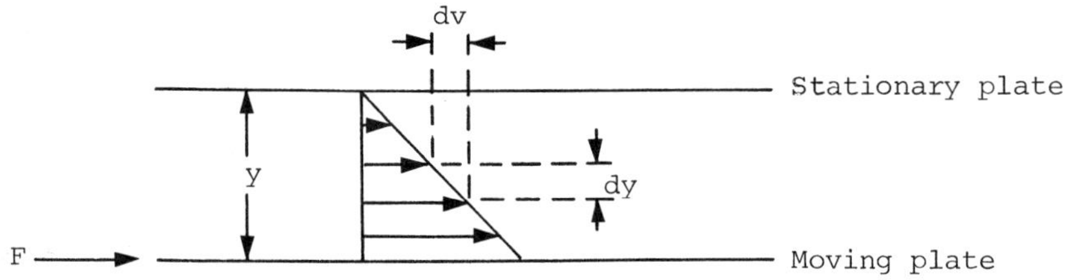

Solution: The shear stress,

$$\tau = -\mu\frac{dv}{dy}$$

Also,

$$\tau = \frac{\text{FORCE}}{\text{SHEAR AREA}} = \frac{0.002}{1.0}$$

$$= 0.002 \text{ poundals/ft}^2$$

Since the velocity profile is linear,

$$\frac{dv}{dy} = \frac{\Delta v}{\Delta y} = \frac{0.1 - 0}{0 - 0.1}$$

$$= -1.0 \text{ sec}^{-1}$$

Substituting the value of the velocity gradient in the expression for τ and solving for μ

$$\mu = \frac{\tau}{-(dv/dy)}$$

$$= \frac{0.002}{1.0}$$

$$= 0.002 \ \frac{\text{poundals x sec.}}{\text{ft}^2}$$

$$= \frac{0.002}{0.0672} = 0.0298 \text{ poise}$$

or $$= 2.98 \text{ cp.}$$

CHAPTER 2

MASS, ENERGY AND MOMENTUM BALANCE

FLOW THROUGH A NOZZLE

• PROBLEM 2-1

A nozzle meter-manometer combination, as shown in the figure, is used to measure the volumetric flow rate in a pipe of circular cross section A_1. The throat diameter is d_2 and the manometer reads h_m meters. If the specific weight of the fluids in the pipe and in the manometer are γ_f and γ_m respectively, find the flow rate. Assume frictionless flow.

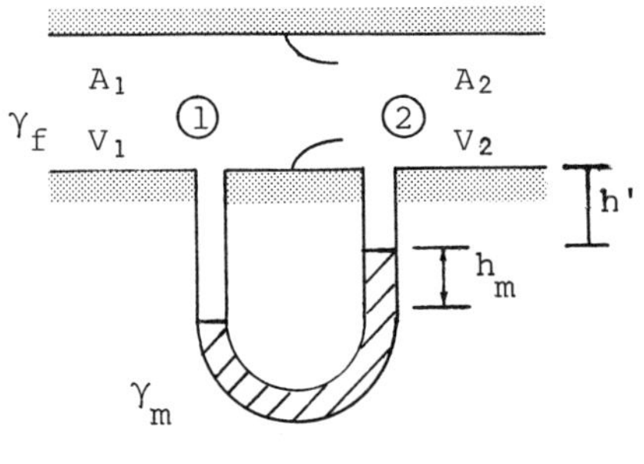

Flow through a nozzle meter.

Solution: Applying Bernoulli's equation at 1 and 2

$$\frac{p_1}{\gamma_f} + \frac{v_1^2}{2g} = \frac{p_2}{\gamma_f} + \frac{v_2^2}{2g}$$

or

$$\frac{p_1 - p_2}{\gamma_f} = \frac{v_2^2 - v_1^2}{2g} \qquad (1)$$

Now equating the pressure between two points at the same level in the manometer, (say at points where the manometer connects with the pipe wall)

$$p_1 + \gamma_f (h' + h_m) = p_2 + \gamma_f h' + \gamma_m h_m$$

or $$p_1 - p_2 = h_m(\gamma_m - \gamma_f)$$

Substituting in (1),

$$\frac{h_m(\gamma_m - \gamma_f)}{\gamma_f} = \frac{v_2^2 - v_1^2}{2g} \qquad (2)$$

The application of the continuity equation $q = v_1A_1 = v_2A_2$ to equation 2 results in the following expression

$$v_2^2\left[1 - \left(\frac{A_2}{A_1}\right)^2\right] = \frac{2g\ h_m(\gamma_m - \gamma_f)}{\gamma_f}$$

i.e. $$v_2 = \sqrt{\frac{2g\ h_m(\gamma_m - \gamma_f)}{\gamma_f\left[1 - (A_2/A_1)^2\right]}}$$

Therefore

$$q = A_2v_2$$

$$= \frac{A_2}{\sqrt{1 - (A_2/A_1)^2}}\sqrt{\frac{2g\ h_m(\gamma_m - \gamma_f)}{\gamma_f}}$$

• PROBLEM 2-2

In a nozzle flow, the inlet conditions are p_1 = 365 kPa gage and d_1 = 100 mm and the outlet conditions are p_2 = 0 kPa gage and d_2 = 50 mm. Find the flow rate. Neglect viscous effects.

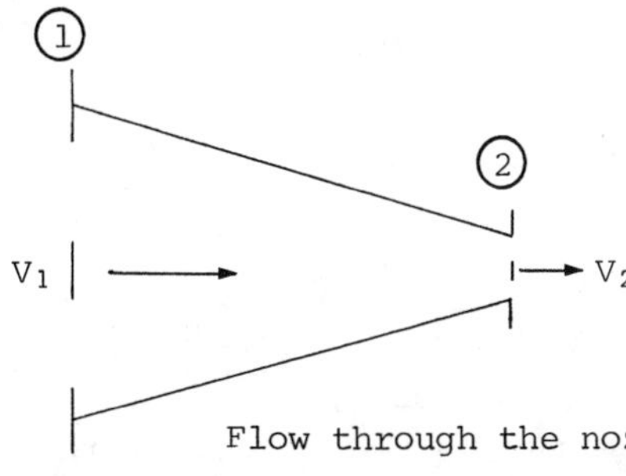

Flow through the nozzle

Solution: Applying Bernoulli's equation between inlet and outlet,

$$\frac{p_1}{\rho g} + \frac{v_1^2}{2g} = \frac{p_2}{\rho g} + \frac{v_2^2}{2g}$$

or

$$\frac{p_1}{\rho} + \frac{1}{2} v_1^2 = \frac{p_2}{\rho} + \frac{1}{2} v_2^2$$

or

$$\frac{v_2^2 - v_1^2}{2} = \frac{p_1 - p_2}{\rho}$$

Applying the continuity equation to (1)

$$A_1 v_1 = A_2 v_2$$

$$v_1 = v_2 \frac{A_2}{A_1}$$

$$v_2 = \sqrt{\frac{2(p_1 - p_2)}{\rho\left[1 - \left(\frac{A_2}{A_1}\right)^2\right]}}$$

$$= \sqrt{\frac{(2)(365{,}000 - 0)}{1000\left[1 - \left(\frac{50}{100}\right)^4\right]}}$$

$$= 27.9 \text{ m/s}$$

Hence,

$$q = A_2 v_2$$

$$= \left(\frac{\pi}{4}\right)(0.050)^2 \ (27.9)$$

$$= 0.055 \text{ m}^3/\text{s}$$

• PROBLEM 2-3

Determine the resultant force on a converging nozzle discharging water to the atmosphere at a rate of 150 gal/min. The inlet internal diameter is 3 in and that of outlet is 1 in. Neglect frictional losses.

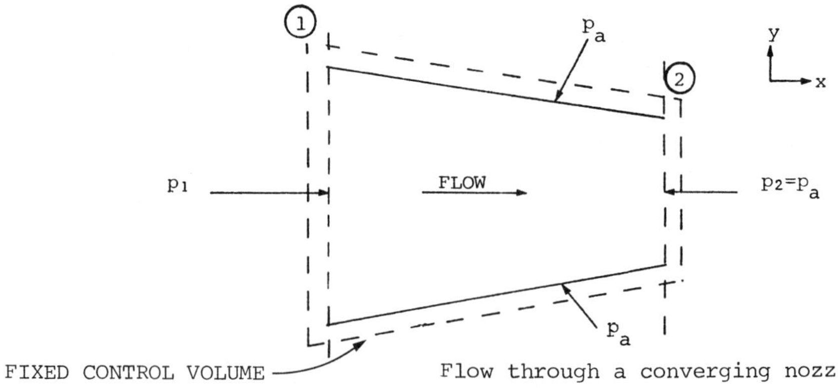

Flow through a converging nozzle

Solution: The momentum balance in x-direction is given by

$$\Sigma \vec{F}_x = \frac{d(mu)}{dt}$$

or $$p_1A_1 - p_2A_2 - p_a(A_1 - A_2) + \vec{R}_x = \dot{m}\,(u_2 - u_1)$$

where R_x is the reaction in the x-direction.

or $$p_1A_1 - p_aA_1 + \vec{R}_x = \dot{m}\,(u_2 - u_1) \quad \text{since } p_2 = p_a$$

or $$A_1(p_1 - p_a) + \vec{R}_x = \dot{m}\,(u_2 - u_1)$$

or $$\vec{R}_x = \dot{m}\,(u_2 - u_1) - A_1(p_1 - p_a) \qquad (1)$$

Applying Bernoulli's equation between inlet and outlet

$$\frac{p_1}{\gamma} + \frac{u_1^2}{2g} = \frac{p_2}{\gamma} + \frac{u_2^2}{2g} = \frac{p_a}{\gamma} + \frac{u_2^2}{2g} \qquad (2)$$

From (1) and (2)

$$\frac{p_1 - p_a}{\gamma} = \frac{u_2^2 - u_1^2}{2g}$$

or $$(p_1 - p_a) = \left(\frac{u_2^2 - u_1^2}{2g}\right)\gamma \qquad (3)$$

The continuity equation is used to calculate the velocities

$$w = \frac{(150)(8.33)}{60} = 20.825 \text{ lb/sec}$$

$$u_1 = \frac{w}{\rho A_1} = \frac{(20.825)(4)(144)}{(62.4)(3.14)(9)}$$

$$= 6.80 \text{ ft/sec}$$

and

$$u_2 = 6.80\,(3/1)^2$$

$$= 61.2 \text{ ft/sec}$$

Substituting in (3)

$$(p_1 - p_a) = \frac{[(61.2)^2 - (6.8)^2]}{(2)(32.2)}(62.4)$$

$$= 3584 \text{ lb}_f/\text{ft}^2$$

or $$(p_1 - p_a) = 24.9 \text{ psi}$$

Substituting in (1),

$$\vec{R}_x = \frac{(20.825)}{32.2}(61.2 - 6.8) - \frac{(3.14)(9)}{4}(24.9)$$

$$= -140.7 \text{ lb}_f$$

The negative sign indicates the resultant is acting in the negative x-direction.

• PROBLEM 2-4

A rocket is moving with a velocity of 1000 ft/sec. The exhaust gases at atmospheric pressure leaves the nozzle with a velocity of 2000 ft/sec. relative to the rocket body. The jet diameter is 8 in., and the fuel consumption rate is 36,000 lb_m/hr. Calculate the engine thrust and the instantaneous horsepower developed.

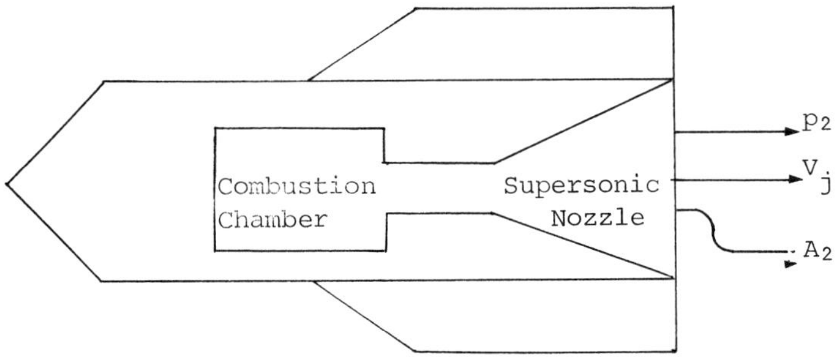

ROCKET

Solution: The fuel rate is,

$$\dot{m}_f = 36{,}000 \ lb_m/hr.$$

$$= \frac{36{,}000}{3600}$$

$$= 10 \ lb_m/sec.$$

Thrust is given by,

$$F_T = \frac{\dot{m}_f}{g} V_j + p_2 A_2$$

but $\quad p_2 = 0$ (atmospheric)

Therefore,

$$F_T = \frac{10 \times 2000}{32.2}$$

$$= 621 \ lb_f$$

Finally, the power developed can be obtained

power = force x velocity

$$= \frac{621 \times 1000}{550} = 1129 \text{ hp.}$$

• PROBLEM 2-5

Water is flowing at a velocity of 3 m/s in a constant-area pipe (540 cm^2). A water jet with a velocity of 27 m/sec enters the pipe at section 1 as shown in the fig. Jet area may be taken as A_j = 45 cm^2. Assume one dimensional frictionless flow and the pressure of the jet and water flow in the pipe to be same at section 1.

Calculate at a section 2, far away from the jet, the average velocity and the pressure gain $(p_2 - p_1)$.

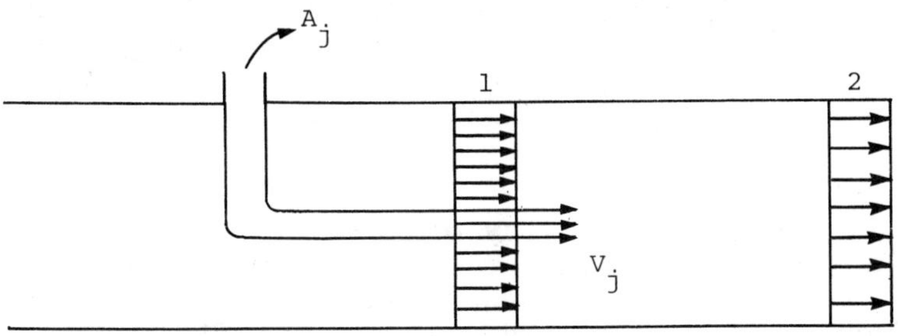

WATER JET PUMP

<u>Solution</u>: By continuity considerations, the flow rate at 1 and 2 are equal. Thus,

$$V_1A_1 + V_jA_j = V_2A_2$$

or
$$V_2 = \frac{(27)(0.0045) + (3)(0.0495)}{0.0540}$$

$$= 5.0 \text{ m/s}$$

Note that A_1 is equal to the difference between the area of the pipe and the area of the jet.

Writing the momentum equation between sections 1 and 2,

$$p_1A_1 - p_2A_2 = \dot{m}_2V_2 - (\dot{m}_jV_j + \dot{m}_1V_1)$$

or
$$(p_1 - p_2)A = \dot{m}_2V_2 - (\dot{m}_jV_j + \dot{m}_1V_1)$$

or
$$(p_1 - p_2) = \frac{(1000)[(0.0540)(5)^2 - (0.0045 \text{x} 27^2 + 0.0495 \text{x} 3^2)]}{0.0540}$$

$$= -44 \text{ kPa}$$

Hence, the pressure gain = 44 kPa.

• PROBLEM 2-6

Liquid contained in a cylinder is pushed through a spout by a leak proof piston as shown in the figure. If the piston velocity is V_p, calculate the liquid velocity through the spout exit. Assume that the cylinder is completely filled with liquid and there is no air trapped inside the cylinder. The cylinder cross sectional area may be taken as A_c and that of spout as A_s.

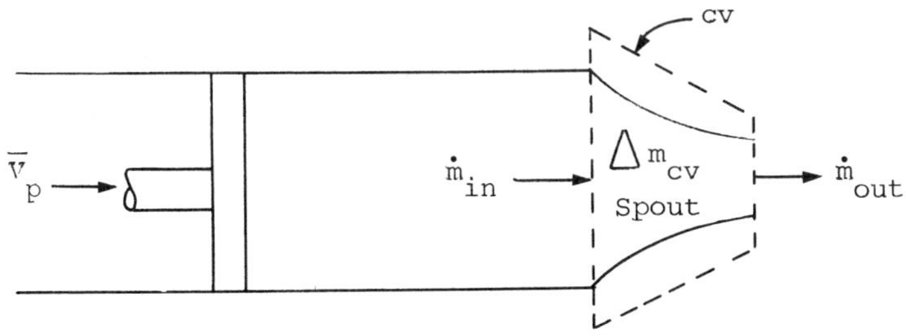

Solution: Assume the density of the liquid to be constant. Consider a control volume around the spout. The mass inside the control volume is not changing with time because the spout is always full of fluid and hence the flow across the spout (control volume) is steady.

From continuity considerations,

$$\dot{m}_{in} = \dot{m}_{out}$$

or $$\rho A_c V_p = \rho A_s V_s$$

or $$V_s = \frac{A_c}{A_s} \bar{V}_p$$

• PROBLEM 2-7

A liquid at 90°F is flowing at a rate of 40 gal/min through a horizontal pipe line of constant diameter 1.61 in. The pipe length is 50 ft. The system contains two 90° standard elbows, two valves and a tee joint across the flow. The density and viscosity of the fluid flowing at 90°F are 53 lb_m/ft^3 and 0.5 cp respectively. Calculate the pressure loss in the system with gate valves and then with globe valves. Assume the valves are fully opened.

Solution: A control volume is chosen to include the entire interior of the pipe as well as the valves, tee and the elbows. The energy balance is:

$$\frac{p_1}{\rho} + \frac{v_1^2}{2} + gz_1 + w + (h_1)_p + (h_1)_m = \frac{p_2}{\rho} + \frac{v_2^2}{2} + gz_2$$

where,

$$v_1 = v_2$$

$$z_1 = z_2$$

$$w = \text{work done} = 0$$

or $$\frac{p_1 - p_2}{\rho} = \frac{\Delta p}{\rho} = -\left[(h_1)_p + (h_1)_m\right]$$

$$= -(h_1)_{TOTAL} \qquad (1)$$

Velocity,

$$v = \frac{Q}{A} = \frac{40}{7.48 \times 60} \times \frac{1}{\frac{\pi}{4}\left(\frac{1.61}{12}\right)^2}$$

$$= 6.31 \text{ ft/sec.}$$

Reynolds number,

$$Re = \frac{\rho v D}{\mu}$$

$$= \frac{(53)(6.31)\left(\frac{1.61}{12}\right)}{(0.5)(6.72 \times 10^{-4})}$$

$$= 1.34 \times 10^5$$

Using the above Reynolds number, the friction factor for head-loss computations is obtained from the Moody chart. It comes out to be approximately 0.0055.

The head loss due to friction in the straight pipe is,

$$(h_1)_p = \frac{2fLv^2}{D}$$

$$= \frac{(2)(0.0055)(50)(6.31)^2}{\left(\frac{1.61}{12}\right) 32.2}$$

$$= 5.08 \text{ ft } lb_f/lb_m$$

The total head loss in fittings is given by,

$$(h_1)_m = \frac{2fL_{EQ.}v^2}{D} \qquad (2)$$

where the equivalent length of fittings is calculated as follows:

Equivalent length when gate valves are used

2 elbows = 2 x 4 = 8

1 tee = 8

2 gate valves (open) = 2 x 1 = 2

Equivalent length = 18 ft

Equivalent length when globe valves (open) are used

2 elbows = 2 x 4 = 8

1 tee = 8

2 globe valves (open) = 2 x 40.5 = 81

Equivalent length = 8 + 8 + 81 = 97 ft

Substituting in (2)

$$(h_1)_m = \frac{(2)(0.0055)(18)(6.31)^2}{\left(\frac{1.61}{12}\right)(32.2)}$$

$$= 1.83 \text{ ft } lb_f/lb_m \text{ (gate valves)}$$

$$= 9.85 \text{ ft } lb_f/lb_m \text{ (globe valves)}$$

Total head loss is

$$(h_1)_T = (h_1)_p + (h_1)_m$$

$$= 5.08 + 1.83$$

$$= 6.9 \text{ ft } lb_f/lb_m \text{ (gate valve)}$$

$$= 14.9 \text{ ft } lb_f/lb_m \text{ (globe valve)}$$

Substituting in (1),

$$\Delta p = -(6.9)(53)$$

$$= -2.54 \ lb_f/in^2 \text{ (gate valve)}$$

$$= -(14.9)(53)$$

$$= -5.52 \ lb_f/in^2 \text{ (globe valve)}$$

• PROBLEM 2-8

Compute the reaction force on a reducing elbow, when water flows through it at a rate of $0.25 \ m^3/s$.

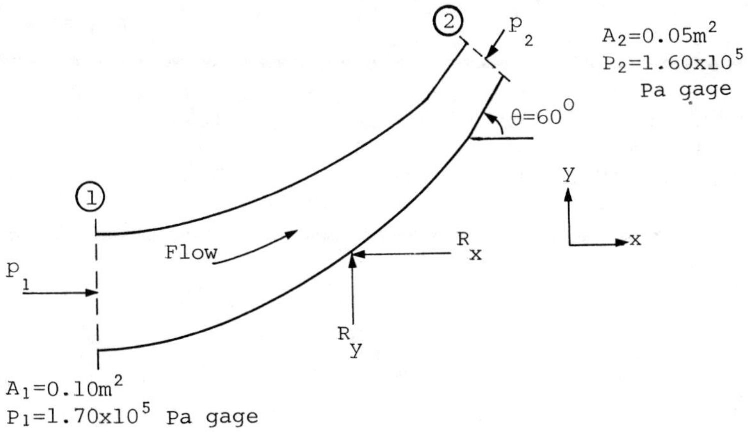

Solution: The momentum equations in x and y directions are,

$$p_1A_1 - R_x - p_2A_2\cos\theta = \rho AV(V_{OUT} - V_{IN})$$

$$= \rho AV(V_2\cos\theta - V_1)$$

and $R_y - p_2A_2\sin\theta = \rho AV(V_2\sin\theta - 0)$

Solving for R_x and R_y,

$$R_x = p_1A_1 - p_2A_2\cos\theta - \rho A_1V_1\left[V_2\cos\theta - V_1\right]$$

and $R_y = p_2A_2\sin\theta + \rho A_1V_1(V_2\sin\theta - 0)$

Inserting numerical values in the above equation we get,

$$R_x = (1.7 \times 10^5)(0.10) - (1.6 \times 10^5)(0.05)(0.5)$$

$$- (1000)(0.1)(2.5)\left[(5)(0.5) - 2.5\right]$$

$$= 13.0 \text{ kN}$$

and $R_y = (1.6 \times 10^5)(0.05)(0.866) + (0.25)(1000)(5)(0.8666)$

$$= 8.0 \text{ kN}$$

The reaction force is the resultant of R_x and R_y

$$R = \left[R_x^2 + R_y^2\right]^{\frac{1}{2}}$$

$$= (13.0^2 + 8.0^2)^{\frac{1}{2}}$$

$$= 15.3 \text{ kN}$$

• **PROBLEM 2-9**

Water flows through a reducer at a rate of 3.14 cfs. The area reduction is from 12 in. at inlet to 6 in. at exit. The pressure is 4 psi gage at the inlet and the friction loss is equivalent to 6 ft of water. What is the resultant force exerted by the water on the reducer?

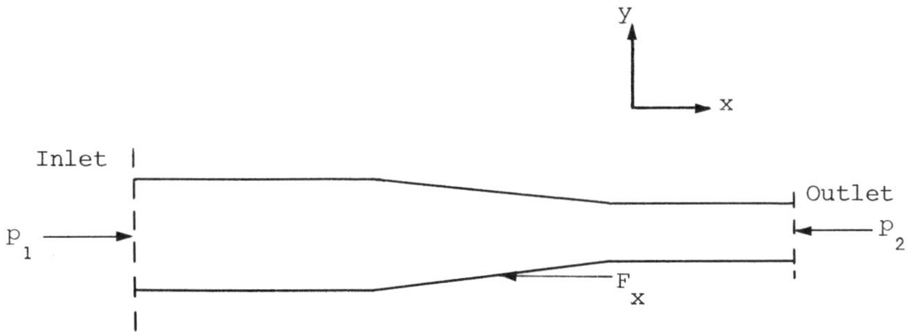

FLOW THROUGH THE REDUCER

Solution: Applying the momentum equation,

$$p_1A_1 - F_x - p_2A_2 = \rho Av(v_2 - v_1) \qquad (1)$$

where,

$$p_1 = 4 \text{ psi}$$

$$A_1 = \frac{\pi}{4} 12^2$$

$$= 36\pi \text{ in}^2$$

$$A_2 = \frac{\pi}{4} 6^2$$

$$= 9\pi \text{ in}^2$$

$$\rho = 1.94 \text{ slugs/ft}^3$$

$$A_1 = \frac{\pi}{4} \left(\frac{12}{12}\right)^2$$

$$= \frac{\pi}{4} \text{ ft}^2$$

$$v_1 = \frac{Q}{A_1} = \frac{3.14}{\pi/4}$$

$$= 4 \text{ fps.}$$

$$v_2 = \frac{3.14}{\frac{\pi}{4}\left(\frac{6}{12}\right)^2}$$

$$= 16 \text{ fps.}$$

$$p_2 = \text{unknown;}$$

Applying Bernoulli's equation

$$\frac{p_1}{\gamma} + \frac{v_1^2}{2g} = \frac{p_2}{\gamma} + \frac{v^2}{2g} + h_L$$

or
$$\frac{p_2}{0.433} = \frac{4}{0.433} + \frac{4^2}{64.4} - \frac{16^2}{64.4} - 6.0$$

or
$$p_2 = -0.212 \text{ psi (vacuum)}$$

Substituting the above values in (1) and solving for F_x,

$$F_x = 4(36\pi) - (-0.212)(9\pi) - (1.94)(\tfrac{\pi}{4})(4)(16 - 4)$$

$$= 385.25 \text{ lb}_f \leftarrow$$

Therefore, the thrust of the water on the pipe is 385.25 $\text{lb}_f \rightarrow$.

FLOW THROUGH PIPE BENDS

• PROBLEM 2-10

Water flows through a curved pipe as shown in the figure. Calculate the force exerted by the liquid on the curved pipe. Assume non-viscous, uniform and steady flow.

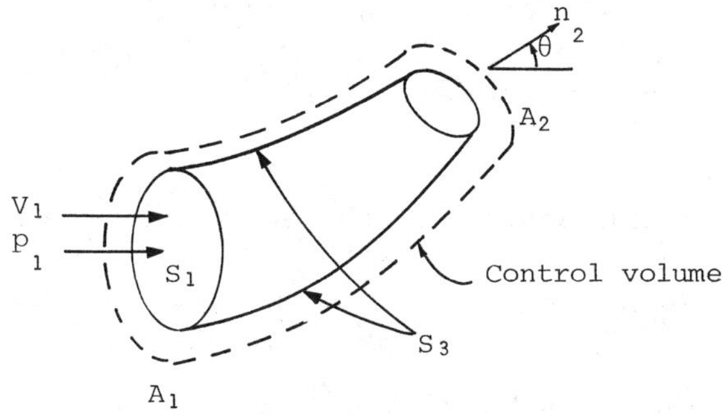

Solution: The general momentum equation for non-viscous, steady flow is

$$\underset{V}{\iiint} \vec{F} d\forall \quad \underset{S}{\iint} \tau dS = \underset{S}{\iint} \frac{\rho}{g_c} \vec{v}(\vec{v} \cdot d\vec{S}) \tag{1}$$

BODY FORCE — SURFACE FORCE — RATE OF CHANGE OF MOMENTUM

Taking the body force, $\vec{F} = -\gamma\vec{k}$
and $\tau = -p\vec{n}$ on surfaces S_1 and S_2.

Since there is no flow across the solid boundary S_3, the equation (1) becomes,

$$-\int_V \gamma\vec{k}\,d\forall - \int_{S_1} p\vec{n}\,dS - \int_{S_2} p\vec{n}\,dS + \int_{S_3} \vec{\tau}\,dS$$

$$= \int_{S_1} \frac{\rho}{g_c}\vec{v}(\vec{v}\cdot d\vec{S}) + \int_{S_2} \frac{\rho}{g_c}\vec{v}(\vec{v}\cdot d\vec{S})$$

For uniform flow the above integrations become

$$-\gamma\forall\vec{k} - p_1(-\vec{i})A_1 - p_2(\vec{n}_2)A_2 + \int_{S_3} \vec{\tau}\,dS$$

$$= \frac{\rho}{g_c}(v_1\vec{i})(-v_1A_1) + \frac{\rho}{g_c}(v_2\vec{n}_2)(v_2A_2)$$

The integral,

$$\int_{S_3} \vec{\tau}\,dS$$

= Resultant force exerted by the pipe wall on the fluid.

$= \vec{R}$ (SAY)

$= (R_1\vec{i} + R_2\vec{j} + R_3\vec{k})$

and let, $\vec{n}_2 = (\cos\theta\vec{i} + \sin\theta\vec{j})$

Substituting and comparing the $\vec{i}$, $\vec{j}$ and $\vec{k}$ components,

$$\vec{i}: \Rightarrow p_1A_1 - p_2A_2\cos\theta + R_1 = -\frac{\rho}{g_c}A_1v_1^2 + \frac{\rho}{g_c}A_2v_2^2\cos\theta$$

$$\vec{j}: \Rightarrow -p_2A_2\sin\theta + R_2 = \frac{\rho}{g_c}A_2v_2^2\sin\theta$$

$$\vec{k}: \Rightarrow -\gamma\forall + R_3 = 0$$

or $R_1 = p_2A_2\cos\theta - p_1A_1 + \frac{\rho}{g_c}(A_2v_2^2\cos\theta - A_1v_1^2)$

$R_2 = p_2A_2\sin\theta + \frac{\rho}{g_c}A_2v_2^2\sin\theta$

and $R_3 = \gamma\forall$

• PROBLEM 2-11

Determine the resultant thrust exerted by the curved pipe fitting in which the diameter changes from 50 mm. to 20 mm. in the direction of water flow. The inlet conditions are $p_1 = 100$ kPa, and $v_1 = 1.0$ m/sec. The water leaves the fitting horizontally, at the same elevation and at an angle of 45° with the entrance direction. Assume the flow to be incompressible and frictionless. Take the momentum and kinetic energy correction factors at both entrance and exit as unity.

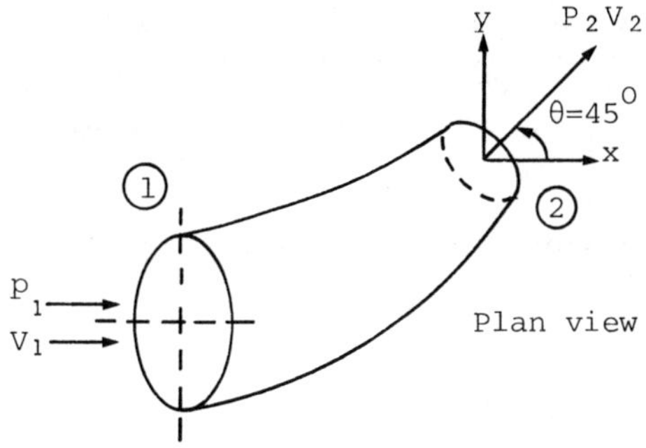

FLOW THROUGH CURVED PIPE FITTING

Solution: The outlet pressure is calculated by applying the Bernoulli's theorem between the inlet and outlet,

$$\frac{p_1}{\rho} + \frac{v_1^2}{2} + gz_1 = \frac{p_2}{\rho} + \frac{v_2^2}{2} + gz_2 + h_L$$

where, $z_1 = z_2$

$h_L = 0$

or $$p_2 = p_1 + \frac{\rho}{2}(v_1^2 - v_2^2) \qquad (1)$$

From continuity considerations, the velocity at the exit is

$$V_2 = \left(\frac{D_1}{D_2}\right)^2 V_1$$

$$= \left(\frac{50}{20}\right)^2 1.0 = 6.25 \text{ m/s}$$

Inserting the numerical values in (1),

$$p_2 = 100 + \frac{998}{2 \times 1000}\left[1^2 - 6.25^2\right]$$

$$= 81.01 \text{ kN/m}^2$$

Considering the momentum balance in x and y directions,

x-direction:

$$p_1 A_{1x} - p_2 A_{2x} + R_x = \dot{m}(\beta_2 V_{2x} - \beta_1 V_{1x}) \qquad (2)$$

y-direction:

$$p_1 A_{1y} - p_2 A_{2y} + R_y = \dot{m}(\beta_2 V_{2y} - \beta_1 V_{1y}) \qquad (3)$$

Note that at inlet there is no flow in the y-direction, thus

$$A_{1y} = V_{1y} = 0.$$

The various terms in equations (2) and (3) are,

A_{1x} = projected area of A_1 on plane normal to flow direction.

$= A_1$ (since there is no flow in y-direction at the inlet)

$= \frac{\pi}{4}(0.050)^2$

$= 0.001964\ m^2$

Similarly,

$$A_{2x} = A_2 \cos\theta$$

$$= \frac{\pi}{4}(0.020)^2 \cos 45^o$$

$$= 0.000222\ m^2$$

and

$$A_{2y} = A_2 \sin\theta$$

$$= 0.000222\ m^2$$

$$V_{2x} = V_2 \cos\theta$$

$$= 6.25 \cos 45^o$$

$$= 4.42\ m/s$$

$$V_{2y} = V_2 \sin\theta = 4.42\ m/s$$

$$\dot{m} = \rho A_1 V_1$$

$$= (998)(0.001964)(1.0)$$

$$= 1.960\ kg/s$$

Inserting the above numerical values in (2) and (3) and solving for R_x and R_y.

$$R_x = 1.96\ (4.42 - 1.0) - 100{,}000 \times 0.001964$$

$$+ 81{,}010 \times 0.000222$$

$$= -171.7\ \text{N}$$

and $$R_y = 1.96(4.42 - 0) - 0 + 81{,}010 \times 0.000222$$

$$= 26.65\ \text{N}$$

• PROBLEM 2-12

Water at 100 kPa gage pressure in the main flows through the nozzle at the rate of 6.5 m^3/sec. and it leaves the nozzle at atmospheric pressure. The pipe diameter is 30 cm. and the nozzle exit diameter is 15 cm. Assuming the velocity to be uniform across the cross section of the pipe, calculate the tension force on the bolts at the water main - filter nozzle joint (elbow joint, see figure).

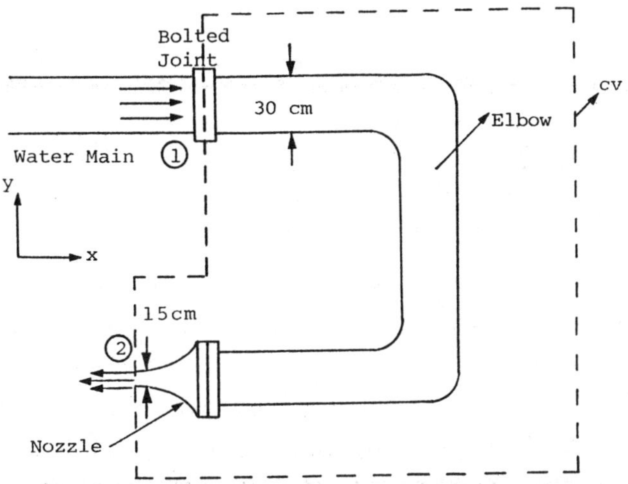

Solution: Consider the control volume through the bolt, nozzle exit and including the elbow. The pressure on the control surface is atmospheric everywhere except where the control surface cuts the main. Considering the momentum balance in x-direction,

$$\Sigma F = R_x + (p_1 - p_{Atm})\ A_1$$

$$= R_x + p_{1g} A_1$$

$$= \rho A_1 V_1\ (-V_2 - V_1)$$

The continuity equation is

$$A_1 V_1 = A_2 V_2 = Q$$

We have,

$$R_x = -\left[p_{1g}A_1 + \rho q^2 \left(\frac{1}{A_1} + \frac{1}{A_2}\right)\right]$$

Inserting the numerical values,

$$R_x = -\left[100 \times 10^3 \times \frac{\pi}{4}\left(\frac{30}{100}\right)^2 + 1000 \quad (6.5)^2 \times \frac{4}{\pi}\left[\left(\frac{100}{30}\right)^2 + \left(\frac{100}{15}\right)^2\right]\right]$$

$$= -7899 \text{ N}$$

Force on the bolts due to flow through the system,

$$= -R_x$$

$$= 7899 \text{ N}.$$

FLOW THROUGH PUMPS AND PIPE FITTINGS

• PROBLEM 2-13

In a liquid-liquid ejector pump, two streams of the same incompressible fluid are mixed at plane 1, one with velocity v_0, with cross sectional area $\frac{1}{3} A_1$ and the other with velocity $\frac{v_0}{2}$ and cross sectional area $\frac{2}{3} A_1$. Section 2 represents a state of uniform mixing of the two streams and the mixture has a uniform velocity v_2. Find an expression for the pressure increase due to the mixing of the two streams. Assume one-dimensional turbulent flow and neglect wall shear.

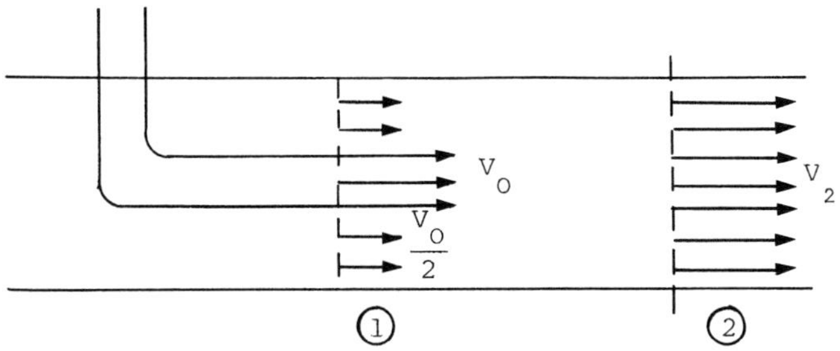

Solution: Steady state continuity equation is,

$$\rho_{Av} = \text{const} = w$$

or $\rho_1 < \bar{v}_1 > A_1 = \rho_2 < \bar{v}_2 > A_2$

but, $\rho_1 = \rho_2 = \rho$ and $A_1 = A_2 = A$

Hence, $< \bar{v}_1 > = < \bar{v}_2 >$

$$= \frac{1}{3} v_0 + \frac{2}{3} (\tfrac{1}{2} v_0)$$

$$= \frac{2}{3} v_0$$

Momentum balance gives the following equation

$$p_1 A_1 - p_2 A_2 + w_1 \frac{< \bar{v}_1^{\,2} >}{< \bar{v}_1 >} - w_2 \frac{< \bar{v}_2^{\,2} >}{< \bar{v}_2 >} = 0 \qquad (1)$$

Assuming flat profiles, the ratios of the averages are

$$\frac{< \bar{v}_1^{\,2} >}{< \bar{v}_1 >} = \frac{\frac{1}{3} v_0^{\,2} + \frac{2}{3}\left(\frac{v_0}{2}\right)^2}{\frac{1}{3} v_0 + \frac{2}{3}\frac{v_0}{2}}$$

$$= \frac{3}{4} v_0$$

and $$\frac{< \bar{v}_2^{\,2} >}{< \bar{v}_2 >} = \frac{2}{3} v_0$$

Substituting $w_1 = w_2 = \rho A(\frac{2}{3} v_0)$ in equation (1) we get

$$p_2 - p_1 = \frac{1}{18} \rho v_0^{\,2}$$

• PROBLEM 2-14

A pump with an overall efficiency of 60% pumps an acid (sp. gr. = 1.8) from an open tank to a process column at the rate of 18 lb/sec. The column operates at 19.65 psia and the fluid is discharged into it with a velocity of 8 fps at a point 60 ft above the acid surface level in the tank. Determine the power required to run the pump if the energy losses are equivalent to 9 ft of water head.

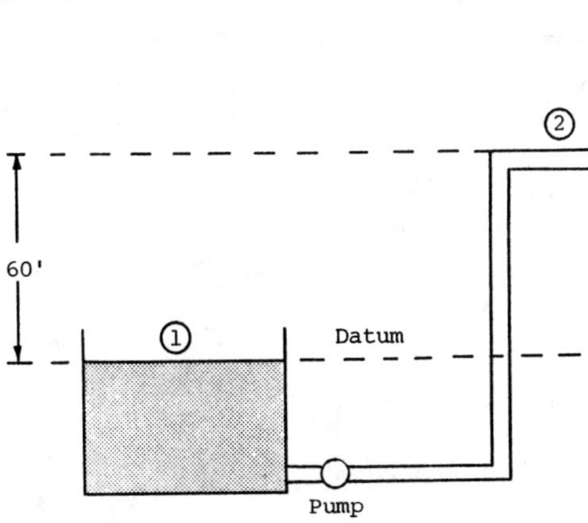

Solution: Applying energy equation between (1) and (2),

$$\frac{p_1}{\gamma} + \frac{v_1^2}{2g} + Z_1 + W = \frac{p_2}{\gamma} + \frac{v_2^2}{2g} + Z_2 + h_f$$

where $v_1 = 0$

W = pump work

$$Z_2 - Z_1 = 60.0$$

$$\frac{v_2^2}{2g} = \frac{8^2}{64.4} = 1.0$$

$$h_f = \frac{9.0}{1.8} \text{ (ft. of water)}$$

$$= 5.0 \text{ ft.}$$

$$\frac{p_2 - p_1}{\gamma} = \frac{(19.65 - 14.65)}{(1.8)(62.4)} 144 = 6.4$$

Substituting and simplifying

$$W = 60 + 6.4 + 1.0 + 5.0$$

$$= 72.4 \text{ ft.}$$

Therefore the work done in pumping 18 lb (lb-wt)/sec of the acid is,

$$= (72.4)(18)$$

Hence the horse-power required

$$= \frac{72.4(18)}{(0.6)550}$$

$$= 3.95 \text{ hp.}$$

• PROBLEM 2-15

The horsepower required to pump oil (ρ = 60 lb/ft^3, ν = 0.02 ft^2/sec) through a 4 in. diameter and 250 ft. long pipe is 6. If the efficiency of the pump is 75%, calculate the mass flow rate through the pipe.

Solution: Since the velocity of the flow is unknown, this problem has to be solved by trial and error method.

The water horsepower is given by,

$$\text{W.H.P.} = \eta \times \text{B.H.P.}$$

or $$\frac{wQh}{550} = 0.75 \text{ x } 6$$

or $$h = \frac{0.75 \text{ x } 6 \text{ x } 550}{60\ Q}$$

or $$h = \frac{41.25}{Q} \qquad (1)$$

We are left with two unknowns and one equation, hence to solve, assume the type of flow to be laminar. Thus,

$$h = \frac{fLv^2}{2gD}$$

or $$h = \frac{64}{Re}\left(\frac{L}{D}\right)\frac{v^2}{2g}$$

where,

$$Re = \frac{vD}{\nu}$$

$$= \frac{Q}{A}\left(\frac{D}{\nu}\right)$$

$$= \frac{Q\left(\frac{4}{12}\right)}{\frac{\pi}{4}\left(\frac{4}{12}\right)^2(0.02)}$$

or $$Re = \frac{600Q}{\pi}$$

and $$v = \frac{Q}{A} = \frac{Q}{\frac{\pi}{4}\left(\frac{1}{3}\right)^2}$$

or $$v = \frac{36Q}{\pi}$$

Substituting,

$$h = \frac{64}{\frac{600Q}{\pi}} \text{ x } \frac{250}{1/3} \text{ x } \frac{(36Q)^2}{\pi^2(2g)}$$

or $$h = 512.459Q \qquad (2)$$

Comparing (1) and (2),

$$\frac{41.25}{Q} = 512.459Q$$

or $$Q = 0.2837 \text{ ft}^3/\text{sec.}$$

Working backwards and finding Re with this value of Q

$$Re = \frac{\quad}{\pi}$$

$$= \frac{600 \text{ x } 0.2837}{\pi}$$

or $$Re = 54.18 < 2300$$

Hence, the assumption that the flow is laminar is reasonable.

$$\text{mass flow rate} = \rho Q$$
$$= 60 \times 0.2837$$
$$= 17.02 \text{ lb/sec.}$$
$$= 17.02 \times \frac{3600}{2240}$$

or $$\dot{m} = 27 \text{ tons/hr.}$$

• PROBLEM 2-16

A pump is used to lift water ($\rho = 62.4\ \text{lb}_m\ \text{ft}^{-3}$, $\mu = 1.0$ cp) from one tank to the other at a rate of 12 $\text{ft}^3\ \text{min}^{-1}$. If the pipe diameter is 4 in, calculate the horsepower required to run the pump.

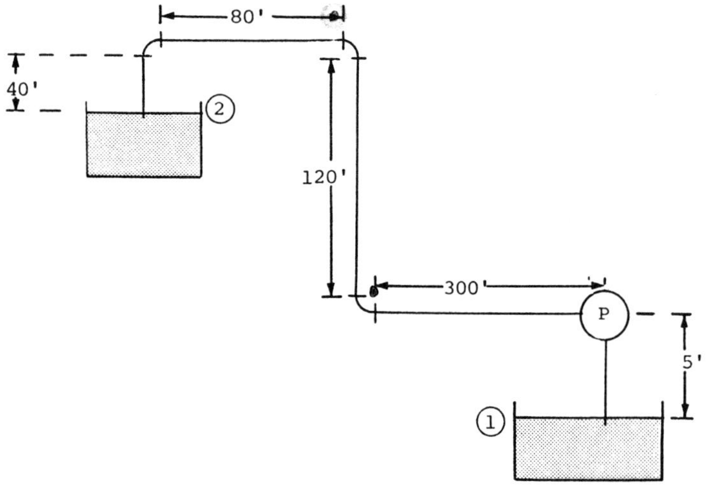

Solution: Applying the energy equation,

$$\frac{p_1}{\rho} + \frac{v_1^2}{2} + gz_1 + w = \frac{p_2}{\rho} + \frac{v_2^2}{2} + gz_2 + (h_1)_T$$

where,

$$p_1 = p_2 = p_{atm}.$$

$$v_1 = v_2 = 0$$

or $$w = g(z_2 - z_1) + (h_1)_T \qquad (1)$$

The flow characteristic, i.e., whether the flow is laminar or turbulent, must be known in order to calculate the head loss quantities.

Computing the Reynolds number,

$$Re = \frac{\rho v D}{\mu}$$

$$= \frac{(62.4)(12/60)(\frac{4}{12})}{(1.0 \times 6.72 \times 10^{-4})(\frac{\pi}{4})\left(\frac{4}{12}\right)^2}$$

$$= 7.11 \times 10^4$$

It is clear that the flow is well into the turbulent range. From the Moody roughness chart and the Moody diagram for commercial steel pipe, the friction factor f, comes out to be 0.021.

The major pipe head loss,

$$(h_l)_p = \frac{fLv^2}{2D}$$

where $v = \dfrac{12/60}{\pi\left(\frac{1}{6}\right)^2} = 2.30$ ft/sec.

$$(h_l)_p = \frac{(0.021)(2.30)^2}{2\left(\frac{1}{3}\right)}(5 + 300 + 120 + 80 + 40)$$

$$= 90.82 \text{ ft}^2/\text{sec}^2$$

And the minor loss is,

$$(h_l)_m = \frac{\Sigma kv^2}{2}$$

$$= \left[0.45 + 3(\tfrac{1}{2}) + 1\right]\frac{(2.30)^2}{2}$$

$$= 8 \text{ ft}^2/\text{sec}^2$$

Substituting in (1)

$$w = 32.2\ (125 - 40) + 90.82 + 8$$

$$= 2835.82 \text{ ft}^2/\text{sec}^2$$

$$= \frac{2835.82}{32.2} \text{ lb}_f/\text{lb}_m$$

$$= 88 \text{ ft lb}_f/\text{lb}_m$$

$$= (88)(\rho Q) \text{ ft lb}_f/\text{sec}$$

$$= (88)(62.4)(\frac{12}{60})$$

$$= \frac{1100}{500}$$

$$= 2 \text{ h.p.}$$

• PROBLEM 2-17

A centrifugal pump with an efficiency of 75 percent is used to lift kerosine at 30 °C from one tank to the other. The total length of the steel piping is 100 m. and its nominal diameter is 5 cm. If the power required to run the pump is 50 kW, calculate the volume flow rate of the kerosine. Assume steady flow.

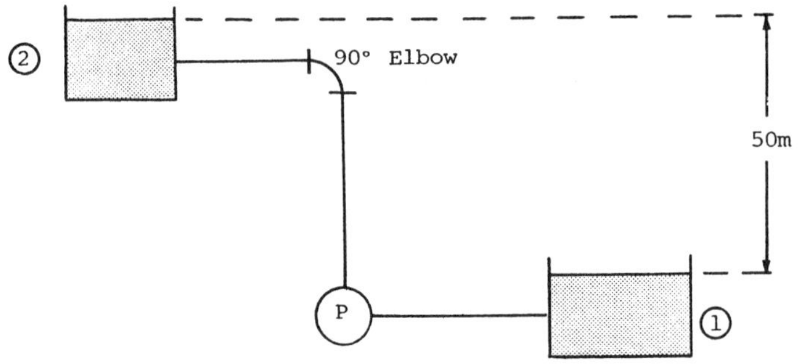

Solution: Writing the Bernoulli's equation between the free surfaces of the tanks,

$$\frac{p_1}{\gamma} + \frac{v_1^2}{2g} + z_1 + H_p = \frac{p_2}{\gamma} + \frac{v_2^2}{2g} + z_2 + h_f$$

or $$H_p = \Delta z + h_f \tag{1}$$

where,

$$W = \gamma Q H_p = \eta(\text{Power})$$

or $$H_p = \text{Pump Head}$$

$$= \frac{0.75 \times 50 \times 1000}{820 \times 9.81 \times Q}$$

$$= \frac{4.6617}{Q}$$

$$h_f = \frac{V^2}{2g}\left[\frac{fL}{D} + k_{entrance} + k_{elbow} + k_{exit}\right]$$

$$= \frac{Q^2}{2A^2 g}\left[\frac{fL}{D} + k_{entrance} + k_{elbow} + k_{exit}\right]$$

$$= \frac{Q^2}{2\left[\frac{\pi}{4}(0.05)^2\right]^2 \times 9.81}\left[f\,\frac{100}{0.05} + 0.58 + 0.75 + 1.0\right]$$

$$= 13{,}220.2Q^2\left[2.33 + 2000\ f\right]$$

and $\Delta z = 50$ m

Substituting the numerical values in (1),

$$\frac{4.6617}{Q} = 50 + 13220.2\ Q^2\left[2.33 + 2000\ f\right]$$

or $$\frac{0.0933}{Q} - 264.7\ (2.33 + 2000\ f)Q^2 = 1.0$$

or $$264.7\ (2.33 + 2000\ f)Q^2 = \frac{0.0933 - Q}{Q}$$

or $$Q = \left[\frac{0.0933 - Q}{264.7\ (2.33 + 2000\ f)}\right]^{1/3} \qquad (2)$$

where "f" depends on Reynolds number

$$Re = \frac{\rho v D}{\mu}$$

$$= \frac{\rho Q/\frac{\pi}{4}D^2\ (D)}{\mu} = \frac{4\rho Q}{\pi\mu D}$$

$$= \frac{4(820)Q}{\pi(0.0015)(0.05)} = 1.39x(10)^7 Q$$

This problem can be solved by the Hit and Trial Method. Assume a value of Q and calculate Re using this value of Q. Then find "f" from the Moody chart and substitute this value of "f" in equation (2) to calculate Q. Different values of Q are assumed till we obtain a case for which $Q_{assumed} = Q_{calculated}$.

As an example, let $Q = 0.0158\ m^3/s$ (assume)

gives,

$$Re = 2.20 \times 10^5$$

and

$$f = 0.0206$$

Substituting the value of "f" in (2),

$$Q_{calculated} = 0.0189$$

$$\neq Q_{assumed}$$

By trial and error, $Q_{exact} = 0.0186\ m^3/sec.$

FLOW THROUGH MOVING VANES, CONTROL VOLUME, TURBINE AND HEATER

• PROBLEM 2-18

A water jet at a rate of 3 cfs impinges on a curved vane moving at 60 ft/sec in the same direction as that of the jet. The jet area is 0.03 ft^2. Calculate the the horsepower developed. Also determine the energy remaining in the jet.

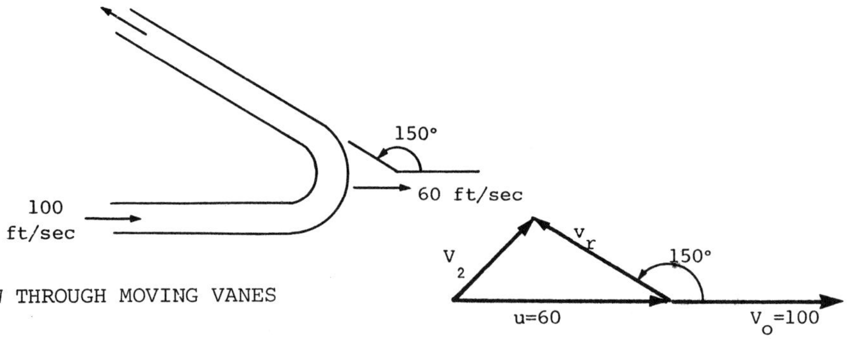

FLOW THROUGH MOVING VANES

Solution: Assume the vane surface is frictionless.

Jet velocity,

$$V_0 = \frac{3}{0.03} = 100 \text{ ft/sec.}$$

Applying the momentum equation,

$$F = \rho AV\,(V_\gamma - V_\gamma \cos 150^0)$$

$$= (1.94)(3)40(1 - \cos 150^0)$$

$$= 434 \text{ lb}_f$$

The horse power developed is,

$$= \frac{(434)(60)}{550}$$

$$= 47.4 \text{ hp.}$$

Absolute velocity leaving the vane is,

x-component: $V_{2x} = 60 - 40 \cos 30^0$

$$= 25.4 \text{ ft/s}$$

y-component: $V_{2y} = 40 \sin 30^0$

$$= 20 \text{ ft/sec.}$$

The energy remaining in the jet is,

$$= \tfrac{1}{2}\,\dot{m}V_2{}^2$$

$$= \tfrac{1}{2}\,\rho QV_2{}^2 = \tfrac{1}{2}\,(1.94)(3)\left[25.4^2 + 20^2\right]$$

$$= 3041 \text{ ft. lb/sec}$$

• PROBLEM 2-19

In an unmixed counter-flow heat exchanger heat is transferred from saturated steam to air. The inlet conditions are: saturated steam at 66.98 psia and at 300^{0}F, air at 14.7 psia and at 85^{0}F.

The outlet conditions are: saturated water at 300^oF and 66.98 psia, air at $T_2\ ^oF$ and 14.7 psia.

If there is no heat loss in the exchanger, compute the outlet temperature of air. Take the mass of air as 5.55 lbmol and that of steam as 5.0 lb.

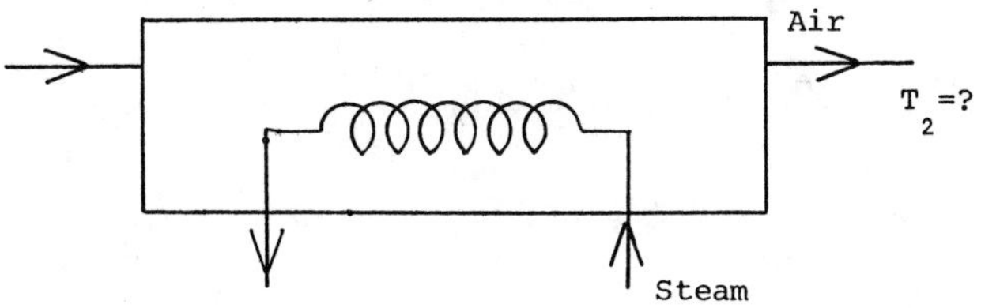

Solution: For 100 percent efficiency,

Heat lost = Heat gain

or
$$\dot{m}_{air}\, c_p(T_2 - 85) = \dot{m}_{H_2O}\,(H_2 - H_1)$$

Substituting $5.55\, c_p\,(T_2 - 85) = 5\,[1180.2 - 269.73]$

or $c_p\,(T_2 - 85) = 820.24$

Two unknowns and one equation. The solution is trial and error.

Trial: 1 Assume $t = 250^oF$

$c_p = 7.01$ (from table)

Solving, $T_2 = 201.8^oF$

Finally, $T_2 \simeq 202.0^oF$

$c_p = 7.0$ btu/lbmol^oF.

FLOW THROUGH OR FROM A TANK

• PROBLEM 2-20

Compute the height of the water in an open tank if it delivers water through a 0.5 in. ID, 200 ft. long, smooth brass pipe at a rate of 0.01 ft^3/sec.

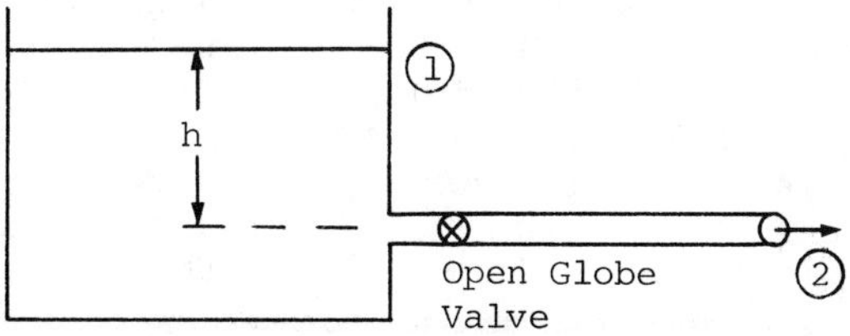

Solution: The cross sectional area is:

$$A = \pi/4 \frac{(0.5)^2}{(12)^2}$$

$$= 0.1364 \times 10^{-2} \text{ ft}^2$$

The average fluid velocity in the pipe is:

$$V = \frac{q}{A} = \frac{0.01}{0.1364 \times 10^{-2}}$$

$$= 7.33 \text{ ft/s.}$$

$$Re = \frac{VD}{\nu}$$

$$= \frac{7.33\left(\frac{0.5}{12}\right)}{1.4 \times 10^{-5}}$$

$$= 22{,}000$$

From the Moody diagram for smooth pipes,

$$f = 0.0255$$

Applying energy equation between (1) and (2)

$$\frac{p_1}{\gamma} + \frac{V_1^2}{2g} + z_1 = \frac{p_2}{\gamma} + \frac{V_2^2}{2g} + z_2 + (h_f)_T$$

or $$z_1 - z_2 = \frac{V^2}{2g}\left[1 + \frac{fL}{D} + k_{globe} + k_{ent.} + k_{exit}\right]$$

$$= \frac{(7.33)^2}{64.4}\left[1 + \frac{0.0255(200)}{\frac{0.5}{12}}\right.$$

$$\left. + 6.9 + 0.78 + 1.0\right]$$

or $$z_1 - z_2 = 110.2 \text{ ft.}$$

• PROBLEM 2-21

Two cylindrical open tanks are connected by two steel pipes of different diameters. Pipe 1 is 200 m in length and 60 cm. in diameter. Pipe 2 is 100 m in length and 30 cm. in diameter. The difference in water surface level in the tanks is 20 m. If the change in diameter from pipe 1 to pipe 2 is an abrupt contraction, compute the volume flow rate.

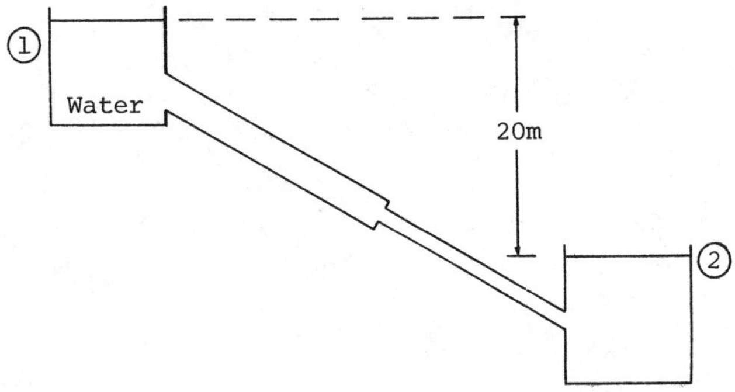

Solution: From continuity equation,

$$q_1 = q_2$$

or $$A_1V_1 = A_2V_2$$

or $$V_1 \frac{\pi}{4} (60)^2 = \frac{\pi}{4} (30)^2 V_2$$

or $$V_2 = 4 V_1$$

Writing the energy equation,

$$\frac{p_1}{\gamma} + \frac{V_1^2}{2g} + z_1 = \frac{p_2}{\gamma} + \frac{V_2^2}{2g} + z_2 + (h_f)_T$$

or $$(h_f)_T = z_1 - z_2$$

or $$(h_f)_T = 20 \qquad (1)$$

where $$(h_f)_T = (h_f)_p + (h_f)_m$$

$$= \frac{f_1L_1}{D_1}\frac{V_1^2}{2g} + \frac{f_2L_2V_2^2}{2gD_2} + \frac{V_1^2}{2g}(k_{ent.}) +$$

$$\frac{V_2^2}{2g}(k_{com.} + k_{exit})$$

$$= \frac{V_1^2}{2g}\left(\frac{f_1(200)}{0.6} + 0.5\right) +$$

$$\frac{V_2^2}{2g}\left(\frac{f_2(100)}{0.3} + 0.35 + 1\right)$$

$$= \frac{V_1^2}{2g}(333.3\ f_1 + 0.5) + \frac{16V_1^2}{2g}(333.3f_2+1.35)$$

$$= \frac{V_1^2}{2g}\Big[333.3f_1 + 0.5 + 16(333.3f_2)$$

$$+ 16\,(1.35)\Big]$$

$$= \frac{V_1^2}{2g}\left[333.3f_1 + 0.5 + 5333.3f_2 + 21.6\right]$$

or $$(h_f)_T = \frac{V_1^2}{2g}\left[333.3f_1 + 5333.3f_2 + 22.1\right] \qquad (2)$$

Comparing (1) and (2),

$$20 = \frac{V_1^2}{2g}\left[333.3f_1 + 5333.3f_2 + 22.1\right] \qquad (3)$$

Here, f_1 and f_2 are unknown along with V_1. Assuming large Reynolds numbers we can obtain friction factors to determine the approximate velocity. For commercial steel pipes with known diameters and large Reynolds numbers, the Moody chart yields:

$$f_1 = 0.0115$$

$$f_2 = 0.0128$$

Substituting and solving for V_1:

$$V_1 = 2.04 \text{ m/s}$$

and $$V_2 = 8.16 \text{ m/s}$$

Now checking for exact friction factors,

$$Re_1 = \frac{(2.04)(0.60)}{10^{-6}} = 1.22 \times 10^6$$

$$Re_2 = \frac{(0.30)(8.16)}{(10^{-6})}$$

$$= 2.45 \times 10^6$$

Thus from Moody diagram,

$$f_1 = 0.013$$

$$f_2 = 0.0135$$

Therefore the new velocity,

$$V_1 = 2.0 \text{ m/s}$$

$$V_2 = 8.0 \text{ m/s}$$

which verify with the new friction factors.

Thus flow rate is,

$$q = VA = 0.565 \text{ m}^3/\text{s}$$

• PROBLEM 2-22

A cylindrical tank 1 ft in diameter discharges through a nozzle connected at the base. Find the time needed for the water level in the tank to drop from 4 ft. to 2 ft. above the nozzle. Take the nozzle diameter as 1 in., and the velocity of water in the jet as $(2gh)^{\frac{1}{2}}$.

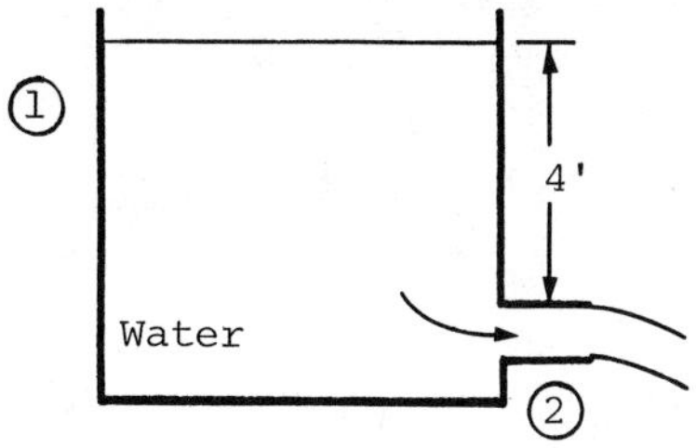

DISCHARGE OF A TANK THROUGH A NOZZLE

Solution: Applying the continuity equation between (1) and (2)

$$\dot{m}_2 - \dot{m}_1 = -\Delta\dot{m}_{cv}$$

or $$\dot{m}_2 - 0 = -\Delta\dot{m}_{cv}$$

or $$\rho AV - 0 = -\frac{d}{dt}\int_{cv}\rho d\forall$$

$$= -\frac{d}{dt}\left[\rho A_T(h + x)\right]$$

where

A_T = cross-sectional area of the tank.

x = depth of water in the tank below outlet. [CONSTANT]

h = depth of water in the tank above outlet.

V = velocity of jet.

Now,

$$\rho AV = -\rho A_T \frac{dh}{dt}$$

or $$AV = -A_T \frac{dh}{dt}$$

or $$dt = \frac{-A_T dh}{A\sqrt{2gh}}$$

$$= \frac{-A_T}{A\sqrt{2g}}\, dh(h)^{-\frac{1}{2}}$$

Integrating,

$$t = \frac{-2A_T\ h^{\frac{1}{2}}}{\sqrt{2g}\ A} + c$$

when $t = 0, \quad h = 4$

$$c = \frac{2A_T}{\sqrt{2g}\ A}\ 4^{\frac{1}{2}}$$

Thus, $t = \dfrac{2A_T}{\sqrt{2g}\ A}\ (2 - h^{\frac{1}{2}})$

when $h = 2$ ft

$$t = \frac{2\ \frac{\pi}{4}\ 1^2\ (2 - 2^{\frac{1}{2}})}{\left[2(32.2)\right]^{\frac{1}{2}}(\frac{\pi}{4})(\frac{1}{12})^2}$$

or $t = 21$ sec.

• PROBLEM 2-23

> Two large open tanks are filled with the same liquid. Flow from both the tanks mixes together and moves through a common pipe. If the common pipe discharges to the atmosphere, find an expression for the flow rate through the common pipe. Assume smooth frictionless flow.

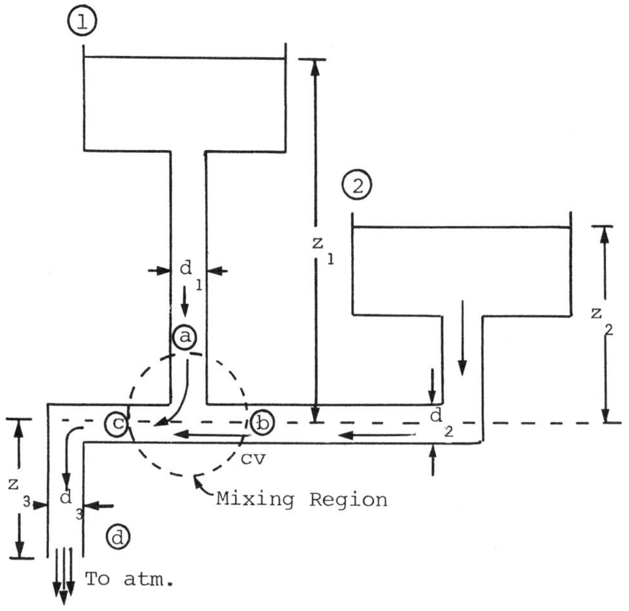

Solution: Consider a control volume around the mixing zone. By applying the Bernoulli equation between different points, the flow rate can be calculated. First between (1) and (a), with $V_1 \simeq 0$

$$\frac{p_1}{\gamma} + 0 + z_1 = p_a + \left(\frac{1}{2g}\right)(V_a^{\,2}) \tag{1}$$

Since the pressure variation in the mixing region is negligible, assume $p_a \simeq p_b \simeq p_c$. Also $p_1 \simeq p_2 \simeq p_d \simeq p_{atm}$. Between (2) and (b)

$$\frac{p_2}{\gamma} + z_2 = p_b + \left(\frac{1}{2g}\right)(V_b^{\,2}) \tag{2}$$

Finally, between (c) and (d)

$$\frac{p_c}{\gamma} + \frac{V_c^{\,2}}{2g} + z_3 = \frac{p_d}{\gamma} + \frac{V_d^{\,2}}{2g}$$

But $\quad V_c = V_d$

Hence, $$\frac{p_c}{\gamma} + z_3 = \frac{p_d}{\gamma} \tag{3}$$

Solving for V_a and V_b from the equations (1), (2) and (3),

$$V_a = \sqrt{2g(z_1 + z_3)}$$

$$V_b = \sqrt{2g(z_2 + z_3}$$

By continuity, for steady flow analysis,

$$\dot{q}_{IN} = \dot{q}_{OUT}$$

or

$$\dot{Q} = AV$$

or

$$\dot{Q} = \frac{\pi}{4}\left[d_1^{\,2}\sqrt{2g(z_1 + z_3)} + d_2^{\,2}\sqrt{2g(z_2 + z_3)}\right]$$

FLOW THROUGH PIPES

• PROBLEM 2-24

The tank shown in the figure is filled with oil. Calculate the rate of flow of the oil in the pipe. Take the pipe diameter to be 6mm and the length to be 100 m. The height of the oil level from the pipe level is 1 m. Assume for oil $\mu = 3.2 \times 10^{-3}$ N·s/m^2, $\nu = 3.9 \times 10^{-6}$ m^2/s, $\gamma = 814$ N/m^3.

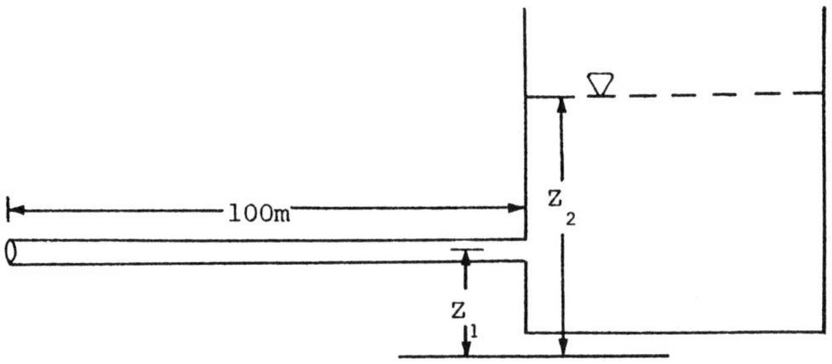

Solution: Assume initially, the flow of oil inside the pipe is laminar, because of the very small diameter of the pipe and also because of the very small head $(z_2 - z_1)$. Also assume the exit velocity to be very small so that $\frac{V_1^2}{2g}$ is negligibly small. Writing the Bernoulli equation between the surface of oil in the tank and the outlet section of the pipe yields:

$$\frac{32\mu LV}{\gamma D^2} + \frac{p_1}{\gamma} + \frac{\alpha_1 V_1^2}{2g} + z_1 = \frac{p_2}{\gamma} + \frac{\alpha_2 V_2^2}{2g} + z_2$$

Here $p_1 = p_2 = p_{atm}$

$$V_2 = 0, \qquad \frac{V_1^2}{2g} \simeq 0$$

Therefore,

$$\frac{32\mu LV_1}{\gamma D^2} = z_2 - z_1$$

or

$$\frac{32\mu LV_1}{\gamma D^2} = 1$$

or

$$V_1 = \frac{\gamma D^2}{32\mu L}$$

Substituting the values in the right hand side of the equation yields:

$$V_1 = \frac{814 \times (0.006)^2}{32 \times 3.2 \times 10^{-3} \times 100}$$

$$= 0.00286 \text{ m/s}$$

or $\qquad V_1 = 2.86$ mm/s

This is the velocity in the pipe with the assumption that the flow is laminar and $\frac{V_1^2}{2g} \simeq 0$. This can be verified by the Reynolds number, which is given by:

$$Re = \frac{V_1 D}{\nu}$$

where Re = Reynolds number

V_1 = velocity in the pipe

ν = kinematic viscosity of oil.

Substituting yields:

$$Re = \frac{0.00286 \times 0.006}{3.9 \times 10^{-6}} = 4.4$$

This shows that the flow is in the laminar region.

Also

$$\frac{V_1^2}{2g} = \frac{(0.00286)^2}{2 \times 9.81} = 4.17 \times 10^{-7} \text{ m}$$

$$\simeq 0$$

Hence, the assumptions are true.

Therefore the rate of flow is

$$Q = VA$$

$$= 0.00286 \times \frac{\pi}{4}(0.006)^2$$

or $$Q = 8.09 \times 10^{-8} \text{m}^3/\text{s}$$

• PROBLEM 2-25

Develop the expressions for the velocity, pressure and temperature of a stream formed by mixing two steady turbulent streams of the same ideal gas which have different velocities, temperatures and pressures.

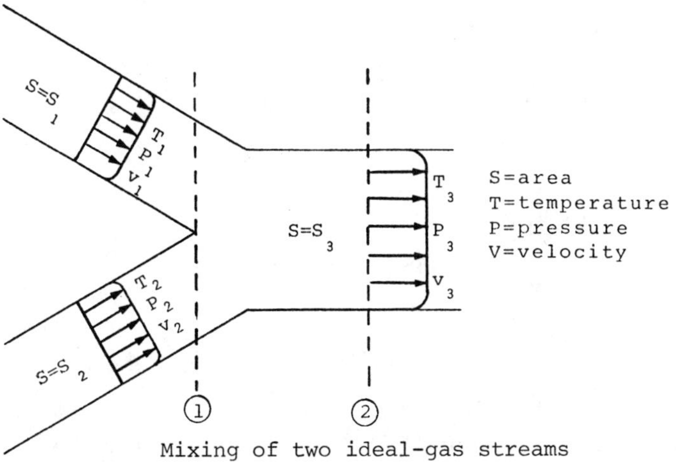

Mixing of two ideal-gas streams

Solution: In this system the changes in density and temperature are very significant. Therefore in addition to the mass and momentum balance equations, the steady-state macroscopic energy balance and the ideal gas equation of state have to be used.

The first reference plane is at the cross section at which the streams first begin to mix (plane (1)) and the second reference plane is far enough downstream that complete mixing has taken place (plane (2)). Assume the shear stress on the pipe wall is negligible, there are no changes in potential energy, the velocity profiles are flat, changes in the heat capacity of the fluid are negligible, and the mixing process is adiabatic.

Then the required equations are given by:

$$w_3 = w_1 + w_2 \qquad (1) \text{ (mass balance)}$$

$$w_3 v_3 + p_3 S_3 = w_1 v_1 + p_1 S_1 + w_2 v_2 + p_2 S_2 \qquad (2) \text{ (momentum balance)}$$

$$w_3\left[C_p(T_3 - T^o) + \tfrac{1}{2}v_3^2\right] = w_1\left[C_p(T_1 - T^o) + \tfrac{1}{2}v_1^2\right] + w_2\left[C_p(T_2 - T^o) + \tfrac{1}{2}v_2^2\right] \qquad (3) \text{ (energy balance)}$$

$$p_3 = \frac{\rho_3 R T_3}{M} \qquad (4) \text{ (equation of state)}$$

where T^o is the reference temperature for the enthalpy.

S = cross sectional area, T = temperature, p = pressure,

v = velocity.

Multiplying equation (1) by $C_p T^o$ gives:

$$w_3 C_p T^o = w_1 C_p T^o + w_2 C_p T^o \qquad (5)$$

Subtracting equation (5) from equation (3) gives:

$$w_3\left[C_p T_3 + \tfrac{1}{2}v_3^2\right] = w_1\left[C_p T_1 + \tfrac{1}{2}v_1^2\right] + w_2\left[C_p T_2 + \tfrac{1}{2}v_2^2\right] \qquad (6)$$

The right hand side of equations (1), (2) and (6) are known and are designated by w, p and E respectively. Now eq. (2) can be written as

$$w_3 v_3 + p_3 S_3 = P$$

Substituting for p_3 from the equation of state gives:

$$w_3 v_3 + \frac{\rho_3 R T_3}{M} \cdot S_3 = P$$

But $w_3 = w$ from equation (1) and dividing the previous equation by w gives:

$$v_3 + \frac{RT_3}{M} \cdot \frac{\rho_3 S_3}{w} = \frac{P}{w}$$

As $w = \rho_3 v_3 S_3$, then $\frac{\rho_3 S_3}{w} = \frac{1}{v_3}$

Therefore,

$$v_3 + \frac{RT_3}{Mv_3} = \frac{P}{w} \qquad (7)$$

Solving equation (7) for T_3 and then substituting in equation (6), and simplifying gives:

$$v_3^2 - \left[2\left(\frac{\gamma}{\gamma + 1}\right)\frac{P}{w}\right] v_3 + 2\left(\frac{\gamma - 1}{\gamma + 1}\right)\frac{E}{w} = 0 \qquad (8)$$

where $\gamma = C_p/C_v$

Eq. (8) is a quadratic equation of v_3, hence v_3 is given by:

$$v_3 = \frac{P}{w}\left(\frac{\gamma}{\gamma + 1}\right)\left[1 \pm \sqrt{1 - 2\left(\frac{\gamma^2 - 1}{\gamma^2}\right)\frac{wE}{P^2}}\right] \qquad (9)$$

One of the solutions for v_3 is supersonic and the other is subsonic. If the quantity in brackets is unity the velocity of the final stream is sonic. The supersonic flow is unstable in the presence of any significant disturbance. Therefore only the subsonic solution can be obtained in the mixing process under consideration. The pressure and temperature of the final stream can be obtained from equations (2) and (6) respectively.

FLOW THROUGH SIPHON, PITOT TUBE, AND MOMENTUM BALANCE ON A JET PLANE

• PROBLEM 2-26

Water is drained from a large open reservoir by means of a frictionless siphon tube. If the distance between the liquid level in the tank and the end of the tube is h = 6 ft., calculate the fluid velocity in the tube. Assume the cross sectional area of the tube is uniform.

Solution: Applying the Bernoulli equation between (2) and (3)

$$\frac{p_2}{\gamma} + \frac{V_2^2}{2g} + z_2 = \frac{p_3}{\gamma} + \frac{V_3^2}{2g} + z_3$$

where $p_3 = p_{atm}$

$V_2 \simeq V_3$

or $$\frac{p_3 - p_2}{\gamma} = z_2 - z_3 = h$$

or $$\frac{p_{atm} - p_2}{\gamma} = h \qquad (1)$$

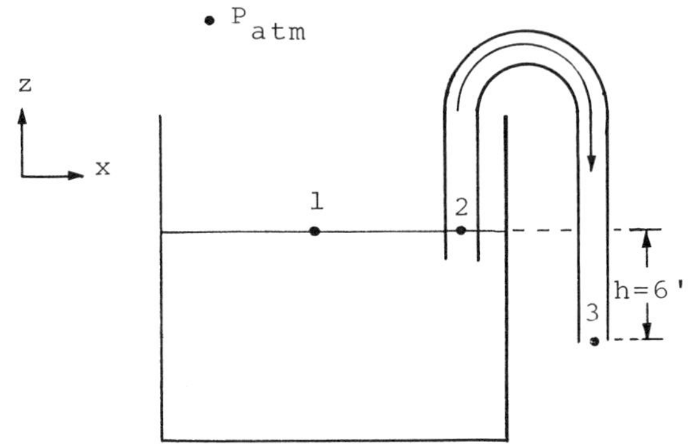

Now writing the energy equation between sections (1) and (2)

$$\frac{p_1}{\gamma} + \frac{V_1^2}{2g} + z_1 = \frac{p_2}{\gamma} + \frac{V_2^2}{2g} + z_2$$

where $z_2 = z_1$

$V_1 \simeq 0$ [large cross sectional area compared to the tube]

$p_1 = p_{atm}$

or $$\frac{p_{atm} - p_2}{\gamma} = \frac{V_2^2}{2g} \qquad (2)$$

Comparing (1) and (2)

$$V_2 = \sqrt{2gh}$$

$$= \sqrt{2(32.2)(6)}$$

or $$V_2 = 19.66 \text{ ft/sec}$$

Here, an interesting point to note, that if the end of the tube is above the liquid level in the tank, then no real value exists for V_2, because "h" will be negative.

• PROBLEM 2-27

A plane engine develops 10,000 lb_f of thrust. The air intake is 60 lb_m per lb_m of fuel, and the fuel burning rate is 3 lbm/sec. If a plane, to which this engine is mounted, flies at a speed of 600 mph, compute the jet outlet velocity.

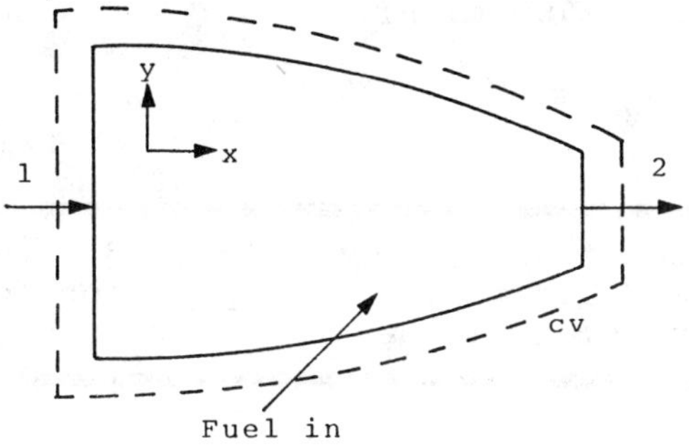

Solution: Choosing a control volume around the engine and applying the steady state momentum equation between (1) and (2):

$$\Sigma\vec{F} = m\vec{a}$$

or
$$\vec{F}_s = \oiint_{cs.} \vec{v}(\rho\vec{v}\cdot d\vec{A})$$

for steady flow with negligible body forces.

or
$$F_x = v_2(\rho_2 v_2 A_2) - v_1(\rho_1 v_1 A_1)$$

But by continuity,

$$\dot{m}_{in} = \dot{m}_{out} \quad \text{for steady flow,}$$

or
$$\dot{m}_a + \dot{m}_f = \dot{m}_2$$

or
$$F_x = v_2\dot{m}_2 - \dot{m}_a v_1 \tag{1}$$

In the above equation the momentum given by the fuel is neglected.

$$\dot{m}_2 = \dot{m}_a + \dot{m}_f$$

$$= 3(60) + 3 = 183 \text{ lb}_m/\text{sec.}$$

$$\dot{m}_a = 60\ (\dot{m}_f) = 60(3) = 180 \text{ lb}_m/\text{sec.}$$

$$v_1 = 600 \text{ mi/hr.} = 600\left(\frac{5280}{3600}\right) = 880 \text{ ft/sec.}$$

$$F_x = 10,000 \text{ lb}_f$$

Substituting in (1),

$$10,000 = \left[\frac{183}{32.2} v_2 - \frac{180}{32.2}(880)\right]$$

or $$v_2 = 2625.14 \text{ ft/sec}$$

$$= 1790 \text{ mi/hr.}$$

• PROBLEM 2-28

In a pipe a pitot tube-manometer is used to measure the velocity of the fluid. Find an expression for the velocity of flow in terms of the manometer reading, h.

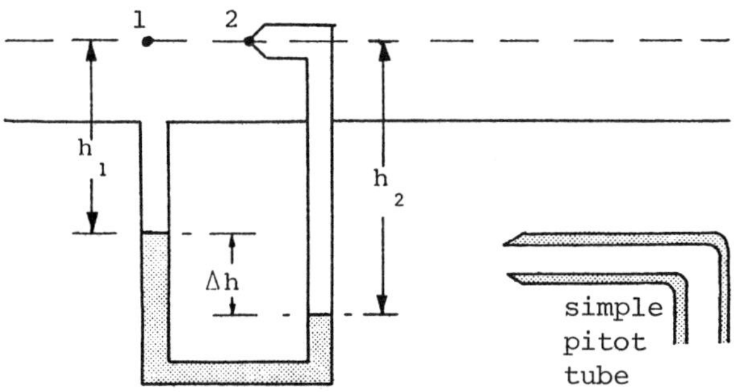

Velocity measurement using pitot tube

Solution: The pressure measurement at 2 gives the total pressure or stagnation pressure. The pressure measurement at 1 gives the undisturbed or static pressure, and the difference clearly determines the dynamic pressure. Apply the Bernoulli equation between (1) and (2), with $z_1 = z_2$ and $v_2 = 0$.

That is, $$\frac{p_1}{\gamma} + \frac{v_1^2}{2g} = \frac{p_2}{\gamma}$$

or $$\frac{v_1^2}{2g} = \frac{(p_2 - p_1)}{\gamma}$$

or $$\frac{v_1^2}{2} = \frac{p_2 - p_1}{\rho}$$

or $$v_1^2 = \frac{2(p_2 - p_1)}{\rho} \qquad (1)$$

Comparing the equal pressure points in the manometer,

$$p_1 + \gamma h_1 + \gamma_{Hg} h = p_2 + \gamma h_2$$

or
$$p_2 - p_1 = \gamma(h_1 - h_2) + \gamma_{Hg} h$$
$$= -\gamma h + \gamma_{Hg} h$$

or
$$(p_2 - p_1) = h(\gamma_{Hg} - \gamma) \qquad (2)$$

Substituting in (1),

$$v_1^{\,2} = \frac{2h}{\rho}(\gamma_{Hg} - \gamma)$$

or
$$v_1^{\,2} = \frac{2gh}{\gamma}(\gamma_{Hg} - \gamma)$$

or
$$v_1 = \left[2gh\left(\frac{\gamma Hg}{\gamma} - 1\right)\right]^{\frac{1}{2}}$$

• PROBLEM 2-29

For the system illustrated, develop expressions for the velocity profile, ratio of maximum velocity to average velocity and the volumetric flow rate through shell balance technique.

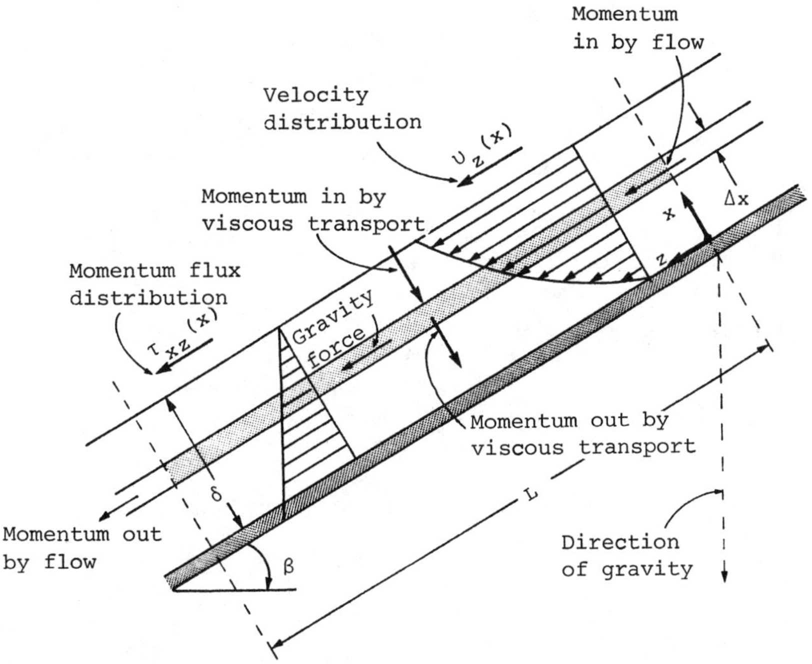

Solution: Making a momentum balance over a differential section of thickness Δx as shown in the figure, extending a distance W in the y-direction, we get

Rate of momentum in across surface at $x + \Delta x$, $LW\tau_{xz}\Big|_{x+x}$

Rate of momentum out across surface at $x = LW\tau_{xz}\Big|_{x}$

Rate of momentum in across surface at $(z = 0) = (W\Delta x v_z)\rho v_z\Big|_{z=0}$

Rate of momentum out across surface at $(z = L) = (W\Delta x v_z)\rho v_z\Big|_{z+\Delta z}$

Gravity force acting on fluid = $(LW\Delta x)\rho_g \sin\beta$

Since in - out = accumulation = 0, we get

$$LW\left(\tau_{xz}\Big|_{x+\Delta x} - \tau_{xz}\Big|_{x}\right) + (LW\Delta x)\rho_g \sin\beta = 0$$

Since v_z at $z = 0$ is the same as v_z at $z = L$ for each value of x.

Dividing throughout by $Lw\Delta x$ and taking the limit as $\Delta x \to 0$,

$$\frac{d}{dx}(\tau_{xz}) = -\rho_g \sin\beta$$

Integrating, we get, $\tau_{xz} = -(\rho_g \sin\beta)\, x + C_1$

B.C.: At $x = L, \delta$, $\tau_{xz} = 0$ $\therefore$ $C_1 = (\rho_g \sin\beta)\delta$

$$\therefore \quad \tau_{xz} = \rho_g \sin\beta \left[\delta - x\right]$$

Assuming the fluid to be Newtonian,

$$\tau_{xz} = -\mu \frac{dv_z}{dx} = \rho_g \sin\beta \left[\delta - x\right]$$

$$\therefore \quad v_z = \frac{\rho_g \sin\beta}{\mu}\left[\delta x - \frac{x^2}{2}\right] + C_2$$

B.C.: At $x = 0$, $v_z = 0$ $\therefore$ $C_2 = 0$

$$\therefore \quad v_z = \frac{\rho_g \sin\beta}{\mu}\left[\delta x - \frac{x^2}{2}\right]$$

This is the velocity profile. Its parabolic.

Maximum velocity as is obvious from the figure occurs at $x = \delta$

$$(v_z)_{max} = \frac{\rho_g \sin\beta}{\mu}\left[\delta^2 - \frac{\delta^2}{2}\right] = \frac{\rho_g \sin\beta\delta^2}{2\mu}$$

$$\text{Average velocity} = \langle v_z \rangle \frac{\int_0^W \int_0^\delta v_z dxdy}{\int_0^W \int_0^\delta dxdy}$$

$$= \frac{1}{\delta}\int_0^\delta v_z dx = \frac{1}{\delta}\int_0^\delta \frac{\rho_g \sin\beta}{\mu}\left(\delta x - \frac{x^2}{2}\right)dx$$

$$= \frac{\rho_g \sin\beta}{\delta\mu}\left[\frac{\delta x^2}{2} - \frac{x^3}{6}\right]_0^\delta = \frac{\rho_g \sin\beta}{\delta\mu}\left[\frac{1}{3}\delta^3\right] = \frac{\rho_g \sin\beta\delta^2}{3\mu}$$

$$\text{Volumetric flow rate} = \langle v_z \rangle A = \langle v_z \rangle \delta W = \frac{\rho_g \sin\beta\delta^3 W}{3\mu}$$

• PROBLEM 2-30

A Newtonian fluid flows through a slit made up of two parallel flat plates a distance 2B apart. Obtain the momentum and velocity profiles.

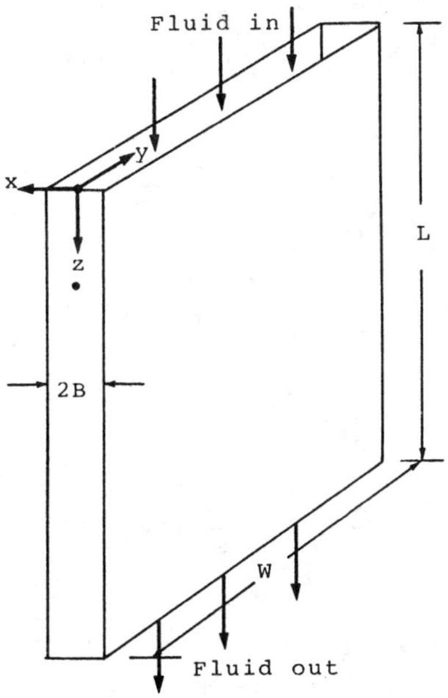

Solution: Consider a differential element of thickness x and width W and length L.

Making a momentum balance,

$$LW\tau_{xz}\Big|_{x=x} - LW\tau_{xz}\Big|_{x=x+\Delta x} + (\Delta xWv_z)(\rho v_z)\Big|_{z=0} -$$

$$(\Delta xWv_z)(\rho v_z)\Big|_{z=z+\Delta z} + L\Delta xW\rho_g + \Delta xWP_o - \Delta xWP_L = 0$$

Since v_z = the same at every x, this reduces to

$$LW\left(\tau_{xz}\Big|_{x=x} - \tau_{xz}\Big|_{x=x+\Delta x}\right) + \Delta xW\left[L\rho_g + P_o - P_L\right] = 0$$

Dividing throughout by $LW\Delta x$, and taking the limit as $\Delta x \to 0$, we get

$$\frac{d}{dx}(\tau_{xz}) = \left[\rho_g + \frac{P_o - P_L}{L}\right]$$

Defining $P = p - \rho_g L$, this reduces to

$$\frac{d}{dx}(\tau_{xz}) = \frac{P_o - P_L}{L}$$

or
$$\tau_{xz} = \left(\frac{P_o - P_L}{L}\right)x + C_1$$

B.C.: At $x = 0$, $\tau_{xz} = 0$ $\quad\therefore\quad C_1 = 0$

$$\therefore \quad \tau_{xz} = \left(\frac{P_o - P_L}{L}\right)x.$$

Since the fluid is Newtonian,

$$\tau_{xz} = -\mu\frac{dv_z}{dx} = \left(\frac{P_o - P_L}{L}\right)x$$

or
$$dv_z = -\frac{P_o - P_L}{\mu L}\,xdx$$

or
$$v_z = -\frac{P_o - P_L}{\mu L}\frac{x^2}{2} + C_1$$

B.C.: At $x = \pm B$, $v_z = 0$ $\quad\therefore\quad C_1 = +\frac{P_o - P_L}{\mu L}\frac{B^2}{2}$

$$\therefore \quad v_z = \frac{P_o - P_L}{2\mu L}\left[B^2 - x^2\right] = \frac{(P_o - P_L)B^2}{2\mu L}\left[1 - \frac{x}{B}^2\right]$$

UNSTEADY STATE MASS BALANCE

• PROBLEM 2-31

A well-stirred tank of 100 ft^3 volume initially contains 5 lbm/ft^3 of a substance A in a liquid form. An inlet stream with 15 lbm/ft^3 of A flows into the tank at a rate of 10 ft^3/min. If the reaction $A \rightarrow C$ is a constant volume, steady flow process, how does the concentration of A in the tank vary with time? Assume the generation of A in lbm/ft^3 sec. can be expressed as $\nu_A = -k\rho_A$ with $k = 0.1/min$.

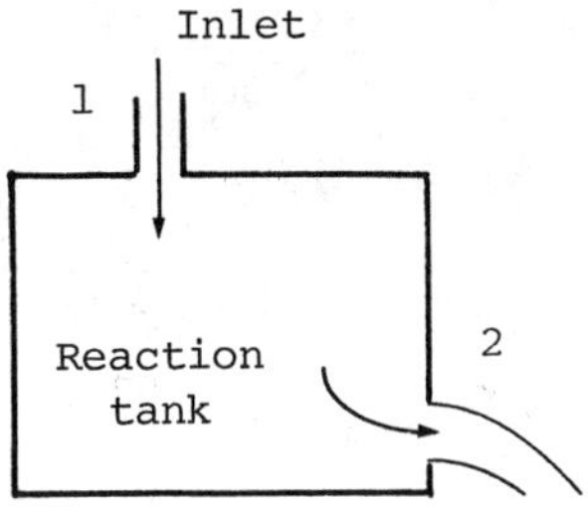

Solution: Applying the mass balance equation for A,

$$\int_{c.s.} d\dot{m}_A + \int_{c.v.} d\dot{m}_A = \int_V \nu_A \, dV$$

$$= -\int_V k\rho_A \, dV \qquad (1)$$

where,

$$\int_{c.s.} d\dot{m}_A = \int_{A_1} \rho_A(\vec{v}\cdot\vec{n})dA + \int_{A_2} \rho_A(\vec{v}\cdot\vec{n})dA$$

$$+ 0 \text{ (remaining surface)}$$

Assume that ρ_A is constant across the inlet and outlet cross section,

$$\int_{c.s.} d\dot{m}_A = -\rho_{A_1} q_1 + \rho_{A_2} q_2$$

$$= \rho_{A_2} q_2 - \rho_{A_1} q_1$$

$$= \rho_{A_2}(10) - (15)(10)$$

Also ρ_{A_2}, the outlet concentration will be the same as that in the tank ρ_A, or $\rho_{A_2} = \rho_A$ = const. for uniform mixing. Therefore:

$$\int_{c.s.} d\dot{m}_A = \rho_A (10) - 150 \qquad (2)$$

Now,

$$\int_{c.v} d\dot{m}_A = \frac{d}{dt}\int_V \rho_A \, dV$$

$$= \frac{d}{dt}\left(\rho_A \int_V dV\right) = \frac{d}{dt}(\rho_A v)$$

$$= \rho_A \frac{dV}{dt} + V\frac{d\rho_A}{dt}$$

But for steady flow,

$$\frac{dV}{dt} = 0$$

and
$$\int_{c.v.} d\dot{m}_A = V\frac{d\rho_A}{dt}$$

or
$$\int_{c.v.} d\dot{m}_A = 100 \frac{d\rho_A}{dt} \qquad (3)$$

Finally,

$$-\int_V k\rho_A \, dV = -(0.1)\rho_A(100)$$

or
$$-\int_V k\rho_A \, dV = -10\rho_A \qquad (4)$$

Substituting (2), (3) and (4) in (1) yields:

$$10\rho_A - 150 + 100 \frac{d\rho_A}{dt} = -10\rho_A$$

or
$$\int_5^{\rho_A} \frac{d\rho_A}{(15-2\rho_A)} = \int_o^t \frac{dt}{10}$$

Multiplying and dividing by -2,

$$-\tfrac{1}{2}\int_5^{\rho_A} \frac{(-2)d\rho_A}{(15 - 2\rho_A)} = \int_o^t \frac{dt}{10}$$

$$\text{or} \quad \ln\left(\frac{15 - 2\rho_A}{5}\right) = -\frac{2}{10}t$$

$$\text{or} \quad \rho_A = 2.5\,(3 - e^{-0.2t})$$

Note that as $t \to \infty$ $\rho_A \to 7.5$

• PROBLEM 2-32

Consider a thoroughly mixed vessel where a salt is dissolved in water. The volume of the fresh water initially in the tank is 100 lbm. The inlet conditions are, $\dot{m}_w$ = 150 lb/hr. and $\dot{m}_s$ = 30 lb/hr. The resulting solution leaves at a rate of 120 lb/hr. If the flow in and out remain constant, compute the outlet concentration after one hour.

Solution: Applying the mass balance equation for salt,

$$\dot{m}_{s1} = \dot{m}_{s2} + \frac{d\dot{m}_s}{dt}$$

where "s" stands for salt

$$\text{or} \quad \dot{m}_{s2} - \dot{m}_{s1} + \frac{d\dot{m}_s}{dt} = 0$$

Let,

$\dot{m}_w$ = mass flow rate of water

m = total mass (H_2O + salt)

$$\text{and} \quad r = \frac{\dot{m}_s}{m}$$

$$\text{or} \quad \dot{m}_s = rm$$

Therefore we can rewrite the equation:

$$(\dot{m}_2)(r) - \dot{m}_{s1} + \frac{d(mr)}{dt} = 0$$

$$\text{or} \quad (120)r - 30 + r\frac{dm}{dt} + m\frac{dr}{dt} = 0 \qquad (1)$$

Writing the total mass balance,

$$m_2 - m_1 + \frac{dm}{dt} = 0$$

or $$120 - (150 + 30) = -\frac{dm}{dt}$$

or $$\frac{dm}{dt} = 60 \text{ lb/hr.} \tag{2}$$

Integrating,

$$m = 60t + C$$

when $t = 0$

$$m = 100 = 0 + C$$

or $C = 100$

Therefore,

$$m = 60t + 100 \tag{3}$$

Substituting (2) and (3) in (1) yields:

$$120r - 30 + 60r + (60t + 100)\frac{dr}{dt} = 0$$

or $$\frac{dt}{(60t + 100)} = -\frac{dr}{(180r - 30)}$$

Integrating between 0 and t, and 0 to r:

$$r = \frac{1}{6}\left[1 - \left(\frac{10}{6t + 10}\right)^3\right]$$

For $t = 1$ hr.

$$r = 0.126$$

Note that as $t \to \infty$ $\quad r \to \frac{1}{6}$

• PROBLEM 2-33

Brine containing 20% salt by mass flows into a well-stirred tank at a rate of 20 kg/min. The tank initially contains 1000 kg of brine containing 10% salt by mass, and the resulting solution leaves the tank at a rate of 10 kg/min. Find an expression for the amount of salt in terms of time θ.

Solution: Writing the mass balance equation,

$$(1) \quad \int_A \rho(\vec{v}\cdot\vec{n})dA + \frac{d}{d\theta}\int_V \rho dV = 0 \qquad \text{for no chemical reaction}$$

The first term on the left-hand side is

$$\dot{m}_{out} - \dot{m}_{in} = 10 - 20$$

$$= -10 \text{ kg/min.}$$

That is,

$$\int_A \rho(\vec{v}\cdot\vec{n})dA = -10$$

Considering the second term on the left in equation (1),

$$\frac{d}{d\theta}\int_V \rho dV = \frac{d}{d\theta}\int_{1000}^{M} dM$$

$$= \frac{d}{d\theta}(M - 1000)$$

where M = total mass of brine.

Substituting the simplified expressions above into equation (1) yields:

$$-10 + \frac{d}{d\theta}(M - 1000) = 0$$

Separating the variables and integrating,

$$M = 10\theta + 1000 \text{ (kg)}$$

Writing a balance on the salt gives:

$$\int_A \rho(\vec{v}\cdot\vec{n})dA + \frac{\partial}{\partial\theta}\int_{c.v.} \rho\, dV = 0$$

where,

$$\int_A \rho(\vec{v}\cdot\vec{n})dA = (\dot{m}_S)_{out} - (\dot{m}_S)_{in}$$

Now, let S be the amount of salt in the tank at any time. The concentration by weight of salt is given by,

$$\frac{S}{M}$$

$$= \frac{S}{(1000 + 10\theta)} \frac{\text{kg salt}}{\text{kg brine}}$$

Therefore,

$$\int_A \rho(\vec{v}\cdot\vec{n})dA = (10)\left(\frac{S}{1000 + 10\theta}\right) - (0.2)(20)$$

The second expression is:

$$\frac{\partial}{\partial\theta}\int_V \rho dV = \frac{d}{d\theta}\int dS = \frac{dS}{d\theta} \text{ kg salt/min.}$$

The complete expression is,

$$\int_A \rho(\vec{v}\cdot\vec{n})dA + \frac{\partial}{\partial\theta}\int_V \rho dV = \frac{10S}{1000 + 10\theta} - 4 + \frac{dS}{d\theta} = 0$$

or $\frac{dS}{d\theta} + \frac{S}{100 + \theta} = 4$

or

$$S = \frac{2\theta(200 + \theta)}{(100 + \theta)} + \frac{C}{100 + \theta}$$

At $\theta = 0$, $S = 100$ gives, $C = 10000$

or $S = \frac{2\theta^2 + 400\theta + 10000}{100 + \theta}$

CHAPTER 3

APPLICATION OF EQUATION OF MOTION AND CONTINUITY

PIPE FLOW, JETS, NOZZLES, VISCOMETER AND MOVING PLATE

• PROBLEM 3-1

Using the continuity equation show that the flow defined by the velocity field

$$\vec{v} = (2t + 2x + 2y)\vec{i} + (t - y - z)\vec{j} + (t + x - z)\vec{k}$$

is possible.

Solution: The continuity equation for an incompressible fluid is,

$$\frac{\partial u}{\partial x} + \frac{\partial v}{\partial y} + \frac{\partial w}{\partial z} = 0 \quad (1)$$

The partial derivatives are calculated from,

$$u = 2t + 2x + 2y$$

or $$\frac{\partial u}{\partial x} = 2$$

$$v = t - y - z$$

or $$\frac{\partial v}{\partial y} = -1$$

and, $$w = t + x - z$$

or $$\frac{\partial w}{\partial z} = -1$$

Inserting the numerical values in (1),

$$2 - 1 - 1 = 0$$

Thus, the equation of continuity is verified and the given velocity field is possible.

• PROBLEM 3-2

Consider a 20 mm diameter manifold with seven identical orifices. Water enters the manifold with an average velocity of 0.15 m/sec. If the flow through the orifices are such that each orifice has 2% less flow through it than the one to its left, compute the flow rates through the orifices at the extreme ends. Take the diameter of the orifices as 0.1 cm.

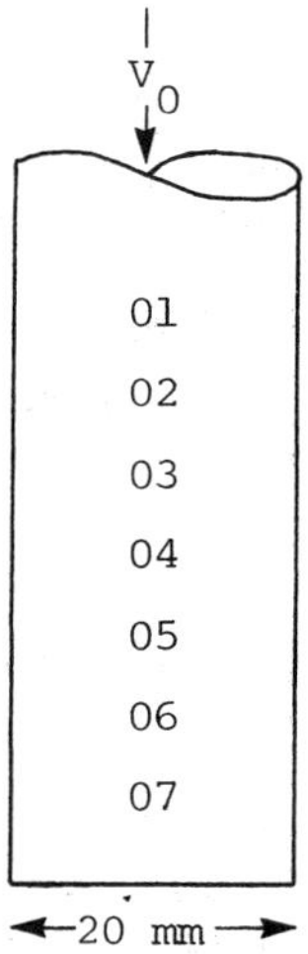

Solution: Writing the continuity equation,

$$A_0V_0 = A_1V_1 + A_2V_2 + ----A_7V_7$$

where,

$$A_1 = A_2 ------ = A_7$$

and

$$V_2 = 0.98V_1$$

$$V_3 = 0.98V_2 = (0.98)(0.98)V_1$$

or $$V_3 = (0.98)^2 V_1$$

$$\vdots$$

$$V_7 = (0.98)^6 V_1$$

Thus,

$$A_0V_0 = [1 + 0.98 + (0.98)^2 + (0.98)^3 --- + (0.98)^6]A_1V_1$$

or

$$(0.15)\left[\left(\frac{\pi}{4}\right)(0.02)^2\right] = \left[1 + 0.98 + ---(0.98)^6\right]\left[\left(\frac{\pi}{4}\right)(0.001)^2\right]V_1$$

Solving,

$$V_1 = 9.1 \text{ m/sec.}$$

and $\quad V_7 = (0.98)^6(9.1)$

or $\quad V_7 = 8.06$ m/sec.

• PROBLEM 3-3

Water flows at a uniform rate of 2 m/s from a 0.75 cm internal diameter pipe into a cylindrical tank of diameter 100 cm and height 60 cm. If the initial height of water in the tank is 10 cm., compute the time required to fill the tank to its top.

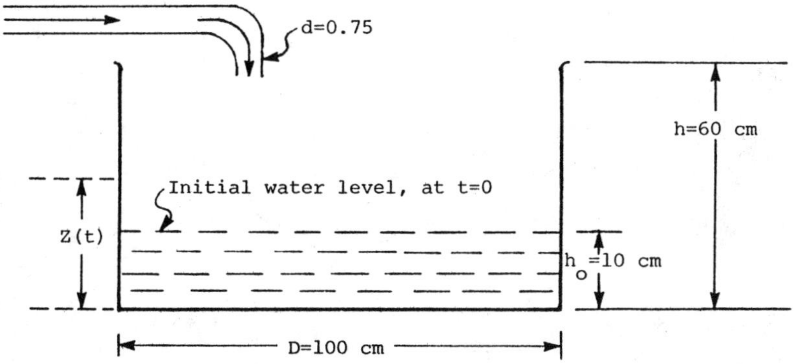

Application Of Continutiy To Tank Filling

Solution: Applying the continuity equation to the entire volume of the tank,

$$\int_S \rho(\vec{v}.\vec{n})dA + \frac{\partial}{\partial t}\int_V \rho\, dV = 0 \quad (1)$$

The first term on the left hand side of the equation is,

$$\int_S \rho(\vec{v} . \vec{n})\, dA = \dot{m}_{out} - \dot{m}_{in}$$
$$= 0 - \dot{m}_{in}$$

or $$\int_s \rho(\vec{v} \cdot \vec{n})\, dA = -\rho AV$$

$$= -\rho v \left(\frac{\pi}{4} d^2\right)$$

The second term is,

$$\frac{\partial}{\partial t}\int_v \rho dv = \rho\frac{\partial}{\partial t}\int_v dv$$

$$= \rho \frac{\partial}{\partial t}\int_v A[dz(t)]$$

$$= \rho \frac{\pi D^2}{4} \frac{\partial}{\partial t}\int_t [dz(t)]$$

or $$\frac{\partial}{\partial t}\int_v \rho dv = \rho\frac{\pi D^2}{4}\frac{dz}{dt}$$

Substituting back into the continuity equation,

$$-\rho v \frac{\pi d^2}{4} + \rho\frac{\pi D^2}{4}\frac{dz}{dt} = 0$$

or $$\frac{dz}{dt} = \left(\frac{d}{D}\right)^2 v$$

Integrating,

$$z = \left(\frac{d}{D}\right)^2 vt + \text{const}$$

Applying the boundary condition, at $t = 0$,

$$z = 10 \text{ cm} = \text{const.} = 0.1 \text{ m}$$

Thus $$z = \left(\frac{d}{D}\right)^2 vt + 0.1$$

Inserting numerical values,

$$0.6 = \left(\frac{0.75}{100}\right)^2 (2.0)t + 0.1$$

or $t = 4444.44$ sec.

or $t = 1.23$ hrs.

A jet of water flows from a 4 in. diameter nozzle such that the velocity at point 1, the top of the jet, which is at a distance of 50 ft. vertically above the nozzle outlet, is equal to 70 ft./sec. Determine the flow rate and the pressure at point 2 (as shown in the figure). Assume the flow is steady.

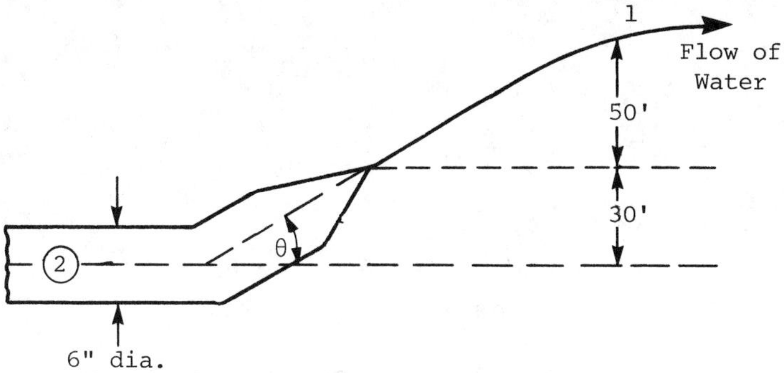

Water Flows from an Inclined Nozzle

Solution: The vertical distance "S" for constant acceleration (gravity) is given by,

$$S = u_0 t + \frac{1}{2} at^2$$

where $u_0 = 0$ initial velocity.

and $a = g$

or $50 = \frac{1}{2}(32.2)t^2$

or $t = 1.76$ sec.

Let the nozzle exit velocity be V, then,

$$V_H = \text{the horizontal component} = V\cos\theta = 70 \qquad (1)$$

and V_V = the vertical component $= V\sin\theta = gt = (32.2)(1.76)$

or $$\tan\theta = \frac{(32.2)(1.76)}{70}$$

or $\tan\theta = 0.8096$ gives,

$$\theta = 38.99°$$

Substituting in (1),

$$V = \frac{70}{\cos(38.99)} = 90.1 \text{ ft/sec}$$

The flow rate is,

$$Q = AV$$

$$= \frac{\pi}{4}\left(\frac{4}{12}\right)^2 (90.1)$$

or $$Q = 7.8 \text{ ft}^3/\text{sec.}$$

The discharge at 1 and 2 are equal for steady flow,

$$Q_1 = Q_2$$

or $$A_1V_1 = A_2V_2$$

or $$V_2 = \frac{A_1}{A_2} V_1$$

$$= \left(\frac{4}{6}\right)^2 90.1$$

or $$V_2 = 40.04 \text{ ft/sec.}$$

Writing the Bernoulli's equation between the points 2 and 1,

$$\frac{p_2}{\gamma} + \frac{V_2^{\,2}}{2g} + Z_2 = \frac{p_1}{\gamma} + \frac{V_1^2}{2g} + Z_1$$

Inserting numerical values,

$$\frac{p_2}{\gamma} + \frac{(40.04)^2}{2(32.2)} = 0 + \frac{(90.1)^2}{2(32.2)} + 80$$

or $$\frac{p_2}{\gamma} = 181.16 \text{ ft. of water.}$$

• PROBLEM 3-5

Water is filled to a distance x in a constant internal diameter steel pipe. A jet of water at a constant speed u_1 strikes against the filled portion. If the pipe wall shear τ, is equal to $\frac{\rho f u_2^2}{8}$, find expressions for the time rate of change of u_2 and x.

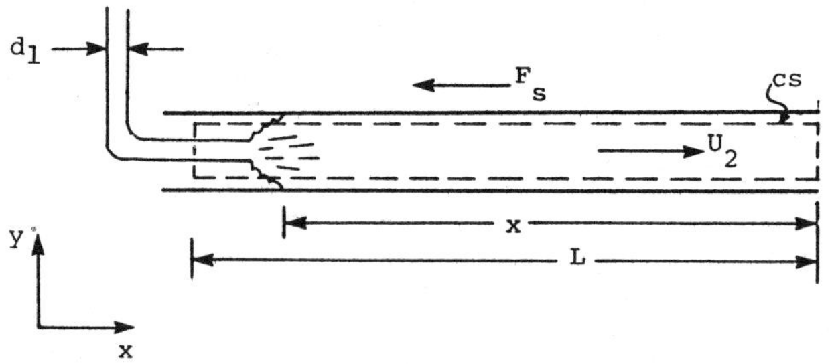

Solution: Consider a control volume with a length of L ft. The wall shear force or frictional force is,

$$F_s = -\tau A$$

where A = pipe wall shear area

$$= \pi D_2 x$$

substituting,

$$F_s = \frac{-\rho f u_2^2 \pi D_2 x}{8}$$

This is the only force acting in the x-direction.

Writing the momentum equation for the x-direction,

$$\Sigma F_x = \int_A \rho u_x (\vec{v} \cdot \vec{n}) dA + \frac{\partial}{\partial t} \int_V \rho u_x dv$$

or $$\frac{-\rho f u_2^2 \pi D_2 x}{8} = (\rho A_2 u_2^2 - \rho A_1 u_1^2) + \frac{\partial}{\partial t} \left[\rho A_2 u_2 x + \rho A_1 u_1 (L - x)\right]$$

After simplifying,

$$\frac{f u_2^2 \pi D_2 x}{8} + A_2 \left[x \frac{du_2}{dt} + u_2 \frac{dx}{dt}\right]$$

$$-A_1 u_1 \frac{dx}{dt} + A_2 u_2^2 - A_1 u_1^2 = 0$$

The term $\frac{dx}{dt}$ can be obtained from the continuity equation,

$$\int_{cs} \rho \vec{v} \cdot d\vec{A} + \frac{\partial}{\partial t} \int_{cv} \rho\, dv = 0$$

or $$\rho(u_2 A_2 - u_1 A_1) + \frac{\partial}{\partial t} [\rho A_2 x + \rho A_1 (L - x)] = 0$$

where L = constant

or $$\frac{dx}{dt} (A_2 - A_1) + u_2 A_2 - u_1 A_1 = 0$$

or $$\frac{dx}{dt} = \frac{A_1 u_1 - A_2 u_2}{A_2 - A_1} \tag{2}$$

Substituting in the momentum equation,

$$\frac{du_2}{dt} = \frac{1}{A_2 x} \left[A_1 u_1^2 - A_2 u_2^2 - \frac{f u_2^2 \pi D_2 x}{8} + \frac{(A_1 u_1 - A_2 u_2)^2}{A_2 - A_1}\right]$$

As an example, if

$$u_1 = 20 \text{ m/s}$$
$$d_1 = 0.06 \text{ m}$$
$$U_{20} = 0.5 \text{ m/sec at } t = 0$$
$$D_2 = 0.25 \text{ m}$$
$$x_0 = 100 \text{ m} \quad \text{at } t = 0$$
$$f = 0.02$$
$$\rho = 1000 \text{ kg/m}^3,$$

then,

$$\frac{dx}{dt} = 0.692 \text{ m/sec}$$

and

$$\frac{du_2}{dt} = 0.0496 \text{ m/sec}^2$$

• PROBLEM 3-6

A jet of water 7 in^2 in cross section is directed out at a speed of 40 ft/sec.towards a stationary inclined flat plate. If the angle of inclination is 35°, what is the total force on the plate from the fluid in contact with it? Solve again with the plate moving at a velocity of 10 ft/sec. in the direction of the jet.

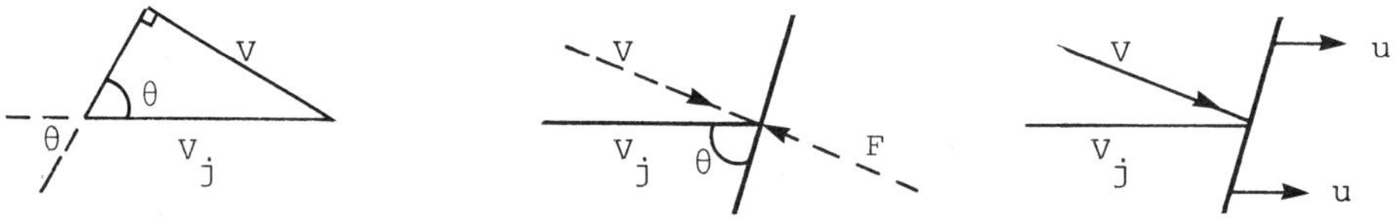

Velocity Triangle | Stationary Plate | Moving Plate

Solution: Writing the momentum equation for steady flow,

$$\Sigma F = \dot{m}(V_{out} - V_{in})$$

where

$$\dot{m} = \rho AV$$
$$= (62.4)\left(\frac{7}{144}\right) 40$$

or

$$\dot{m} = 121.3 \text{ lb/sec.}$$

V_{in} = velocity normal to the plate

$$= V_j \sin\theta$$

$$= (40) \sin 35°$$

$$= 22.94 \text{ ft/sec.}$$

and $V_{out} = 0$ [Because after striking there is no flow normal to the plate.]

Inserting numerical values,

$$F = 121.3(0 - 22.94)$$

$$= -2782.6 \text{ poundals}$$

$$= \frac{-2782.6}{32.2}$$

or $$F = -86.4 \text{ lb}_f$$

Thus, the force exerted by the plate is:

$$F = 86.4 \text{ lb}_f$$

For the moving plate the relative velocity is,

$$V_j^1 = V_j - u$$

$$= 40 - 10 = 30 \text{ ft/sec.}$$

$$\dot{m}^1 = \rho A V_j^1$$

$$= (62.4)\left(\frac{7}{144}\right)(30)$$

or $$\dot{m}^1 = 91 \text{ lb/sec.}$$

$$V_{in} = (30) \sin 35$$
$$= 17.21 \text{ ft/sec.}$$

$$V_{out} = 0$$

Thus,

$$F = (91)(17.21)$$

$$= 1565.66 \text{ poundals}$$

or $$F = 48.6 \text{ lb}_f$$

Water with a constant density 62.4 lb/ft^3 is flowing at a rate of 500 gpm through a horizontal pipe of internal diameter 2 in. at a pressure 1000 psi. It then passes to a section of the pipe of diameter 1 in. If the diameter is reduced gradually, calculate the pressure P_2. Assume frictionless flow.

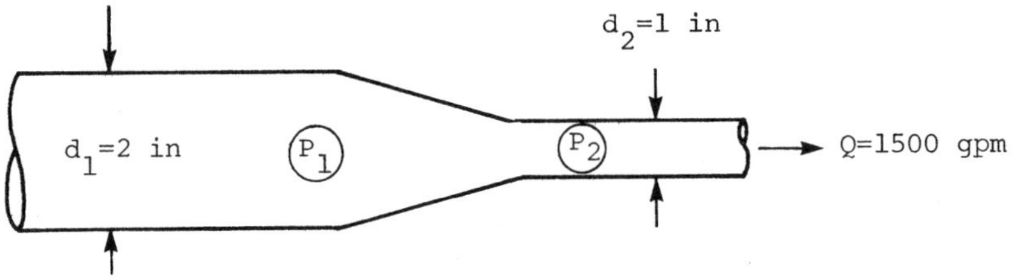

Solution: The velocities at sections (1) and (2), (from the continuity equation) are:

$$V_1 = \frac{Q}{A_1}$$

$$V_2 = \frac{Q}{A_2}$$

or $$V_1 = \frac{500 \times 2.228 \times 10^{-3}}{\frac{\pi}{4}\left(\frac{2}{12}\right)^2}$$

or $$V_1 = 51.1 \text{ ft/sec.}$$

and $$V_2 = \frac{500 \times 2.228 \times 10^{-3}}{\frac{\pi}{4}\left(\frac{1}{12}\right)^2}$$

or $$V_2 = 204.2 \text{ ft/sec.}$$

Applying the Bernoulli equation between (1) and (2)

$$\frac{P_1}{\gamma} + \frac{V_1^2}{2g} + Z_1 = \frac{P_2}{\gamma} + \frac{V_2^2}{2g} + Z_2$$

where $$Z_1 \approx Z_2$$

Substituting the known values,

$$\frac{1000 \cdot \times 144}{62.4} + \frac{(51.1)^2}{2(32.2)} = \frac{P_2 \times 144}{62.4} + \frac{(204.2)^2}{2(32.2)}$$

or $$P_2 = 737 \text{ psi}$$

A differential manometer is used to measure the pressure difference between two points in a pipe of varying cross-sectional area. If the manometric height is Δh, determine the velocities V_1 and V_2. Assume frictionless, steady, constant density flow.

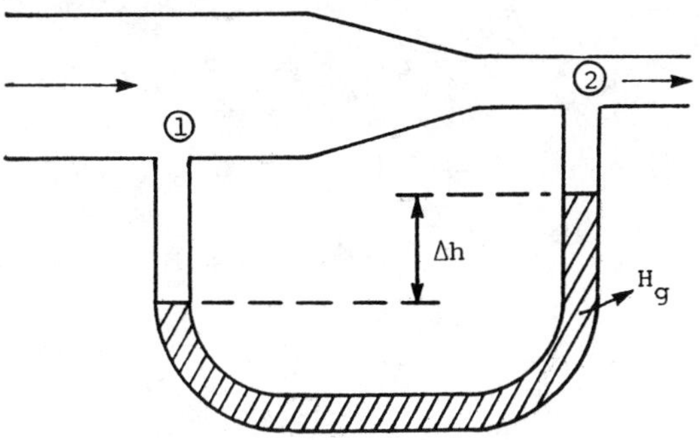

Flow Through a Pipe of Varying Cross-Sectional Area.

Solution: Writing the steady flow Bernoulli energy equation between (1) and (2)

$$\frac{P_1}{\gamma} + \frac{V_1^2}{2gc} + Z_1 = \frac{P_2}{\gamma} + \frac{V_2^2}{2gc} + Z_2$$

where,

$$Z_1 \approx Z_2$$

$$V_1 = \frac{V_2 A_2}{A_1} \quad \text{(from the continuity equation)}$$

$$\frac{P_1 - P_2}{\gamma} = \Delta h$$

Thus,

$$\frac{P_1 - P_2}{\gamma} + \left(\frac{V_2^2 A_2^2}{A_1^2}\right) \frac{1}{2g_c} = \frac{V_2^2}{2g_c}$$

or $$\frac{V_2^2}{2g_c}\left[\frac{A_2^2}{A_1^2} - 1\right] = \frac{-(P_1 - P_2)}{\gamma}$$

or $$\frac{V_2^2}{2g_c}\left[1 - \left(\frac{A_2}{A_1^2}\right)^2\right] = \frac{P_1 - P_2}{\gamma} = \Delta h$$

or $$V_2^2 = \frac{2g_c \ \Delta h}{1 - \left(\frac{A_2}{A_1}\right)^2}$$

or $$V_2 = \left[\frac{2g_c \;\Delta h}{1 - \left(\frac{A_2}{A_1}\right)^2} \right]$$

Now,

$$V_1 = \frac{V_2 A_2}{A_1}$$

or $$V_1 = \left[\frac{2g_c \;\Delta h}{1 - \left(\frac{A_2}{A_1}\right)^2} \left(\frac{A_2^2}{A_1^2} \right) \right]^{\frac{1}{2}}$$

or $$V_1 = \left[\frac{2g_c \;\Delta h}{\left(\frac{A_1}{A_2}\right)^2 - 1} \right]^{\frac{1}{2}}$$

• PROBLEM 3-9

If friction is neglected, what is the discharge rate of glycerine at 68°F (γ = 78 lbf/ft^3, μ = 3.12 × 10^{-5} lbf sec/ft^2) from the large tank shown in Figure (1)?

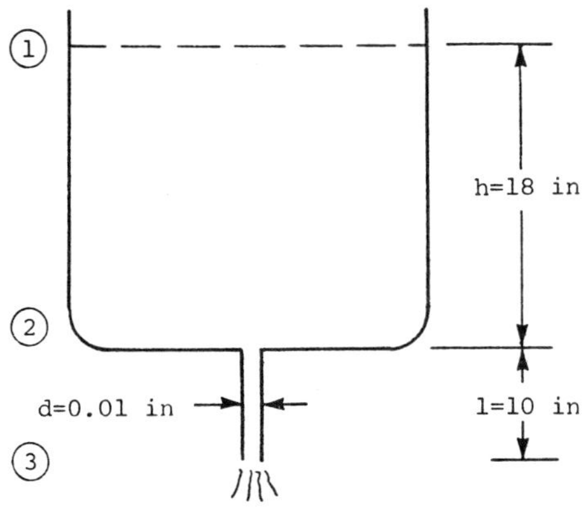

Flow Through a Capillary Tube.

Solution: The effect of the variation of h can be neglected in the case of large tanks and hence, the flow is at steady state.

The hydrostatic pressure at 2 is,

$$P_2 = P_1 + \gamma h$$

or $$P_2 - P_1 = \gamma h$$

But $$P_1 \approx P_3$$

Thus, $$P_2 - P_3 = \gamma h$$

Now,

$$P_2 - P_3 + \gamma h = \frac{32\mu\ VL}{D^2}$$

or $$P_2 - P_3 + \gamma h = \frac{128\mu\ QL}{\pi D^4}$$

which is Poiseuille's equation.

Since $P_3 = P_1 = Q = \frac{\pi\gamma D^4}{128\mu}\left(\frac{L + h}{L}\right)$

$$= \frac{\pi(78)\left(\frac{0.01}{12}\right)^4}{128 \times 3.12 \times 10^{-5}} \left(\frac{18 + 10}{10}\right)$$

$$= 8.285 \times 10^{-8}\ ft^3/sec$$

$$= 8.285 \times 10^{-8} \times 3600$$

$$= 2.98 \times 10^{-4}\ ft^3/hr$$

• PROBLEM 3-10

A jet of water with a velocity of V_j = 25 m/sec. and a diameter of d = 3 cm ejects from a stationary nozzle and strikes a flat plate. The plate is at 90° and is moving in the direction of the jet at a constant velocity of V_p = 17 m/sec. If the jet divides into two equal parts after inpinging (as shown in figure (1)) calculate the thrust produced for steady flow. Assume the weight of the jet and the plate are negligible.

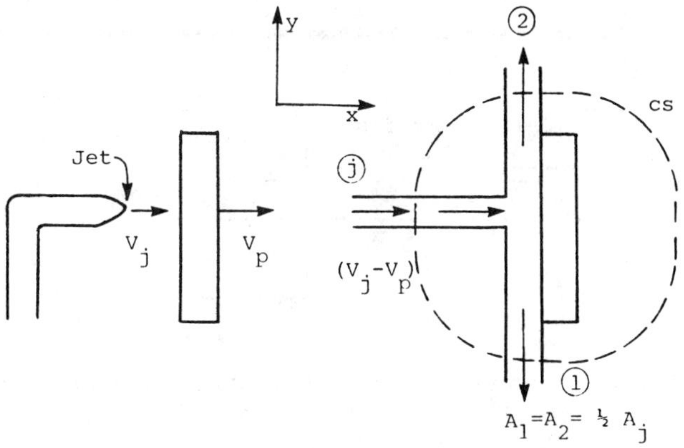

Momentum Principle on a Moving Plate

Solution: Consider a control surface fixed relative to the plate and thus moving at speed V_p. The resultant force in the Y-direction is zero due to the symmetry of jet deflection. Writing the steady-state momentum equation,

$$\Sigma F_x = \dot{m}_j u_j - \dot{m}_1 u_1 - \dot{m}_2 u_2$$

where, $u_j = V_j - V_p$

$u_1 = u_2 = 0$ (No flow in the X-direction after striking the plate)

Thus,

$$\Sigma F_x = \dot{m}_j (V_j - V_p) \quad (1)$$

where $\dot{m}_j = \rho A_j (V_j - V_p)$

Therefore:

$$\Sigma F_x = \rho A_j (V_j - V_p)(V_j - V_p)$$

$$= (1000)\left(\frac{\pi}{4}\right)\left(\frac{3}{100}\right)^2 (25 - 17)^2$$

or $\Sigma F_x = 45\text{N}$

or $R = -45\text{N}$

• PROBLEM 3-11

Using the continuity equation and the equation of motion, deduce expressions for the velocity distribution and the volumetric flow rate for the situation illustrated in the figure.

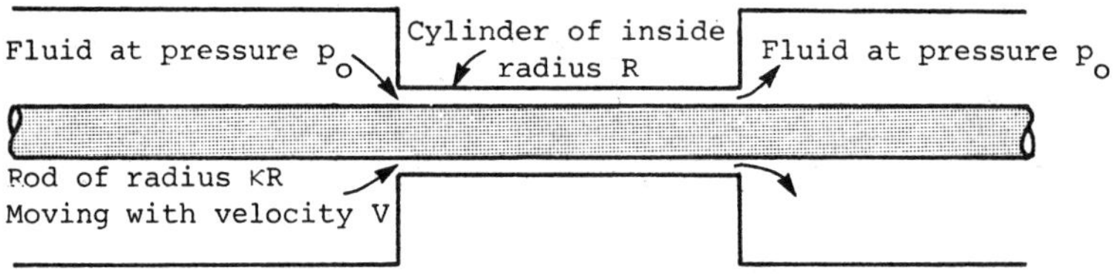

Solution: The continuity equation for the cylindrical coordinate system is

$$\frac{\partial \rho}{\partial t} + \frac{1}{r}\frac{\partial}{\partial r}(\rho_r v_r) + \frac{1}{r}\frac{\partial}{\partial \theta}(\rho v_\theta) + \frac{\partial}{\partial z}(\rho v_z) = 0$$

Assuming $v_r = 0 = v_z$, we get

$$\frac{\partial}{\partial z}(\rho v_z) = 0$$

Assuming incompressible flow $\frac{\partial v_z}{\partial t} = 0$ ∴ v_z is a function of only r.

The equation of motion reduces to, for the z-component,

$$0 = -\frac{\partial \not{\wp}}{\not{\partial} z}^{\,0} + \mu\left[\frac{1}{r}\frac{\partial}{\partial r}\left(r\frac{\partial v_z}{\partial r}\right)\right] + \rho g_z$$

Neglecting gravity effects, $\frac{\partial}{\partial r}\left(r\frac{\partial v_z}{\partial r}\right) = 0$

or $\frac{\partial v_z}{\partial r} = \frac{C_1}{r}$ and hence $v_z = C_1 \ln r + C_2$

B.C.: At $r = \kappa R$, $v_z = v$

$r = R \quad v_z = 0$

$$\therefore \quad C_1 \ln \kappa R + C_2 = v$$

$$C_1 \ln R + C_2 = 0$$

$$\therefore \quad C_1 \ln \kappa = v \qquad \therefore \quad C_1 = \frac{v}{\ln \kappa}$$

$$\therefore \quad C_2 = -\frac{v}{\ln \kappa} \cdot \ln R$$

$$\therefore \quad v_z = \frac{v}{\ln \kappa}\ln r - \frac{v}{\ln \kappa}\ln R$$

$$= \frac{v}{\ln \kappa}\ln r/R$$

$$\therefore \quad \left(\frac{v_z}{v}\right) = \frac{\ln r/R}{\ln \kappa}$$

volumetric flow rate $= Q \int_{\kappa R}^{R} v_z \, 2\pi r \, dr$

$$= \frac{2\pi v}{\ln \kappa}\int_{\kappa R}^{R} r \ln r/R \, dr = \frac{2\pi v}{\ln \kappa}\left\{\left[\frac{r^2}{2}\ln\left(\frac{r}{R}\right) - \frac{r^2}{4}\right]_{\kappa R}^{R}\right\}$$

$$= \frac{2\pi v}{2\ln \kappa}\left[-\frac{R^2}{2} - \kappa^2 R^2 \ln \kappa + \frac{\kappa^2 R^2}{2}\right]$$

$$Q = \frac{\pi v}{\ln\kappa}\left[\frac{\kappa^2 R^2}{2} - \frac{R^2}{2} - \kappa^2 R^2 \ln\kappa\right]$$

$$Q = \frac{\pi R^2 v}{2}\left[\frac{1}{\ln\kappa}(\kappa^2 - 1) - 2\kappa^2\right]$$

APPLICATION OF NAVIER-STOKES EQUATION TO VERTICAL, HORIZONTAL PARALLEL PLATES, PIPE FLOW AND ROTATING LIQUID BODY

• PROBLEM 3-12

Starting with the Navier-Stokes equation, obtain the velocity profile which describes the incompressible flow between two parallel vertical plates. The right plate is at rest, while the left is moving upward at a constant velocity, v_s (see figure (1)). Assume the flow is laminar.

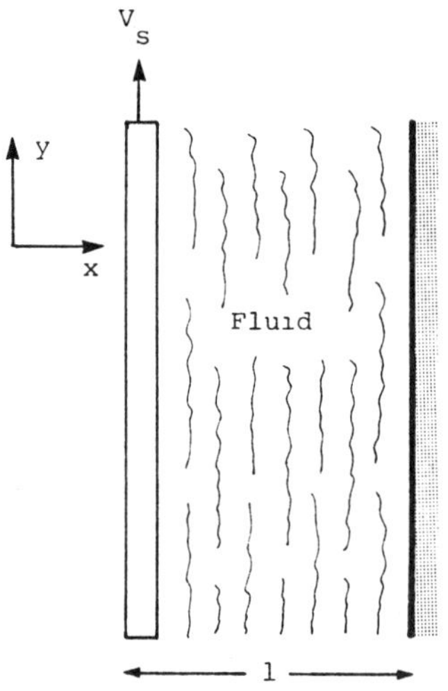

Incompressible fluid between two vertical surfaces.

Figure (1)

Solution: The Navier-Stokes equation in the y-direction is,

$$\rho\left(\frac{\partial v}{\partial t} + u\frac{\partial v}{\partial x} + v\frac{\partial v}{\partial y} + w\frac{\partial v}{\partial z}\right) = -\frac{\partial p}{\partial y} + \mu\left(\frac{\partial^2 v}{\partial x^2} + \frac{\partial^2 v}{\partial y^2} + \frac{\partial^2 v}{\partial z^2}\right) - \rho g \quad (1)$$

where,

$$\frac{\partial v}{\partial t} = 0 \text{ for steady flow.}$$

$$u = 0 = w$$

$$\frac{\partial v}{\partial y} = 0 = \frac{\partial v}{\partial z}$$

$$\frac{\partial p}{\partial y} = \frac{dp}{dy} = \text{const.}$$

Substituting in (1)

$$0 = -\frac{dp}{dy} + \mu \frac{d^2 v}{d^2 x} - \rho g$$

or $$\frac{d^2 v}{dx^2} = \frac{1}{\mu}\left[\rho g + \frac{dp}{dy}\right]$$

Integrating,

$$v = \frac{x^2}{2\mu}\left[\rho g + \frac{dp}{dy}\right] + Ax + B \qquad (2)$$

Applying the boundary conditions,

At $x = 0$, $v = v_s$ gives,

$$v_s = B$$

At $x = \ell$, $v = 0$ gives,

$$0 = \frac{\ell^2}{2\mu}\left(\rho g + \frac{dp}{dy}\right) + A\ell + v_s$$

or $$A = -\left[\frac{v_s}{\ell} + \frac{\ell}{2\mu}\left(\rho g + \frac{dp}{dy}\right)\right]$$

Substituting for A and B in equation (2) gives:

$$v = \underbrace{\frac{1}{2\mu}\left[\rho g + \frac{dp}{dy}\right](x^2 - \ell x)}_{ⓐ} + \underbrace{V_s\left(1 - \frac{x}{\ell}\right)}_{ⓑ}$$

Note: the term "a" is the equation for a symmetric parabola and the term "b" is the equation of a straight line with negative slope.

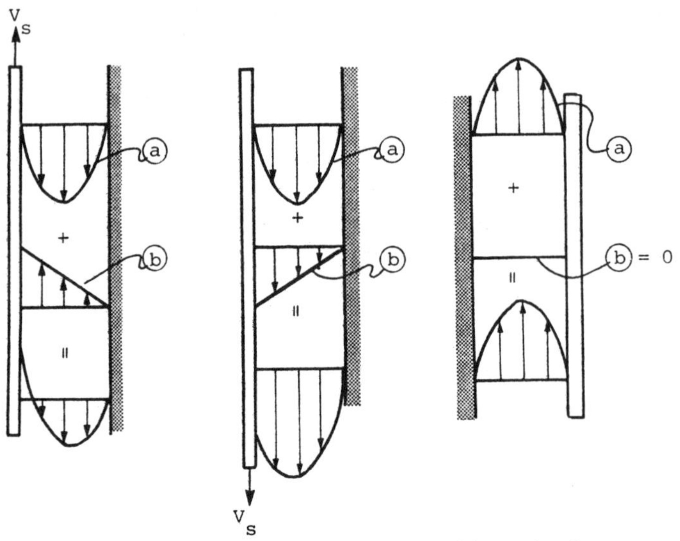

(A) Plate Moving Upward (B) Plate Moving Downward (C) Both Plates are at Rest

Figure(2)

The terms a and b may be individually evaluated for the three possible cases ($v_s > 0$, $v_s < 0$, $v_s = 0$) and then combined to produce the velocity profile as shown in figure (2).

• PROBLEM 3-13

Derive the differential equations of motion for a fluid of constant viscosity and density which is flowing over an impulsively accelerated, infinitely long horizontal flat plate. Assume that the flow is laminar.

Solution: Writing the Navier-Stokes equation for the x-direction,

$$\rho\left(\frac{\partial u}{\partial t} + u\frac{\partial u}{\partial x} + v\frac{\partial u}{\partial y} + w\frac{\partial u}{\partial z}\right) = -\frac{\partial p}{\partial x} + \mu\left(\frac{\partial^2 u}{\partial x^2} + \frac{\partial^2 u}{\partial y^2} + \frac{\partial^2 u}{\partial z^2}\right) + \rho B_x \quad (1)$$

Assuming the following,

1. No body forces in the x-direction; $B_x = 0$
2. One dimensional flow; $v = w = 0$
3. No change of flow variables in the z-direction;

$$\frac{\partial}{\partial z} = \frac{\partial^2}{\partial z^2} = 0$$

Then,

$$\frac{\partial}{\partial x} = \frac{\partial^2}{\partial x^2} = 0 \quad \text{for the long plate in the x-direction.}$$

Substituting these conditions into equation (1) yields:

$$\rho \frac{\partial u}{\partial t} = \mu \frac{\partial^2 u}{\partial y^2}$$

Similarly for the y-direction, the y component of the Navier-Stokes equation becomes,

$$\frac{\partial p}{\partial y} = \rho B_y$$

$$= -\rho g$$

or $$\frac{\partial p}{\partial y} = -\rho g$$

and the z-direction gives,

$$0 = \rho B_z$$

Thus, there is no body force component in the z-direction.

• PROBLEM 3-14

Consider a fluid with constant viscosity and density which is flowing between two fixed parallel plates. The velocity profile is given by $u = c(bz - z^2)$, where b is the distance between the plates and c is a constant. If the pressure at the point (0,0,0) is p_0, find the pressure distribution at any point in the flow region. Assume that v = w = 0.

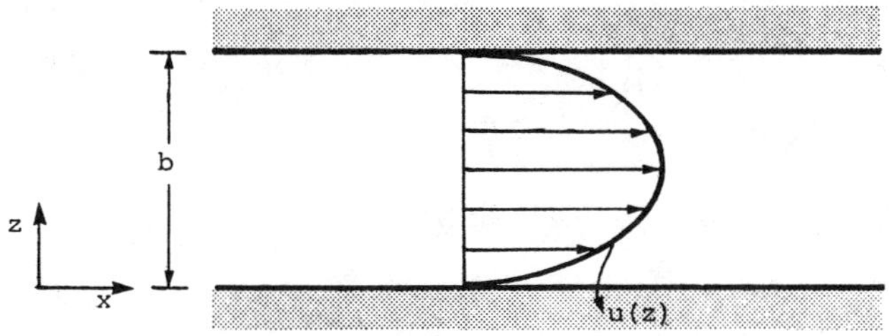

Laminar Flow Between Two Parallel Plates.

Solution: Writing the Naiver-Stokes equation for steady flow in the x-direction,

$$\rho\left(u\frac{\partial u}{\partial x} + v\frac{\partial u}{\partial y} + w\frac{\partial u}{\partial z}\right) = -\frac{\partial p}{\partial x} + \mu\left(\frac{\partial^2 u}{\partial x^2} + \frac{\partial^2 u}{\partial y^2} + \frac{\partial^2 u}{\partial z^2}\right) + \rho g_x \quad (1)$$

where,

$$\rho g_x = 0 \quad \text{(no body forces in x-direction)}$$

$$v = w = 0 \quad \text{(given)}$$

$$\frac{\partial u}{\partial x} = 0 = \frac{\partial u}{\partial y} \quad \text{(given)}$$

and

$$\frac{\partial^2 u}{\partial z^2} = -2c$$

Substituting in equation (1)

$$\frac{\partial p}{\partial x} = -2\mu c \qquad (2)$$

The y and z components of the Navier-Stokes equation are:

$$\frac{\partial p}{\partial y} = 0 \qquad (3)$$

Thus p is not a function of y.

$$\frac{\partial p}{\partial z} = -\rho g \qquad (4)$$

Integrating equation (4) with respect to z,

$$p = -\rho g z + f(x) \qquad (5)$$

To find f(x), differentiate (5) with respect to x,

$$\frac{\partial p}{\partial x} = f'(x) \qquad (6)$$

Comparing to (6) with (2) gives:

$$f'(x) = -2\mu c$$

or

$$f(x) = -2\mu c x + c' \qquad (7)$$

Substituting (7) into (5) yields:

$$p(x,z) = c' - 2\mu c x - \rho g z$$

Substituting $p = p_0$ at (0,0,0) gives

$$c' = p_0$$

and the final result is:

$$p(x,z) = p_0 - 2\mu c x - \rho g z$$

Using the Navier-Stokes equation, determine the velocity profile for the incompressible steady flow of water between two parallel plates at rest. Assume one dimensional laminar flow with constant viscosity.

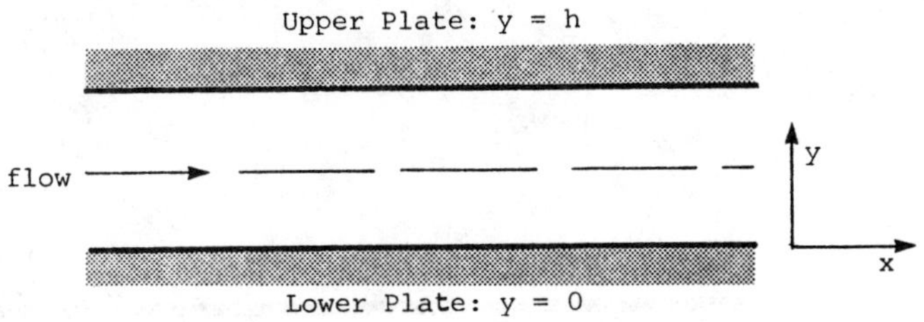

Flow between two parallel plates of infinite width.

Solution: For one dimensional flow,

$$v = w = 0$$

Thus, $\frac{\partial u}{\partial x} = 0$ (from the continuity equation)

Also, $\frac{\partial u}{\partial t} = 0$ for steady flow
(no body forces in the x-direction)

Substituting the above in the x-direction of the Naiver-Stokes equation and simplifying,

$$\frac{\partial p}{\partial x} = \mu \frac{\partial^2 u}{\partial y^2} \tag{1}$$

Similarly for the y and z direcitons:

$$\frac{\partial p}{\partial y} = -\rho g$$

and $\frac{\partial p}{\partial z} = 0$

For small "h" the variation of p in the y-direction will be negligible and hence,

$$\frac{\partial p}{\partial y} = 0$$

Thus, $\frac{\partial p}{\partial x} = \frac{dp}{dx} = \text{const.}$ (because $u \neq f(x)$)

Substituting in (1) and integrating twice,

$$u = \frac{1}{2\mu}\left(\frac{dp}{dx}\right) y^2 + c_1 y + c_2$$

At $y = 0 \quad u = 0$ gives, $c_2 = 0$

At $y = h \quad u = 0$ gives,

$$c_1 = -\frac{1}{2\mu}\left(\frac{dp}{dx}\right)\frac{h^2}{h} = -\frac{1}{2\mu}\left(\frac{dp}{dx}\right)h$$

Substituting,

$$u = \frac{1}{2\mu}\left(\frac{dp}{dx}\right)(y^2 - hy)$$

• PROBLEM 3-16

> A liquid ($\mu = 6.98 \times 10^{-3}$ lb-s/ft^2) is flowing at a rate of 0.2 ft^3/sec/ft. of width of the plate between two flat parallel plates. If the distance between the plates is 1 in., calculate: 1) the maximum velocity 2) the shear stress at the boundaries and 3) the pressure drop in 10 ft. of length. Assume laminar flow.

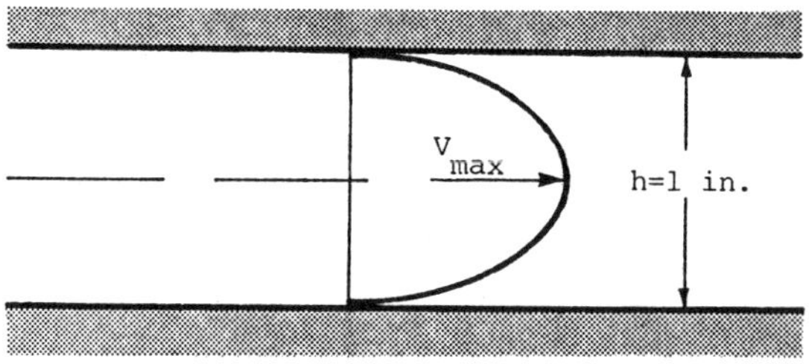

Fully Developed Laminar Flow.

Solution: The maximum velocity is,

$$V_{max} = 1.5\,(V_{av})$$

$$= 1.5\left(\frac{Q}{h}\right)$$

$$= 1.5\left(\frac{0.2}{1/12}\right)$$

or $$V_{max} = 3.6 \text{ ft/sec.}$$

The pressure difference between two points at a distance of L is,

$$p_1 - p_2 = \frac{12\mu V L}{h^2} \tag{1}$$

where V = average velocity

$$= \frac{Q}{h}$$

$$= \frac{0.2}{1/12} = 2.4 \text{ ft/sec.}$$

Inserting numerical values in equation (1) gives;

$$p_1 - p_2 = \frac{12(6.98 \times 10^{-3})(2.4)10}{(1/12)^2}$$

$$= 289.5 \text{ lbf/ft}^2$$

The pressure gradient is

$$\frac{dp}{dx} = \frac{p_1 - p_2}{L}$$

$$= \frac{289.5}{10} = 28.95 \text{ psf/ft}$$

Finally, the shear stress at the boundary is:

$$\tau = -\frac{h}{2}\frac{dp}{dx}$$

$$\tau = \frac{1}{2(12)}(28.95)$$

or $\tau = 1.21 \text{ lbf/ft}^2$

• PROBLEM 3-17

Consider a binary flowing stream which consists of a water phase and an oil phase that is moving between two parallel plates. The flow rates at the inlet and the absolute viscosities of oil and water are 0.1 ft^3/sec/ft. and 0.1 ft^3/sec/ft. of width of the plate and 100 and 0.89 centipoises, respectively. If the distance between the plates is 2 in., find 1) the elevation of the oil-water interface, 2) the pressure gradient, and 3) the velocity distribution. Assume the flow is steady, uniform and laminar.

Solution: For each phase,

water: $$\tau_{yx,1} = \mu_1 \frac{du_{x,1}}{dy}$$

oil: $$\tau_{yx,2} = \mu_2 \frac{du_{x,2}}{dy}$$

In general $$\tau_{yx} = \mu \frac{du_x}{dy} \qquad (1)$$

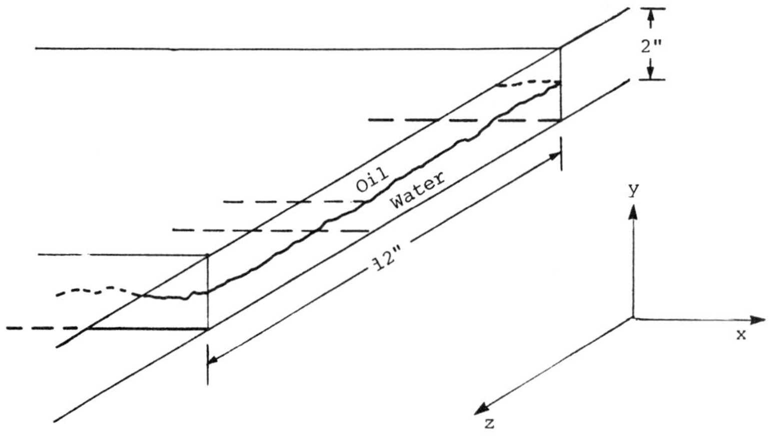

Fig. 1 Laminar Flow of Water and Oil between Two Parallel Plates.

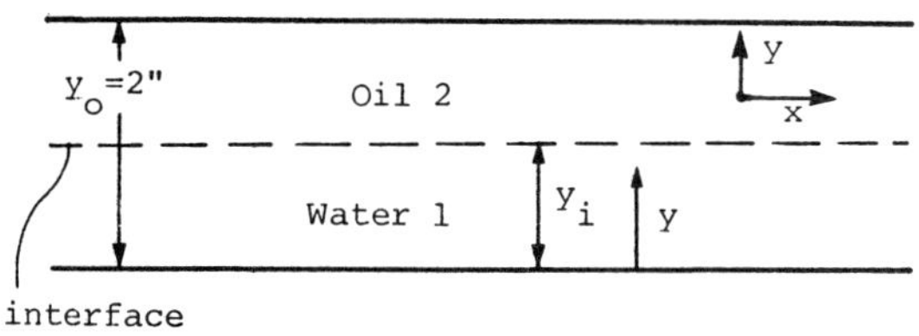

Fig. 2 Two Dimensional Flow of Oil and Water.

Consider a differential element of the fluid with unit width. The net shearing stress on the element is:

$$d\tau_{yx} = \left(\tau_{yx} + \frac{d\tau_{yx}}{dy}\,dy\right) - \tau_{yx}$$

$$= \frac{d\tau_{yx}}{dy}\,dy$$

Thus, the net shearing force is,

$$dF_s = \left(\frac{d\tau_{yx}}{dy}\,dy\right)(dx)$$

Similarly, the net pressure is given by,

$$dp = \left(P + \frac{dP}{dx}\,dx\right) - P$$

$$= \frac{dP}{dx}\,dx$$

and the pressure force is,

$$dF_P = \left(\frac{dP}{dx}\,dx\right)(dy)$$

For steady uniform flow,

$$dF_P = dF_S$$

or $$\frac{dP}{dx}\,dx\,dy = \frac{d\tau_{yx}}{dy}\,dx\,dy$$

or $$\frac{d\tau_{yx}}{dy} = \frac{dP}{dx}$$

Neglecting any solubility or dispersion of one phase in the other and assuming isothermal conditions, integrating the above equation gives,

$$\tau_{yx} = \frac{dP}{dx}\,y + c$$

At $y = y_i$ (interface)

$\tau_{yx} = \tau_{yx,i}$ gives,

$$c = \tau_{yx,i} - \frac{dP}{dx}\,y_i$$

Substituting,

$$\tau_{yx} = \left(\tau_{yx}\right)_i + \frac{dP}{dx}\,(y - y_i)$$

Comparing with equation (1),

$$\left(\tau_{yx}\right)_i + \frac{dP}{dx}\,(y - y_i) = \mu\,\frac{du_x}{dy}$$

where $\frac{dP}{dx}$ is not a function of y.

Integrating the above equation with respect to y,

$$y\left(\tau_{yx}\right) + \frac{dP}{dx}\left(\frac{y^2}{2} - y\,y_i\right) = \mu u_x + c_1 \qquad (2)$$

First considering the oil phase,

at $y = y_0$ (top surface)

$u_x = 0$

Also $\mu = \mu_2$ (oil)

Substituting the boundary condition and rewriting,

$$\left(\tau_{yx}\right)_i\,(y - y_0) + \frac{dP}{dx}\left(\frac{y^2}{2} - \frac{y_0^2}{2} + y_i y_0 - y\,y_i\right) = \mu_2 u_x$$

or $$u_x = \frac{1}{\mu_2}\left[\left(\tau_{yx}\right)_i(y - y_0) + \frac{dP}{dx}\left(\frac{y^2}{2} - \frac{y_0^2}{2} + y_i y_0 - y\,y_i\right)\right] \qquad (3)$$

The volume flow rate is,

$$\dot{Q}_2 = \int_{y_i}^{y_0} u_x dy$$

or $$\dot{Q}_2 = \left(\tau_{yx}\right)_i \frac{(y_i - y_0)^2}{2} - \frac{dP}{dx}\frac{(y_0 - y_1)^3}{3}$$

Now similarly for the water phase, applying the boundary condition at $y = 0$, $u_x = 0$ to equation (2) gives, $c_1 = 0$. Thus, equation (2) becomes,

$$y\left(\tau_{yx}\right)_i + \frac{dP}{dx}\left(\frac{y^2}{2} - y\, y_i\right) = \mu_1 u_x$$

or $$u_x = \frac{1}{\mu}\; y\left[\left(\tau_{yx}\right)_i + \frac{dP}{dx}\left(\frac{y^2}{2} - y\, y_i\right)\right] \tag{5}$$

Likewise,

$$\dot{Q}_1 = \int_0^{y_i} u_x dy = \frac{1}{\mu_1}\left[\frac{\left(\tau_{yx}\right)_i y_i^2}{2} - \frac{dP}{dx}\frac{y_i^3}{3}\right] \tag{6}$$

At the interface,

$$u_x = u_{i,1} = u_{i,2}$$

Thus, equations (3) and (5) become equal. Combining and rearranging,

$$\frac{\mu_2}{\mu_1}\left[\left(\tau_{yx}\right)_i y_i - \frac{y_i^2}{2}\frac{dP}{dx}\right] = \left(\tau_{yx}\right)_i \left(y_i - y_0\right) - \frac{dP}{dx}\frac{\left(y_i - y_0\right)^2}{2} \tag{7}$$

Solving equations (4), (6) and (7) simultaneously for y_i, $\frac{dP}{dx}$ and $\tau_{yx\,i}$,

$$\left(\tau_{yx}\right)_i = -\,0.00460 \text{ lb/ft}^2$$

$$y_i = 0.0404 \text{ ft}$$

$$\frac{dP}{dx} = -\,0.256 \text{ lb/ft}^3$$

From equations (3) and (5), the velocity distribution in water and oil,

$$u_{x,1} = 307y - 6.840y^2,\ 0 \le y \le 0.0404 \text{ ft}$$

$$u_{x,2} = 1.24 + 2.74y - 61.2y^2\ 0.040 \le y \le 0.1667 \text{ ft}$$

• PROBLEM 3-18

An incompressible viscous fluid undergoes steady, laminar flow through a circular pipe of radius R. Derive the equation relating the velocity at any point to the maximum velocity. Assume one dimensional flow.

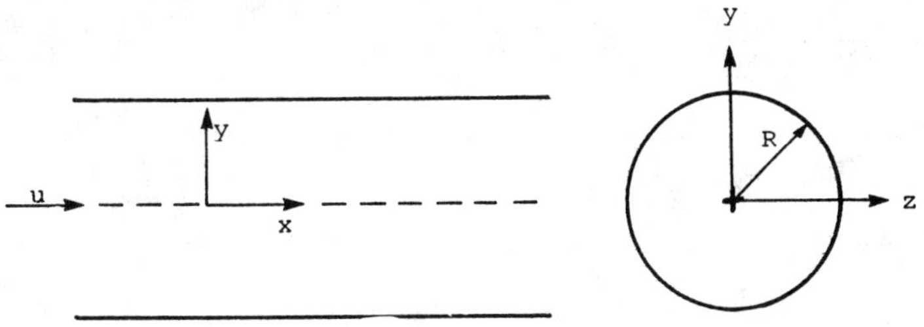

Laminar Flow in a Circular Pipe.

Solution: Writing the Naiver-Stokes equation in cylindrical coordinates for steady, laminar, constant property, with fully developed flow within a circular pipe,

$$\frac{1}{r}\frac{\partial}{\partial r}\left(r\frac{\partial u}{\partial r}\right) = \frac{1}{\mu}\frac{\partial p}{\partial x} \qquad (1)$$

Since the flow is fully-developed,

$$\frac{\partial u}{\partial x} = 0$$

Thus, u is a function of r alone. In addition, since p is not a function of r and the left-hand side of equation (1) cannot depend on x (since u depends upon r, but not x),

$$\frac{\partial p}{\partial x} = \frac{dp}{dx} = \text{const.}$$

Thus, equation (1) becomes,

$$\frac{1}{r}\frac{d}{dr}\left(r\frac{du}{dr}\right) = \frac{1}{\mu}\frac{dp}{dx}$$

Integrating twice,

$$u = \frac{1}{4\mu}\frac{dp}{dx}(r^2) + c_1 r + c_2$$

At $r = \pm R$ $u = 0$, which gives,

$$0 = \frac{1}{4\mu}\left(\frac{dp}{dx}\right)R^2 + c_1 R + c_2$$

$$0 = \frac{1}{4\mu}\left(\frac{dp}{dx}\right)R^2 - c_1 R + c_2$$

Solving,

$$c_1 = 0$$

$$c_2 = -\frac{1}{4\mu}\left(\frac{dp}{dx}\right) R^2$$

Substituting,

$$u = \frac{1}{4\mu}\left(\frac{dp}{dx}\right)(r^2 - R^2) \qquad (2)$$

Now, the maximum velocity occurs at r = 0,

$$u_{max} = U = -\frac{R^2}{4\mu}\left(\frac{dp}{dx}\right)$$

Substituting in (2) and simplifying,

$$u = U\left[1 - \left(\frac{r}{R}\right)^2\right]$$

• PROBLEM 3-19

In idealized laminar flow, as defined for the circular pipe shown in fig. (1), the temperature is constant. Velocities in the z-direction are not zero, the viscosity and density are functions of temperature only, the potential Ω is zero and the flow is at steady state. Also, the pressure drop per unit length of conduit is taken to be a constant. Determine the equations of motion for idealized laminar flow.

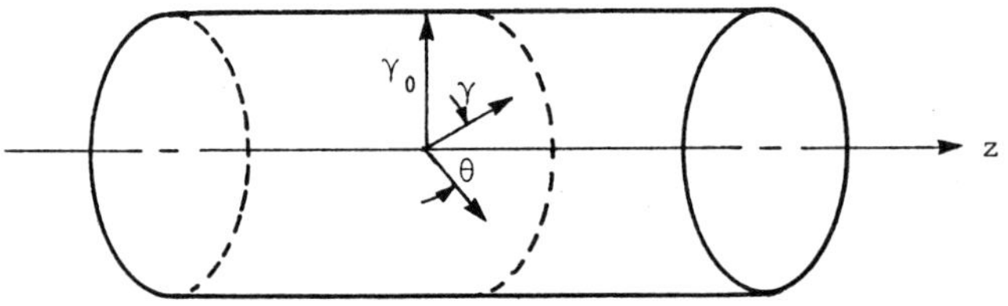

Coordinate System for Flow in Circular Pipe.

Solution: The continuity equation in cylindrical coordinates is,

$$\left(\frac{\partial \rho}{\partial t}\right)_{r,\theta,z} + \frac{1}{r}\left\{\left(\frac{\partial r\rho v_x}{\partial r}\right)_{\theta,z,t} + \left(\frac{\partial \rho v_\theta}{\partial \theta}\right)_{r,z,t} + \left(\frac{\partial r\rho v_z}{\partial z}\right)_{r,\theta,t}\right\} = 0$$

where r is the radial direction, θ the azimuth, and z the axial direction. The designations v_r, v_θ and v_z denote the components of the velocity in the radial, azimuthal, and axial direction, respectively. For idealized flow, the above equation becomes,

$$\frac{\partial \rho}{\partial t} + v_r \frac{\partial \rho}{\partial r} + v_\theta \frac{\partial \rho}{\partial \theta} + v_z \frac{\partial \rho}{\partial z} + \frac{\rho}{r}\left[\frac{\partial r v_r}{\partial r} + \frac{\partial v_\theta}{\partial \theta} + \frac{\partial r v_z}{\partial z}\right] = 0 \qquad (1)$$

Since ρ is a constant,

$$\frac{\partial r v_r}{\partial r} + \frac{\partial v_\theta}{\partial \theta} + \frac{\partial r v_z}{\partial z} = 0 \qquad (2)$$

There are no radial or azimuthal components of velocity. Therefore:

$$\frac{\partial v_z}{\partial z} = 0 \qquad (3)$$

Since the potential is zero, the following equation,

$$\rho \frac{dv_r}{dt} = \rho\phi_r - \frac{\partial p}{\partial r} + \frac{1}{3}\frac{\partial}{\partial r}\left[\frac{\mu}{r}\left(\frac{\partial r v_r}{\partial r} + \frac{\partial v_\theta}{\partial \theta} + \frac{\partial r v_z}{\partial z}\right)\right]$$
$$+\left[\frac{1}{r}\quad \frac{\partial}{\partial r}\left(\mu r \frac{\partial v_r}{\partial r}\right) + \frac{1}{r}\frac{\partial}{\partial \theta}\left(\mu \frac{\partial v_r}{\partial \theta}\right) + r\frac{\partial}{\partial z}\left(\mu \frac{\partial v_r}{\partial z}\right)\right]$$
$$- \frac{1}{r^2}\left[\mu v_r + 2\mu \frac{\partial v_\theta}{\partial \theta}\right]$$

where μ = absolute viscosity, becomes

$$\frac{\partial p}{\partial r} = 0 \qquad (4)$$

when Eqs. (2) and (3) are used along with the fact that $v_r = 0$.

Similarly, the following equation

$$\rho \frac{\partial v_\theta}{\partial t} = \rho\phi_\theta - \frac{1}{r}\frac{\partial p}{\partial \theta} + \frac{1}{3r}\frac{\partial}{\partial \theta}\left[\frac{\mu}{r}\left(\frac{\partial r v_r}{\partial r} + \frac{\partial v_\theta}{\partial \theta} + \frac{\partial r v_z}{\partial z}\right)\right]$$
$$+ \frac{1}{r}\left[\frac{\partial}{\partial r}\left(\mu r \frac{\partial v_\theta}{\partial r}\right) + \frac{1}{r}\frac{\partial}{\partial \theta}\left(\mu \frac{\partial v_\theta}{\partial \theta}\right) + r\frac{\partial}{\partial z}\left(\mu \frac{\partial v_z}{\partial z}\right)\right]$$
$$- \frac{1}{r^2}\left[\mu v_\theta - 2\mu \frac{\partial v_r}{\partial \theta}\right]$$

becomes

$$\frac{\partial p}{\partial \theta} = 0 \qquad (6)$$

since

$$v_\theta = 0 \qquad (7)$$

Since steady-state conditions are assumed, the following equations,

$$\rho \frac{\partial v_z}{\partial t} = \rho \phi_z - \frac{\partial p}{\partial z} + \frac{1}{3}\frac{\partial}{\partial z}\left[\frac{\mu}{r}\left(\frac{\partial r v_r}{\partial r} + \frac{\partial v_\theta}{\partial \theta} + \frac{\partial r v_z}{\partial z}\right)\right]$$

$$+ \frac{1}{r}\left[\frac{\partial}{\partial r}\left(\mu r \frac{\partial v_z}{\partial r}\right) + \frac{1}{r}\frac{\partial}{\partial \theta}\left(\mu \frac{\partial v_z}{\partial \theta}\right) + r\frac{\partial}{\partial z}\left(\mu \frac{\partial v_z}{\partial z}\right)\right]$$

and

$$\frac{\partial v_z}{\partial t} = \frac{\partial v_z}{\partial t} + v_r \frac{\partial v_z}{\partial r} + \frac{v_\theta}{r}\frac{\partial v_z}{\partial \theta} + v_z \frac{\partial v_z}{\partial z}$$

gives:

$$-\frac{\partial p}{\partial z} + \frac{1}{r}\frac{\partial}{\partial r}\left(\mu r \frac{\partial v_z}{\partial r}\right) = 0 \qquad (8)$$

The fact that v_r and v_θ are zero and the symmetry of the flow conditions gives:

$$\frac{\partial v_z}{\partial \theta} = 0 \qquad (9)$$

Thus, for idealized laminar flow in a pipe the pressure gradient may be expressed in terms of the viscous forces in the following manner:

$$\frac{\partial p}{\partial z} = \frac{1}{r}\frac{\partial}{\partial r}\left(\mu r \frac{\partial v_z}{\partial r}\right) \qquad (10)$$

Equation (10) may be solved for the idealized flow by integrating once with respect to r so that

$$\frac{r^2}{2}\frac{\partial p}{\partial z} = \mu r \frac{\partial v_z}{\partial r} + A(z) \qquad (11)$$

where A(z) is an arbitrary function of z and corresponds to a constant of integration in ordinary integration. Since the flow is symmetrical about the axis,

$$\frac{\partial v_z}{\partial r} = 0 \qquad (12)$$

at $r = 0$

so that $A(z) = 0$

In the idealized flow T has been taken as a constant and

$$\left(\frac{\partial \mu}{\partial p}\right)_T = 0$$

and thus μ is also a constant. Therefore, a second radial integration may be made to give

$$\frac{r^2}{4}\frac{dp}{dz} = \mu v_z + B(z) \tag{13}$$

The velocity v_z is zero when

$$r = r_0$$

and so

$$B(z) = \frac{r_0^2}{4}\frac{dp}{dz}$$

Thus finally, (14)

$$v_z = \frac{dp}{dz}\frac{(r^2 - r_0^2)}{4\mu}$$

• PROBLEM 3-20

> Consider an incompressible liquid in a cylindrical vessel which has been undergoing constant angular motion for a time interval which is of such a duration that the liquid has assumed a fixed orientation in the vessel. Show that at steady-state, the free surface forms a paraboloidal surface given by $Z - Z_0 = \left(\frac{\omega^2}{2g}\right) r^2$. Assume that the viscosity of the fluid is constant.

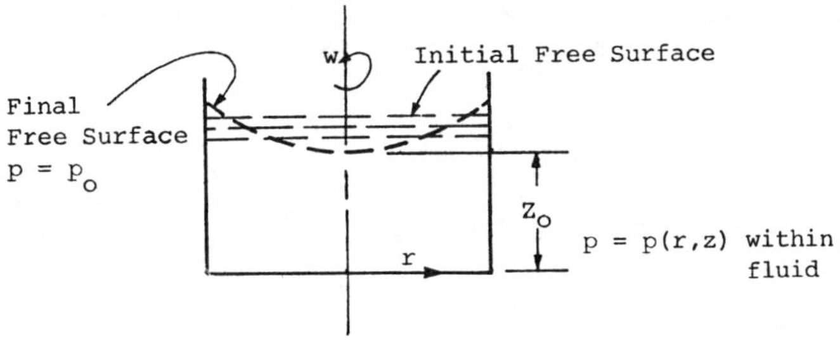

Solution: Writing the Naiver-Stokes equation in cylindrical coordinates for laminar flow,

r-component
$$\rho\left(\frac{\partial v_r}{\partial t} + v_r\frac{\partial v_r}{\partial r} + \frac{v_\theta}{r}\frac{\partial v_r}{\partial \theta} - \frac{v_\theta^2}{r} + v_z\frac{\partial v_r}{\partial z}\right) = -\frac{\partial p}{\partial r}$$

$$+ \mu\left[\frac{\partial}{\partial r}\left(\frac{1}{r}\frac{\partial}{\partial r}(rv_r)\right) + \frac{1}{r^2}\frac{\partial^2 v_r}{\partial \theta^2} - \frac{2}{r^2}\frac{\partial v_\theta}{\partial \theta}\right.$$

$$\left. + \frac{\partial^2 v_r}{\partial z^2}\right] + \rho g_r$$

θ-component $\rho\left(\frac{\partial v_\theta}{\partial t} + v_r \frac{\partial v_\theta}{\partial r} + \frac{v_\theta}{r}\frac{\partial v_\theta}{\partial \theta} + \frac{v_r v_\theta}{r} + v_z \frac{\partial v_\theta}{\partial z}\right)$

$$= -\frac{1}{r}\frac{\partial p}{\partial \theta} + \mu\left[\frac{\partial}{\partial r}\left(\frac{1}{r}\frac{\partial}{\partial r}(r v_\theta)\right) + \frac{1}{r^2}\frac{\partial^2 v_\theta}{\partial \theta^2} + \frac{2}{r^2}\frac{\partial v_r}{\partial \theta} + \frac{\partial^2 v_\theta}{\partial z^2}\right] + \rho g_\theta$$

z-component $\rho\left(\frac{\partial v_z}{\partial t} + v_r \frac{\partial v_z}{\partial r} + \frac{v_\theta}{r}\frac{\partial v_z}{\partial \theta} + v_z \frac{\partial v_z}{\partial z}\right)$

$$= -\frac{\partial p}{\partial z} + \mu\left[\frac{1}{r}\frac{\partial}{\partial r}\left(r\frac{\partial v_z}{\partial r}\right) + \frac{1}{r^2}\frac{\partial^2 v_z}{\partial \theta^2} + \frac{\partial^2 v_z}{\partial z^2}\right] + \rho g_z$$

For steady state,

$$v_z = v_r = 0$$

and $\quad v_\theta = f(r)$ only.

Therefore, the above equations reduce to:

$$\rho\frac{v_\theta^2}{r} = \frac{\partial p}{\partial r} \qquad (1)$$

$$0 = \mu\frac{\partial}{\partial r}\left(\frac{1}{r}\frac{\partial}{\partial r}(r v_\theta)\right) \qquad (2)$$

$$0 = -\frac{\partial p}{\partial z} - \rho g$$

or

$$\frac{\partial p}{\partial z} = -\rho g \qquad (3)$$

Integrating equation (2),

$$v_\theta = \frac{1}{2}c_1 r + \frac{c_2}{r}$$

where $c_2 = 0$ for a finite value of v_θ at $r = 0$

At $r = R$, the vessel radius,

$$v_\theta = \omega R = \frac{c_1 R}{2}$$

or

$$c_1 = 2\omega$$

Thus, $\quad v_\theta = \omega r$

Substituting in (1),

$$\frac{\omega^2 r^2}{r} = \frac{\partial p}{\partial r}$$

or

$$\frac{\partial p}{\partial r} = \rho\omega^2 r$$

Integrating,

$$p = \frac{1}{2} \rho\omega^2 r^2 + f(z) \qquad (4)$$

To find the unknown function f(z), differentiate the above expression with respect to z,

$$\frac{\partial p}{\partial z} = f'(z)$$

comparing with equation (3),

$$f'(z) = -\rho g$$

Thus, $f(z) = -\rho gz + c$

Substituting in equation (4),

$$p = - -\rho gz + \frac{1}{2} \rho\omega^2 r^2 + c$$

At $r = 0$, $p = p_0$ and $z = z_0$ gives,

$$c = p_0 + \rho g z_0$$

Thus,

$$p = \rho g(z_0 - z) + \frac{1}{2} \rho\omega^2 r^2 + p_0$$

or $p - p_0 = -\rho g(z - z_0) + \frac{1}{2} \rho\omega^2 r^2$

Note that $p = p_0 = p_{atm}$ (for open vessel) at all radii on the free surface, and hence the equation for the free surface is,

$$0 = -\rho g(z - z_0) + \frac{1}{2} \rho\omega^2 r^2$$

or $z - z_0 = \left(\frac{\omega^2}{2g}\right) r^2$

• PROBLEM 3-21

Consider the steady-state tangential laminar flow of a constant density and viscosity fluid between two vertical concentric cylinders. If the outer cylinder is rotating with an angular velocity ω, find: 1) the velocity and shear stress distributions and 2) the torque required to turn the outer shaft. Assume that the inner cylinder is at rest.

Solution: For steady state laminar flow in a cylindrical coordinate system,

$$V_r = V_z = 0$$

and $\frac{\partial p}{\partial \theta} = 0$ (based on physical grounds)

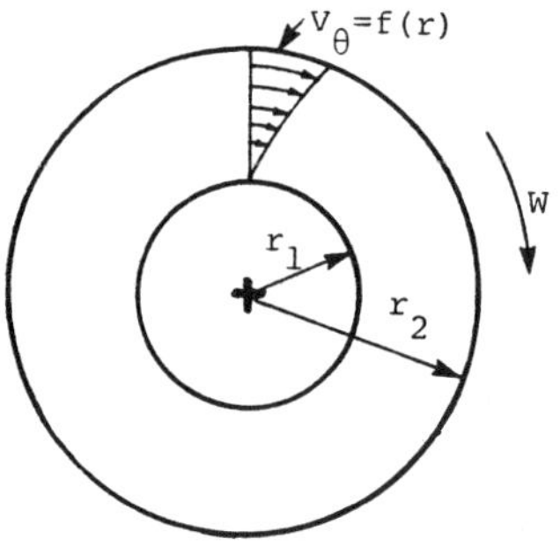

The Naiver-Stokes equation reduces to:

$$0 = \frac{d}{dr}\left(\frac{1}{r}\frac{d}{dr}(rV_\theta)\right) \qquad \theta \text{ - direction}$$

The boundary conditions are,

At $r = r_1$ $V_\theta = 0$

At $r = r_2$ $V_\theta = \omega r_2$

Integrating and applying the boundary conditions,

$$V_\theta = \omega r_2 \frac{\left(\frac{r_1}{r} - \frac{r}{r_1}\right)}{\left(\frac{r_1}{r_2} - \frac{r_2}{r_1}\right)} \tag{1}$$

Now determine the torque, T, required to turn the outer shaft.

$$T = \text{force} \bullet \text{lever arm}$$

$$= (\text{area} \bullet \text{shear stress}) \text{ lever arm}$$

or $$T = \left[A \bullet (-\tau_{r\theta})\Big|_{r = r_2}\right] \bullet r_2$$

or $$T = (2\pi r_2 L) \bullet (-\tau_{r\theta})\Big|_{r = r_2} \bullet r_2 \tag{2}$$

where, the shear stress $\tau_{r\theta}$ is given by

$$\tau_{r\theta} = \tau_{\theta r} = -\mu\left[r\frac{\partial}{\partial r}\left(\frac{V_\theta}{r}\right) + \frac{1}{r}\frac{\partial v_r}{\partial \theta}\right]$$

But $V_r = 0$

hence, $$\tau_{r\theta} = -\mu\left[r\frac{\partial}{\partial r}\left(\frac{V_\theta}{r}\right)\right]$$

Substituting the value of V_θ from (1) into the above expression and differentiating,

$$\tau_{r\theta} = -2\mu\omega r_2^2 \left(\frac{1}{r^2}\right)\left[\frac{\left(\frac{r_1}{r_2}\right)^2}{1 - \frac{r_1^2}{r_2^2}}\right]$$

Substituting the above expression into (2),

$$T = 4\pi\mu L\omega r_2^2 \left[\frac{\left(\frac{r_1}{r_2}\right)^2}{1 - \left(\frac{r_1}{r_2}\right)^2}\right]$$

• PROBLEM 3-22

Consider the system illustrated in the figure. An inverted cone rests on a stationary flat plate such that its apex just touches the plate. The set-up is placed in a puddle of a sample of the liquid whose viscosity needs to be determined. The cone rotates at an angular velocity Ω. Assuming that the torque required to turn the cone can be determined, develop expressions for the torque $\tau_{\theta\phi}$ as a function or r and θ. Assume only one stress component $\tau_{\theta\phi}$ is significant and that it is constant throughout the fluid. End effects can almost be eliminated.

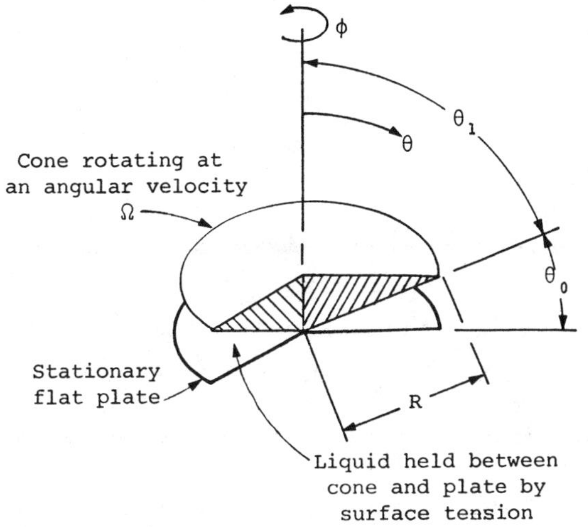

Solution: Assume tangential flow. Therefore, $v_r = v_\theta = 0$ and $v_\theta = f(\theta, r)$ only.

The three components of the equation of motion reduce to

$$\frac{-\rho v_\phi^2}{r} = -\frac{\partial p}{\partial r} \tag{1}$$

$$-\rho\cot\theta\,\frac{v_\phi^2}{r} = -\frac{1}{r}\frac{\partial p}{\partial \theta} \tag{2}$$

$$0 = -\left(\frac{1}{r^2}\frac{\partial}{\partial r}\left(r^2\tau_{r\phi}\right) + \frac{1}{r}\frac{\partial \tau_{\theta\phi}}{\partial \theta} + \frac{\tau_{r\phi}}{r} + 2\cot\theta\,\frac{\tau_{\theta\phi}}{r}\right) \tag{3}$$

Assuming creep flow, i.e. $v_\phi^2 = 0$, which eliminates equations (1) and (2), since $\tau_{\theta\phi}$ is the only important stress vector, (3) reduces to

$$\frac{1}{r}\frac{\partial \tau_{\theta\phi}}{\partial \theta} = -\frac{2\cot\theta}{r}\tau_{\theta\phi}$$

or

$$\frac{\partial \tau_{\theta\phi}}{\partial \theta} = -2\tau_{\theta\phi}\cot\theta$$

or

$$\tau_{\theta\phi} = \frac{c_1}{\sin^2\theta}$$

B.C:- at $\theta = \frac{\pi}{2}$, $\tau_{\theta\phi} = f(\tau)$ = the measured torque transmitted by the fluid to the stationary plate.

$$\tau = \int_0^{2\pi}\int_0^{R} \tau_{\theta\phi}\Big|_{\theta=\pi/2} r^2 dr d\phi$$

$$= 2\pi\left(\frac{R^3}{3}\right)\frac{c_1}{\sin^2\pi/2} \quad \text{or} \quad c_1 = \frac{\tau\sin^2\pi/2}{2\pi(R^3/3)}$$

$$\therefore \quad \tau_{\theta\phi} = \frac{c_1}{\sin^2\theta} = \frac{\tau\sin^2\pi/2}{2\pi(R^3/3)\sin^2\theta} = \frac{3\tau\sin^2\pi/2}{2\pi R^3\sin^2\theta}$$

• PROBLEM 3-23

Two coaxial cylinders with radii R_0 and R_i rotate at angular velocities of ω_0 and ω_i respectively. Develop the velocity profile of the fluid filling the space between them. Assume isothermal laminar flow.

Solution: There is only velocity in the θ direction. $V_r = V_z = 0$. The continuity equation at steady state reduces to

$$\frac{dV_\theta}{d\theta} = 0 \quad \text{or } V_\theta \text{ is not a function of } \theta.$$

The equation of motion reduces to, for the θ component,

$$\mu \frac{\partial}{\partial r}\left(\frac{1}{r}\frac{\partial}{\partial r}(rV_\theta)\right) = 0$$

or $$\frac{\partial}{\partial r}\left[rV_\theta\right] = c_1 r$$

or $$rV_\theta = \frac{c_1 r^2}{2} + c_2$$

$$\therefore \quad V_\theta = \frac{c_1 r}{2} + \frac{c_2}{r}$$

Boundary conditions: at $r = R_i$, $V_\theta = \omega_i R_i$

$r = R_0$, $V_\theta = \omega_0 R_0$

$$\therefore \quad \omega_i R_i = \frac{c_1 R_i}{2} + \frac{c_2}{R_i}$$

and $$\omega_0 R_0 = \frac{c_1 R_0}{2} + \frac{c_0}{R_0}$$

c_1 and c_2 can be determined to be

$$c_1 = \frac{2(\omega_i R_i^2 - \omega_0 R_0^2)}{R_i^2 - R_0^2}$$

and

$$c_2 = \frac{R_i^2 R_0^2(\omega_0 - \omega_i)}{R_i^2 - R_0^2}$$

$$\therefore \quad V_\theta = \left[\left(\omega_i R_i^2 - \omega_0 R_0^2\right) r + \frac{R_i^2 R_0^2}{r}(\omega_0 - \omega_i)\right]\frac{1}{R_i^2 - R_0^2}$$

CHAPTER 4

LAMINAR AND TURBULENT FLOW IN PIPES

LAMINAR FLOW: PRESSURE DROP, VISCOUS SUBLAYER AND BUFFER ZONE THICKNESS AND VELOCITY DISTRIBUTION

• PROBLEM 4-1

In the figure shown below, P, Q and R are standard steel pipes of schedule 40. The nominal sizes of P, Q and R are 2 in., 3 in. and $1\frac{1}{2}$ in. respectively. If 15 gal/min of oil of density 55.3 lb/ft^3 is flowing out through each of the pipes R, calculate (a) the mass flow rate in each pipe, (b) the mass velocity in each pipe, and (c) the average velocity in each pipe.

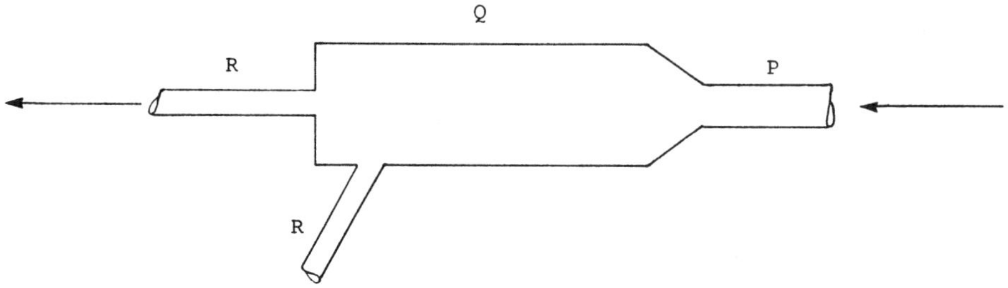

Solution: The cross-sectional areas for the standard steel pipes can be taken from the properties table, for pipes and tubes.

The cross-sectional areas of 2 in., 3 in., and $1\frac{1}{2}$ in. pipes are 0.0233 ft^2, 0.0513 ft^2 and 0.01414 ft^2 respectively.

Since equal quantities of oil are flowing through both pipes R, the total volumetric flow rate through the pipe P is 15×2.

i.e., $q = 30$ gal/min

where q = total volumetric flow rate

or $$q = \frac{30 \times 60}{7.48} \text{ ft}^3\text{/h}$$

or $$q = 240.7 \text{ ft}^3\text{/h}$$

The mass flow rate is given by

$$\overset{\circ}{m} = q \times \rho$$

where $\overset{\circ}{m}$ = mass flow rate in lb/h

q = volumetric flow rate in ft^3/h

ρ = density of oil in lb/ft^3

Therefore, the mass flow rate through pipe P is,

$$\overset{\circ}{m}_P = 240.7 \times 55.3 \text{ lb/h}$$

$$= 13{,}300 \text{ lb/h}$$

The mass flow rate through pipe Q is the same as that through pipe P.

Therefore, the mass flow rate through pipe Q is,

$$\overset{\circ}{m}_Q = 13{,}300 \text{ lb/h}$$

The mass flow rate through each of the pipes R is one-half of that through pipe Q.

Therefore, the mass flow rate through pipe R is,

$$\overset{\circ}{m}_R = \frac{13{,}300}{2} \text{ lb/h}$$

or $$\overset{\circ}{m}_R = 6{,}650 \text{ lb/h}$$

(b) The mass velocity through a pipe is given by

$$G = \frac{\overset{\circ}{m}}{s}$$

where G = mass velocity in lb/ft^2-h

$\overset{\circ}{m}$ = mass flow rate in lb/h

s = cross-sectional area of the pipe in ft^2

The mass velocity through pipe P is,

$$G_P = \frac{13{,}300}{0.0233} \text{ lb/ft}^2\text{-h}$$

or $$G_P = 571{,}000 \text{ lb/ft}^2\text{-h}$$

The mass velocity through pipe Q is,

$$G_Q = \frac{13,300}{0.0513} \text{ lb/ft}^2\text{-h}$$

or $$G_Q = 259,000 \text{ lb/ft}^2\text{-h}$$

The mass velocity through pipe R is,

$$G_R = \frac{6,650}{0.01414} \text{ lb/ft}^2\text{-hr}$$

$$= 470,000 \text{ lb/ft}^2\text{-h}$$

(c) The average velocity $\bar{V}$ of a stream flowing through an area s is,

$$\bar{V} = \frac{\overset{\circ}{m}}{\rho s}$$

The average velocity through pipe P is,

$$\bar{V}_P = \frac{13,300}{55.3 \times 0.0233} \text{ ft/h}$$

or $$\bar{V}_P = \frac{13,300}{55.3 \times 0.0233} \times \frac{1}{3600} \text{ ft/s}$$

or $$\bar{V}_P = 2.87 \text{ ft/s}$$

The average velocity through pipe Q is,

$$\bar{V}_Q = \frac{13,300}{55.3 \times 0.0513} \times \frac{1}{3600} \text{ ft/s}$$

or $$\bar{V}_Q = 1.30 \text{ ft/s}$$

The average velocity through pipe R is,

$$\bar{V}_R = \frac{6,650}{55.3 \times 0.01414} \times \frac{1}{3600} \text{ ft/s}$$

or $$\bar{V}_R = 2.36 \text{ ft/s}$$

• PROBLEM 4-2

Oil is flowing at an average velocity of 1.2 ft/s, through a pipe of ½ in. inside diameter and 100 ft long. Determine the pressure drop over the length of tube if the inlet and exit losses are neglected. Determine the pressure drop, if the tube is of 1 in. inside diameter. For oil assume $\rho = 56 \text{ lb/ft}^3$ and $\nu = 5 \times 10^{-4} \text{ ft}^2\text{/s}$.

Solution: The only pressure drop that is involved here, is frictional pressure drop.

The frictional pressure drop for a fluid flowing inside a pipe is given by

$$\Delta p = f \frac{L\rho u_m^2}{D\ 2g}$$

where Δp = pressure drop in lbf/ft^2

f = friction coefficient

L = length of the pipe in ft.

D = Inside diameter of the pipe in ft.

ρ = density of the liquid flowing in lb/ft^3

u_m = average flow velocity in ft/s

Considering the flow to be laminar flow, the friction coefficient and Reynolds number are given by

$$f = \frac{64}{R_e}\ ;\ R_e = \frac{u_m D}{\nu}$$

(a) For a pipe of ½ in. inside diameter.

The Reynolds number is

$$R_e = \frac{1.2 \times 1}{5 \times 10^{-4} \times 2 \times 12}$$

or

$$R_e = 100$$

Substituting the value of Reynolds number, the friction coefficient is

$$f = \frac{64}{100}$$

or

$$f = 0.64$$

Therefore the frictional pressure drop in a pipe of ½ in. inside diameter is

$$\Delta p = 0.64 \times 100 \times (2 \times 12)\ \frac{56 \times (1.2)^2}{2 \times 32.2}\ lbf/ft^2$$

or

$$\Delta p = 1925\ lbf/ft^2$$

(b) For a pipe of 1 in. inside diameter

The Reynolds number is

$$R_e = \frac{1.2}{5 \times 10^{-4}(12)}$$

or $$R_e = 200$$

Substituting the value of Reynolds number, the friction coefficient is

$$f = \frac{64}{200}$$

or $$f = 0.32$$

Therefore the frictional pressure drop in a pipe of 1 in. inside diameter is

$$\Delta p = 0.32 \times 100(12) \times \frac{56 \times (1.2)^2}{2 \times 32.2} \text{ lbf/ft}^2$$

or $$\Delta p = 481.3 \text{ lbf/ft}^2$$

The pressure drop is inversely proportional to the square of the inside diameter of the pipe, provided the flow is laminar.

• PROBLEM 4-3

Oil is flowing at 6 gal/min, inside a pipe of $\frac{1}{2}$ in. inside diameter. If the flow is laminar, determine

(a) the pressure lost per foot length

(b) the velocity at the center of the pipe

(c) the shear stress at the wall

(d) the radial position of the point at which the flow velocity is equal to the average velocity.

For oil take the density to be 60 lb/ft^3 and its viscosity to be 0.2016 lbm/ft-s.

Solution: This problem involves laminar flow inside a pipe. The Hagen-Poiseuille's law for a laminar flow can be used to find the pressure drop per unit length of flow.

The average velocity of flow is given by

$$\bar{v} = \frac{q}{A}$$

where $\bar{v}$ = average velocity in ft/sec.

q = volumetric flow rate in ft^3/sec.

A = cross-sectional area in ft^2

Therefore, the average velocity is,

$$\bar{v} = \frac{6}{7.48 \times 60} \times \frac{4}{\pi\left(\frac{1}{2} \times \frac{1}{12}\right)^2} \text{ ft/sec.}$$

or $$\bar{v} = 9.8 \text{ ft/sec.}$$

(a) The Hagen-Poiseuille's law for a laminar flow is

$$\bar{v} = -\frac{\Delta P g_c D^2}{32 \Delta y \mu}$$

rearranging

$$-\frac{\Delta P}{\Delta y} = \frac{32 \bar{v} \mu}{D^2 g_c}$$

where $\frac{\Delta P}{\Delta y}$ = Pressure gradient

$\bar{v}$ = average velocity

μ = viscosity of oil

D = inside diameter.

Substituting the values in the right hand side of the equation yields,

$$\frac{-\Delta P}{\Delta y} = \frac{32 \times 9.8 \times 0.2016}{\left(\frac{1}{2} \times \frac{1}{12}\right)^2 \times 32.2} \text{ lbf/ft}^2 \text{ per foot}$$

$$\frac{-\Delta P}{\Delta y} = 1130 \text{ lbf/ft}^2 \text{ per foot}$$

Therefore the pressure drop = 1130 lbf/ft^2 per foot

(b) The point velocity is defined by

$$\frac{v}{\bar{v}} = 2\left(\frac{\gamma_1^2 - \gamma^2}{\gamma_1^2}\right)$$

or $$\frac{v}{\bar{v}} = 2\left[1 - \left(\frac{\gamma}{\gamma_1}\right)^2\right]$$

or $$v = 2\bar{v}\left[1 - \left(\frac{\gamma}{\gamma_1}\right)^2\right]$$

where v = velocity at any radial point

γ_1 = radius of the pipe

$\bar{v}$ = average velocity

Substituting the values, $\gamma = 0$ for center of the pipe and

$$\bar{v} = 9.8 \text{ ft/sec.}$$

the velocity at the center of the pipe is

$$v = 2 \times 9.8 \; [1-0] \; \text{ft/sec}$$

or $$v = 19.6 \text{ ft/sec}$$

Therefore the velocity at the center of the pipe is twice the average velocity.

(c) The shear stress at the wall is given by

$$\tau_y = -\frac{1}{2}\frac{\Delta P}{\Delta y}$$

where τ_y = shear stress at radial distance γ

$\frac{\Delta P}{\Delta y}$ = pressure gradient

γ = radial location

Therefore the shear stress at the wall is

$$\tau = \frac{1130}{2} \times \frac{1}{4 \times 12} \text{ lbf/ft}^2$$

or $$\tau = 11.8 \text{ lbf/ft}^2$$

(d) The point velocity is defined by

$$v = 2\bar{v}\left[1 - \left(\frac{\gamma}{\gamma_1}\right)^2\right]$$

To find the radial location where the point velocity is equal to average velocity, substitute $v = \bar{v}$ into the above equation.

$$\bar{v} = 2\bar{v}\left[1 - \left(\frac{\gamma}{\gamma_1}\right)^2\right]$$

or $$1 - \left(\frac{\gamma}{\gamma_1}\right)^2 = \frac{1}{2}$$

or $$\frac{\gamma}{\gamma_1} = \frac{1}{\sqrt{2}}$$

or $$\gamma = \frac{\gamma_1}{\sqrt{2}}$$

or $$\gamma = 0.177 \text{ in.}$$

Therefore at $\gamma = 0.177$ in. the velocity of oil is equal to the average velocity.

Benzene flows steadily through a 150 m. long horizontal pipe of 5.5 cm inside diameter. If the flow rate is 15 L/min, calculate the pressure drop. Compare the pressure drop of the benzene flow with that of kerosine flow, if same amount of kerosine is flowing through the same pipe.

For kerosine take $\rho_K = 820\ kg/m^3$, $\mu_K = 0.0025\ N.s/m^2$

For benzene take $\rho_B = 899\ kg/m^3$, $\mu_B = 0.0008\ N.s/m^2$

The equivalent roughness for the pipe $\varepsilon = 0.00085$ ft.

Solution: In order to calculate the pressure drop, it must be known whether the flow in the pipe is laminar or turbulent.

The type of flow can be found out by calculating the Reynolds number of the liquid flow.

The average velocity of benzene flow is given by

$$\bar{v} = \frac{q}{A}$$

where q = flow rate in cm^3/s

A = cross-sectional area in cm^2

Therefore $$\bar{v} = \left(\frac{15 \times 1000}{60}\right) \times \frac{1}{\frac{\pi}{4}(5.5)^2}\ cm/s$$

or $$\bar{v} = 10.5\ cm/s$$

or $$\bar{v} = 0.105\ m/s$$

The Reynolds number is given by

$$R_e = \frac{D\bar{v}\rho}{\mu}$$

where R_e = Reynolds number

D = diameter of the pipe in m.

$\bar{v}$ = average velocity in m/s

ρ = density in kg/m^3

μ = viscosity in $N.s/m^2$

Therefore the Reynolds number of benzene flow is

$$R_{e_B} = \frac{0.055 \times 0.105 \times 899}{0.0008}$$

or $$R_{e_B} = 6490$$

Reynolds number of benzene shows that the benzene flow is turbulent, since it is greater than 2100 (critical Reynolds number).

The pressure drop for turbulent flow inside a pipe can be calculated by the equation

$$\Delta p = f \frac{L}{D} \frac{1}{2} \rho (\bar{v})^2$$

where Δp = pressure drop in Pa.

f = friction coeff., to be found out from Moody diagram.

L = length of the pipe in m.

D = diameter of the pipe in m.

ρ = density of benzene in kg/m^3

$\bar{v}$ = average velocity in m/s.

The friction coefficient can be found out from Moody diagram by knowing Reynolds number of the flow and the relative roughness of the pipe. The relative roughness of the pipe is given by

$$\frac{\varepsilon}{D}$$

Therefore relative roughness of the pipe is

$$\frac{(0.00085 \times 30.48)}{5.5} = 0.0047$$

From the Moody diagram, with $R_{e_B} = 6490$ and $\varepsilon/D = 0.0047$, $f = 0.04$

Substituting the values into the pressure drop relation, yields

$$\Delta p_B = 0.04 \times \frac{150}{0.055} \times \frac{1}{2} \times 899 \times (0.105)^2 \text{ Pa}$$

or $$\Delta p_B = 540.6 \text{ Pa}$$

Therefore the pressure drop for benzene is 540.6 Pa.

To calculate the pressure drop for kerosine, the Reynolds number of the kerosine flow is

$$R_{e_K} = \frac{D\bar{V}\rho_K}{\mu_K}$$

or $$R_{e_K} = \frac{0.055 \times 0.105 \times 820}{0.0025}$$

or $$R_{e_K} = 1894$$

The Reynolds number for kerosine shows that the kerosine flow is laminar, since it is less than 2100.

The pressure drop in a laminar flow can be found out from the equation

$$\Delta p = \frac{8\mu \overline{V} L}{\gamma_0^2}$$

For kerosine

$$\Delta p_K = \frac{8\upsilon_k \overline{V} L}{\gamma_0^2} \text{ Pa}$$

or $$\Delta p_K = \frac{8 \times 0.0025 \times 0.105 \times 150}{(0.0275)^2} \text{ Pa}$$

$$\Delta p_K = 416.5 \text{ Pa}$$

Therefore the pressure drop for kerosine 416.5 Pa is much less than that for benzene 540.6 Pa, even though the viscosity of kerosine is more.

The pressure drop for kerosine is less than that for benzene, because of the fact that the viscosity of kerosine is high enough to give laminar flow.

• PROBLEM 4-5

Calculate the pressure drop in water over a length of 10 ft. if water is flowing at a steady speed of 1 fps through a pipe of 0.25 in. diameter. Density and viscosity of water are 62.4 lb/ft^3 and 0.000672 lbm/ft.sec. respectively.

Solution: The pressure drop in water depends upon the type of flow i.e., laminar or turbulent.

The type of flow can be found out from the Reynolds number of the water flow. The Reynolds number is given by

$$R_e = \frac{Dv\rho}{\mu}$$

where R_e = Reynolds number

D = diameter of the pipe

v = velocity of water flow

ρ = density of water

μ = viscosity of water

Therefore the Reynolds number of water flow is

$$R_e = \left(\frac{0.25}{12}\right) \times \frac{1.0 \times 62.4}{0.000672}$$

or $$R_e = 1935$$

The Reynolds number is less than the critical Reynolds number (2100). Therefore the flow is laminar. The pressure drop in a laminar flow is given by

$$\Delta p = \frac{32\mu\bar{v}L}{g_c D^2}$$

Therefore the pressure drop in a length of 10 ft. is

$$\Delta p = \frac{32 \times 0.000672 \times 1.0 \times 10}{\left(\frac{0.25}{12}\right)^2 \times 32.2} \text{ lbf/ft}^2$$

or $$\Delta p = 15.38 \text{ lbf/ft}^2$$

The frictional pressure drop in a laminar flow inside a pipe can also be calculated using friction factor. The friction factor is given by

$$f = \frac{16}{R_e}$$

Therefore friction factor is $f = \dfrac{16}{1935} = 0.00827$

The pressure drop is related to friction factor by

$$\Delta p = 4f\frac{L\rho}{D}\ \frac{v^2}{2g}$$

Therefore pressure drop in a laminar flow for a length of 10 feet is

$$\Delta p = \frac{4 \times 0.00827 \times 10 \times 62.4 \times 12}{0.25}\ \frac{1}{2 \times 32.2}$$

or $$\Delta p = 15.38 \text{ lbf/ft}^2$$

• PROBLEM 4-6

Oil of viscosity 0.2248 lbm/ft-sec. is pumped through a horizontal pipe of 4-in. inside diameter. If there is a pressure drop of 24,000 lbf/ft^2 per mile of flow, calculate the average velocity of flow and the power necessary to maintain the oil flow. Also calculate the velocity and shear stress at $\frac{3}{2}$ in. from the center.

Solution: The Hagen-Poiseville's equation for a laminar flow inside a pipe is

$$V = \frac{\Delta p D^2 g_c}{32 \mu L}$$

where V = average velocity in ft/s

ΔP = Pressure loss in lbf/ft^2

D = inside diameter of pipe in ft.

μ = viscosity in lb/ft-sec.

L = length of fluid flow in ft.

Therefore the average velocity of flow of oil inside the pipe is

$$V = \frac{24000 \times \left(\frac{4}{12}\right)^2 \times 32.2}{32 \times 0.2248 \times 5280} \text{ ft/s}$$

or $V = 2.26$ ft/s

The power consumed in pumping the oil for a pressure drop of 24,000 psf is given by

$$P = \frac{V \pi \gamma_0^{\,2} (P_1 - P_2)}{550}$$

where P = power consumed in hp

V = average velocity in ft/s

γ_0 = radius of the pipe in ft.

$(P_1 - P_2)$ = Pressure drop

Therefore the power consumed is

$$P = 2.26 \times \pi \times \left(\frac{2}{12}\right)^2 \times 24{,}000 \times \frac{1}{550} \text{ hp/mile}$$

or $P = 8.61$ hp/mile

The velocity at any point is given by the equation

$$V = -\frac{g_c}{4\mu}\left(\frac{dp}{dx}\right)\left(\gamma_0^{\,2} - \gamma^2\right)$$

where V = velocity at any radial location γ from the center

$-\frac{dp}{dx}$ = Pressure gradient

γ_0 = radius of the pipe

Therefore the velocity at $\gamma = \frac{3}{2}$ in. is

$$V = \frac{1}{4} \times \frac{32.2}{0.2248} \times \frac{24000}{5280} \times \left[\left(\frac{2}{12}\right)^2 - \left(\frac{1.5}{12}\right)^2 \right] \text{ ft/s}$$

or $\qquad V = 1.98$ ft/s

The equation for the shear stress is

$$\tau = -\frac{\gamma}{2} \frac{dp}{dx}$$

Therefore the shear stress at $\gamma = \frac{3}{2}$ in. is

$$\tau = \frac{3}{4 \times 12} \times \frac{24000}{5280} \text{ lb/ft}^2$$

or $$\tau = 0.284 \text{ lb/ft}^2$$

• PROBLEM 4-7

Water with viscosity $\mu = 7.59 \times 10^{-4}$ lbm/ft-s and density $\rho = 62.4$ lb/ft^3, is flowing through a pipe of 1 in. inside diameter at an average velocity of 5 ft/sec. If in a length of 500 ft of the pipe, the pressure drop is 15 lbf/in^2, calculate the thickness of the viscous sublayer.

Solution: Viscous sublayer occurs only in turbulent flow. To know the type of flow, the Reynolds number of the flow has to be compared with the critical Reynolds number.

The Reynolds number of the flow is given by

$$Re = \frac{\rho VD}{\mu}$$

where ρ = density of water = 62.4 lb/ft^3

V = velocity of flow = 5 ft/s

D = diameter of the pipe = $\frac{1}{12}$ ft

μ = viscosity of water = 7.59×10^{-4} lbm/ft-s

Substituting the values yield,

$$Re = 62.4 \times 5 \times \left(\frac{1}{12}\right) \times \frac{1}{7.59 \times 10^{-4}}$$

$$= 34{,}256.$$

Since the Reynolds number is much greater than critical Reynolds number, the flow is turbulent. The thickness of a viscous sublayer is given by

$$y = \frac{5\nu}{\nu*}$$

where ν = kinematic viscosity = μ/ρ

$$\nu* = \sqrt{\frac{\tau_0}{\rho}}$$

The shear stress τ_0 is given by the force balance on the fluid in the pipe

$$\tau_0\ (\pi DL) = \Delta P\ \frac{\pi}{4}\ D^2$$

or $$\tau_0 = \frac{\Delta P.D}{4L}$$

Substituting into the equation for y

$$y = 5\ \frac{\mu}{\rho}\left(\frac{4L\rho}{\Delta P.D}\right)^{\frac{1}{2}}$$

$$= 5^{\mu}\left(\frac{4L}{\Delta P.D\rho}\right)^{\frac{1}{2}}$$

Substituting the values yield,

$$y = 5 \times 7.59 \times 10^{-4}\left(\frac{4 \times 500}{(15 \times 144)\left(\frac{1}{12}\right)(62.4)(32.2)}\right)^{\frac{1}{2}}$$

$$= 0.00028 \text{ ft.}$$

or $y = 0.0034$ in.

Therefore, the thickness of the viscous sublayer is $y = 0.0034$ in.

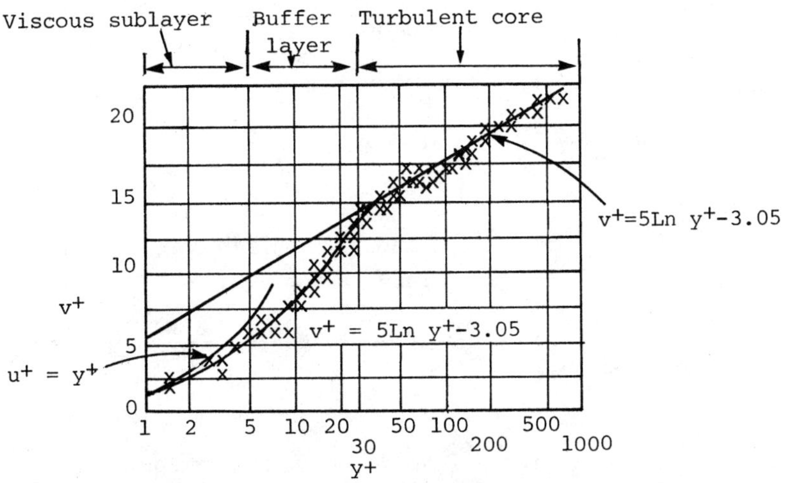

Universal velocity profile.

Consider a steady, two-dimensional, laminar, constant property, fully developed flow between two parallel plates, flowing at an average velocity U_m. If the pressure is independent of y and body forces are neglected, obtain an expression for the velocity distribution.

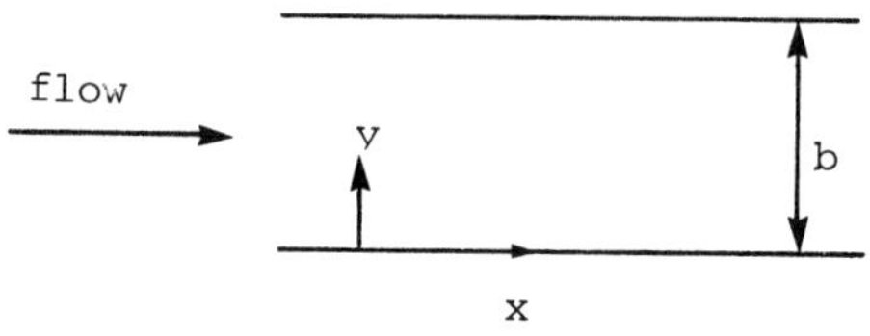

LAMINAR FLUID FLOW BETWEEN THE PARALLEL PLATES.

Solution: As the flow is two-dimensional, there is no velocity component in the Z direction.

Now the continuity equation for incompressible flow reduces to

$$\frac{\partial u}{\partial x} + \frac{\partial v}{\partial y} = 0 \tag{1}$$

The flow is fully developed, i.e. $\frac{\partial u}{\partial x} = 0$.

Then
$$\frac{\partial v}{\partial y} = 0 \tag{2}$$

Integrating equation (2) partially with respect to y gives

$$v = F(x) \tag{3}$$

The plates are solid and impervious to mass. Then, at all x

$$\left.\begin{array}{l} y = 0 \\ y = b \end{array}\right\} \quad v = 0$$

Then from equation (3)

$$F(x) = 0$$

This gives v = 0 for all x and y. The Navier-Stokes equation in the Z direction is

$$\rho\left(\frac{\partial w}{\partial t} + u\,\frac{\partial w}{\partial x} + v\,\frac{\partial w}{\partial y} + w\,\frac{\partial w}{\partial z}\right) = -\,\frac{\partial P}{\partial z} + \mu\left(\frac{\partial^2 w}{\partial x^2} + \frac{\partial^2 w}{\partial y^2} + \frac{\partial^2 w}{\partial z^2}\right) + f_z \tag{4}$$

where u, v and w are the local velocity components in the x, y and z direction. All the terms in equation (4) are zero, because the flow is two-dimensional. All the terms of the Navier-Stokes equation in the y-direction will be zero. Since

$$\frac{\partial P}{\partial y} = 0; \; f_y = 0$$

$$\text{and} \; \frac{\partial^2 u}{\partial x^2} = \frac{\partial^2 u}{\partial z^2} = \frac{\partial u}{\partial t} = u\frac{\partial u}{\partial x} = v\frac{\partial u}{\partial y} = w\frac{\partial u}{\partial z} = f_x = 0$$

The Navier-Stokes equation in the x-direction reduces to

$$0 = -\frac{\partial P}{\partial x} + \mu\frac{\partial^2 u}{\partial y^2}$$

$$\frac{\partial^2 u}{\partial y^2} = \frac{1}{\mu}\frac{\partial P}{\partial x} \qquad (5)$$

Given that pressure is independent of y. Then both sides of equation (5) are constant. Since u is a function of only one variable, then equation (5) can be written as

$$\frac{d^2 u}{dy^2} = \frac{1}{\mu}\frac{\partial P}{\partial x}$$

Integrating both sides twice with respect to y gives

$$u = \frac{1}{2\mu}\frac{\partial P}{\partial x}y^2 + c_1 y + c_2 \qquad (6)$$

The boundary conditions are:

$$\text{at} \quad y = 0, \quad u = 0 \qquad (7)$$

$$\text{at} \quad y = b, \quad u = 0 \qquad (8)$$

Applying the boundary condition (7) to equation (6) gives

$$0 = 0 + 0 + c_2$$

Therefore $c_2 = 0$.

Applying the boundary condition (8) to equation (6) gives

$$0 = \frac{1}{2\mu}\frac{\partial P}{\partial x}b^2 + c_1 b + 0$$

Then

$$C_1 = -\frac{b}{2\mu}\frac{\partial P}{\partial x}$$

substituting constants c_1 and c_2 in equation (6) gives

$$U = \frac{1}{2\mu}\frac{\partial P}{\partial x}(y^2 - by) \qquad (9)$$

In equation (9) the pressure gradient is an unknown quantity. This can be eliminated by relating pressure gradient to average velocity U_m. The total mass flow rate past any station x per foot in the z-direction is

$$w = \rho A U_m = \rho b(1) U_m \tag{10}$$

The mass flow rate across the area dy × 1 ft at position x is

$$dw = \rho u \, dy \tag{11}$$

Substituting equation (9) in equation (11) gives

$$dw = \frac{\rho}{2\mu} \frac{\partial P}{\partial x} (y^2 - by) dy \tag{12}$$

Integrating equation (12) from y=0 to y=b gives the total mass flow rate

$$\int dw = w = \int_0^b \frac{\rho}{2\mu} \frac{\partial P}{\partial x} (y^2 - by) \, dy$$

$$w = \frac{\rho}{2\mu} \frac{\partial P}{\partial x} \left(- \frac{b^3}{6} \right) \tag{13}$$

Equating (11) and (13) gives

$$\rho b U_m = \frac{\rho}{2\mu} \frac{\partial P}{\partial x} \left(- \frac{b^3}{6} \right)$$

Solving for $\partial P/\partial x$ gives

$$\frac{\partial P}{\partial x} = - \frac{12 \mu U_m}{b^2} \tag{14}$$

The negative sign in equation (14) indicates that the pressure is dropping in the direction of flow. This agrees with what is to be expected since the pressure drop is the sole driving potential for fluid flow in the given situation.

Substituting equation (14) in equation (10) gives the velocity distribution as

$$u = 6 \, U_m \left(\frac{y}{b} - \frac{y^2}{b^2} \right) \tag{15}$$

• PROBLEM 4-9

Calculate the loss of head in a pipe ¼ in. in diameter and 16 ft. long, when water flows at half the critical velocity. The critical velocity occurs when Reynolds number is 2500. Take viscosity μ = 1.01 centipoise = 0.679×10^{-3} lbm/ft-sec.

Solution: The actual velocity of flow through the pipe corresponds to a Reynolds number

$$Re = \frac{2500}{2} = \frac{Re_c}{2}$$

where Re_c = Reynolds number corresponding to critical velocity.

Therefore

$$Re = 1250$$

Since the velocity of flow is less than critical velocity, the flow is laminar flow.

The Reynolds number is given by

$$Re = \frac{\rho VD}{\mu}$$

where ρ = density of water

V = mean velocity of flow

D = diameter of the pipe

μ = viscosity of water.

From this expression,

$$V = \frac{R_e \mu}{\rho D}$$

Substituting the values in the R.H.S. of the expression

$$V = \frac{1250 \times 0.679 \times 10^{-3}}{62.4 \times \frac{1}{4} \times \frac{1}{12}}$$

$$= 0.653 \text{ ft/sec.}$$

The mean velocity of flow is 0.653 ft/sec.

The frictional pressure loss for a laminar flow in a circular pipe is given by

$$h = \frac{fLV^2}{2gD}$$

where h = pressure loss

f = friction factor

L = length of the pipe

V = velocity of flow

D = diameter of the pipe.

In this problem, the friction factor is given by the relation

$$f = \frac{64}{Re}$$

$$= \frac{64}{1250}$$

or $$f = 0.0512$$

Substituting the values,

$$h = \frac{0.0512 \times 16 \times (0.653)^2}{2 \times 32.2 \times \frac{1}{4} \times \frac{1}{12}}$$

$$= 0.26 \text{ ft.}$$

or $$h = 3.12 \text{ in.}$$

Therefore the head loss is 3.12 in.

FLOW THROUGH BRANCHED PIPES

• PROBLEM 4-10

Three reservoirs of water are located and connected by a piping system. If 18 ft^3/min. of water is flowing out of the reservoir A, and equal amounts of water are flowing into the reservoirs B and C, calculate the diameters of the pipes b and c.

Take dimensions of the pipes as

Pipe 'a' - 200 ft. long and 3.068 in. diameter

Pipe 'b' - 100 ft. long

Pipe 'c' - 150 ft. long

Take Darcy friction factor f = 0.008

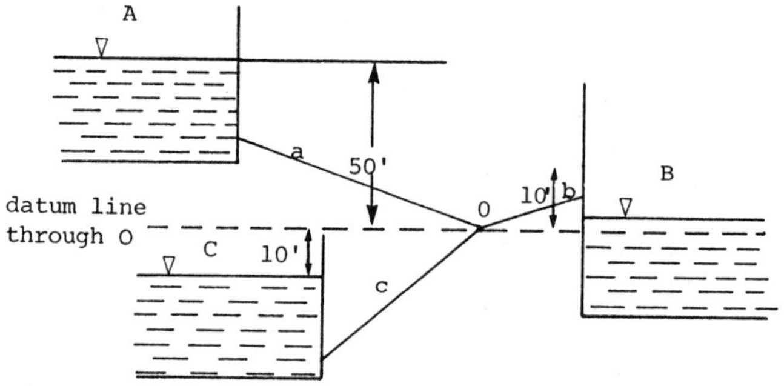

Solution: The water surface in the reservoirs is at the atmospheric pressure, since they are exposed to atmospheric conditions.

Therefore $$P_A = P_B = P_C = P_{Atm}$$

Taking the pressure at the junction '0' as P_0 and ignoring the velocity head terms, the following flow equations can be written with reference to the figure:

Between (A) and (O)

$$Z_A + \frac{P_A}{\gamma} = Z_0 + \frac{P_0}{\gamma} + h_{fa}$$

where Z_a = vertical height of the water level in A from the datum

P_A = pressure at the surface A

γ = density of water

P_0 = pressure of the water at junction 0

h_{fa} = frictional head loss due to flow through the pipe 'a'

But $Z_A - Z_0 = 50'$

then $$\frac{P_0 - P_A}{\gamma} = 50 - h_{fa} \quad (1)$$

Similarly between (0) and (B)

$$Z_0 + \frac{P_0}{\gamma} = Z_B + \frac{P_B}{\gamma} + h_{fb}$$

But $Z_B - Z_0 = 10'$

then $$\frac{P_0 - P_B}{\gamma} = 10 + h_{fb} \quad (2)$$

Between (0) and (C)

$$Z_0 + \frac{P_0}{\gamma} = Z_c + \frac{P_c}{\gamma} + h_{fc}$$

here $$Z_0 - Z_c = 10'$$

then $$\frac{P_0 - P_c}{\gamma} = h_{fc} - 10 \quad (3)$$

Given the volume flow rate through the pipe 'a'

$$q_a = 18 \text{ ft}^3/\text{min.}$$

or $$q_a = \frac{18}{60} \text{ cfs}$$

$$= 0.3 \text{ cfs}$$

The volume flow rate through the pipes b and c

$$q_b = q_c = \frac{q_a}{2} = 0.15 \text{ cfs}$$

The head loss due to friction is given by

$$h_f = \frac{fLq^2}{10D^5}$$

Therefore the frictional head loss due to water flow through pipe 'a' is given by

$$h_{fa} = \frac{fL_a q_a^2}{10D_a^5}$$

where L_a = length of pipe 'a' in ft.

q_a = flow rate through pipe 'a' in cfs

D_a = diameter of pipe 'a' in ft.

Substituting the values, yield

$$h_{fa} = \frac{(0.008)(200)(0.3)^2}{(10)(3.068/12)^5}$$

or $$h_{fa} = 13.19 \text{ ft.}$$

Similarly $$h_{fb} = \frac{fL_b q_b^2}{10D_b^5}$$

$$= \frac{(0.008)(100)(0.15)^2}{10\ (D_b)^5}$$

or $$h_{fb} = \frac{0.0018}{(D_b)^5}$$

Similiarly $$h_{fc} = \frac{fL_c q_c^2}{10D_c^5}$$

$$= \frac{(0.008)(150)(0.15)^2}{10\ (D_c)^5}$$

$$h_{fc} = \frac{0.0027}{(D_c)^5}$$

Substituting the frictional head losses in the respective

equations (1), (2) and (3), yields

$$\frac{P_0 - P_A}{\gamma} = 50 - 13.19$$

or

$$\frac{P_0 - P_A}{\gamma} = 36.81 \qquad (4)$$

$$\frac{P_0 - P_B}{\gamma} = 10 + \frac{0.0018}{(D_b)^5} \qquad (5)$$

$$\frac{P_0 - P_C}{\gamma} = \frac{0.0027}{(D_c)^5} - 10 \qquad (6)$$

But since $P_A = P_B = P_C = P_{Atm.}$

From equations (4) and (5)

$$10 + \frac{0.0018}{(D_b)^5} = 36.81$$

Therefore $D_b = 0.1463$ ft.

$$D_b = 1.756 \text{ in.}$$

From equations (4) and (6)

$$\frac{0.0027}{(D_c)^5} - 10 = 36.81$$

Therefore $D_c = 0.1420$ ft.

or

$$D_c = 1.704 \text{ in.}$$

The nearest nominal sizes would be taken for the branched pipes.

• PROBLEM 4-11

Two reservoirs A and B are connected by a piping system, as shown in the figure below. The water level in reservoir B is 100 ft. below that in the reservoir A. Water at 59°F is flowing from reservoir A to reservoir B. Calculate the volumetric flow rate (1) in the 12 in. diameter branch (2) in the 6 in. diameter branch and (3) the main line. In the figure the pipes in branch 3 are of 6 in. diameter and all other pipes are of 12 in. diameter. Assume for pipe $K_s = 0.010$ in.

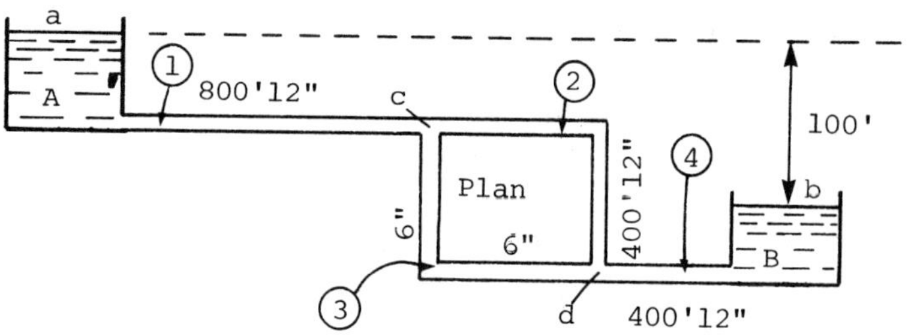

Solution: The pressure at a joint will be the same for each pipe entering that joint, which implies that the head loss in each branch will be the same.

From the equations of continuity

$$q_1 = q_2 + q_3$$

i.e., the volumetric flow rate through section 1 = sum of the volumetric flow rates through sections 2 and 3.

i.e.,
$$a_1 v_1 = a_2 v_2 + a_3 v_3$$

where a = cross-sectional area

v = velocity of flow

but $a_1 = a_2 = 4a_3$

hence
$$v_1 = v_2 + \frac{v_3}{4} \tag{1}$$

Apply the Bernoulli equation to the two branches 2 and 3.

For branch 2:

$$\frac{P_c}{\gamma} + \frac{V_2^2}{2g} + Z_c = \frac{P_d}{\gamma} + \frac{V_2^2}{2g} + Z_d + f_2(800)\frac{V_2^2}{2g} \tag{2}$$

For branch 3:

$$\frac{Pc}{\gamma} + \frac{V_3{}^2}{2g} + Zc = \frac{P_d}{\gamma} + \frac{V_3{}^2}{2g} + Zd + f_3(1600)\frac{V_3{}^2}{2g} \tag{3}$$

Rewriting the equations 2 and 3,

$$\frac{P_c}{\gamma} + Z_c - \frac{P_d}{\gamma} - Z_d = 800\ f_2 \frac{V_2^2}{2g}$$

$$\frac{P_c}{\gamma} + Z_c - \frac{P_d}{\gamma} - Z_d = 1600\ f_3 \frac{V_3^2}{2g}$$

Therefore
$$800\ f_2 \frac{V_2^2}{2g} = 1600\ f_3 \frac{V_3^2}{2g}$$

or
$$f_2 V_2^2 = 2 f_3 V_3^2 \tag{4}$$

The Bernoulli's equation from point a to point b, through section 2 is given by

$$\frac{P_a}{\gamma} + \frac{V_a^2}{2g} + Z_a = \frac{P_b}{\gamma} + \frac{V_b^2}{2g} + Z_b + f_1(800)\,\frac{V_1^2}{2g} + f_2\frac{(800)V_2^2}{2g}$$

$$+ f_4(400)\,\frac{V_4^2}{2g}$$

Substituting the values, $v_1 = v_4$ and $f_1 = f_4$

$$100 = 1200\, f_1 \frac{V_1^2}{2g} + 800\, f_2 \frac{V_2^2}{2g} \qquad (5)$$

Assume the value of f = 0.02 for all the sections. Substituting the value f = 0.02 in (4) yields

$$v_2^2 = 2v_3^2$$

or

$$v_3 = v_2/(2)^{\frac{1}{2}} \qquad (6)$$

Equation (5) yields

$$64.4 = 12 \times 0.02\, v_1^2 + 8 \times 0.02\, v_2^2$$

or

$$402.5 = 1.5\, v_1^2 + v_2^2 \qquad (7)$$

Substituting the value of V_3 in equation (6) into equation (1)

$$v_1 = v_2 + \frac{1}{4}\left(\frac{v_2}{(2)^{\frac{1}{2}}}\right)$$

or

$$v_1 = 1.177\, v_2$$

or

$$v_1^2 = 1.38\, v_2^2$$

Substituting this value into equation (7) yields

$$402.5 = 1.5\,(1.38\, v_2^2) + v_2^2$$

or

$$v_2 = 11.4 \text{ ft/s}$$

Therefore

$$v_1 = 13.42 \text{ ft/s}$$

and

$$v_3 = \frac{11.4}{1.414}$$

$$v_3 = 8.08 \text{ ft/s}$$

In calculating these velocities, it was assumed that the value of f = 0.02 for all sections of the pipe. Reynolds number for flow in each section can be used to verify the assumed value of f.

Reynolds number for section 1 is given by

$$R_{e_1} = \frac{1.937(13.42)10^6}{23.83}$$

or $$R_{e_1} = 1{,}090{,}000$$

and the relative roughness $\frac{k}{d} = \frac{0.01}{12} = 0.00083$

Therefore the friction factor from Moody diagram is

$$f_1 = 0.0191$$

Similarly for section 2

$$R_{e_2} = \frac{1.937(11.40)10^6}{23.83}$$

$$= 926{,}000$$

and the corresponding value of $f_2 = 0.0191$

For the section 3,

$$R_{e_3} = \frac{1.937(8.08)10^6}{23.83}$$

$$= 657{,}500$$

and the relative roughness $\frac{k}{d} = \frac{0.01}{6} = 0.0017.$

The corresponding friction factor f is

$$f_3 = 0.0228$$

Since the value of f_3 varies a lot from the assumed value of 0.02, using the new values of f, yields

From equation (4)

$$0.0191\ v_2^2 = 0.0456\ v_3^2$$

or $$v_3 = v_2/(2.39)^{\frac{1}{2}} \qquad (8)$$

From equation (5)

$$64.4 = 0.229\ v_1^2 + 0.1526\ v_2^2$$

or $$422 = 1.5\ v_1^2 + v_2^2 \qquad (9)$$

Again substituting the values in equation (1)

$$v_1 = v_2 + \frac{1}{4}\ \frac{v_2}{(2.39)^{\frac{1}{2}}}$$

or $$v_1^2 = 1.35\ v_2^2$$

Substituting this value into equation (9)

$$422 = 1.5\ (1.35\ v_2^2) + v_2^2$$

or $$v_2 = 11.81\ \text{ft/s}$$

Therefore $v_1 = 1.162\ (11.81)$

$$= 13.72 \text{ ft/s}$$

and $$v_3 = 4(13.72-11.81)$$

$$= 7.64 \text{ ft/s}$$

Check the values of f for these values of v or the Reynolds number corresponding to these values of v

$$R_{e_1} = \frac{1.937(13.72)10^6}{23.83}$$

$$= 1,115,000$$

and relative roughness $\frac{k}{d} = 0.00083$

The corresponding value of f from Moody diagram is

$$f_1 = 0.0191$$

$$R_{e_2} = \frac{1.937(11.81)10^6}{23.83}$$

$$= 960,000$$

The corresponding value of f is $f_2 = 0.0191$

and $$R_{e_3} = \frac{1.937(7.64)10^6}{23.83}$$

$$= 620,000$$

the relative roughness $\frac{k}{d} = 0.0017.$

Therefore the value of $f_3 = 0.0228.$

Since all the values of f tally with the used values of f, there is no need to iterate further.

The velocities in the 3 sections are

$$v_1 = 13.72 \text{ ft/s}$$

$$v_2 = 11.81 \text{ ft/s}$$

$$v_3 = 7.64 \text{ ft/s}$$

Therefore the flow rate through

(1) 12 in. diameter branch i.e. section 2 is

$$\frac{\pi}{4} \times 11.81 = 9.28 \text{ ft}^3/\text{s}$$

(2) 6 in. diameter branch i.e., section 3 is

$$\frac{\pi}{4} \times \left(\frac{1}{2}\right)^2 \times 7.64 = 1.50 \text{ ft}^3/\text{s}$$

(3) Main line-section 1 is

$$\frac{\pi}{4} \times 13.72 = 10.78 \text{ ft}^3/\text{s}$$

The flow rate through the main line = sum of the flow rates through sections 2 and 3.

• PROBLEM 4-12

A 42 ft. long pipe of 4 in. inside diameter, discharges water from a tank of 16 ft. diameter into a reservoir. Initially, if the height of the water surface in the tank from the water surface in the reservoir is 26 ft., calculate the time taken to discharge 1500 ft^3 of water. Take the Darcy friction factor f = 0.008.

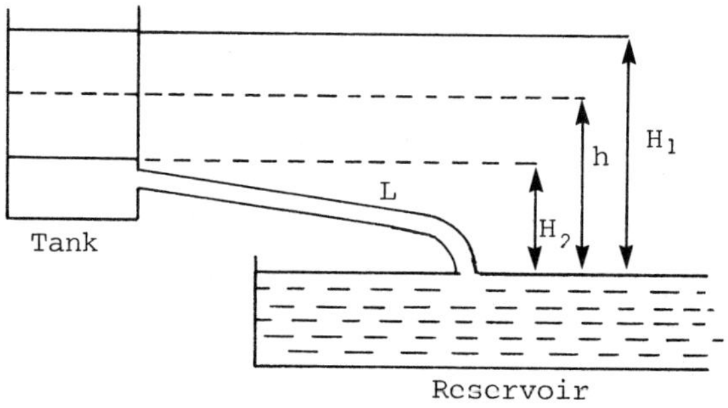

Solution: Since the cross-sectional area of the water tank is small, the discharge of 1500 ft^3 of water lowers the level of water in it.

Therefore, the discharge has variable head.

The height occupied by 1500 ft^3 of water in the water tank is given by

$$\frac{1500}{\frac{\pi}{4}(16)^2} = 7.44 \text{ ft.}$$

Original height of water level in the tank from the water level in the reservoir, H_1 = 26 ft.

Final height of water level is given by $H_2 = H_1 - 7.44$ ft.

or $$H_2 = 26 - 7.44$$

$$= 18.56 \text{ ft.}$$

The total head loss is given by

$$H_f = \frac{0.5V^2}{2g} + \frac{V^2}{2g} + 4f\left(\frac{L}{D}\right)\frac{V^2}{2g}$$

where H_f = Total pressure loss in the pipe

$$\frac{0.5V^2}{2g} = \text{entry pressure loss}$$

$$\frac{V^2}{2g} = \text{exit pressure loss}$$

$4f\left(\frac{L}{D}\right)\frac{V^2}{2g}$ = frictional pressure loss during the flow through the pipe of length L.

V = velocity of water in the pipe

Substituting the values into the equation,

$$H_f = \frac{V^2}{2 \times 32.2}\left[0.5 + 1.0 + 4(0.008)\frac{42}{4/12}\right]$$

or $$h = H_f = 0.0859\ V^2$$

or $$V = 3.41\ (h)^{\frac{1}{2}}$$

The flow rate is given by

$$q = \frac{\pi}{4}\ D^2.V$$

or $$q = \frac{\pi}{4}\left(\frac{4}{12}\right)^2(3.41)(h)^{\frac{1}{2}}$$

In a differential time dt the amount of flow is given by

$$q(dt) = A(dh)$$

where dh is the differential height of the water level in the tank.
Substituting the values into this equation,

$$\frac{\pi}{4}\left(\frac{4}{12}\right)^2(3.41)(h)^{\frac{1}{2}}\ dt = \frac{\pi}{4}\ (16)^2.dh$$

Therefore $dt = 675(h)^{-\frac{1}{2}}\ dh$

Therefore the total time taken to discharge 1500 ft^3 of water or to decrease the water level from 26 ft. to 18.56 ft. is

$$T = 675\int_{H_2}^{H_1}(h)^{-\frac{1}{2}}\ dh \text{ secs.}$$

The $$\int_{H_2}^{H_1}(h)^{-\frac{1}{2}}\ dh = 2\left[(H_1)^{\frac{1}{2}}-(H_2)^{\frac{1}{2}}\right]$$

Therefore $$T = 2 \times 675\left[(26)^{\frac{1}{2}} - (18.56)^{\frac{1}{2}}\right]$$

$$T = 1067.7 \text{ secs.}$$

TURBULENT FLOW: PRESSURE DROP, FRICTION FACTOR, MINIMUM PIPE DIAMETER AND VELOCITY DISTRIBUTION

• PROBLEM 4-13

Air at 75°F and 14.6 psia flows through a rectangular duct of 1 × 2 ft cross-section. If the flow rate is 4800 cfm, determine the pressure drop per 100 ft of flow. For duct K_s = 0.00015 ft.

Solution: The density of air at the given temperature and pressure can be found by using the perfect gas equation.

The density is given by

$$\rho = \frac{P}{RT}$$

$$= \frac{14.6 \times 144}{1716 \times 535}$$

or
$$\rho = 2.3 \times 10^{-3} \text{ slugs/ft}^3$$

The flow velocity V is given by

$$V = \frac{q}{A}$$

where q = flow rate in ft^3/s

A = cross-sectional area of the duct in ft^2

Therefore the flow velocity

$$V = \left(\frac{4800}{60}\right) \times \frac{1}{1 \times 2}$$

or
$$V = 40 \text{ ft/s}$$

Since the cross-section of the duct is not circular, the hydraulic radius is given by

$$R = \frac{A}{P}$$

where R = Hydraulic radius in ft.

A = cross-sectional area in ft^2

P = wetted perimeter of the duct in ft.

$$R = \frac{1 \times 2}{6}$$

Therefore
$$R = 0.333 \text{ ft.}$$

The Reynolds number for the air flow through a rectangular duct is given by

$$R_e = \frac{V(4R)}{\nu}$$

where R_e = Reynolds number

V = average velocity of air

R = Hydraulic radius

ν = kinematic viscosity of air = 1.6×10^{-4} ft^2/s

Substituting the values, yield

$$R_e = \frac{40 \times 4 \times 0.333}{1.6 \times 10^{-4}}$$

$$= 3.33 \times 10^5$$

The ratio $\frac{K_s}{4R} = \frac{0.00015}{4 \times 0.333}$

$= 0.000113$

Therefore, from the Moody diagram

Corresponding to $R_e = 3.33 \times 10^5$ and $\frac{K_s}{4R} = 0.000113$

the friction factor

$$f = 0.015$$

The pressure drop is given by

$$h_f = \frac{fL\rho V^2}{4R\ 2}$$

where h_f = pressure drop

f = friction factor = 0.015

L = length of flow = 100 ft.

ρ = density of air = 2.3×10^{-3} $slugs/ft^3$

V = flow velocity = 40 ft/s

R = hydraulic radius = 0.333 ft.

Substituting the values, yield

$$h_f = \frac{0.015 \times 100 \times (40)^2 \times 2.3 \times 10^{-3}}{4 \times 0.333 \times 2}$$

$$= 2.07 \text{ psf.}$$

• PROBLEM 4-14

Consider a horizontal pipe of 1.2 in. inside diameter and of roughness k = 0.002 ft. If water flows through it at 9.3 ft/s, calculate the pressure loss per 10 ft. of the pipe length. Kinematic viscosity of water $\nu = 0.93 \times 10^{-5}$ ft²/s.

Solution: The pressure loss in a liquid flowing through a pipe is given by the Darcy Equation

$$H_f = f \frac{L}{D} \rho \frac{V^2}{2g}$$

where H_f = pressure loss

f = friction factor from Moody diagram

L = length of the pipe = 10 ft.

D = diameter of the pipe = 0.1 ft.

ρ = density of water = 62.2 lb/ft³

V = velocity of flow = 9.3 ft/s

The Reynolds number for a liquid flowing in a pipe is given by

$$R_e = \frac{VD}{\nu}$$

where V = velocity of flow

D = diameter of the pipe

ν = kinematic viscosity of water

Therefore $$R_e = \frac{9.3 \times}{0.93 \times 10^{-5}}\left(\frac{1.2}{12}\right)$$

or $$R_e = 1 \times 10^5$$

The relative roughness is given by $\frac{0.002}{1.2} \times 12$

$$= 0.02$$

From the Moody diagram,

corresponding to the value of $R_e = 1 \times 10^5$ and relative roughness = 0.02, the friction factor f = 0.048.

Substituting the values into the Darcy equation, the pressure loss is

$$H_f = (0.048)\,\frac{10}{0.10}\,\frac{(62.2)(9.3)^2}{64.4}$$

$$= 402 \text{ lbf/ft}^2$$

or $$H_f = 2.78 \text{ psi.}$$

• PROBLEM 4-15

Diethylaniline $C_6H_5N(C_2H_5)_2$ at 20°C (density $\rho = 0.935$ g/cm^3 and viscosity $\mu = 1.95$ CP) is flowing through a horizontal smooth pipe of inside diameter 3 cm. If the volumetric flow rate is 66 liters/min, determine the pressure gradient.

Solution: The pressure gradient in the flow is given by

$$\frac{\Delta P}{L} = 4\ f\ \frac{1}{2D}\ \rho\ v^2$$

where $\frac{\Delta P}{L}$ = pressure gradient

f = friction factor (from Moody diagram)

ρ = density

v = flow velocity

The flow velocity is given by

$$v = \frac{q}{A} \text{ cm/sec}$$

where q = volumetric flow rate in cm^3/s

A = cross-sectional area in cm^2

Therefore $$v = \left(\frac{66 \times 1000}{60}\right)\frac{4}{\pi(3)^2}$$

$$= 155.62 \text{ cm/sec.}$$

To find the friction factor 'f' from the Moody diagram, the Reynolds number of the flow and relative roughness of the pipe are needed.

The Reynolds number is given by

$$R_e = \frac{\rho v D}{\mu}$$

Substituting, $\rho = 0.935\ g/cm^3$

$v = 155.62$ cm/sec.

$D = 3$ cm.

$\mu = 1.95 \times 10^{-2}$ g/cm-sec.

yield

$$R_e = \frac{0.935 \times 155.62 \times 3}{1.95 \times 10^{-2}}$$

$$= 22,385$$

Therefore from the Moody diagram, corresponding to Reynolds number 22,385 and for a smooth pipe, the friction factor $f = 0.0063$.

Substituting the values into the pressure gradient equation, yield

$$\frac{\Delta P}{L} = 4 \times 0.0063 \times \frac{1}{2 \times 3} \times 0.935 \times (155.62)^2$$

$$= 95\ (\text{dynes cm}^{-2})/\text{cm length}$$

or $$\frac{\Delta P}{L} = 0.071 \text{ mm of Hg/cm length}$$

• PROBLEM 4-16

Can the wall shear stress (τ_w), be determined from the plot of experimental data of u^+ Vs. y^+? For Reynolds numbers between 10,000 and 100,000, the law of the wall relates u^+ and y^+ by $u^+ = 87(y^+)^{1/7}$ and the corresponding elation between average velocity and centerline velocity is $u_{av} = 0.81\ U_0$.

Use these two equations to get wall shear stress and large friction factor. Compare this friction factor with the friction factor of the Blasius equation for fully developed pipe flow $f = \dfrac{0.3164}{(R_e)^{\frac{1}{4}}}$

Solution: Wall shear stress (τ_w) can be determined from u^+ and y^+, because both u^+ and y^+ are functions of shear velocity u* given by

$$u^+ = u/u^* \tag{1}$$

$$y^+ = y\,u^*/\nu \tag{2}$$

where u = velocity at distance y from the wall.

ν = kinematic viscosity

The shear velocity u^* is related to τ_w by the equation

$$u^* = \sqrt{(\tau_w/\rho)} \tag{3}$$

where ρ = density of the fluid.

Hence the shear stress at the wall (τ_w) can be found from the plot of experimental data of u^+ and y^+

The law of the wall is given by

$$u^+ = 8.7(y^+)^{1/7}$$

Substituting equations (1) and (2) into the above equation yields,

$$\frac{u}{u^*} = 8.7\ (yu^*/\nu)^{1/7}$$

Simplifying for u^* yields,

$$u^* = \left[\frac{u^7\nu}{y}\right]^{1/8} \times 0.1506$$

from equation (3)

$$\left(\frac{\tau_w}{\rho}\right)^{\frac{1}{2}} = 0.1506\ \left(\frac{u^7\nu}{y}\right)^{1/8}$$

or

$$\frac{\tau_w}{\rho} = 0.0227\ \left(\frac{u^7\nu}{y}\right)^{1/4}$$

At $y = R = D/2$

$$u = U_0$$

i.e., the centerline velocity

or $u = 1.235\ U_{av}$ in terms of average velocity.

Substituting $y = D/2$ and $u = 1.235\ U_{av}$ into the above equation

$$\frac{\tau_w}{\rho} = 0.0227\ (1.235\ U_{av})^{7/4}\ (\nu)^{1/4} \times \left(\frac{2}{D}\right)^{1/4}$$

or

$$\tau_w = \frac{0.039\rho U_{av}^{7/4}\ \nu^{1/4}}{(D)^{\frac{1}{4}}}$$

or $$\tau_w = \frac{0.039 \rho U_{av}^2}{(R_e)^{\frac{1}{4}}} \quad \text{where } R_e = \frac{U_{av}.D}{\nu}$$

Therefore the wall shear stress is

$$\tau_w = \frac{0.039\ \rho\ U_{av}^2}{(R_e)^{\frac{1}{4}}}$$

The large friction factor f is given by

$$f = 4\tau_w/\tfrac{1}{2}\ \rho\ U_{av}^2$$

substituting τ_w into the above equation

$$f = \frac{8 \times 0.039\ \rho\ U_{av}^2}{(R_e)^{\frac{1}{4}}\ \rho\ U_{av}^2}$$

or $$f = \frac{0.312}{(R_e)^{\frac{1}{4}}}$$

But from the Blasius result

$$f = \frac{0.3164}{(R_e)^{\frac{1}{4}}}$$

Therefore the obtained value of the large friction factor is very close to the Blasius result i.e., within 1.5% of the Blasius result.

• PROBLEM 4-17

Consider a big water tank connected to the piping system as shown in figure 1. If water at 180°F is discharged at the rate of 100 gal/min. through the end B, what is the water level in the tank. The pipe sizes shown in the figure 1 are standard nominal sizes. The actual inside diameters of 4 in. and 2 in. pipes are 4.026 in. and 2.067 in. respectively. For water take ρ = 60.58 lb/ft^3 and μ = 0.000233 lb/ft-s.

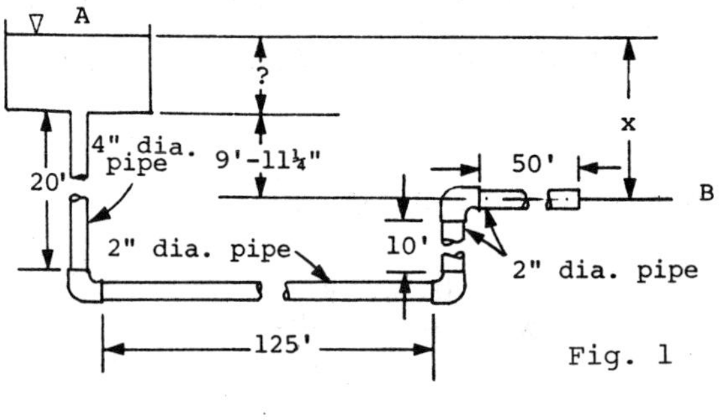

Fig. 1

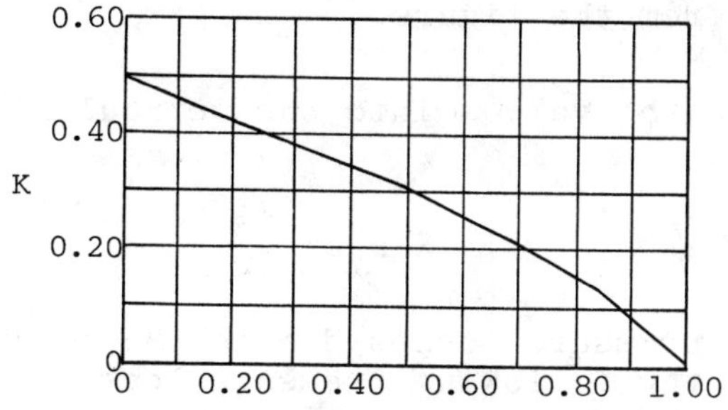

FIG. 2 CONTRACTION COEFFICIENTS

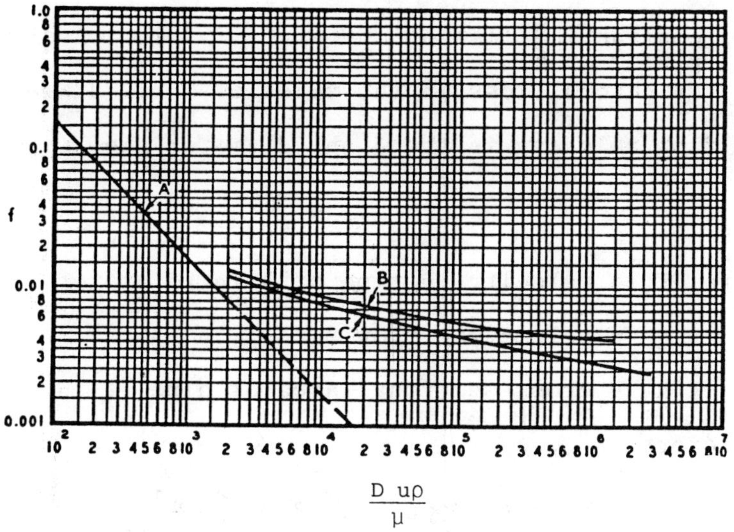

FIG. 3 FRICTION FACTORS FOR FLUIDS INSIDE PIPES.

Solution: The Bernoulli's theorem describing the flow between the points A and B is given by

$$\frac{P_A}{\rho} + \frac{u_A^2}{2g} + Z_A = \frac{P_B}{\rho} + \frac{u_B^2}{2g} + Z_B + H_f - W$$

where P = pressure

ρ = density of water

u = velocity of water

Z = vertical height from datum

H_f = frictional losses

W = external work

In this case $w = 0$, since no work is done on or by the liquid. The pressure at points A and B is atmospheric pressure, since both are open to atmosphere.

Since the diameter of the tank is large, $u_A \cong 0$

$Z_A - Z_B = X$, from the figure.

Substituting the values into the Bernoulli's equation, yields

$$X - H_f = \frac{u_B^2}{2g}$$

Neglect the pressure losses due to change in direction. H_f includes the following pressure losses:

(1) contraction loss at the exit of tank (H_{f_1})

(2) frictional loss in the pipe of 4 in. diameter (H_{f_2})

(3) contraction loss at the exit of 4 in. pipe (H_{f_3})

(4) frictional loss in the pipes of 2 in. diameter (H_{f_4})

The flow velocity in the 4 in. diameter pipe is given by

$$V_4 = \frac{q}{A_4}$$

where V_4 = velocity in pipe of 4 in. diameter

q = volumetric flow rate

A_4 = cross-sectional area of pipe (4 in. diameter).

Therefore

$$V_4 = (100 \times 0.002228) \times \frac{4 \times (12)^2}{\pi \times (4.026)^2}$$

$$= 2.52 \text{ ft/s}$$

The area of the tank is so large in proportion to the area of the 4 in. pipe, that the ratio of the areas is practically zero.

Therefore from the figure 2, the value of k = 0.5.

The head loss due to contraction is given by

$$H_c = \frac{k u_2^2}{2g}$$

where k = contraction coefficient

u_2 = velocity in the smaller diameter pipe.

Therefore

$$H_{f_1} = \frac{0.5 \times (2.52)^2}{2 \times 32.2}$$

$$= 0.05 \text{ ft.}$$

The effective length of a pipe with an elbow is

$$L_E = L + \frac{32D}{12}$$

where L_E = effective length in ft.

L = actual length in ft.

D = diameter in inches.

Therefore the effective length of the 4 in. pipe is

$$L_E = 20 + \frac{32 \times 4}{12}$$

$$= 30.7 \text{ ft}$$

The Reynolds number for the flow in the 4 in. pipe is given by

$$\frac{\rho D u}{\mu}$$

$$R_{e_4} = 60.58 \times \frac{4.026}{12} \times 2.52 \times \frac{1}{0.000233}$$

$$= 219{,}700$$

Therefore, from the figure 3, with $\frac{\rho D u}{\mu} = 219{,}700$ and curve B for commercially clean steel pipe, the friction factor f = 0.0048.

The frictional pressure loss in the pipe is

$$H_f = \frac{2fLu^2}{gD}$$

Therefore $$H_{f_2} = \frac{2 \times 0.0048 \times 30.7 \times (2.52)^2}{32.2 \times 4.026} \times 12$$

or $$H_{f_2} = 0.173 \text{ ft.}$$

The flow velocity in the 2 in. diameter pipe

$$V_2 = 100 \times 0.002228 \times \frac{4 \times (12)^2}{\pi \times (2.067)^2}$$

$$= 9.58 \text{ ft/s}$$

The ratio of the areas of the 2 in. diameter and 4 in. diameter pipes is

$$\left(\frac{2.067}{4.026}\right)^2 = 0.263$$

Therefore from the figure 2, the value of k is 0.40.

Therefore $$H_{f_3} = \frac{0.40 \times (9.58)^2}{2 \times 32.2}$$

$$= 0.57 \text{ ft.}$$

The effective length of the 2 in. diameter pipe is

$$L_E = L + \frac{2(32)D}{12} \text{ because of 2 elbows}$$

$$= 125 + 10 + 50 + \frac{2 \times 32 \times 2}{12}$$

$$= 196 \text{ ft.}$$

The Reynolds number $\frac{\rho Du}{\mu}$ is

$$\frac{\rho Du}{\mu} = 60.58 \times \frac{2.067}{12} \times 9.58 \times \frac{1}{0.000233}$$

$$= 428{,}400.$$

Therefore, from the figure 3, with $\frac{\rho Du}{\mu} = 428{,}400$ and using curve B, the friction factor f = 0.0046.

Therefore the frictional pressure loss in the 2 in. diameter pipe is

$$H_{f_4} = \frac{2 \times 0.0046 \times 196 \times (9.58)^2}{32.2 \times 2.067} \times 12$$

$$= 29.9 \text{ ft.}$$

Therefore the total frictional pressure loss in the piping unit is the sum $H_{f_1} + H_{f_2} + H_{f_3} + H_{f_4}$

i.e., $$H_f = 0.05 + 0.17 + 0.57 + 29.9$$

$$= 30.7 \text{ ft.}$$

Substituting H_f into the Bernoulli's equation

$$X - 30.7 = \frac{(9.58)^2}{2 \times 32.2}$$

or $$X = 32.1 \text{ ft.}$$

Therefore the level of water in the tank is 32.1-9.9 = 22.2 ft. above the bottom surface of tank.

• **PROBLEM 4-18**

Water at 70°F is flowing through an R.C.C. pipe, at a volumetric flow rate of 15 ft^3/s. Determine the diameter of the pipe, if the pressure loss must not exceed 4.8 ft. in a length of 1000 ft.

Solution: The maximum value of surface roughness for an R.C.C. pipe is k = 0.01 ft. By taking this maximum value, it can be assured that the pressure loss will not exceed the given value.

The Reynolds number for water flow through a pipe is given by

$$R_e = \frac{VD}{\nu} = \frac{4q}{\pi D \nu}$$

where q = volumetric flow rate

ν = kinematic viscosity of water

D = diameter of the pipe

Substituting the known values into the above equation yield,

$$R_e = \frac{4 \times 15}{\pi \times D \times 1.05 \times 10^{-5}}$$

or
$$R_e = \frac{1.82}{D} \times 10^6$$

The frictional pressure drop in a fluid flowing inside a pipe is

$$h_1 = f \frac{L}{D} \frac{V^2}{2g}$$

or
$$h_1 = f \frac{L}{D} \frac{q^2}{2g\left(\frac{\pi}{4} D^2\right)^2}$$

or
$$D = f^{1/5} \left(\frac{8Lq^2}{\pi^2 g h_1}\right)^{1/5}$$

Substituting the known values into the above equation yield,

$$D = f^{1/5} \left(\frac{(8)(1000)(15)^2}{\pi^2 \times 32.2 \times 4.8}\right)^{1/5}$$

$$= 4.12\ f^{1/5}$$

This has to be evaluated by iterative method.

Initially, assume f = 0.025

then
$$D = 4.12 \times (0.025)^{1/5}$$

$$= 1.97 \text{ ft.}$$

The relative roughness of the pipe is the ratio

$$\frac{k}{D} = \frac{0.01}{1.97}$$

$$= 0.0051$$

The Reynolds number is

$$R_e = \frac{1.82}{1.97} \times 10^6 = 9.24 \times 10^5$$

The Reynolds number and the relative roughness can be used to find the corresponding friction factor, from the Moody diagram.

Therefore, the corresponding value of f = 0.03

This value of f is different from the assumed value of 0.025.

Substituting the new value of f = 0.03

$$D = 4.12 \times (0.03)^{1/5}$$

$$= 2.04 \text{ ft.}$$

The relative roughness $= \frac{k}{D}$

$$= \frac{0.01}{2.04} = 0.0049$$

The Reynolds number $R_e = \frac{1.82}{2.04} \times 10^6$

$$= 8.92 \times 10^5$$

From the Moody diagram the friction factor is f = 0.03, corresponding to the $R_e = 8.91 \times 10^5$ and relative roughness = 0.0049.

This value of f = 0.03 is same as the one used before.

Therefore this is the correct value of f.

Therefore the required diameter of the pipe is 2.04 ft.

• PROBLEM 4-19

Water flows through a galvanized iron pipe at a rate of $3 \text{ ft}^3/\text{s}$. If the pressure loss is 5 ft. per 1000 ft. of flow, determine the size of the pipe.

Solution: The frictional pressure loss in a liquid flowing through a circular pipe is given by the relation

$$h_f = f\left(\frac{L}{D}\right)\frac{V^2}{2g}$$

substituting $V = q/A$

$$= \frac{q}{\frac{\pi}{4}D^2}$$

$$h_f = \frac{fLq^2}{2g\pi^2 D^5} \times 16$$

or
$$D^5 = \frac{8fLq^2}{g\pi^2 h_f} \qquad (1)$$

Initially assume f = 0.015

Substituting the values, in equation (1) gives

$$D^5 = \frac{8(0.015)(1000)(3)^2}{32.2(\pi)^2(5)}$$

$$= 0.67967$$

or
$$D = 0.926 \text{ ft.}$$

For a galvanized iron pipe, the relative roughness factor is $\frac{k}{D}$ = 0.0005 (for diameter in the range-11 inches).

The flow velocity $V = \frac{q}{A}$

or
$$V = \frac{3}{\frac{\pi}{4}(0.926)^2}$$

or
$$V = 4.45 \text{ ft/s}$$

The Reynolds number R_e is given by

$$R_e = \frac{VD}{\nu}$$

where V = velocity

D = diameter

ν = kinematic viscosity

Therefore

$$R_e = \frac{4.45 \times 0.926}{1.21 \times 10^{-5}}$$

$$= 3.4 \times 10^5$$

From the Moody diagram, corresponding to a $R_e = 3.4 \times 10^5$ and $\frac{k}{D} = 0.0005$, the friction factor f = 0.0185

Substituting the correct value of f (instead of assumed value f = 0.015) in equation (1) gives the value of D.

$$D^5 = \frac{8(0.0185)(1000)(3)^2}{32.2\ (\pi)^2(5)}$$

$$= 0.8383$$

or $$D = 0.965 \text{ ft.}$$

$$11\tfrac{5}{8}''$$

• PROBLEM 4-20

Air at 150°F and 20 psig is flowing through a wrought iron pipe at a rate of 900 cfm. Calculate the smallest diameter of the pipe, if the maximum pressure loss in 200 ft. of the air flow is 6 psi. The relative roughness for a wrought iron pipe (ε/D) = 0.0004.

Solution: The equation relating the pressure drop to the friction factor will be solved simultaneously with the Moody diagram. Assume an initial value for D and calculate the Reynolds number to find the friction factor from the Moody diagram. This friction factor will then be used to find D from the pressure drop equation.

The frictional pressure loss in a fluid flowing through a circular pipe is given by the relation.

$$\Delta p = f \left(\frac{L}{D}\right) \frac{\rho V^2}{2g}$$

substituting

$$V = \frac{q}{\frac{\pi}{4} D^2}$$

$$\Delta p = \frac{8 f L \rho q^2}{g \pi^2 D^5}$$

or $$D = \left(\frac{8\rho L q^2}{\pi^2 \Delta p g}\right)^{1/5} f^{1/5} \qquad (1)$$

The Reynolds number is given by

$$R_e = \frac{\rho V D}{\mu}$$

or $$R_e = \frac{4\rho q}{\pi \mu D} \quad (2)$$

The density of air (ρ) is calculated from the equation of state for a perfect gas.

$$\rho = \frac{pm}{RT}$$

where p = pressure in lbf/ft^2

m = molecular wt. lb/lb-mol

R = gas constant ft-lbf/lb-mol.°R

T = temperature in °R

substituting the values

$$\rho = \frac{(20 + 14.7)(144) \times 28.97}{(1545) \times (460 + 150)}$$

$$= 0.1536 \ lb/ft^3$$

Substituting the values in equation (1) yields

$$D = \left[\frac{8 \times 0.1536 \times 200}{\pi^2 \times 6 \times 144 \times 32.17} \times \left(\frac{900}{60}\right)^2\right]^{1/5} f^{1/5}$$

Simplifying yields

$$D = 0.7259 \ f^{1/5} \quad (3)$$

Substituting the values in equation (2) for Reynolds number,

$$R_e = \frac{4 \times 0.1536}{\pi \times (1.364 \times 10^{-5})} \times \left(\frac{900}{60}\right) \times \frac{1}{D}$$

simplifying yields

$$R_e = \frac{2.15 \times 10^5}{D} \quad (4)$$

To find the value of D from equations (3) and (4), initially assume D = 0.5 ft.

Substituting the value of D in equation (4) and finding out the friction factor from the Moody diagram and then substituting f into equation (3) yields another value of D.

This process continues until the value of D obtained from equation (3) is equal to or very close to the value of D taken to calculate R_e and hence f. The calculations are shown in the table.

D	$Re = \frac{2.15\times10^5}{D}$	f friction factor	$D = 0.7259\ f^{1/5}$
0.5	4.3×10^5	0.0175	0.3232
0.3232	6.6×10^5	0.0170	0.3213
0.3213	6.7×10^5	0.0170	0.3213

Therefore the solution is

$$D = 0.3213 \text{ ft.}$$

or

$$D = 3.86 \text{ in.}$$

• PROBLEM 4-21

Determine the velocity profile of gasoline flowing in a 7 in. cast-iron pipe at the rate of 400 cfm. The kinematic viscosity and density of gasoline are 0.42×10^{-5} ft^2/sec. and 1.35 slugs/ft^3 respectively. Also find the drag induced by the flow on a unit length of the pipe.

Solution: The velocity profile is dependent on the type of flow in the pipe. To determine the type of flow the Reynolds number has to be calculated.

The Reynolds number is given by

$$R_e = \frac{VD}{\nu}$$

where V = velocity of gasoline

D = diameter of pipe

ν = kinematic viscosity.

Substituting the known values gives

$$R_e = \frac{\left(\dfrac{400}{(60)\ \frac{\pi}{4}\ (7/12)^2}\right)\dfrac{7}{12}}{0.42\times10^{-5}}$$

$$= 3{,}465{,}278 \cong 3.47\times10^6$$

This implies the flow is turbulent. The high Reynolds number necessitates the use of universal formulations to compute the velocity profile.

The equations used are

$$\frac{v_Z}{\sqrt{\tau_0/\rho}} = \frac{1}{0.4}\left(\ln \frac{y\sqrt{\tau_0/\rho}}{\nu} - \ln\beta\right) \qquad (1)$$

where

$$\ln\beta = \ln \frac{\varepsilon\sqrt{\tau_0/\rho}}{\nu} - 3.4 \qquad (2)$$

To find the zone of the pipe ε/D has to be read from the Moody chart. From the Moody chart for 7 in. cast iron pipe $\varepsilon/D = 0.0017$ is obtained. This signifies that it is in the rough pipe zone of flow.

The shear stress (τ_0) is given by

$$\tau_0 = \frac{f}{4}\frac{\rho v^2}{2}$$

$$\tau_0 = \frac{f}{4}\left(\frac{1.35(24.95)^2}{2}\right)$$

$$= 105.05\ f \qquad (3)$$

From Moody diagram for $R_e = 3.47 \times 10^6$ and $\varepsilon/D = 0.0017$ we find the friction factor $f = 0.040$.

Then from equation (3)

$$\tau_0 = 105.05\ (0.040)$$

$$= 4.202 \text{ psf.}$$

From equation (2)

$$\ln\beta = \ln \frac{(0.000992)\sqrt{\left(\frac{4.202}{1.35}\right)}}{0.42 \times 10^{-5}} - 3.4$$

$$= 2.63$$

Then from equation (1)

$$v_Z = \sqrt{\left(\frac{4.202}{1.35}\right)}\left(\frac{1}{0.4}\right)\left[\ln \frac{\sqrt{\left(\frac{4.202}{1.35}\right)}y}{0.42 \times 10^{-5}} - 2.63\right]$$

$$= 4.41\ [\ln\ (4.2 \times 10^5\ y) - 2.63]$$

The maximum velocity occurs at $y = 0.29$. Then

$$(v_Z)_{max} = 4.41\ [\ln(4.2 \times 10^5 \times 0.29) - 2.63]$$

$$= 40.04 \text{ fps.}$$

The profile will be flatter because of turbulent flow. If it would have been laminar flow the profile would be parabolic. The maximum velocity in laminar flow would have been 50 fps.

The drag per unit length of pipe is given by

$$\text{Drag} = (\tau_w)(\pi D)$$

$$= (4.202)(\pi)(7/12)$$

$$= 7.7 \text{ lb/ft.}$$

• PROBLEM 4-22

Water flows through a pipe of 1 ft. inside diameter. The kinematic viscosity of water $\nu = 1 \times 10^{-5}$ ft^2/s, the wall roughness of the pipe $\varepsilon = 0.001$ ft. and the velocity distribution is as shown in the figure below.

(a) Assume the pipe surface is rough and find the shear stress at the pipe wall.

(b) Show that the pipe surface is rough.

(c) Find the velocity distribution corresponding to the maximum flow rate for which the pipe can be considered as a smooth pipe.

(d) Find the velocity at y = 0.2 ft. and y = 0.5 ft. (center line) for both the velocity profiles - rough and smooth.

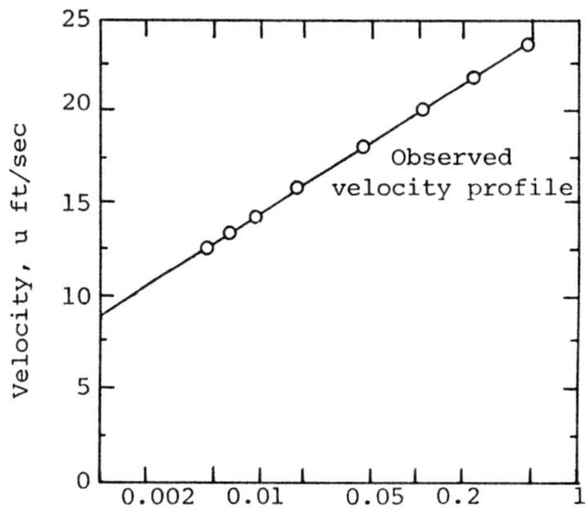

Distance from pipe wall, y, ft. Turbulent velocity profiles

Solution: The velocity distribution of water in a rough pipe is given by the empirical relation,

$$\frac{u}{u^*} = 5.75 \log_{10}\left(\frac{y}{\varepsilon}\right) + 8.5 \qquad (1)$$

From the actual velocity distribution given in the figure

$$u = 5.71 \log_{10} y + 25.53 \qquad (2)$$

Comparing equations (1) and (2) yields, the shear velocity

$$u^* = 0.992 \text{ ft/s}$$

But the shear velocity is given by

$$u^* = \sqrt{\frac{\tau_0}{\rho}}$$

where τ_0 = shear stress at wall

ρ = density of water.

rearranging

$$\tau_0 = \rho u^{*2}$$

substituting the values,

$$\tau_0 = \frac{62.4}{32.2} \times (0.992)^2$$

$$= 1.91 \text{ lbf/ft}^2$$

Therefore the wall shear stress = 1.91 lbf/ft^2.

(b) For the pipe surface to be rough, the shear velocity/ roughness Reynolds number

i.e., $\frac{u^*\varepsilon}{\nu}$ should be greater than 70.

substituting the values into the ratio

$$\frac{0.992 \times 0.001}{1 \times 10^{-5}}$$

$$= 99.2$$

Since the value of the ratio is greater than 70, the pipe surface is rough.

(c) The pipe can be considered smooth, if the shear velocity satisfies the relation

$$\frac{u^*\varepsilon}{\nu} = 5$$

or

$$u^* = \frac{5\nu}{\varepsilon}$$

substituting the values

$$u^* = \frac{5 \times 1 \times 10^{-5}}{0.001}$$

$$= 0.05$$

Then, the velocity distribution for a smooth pipe is

$$\frac{u}{u*} = 5.75 \log\left(\frac{u*y}{\nu}\right) + 5.5$$

Substituting the values and solving for u yields,

$$u = 0.288 \log_{10} y + 1.338$$

This is the equation of velocity distribution for maximum flow rate, for which the pipe can be considered as a smooth pipe.

(d) The velocity distribution for a rough flow is

$$u_r = 5.71 \log_{10} (y) + 25.53$$

and for a smooth flow

$$u_s = 0.288 \log_{10} (y) + 1.338$$

substituting y = 0.2 ft. and y = 0.5 ft. in both of these equations

$$u_{r(0.2)} = 5.71 \log_{10} (0.2) + 25.53$$

$$= 21.54 \text{ ft/s}$$

$$u_{r(0.5)} = 5.71 \log_{10} (0.5) + 25.53$$

$$= 23.81 \text{ ft/s}$$

$$u_{s(0.2)} = 0.288 \log_{10}(0.2) + 1.338$$

$$= 1.14 \text{ ft/s}$$

$$u_{s(0.5)} = 0.288 \log_{10} (0.5) + 1.338 = 1.25 \text{ ft/sec.}$$

• PROBLEM 4-23

Air of density $\rho = 0.07 \text{ lb/ft}^3$ and viscosity $\mu = 12.9 \times 10^{-6}$ lb/ft.sec is flowing through a pipe of 10 in. inside diameter. The mean velocity of the air is 50 ft/sec. Find the velocity at points 0.4 in and 3 in. from the wall. Also find the thickness of the laminar sub-layer if this extends up to $u^+ = y^+ = 5$.

u^+ and y^+ are dimensionless quantities defined as uy/u* and $y\rho u*/\mu$ respectively, where y is the distance from the surface.

Solution: The velocity at any point inside the pipe is given by the velocity defect law. The velocity defect law is given by

$$\frac{u_s - u_x}{u^*} = -2.5 \ln(y/r)$$

or $$u_x = u_s + u^* \left(2.5 \ln(y/r)\right) \qquad (1)$$

where u_x = velocity at the required point

$u_s = \frac{u}{0.82}$ where u = mean velocity of flow

$u^* = u\sqrt{\phi}$ where ϕ = friction factor

y = distance of the point from the pipe surface

r = radius of the pipe

$$u_s = \frac{u}{0.82}$$

or $$u_s = \frac{50}{0.82} = 61 \text{ ft/sec.}$$

The Reynolds number is given by

$$R_e = \frac{\rho VD}{\mu}$$

where R_e = Reynolds number

ρ = density of the air = 0.07 lb/ft^3

V = mean velocity of flow = 50 ft/sec.

μ = viscosity of air = 12.9×10^{-6} lb/ft-sec.

D = diameter of the pipe = $\frac{10}{12}$ ft.

substituting the values gives

$$R_e = \frac{0.07 \times 50 \times (10/12)}{12.9 \times 10^{-6}}$$

or $$R_e = 2.3 \times 10^5$$

Therefore the corresponding friction factor ϕ is

$$\phi = \frac{R}{\rho u^2} = 0.00185$$

Substituting ϕ = 0.00185 in the equation for u* gives

$$u^* = 50\sqrt{0.00185}$$

$$= 2.15 \text{ ft/sec.}$$

For the point y = 0.4 in. from the wall the ratio y/r = 0.4/5

$$= 0.08$$

Substituting the values into equation (1) gives

$$u_{x_{0.4}} = 61 + [2.15 \times 2.5 \ln (0.08)]$$

or $$u_{x_{0.4}} = 47.42 \text{ ft/sec.}$$

where $u_{x_{0.4}}$ = fluid velocity at 0.4 in. from the pipe wall.

For the point y = 3 in. from the pipe wall the ratio

$$y/r = 3/5$$
$$= 0.6$$

Then substituting the values into equation (1) gives

u_{x_3} = fluid velocity at 3 in from the pipe wall

$$= 61 + 2.15 \times 2.5 \ln (0.6)$$

or $$u_{x_3} = 58.25 \text{ ft/sec.}$$

The thickness of the laminar sub-layer is

$$\delta_1 = 5d/R_e(\phi)^{\frac{1}{2}}$$

where δ_1 = thickness of laminar sub-layer in inches

d = diameter of pipe in inches

R_e = Reynolds number

ϕ = friction factor

Substituting the values gives

$$\delta_1 = \frac{5 \times 10}{(2.3 \times 10^5) \times (0.00185)^{\frac{1}{2}}}$$

or $$\delta_1 = 0.005 \text{ in.}$$

APPLICATION OF BERNOULLI EQUATION TO FLUID FLOW

• PROBLEM 4-24

Water is flowing through a 4 in. inside diameter, wrought iron pipe of 100 ft., at a mean velocity of 6 feet/sec. If the outlet of the pipe is 3 ft. higher than the inlet, determine the power required to obtain this flow rate.

Solution: The power required can be found from the Bernoulli's energy equation.

$$\frac{P_1}{\rho} + \frac{V_1^2}{2g} + Z_1 = \frac{P_2}{\rho} + \frac{V_2^2}{2g} + Z_2 + h_f - W \cdot$$

where P = Pressure

ρ = density

V = velocity

Z = height

h_f = frictional losses

W = work done on water

Assume, $P_1 = P_2 = P_{atm}$.

$V_1 = V_2$ for constant cross section of the pipe

$$(Z_2 - Z_1) = 3 \text{ ft.}$$

Substituting these values into the Bernoulli's equation, yields

$$W = 3 + h_f$$

frictional losses h_f is given by

$$\frac{2fLV^2}{Dg}$$

where f = friction factor from Moody diagram

L = length of pipe

V = velocity of flow

D = diameter of the pipe

To find the friction factor from the Moody diagram, the Reynolds number for the flow and relative roughness of the pipe are needed.

Reynolds number for the flow is given by

$$R_e = \frac{\rho VD}{\mu}$$

where ρ = density of water = 62.4 lbm/ft^3

μ = viscosity of water = 0.76×10^{-3} lbm/ft-s

V = velocity of flow = 6 ft/s

D = diameter of the pipe = 0.333 ft.

substituting,

$$R_e = \frac{62.4 \times 6 \times 0.3333}{0.76 \times 10^{-3}}$$

$$R_e = 164{,}194$$

The relative roughness of a 4 in. diameter wrought iron pipe is 0.0004.

The friction factor corresponding to $R_e = 1.6 \times 10^5$ and relative roughness 0.0004 is,

$$f = 0.019$$

Substituting f into the expression for h_f gives

$$h_f = \frac{2 \times 0.019 \times 100 \times (6)^2}{0.3333 \times 32.2}$$

$$h_f = 12.75 \text{ ft.}$$

Therefore the work done

$$W = 3 + 12.75$$

$$W = 15.75 \text{ ft.}$$

or $$W = 15.75 \times \left[62.3 \times \frac{\pi}{4}\left(\frac{1}{3}\right)^2 \times 6 \times \frac{1}{550}\right] \text{hp.}$$

or $$W = 0.934 \text{ hp.}$$

Therefore the power required is 0.934 hp.

• PROBLEM 4-25

Derive an expression for the loss of mechanical energy using the energy and momentum balance equations, for a fluid flow from a small pipe to a large pipe through an abrupt expansion.

Then, find the energy lost due to the abrupt expansion, if 7200 cfm of air at 80°F flows through the pipe. Take $A_0 = \frac{\pi}{4}$ and $A_1 = A_2 = \pi$.

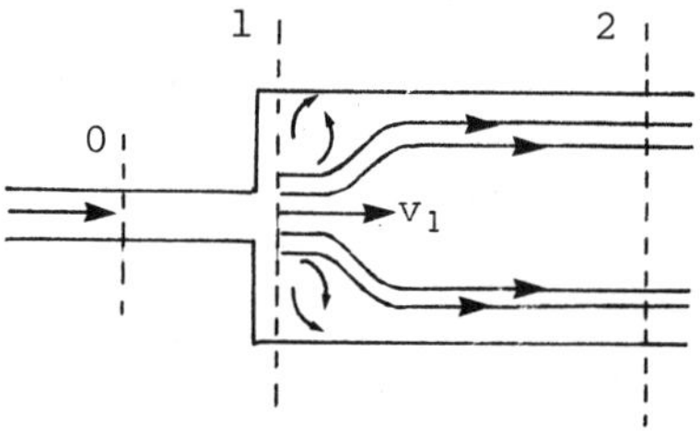

ABRUPT EXPANSION

Fig. 1.

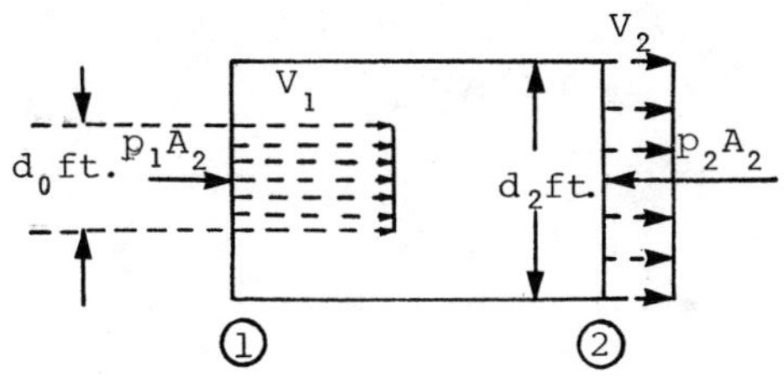

CONTROL VOLUME FOR AN ABRUPT EXPANSION. Fig. 2

Solution: In order to neglect frictional losses at the wall surface, consider a control volume that does not include the pipe wall. Then all the pressure losses are due to eddies in the control volume between sections 1 and 2.

The section 1 is chosen immediately after the abrupt expansion so that the flow area in the section 1 is A_0. Then $p_0 = p_1$; $V_0 = V_1$ and $A_1 = A_2$

Assume pressures p_1 and p_2 to be uniform over the cross-sectional area.

Apply momentum balance between sections 1 and 2,

$$p_1A_1 - p_2A_2 = mv_2 - mv_1$$

or $$(p_1 - p_2)A_2 = m(V_2 - V_1) \qquad (1)$$

The mass flow rate m is given by

$$m = \rho V_0 A_0$$

and from the continuity equation

$$V_2A_2 = V_0A_0$$

or $$V_2 = \left(\frac{A_0}{A_2}\right) V_0$$

Substituting these terms into the equation (1), yields

$$(p_1 - p_2)A_2 = \rho A_0 V_0 \left(\frac{A_0V_0}{A_2} - V_0\right)$$

$$= \rho A_0 V_0^2 \left(\frac{A_0}{A_2} - 1\right)$$

or $$\frac{p_2 - p_1}{\rho} = V_0^2 \frac{A_0}{A_2}\left(1 - \frac{A_0}{A_2}\right) \qquad (2)$$

The mechanical energy balance equation between the sections 1 and 2 is

$$\tfrac{1}{2}(V_2^2 - V_1^2) + (Z_2 - Z_1) + \frac{p_2 - p_1}{\rho} + \Sigma F + W_s = 0$$

here

$$Z_2 - Z_1 = 0$$

$$W_5 = 0; \; V_1 = V_0$$

rewriting

$$\frac{1}{2}(V_0^2 - V_2^2) - \Sigma F = \frac{p_2 - p_1}{\rho} \qquad (3)$$

From equations (2) and (3)

$$\Sigma F = \frac{1}{2}(V_0^2 - V_2^2) - V_0^2 \frac{A_0}{A_2}\left(1 - \frac{A_0}{A_2}\right)$$

$$= \frac{1}{2}\left(V_0^2 - \frac{A_0^2 V_0^2}{A_2^2}\right) - \frac{V_0^2 A_0}{A_2}\left(1 - \frac{A_0}{A_2}\right)$$

Simplifying further yields

$$\Sigma F = \frac{V_0^2}{2}\left(1 - \frac{A_0}{A_2}\right)^2 \qquad (4)$$

or $$F = \frac{\rho}{g}\,\Sigma F = \frac{\rho V_0{}^2}{2g}\left(1 - \frac{A_0}{A_2}\right)^2$$

The volumetric flow rate $q = 7200$ cfm

$$= 120 \text{ ft}^3/\text{s}$$

The velocity V_0 is given by

$$V_0 = \frac{q}{A_0}$$

$$= \frac{120}{\frac{\pi}{4} \times (1)^2}$$

or $$V_0 = 152.79 \text{ ft/s}$$

substituting into equation 4, the mechanical energy lost

$$F = \frac{0.00228}{2} \times (152.79)^2 \left(1 - \left(\frac{1}{2}\right)^2\right)^2$$

$$= 14.97 \text{ ft-lb/ft}^3$$

The total power loss is

$$P = F \times q$$

$$= 14.97 \times 120$$

$$= 1796.4 \text{ ft-lb/s}$$

or $$P = 3.26 \text{ horse power}$$

Water from a reservoir is pumped into a machine, which is at a height of 25 feet from the water level in the reservoir. If 180 cfm of water at 8 psi enters the machine, find the input power required to drive the pump if it is 85 percent efficient. The pressure losses between sections 1 and 2 is given by $h_f = KV_2^2/2g$ where K = 7.5. Take pipe diameter as 3 in.

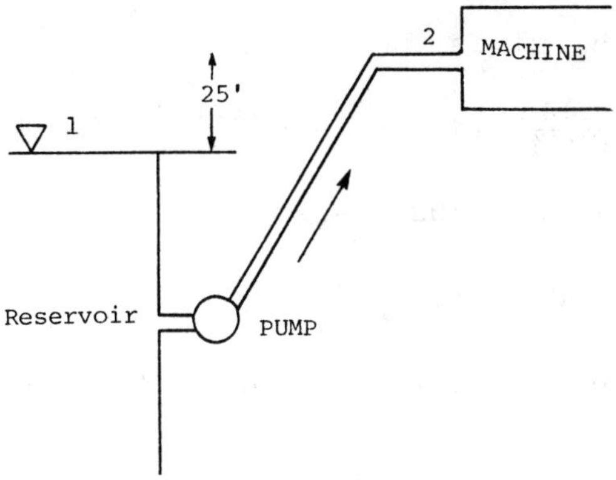

Solution: Assume the reservoir is very large in area, then the velocity of the water surface in the reservoir is approximately zero, i.e., $V_1 \cong 0$.

The velocity V_2 at the entrance to the machine is given by

$$V_2 = \frac{q}{A_2}$$

where q = volumetric flow rate

A_2 = cross-sectional area of the pipe

Substituting the values

$$V_2 = \left(\frac{180}{60}\right) \times \frac{4}{\pi \times (3/12)^2}$$

$$= 61.1 \text{ ft/s}$$

Apply the energy equation between the sections 1 and 2

$$\frac{p_1}{\rho g} + \frac{V_1^2}{2g} + Z_1 = \frac{p_2}{\rho g} + \frac{V_2^2}{2g} + Z_2 + h_s + h_f$$

where p = pressure

ρ = density

V = velocity

Z = height

h_s = shaft head or pump head

h_f = friction head

Substituting $V_1 = Z_1 = 0$, $k = 7.5$, $V_2 = 61.1$; $\rho g = 62.4$

$Z_2 = 25$; $p_1 = 14.7 \times 144$ psf; $p_2 = 8 \times 144$ psf

$$\frac{14.7 \times 144}{62.4} = \frac{8 \times 144}{62.4} + \frac{(61.1)^2}{2 \times 32.2} + 25 + h_s + \frac{7.5 \times (61.1)^2}{2 \times 32.2}$$

Solving for h_s gives

$$h_s = \frac{144}{62.4}(14.7-8) - \frac{(61.1)^2}{2 \times 32.2}(7.5 + 1) - 25$$

$$h_s = 15.5 - 492.7 - 25$$

or $$h_s = -502.2 \text{ ft.}$$

The pump head is negative, showing that work is done on the water.

Therefore the power required is

$$P = \rho g q h_s$$

$$= (1.94)(32.2)\frac{180}{60}(502.2)$$

$$P = 94{,}114 \text{ ft.lbf/s}$$

Considering the efficiency of the pump, the power required to drive the pump is

$$P_{input} = \frac{P}{\text{efficiency}}$$

$$= \frac{94114}{0.85 \times 550}$$

$$P_{input} = 202 \text{ HP}$$

• PROBLEM 4-27

Two reservoirs, A and B, are filled with water to the same height h. The reservoir A discharges water through a circular orifice where as reservoir B discharges through a circular tube of length L. If the diameter of the orifice is same as the diameter of the tube (d), then compare the velocities and rate of flow at points 1 and 2 as shown in figure, in both the reservoirs.

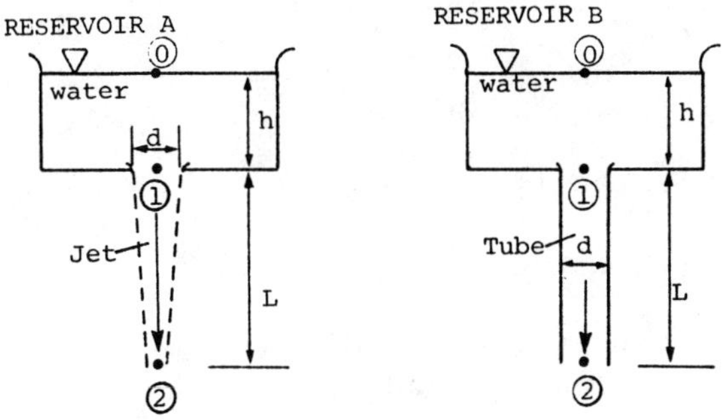

Solution: To get a relationship for velocity at a point in a streamline, apply the Bernoulli's equation along a streamline.

Assume that the reservoirs are large enough to neglect the velocity of the water surface i.e., $V_0 \cong 0$.

Apply the Bernoulli's equation between points 0 and 2 and compare the velocities at points 2.

The Bernoulli's equation is

$$\frac{p_0}{\gamma} + Z_0 + \frac{V_0^2}{2g} = \frac{p_2}{\gamma} + Z_2 + \frac{V_2^2}{2g}$$

where p = pressure

Z = height

V = velocity

subscripts 0 and 2 indicate the points 0 and 2 respectively.

In the case of reservoir A,

$$p_0 = p_2 = p_{atm}$$

since both the ends are open to atmosphere

$$(Z_0 - Z_2) = h + L$$

and

$$V_0 = 0$$

Substituting these values into the above equation, yields

$$\frac{V_2^2}{2g} = h + L$$

or

$$V_2 = \sqrt{2g(h+L)}$$

or

$$(V_2)_A = \sqrt{2g(h+L)}$$

where $(V_2)_A$ = velocity at point 2 in the reservoir A.

Similarly in the case of reservoir B, the same conditions

exists between points 0 and 2 so

$$(V_2)_B = \sqrt{2g(h+L)}$$

where $(V_2)_B$ = velocity at point 2 in the reservoir B.

Therefore $(V_2)_A = (V_2)_B$

To compare the velocities at point 1, apply the Bernoulli's equation between points 0 and 1.

In the case of reservoir A

$$\frac{p_0}{\gamma} + Z_0 + \frac{V_0^2}{2g} = \frac{p_1}{\gamma} + Z_1 + \frac{V_1^2}{2g}$$

here $p_0 = p_1 = p_{atm}$

since both the ends are open to the atmosphere.

$$(Z_0 - Z_1) = h$$

and $$V_0 \cong 0$$

Substituting these values into the above equation yields

$$\frac{V_1^2}{2g} = h$$

or $$(V_1)_A = \sqrt{2gh}$$

where $(V_1)_A$ = velocity at point 1 in the reservoir A.

In the case of reservoir B, the Bernoulli's equation between points 0 and 1 is

$$\frac{p_0}{\gamma} + Z_0 + \frac{V_0^2}{2g} = \frac{p_1}{\gamma} + Z_1 + \frac{V_1^2}{2g}$$

here $$(Z_0 - Z_1) = h$$

$$V_0 = 0$$

but p_0 is not equal to p_1

Since the point 1 is not open to atmosphere

i.e., $$p_1 \neq p_{atm}$$

Therefore the Bernoulli's equation cannot be used to find $(V_1)_B$.

From the equation of continuity between points 1 and 2 in the case of reservoir B,

$$(V_1)_B = (V_2)_B = \sqrt{2g(h+L)}$$

Therefore $(V_1)_B$ is greater than $(V_1)_A$.

The discharge through reservoir A is given by

$$(V_1)_A \times \text{Area of orifice}$$

$$= (\sqrt{2gh}) \times \frac{\pi}{4} d^2 .$$

The discharge through reservoir B is given by

$$(V_1)_B \times \text{Area of tube}$$

$$= (\sqrt{2g(h+L)}) \times \frac{\pi}{4} d^2 .$$

Therefore the discharge through reservoir B is greater than that through reservoir A.

• PROBLEM 4-28

A nozzle attached to a pipe, as shown in the figure, discharges water at a rate of 120 cfm. If the pipe diameter is 6 in. and the nozzle diameter is 3 in., calculate the water pressure in the pipe.

Assume $\alpha_A = 1.1$ at section A.

$\alpha_B = 1.02$ at section B.

Also determine the force acting on the joint of the contracting nozzle.

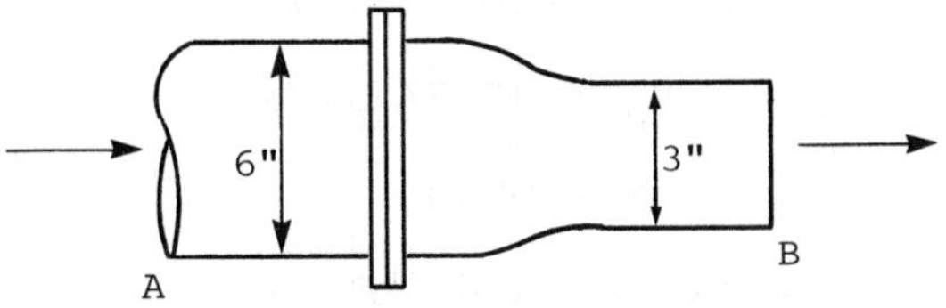

FIG. 1 CONTRACTING NOZZLE

Solution: The water pressure in the pipe can be found out by applying the Bernoulli's equation between the sections A and B.

The volumetric flow rate q = 120 ft^3/min

or

$$q = \frac{120}{60} \ ft^3/s$$

$$= 2 \ ft^3/s$$

The mean velocity at section A is given by

$$V_A = \frac{q}{A_{pipe}}$$

where A_{pipe} = cross-sectional area of the pipe

Therefore
$$V_A = \frac{2}{\frac{\pi}{4}\left(\frac{6}{12}\right)^2}$$
$$= 10.19 \text{ ft/s}$$

Similarly the mean velocity at section B is given by

$$V_B = \frac{q}{A_{Nozzle}}$$

or
$$V_B = \frac{2}{\frac{\pi}{4}\left(\frac{3}{12}\right)^2}$$
$$= 40.74 \text{ ft/s.}$$

The Bernoulli's equation between the two sections A and B is given by

$$\frac{P_A}{\gamma} + Z_A + \alpha_A \frac{V_A^2}{2g} = \frac{P_B}{\gamma} + Z_B + \alpha_B \frac{V_B^2}{2g}$$

here $Z_A = Z_B$ for horizontal pipe

$P_B = 0$ because the end B is open to the atmosphere.

$\alpha_A = 1.1;\ \alpha_B = 1.02$ given

$V_A = 10.19$ ft/s

$V_B = 40.74$ ft/s

$\gamma = 62.4$

Substituting these values and solving for P_A

$$\frac{P_A}{62.4} + \frac{(1.1)(10.19)^2}{2 \times 32.2} = \frac{(1.02)(40.74)^2}{2 \times 32.2}$$

or
$$P_A = 1529.69 \text{ lb/ft}^2$$

or
$$P_A = 10.62 \text{ psi}$$

Therefore the water pressure in the pipe is 10.62 psi.

The force acting on the joint can be found by applying the momentum equation between the sections A and B.

The momentum equation in the horizontal direction is

$$P_A \cdot A_A - F = \rho q(V_B - V_A)$$

where P_A = pressure at section A

A_A = cross-sectional area of the pipe

F = force acting on the joint

ρ = density

q = discharge rate of water

Substituting the values and solving for F, yields

$$(1529.69)\ \frac{\pi}{4} \times \left(\frac{6}{12}\right)^2 - F = 1.94 \times 2\ [40.74 - 10.19]$$

or $$F = 181.82 \text{ lbf}$$

This force on the joint is the tensile stress in the joint.

• PROBLEM 4-29

Water at 25°C is discharged from a reservoir by a siphon as shown in the figure. Determine the maximum value of L that can be used and the maximum rate of discharge such that no cavitation occurs. Take, for pipe d = 8 cm.

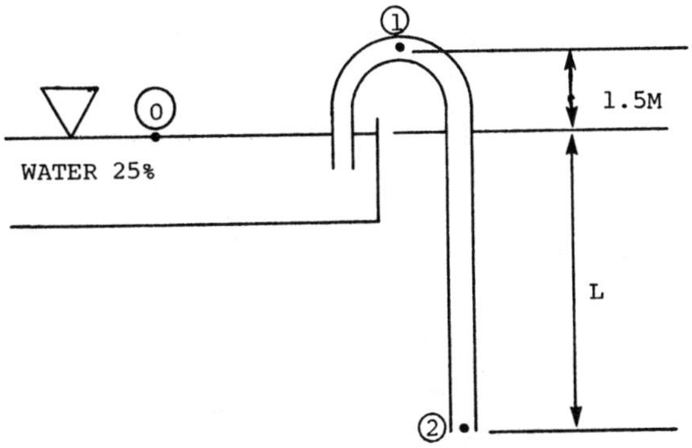

Solution: Applying the Bernoulli's equation between the sections 0 and 2, implies that the velocity at section 2 is related to length L, provided there is no cavitation within the siphon.

From the equation of continuity the velocity at section 1 is equal to the velocity at section 2. Apply the Bernoulli's equation between the two sections 1 and 2. It is

$$\frac{p_1}{\gamma} + Z_1 + \frac{V_1^2}{2g} = \frac{p_2}{\gamma} + Z_2 + \frac{V_2^2}{2g}$$

Substituting

$$(Z_1 - Z_2) = (1.5 + L)\ \text{m}$$

$$V_1 = V_2$$

$$\gamma = 9789\ \text{N/m}^3$$

$p_1 = 3.168\ \text{KN/m}^2$ (vapor pressure of water at 25 C) minimum pressure in siphon pipe.

$$p_2 = p_{atm} = 101.3\ \text{KN/m}^2$$

Substituting these values into the above equation yields

$$\frac{3168}{9789} + (1.5 + L) = \frac{101300}{9789}$$

or

$$L = 8.52\ \text{m}.$$

Therefore the maximum value of L that can be used with no cavitation is 8.52 m.

The maximum value of L also gives the maximum rate of discharge.

Apply the Bernoulli's equation between sections 0 and 2.

$$\frac{p_0}{\gamma} + Z_0 + \frac{V_0^2}{2g} = \frac{p_2}{\gamma} + Z_2 + \frac{V_2^2}{2g}$$

here $p_0 = p_2 = p_{atm}$

$$(Z_0 - Z_2) = L = 8.52\ \text{m}.$$

$$V_0 = 0$$

Substituting these values yields,

$$8.52 = \frac{V_2^2}{2g}$$

or

$$V_2 = \sqrt{2 \times 9.81 \times 8.52}$$

$$= 12.93\ \text{m/s}.$$

Therefore the maximum rate of discharge is

$$q = A \times V$$

$$= \frac{\pi}{4}(0.08)^2 \times 12.93$$

$$= 0.065\ \text{m}^3/\text{sec}.$$

or

$$q = 65\ \text{liters/sec}.$$

Determine the power developed by the turbine, installed as shown in the figure, if the volumetric flow rate is 25 m^3/s. Neglect frictional losses.

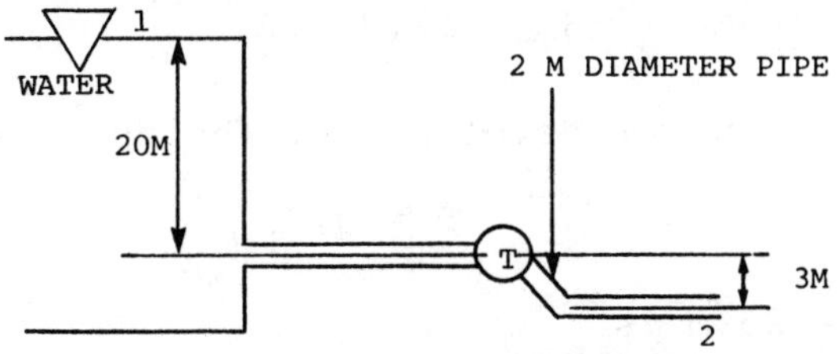

Solution: The pressure head removed by the turbine is given by the Bernoulli's equation. The Bernoulli's equation between the sections 1 and 2 is

$$\frac{p_1}{\gamma} + Z_1 + \frac{V_1^2}{2g} = \frac{p_2}{\gamma} + Z_2 + \frac{V_2^2}{2g} + H_T$$

where p = pressure

γ = density

Z = height

V = velocity

H_T = pressure head of the turbine

here

$$p_1 = p_2 = p_{atm}$$

Since both ends are open to atmosphere

$$(Z_1 - Z_2) = (20 + 3) = 23 \text{ m.}$$

$$V_1 = 0 \text{ reservoir water surface velocity}$$

Substituting the values, yield

$$23 = \frac{V_2^2}{2g} + H_T \qquad (1)$$

The velocity V_2 is related to the volumetric flow rate q by

$$V_2 = \frac{q}{A}$$

where A = cross-sectional area of the pipe

or $$V_2 = 25 \times \frac{1}{\frac{\pi}{4}(2)^2}$$

$$= 7.96 \text{ m/s}$$

Substituting this value into equation (1)

$$H_T + \frac{(7.96)^2}{2 \times 9.81} = 23 \text{ m}$$

or

$$H_T = 19.77 \text{ m}$$

Therefore the power developed by the turbine is given by

$$P = q\gamma H_T$$

where $q = 25 \text{ m}^3/\text{s}$

$\gamma = 9800 \text{ N/m}^3$

$H_T = 19.77$ m.

Therefore

$$P = 25 \times 9800 \times 19.77$$

$$= 4.84 \times 10^6 \text{ N.m/s}$$

or

$$P = 4.84 \text{ MW.}$$

• PROBLEM 4-31

Consider a water jet of diameter 4 in. moving horizontally with a velocity of 60 ft/s. The water jet strikes a fixed blade and is deflected by 60° from its horizontal direction (a) calculate the vertical and horizontal components of the force exerted by the jet on the blade. (b) If the blade is moving horizontally towards the right at a speed of 15 ft/s calculate the force components exerted on the blade and the actual velocity of the jet leaving the blade.

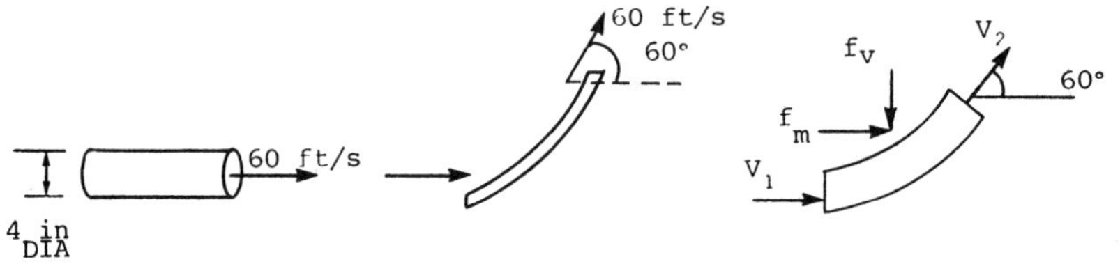

Solution: In this type of problem, the weight component of water and effects of height changes are ignored. The approaching jet is at atmospheric pressure and flowing at 60 ft/s. The jet leaving the blade is also at atmospheric pressure and flowing at 60 ft/s, but the angle between leaving jet and approaching jet is 60° caused by the blade.

This change in direction of the jet, causes a force to be

exerted by the jet on the blade.

This force can be calculated from the momentum equation.

The momentum equation for the horizontal direction is given by

$$F_H = \rho q(V_1 - V_2 \cos\theta)$$

where ρ = density

q = volumetric flow rate = $A \times V$

V = velocity

Substituting these values, yields

$$F_H = (1.94)\left[\frac{\pi}{4} \times \left(\frac{4}{12}\right)^2 \times 60\right](60 - 60 \cos 60°)$$

$$= 304.73 \text{ lb.}$$

Similarly the momentum equation for the vertical direction is given by

$$F_V = \rho q V_2 \sin\theta$$

$$= (1.94)\left[\frac{\pi}{4} \times \left(\frac{4}{12}\right)^2 \times 60\right] 60 \sin 60°$$

or $$F_V = 527.82 \text{ lb.}$$

Therefore the components of the force exerted by the jet on the blade are

$$F_H = 304.73 \text{ lb.}$$

$$F_V = 527.82 \text{ lb.}$$

(b) When the blade is moving at a velocity of 15 ft/s in the same direction as the jet, then the relative velocity of the jet is 60-15 = 45 ft/s.

With this relative velocity, the blade can be considered stationary when calculating the forces on the blade.

The horizontal component of the force

$$F_H = \rho q(V_1 - V_2 \cos\theta)$$

$$= (1.94)\left[\frac{\pi}{4} \times \left(\frac{4}{12}\right)^2 \times 45\right](45 - 45 \cos 60)$$

or $$F_H = 171.41 \text{ lb.}$$

The vertical component of the force

$$F_V = \rho q \, V_2 \sin \theta$$

or $$F_V = (1.94)\left[\frac{\pi}{4}\left(\frac{4}{12}\right)^2 45\right] 45 \sin 60$$

$$= 296.90 \text{ lb.}$$

The actual velocity of water leaving the blade is found by considering the velocity of the blade.

The horizontal component of the actual velocity is equal to the sum of horizontal component of the relative velocity and the velocity of the blade

i.e., $$V_{2H_{\text{actual}}} = V_{2H_{\text{relative}}} + V_{\text{blade}}$$

$$= 45 \cos 60 + 15$$

$$V_{2H_{\text{actual}}} = 37.5 \text{ ft/s}$$

Similarly $$V_{2V_{\text{actual}}} = V_{2V_{\text{relative}}}$$

because there is no vertical component of the blade velocity.

Therefore $$V_{2V_{\text{actual}}} = 45 \sin 60$$

$$= 38.97 \text{ ft/s}$$

Therefore the magnitude of the actual exit velocity is

$$\left[\left(V_{2H_{\text{actual}}}\right)^2 + \left(V_{2V_{\text{actual}}}\right)^2\right]^{1/2}$$

i.e., $$\sqrt{(37.5)^2 + (38.97)^2}$$

$$V_{2\text{actual}} = 54.08 \text{ ft/s}$$

The angle that this velocity makes with the horizontal is

$$\alpha = \tan^{-1} \frac{V_{2V}}{V_{2H}}_{\text{actual}}$$

$$= \tan^{-1} \frac{38.97}{37.5}$$

or $$\alpha = 46.1°$$

CHAPTER 5

FLUID FLOW MEASURING INSTRUMENTS, FLUID MOVING EQUIPMENT AND AGITATION OF FLUIDIZATION

ANALYSIS OF VENTURIMETER, ROTAMETER, NOZZLEMETER

• PROBLEM 5-1

A venturimeter of throat diameter 1 in. is connected to a water pipeline of 2 in. diameter, as shown in the figure. If the mercury manometer shows a head difference of 10.5 in. of Hg, what is the flow velocity in the pipe and in the throat of the venturimeter. Also calculate the volumetric flow rate of water through the water pipe.

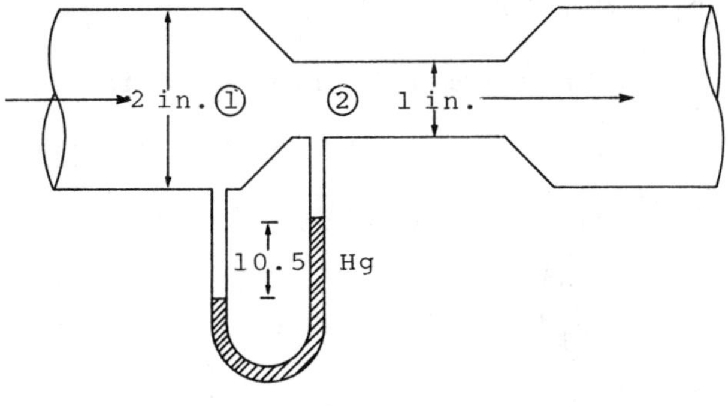

Solution: The Bernoulli equation and the equation of continuity will be used to solve this problem. The head difference shown by the mercury manometer is H = 10.5 in. of Hg.

or, in terms of equivalent head of water

$$H = 10.5 \times 13.6$$

where 13.6 is the specific gravity of Hg

or $\quad H = 142.8$ in. of water

$= 11.9$ ft. of water.

Apply Bernoulli's equation between points 1 and 2,

$$\frac{p_1}{\gamma} + \frac{v_1^2}{2g} + z_1 = \frac{p_2}{\gamma} + \frac{v_2^2}{2g} + z_2$$

where

p = pressure

v = velocity

z = height from datum level.

For a horizontal pipe $z_1 = z_2$

Therefore

$$\frac{v_2^2 - v_1^2}{2g} = \frac{p_1 - p_2}{\gamma}$$

but $\frac{p_1 - p_2}{\gamma} = H$ (measured by the manometer)

Therefore,

$$\frac{v_2^2 - v_1^2}{2g} = 11.9 \qquad (1)$$

The continuity equation states that

$$A_1 v_1 = A_2 v_2$$

indicating that the volumetric flow rate is the same at the sections 1 and 2.

or $$\frac{v_1}{v_2} = \frac{A_2}{A_1} = \left(\frac{D_2}{D_1}\right)^2$$

or $$\frac{v_1}{v_2} = \left(\frac{1}{2}\right)^2 = \frac{1}{4}$$

Therefore $v_1 = \frac{1}{4} v_2$

Substituting into equation (1):

$$\frac{v_2^2 \left[1 - \frac{1}{16}\right]}{2g} = 11.9$$

or $$v_2^2 = 2 \times 32.2 \times (11.9) \times \frac{16}{15}$$

$$= 817.45$$

or $\quad v_2 = 28.59$ ft/s

and $\quad v_1 = \frac{1}{4} v_2$

$$= \frac{1}{4} \times 28.59$$

or, $\quad v_1 = 7.15$ ft/s

The volumetric flow rate of water $= A_1 v_1$

$$= \frac{\pi}{4} \times \frac{4}{144} \times 7.15$$

$$= 0.156 \text{ ft}^3/\text{sec}$$

or

the volumetric rate is $0.156 \times 7.481 \times 60$

$$= 70 \text{ gpm.}$$

• PROBLEM 5-2

Consider a venturimeter connected to a pipeline (see figure (1)). Derive an expression for the volumetric flow rate, q, in terms of the manometer reading, h.

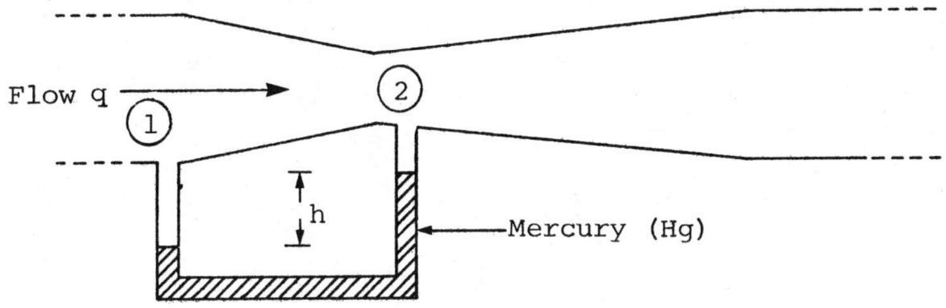

Fig. 1

Solution: An expression for the volumetric flow rate q, in terms of manometer reading h, can be obtained from the Bernoulli energy equation and the continuity equation.

Applying Bernoulli's equation for points 1 and 2 yields,

$$\frac{p_1}{\gamma} + \frac{v_1^2}{2g} + z_1 = \frac{p_2}{\gamma} + \frac{v_2^2}{2g} + z_2$$

For a horizontal pipe, $z_1 = z_2$

Therefore,

$$\frac{v_2^2 - v_1^2}{2g} = \frac{p_1 - p_2}{\gamma}$$

or $$v_2^2 - v_1^2 = \frac{2g}{\gamma}(p_1 - p_2) \qquad (1)$$

The continuity equation states:

$$A_1 v_1 = A_2 v_2$$

where

A = cross-sectional area

v = flow velocity

Rewriting,

$$v_1 = \frac{A_2 v_2}{A_1}$$

or $$v_1 = \left(\frac{D_2}{D_1}\right)^2 v_2$$

where

D = diameter

Substituting this relation into equation (1), and solving for v_2,

$$v_2^2 - \left(\frac{D_2}{D_1}\right)^4 v_2^2 = \frac{2g}{\gamma}(p_1 - p_2)$$

or $$v_2^2 \left[1 - \left(\frac{D_2}{D_1}\right)^4\right] = \frac{2g}{\gamma}(p_1 - p_2)$$

or $$v_2 = \frac{\sqrt{\frac{2g}{\gamma}(p_1 - p_2)}}{\sqrt{1 - (D_2/D_1)^4}}$$

Therefore, the volumetric flow rate

$$q = A_2 v_2$$

$$= \frac{A_2}{\sqrt{1 - (D_2/D_1)^4}} \times \sqrt{\frac{2g}{\gamma}(p_1 - p_2)}$$

Considering viscous effects and other minor losses,

$$q = \frac{A_2 C_D}{\sqrt{1 - (D_2/D_1)^4}} \sqrt{\frac{2g}{\gamma}(p_1 - p_2)} \qquad (2)$$

where

C_D = an empirical coefficient of the venturimeter

To write in terms of the manometer reading h, consider

$$p_1 - p_2 = (\gamma_{hg} - \gamma)h$$

where

γ_{hg} = specific wt. of mercury.

γ = specific wt. of water.

Substiuting this into equation (2)

$$q = \frac{A_2 C_D}{\sqrt{1 - (D_2/D_1)^4}} \sqrt{2gh\left(\frac{\gamma_{hg}}{\gamma} - 1\right)}$$

• PROBLEM 5-3

A tube has a converging section as shown in the figure. If the flow rate of water through it is 2 cfs, determine the head loss in this converging section. The friction factor is f = 0.006 and is assumed constant.

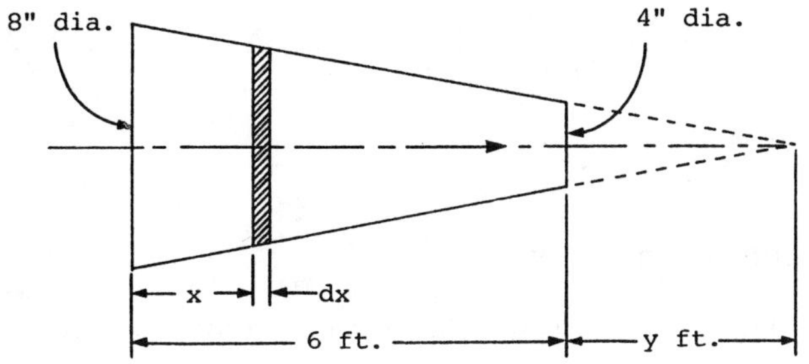

Fig. 1

Solution: The head loss in a straight tube is given by

$$h = \frac{fLq^2}{10D^5}$$

where

h = head loss due to friction

f = friction factor

L = length of the tube

q = volumetric discharge

D = diameter of the tube.

In this problem, D is not constant, but is varying from one end to the other.

i.e., D is a function of the length.

Therefore the above equation should be used in a differential form, writing D as a function of length and then integrating for the whole length of the converging section.

To get D as a function of length, consider an element of the tube of length dx, which is at a distance of x from the larger diameter end.

From the figure, for equivalent triangles

$$\frac{8}{4} = \frac{6 + y}{y} \qquad \text{where y is as shown in the figure.}$$

or $\quad 8y - 4y = 24$

i.e., $\quad y = 6$ ft.

Also from the figure,

$$\frac{D}{4/12} = \frac{6 - x + y}{y}$$

Knowing that y = 6 ft,

$$D = \frac{1}{3}\left[\frac{6 - x + 6}{6}\right]$$

$$= \frac{1}{3}\left[2 - \frac{x}{6}\right]$$

Now, D is a function of x

Substituting this into a differential form of head loss equation yields,

$$d(h) = \frac{0.006 \text{ x } dx \text{ x } (2)^2}{10\left[\frac{1}{3}\left(2 - \frac{x}{6}\right)\right]^5}$$

$$d(h) = 0.5832\left(2 - \frac{x}{6}\right)^{-5} dx$$

For the converging section, integrating from 0 to 6

$$h = 0.5832\int_{x=0}^{x=6}\left(2 - \frac{x}{6}\right)^{-5} dx$$

or
$$h = 0.5832\left[\frac{\left(2 - \frac{x}{6}\right)^{-4}}{-4} \text{ x } (-6)\right]_0^6$$

or $$h = 0.5832 \ \frac{6}{4}\left[\left((1)^{-4} - (2)^{-4}\right)\right]$$

$$= 0.5832 \times \frac{6}{4}\left[1 - \frac{1}{2^4}\right]$$

or $$h = 0.82 \text{ ft.}$$

Therefore, the head loss in the converging section is 0.82 ft. of water.

• PROBLEM 5-4

A horizontal venturimeter of throat diameter 3 in. is connected to water pipeline of 5 in. If the mercury manometer attached to this system shows a reading of 15 in., find out the actual discharge of water through the pipeline. Assume the venturimeter coefficient as 0.98.

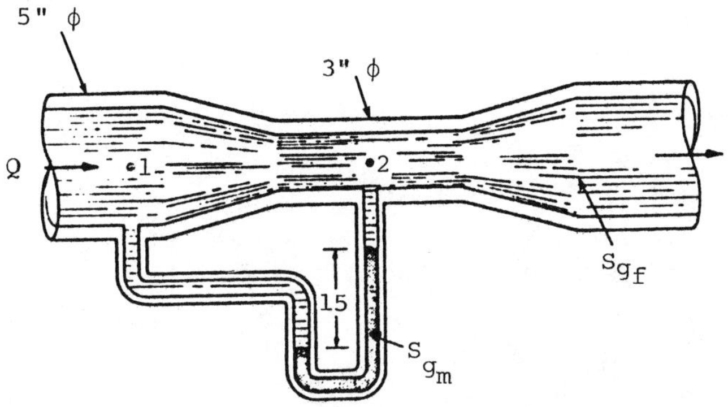

Solution: The manometer equation, Bernoulli's equation, and the equation of continuity will be used to solve the problem.

The manometer equation or hydrostatic equation is applied to points 1 and 2 to obtain

$$p_1 + \gamma_\omega(y + h_m) - \gamma_m h_m - \gamma_\omega y = p_2$$

so that

$$p_1 - p_2 = h_m(\gamma_m - \gamma_\omega)$$

where $(p_1 - p_2)$ = pressure drop

h_m = manometer reading in ft.

γ_m = specific wt. of mercury

γ_ω = specific wt. of water

or $$\frac{p_1 - p_2}{\gamma_\omega} = \frac{15}{12}(13.6 - 1)$$

$$= 15.75 \text{ ft. of water}$$

From Bernoulli's equation

$$\frac{p_1 - p_2}{\gamma} = \frac{v_2^2 - v_1^2}{2g}$$

and from continuity equation

$$A_1v_1 = A_2v_2$$

i.e., the volume flow rate is constant

or, $$\frac{v_1}{v_2} = \frac{A_2}{A_1}$$

$$= \left(\frac{D_2}{D_1}\right)^2$$

Therefore

$$v_2 = \left(\frac{5}{3}\right)^2 v_1^2 = 2.778\ v_1$$

Substituting this into Bernoulli's equation,

$$\frac{p_1 - p_2}{\gamma} = \frac{v_1^2\,(7.716 - 1)}{2 \times 32.2}$$

or $$\frac{p_1 - p_2}{\gamma} = 0.1043\ v_1^2$$

Substituting the value of $\frac{p_1 - p_2}{\gamma}$ obtained from the manometer equation, and solving for v_1

$$v_1^2 = \frac{15.75}{0.1043}$$

or $$v_1 = 12.29 \text{ ft/s}$$

From the continuity equation, the ideal volumetric flow rate is = A_1v_1

Considering the losses due to viscous effect and other, the actual discharge is given by

$$KA_1v_1$$

where

K = venturimeter coefficient

= 0.98

Therefore, the actual discharge of water through the pipeline is

$$0.98 \times \left[\frac{\pi}{4} \times \left(\frac{5}{12}\right)^2\right] \times (12.29)$$

$$= 1.64 \text{ cfs}$$

• PROBLEM 5-5

> A rotameter, used for measuring the volumetric flow rate, consists of a tapered vertical tube 18 inches long. The internal diameters of the top and bottom ends of the tube are 1.5 and 1.0 inches respectively. The floating cork has a 1.0 inch diameter, 0.65 in^3 volume, and a specific gravity of 4.74. If the volumetric flow rate is 1.80 gpm, determine the height of the cork from the bottom end of the tube. Take the coefficient of the rotameter as 0.74.

Solution: The position of the cork can be found from the area of the annulus space between the cork and the tube.

The mass flow rate of water through the rotameter is given by:

$$\dot{m} = C_R A_2 \sqrt{\frac{2gv_c(\rho_c - \rho_\omega)\rho_\omega}{A_c\left[1 - \frac{A_2}{A_1}\right]^2}}$$

where

$\dot{m}$ = mass flow rate

A_1 = cross-sectional area of the tube on the down stream side of the cork.

A_2 = annulus area

v_c = volume of the cork

A_c = max. cross-sectional area of the cork in a horizontal plane.

ρ_c = density of the cork material

ρ_ω = density of water

C_R = coefficient of the rotameter

If the ratio of the areas A_2/A_1 is negligible, the above becomes,

$$\dot{m} = C_R A_2 \sqrt{\frac{2gv_c(\rho_c - \rho_\omega)\rho_\omega}{A_c}}$$

Given the volumetric flow rate is 1.80 gpm

Therefore, $\dot{m} = \frac{1.80}{60} \times 0.13368 \times 62.4$

$$= 0.25 \text{ lb/s}$$

$$A_2 = \frac{\dot{m}}{C_R \sqrt{\frac{2gv_c(\rho_c - \rho_\omega)\rho_\omega}{A_c}}}$$

Substituting the values,

$$A_2 = \frac{0.25}{0.74} \sqrt{\frac{\frac{\pi}{4}\left(\frac{1}{12}\right)^2}{2 \times 32.2 \times \frac{0.65}{(12)^3} (4.74 - 1)62.4 \times 62.4}}$$

$$= 0.00133 \text{ ft}^2$$

$$= 0.1913 \text{ in}^2$$

The annulus area

$$A_2 = \frac{\pi}{4}(D^2 - d^2)$$

where

D = diameter of the tube

d = diameter of the cork

or, $D = \sqrt{\frac{4}{\pi} A_2 + d^2}$

Substituting the values

$$D = \sqrt{\frac{4 \times 0.1913}{\pi} + (1)^2}$$

$$= 1.115 \text{ in.}$$

Correcting for $1 - \left(\frac{A_2}{A_1}\right)^2$ term which was neglected

$$1 - \left(\frac{A_2}{A_1}\right)^2 = 1 - \left(\frac{0.1913}{\frac{\pi}{4}(1.115)^2}\right)^2$$

$$= 0.962$$

Corrected value of A_2 = $0.1913 \times \sqrt{0.962}$

$= 0.1876$ in.

Substituting into the equation for D,

$$D = \sqrt{\frac{4}{\pi} \times 0.1876 + (1)^2}$$

$$= 1.113 \text{ in.}$$

Since there is not much change in the value for D, this is taken as the final value.

Therefore the height of the float from the bottom end is

$$18 \times \left(\frac{1.113 - 1.00}{1.50 - 1.00}\right)$$

$= 4.1$ in.

• PROBLEM 5-6

A flow rate measuring device consisting of a nozzle of 2 in. diameter and a U-tube manometer (manometric liquid is oil of density 50 lb/ft^3), is used to measure the volumetric flow rate of dry chlorine (mol. wt. = 70.5) containing 1.6 mole percent oxygen. The chlorine flows through a tube of 4 in. inside diameter. To calibrate the nozzle, oxygen (mol. wt. = 32) is made to flow in the tube as shown in the figure. When 0.5 lb/min of oxygen is blown, the manometer reading is 8 in. of oil and a test sample on the downstream side of the feed point has 8.1 mole percent of oxygen. Find the coefficient of discharge of the nozzle. The density of chlorine = 0.172 lb/ft^3.

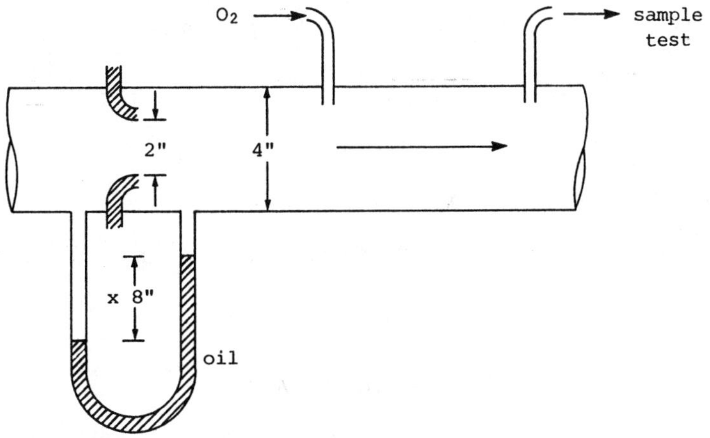

Calibration of a Nozzle Meter

Solution: The coefficient of discharge can be found from the equation for the volumetric flow rate

$$q = C_D A_N \sqrt{\frac{2gh}{(1 - \alpha^4)}} \qquad (1)$$

where

q = volumetric flow rate

C_D = coefficient of discharge

A_N = area of the nozzle

h = manometer reading in terms of ft. of chlorine

α = ratio of the nozzle diameter to the tube diameter.

To get the volumetric flow rate, an overall material balance is needed.

The input rate of oxygen = 0.5 lb/min

$$\text{or } \frac{0.5}{32} \text{ lb-mole/min}$$

$$= 0.0156 \text{ lb-mole/min}$$

From the overall material balance,

$$m + 0.0156 = n$$

where

m = mole-rate of gas flowing upstream

n = mole-rate of gas flowing downstream

From the oxygen balance

$$0.016\, m + 0.0156 = 0.081\, n$$

Solving simultaneously the above two equations

$$m = 0.2206 \text{ lb-mole/min}$$

$$= \frac{0.2206}{60} \times 70.5 \text{ lb/sec.}$$

or $m = 0.259$ lb/sec.

Therefore, the volumetric flow rate of gas flowing upstream is:

$$q = \frac{0.259}{0.172} \text{ ft}^3\text{/sec}$$

$$\text{or,} \qquad q = 1.506 \text{ ft}^3\text{/sec}$$

The manometer reading in terms of ft. of chlorine is given by:

$$h = \frac{x}{12}\left(\frac{\rho_0}{\rho_{Cl}} - 1\right)$$

where

$$x = \text{manometer reading in inches}$$

$$\rho_0 = \text{density of oil (manometric fluid)}$$

$$\rho_{Cl} = \text{density of chlorine}$$

Substituting the values

$$h = \frac{8}{12}\left(\frac{50}{0.172} - 1\right)$$

$$= 193 \text{ ft.}$$

Now, substitute into equation (1) for the rate of flow and solve for C_D.

$$1.506 = C_D \cdot \frac{\pi}{4}\left(\frac{2}{12}\right)^2 \sqrt{\frac{2 \times 32.2 \times 193}{1 - \left(\frac{2}{4}\right)^4}}$$

or
$$C_D = 1.506 \times \frac{4}{\pi} \times 36 \sqrt{\frac{1 - (0.5)^4}{2 \times 32.2 \times 193}}$$

$$= 0.60$$

ANALYSIS OF ORIFICEMETER

• PROBLEM 5-7

An inert gas of specific wt. 0.00062 is flowing through a 3 in. diameter pipe which is equipped with a ½ in. diameter orifice plate. What is the discharge rate of the gas if the water manometer attached to this system indicates a reading of 4 in. The meter coefficient is assumed to be 0.65.

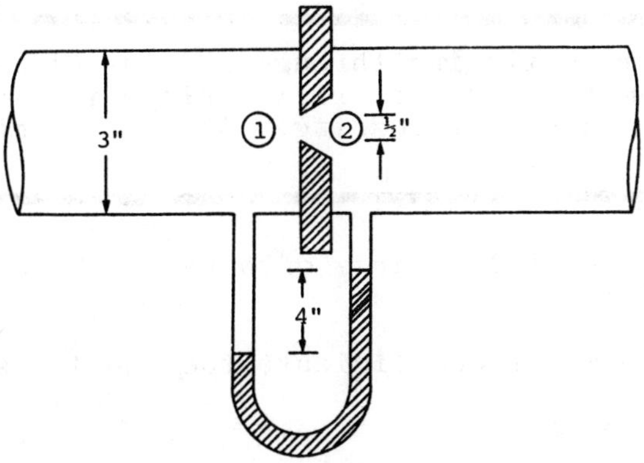

Solution: A good approximate formula for orifices in practical applications may be written in the simplified form as

$$q = CA_2 \sqrt{\frac{2g}{\gamma}(\Delta p)}$$

where

q = actual discharge of fluid through the pipe

A_2 = area of the circular orifice

$\frac{\Delta p}{\gamma} = \frac{p_1 - p_2}{\gamma}$

= pressure drop in terms of ft. of fluid

C = meter discharge coefficient

$\frac{\Delta p}{\gamma}$ is given by the manometer equation

$$\frac{p_1 - p_2}{\gamma} = \frac{\Delta p}{\gamma_g} = h_\omega \frac{(\gamma_\omega - \gamma_g)}{\gamma_g}$$

Substituting the values

$$\frac{\Delta p}{\gamma_g} = \frac{4}{12}\frac{(0.433 - 0.00062)}{0.00062} = 232.46 \text{ ft. of gas}$$

Substituting the values into the equation of discharge, the actual discharge of gas

$$q = 0.65 \times \frac{\pi}{4}\left(\frac{1}{2 \times 12}\right)^2 \times (2 \times 32.2 \times 232.46)^{\frac{1}{2}}$$

$$= 0.1084 \text{ cfs}$$

• PROBLEM 5-8

25 cfm of water is flowing through a 4 in. diameter pipe. If a 1 in. diameter nozzled orifice plate is used, what is the mercury manometer reading? Assume the meter coefficient to be 0.82.

Solution: The actual discharge of water is 25 cfm

or $q_a = \frac{25}{60}$ ft³/s

Considering the meter coefficient, the ideal discharge q_i is given by $q_i = \frac{q_a}{C}$

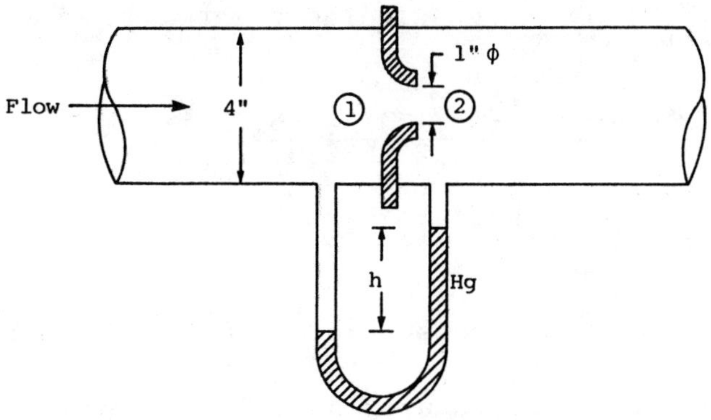

where $C = 0.82$, the meter coefficient

Therefore, $q_i = \dfrac{25}{60 \times 0.82}$

$= 0.508$ cfs

The ideal velocities are given by

$$v = \frac{q}{A}$$

where

v = velocity at the sectional area A

A = cross-sectional area

Therefore

$$v_1 = \frac{q}{A_1} \qquad \text{velocity at section 1.}$$

$$= \frac{0.508}{\frac{\pi}{4}\left(\frac{4}{12}\right)^2}$$

or $v_1 = 5.82$ ft/s

Velocity at section 2,

$$v_2 = \frac{q}{A_2}$$

$$= \frac{0.508}{\frac{\pi}{4}\left(\frac{1}{12}\right)^2}$$

or $v_2 = 93.14$ ft/s

The Bernoulli's equation is applied to points 1 and 2,

$$\frac{p_1 - p_2}{\gamma} = \frac{v_2^2 - v_1^2}{2g}$$

Substituting the values in the right hand side of the equation yields,

$$\frac{p_1 - p_2}{\gamma} = \frac{(93.14)^2 - (5.82)^2}{2 \times 32.2}$$

or $$\frac{p_1 - p_2}{\gamma} = 134.18$$

but $\frac{p_1 - p_2}{\gamma}$ is the pressure drop in ft. of water

Therefore the pressure drop across the orifice plate is 134.18 ft. of water.

From the manometer equation,

$$\frac{p_1 - p_2}{\gamma_\omega} = h(\gamma_{hg} - \gamma_\omega)$$

where

h = mercury manometer reading

γ_{hg} = specific wt. of mercury

γ_ω = specific weight of water

Therefore

$$h(13.6 - 1) = 134.18$$

or, $$h = \frac{134.18}{12.6}$$

$$= 10.65 \text{ ft. of Hg}$$

or, $$h = 127.8 \text{ in. of Hg.}$$

• PROBLEM 5-9

A crude oil with a viscosity of 5.53 cp and a specific gravity of 0.895 is flowing through a 4 in. inside diameter horizontal pipe. An orifice meter consisting of an orifice plate and a differential mercury-glycol manometer (mercury is the manometric liquid and glycol (specific gravity = 1.15) is the sealing liquid) is used to measure the volumetric flow rate of crude oil. If the manometer reading is 25 in., corresponding to a volumetric flow rate of 200 gpm, estimate the diameter of the orifice and also the power lost due to the pressure drop caused by the orifice plate.

Solution: The pressure loss due to the orifice is given by the manometer equation. The manometer equation for a manometer with a sealing liquid reduces to

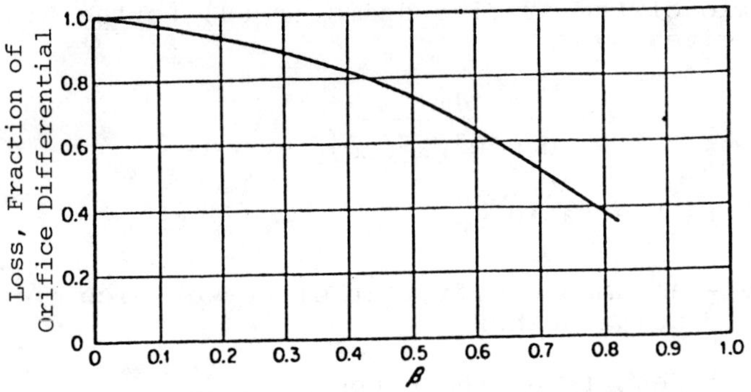

Figure 1.

$$\Delta p = p_1 - p_2 = h_m(\gamma_m - \gamma_g)$$

where

Δp = pressure drop across the orifice

h_m = manometer reading

γ = specific weight

subscripts

m denotes mercury

g denotes glycol

ω denotes water

Therefore, the pressure drop across the orifice

$$\Delta p = h_m\left(\frac{\gamma_m - \gamma_g}{\gamma_\omega}\right)\gamma_\omega$$

$$= \frac{25}{12}\ (13.6 - 1.15) \times 62.4$$

$$= 1618.5 \text{ lb/ft}^2$$

The mass flow rate of the crude oil m is given by

$$m = q \times \rho$$

where

q = volumetric flow rate

ρ = density of the crude oil

Therefore

$$\dot{m} = \left(200 \times \frac{1}{7.481} \times \frac{1}{60}\right) \times 0.895 \times 62.4$$

$$= 24.88 \text{ lb/s}$$

The ratio of the orifice diameter (d) to the pipe diameter (D) is given by

$$\beta^2 = \frac{4\dot{m}}{0.6\pi D^2\sqrt{2g(\Delta p)\rho}}$$

where β is the ratio $\frac{d}{D}$

0.6 = assumed coefficient of the orifice for high Reynolds number

ρ = density of the crude

$\dot{m}$ = mass flow rate

Δp = pressure drop

Substituting the values into the above equation

$$\beta^2 = \frac{4 \times 24.88}{0.6 \times \pi \times \left(\frac{4}{12}\right)^2 \sqrt{2 \times 32.2 \times 1618.5 \times (0.895 \times 62.4)}}$$

$$= 0.19695$$

Therefore

$$\beta = \frac{d}{D} = \sqrt{(0.19695)}$$

$$\text{or } \frac{d}{D} = 0.4438$$

Therefore $d = (0.4438) \times (4)$

$= 1.78$ in.

Now check the Reynolds number to verify that the assumed value of the orifice coefficient is justified.

The Reynolds number is given by

$$Re = \frac{4\dot{m}}{\pi d\mu}$$

Substituting the values

$$Re = \frac{4 \times 24.88}{\pi \times \left(\frac{1.78}{12}\right) \times (5.53 \times 6.72 \times 10^{-4})}$$

$$= 57468$$

The Reynolds number is high enough to justify employing an orifice coefficient of 0.6.

Therefore the diameter of the orifice = 1.78 in.

The overall pressure loss in the orifice, corresponding to $\beta = 0.4438$, is given by figure (1).

From the chart, the fraction of the differential pressure lost is 0.78.

Therefore, the power lost due to the orifice plate is given by

$$W = \frac{\dot{m} \times \Delta p}{\rho \times 550} \text{ Hp}$$

$$= \frac{24.88 \times (0.78 \times 1618.5)}{0.895 \times 62.4 \times 550}$$

or $$W = 1 \text{ Hp}.$$

ANALYSIS OF PITOT TUBE

• PROBLEM 5-10

An oil with a specific gravity of 0.84 and a viscosity of 0.0336 lb/ft-s is flowing downwards in a vertical pipe of inside diameter 3 in. If the water-oil manometer connected to a pitot tube, as shown in the figure, shows a reading of 25 in., calculate the volumetric flow rate of oil.

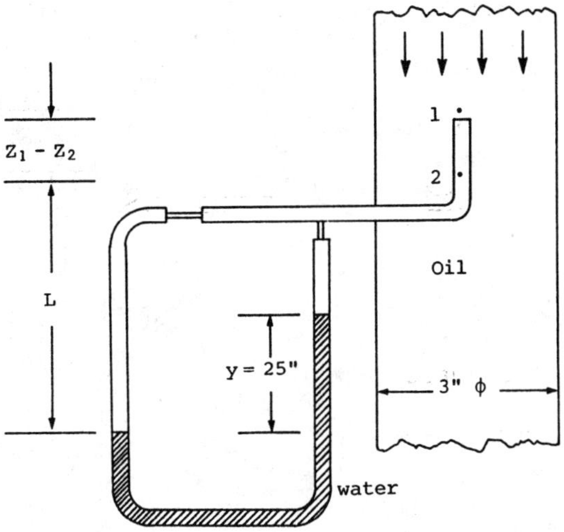

Solution: The piezometric head for the given pitot tube is given by

$$\Delta h = h_1 - h_2$$

$$= \frac{p_1 - p_2}{\gamma} + z_1 - z_2$$

From the manometer equation,

$$p_1 + (z_1 - z_2)\gamma_0 + L\gamma_0 - y\gamma_\omega - (L - y)\gamma_0 = p_2$$

Rearranging,

$$\frac{p_1 - p_2}{\gamma_0} + z_1 - z_2 = y\left(\frac{\gamma_\omega}{\gamma_0} - 1\right)$$

Therefore piezometric head is

$$\Delta h = y\left(\frac{\gamma_\omega}{\gamma_0} - 1\right)$$

Substituting the values

$$\Delta h = \frac{25}{12}\left(\frac{1}{0.84} - 1\right)$$

$$= 0.397 \text{ ft. of oil}$$

The velocity of oil is given by

$$V = \sqrt{2g(\Delta h)}$$

Substituting the values, the velocity of flow is

$$V = \sqrt{2 \times 32.2 \times 0.397}$$

$$= 5.06 \text{ ft/s}$$

Assuming the flow is laminar, the above velocity is the velocity at the center, i.e., the maximum velocity

Assuming $\alpha = 0.65$.

Substituting this value into

$$V = \alpha V_{max}$$

the average velocity is

$$V = 0.65 \times 5.06$$

$$= 3.3 \text{ ft/s}$$

Checking on the Reynolds number

$$Re = \frac{DV\rho}{\mu}$$

$$= \frac{\left(\frac{3}{12}\right) 3.3 \times 0.84 \times 62.4}{0.0336}$$

$$Re = 1287$$

which is less than the critical Reynolds number, hence the assumption that the flow is laminar is correct.

Hence the volumetric flow rate

$$q = A \times V$$

$$= \frac{\pi}{4}\left(\frac{3}{12}\right)^2 \times 3.3$$

$$q = 0.162\ ft^3/s = 73\ gpm$$

• PROBLEM 5-11

A pitot tube with a U-tube water manometer is attached to a horizontal oil pipe of 4" inside diamater, as shown in the figure. If the manometer reading is 15 in., determine the volumetric flow rate of oil in the pipe. The oil has a specific gravity of 0.84 and a viscosity of 0.0336 lb/ft-sec.

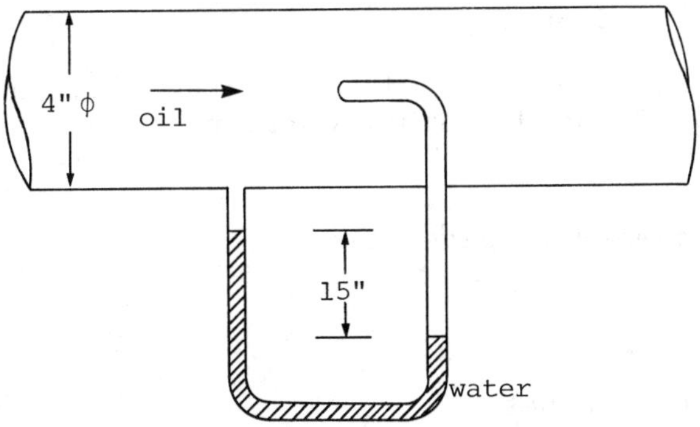

Solution: From the manometer equation, the pressure head is given by

$$\Delta h = \frac{p_1 - p_2}{\gamma_0} = h_\omega\left(\frac{\gamma_\omega}{\gamma_0} - 1\right)$$

where

h_ω = manometer reading

γ_ω = specific weight of water

γ_0 = specific weight of oil.

Substituting the values

$$\Delta H = \frac{15}{12}\left(\frac{1}{0.84} - 1\right)$$

$$= 0.2381\ ft.$$

The velocity of oil at the entry point of the pitot tube is given by:

$$v = \sqrt{2g(\Delta H)}$$

Assume that the pitot tube is attached centrally to the pipe, i.e., along the axis of the pipe. Then the velocity obtained by the above equation is the maximum velocity.

Therefore

$$v_{max} = \sqrt{2g(\Delta H)}$$

Substituting the values

$$v_{max} = \sqrt{2 \times 32.2 \times 0.2381}$$

$$= 3.916 \text{ ft/s}$$

Assume the flow is laminar.

Taking the average velocity as 0.6 v_{max}

$$v_{av} = 0.6 \times 3.916$$

$$= 2.35 \text{ ft/s}$$

Now check the type of flow, i.e., whether laminar or turbulent, from the Reynolds number corresponding to the average velocity v_{av}.

The Reynolds number is given by

$$Re = \frac{\rho v D}{\mu}$$

Substituting the values

$$Re = \frac{(0.84 \times 62.4) \times (2.35) \times (4/12)}{0.0336}$$

$$= 1222$$

This number is less than the critical Reynolds number (2100).

Hence the assumption that the flow is laminar is true.

Therefore the volumetric flow rate of oil is given by

$$q = v_{av} \times A$$

$$q = 2.35 \times \frac{\pi}{4}\left(\frac{4}{12}\right)^2$$

$$= 0.205 \text{ ft}^3\text{/s}$$

or $$q = 0.205 \times 7.481 \times 60 \text{ gpm}$$

$$q = 92 \text{ gpm.}$$

• PROBLEM 5-12

During an experiment to determine the velocity profile of air flowing through a circular flue, a pitot tube attached to a water manometer is traversed across the cross-section. The diameter of the circular flue is 2 ft. If the following readings are obtained, determine the velocity profile.

Take $\rho_{air} = 0.081\ lb_m/ft^3$ and the coefficient of pitot tube as $C_p = 0.98$.

Radial distance from wall (ft)	Manometer reading (in.)
0.1 ft.	1.0
0.2	1.5
0.4	3.0
0.6	4.5
0.8	5.5
0.9	6.0

Solution: Applying the manometer equation, the pressure difference read by the manometer is given by

$$\Delta p = \rho_\omega gh$$

where

ρ_ω = density of the manometric liquid (water)

h = manometer reading in inches of water

Δp = pressure difference.

The velocity is related to the pressure difference Δp by the equation

$$v = C_p \sqrt{\frac{2\Delta p}{\rho_a}}$$

where

v = actual velocity

C_p = coefficient of pitot tube

Δp = pressure difference

ρ_a = density of air.

Writing the velocity v in terms of manometer reading, by substituting for Δp in the equation for velocity:

$$v = C_p \sqrt{\frac{2\rho_\omega gh}{\rho_a}}$$

Substituting the known values

$$v = 0.98 \sqrt{\frac{2 \times 62.4 \times 32.2}{0.081}} \times \sqrt{h}$$

$$= 218.28 \sqrt{h}$$

Substituting the values of h for different radial locations of the pitot tube

Radial location (ft)	h (ft)	Velocity (ft/s)
0.1	0.0833	63.0
0.2	0.125	77.2
0.4	0.25	109.1
0.6	0.375	133.7
0.8	0.458	147.7
0.9	0.50	154.3

• PROBLEM 5-13

Consider a pitot tube attached centrally to a circular air duct of 23 in. inside diameter. When air at 150°F is blown through the duct, the pitot tube reading is 0.38 in. of water and the static pressure at the pitot tube is 19.5 in. of water. Determine the volume of air blown per minute at 70°F and atmospheric pressure. Take the coefficient of the pitot tube as 0.97. The voscosity of air at 150°F = 1.48 x 10^{-5} lb/ft-s.

Solution: The drop in pressure at the pitot tube is given as 0.38 in. of water

or $$(p_s - p_o) = \Delta p = \left(\frac{0.38}{12}\right) \times 62.4$$

$$= 1.976 \ lb_f/ft^2$$

The total pressure at the pitot tube = atmospheric pressure + static pressure

or $$p = 29.92 + \frac{19.5}{13.6} \text{ in. of Hg}$$

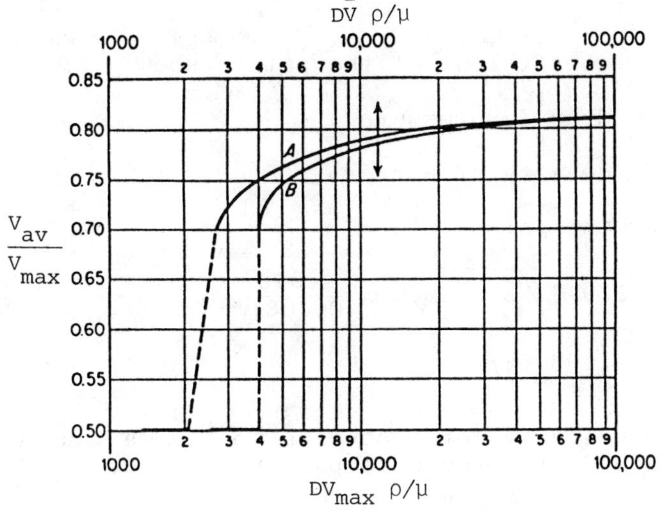

where

$$29.92 = \text{atmospheric pressure in inches of Hg}$$

$$\frac{19.5}{13.6} = \text{static pressure in inches of Hg}$$

Therefore

$$p = 31.354 \text{ in. of Hg}$$

$$= \frac{31.354}{29.92} \times 2116.3 = 2217.73 \ lb_f/ft^2$$

The density of air at $150^{O}F$ and at 2217.73 lb_f/ft^2 is given from the perfect gas law equation

$$\rho = \frac{p}{RT}$$

where

ρ = density of air in lb/ft^3

p = pressure of air in lb_f/ft^2

R = gas constant 53.34 $ft\text{-}lb_f/lb_m{}^{O}R$

T = temperature in Rankine

Substituting the values,

$$\rho = \frac{2217.73}{53.35 \times (460 + 150)}$$

$$= 0.0681 \ lb/ft^3$$

The maximum velocity for incompressible fluids is given by

$$v_{max} = C_{pt}\sqrt{2g\ \frac{\Delta p}{\rho}}$$

where

C_{pt} = coefficient of the pitot tube

Δp = drop in pressure

ρ = density of air

Substituting the values,

$$v_{max} = 0.97 \sqrt{2 \times 32.2 \times \frac{1.976}{0.0681}}$$

$$= 41.93 \text{ ft/s}$$

The average velocity corresponding to the maximum velocity can be obtained from the accompanying figure.

$$\frac{\rho D v_{max}}{\mu} = \frac{0.0681 \times \left(\frac{23}{12}\right) \times 41.93}{1.48 \times 10^{-5}}$$

$$= 370{,}000$$

The corresponding $\dfrac{v_{av}}{v_{max}} = 0.82$

Therefore $\quad v_{av} = 0.82 \times 41.93$

$$= 34.38 \text{ ft/s}$$

Therefore the volumetric flow rate is v x A

$$= 34.38 \times \frac{\pi}{4} \times \left(\frac{23}{12}\right)^2 \text{ ft}^3\text{/s}$$

$$= 99.195 \text{ ft}^3\text{/s}$$

$$= 5951.69 \text{ ft}^3\text{/min.}$$

This is the volume of air blown per minute when the air is at 150°F and 31.354 in. of Hg pressure.

The volume of air measured at 70°F and 29.92 in. of Hg is given by the relationship $\dfrac{p_1 v_1}{T_1} = \dfrac{p_2 v_2}{T_2}$ for a perfect gas.

Therefore the volume/min blown is given by

$$v_2 = \frac{p_1 v_1}{T_1} \times \frac{T_2}{p_2} = \frac{5951.69 \times 31.354 \times (460 + 70)}{(460 + 150) \times 29.92} \text{ ft}^3\text{/min.}$$

$$= 5419 \text{ ft}^3\text{/min.}$$

CALCULATION OF H. P, FRICTION FACTOR EFFICIENCY FOR PUMPS, FANS AND COMPRESSORS

• PROBLEM 5-14

600 gal/hr of water is pumped to a height of 25 ft through a pipe with a 2 in. inside diameter, 0.0007 ft. surface roughness, and a total length of 625 ft. The pipeline has valves and other fittings which may be considered as equivalent to 300 pipe diameters. There is also an additional pressure loss of 8 ft. of water in the pipeline. Determine the power needed to drive the pump if it is 65 percent efficient.

Solution: The power required by the pump can be found from the total head that has to be developed by the pump.

The total head of the pump is the sum of the pressure losses and the height to which water is supplied.

The velocity of flow is given by

$$v = \frac{q}{A}$$

where

q = volumetric flow rate

A = cross-sectional area

Substituting the values

$$v = \left(\frac{600}{3600} \times \frac{1}{7.481}\right) \times \frac{1}{\frac{\pi}{4}\left(\frac{2}{12}\right)^2}$$

$$= 1.02 \text{ ft/s}$$

The Reynolds number for the flow is given by:

$$Re = \frac{\rho v D}{\mu}$$

where

ρ = density of water

v = velocity of flow

D = diameter of the pipe

μ = viscosity of water

Substituting the values

$$Re = \frac{62.4 \times 1.02 \times (2/12)}{4.368 \times 10^{-4}}$$

$$= 2.4 \times 10^4$$

The relative roughness ratio is given by:

$$\frac{\varepsilon}{D} = \frac{0.0007}{(2/12)}$$

$$= 0.0042$$

Therefore from the Moody diagram, corresponding to a Re of 2.4×10^4 and a relative roughness of 0.0042, the Darcy friction factor is f = 0.033.

The equivalent length of the pipe = $625 + 300 \times \left(\frac{2}{12}\right)$

$$L = 675 \text{ ft.}$$

The frictional head loss is given by

$$h_f = \frac{fLv^2}{2dg}$$

$$= \frac{0.033 \times 675 \times (1.02)^2}{2 \times (2/12) \times 32.2}$$

or $\quad h_f = 2.16$ ft.

The total head to be developed by the pump is

$\Delta p = 2.16 + 8 + 25 = 35.16$ ft. of water neglecting the kinetic energy head,

or $\quad \Delta p = 35.16 \times 62.4$

or, $\quad \Delta p = 2194 \ lb_f/ft^2$

The work done on the liquid is equal to the total head generated by the pump.

The power required to generate the pressure head is given by:

$$P = \frac{\dot{m}Wp}{550}$$

$$= 2194 \times \left(\frac{600}{3600} \times \frac{1}{7.481}\right) \times \frac{1}{550}$$

or, $\quad P = 0.089$ hp

Considering the efficiency of the pump, the power required to drive the pump is

$$\frac{0.089}{0.65} = 0.14 \text{ hp}$$

• PROBLEM 5-15

> 500 cfm of water is pumped through a horizontal pipe 10 in. inside diameter and 800 ft. long. If the pump is 65 percent efficient and needs 80 hp of input power, determine the surface roughness of the pipe.

Solution: The surface roughness of the pipe ε, can be obtained from Moody diagram, corresponding to the Reynolds number of the water flow and the friction factor obtained by equating the pressure losses to the frictional pressure losses.

The output power of the pump is given by the product of input power and efficiency of the pump:

$$hp_{output} = hp_{input} \times \eta_{efficiency}$$

$$= 80 \times 0.65$$

$$= 52 \text{ hp.}$$

The output power of the pump is related to the pressure head generated by the following equation,

$$hp_{output} = \frac{q(\Delta p)}{550}$$

where

q = volumetric flow rate

Δp = pressure head generated at the pump

Substituting the values and solving for Δp,

$$\Delta p = \frac{550 \times 51}{\left(\frac{500}{60}\right)}$$

$$= 3432 \text{ lb}_f/\text{ft}^2$$

This is the pressure loss due to friction as water flows in the pipe.

It is known that:

$$h_f = \frac{\Delta p}{\gamma} = \frac{fLq^2}{40D^5}$$

where

γ = specific weight of water

f = friction factor

L = length of the pipe

q = flow rate of water

D = inside diameter of the pipe

Substituting values and solving for f,

$$f = 40 \times \left(\frac{10}{12}\right)^5 \times \left(\frac{3432}{62.4}\right) \times \frac{1}{800} \times \left(\frac{60}{500}\right)^2$$

$$= 0.016$$

The average flow velocity $v_{av} = \frac{q}{A}$

$$= \frac{500}{60} \times \frac{4}{\pi} \left(\frac{12}{10}\right)^2$$

$$= 15.28 \text{ ft/s}$$

The Reynolds number is given by

$$Re = \frac{\rho v D}{\mu}$$

$$= \frac{62.4 \times 15.28 \times 10}{0.00067 \times 12}$$

or, $Re = 1.19 \times 10^6$

Therefore, from the Moody diagram, corresponding to Re = 1.19×10^6 and f = 0.0016, the ratio of relative roughness is 0.00035.

i.e., $\frac{\varepsilon}{D} = 0.00035$

or $\varepsilon = 0.00035 \times 10$

$= 0.0035$ inches

Therefore the roughness of the pipe = 0.0035 inches.

• PROBLEM 5-16

200 gal/min of water is pumped from one reservoir into another through a piping system shown in the figure. If the efficiency of the pump is 50 percent and the cost of electrical energy is 2.25 cents per kilowatt hour, estimate the cost per day for pumping the water. The roughness of the pipe is $\varepsilon = 0.0002$ ft. The viscosity of water is $\mu = 7.5 \times 10^{-4}$ lb/ft-sec. Neglect the connection losses to the pump.

Solution: The work done by the pump on the water is given by

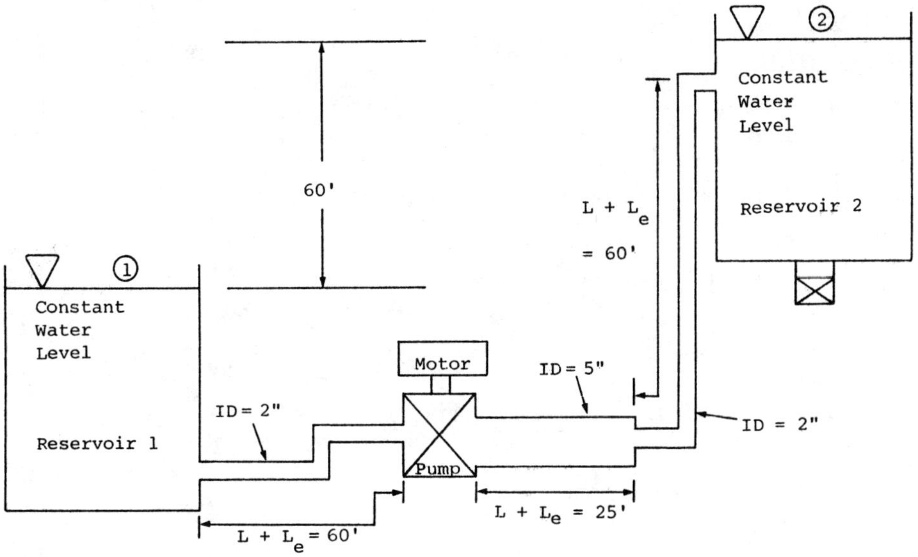

the mechanical energy balance between points 1 and 2.

For an incompressible fluid, the mechanical energy balance equation is:

$$\frac{p_1}{\rho} + \frac{v_1^2}{2g_c\alpha_1} + z_1\frac{g}{g_c} + W_p = \frac{p_2}{\rho} + \frac{v_2^2}{2g_c\alpha_2} + z_2\frac{g}{g_c} + \Sigma F_f + \Sigma F_c + \Sigma F_e \quad (1)$$

where

p = pressure

ρ = density of water

v = velocity

$\alpha_1 = \alpha_2$ = 1 for turbulent flow

z = height

F_f = friction work

F_c = contraction work

F_e = expansion work

W_p = work done by the pump.

The volumetric flow rate q = 200 gal/min

$$= \frac{200}{60} \times \frac{1}{7.48}$$

or $q = 0.4456\ \text{ft}^3/\text{sec.}$

The velocity of flow is given by

$$v = \frac{q}{A}$$

where

$$A = \text{cross-sectional area of the pipe.}$$

Therefore, the velocity in a 2 in diameter pipe is:

$$v_{2d} = \frac{0.4456}{\frac{\pi}{4}\left(\frac{2}{12}\right)^2}$$

$$= 20.42 \text{ ft/s}$$

The velocity in 5 in diameter pipe is:

$$v_{5d} = \frac{0.4456}{\frac{\pi}{4}\left(\frac{5}{12}\right)^2}$$

$$= 3.27 \text{ ft/s}$$

From reservoir 1 to 2 in. diameter pipe, the contraction work is given by:

$$F_c = \frac{K_c v_{2d}^2}{2g}$$

where

$$K_c = \text{contraction coefficient}$$

$$= 0.5$$

Therefore

$$F_{c1} = \frac{0.5 \times (20.42)^2}{2 \times 32.2}$$

$$= 3.237 \text{ ft.lb}_f/\text{lb}_m.$$

From 5 in. diameter to 2 in. diameter pipe the contraction coefficient $K_c = 0.45$

Therefore, the contraction work

$$F_{c2} = \frac{0.45 \times (20.42)^2}{2 \times 32.2}$$

$$= 2.91 \text{ ft.lb}_f/\text{lb}_m.$$

Therefore the total contraction work

$$\Sigma F_c = F_{c1} + F_{c2}$$

$$= 3.237 + 2.91$$

$$= 6.147 \text{ ft.lb}_f/\text{lb}_m.$$

There is only one expansion. It is from 2 in. diameter pipe to reservoir 2.

$$\text{Expansion work} \quad F_e = \frac{(v_{2d} - v_2)^2}{2g}$$

but $v_2 = 0$, the velocity in reservoir 2.

Therefore

$$\Sigma F_e = F_e = \frac{(20.42)^2}{2 \times 32.2}$$

$$= 6.47 \text{ ft.lb}_f/\text{lb}_m.$$

To find the frictional work lost in pipes of 2 in. diameter and 5 in. diameter, the Reynolds number of the flow is required.

The Reynolds number in 2 in. diameter pipe is given by:

$$Re = \frac{\rho v D}{\mu}$$

or,

$$Re_2 = \frac{62.4 \times 20.42 \times \left(\frac{2}{12}\right)}{7.5 \times 10^{-4}}$$

$$= 2.8 \times 10^5$$

Similarly Reynolds number in 5 in. diameter pipe

$$Re_5 = \frac{62.4 \times 3.27 \times (5/12)}{7.5 \times 10^{-4}}$$

or,

$$Re_5 = 1.1 \times 10^5$$

The relative roughness ratio for 2 in. pipe

$$\frac{\varepsilon}{2/12} = \frac{0.0002}{(2/12)}$$

$$= 0.0012$$

The relative roughness ratio for 5 in. diameter pipe

$$\frac{\varepsilon}{5/12} = \frac{0.0002 \times 12}{5} = 0.00048$$

From the Moody diagram, the friction factor for the 2 in. diameter pipe is $f_1 = 0.021$ and the friction factor for the 5 in. diameter pipe is $f_2 = 0.020$.

Therefore $\Sigma F_f = \dfrac{2fv^2L}{gD}$

$$= \frac{2f_1 v_{2d}^2 L_1}{gD_1} + \frac{2f_2 v_{5d}^2 L_2}{gD_2}$$

$$= \frac{2 \times 0.021 \times (20.42)^2(60 + 60)}{32.2 \times (2/12)} +$$

$$\frac{2 \times 0.02 \times (3.27)^2(25)}{32.2 \times (5/12)}$$

$$= 391.6 + 0.8$$

or $\Sigma F_f = 392.4 \text{ ft.lb}_f/\text{lb}_m.$

$$p_1 = p_2 = p_{atm} = 14.7 \times 144 \text{ lb}_f/\text{ft}^2$$

$$= 2116.8 \text{ lb}_f/\text{ft}^2$$

$$(z_2 - z_1) = 60 \text{ ft.}$$

Substituting the values into the mechanical energy balance, equation (1), and solving for W_p:

$$W_p = 60 + 392.4 + 6.147 + 6.47$$

$$= 465$$

where $p_2 - p_1 = 0$ and $v_2 = v_1 = 0$ due to the large volumes of the reservoirs.

Therefore the input power supplied to the pump

$$= \frac{465}{0.5} = 930 \text{ ft.lb}_f/\text{lb}_m.$$

and the cost per day to pump water is:

$$= 930 \frac{\text{ft.lb}_f}{\text{lb}_m}\left(200 \frac{\text{gal}}{\text{min}}\right)\left(\frac{1 \text{ ft}^3}{7.481 \text{ gal}}\right)\left(62.4 \frac{\text{lb}_m}{\text{ft}^3}\right)\left(\frac{1 \text{ min.}}{60 \text{ sec}}\right)\left(\frac{1 \text{ kw}}{738 \frac{\text{ft.lb}_f}{\text{sec}}}\right)$$

$$\left(\frac{\text{hr}}{\text{hr}}\right)\left(\frac{2.25 \text{ cents}}{\text{kwhr}}\right)$$

$$= 78.8 \text{ cents/hr}$$

$$= 1892 \text{ cents/day}$$

$$= 18.92 \text{ dollars/day}$$

• PROBLEM 5-17

In figure (1), a liquid with a specific gravity of 1.65 is pumped to a height of 60 feet from a large reservoir. The rate of discharge from the pump is 70 gal/min. The total frictional pressure loss is 12 $\text{ft.lb}_f/\text{lb}_m$. Determine the power of the pump and the pressure it generates. The efficiency of the pump is $\eta_p = 0.65$.

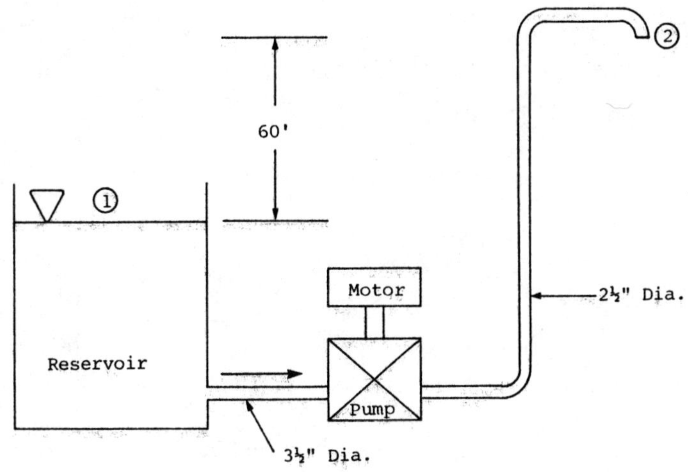

Solution: Bernoulli's equation, corrected for pump work, is to be used to obtain a relationship for the work performed by the pump.

Bernoulli's equation is,

$$\frac{p_1}{\rho} + \frac{v_1^2}{2g_c} + \frac{gz_1}{g_c} + W_p = \frac{p_2}{\rho} + \frac{v_2^2}{2g} + \frac{gz_2}{g_c} + h_f$$

where

p = pressure

ρ = density of the liquid

v = velocity

z = height from datum

W_p = work done by the pump on the liquid

h_f = frictional head loss

In this problem

$p_1 = p_2 = p_{atm}$

$(z_2 - z_1) = 60$ feet

$h_f = 12$ ft.lb_f/lb_m

$v_1 = 0$, because of the large cross-sectional area of the reservoir

v_2 = the exit velocity of the liquid

v_2 can be obtained from the relationship:

$$v = \frac{q}{A}$$

where

$$q = \text{volumetric flow rate}$$

and

$$A = \text{cross=sectional area}$$

Therefore

$$v_2 = \frac{70}{60} \times \left(\frac{1}{7.481}\right) \times \frac{1}{\frac{\pi}{4}\left(\frac{2.5}{12}\right)^2}$$

$$= 4.57 \text{ ft/s}$$

Substituting the values into Bernoulli's equation:

$$W_p = \frac{(4.57)^2}{2 \times 32.2} + 60 + 12$$

$$= 72.32 \text{ ft.lb}_f/\text{lb}_m.$$

The mass flow rate of the liquid is given by: $\dot{m} = \rho q$

where

$$\rho = \text{density of the liquid}$$

$$\rho = \text{specific gravity} \times \text{density of water}$$

$$= 1.65 \times 62.4$$

or, $\rho = 102.96 \text{ lb}_m/\text{ft}^3$

Therefore the mass flow rate

$$\dot{m} = \left(\frac{70}{60} \times \frac{1}{7.481}\right) \times 102.96$$

$$= 16.06 \text{ lb}_m/\text{sec}$$

The output power of the pump is given by:

$$P_p = \frac{\dot{m}W_p}{550 \, \frac{\text{ft.lb}_f/\text{sec}}{1 \text{ hp}}}$$

Substituting the values

$$P_p = \frac{16.06 \times 72.32}{550}$$

$$= 2.11 \text{ hp.}$$

Therefore the input power required to drive the pump is

$\frac{2.11}{0.65} = 3.25$ hp.

The pressure developed by the pump is given by

$$\Delta p = W_p \times \rho$$

neglecting the velocities in the pipe.

Therefore $\Delta p = 72.32 \times 102.96$

$$= 7446 \ lb_f/ft^2$$

$$= 51.7 \ psi$$

• PROBLEM 5-18

60 gal/min of a liquid (sp. gr. = 0.85, vapor pressure = 4.2 lb_f/in^2) is pumped from an open reservoir to a height of 15 feet, as shown in figure (1). The frictional pressure losses in the inlet and outlet pipes of the pump are 0.8 lb_f/in^2 and 7.5 lb_f/in^2 respectively. The liquid pressure at point 2 is 45 lb_f/in^2 gauge. If the pump efficiency is 0.65 (η_p), determine

1) the pressure head developed by the pump.

2) the horsepower needed to drive the pump.

3) the net positive suction head.

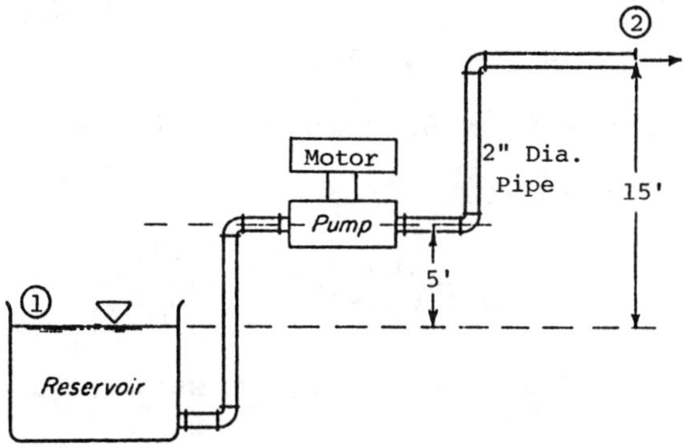

Fig. 1

Solution: The volumetric flow rate q = 60 gal/min

$$= \frac{60}{60} \times \frac{1}{7.481}$$

$$q = 0.1337 \ ft^3/s$$

The exit velocity at point 2 is given by:

$$v_2 = \frac{q}{A}$$

$$= \frac{0.1337}{\frac{\pi}{4}\left(\frac{2}{12}\right)^2}$$

or, $v_2 = 6.13$ ft/s

The pressure head developed by the pump is equivalent to the work done by the pump on the liquid.

The work done by the pump can be found from Bernoulli's equation applied between points 1 and 2.

Bernoulli's equation is:

$$\frac{p_1}{\rho} + \frac{v_1^2}{2g_c} + z_1 \frac{g}{g_c} + W_p = \frac{p_2}{\rho} + \frac{v_2^2}{2g_c} + z_2 \frac{g}{g_c} + h_f$$

where

p = pressure

ρ = density of the liquid

v = velocity

z = height from datum

W_p = work done by the pump on the liquid

h_f = frictional head loss.

In this problem

$p_1 = 14.7 \times 144 \ lb_f/ft^2$

$\rho = 0.85 \times 62.4 \ lb_m/ft^3$

$(z_2 - z_1) = 15$ ft.

$$h_f = \frac{(7.5 + 0.8) \times 144}{0.85 \times 62.4} \ \frac{ft.lb_f}{lb_m}$$

$v_1 = 0$ due to the large surface area of the reservoir

$v_2 = 6.13$ ft/s

Substituting into Bernoulli's equation, and solving for W_p:

$$W_p = \frac{(45 + 14.7) \times 144}{0.85 \times 62.4} + \frac{(6.13)^2}{2 \times 32.2} + 15 + \frac{(7.5 + 0.8) \times 144}{0.85 \times 62.4} - \frac{14.7 \times 144}{0.85 \times 62.4}$$

$= 162.08 + 0.58 + 15 + 22.53 - 39.91$

$= 160.3 \ ft.lb_f/lb_m$

Therefore, the pressure head developed is:

$$\Delta p = W_p \times \rho$$

$$= 160.3 \times 0.85 \times 62.4 \times \frac{1}{144}$$

or, $\Delta p = 59 \text{ lb}_f/\text{in}^2$.

2) The horsepower needed to drive the pump is given by

$$P_p = \frac{W_p}{\eta_p} \times \frac{\dot{m}}{550} \qquad (1)$$

where

$\dot{m}$ = mass flow rate

$= \rho q$.

Therefore $\dot{m} = (0.85 \times 62.4) \times 0.1337$

$= 7.09 \text{ lb}_m/\text{sec}$

Substituting the values into equation (1):

$$P_p = \frac{160.3}{0.65} \times \frac{7.09}{550}$$

$$= 3.18 \text{ hp}.$$

3) The net positive suction head is given by

$$\text{NPSH} = \frac{p_1 - p_v}{\rho} - h_{fs} - z_p \frac{g}{g_c}$$

where

p_1 = pressure at point 1 = 1 atm.

p_v = vapor pressure of the liquid = 4.2 psi

ρ = density of the liquid

h_{fs} = frictional pressure loss in suction pipe

z_p = height of the pump from the level of liquid in reservoir

Substituting the values,

$$\text{NPSH} = \frac{14.7 \times 144}{0.85 \times 62.4} - \frac{4.2 \times 144}{0.85 \times 62.4} - \frac{0.8 \times 144}{0.85 \times 62.4} - 5$$

$$= 21.33 \text{ ft.lb}_f/\text{lb}_m$$

A centrifugal fan with an efficiency of 60% is used to pump flue gas at a rate of 150 cfs. The flue gas (mol. wt. = 31.5, molar specific volume = 378.5 ft^3/lbmol) is initially at rest at 220 ^oF and 28.5 in. Hg. At the exit of the fan, the flue gas is at a pressure of 31.0 in. of Hg and a velocity of 170 ft/s. Determine the power needed to drive the fan.

Solution: The work done by the centrifugal fan on the gas can be obtained from Bernoulli's equation.

Bernoulli's equation is written across the fan, noting that $h_f = 0$ because the friction is accounted for by the mechanical efficiency of the fan.

$$\frac{p_1}{\rho_1} + \frac{v_1^2}{2g_c} + \frac{g}{g_c} z_1 + W_p = \frac{p_2}{\rho_2} + \frac{v_2^2}{2g_c} + z_2 \frac{g}{g_c}$$

where

p = pressure

ρ = density

v = velocity

z = height from datum

W_p = work done by the fan.

Subscripts: 1 relates to the inlet conditions

2 relates to the outlet conditions

The density at the inlet is $\rho_1 = \rho_s \frac{T_s P_1}{T_1 P_s}$

where subscript s denotes standard conditions

Substituting the values,

$$\rho_1 = \left(\frac{31.5}{378.5}\right) \times \frac{(460 + 60) \times 28.5}{(460 + 220) \times 29.92}$$

$$= 0.0606 \text{ lb/ft}^3$$

Similarly the density at outlet $\rho_2 = \frac{\rho_s T_s P_2}{T_2 P_s}$

$$= \left(\frac{31.5}{378.5}\right) \times \frac{(460 + 60) \times 31.0}{(460 + 220) \times 29.92}$$

$$\rho_2 = 0.066 \text{ lb/ft}^3$$

Substituting the values into Bernoulli's equation:

$$\frac{28.5 \times 144 \times 14.7}{29.92 \times 0.0606} + W_p = \frac{31 \times 144 \times 14.7}{29.92 \times 0.066} + \frac{(170)^2}{2 \times 32.2}$$

or $$33272.89 + W_p = 33230.43 + 448.76$$

or $$W_p = 406.3 \text{ ft.lb}_f/\text{lb.}$$

Considering the efficiency of the fan, the power needed to drive the fan is: $\frac{406.3}{0.6} = 677.17 \text{ ft.lb}_f/\text{lb}_m$.

The mass flow rate is given by:

$$\dot{m} = \rho \times q.$$

Therefore

$$\dot{m} = \frac{31.5}{378.5} \times 150$$

$$= 12.48 \text{ lb/s}$$

Therefore the horsepower required to drive the fan is

$$= \frac{\dot{m}W_p}{550}$$

$$= \frac{12.48 \times 677.17}{550}$$

$$= 15.37 \text{ hp.}$$

• PROBLEM 5-20

200 std ft^3/min of ethane at 70°F (C_p = 13.3 Btu/lb-mol $^\circ$F, γ = specific heat ratio = 1.22) is compressed from 11 psia to 1,000 psia in a three stage reciprocating compressor of 85 percent mechanical efficiency. Cooling water is used in the intercoolers and aftercooler to bring the compressed gas to 70°F. If 20 gal/min of water is used in the coolers, determine the change in temperature of the water.

Also determine the power required to drive the compressor.

Solution: The power required to drive a multistage compressor is a minimum when each stage does same amount of work, meaning that each stage has the same compression ratio. Given that the compressor is a three stage compressor, the compression ratio of each stage is

$$\frac{p_o}{p_i} = \left(\frac{1000}{11}\right)^{1/3}$$

$= 4.5$

As a result of isentropic compression in each stage, the compressed gas at the outlet of each stage is at a higher temperature than at the inlet. But this compressed gas which is at a higher temperature, is again cooled back to $70^{\circ}F$ in the intercoolers. Hence the inlet gas to all stages is at the same temperature.

The temperature relation for the isentropic pressure change of an ideal gas is:

$$\frac{T_o}{T_i} = \left(\frac{p_o}{p_i}\right)^{1 - \frac{1}{\gamma}}$$

Hence, the temperature at the exit of each stage is

$$T_o = T_i\left(\frac{p_o}{p_i}\right)^{1 - \frac{1}{\gamma}}$$

Substituting the values,

$$T_o = (460 + 70)(4.5)^{1 - \frac{1}{1.22}}$$

$$= 695^{\circ}R$$

or, $T_o = 235^{\circ}F.$

Now, determine the change in temperature of the water.

The mass flow rate of ethane is given by

$$\dot{m} = \frac{q}{378.7}$$

where

q = volumetric flow rate

378.7 std ft^3/lbmole = molar specific volume.

Substituting the values,

$$\dot{m} = \frac{200}{378.7} \text{ lb-mol/min}$$

$$= 0.528 \text{ lb-mol/min.}$$

Therefore the amount of heat absorbed by the water from the compressed gas of each stage is given by:

$$Q = \dot{m}C_p\Delta T$$

where

Q = amount of heat absorbed by the water

$\dot{m}$ = mass flow rate of ethane

C_p = specific heat of ethane at constant pressure

ΔT = change in temperature of ethane during cooling

Substituting the values,

$$Q = 0.528 \times 13.3 \times (235 - 70)$$

$$= 1158.7 \text{ Btu/min.}$$

Therefore the total amount of heat absorbed in the intercoolers and aftercooler is 3 x 1158.7 = 3476 Btu/min.

The change in the temperature of 20 gal/min of water due to the absorption of 3476 Btu/min is given by

$$\Delta T = \frac{Q}{\dot{m}C_p}$$

$$= \frac{3476}{(20 \times \frac{1}{7.481} \times 62.4) \times 1}$$

or

$$\Delta T = 20.84^{\circ}F.$$

The power required for each stage of compression is given by

$$P = \frac{0.0643\ T_i\ q}{520(\gamma - 1)} \left[\left(\frac{p_o}{p_i}\right)^{1 - \frac{1}{\gamma}} - 1\right]$$

where

p = power required in hp.

T_i = inlet temperature of ethane in $^{\circ}R$

q = volumetric flow rate in std ft^3/min

γ = specific heat ratio

Substituting the values,

$$P = \frac{0.0643(460 + 70) \times 1.22 \times 200}{520(1.22 - 1)} \times \left[(4.5)^{1 - \frac{1}{1.22}} - 1\right]$$

$$= 22.65 \text{ hp.}$$

The total output of the three stage compressor is

$$3 \times 22.65 = 67.95 \text{ hp.}$$

Considering the efficiency of the compressor, the power required to drive the compressor is $67.95 \times \frac{1}{0.85}$

$$= 80 \text{ hp.}$$

AGITATION AND MIXING OF FLUIDS

• PROBLEM 5-21

Derive an expression for the power required to mix a liquid if it depends on the density ρ and viscosity μ of the liquid, the diameter of the mixer D, the rotational speed of the mixer N, and the acceleration due to gravity g.

Solution: The power required to mix a liquid is a function of the density ρ and the viscosity μ of the liquid, the diameter of the mixer D, the rotational speed of the mixer N, and the acceleration due to gravity g.

$$P = f(\rho, \mu, D, N, g)$$

or

$$P = K\rho^a \mu^b D^c N^d g^e \qquad (1)$$

where

$$K = \text{constant}$$

Expressing each variable in terms of the fundamental units of mass M, length L, and time T, equation (1) becomes:

$$\frac{ML^2}{T^3} = \left(\frac{M}{L^3}\right)^a \cdot \left(\frac{M}{LT}\right)^b \cdot (L)^c \cdot \left(\frac{1}{T}\right)^d \cdot \left(\frac{L}{T^2}\right)^e$$

equating the powers of M, L and T,

For M

$$1 = a + b$$

For L

$$2 = -3a - b + c + e$$

For T

$$-3 = -b - d - 2e$$

Simplifying the three relations

$$a = 1 - b$$

$$c = 5 - 2b - e$$

$$d = 3 - b - 2e$$

Substituting the values of a, c and d into equation (1) yields,

$$P = K\rho^{(1-b)} \cdot \mu^b \cdot D^{(5-2b-e)} \cdot N^{(3-b-2e)} \cdot g^e$$

Rewriting,

$$P = K\rho N^3 D^5 \cdot \left(\frac{\mu}{\rho N D^2}\right)^b \left(\frac{g}{N^2 D}\right)^e$$

or

$$\left(\frac{P}{\rho N^3 D^5}\right) = K\left(\frac{\rho N D^2}{\mu}\right)^{-b} \left(\frac{N^2 D}{g}\right)^{-e}$$

but $\frac{P}{\rho N^3 D^5}$ = dimensionless power.

$\frac{\rho N D^2}{\mu}$ = Reynolds number.

$\frac{N^2 D}{g}$ = Froude number.

Therefore the power is a function of the Reynolds number and the Froude number.

Thus

$$N_p = f(\text{Re}, \text{Fr}).$$

• PROBLEM 5-22

a) Calculate the horsepower required to run a 22 in. diameter, flat blade turbine with 6 blades installed centrally in a vertical, unbaffled tank of 65 in. diameter. The tank contains a liquid with a density of 95 lb/ft^3 and a viscosity of 15 cp. The rotational speed of the impeller of the turbine is 100 rpm. The height of the liquid in the tank is 60 inches and the turbine is located 20 inches from the bottom of the tank.

b) If the same unit is used to mix a rubber compound with a density of 75 lb/ft^3 and a viscosity of 1000 poises, determine the power required to run the turbine.

c) If in problem a, the tank is fitted with 4 baffles, each of width 8 in., determine the power required to run the turbine.

Solution:

a) The power required to run the turbine is given by the relation

$$P = \frac{\phi N_{Fr}^m \cdot n^3 D_t^5 \rho}{g_c} \qquad (1)$$

where

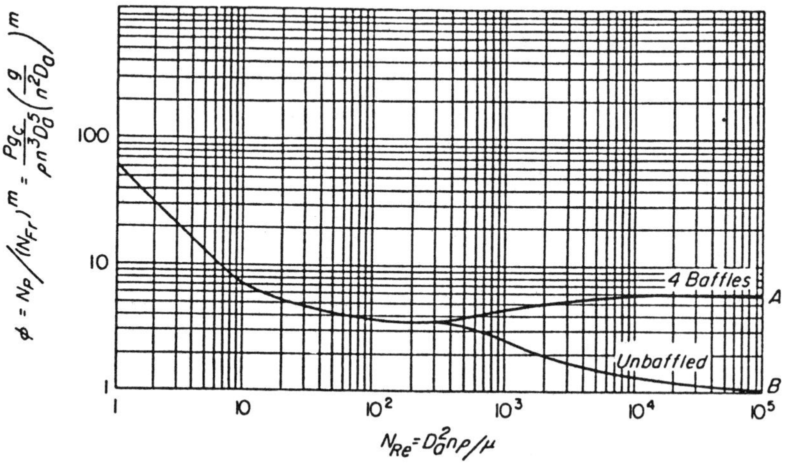

Power function ϕ versus N_{Re} for six-blade turbine.

Figure 1.

ϕ = power function obtained from the figure (1), by using the Reynolds number.

N_{Fr} = Froude number

m = exponent of the Froude number.

n = revolutions per second of the impeller

D_t = diameter of the turbinc

ρ = density of the liquid

The term m depends on the shape factor and is empirically related to the Reynolds number by

$$m = \frac{a - \log_{10} Re}{b} \qquad (2)$$

The values of a and b are given by the table in figure (2).

For a mixer operating at low Reynolds numbers and also for baffled tanks, the Froude number can be dropped from the power equation.

The Reynolds number is given by

$$Re = \frac{\rho n D_t^2}{\mu}$$

Substituting the values,

$$Re = 95 \times (100/60) \times \left(\frac{22}{12}\right)^2 \times \frac{1}{15 \times 6.72 \times 10^{-4}}$$

$$= 52{,}800 = 5.3 \times 10^4$$

Since the Reynolds number is above 300, vortexing is present in the system.

Therefore the power required is given by

$$P = \frac{\phi N_{Fr}^{m} \cdot n^3 D_t^5 \rho}{g_c} \qquad (1)$$

where the value of the power function, ϕ, from figure (1) is:

$\phi = 1.1$ corresponding to Re = 5.3×10^4 for unbaffled tank. (curve B)

The Froude number

$$N_{Fr} = \frac{D_t n^2}{g}$$

$$= \left(\frac{22}{12}\right)\left(\frac{100}{60}\right)^2 \times \frac{1}{32.2}$$

$$= 0.158$$

The constants a and b in the relation for m are obtained from figure (2):

Values for the Froude Number Exponent y at Reynolds Numbers Above 300

Propeller Diameter (in.)	D_i/D_T Ratio	a	b
4	0.48	2.6	18.0
20	0.37	2.3	18.0
18	0.33	2.1	18.0
4	0.30	1.7	18.0
12	0.22	0	18.0

6 Blade Flat Blade Turbine Diameter (in.)	D_i/D_T Ratio	a	b
4	0.30	1.0	40.0
6	0.33	1.0	40.0

$y = (Q - \log_{10} N_{Re})/b$ when y = 0 no vortexing is present and gravitational effects are negligible.

$$a = 1.0$$

$$b = 40.0$$

Substituting in equation (2) yields:

$$m = \frac{1.0 - \log_{10} 5.3 \times 10^4}{40}$$

$$= -0.093$$

Substituting into equation (1):

$$P = \frac{1.1 \times (0.158)^{-0.093} \times \left(\frac{100}{60}\right)^3 \times \left(\frac{22}{12}\right)^5 \times 95}{32.2}$$

$$= 369.44 \text{ ft.lb}_f/\text{s}$$

$$= \frac{369.44}{550} = 0.67 \text{ hp.}$$

b) The Reynolds number is given by

$$Re = \frac{\rho n D_t^2}{\mu}$$

Substituting the values,

$$Re = 75 \times \left(\frac{100}{60}\right) \times \left(\frac{22}{12}\right)^2 \times \frac{1}{1000 \times 100 \times 6.72 \times 10^{-4}}$$

$$= 6.25$$

Since the Reynolds number is much less than 300, vortexing is absent in the system.

Therefore, the power requirement is independent of whether or not the tank is baffled.

The power required is given by

$$P = \frac{\phi n^3 D_t^5 \rho}{g_c}$$

where the Froude number has been dropped due to the low value of the Reynolds number.

From the graph $\phi = 10.5$ corresponding to $Re = 6.25$

Substituting the values into the equation for the power,

$$P = 10.5 \times \left(\frac{100}{60}\right)^3 \times \left(\frac{22}{12}\right)^5 \times 75 \times \frac{1}{32.2}$$

$$= 2345 \text{ ft.lb}_f/\text{s}$$

or $$P = \frac{2345}{550} = 4.26 \text{ hp.}$$

c) Since the tank is now fitted with baffles, curve A in figure (1) is used to find the power factor corresponding to the calculated Reynolds number.

The Reynolds number calculated in part a, was

$$Re = 5.3 \times 10^4$$

The power factor ϕ from figure (1) is $\phi = 6.0$.

The power required is given by:

$$P = \frac{\phi n^3 D_t^5 \rho}{g}$$

Substituting the values,

$$P = 6 \times \left(\frac{100}{60}\right)^3 \times \left(\frac{22}{12}\right)^5 \times 95 \times \frac{1}{32.2}$$

$$= 1697 \text{ ft.lb}_f/\text{s}$$

or $$P = \frac{1697}{550} = 3.1 \text{ hp.}$$

By fitting baffles to the tank, the power required to operate the turbine, which mixes the liquid, has increased as has the effectiveness of the mixer. When fitting baffles to an unbaffled tank that is operating at a high Reynolds number, always check whether the motor driving the mixer is powerful enough to supply the additional power requirement.

• PROBLEM 5-23

A 24 in. diameter turbine is used to agitate a liquid with a density of 65 lb/ft^3 and a viscosity of 550 poise (36.96 lb$_m$/ft-s) that is contained in a tank with a 6 ft. diameter. The turbine operates at three different speeds, low, medium and high. The corresponding tip speeds are 600, 800 and 1000 ft/min. respectively. The correction factors for the horizontal and vertical components are 0.5 and 0.25 respectively. Determine the effective radii at the three different speeds.

Solution: The theoretical effective radius of agitation can be obtained from figure 2. The parameters are the input power, obtained from power relationship, and the viscosity of the liquid.

The power relationship is given by equation (1):

$$P = \frac{\phi \rho n^3 D_t^5}{g_c} \tag{1}$$

where

P = input power

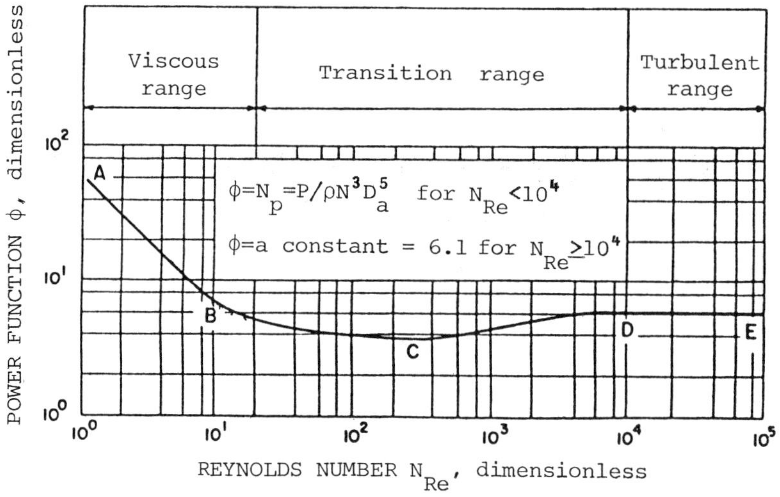

Power Curve for Standard Tank Configuration

Figure 1.

ϕ = power factor

ρ = density of the liquid

n = rotational speed of the turbine impeller

D_t = diameter of the turbine.

The rotational speed of the impeller is related to the tip speed by the relation,

$$\text{Rotational speed} = \frac{\text{Tip speed}}{\text{Turbine circumference}}$$

let n_1, n_2 and n_3 be the rotational speeds corresponding to the low, medium and high tip speeds of the turbine.

Therefore

$$n_1 = \frac{600}{60 \times \pi \times 2} = 1.59 \text{ rps}$$

$$n_2 = \frac{800}{60 \times \pi \times 2} = 2.12 \text{ rps}$$

$$n_3 = \frac{1000}{60 \times \pi \times 2} = 2.65 \text{ rps}$$

The power factor ϕ can be found from figure 1 corresponding to the Reynolds number.

The Reynolds number is given by

$$Re = \frac{\rho n D_t^2}{\mu}$$

For different values of n

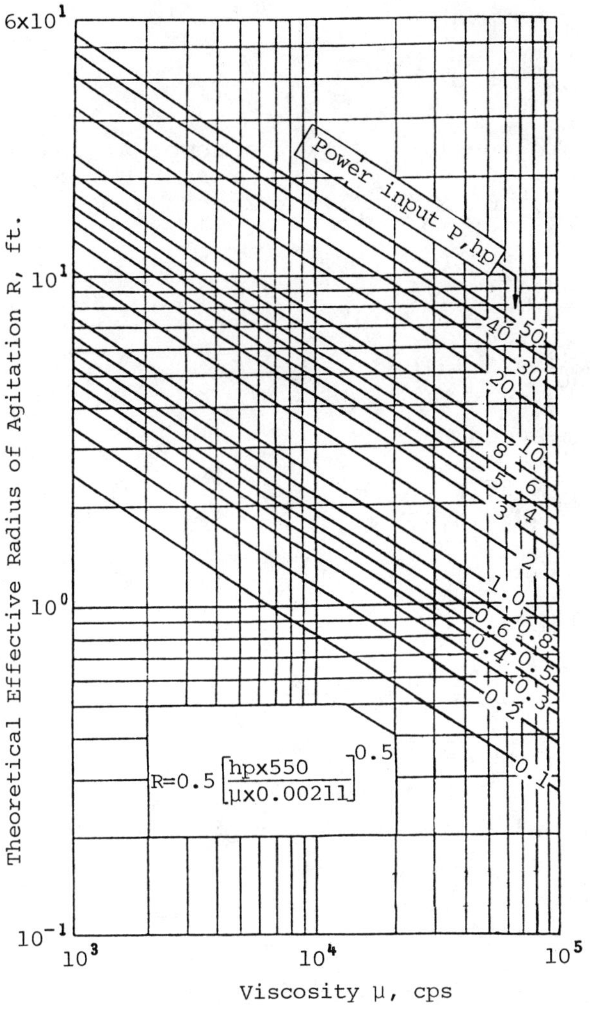

Theoretical effective radius of agitation as a function of viscosity and power input.

Substituting the values,

$$Re_1 = \frac{65 \text{ x } 1.59 \text{ x } \left(\frac{24}{12}\right)^2}{36.96}$$

$$= 11.2$$

$$Re_2 = \frac{65 \text{ x } 2.12 \text{ x } 2^2}{36.96} = 14.9$$

$$Re_3 = \frac{65 \text{ x } 2.65 \text{ x } 2^2}{36.96} = 18.6$$

Then from figure 1, the corresponding power functions are:

$$\phi_1 = 6.75$$

$$\phi_2 = 6.0$$

$$\phi_3 = 5.5$$

Substituting into equation (1), the power at low speed is:

$$P_1 = \frac{6.75 \times 65 \times (1.59)^3 \times 2^5}{32.2}$$

$$= 1753 \text{ ft.lb}_f/\text{s}$$

or $$P_1 = \frac{1753}{550} = 3.19 \text{ hp.}$$

Power at medium speed

$$P_2 = \frac{6.0 \times 65 \times (2.12)^3 \times 2^5}{32.2 \times 550}$$

$$P_2 = 6.71 \text{ hp.}$$

Power at high speed

$$P_3 = \frac{5.5 \times 65 \times (2.65)^3 \times 2^5}{32.2 \times 550}$$

$$P_3 = 12.02 \text{ hp.}$$

The theoretical effective radii are obtained from figure 2:

$$R_1 = 1.9 \text{ ft.}$$

$$R_2 = 2.8 \text{ ft.}$$

$$R_3 = 3.8 \text{ ft.}$$

The actual radii of agitation R', considering the correction factor 0.5 for the horizontal component and 0.25 for the vertical component, are at tip speed = 600 ft/min.

$$R_1' \text{ (horizontal)} = 0.5 \times 1.9 \text{ ft.}$$

$$= 0.95 \text{ ft.}$$

$$R_1' \text{ (vertical)} = 0.25 \times 1.9 \text{ ft.}$$

$$= 0.475 \text{ ft.}$$

at tip speed = 800 ft/min

$$R_2' \text{ (horizontal)} = 0.5 \times 2.8 \text{ ft.}$$

$$= 1.4 \text{ ft.}$$

$$R_2' \text{ (vertical)} = 0.25 \times 2.8$$

$$= 0.7 \text{ ft.}$$

at tip speed = 1000 ft/min

$$R_3' \text{ (horizontal)} = 0.5 \times 3.8$$

$$= 1.9 \text{ ft.}$$

$$R_3' \text{ (vertical)} = 0.25 \times 3.8$$

$$= 0.95 \text{ ft.}$$

FLUIDIZATION AND SETTLING

• PROBLEM 5-24

A vertical tank with an 8 ft. inside diameter contains 20 tons of ground coke. The ground coke is 60-mesh (0.0098 in. diameter) and has a density of 80 lb/ft^3. If the coke is to be fluidized with air of density $\rho = 0.583\ lb/ft^3$ and viscosity $\mu = 2.2 \times 10^{-5}$ lb/ft-s, determine:

a) the minimum porosity for fluidization.

b) the minimum height of the bed.

c) the pressure drop in the bed.

d) the critical velocity of air for the fluidization.

Solution:

a) The graph in figure (1) shows the minimum porosity for fluidization versus particle sizes of various materials.

The graph h corresponds to coke particles. Therefore, for a particle size of 60-mesh (0.0098 in. diameter), the corresponding value of the minimum porosity is $\varepsilon_f = 0.6$.

b) Given that the mass of grounded coke = 20 tons

$$= 20 \times 2000 \text{ lbs.}$$

$$\text{The volume occupied} = \frac{20 \times 2000}{80}\ ft^3$$

$$= 500\ ft^3$$

Therefore, the initial height of coke in the tank, with no porosity is given by:

$$h_i = \frac{\text{volume}}{\text{cross-sectional area of tank}}$$

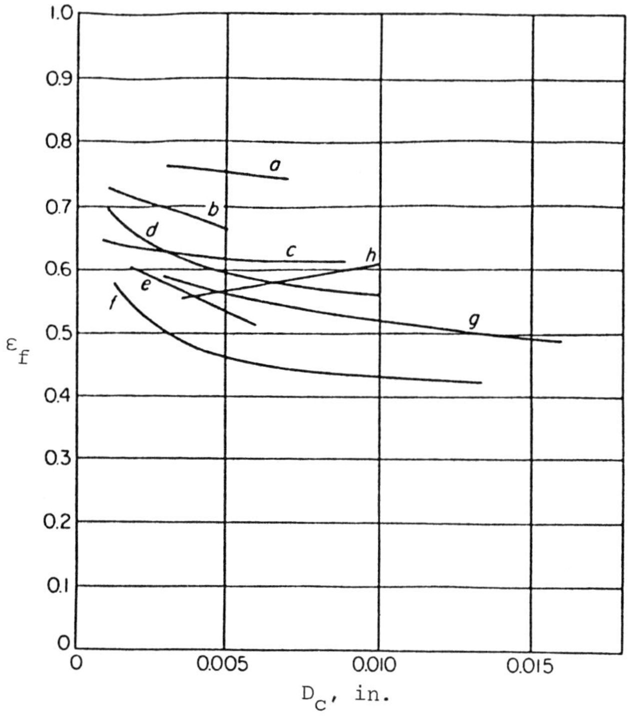

Minimum porosity for fluidization versus particle size: (a) soft brick; (b) adsorption carbon; (c) broken Raschig rings; (d) coal and glass powder; (e) carborundum; (f) round sand; (h) coke.

Figure 1.

$$= \frac{500}{\frac{\pi}{4}(8)^2}$$

or, $h_i = 9.95$ ft. this corresponds to $\varepsilon_i = 0$

The minimum height of the fluidized bed is given by:

$$h_f = h_i \frac{(1 - \varepsilon_i)}{(1 - \varepsilon_f)}$$

Substituting the values,

$$h_f = 9.95 \times \frac{1}{1 - 0.6}$$

$$= 24.88 \text{ ft.}$$

c) The pressure drop in the fluidized bed is given by:

$$\frac{-\Delta p}{h_f} = \frac{g}{g_c}(1 - \varepsilon_f)(\rho_c - \rho_a)$$

where

$-\Delta p$ = pressure drop

h_f = minimum height of the fluidized bed

ρ_c = density of coke

ρ_a = density of air

$\frac{g}{g_c}$ = gravitational units conversion

Substituting the values and solving for $-\Delta p$

$$-\Delta p = 24.88(1 - 0.6)(80 - 0.583)$$

$$= 790.4 \text{ lb}_f/\text{ft}^2$$

$$= 5.5 \text{ psi}$$

Therefore, the pressure drop is 5.5 psi.

d) The critical velocity of air for fluidization is given by:

$$v_{cr} = \frac{D_c^2 g(\rho_c - \rho_a)}{150\mu_a} \times \frac{\varepsilon_f^{\,3}}{1 - \varepsilon_f}$$

where

D_c = size of the grounded coke particles

μ_a = viscosity of air

Substituting the values into the previous equation,

$$v_{cr} = \left(\frac{0.0098}{12}\right)^2 \times \frac{32.2(80 - 0.583)}{150 \times 2.2 \times 10^{-5}} \times \frac{(0.6)^3}{(1 - 0.6)}$$

$$= 0.279 \text{ ft/s.}$$

• PROBLEM 5-25

A mixture of oil (sp. gr. = 0.88) and air consists of drops of oil with a diameter of 3.5×10^{-5} ft. If a settling time of 90 seconds is allowed, find the maximum height of the chamber required for the oil drops to settle. Take density and viscosity of air as 0.075 lb/ft^3 and 1.2×10^{-5} lb/ft-s respectively.

Solution: The equation defining the criteria for the settling of the oil drop is given by:

$$K = D_o \left[\frac{g\rho_a(\rho_o - \rho_a)}{\mu_a^2}\right]^{1/3} \qquad (1)$$

where

D_o = diameter of the oil drop

ρ_a = density of air

ρ_o = density of oil

μ_a = viscosity of air.

The density of air ρ_a is very small compared to the density of oil ρ_o.

Hence $(\rho_o - \rho_a)$ can be considered as ρ_o.

The density of oil = 0.88 x 62.4

or, $\rho_o = 54.9\ \text{lb/ft}^3$

Substituting the values into equation (1):

$$K = 3.5 \times 10^{-5}\left[\frac{32.2 \times 0.075 \times 54.9}{(1.2 \times 10^{-5})^2}\right]^{1/3}$$

$$= 0.34.$$

Thus the settling occurs in the Stoke's-law range where:

$$K < 3.3$$

Therefore the equation for the terminal velocity of the particle is:

$$v_t = \frac{D_o^2 g(\rho_o - \rho_a)}{18\ \mu_a} = \frac{D_o^2 g\rho_o}{18\ \mu_a} \qquad (2)$$

Substituting the values,

$$v_t = \frac{(3.5 \times 10^{-5})^2 \times 32.2 \times 54.9}{18 \times 1.2 \times 10^{-5}}$$

$$= 0.01\ \text{ft/s}$$

Therefore, in the settling time of 90 seconds, the drops would move down by 0.01 x 90 ft.

= 0.9 ft.

and the maximum height of the chamber is 0.9 ft.

• **PROBLEM 5-26**

A zinc mineral slurry consists of ore particles and water in the volumetric ratio of 1:3. The volumetric ratio of zinc mineral (sp. gr. = 3.8) to ore particles (sp. gr. = 2.6) is 0.2. The mineral particles are 0.007 in. in diameter. If the particles of zinc mineral are settling under gravity, determine the terminal velocity of the particles. Take viscosity of water as $\mu = 8.1 \times 10^{-4}$ lb/ft-s.

Solution: The density of the settling medium (the slurry) is given by:

$$\left[\frac{1}{4} \text{ x sp. gr. of ore particles} + \frac{3}{4} \text{ sp. gr. of water}\right] \text{ x (density of water)}$$

$$\rho_m = \left(\frac{1}{4} \times 2.6 + \frac{3}{4} \times 1\right) 62.4$$

$$= 87.36 \text{ lb/ft}^3.$$

The porosity ε is $\quad \varepsilon = 1 - 0.2$

$$= 0.8$$

The correction factor ψ_p is given by the empirical relation

$$\psi_p = e^{-4.19(1-\varepsilon)}$$

$$= e^{-4.19(1-0.8)}$$

or $\quad \psi_p = 0.43$

The equation defining the criterion for settling is:

$$K = D_p \left[\frac{g\rho_m(\rho_p - \rho_m)(\psi_p)^2}{\mu_\omega^2}\right]^{1/3}$$

where

D_p = diameter of the settling particles

g = acceleration due to gravity

ρ_m = density of the slurry

ρ_p = density of the settling particles

μ_ω = viscosity of water

ψ_p = correction factor.

Substituting the values,

$$K = \left(\frac{0.007}{12}\right)\left[\frac{32.2 \times 87.36 \times (3.8 \times 62.4 - 87.36) \times (0.43)^2}{(8.1 \times 10^{-4})^2}\right]^{1/3}$$

$$= 2.87$$

Thus the settling occurs in the Stoke's-law range where

$$K < 3.3$$

Therefore, the equation for the terminal velocity of the mineral is

$$v_t = \left[\frac{4g\, D_p^{1+n}\cdot{}^{2-n}(\psi_p)^n(\rho_p - \rho_m)}{3b_1\rho_m^{1-n}\mu_\omega^n}\right]^{\frac{1}{2-n}}$$

taking $n = 1$ and $b_1 = 24$

$$v_t = \left[\frac{4 \times 32.2 \times (0.007/12)^2 \times (0.43) \times (0.8) \times (62.4 \times 3.8 - 87.36)}{3 \times 24 \times 8.1 \times 10^{-4}}\right]^1$$

$$= 0.039 \text{ ft/s}$$

CHAPTER 6

BOUNDARY LAYER FLOW AND DRAG FORCE

BOUNDARY LAYER THICKNESS AND SHEAR STRESS

• PROBLEM 6-1

Oil (sp. gr. = 0.96, viscosity μ = 50 cp) flows past a flat plate with a free-stream velocity of 1.1 ft/s. What is the thickness of the boundary layer, and the displacement thickness 6 inches from the leading edge?

Solution: The Reynolds number for the flow is given by

$$Re_x = \frac{vx}{\nu}$$

where

Re_x = Reynolds number of the flow at a distance x feet from the leading edge.

v = velocity of flow

ν = kinematic viscosity of oil.

The kinematic viscosity of oil is given by

$$\nu = \frac{\mu}{\rho} = \frac{50 \times 6.72 \times 10^{-4}}{0.96 \times 62.4}$$

$$= 5.61 \times 10^{-4} \text{ ft}^2/\text{s}$$

Substituting the values into the relationship for the Reynolds number,

$$Re_x = \frac{1.1 \times 0.5}{5.61 \times 10^{-4}} = 980$$

Thus the boundary layer may be assumed to be laminar. Then the thickness of the boundary layer is given by:

$$\frac{\delta}{x} = 4.64\ (Re_x)^{-0.5}$$

where

δ = boundary layer thickness at a distance x feet from the leading edge

Substituting the values and solving for δ,

$$\delta = 4.64 \times \frac{6}{12} \times (980)^{-0.5}$$

$$\delta = 0.074 \text{ ft.}$$

$$= 0.90 \text{ inches.}$$

The displacement thickness δ^* is related to boundary layer thickness by

$$\delta^* = 0.375\delta$$

Thus, the displacement thickness is

$$\delta^* = 0.375 \times 0.074$$

$$= 0.0278 \text{ ft}$$

$$\text{or } \delta^* = 0.333 \text{ inches}$$

• PROBLEM 6-2

Calculate the thickness of the boundary layer at a distance of 3 in. from the leading edge of a flat surface over which air at 80°F is flowing with a free-stream velocity of 35 ft/sec. Also estimate the rate of growth of the boundary layer. For air, take $\rho = 0.0735\ lb/ft^3$ and $\nu = 1.69 \times 10^{-4}\ ft^2/sec$.

Solution: The Reynolds number for the flow is given by

$$Re_x = \frac{vx}{\nu}$$

Substituting the values,

$$Re_x = \frac{35 \times \left(\frac{3}{12}\right)}{1.69 \times 10^{-4}}$$

$$= 51,775$$

The transition from laminar to turbulent flow on a smooth plate occurs in the range of Re from 2×10^5 to 3×10^6.

Thus the boundary layer may be taken as laminar.
The thickness of the boundary layer is given by

$$\frac{\delta}{x} = \frac{5}{\sqrt{Re_x}}$$

where

δ = boundary layer thickness at a distance of x from the leading edge

Substituting the values,

$$\delta = \frac{5 \times 3}{\sqrt{51775}}$$

or, $\delta = 0.066$ in.

The rate of growth of the boundary layer is obtained by differentiating δ with respect to x.

$$\delta = \frac{5x}{\sqrt{Re_x}}$$

$$= 5x\sqrt{\frac{\nu}{Vx}}$$

or, $$\delta = 5\sqrt{\frac{\nu}{V}} \cdot \sqrt{x}$$

Differentiating with respect to x

$$\frac{d\delta}{dx} = \frac{5}{2}\sqrt{\frac{\nu}{V}} \cdot \frac{1}{\sqrt{x}}$$

$$= \frac{5}{2}\sqrt{\frac{\nu}{Vx}}$$

$$\frac{d\delta}{dx} = \frac{5}{2\sqrt{Re_x}}$$

$$= \frac{5}{2 \times \sqrt{51775}}$$

and

$$\frac{d\delta}{dx} = 0.011 \text{ in./in.}$$

• **PROBLEM 6-3**

Water at 70°F (μ = 1 cp) is flowing at a velocity of 15 ft/s over a long (in the direction of the flow) thin flat plate. Find the distance from the leading edge at which the boundary layer thickness is 0.75 in.

Solution: Since neither the Reynolds number nor the type of flow has been specified in the problem, the applicable boundary layer equation must first be determined.

Assuming the flow to be laminar, the boundary layer thickness is given by equation (1).

$$\frac{\delta}{x} = \frac{5}{\sqrt{Re_x}} = 5\sqrt{\frac{\nu}{vx}} \tag{1}$$

or $$x = \frac{\delta^2}{25} \times \left(\frac{v}{\nu}\right)$$

where

x = distance from the leading edge

δ = boundary layer thickness at 'x'

v = velocity of flow

ν = kinematic viscosity = μ/ρ

Substituting the values,

$$x = \left(\frac{0.75}{12}\right)^2 \times \frac{1}{25} \times \frac{15 \times 62.4}{1 \times 6.72 \times 10^{-4}}$$

$$= 218 \text{ ft.}$$

Substituting this value of x into the equation for the Reynolds number to check whether the assumption of laminar flow is correct yields:

$$Re_x = \frac{vx}{\nu} = \frac{15 \times 218 \times 62.4}{1 \times 6.72 \times 10^{-4}}$$

$$= 3.0 \times 10^8$$

The maximum Reynolds number for a laminar flow past a flat plate is 3×10^6.

Since the Reynolds number obtained above is greater than 3×10^6 the assumption that the flow is laminar is incorrect.

Assume the flow to be turbulent. Then the boundary layer thickness is given by the equation:

$$\frac{\delta}{x} = \frac{0.16}{\left(Re_x\right)^{1/7}}$$

$$\frac{\delta}{x} = 0.16\left(\frac{\nu}{vx}\right)^{1/7}$$

or $$x = \left(\frac{\delta}{0.16}\right)^{7/6} \times \left(\frac{v}{\nu}\right)^{1/6}$$

Substituting the values,

$$x = \left(\frac{0.75/12}{0.16}\right)^{7/6} \times \left(\frac{15 \times 62.4}{6.72 \times 10^{-4}}\right)^{1/6}$$

$$x = 3.53 \text{ ft.}$$

Now use this value of x in the Reynolds number equation to verify the assumption of turbulent flow.

$$Re_x = \frac{vx}{\nu}$$

$$= 15 \times 3.53 \times \frac{62.4}{6.72 \times 10^{-4}}$$

$$Re_x = 4.9 \times 10^6$$

This value of Reynolds number lies in the turbulent zone. Hence the assumption that the flow is turbulent is correct.

Therefore, the distance from the leading edge at which the boundary layer thickness is 0.75 in. is

$$x = 3.53 \text{ ft.}$$

• PROBLEM 6-4

A liquid (ρ = 62.4 lb/ft^3 and μ = 7.5 x 10^{-4} lb/ft-s) flows past a flat plate with a free-stream velocity of 12 ft/s. For a point at a distance of 2 in. from the leading edge of the plate, determine:

a) the laminar boundary layer thickness.

b) the shear stress.

c) the shear force per unit width of flow, acting on the plate between the leading edge and the given point.

Solution:

a) For laminar flow, an exact expression for the boundary layer thickness is given by Blasius.

$$\frac{\delta}{x} = \frac{4.91}{Re_x^{\frac{1}{2}}} = 4.91\left(\frac{\nu}{vx}\right)^{\frac{1}{2}} \qquad (1)$$

Substituting into equation (1) with $\nu = \frac{\mu}{\rho}$ gives:

$$\delta = 4.91 \times \left(\frac{2}{12}\right)\left(\frac{7.5 \times 10^{-4}}{62.4} \times \frac{12}{2} \times \frac{1}{12}\right)^{\frac{1}{2}}$$

$$= 0.002 \text{ ft.}$$

Therefore the boundary layer thickness is

$$\delta = 0.002 \text{ ft.}$$

b) The shear stress at the point of interest is given by:

$$\tau = \frac{0.332\rho V^2}{g_c} \times (Re_x)^{-\frac{1}{2}}$$

$$= \frac{0.332 \times 62.4 \times (12)^2}{32.2} \times$$

$$\left(12 \times \frac{2}{12} \times \frac{62.4}{7.5 \times 10^{-4}}\right)^{-0.5}$$

$$= 0.227 \text{ lb}_f/\text{ft}^2$$

c) The shear force per unit width of flow, acting on the plate between the leading edge and 2 inches beyond is obtained from the integral

$$F = w \int_0^x \tau dx$$

$$\text{or} \quad \frac{F}{w} = \int_0^x \tau dx$$

where $\frac{F}{w}$ = shear force per unit width.

$$\text{Therefore} \quad \frac{F}{w} = \int_0^x \frac{0.332\rho V^2}{g_c} \left(\frac{\nu}{Vx}\right)^{\frac{1}{2}} dx$$

$$= \frac{0.332\rho V^2}{g_c} \cdot \left(\frac{\nu}{V}\right)^{\frac{1}{2}} \int_0^x x^{-\frac{1}{2}} dx$$

$$\frac{F}{w} = \frac{0.332\rho V^2}{g_c} \left(\frac{\nu}{V}\right)^{\frac{1}{2}} . \; 2x^{\frac{1}{2}}$$

Substituting gives:

$$\frac{F}{w} = \frac{0.332 \times 62.4 \times (12)^2}{32.2} \times \left(\frac{7.5 \times 10^{-4}}{62.4 \times 12}\right)^{\frac{1}{2}} \times 2\left(\frac{2}{12}\right)^{\frac{1}{2}}$$

$$= 0.0757 \text{ lb}_f/\text{ft.}$$

Air at 80 °F flows over a 50 x 150 ft. flat plate with a velocity of 75 ft/s. Air is flowing along the length of the plate (parallel to the 150 foot side). If there is an initial laminar boundary layer along the length of the plate followed by a turbulent boundary layer, calculate:

a) the length of the laminar boundary layer region.

b) the boundary layer thickness at the end of laminar region

c) the shear stress at the end of the laminar boundary layer region and at the end of 150 ft.

d) the force acting on the first 75 ft. of the plate.

Solution: At 80 °F, the properties of air are:

$$\rho = 0.0735 \ lb_m/ft^3$$

$$\nu = 1.69 \times 10^{-4} \ ft^2/s$$

a) The maximum Re_x (Reynolds number) for laminar flow past a flat plate is 500,000. From the definition of Reynolds number

$$Re_x = \frac{vx}{\nu}$$

where

v = velocity of flow

x = distance from the leading edge

ν = kinematic viscosity of the flowing fluid.

In the above equation v and ν can be considered as constants.

Therefore the Reynolds number is directly proportional to x.

Therefore, to get the length of the laminar boundary layer, substitute the maximum value of Re_x for a laminar flow, which is:

$$\frac{vx}{\nu} = 500{,}000$$

or $$\frac{75 \times x}{1.69 \times 10^{-4}} = 500{,}000$$

or $$x = 1.13 \ ft.$$

Thus, the length of the laminar boundary layer is 1.13 ft.

b) The boundary layer thickness is given by the equation

$$\frac{\delta}{x} = \frac{5.2}{\left(Re_x\right)^{\frac{1}{2}}} \tag{1}$$

where

δ = boundary layer thickness at a distance x from the leading edge

Re_x = Reynolds number at the corresponding point.

Since the boundary layer thickness at the end of the laminar region is required,

substitute $x = 1.13$ ft

and $Re_x = 500{,}000$

into equation (1).

$$\delta = \frac{1.13 \times 5.2}{(500{,}000)^{\frac{1}{2}}}$$

$$= 0.0083 \text{ ft.}$$

Thus, the boundary layer thickness at the end of the laminar region is 0.0083 ft.

c) The shear stress is given by

$$\tau = C_f \frac{\rho V^2}{2g_c} \tag{2}$$

where

τ = shear stress

C_f = local drag coefficient

$= \frac{0.664}{\sqrt{Re_x}}$ for a laminar boundary layer

$C_f = \frac{0.059}{(Re_x)^{1/5}}$ for turbulent boundary layer.

The shear stress at the end of the laminar boundary layer region is $\tau = \frac{0.664}{\sqrt{Re_x}} \times \frac{\rho V^2}{2g_c}$

$$= \frac{0.664}{(5 \times 10^5)^{\frac{1}{2}}} \times \frac{0.0735 \times (75)^2}{2 \times 32.2}$$

or $\tau = 0.00603 \ lb_f/ft^2$

To obtain the shear stress at the end of 150 ft, the Reynolds number at that point is required to calculate the local drag coefficient.

$$Re_x = \frac{vx}{\nu}$$

$$= \frac{75 \times 150}{1.69 \times 10^{-4}}$$

$$= 6.66 \times 10^7$$

The local drag coefficient for turbulent boundary layer is

$$C_f = \frac{0.059}{(Re_x)^{1/5}}$$

$$= \frac{0.059}{(6.66 \times 10^7)^{1/5}}$$

$$C_f = 0.0016$$

Substituting into equation (2), the shear stress at 150 ft. is:

$$\tau = 0.0016 \times \frac{0.0735 \times (75)^2}{2 \times 32.2}$$

$$= 0.0103 \ lb_f/ft^2$$

d) The force acting on the plate is given by

$$F = CA \frac{\rho V^2}{2g_c}$$

where

F = the force acting on the plate

C = drag coefficient given by $\frac{1}{\sqrt{C}} = 4.13 \log_{10}(ReC)$

A = area of the plate considered

For the first 75 feet,

$$Re_x = \frac{vx}{\nu}$$

$$= \frac{75 \times 75}{1.69 \times 10^{-4}} = 3.33 \times 10^7$$

Calculating the value of C by iteration

$$C = 0.0024$$

Substituting the values into the equation for F

$$F = 0.0024 \times (50 \times 75) \times \frac{0.0735 \times (75)^2}{2 \times 32.2}$$

$$= 57.78 \ lb_f$$

Therefore, the force acting on the first half of the plate = 57.78 lb_f.

For a steady, turbulent, constant property, two dimensional boundary layer-type flow over a flat plate at zero angle of approach, the velocity profile is given by

$$u = v\left(\frac{y}{\delta}\right)^{1/7} \qquad (1)$$

where

v = free stream velocity

δ = boundary layer thickness

and the local skin friction coefficient is given by

$$C_f = \frac{\tau}{\frac{1}{2}\rho V^2} = 0.045\left(\frac{\nu}{\delta V}\right)^{1/4} \qquad (2)$$

where

τ = local shear stress

ρ = density of the flowing fluid

ν = kinematic viscosity

Determine the local boundary layer thickness δ, as a function of x, by substituting the given equations into the integral form of the momentum equation.

Solution: The integral momentum equation for a steady, planar, two-dimensional, constant property, boundary layer-type flow is:

$$\frac{d}{dx}\int_0^\delta u(V - u)dy + \frac{dV}{dx}\int_0^\delta (V - u)dy = \frac{\tau}{\rho}$$

but for a flat plate,

$$\frac{dV}{dx} = 0$$

Therefore, the momentum equation becomes:

$$\frac{d}{dx}\int_0^\delta u(V - u)dy = \frac{\tau}{\rho} \qquad (3)$$

Substituting equations (1) and (2) into equation (3):

$$\frac{d}{dx}\int_0^{\delta} V^2\left[\left(\frac{y}{\delta}\right)^{1/7} - \left(\frac{y}{\delta}\right)^{2/7}\right]dy = \tfrac{1}{2} \times 0.045V^2\left(\frac{\nu}{V}\right)^{\frac{1}{4}} \delta^{-\frac{1}{4}}$$

or:

$$V^2 \frac{d}{dx}\int_0^{\delta} \left[\left(\frac{y}{\delta}\right)^{1/7} - \left(\frac{y}{\delta}\right)^{2/7}\right]dy = V^2 \times \tfrac{1}{2} \times 0.045\left(\frac{\nu}{V}\right)^{\frac{1}{4}} \delta^{-\frac{1}{4}}$$

$$\frac{d}{dx}\int_0^{\delta} \left[\left(\frac{y}{\delta}\right)^{1/7} - \left(\frac{y}{\delta}\right)^{2/7}\right]dy = 0.0225 \left(\frac{\nu}{V}\right)^{\frac{1}{4}} \delta^{-\frac{1}{4}}$$

Integrating and evaluating the limits yields:

$$\frac{7}{72}\frac{d\delta}{dx} = 0.0225\left(\frac{\nu}{V}\right)^{\frac{1}{4}} \delta^{-\frac{1}{4}}$$

and separating variables:

$$\delta^{\frac{1}{4}}\, d\delta = \frac{72}{7} \times 0.0225\left(\frac{\nu}{V}\right)^{\frac{1}{4}} dx \qquad (4)$$

Assuming that the boundary layer is turbulent over the entire plate, i.e., the boundary layer thickness $\delta = 0$ at $x = 0$, integrate equation (4).

$$\int_0^{\delta} \delta^{\frac{1}{4}}\, d\delta = \int_0^{x} \frac{72}{7} \times 0.0225\left(\frac{\nu}{V}\right)^{\frac{1}{4}} dx$$

Simplifying,

$$\frac{4}{5}\,\delta^{5/4} = 0.231\left(\frac{\nu}{V}\right)^{\frac{1}{4}} x$$

or,

$$\delta = 0.37\left(\frac{\nu}{V}\right)^{1/5} x^{4/5}$$

$$= 0.37\left(\frac{\nu}{Vx}\right)^{1/5} \cdot x$$

$$\delta = \frac{0.37x}{(Re_x)^{1/5}}$$

Therefore, the local boundary layer thickness δ, in terms of x, is:

$$\delta = \frac{0.37x}{(Re_x)^{1/5}}$$

Consider a steady, laminar, two dimensional flow over a flat plate at zero angle of approach to the flow. If the local skin friction coefficient can be expressed as $C_f = \frac{0.664}{\sqrt{Re_x}}$, derive an expression for the average skin friction coefficient defined by:

$$\bar{C}_f = \frac{\tau_{av}}{\frac{1}{2}\rho V^2}$$

where

τ_{av} = the average shear stress.

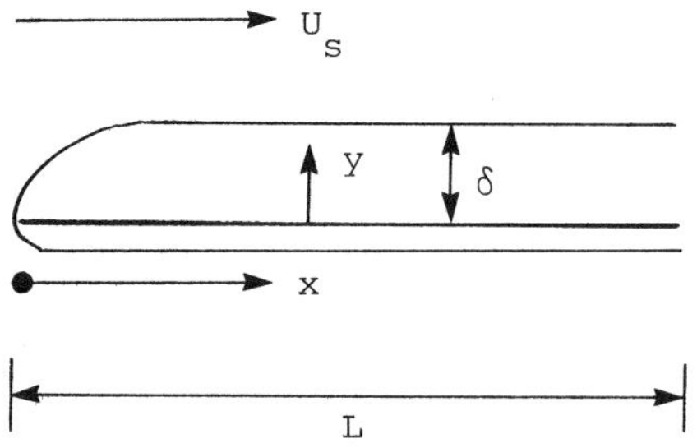

Fig. Hydrodynamic boundary layer development on a flat plate.

Solution: Assume that the width of the flat plate (z-direction) is of unit length. Consider a differential strip of length dx. The differential shear force, dF, acting on this strip is given by the product of the local shear stress and the area of the strip:

$$dF = \tau(dx \times 1)$$

$$= \tau dx$$

The total shear force acting on the plate is obtained by integrating dF over the length L of the plate.

Thus

$$F = \int_0^L dF$$

$$= \int_0^L \tau\, dx$$

The local shear stress is given by

$$\tau = C_f \tfrac{1}{2}\rho V^2$$

where

C_f = skin friction coefficient

ρ = density of fluid flowing

V = velocity of the fluid

but

$$C_f = \frac{0.664}{\sqrt{Re_x}}$$

$$= 0.664\sqrt{\frac{\mu}{\rho Vx}}$$

Therefore,

$$\tau = \frac{0.664}{2}\ \rho V^2\sqrt{\frac{\mu}{\rho Vx}}$$

$$F = \int_0^L \frac{0.664\rho V^2}{2}\sqrt{\frac{\mu}{\rho V}}\ .\ x^{-\frac{1}{2}}\ dx$$

$$= \frac{0.664}{2}\ \rho V^2\sqrt{\frac{\mu}{\rho V}}\int_0^L x^{-\frac{1}{2}}\ dx$$

$$\text{or,}\quad F = \frac{0.664}{2}\ \rho V^2\sqrt{\frac{\mu}{\rho V}}\cdot 2\sqrt{L}$$

$$= 0.664\ \rho V^2\sqrt{\frac{\mu L}{\rho V}} \qquad (1)$$

The total shear force on the plate can also be obtained from the average shear stress τ_{av}.

$$F = \tau_{av}\ x\ (L\ x\ 1) \qquad (2)$$

$$= \tau_{av}\ x\ L$$

From the definition of the average skin friction coefficient

$$\tau_{av} = \tfrac{1}{2}\ \rho V^2\overline{C}_f$$

Substituting into equation (2):

$$F = \tfrac{1}{2}\ \rho V^2\overline{C}_f\ x\ L \qquad (3)$$

Equations (1) and (3) represent the same shear force acting on the plate.

Therefore, $\tfrac{1}{2}\ \rho V^2\overline{C}_f\ x\ L = 0.664\ \rho V^2\sqrt{\frac{\mu L}{\rho V}}$

Solving for $\overline{C}_f$

$$\overline{C}_f = 0.664 \times \frac{2}{L}\sqrt{\frac{\mu L}{\rho V}}$$

$$= 0.664 \times 2\sqrt{\frac{\mu}{\rho VL}}$$

$$\overline{C}_f = \frac{1.328}{(Re_L)^{\frac{1}{2}}}$$

Therefore, the expression for the average skin friction coefficient is

$$\overline{C}_f = \frac{1.328}{(Re_L)^{\frac{1}{2}}}$$

• PROBLEM 6-8

Consider a steady, constant property, laminar, two dimensional, boundary layer-type flow. For a control volume as shown in part a of figure (1), apply the momentum theorem and the boundary layer approximations to derive the momentum equation for the x direction.

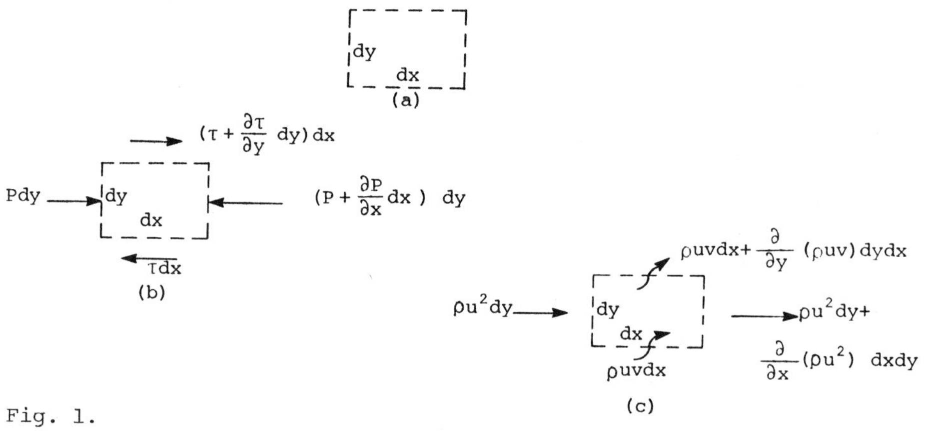

Fig. 1.

Solution: The forces acting on the control volume in the x-direction are shown in part b of figure (1). The shear force on the top surface and the normal force on the right surface are the first two terms of a Taylor series expansion. The normal force due to viscosity is negligible compared to the shear force due to viscosity for a thin boundary layer, thus it is neglected. Therefore, the sum of the forces on the control volume in the x-direction is:

$$\Sigma F_x = Pdy + (\tau + \frac{\partial \tau}{\partial y} dy)dx - \tau dx - (P + \frac{\partial P}{\partial x} dx)dy$$

$$= \left(\frac{\partial \tau}{\partial y} - \frac{\partial P}{\partial x}\right)dxdy \qquad (1)$$

Part c of figure (1) shows the momentum flux across the control surface.

Momentum flux is defined as the product of mass flow rate and velocity.

The x-momentum flux crossing the left face is $(\rho u dy)u = \rho u^2 dy$ Similarly the x-momentum flux crossing the right face is the Taylor series expansion of $\rho u^2 dy$:

$$\rho u^2 dy + \frac{\partial}{\partial x}(\rho u^2)dxdy$$

$$= \rho u^2 dy + \rho\frac{\partial(u^2)}{\partial x} dxdy.$$

The x-momentum flux crossing the bottom face is:

$$\rho v dx \cdot u$$

and that crossing the top face is the Taylor series expansion of $\rho v dx \cdot u$

$$= \rho uvdx + \rho\frac{\partial}{\partial y}(uv)dxdy$$

Hence the net momentum flux is:

$$\rho uvdx + \rho\frac{\partial}{\partial y}(uv)dxdy + \rho u^2 dy + \rho\frac{\partial}{\partial x}(u^2)dxdy - \rho uvdx - \rho u^2 dy$$

Simplifying, $\rho\left[\frac{\partial}{\partial y}(uv) + \frac{\partial}{\partial x}(u^2)\right]dxdy$ (2)

From the momentum theorem, the sum of the forces in the x direction is equal to the net momentum flux in the x-direction. Equating equations (1) and (2) gives:

$$\left(\frac{\partial \tau}{\partial y} - \frac{\partial P}{\partial x}\right)dxdy = \rho\left[\frac{\partial}{\partial y}(uv) + \frac{\partial}{\partial x}(u^2)\right]dxdy$$

or $\frac{\partial \tau}{\partial y} - \frac{\partial P}{\partial x} = \rho\left[\frac{\partial}{\partial y}(uv) + \frac{\partial}{\partial x}(u^2)\right]$ (3)

From the Newtons law of viscosity, the shear stress τ is defined as $\tau = \mu\frac{\partial u}{\partial y}$, for a thin boundary layer ($\partial v/\partial x << \partial u/\partial y$):

where

μ = viscosity

$\frac{\partial u}{\partial y}$ = velocity gradient

Therefore, $\frac{\partial \tau}{\partial y} = \mu\frac{\partial^2 u}{\partial y^2}$

Substituting into equation (3) and simplifying,

$$\mu\frac{\partial^2 u}{\partial y^2} - \frac{\partial P}{\partial x} = \rho\left[v\frac{\partial u}{\partial y} + u\frac{\partial v}{\partial y} + 2u\frac{\partial u}{\partial x}\right]$$

$$= \rho\left[u\frac{\partial u}{\partial x} + v\frac{\partial u}{\partial y} + u\left(\frac{\partial u}{\partial x} + \frac{\partial v}{\partial y}\right)\right]$$

$$= \rho\left[u\frac{\partial u}{\partial x} + v\frac{\partial u}{\partial y}\right] + \rho u\left(\frac{\partial u}{\partial x} + \frac{\partial v}{\partial y}\right)$$

From the continuity equation

$$\frac{\partial u}{\partial x} + \frac{\partial v}{\partial y} = 0$$

Therefore,

$$\mu\frac{\partial^2 u}{\partial y^2} - \frac{\partial P}{\partial x} = \rho\left[u\frac{\partial u}{\partial x} + v\frac{\partial u}{\partial y}\right]$$

Therefore, the momentum equation in the x-direction is:

$$\rho\left[u\frac{\partial u}{\partial x} + v\frac{\partial u}{\partial y}\right] = -\frac{\partial P}{\partial x} + \mu\frac{\partial^2 u}{\partial y^2}$$

• PROBLEM 6-9

a) Consider a thin flat plate which is 10 ft wide and 20 ft long, over which air at 70 °F flows along the length with a free stream velocity of 100 ft/s. If the boundary layer is turbulent from the leading edge, calculate the boundary layer thickness, the shear stress, and the thickness of the laminar sub-layer at a point 15 ft from the leading edge. Also determine the total drag on the plate.

Solution:

a) The Reynolds number for flow on a plate is given by:

$$Re_x = \frac{vx}{\nu}$$

where

v = the free stream velocity

ν = the kinematic viscosity of air

x = the distance from the leading edge

Therefore, the Reynolds number at 15 ft from the leading edge is:

$$Re_x = \frac{100 \times 15}{1.6 \times 10^{-4}}$$

$$= 9.4 \times 10^6$$

The boundary layer thickness, δ, for a turbulent boundary layer is given by:

$$\frac{\delta}{x} = \frac{0.37}{(Re_x)^{1/5}}$$

Therefore, $\delta = \dfrac{0.37 \times 15}{(9.4 \times 10^6)^{1/5}}$

$= 0.224$ ft $= 2.7$ in.

Therefore, the thickness of the boundary layer at 15 ft from the leading edge is 2.7 in.

The shear stress acting on the plate is given by

$$\tau = C_f \rho \frac{v^2}{2g_c}$$

where

C_f = the shear stress coefficient

ρ = the density of air

v = the velocity of flow.

For a turbulent boundary layer

$$C_f = \frac{0.058}{Re_x^{1/5}}$$

Therefore, the shear stress at a point 15 ft from the leading edge is:

$$\tau = \frac{0.058}{(9.4 \times 10^6)^{1/5}} \times 0.0735 \times \frac{(100)^2}{2 \times 32.2}$$

$$= 0.0267 \ lb_f/ft^2$$

where an air density of 0.0735 lb/ft^3 has been employed.

The thickness of the laminar sub-layer is given by:

$$\delta' = \frac{5\nu}{u_*}$$

where

ν = the kinematic viscosity

u_* = the shear stress velocity

$= \sqrt{\dfrac{\tau g_c}{\rho}}$

Therefore

$$\delta' = 5\nu\sqrt{\frac{\rho}{\tau g_c}}$$

The thickness of the laminar sub-layer at a point 15 ft from the leading edge is:

$$\delta' = 5 \times 1{\cdot}6 \times 10^{-4}\sqrt{\frac{0.0735}{0.0267 \times 32.2}}$$

$$= 2.34 \times 10^{-4} \text{ ft.}$$

The drag force on one side of the plate is given by

$$F = C_f A \frac{\rho v^2}{2g_c}$$

where

C_f = the shear stress coefficient

A = the area of the plate

ρ = the density of air

v = the velocity of flow

The shear stress coefficient C_f is related to the Reynolds number by $C_f = \dfrac{0.058}{Re_x^{1/5}}$.

The Reynolds number at the end of the plate is:

$$Re_x = \frac{vx}{\nu}$$

$$= \frac{100 \times 20}{1.6 \times 10^{-4}}$$

$$= 1.25 \times 10^7$$

Therefore $C_f = \dfrac{0.058}{(1.25 \times 10^7)^{1/5}}$

$$= 2.21 \times 10^{-3}$$

The total drag force on the plate (considering both sides) is:

$$F = C_f \frac{A\rho v^2}{2g_c} \times 2 = C_f \frac{A\rho v^2}{g_c}$$

Substituting yields:

$$F = 2.21 \times 10^{-3} \times (10 \times 20) \times \frac{0.0735 \times (100)^2}{32.2}$$

$$= 10.1 \text{ lb}_f$$

A 6 foot long thin flat plate is placed parallel to a 10 ft/s stream of oil (ν = 10^{-4} ft^2/s, sp. gr. = 0.86). Determine the boundary layer thickness and the shear stress in terms of the distance from the leading edge and plot them.

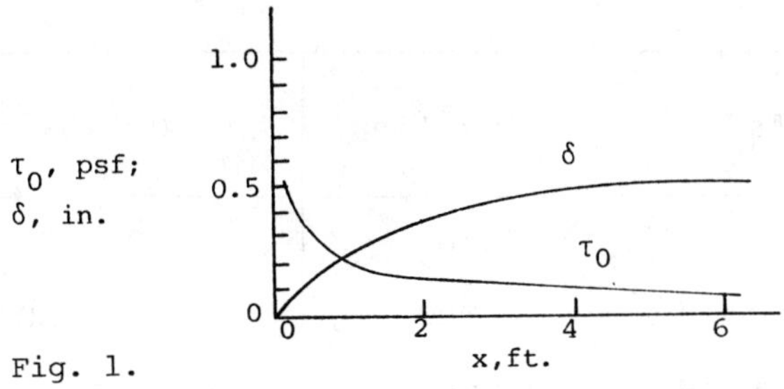

Fig. 1.

Solution: The Reynolds number for flow on a flat surface is given by:

$$Re_x = \frac{vx}{\nu}$$

where

v = velocity of flow

x = distance from the leading edge

ν = kinematic viscosity.

Substituting for v and ν yields Re_x as a function of x.

$$Re_x = \frac{10x}{10^{-4}} = 10^5 x$$

The boundary layer thickness is given by:

$$\frac{\delta}{x} = \frac{5}{\sqrt{Re_x}}$$

or $$\delta = \frac{5x}{(10^5 x)^{\frac{1}{2}}}$$

$$= 0.0158x^{\frac{1}{2}}$$

If x is expressed in ft, then

$$\delta = 0.0158 \times 12x^{\frac{1}{2}} \text{ in.}$$

$$= 0.19x^{\frac{1}{2}} \text{ in.}$$

The shear stress is given by:

$$\tau = 0.332 \frac{\mu v}{g_c x} (Re_x)^{\frac{1}{2}}$$

$$= 0.332 \frac{\rho\nu v}{g_c x} (Re_x)^{\frac{1}{2}}$$

Substituting and writing τ in terms of x gives:

$$\tau = 0.332 \times \left(\frac{0.86 \times 62.4}{32.2}\right) \times 10^{-4} \times \frac{10}{x} \times (10^5 x)^{\frac{1}{2}}$$

$$\tau = 0.175x^{-\frac{1}{2}} \ lb_f/ft^2$$

Calculating the values of δ and τ corresponding to different values of x allows the graph in figure (1) to be plotted.

x(ft)	$x^{\frac{1}{2}}(ft^{\frac{1}{2}})$	$\delta = 0.19x^{\frac{1}{2}}$(in)	$\tau = 0.175x^{-\frac{1}{2}} \ \frac{lb_f}{ft^2}$
0.1	0.3163	0.0601	0.5534
1.0	1.0000	0.1900	0.1750
2.0	1.4142	0.2687	0.1237
3.0	1.7321	0.3291	0.1010
4.0	2.0000	0.3800	0.0875
5.0	2.2361	0.4249	0.0783
6.0	2.4495	0.4654	0.0714

• PROBLEM 6-11

Determine the total drag force acting on a thin flat plate, 6 m long and 1 m wide, when air is flowing past it at a velocity of 3 m/s. The laminar boundary layer terminates at the critical Reynolds number of $Re_{c\gamma} = 5 \times 10^5$. The situation is shown in figure (1).

For air, take $\rho = 1.12 \ kg/m^3$; $\nu = 0.768 \times 10^{-5} \ m^2/s$

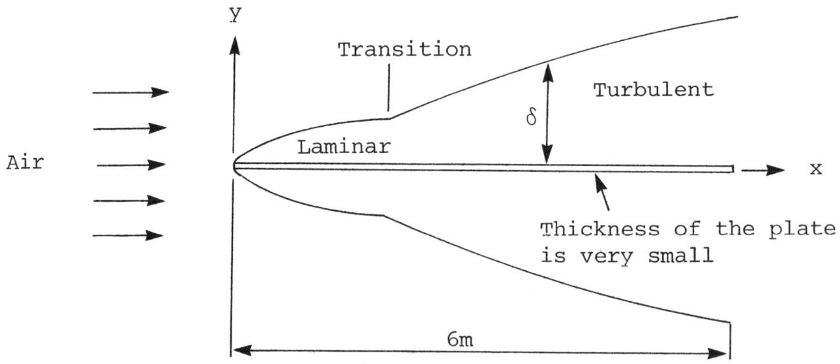

Fig. 1.

Solution: The total drag force acting on the plate is the sum of the drag force in the laminar boundary layer region and the drag force in the turbulent boundary layer region.

The drag force in each of the regions is the product of the average local shear stress and the area of the respective region.

The length of the laminar boundary layer region is obtained by substituting the value of $Re_{c\gamma}$ in the equation for Reynolds number.

$$Re = \frac{vx}{\nu}$$

or

The length of the laminar region is $x = \frac{\nu}{v} Re_{c\gamma}$

$$= \frac{0.768 \times 10^{-5}}{3} \times 5 \times 10^5$$

$$= 1.28 \text{ m.}$$

Hence, the length of turbulent region is $(6 - 1.28)$

$$= 4.72 \text{ m.}$$

The average local shear stress in the laminar boundary layer region is given by

$$\tau_1 = 1.292 \frac{\rho v^2}{2g_c} \times \frac{1}{(Re_{c\gamma})^{\frac{1}{2}}}$$

Substituting

$$\tau_1 = 1.292 \times \frac{1.12 \times (3)^2}{2 \times 1} \times \frac{1}{(5 \times 10^5)^{\frac{1}{2}}}$$

$$\tau_1 = 0.0092 \text{ N/m}^2$$

Therefore, the drag force in the laminar boundary layer region is τ_1 x Area of the region.

$$F_{lam} = \tau_1 \times (1.28 \times 1) \times (2 \text{ sides})$$

$$F_{lam} = 0.0092 \times 1.28 \times 2 = 0.0236 \text{ N.}$$

The average local shear stress in the turbulent boundary layer region is given by:

$$\tau_t = \frac{1}{(L - L_{cr})} \int_{L_{cr}}^{L} 0.02915 \frac{\rho v^2}{g_c} \left(\frac{\nu}{v}\right)^{1/5} x^{-1/5} \, dx$$

where

L = total length of the plate

L_{cr} = length of laminar boundary layer

ρ = density of air

ν = kinematic viscosity of air

v = velocity of air

Substituting and simplifying,

$$\tau_t = \frac{1}{(6 - 1.28)} \times 0.02915 \times \frac{1.12 \times (3)^2}{1} \times \left(\frac{0.768 \times 10^{-5}}{3}\right)^{\frac{1}{5}} \int_{1.28}^{6} x^{-1/5}\, dx$$

$$= 4.74 \times 10^{-3} \int_{1.28}^{6} x^{-1/5}\, dx$$

Integrating,

$$\tau_t = 4.74 \times 10^{-3} \left[\frac{x^{4/5}}{4/5}\right]_{1.28}^{6}$$

$$\tau_t = 4.74 \times 10^{-3} \left[6^{4/5} - (1.28)^{4/5}\right] \times \frac{5}{4}$$

$$= 0.0176 \text{ N/m}^2$$

Therefore, the drag force in the turbulent region is:

$$F_{tur} = \tau_t \times \text{Area of the region}$$

$$= 0.0176 \times (4.72 \times 1) \times 2$$

$$= 0.1661 \text{ N}$$

Therefore, the total drag force acting on the plate is:

$$= F_{lam} + F_{tur}$$

$$= 0.0236 + 0.1661$$

$$= 0.1897 \text{ N.}$$

If air is passing over a flat, hot plate, then find the quantity of heat picked up by the air per hour. Use the following data.

Temperature of air = 50 °F

Temperature of the plate = 150 °F

Length of the plate = 1.5 ft

Width of the plate = 2.5 ft

Velocity of air = 15 ft/sec.

Solution: The properties of air at the average temperature:

$$t = \frac{50 + 150}{2} = 100\,^{\circ}\text{F} \quad \text{are}$$

$$\rho = 0.071\ \text{lb}_m/\text{ft}^3$$

$$C_p = 0.24\ \text{Btu/lb}_m\,^{\circ}\text{F}$$

$$\mu = 0.019\ \text{cp} = 1.276 \times 10^{-5}\ \text{lb}_m/\text{ft.sec.}$$

$$k = 0.0156\ \text{Btu/hr.ft.}\,^{\circ}\text{F}$$

$$N_{Pr} = 0.705$$

Therefore

$$N_{Re} = \frac{Lv\rho}{\mu} = \frac{1.5 \times 15 \times 0.071}{1.276 \times 10^{-5}}$$

$$= 125{,}196$$

It is less than 500,000. Hence it is a laminar flow.

Therefore

$$h = 0.664\,(N_{Re})^{\frac{1}{2}}\,(N_{Pr})^{1/3}\,\frac{k}{L}$$

Substituting the numerical values and calculating

$$h = 0.664\,(125{,}196)^{\frac{1}{2}}\,(0.705)^{1/3}\left(\frac{0.0156}{1.5}\right)$$

$$h = 2.175\ \text{Btu/hr ft}^2\,^{\circ}\text{F}$$

Hence, the heat picked up by air is

$$Q = hA\,(T_s - T_a)$$

where Q = heat transferred

A = area of the plate

T_s = surface temperature of the plate

T_a = temperature of air.

Therefore,

$$Q = 2.175 \times 1.5 \times 2.5 \times (150 - 50)$$

$$Q = 816 \text{ Btu/hr}$$

• PROBLEM 6-13

Air (100 °F, 1 atm) is flowing at a velocity of 20 fps over a flat plate (200°F) of 2 ft width. At x = 2 ft find the local convective heat transfer coefficient, rate of heat transfer by convection, local friction coefficient, local drag due to friction and the boundary layer thickness.

Solution: Properties of air at the average temperature $t = \frac{100 + 200}{2} = 150\,^{\circ}F$ are

$$\rho = 0.0651 \text{ lb}_m/\text{ft}^3$$

$$C_p = 0.241 \text{ Btu/lb}_m\,^{\circ}F$$

$$\mu = 0.0203 \text{ cp} = 1.364 \times 10^{-5} \text{ lb}_m/\text{ft-sec}$$

$$k = 0.0169 \text{ Btu/hr.ft.}\,^{\circ}F$$

$$N_{Pr} = 0.702$$

The local Reynolds number at x = 2 ft is

$$N_{Re} = \frac{Dv\rho}{\mu} = \frac{xv\rho}{\mu}$$

$$= \frac{2 \times 20 \times 0.0651}{1.364 \times 10^{-5}}$$

$$= 190{,}909$$

The local convective heat transfer coefficient is given by

$$h = \frac{q}{A(T_s - T_\infty)} = 0.332\,\frac{k}{x}\,N_{Re}^{\frac{1}{2}}\,N_{Pr}^{1/3}$$

$$= 0.332 \times \frac{0.0169}{2} \times (190{,}909)^{\frac{1}{2}}\,(0.702)^{1/3}$$

$$h = 1.09 \text{ Btu/hr ft}^{2\,\circ}F$$

The rate of heat transfer by convection is given by

$$q = 0.664\,N_{Re}^{\frac{1}{2}}\,N_{Pr}^{1/3}\,b(T_s - T_\infty)$$

where q = rate of heat transfer

N_{Re} = Reynolds number

Pr = Prandtl number

T_s = plate surface temperature

T_∞ = air temperature

b = width of the plate

Substituting the numerical values

$$q = 0.664\ (190{,}909)^{\frac{1}{2}}\ (0.702)^{1/3}\ (2)\ (200 - 100)$$

$$= 0.664\ (436.93)\ (0.888)\ (2)\ (100)$$

$$q = 51{,}569 \text{ Btu/hr}$$

The local friction coefficient is given by

$$C_f = \frac{\tau_s}{\rho u^2/2g_c} = 0.664/\sqrt{N_{Re}}$$

$$= \frac{0.664}{\sqrt{190909}} = 0.0015$$

The local drag due to friction is given by:

$$\tau_s = \frac{\mu}{g_c} \left.\frac{\partial u}{\partial y}\right|_{y=0} = 0.332\ \frac{\mu}{g_c} \cdot \frac{u}{x} \sqrt{N_{Re}}$$

$$= 0.332 \times \frac{1.364 \times 10^{-5}}{32} \times \frac{20}{2} \times \sqrt{190909}$$

$$= 6.18 \times 10^{-4}\ lb_f/ft^2$$

The boundary layer thickness is given by

$$\delta = \frac{5x}{\sqrt{N_{Re}}} = \frac{5 \times 2}{\sqrt{190909}}$$

$$\delta = 0.023 \text{ ft}$$

• PROBLEM 6-14

A system consists of two porous concentric spherical shells and a gas is blown outward radially from the inner shell to the outside through the outer shell. Express the rate of heat removal from the inner sphere as a function of the mass flow rate of gas for steady state laminar flow and low gas velocity. The following data is given.

The radius of the outer shell: R

The radius of inner shell: kR

The temperature of inner surface of the outer shell: T_1

The temperature of outer surface of inner shell: T_k.

The temperature of gas: T_k ($T_k < T_1$)

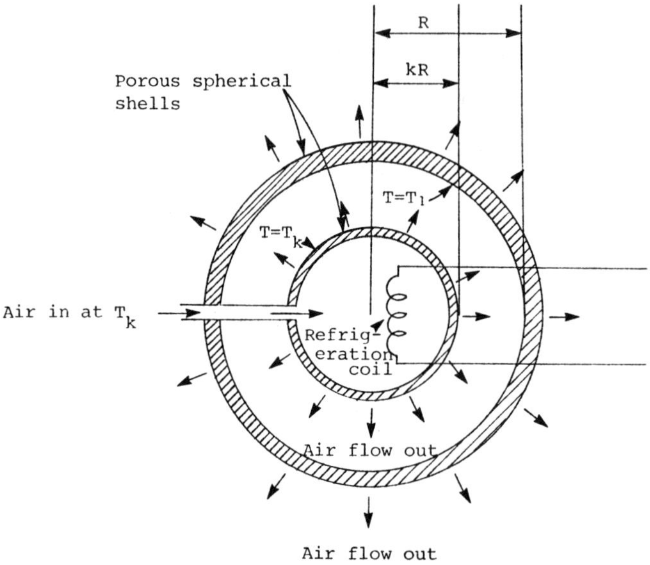

Fig. Transpiration cooling. The inner sphere is being cooled by means of the refrigeration coil to maintain its temperature at T_k. When air is blown outward, as shown, less refrigeration is required.

Solution: Velocity is in the radial direction only; v_r.

Hence

$$v_\theta = v_\phi = 0$$

Applying equation of continuity

$$\frac{1}{r^2}\frac{d}{dr}(r^2 \rho v_r) = 0$$

Integrating

$$r^2 \rho v_r = \text{constant} = \frac{w_r}{4\pi}$$

where w_r is the radial mass flow rate of gas.

Applying equation of energy:

$$\rho C_p v_r \frac{dT}{dr} = k \frac{1}{r^2}\frac{d}{dr}\left(r^2 \frac{dT}{dr}\right)$$

$$\frac{dT}{dr} = \frac{k}{\rho C_p v_r r^2} \frac{d}{dr} \left(r^2 \frac{dT}{dr} \right)$$

Note that $\frac{k}{\rho v_r r^2 C_p} = \frac{4\pi k}{w_r C_p}$ and since it is constant, let it be equal to 1/N

Then

$$\frac{dT}{dr} = \frac{4\pi k}{w_r C_p} \frac{d}{dr} \left(r^2 \frac{dT}{dr} \right)$$

$$\frac{dT}{dr} = \frac{1}{N} \frac{d}{dr} \left(r^2 \frac{dT}{dr} \right)$$

Integrating once

$$T = \frac{1}{N} \left(r^2 \frac{dT}{dr} \right) + C_1$$

where C_1 is the integration constant

$$N(T - C_1) = r^2 \frac{dT}{dr}$$

$$N \cdot \frac{1}{r^2} dr = \frac{1}{(T - C_1)} dT$$

or

$$\frac{dT}{(T - C_1)} = N \cdot (\frac{1}{r^2} dr)$$

Integrating again:

$$Ln(T - C_1) = N \cdot (- \frac{1}{r}) + C_2$$

where C_2 is again an integration constant.

$$T - C_1 = e^{\left(-N/r + C_2\right)}$$

$$T - C_1 = e^{-N/r} \cdot e^{C_2}$$

Let e^{C_2} be another constant C_3.

$$T - C_1 = C_3 e^{-N/r}$$

$$T = C_3 e^{-N/r} + C_1$$

Applying the boundary conditions in order to evaluate the constants

$$\text{At } r = R \quad ; \quad T = T_1$$

$$\text{At } r = kR \quad ; \quad T = T_k$$

Substituting the first boundary condition

$$T_1 = C_3 e^{-N/R} + C_1$$

Substituting the second boundary condition

$$T_k = C_3 e^{-N/kR} + C_1$$

Solving these two equations simultaneously

$$C_3 = \frac{T_1 - T_k}{\left(e^{-N/R} - e^{-N/kR}\right)}$$

and

$$C_1 = T_1 - \frac{T_1 - T_k}{\left(e^{-N/R} - e^{-N/kR}\right)} e^{-N/R}$$

Substituting the values of C_1 and C_3 into the equation

$$T = C_3 e^{-N/r} + C_1$$

$$T = \frac{T_1 - T_k}{\left(e^{-N/R} - e^{-N/kR}\right)} e^{-N/r} + T_1 - \frac{(T_1 - T_k)}{\left(e^{-N/R} - e^{-N/kR}\right)} e^{-N/R}$$

Rearranging

$$T - T_1 = \frac{T_1 - T_k}{e^{-N/R} - e^{-N/kR}} \left[e^{-N/r} - e^{-N/R}\right]$$

$$\frac{T - T_1}{T_1 - T_k} = \frac{e^{-N/r} - e^{-N/R}}{e^{-N/R} - e^{-N/kR}}$$

The rate of heat flow to the inner sphere in the negative r-direction is

$$Q = -4\pi k^2 R^2 q_r \Big|_{r=kR}$$

But $\quad q_r = - K\dfrac{dT}{dr}$

Therefore

$$Q = +4\pi K k^2 R^2 \left.\frac{dT}{dr}\right|_{r=kR}$$

It is known that

$$\frac{T - T_1}{T_1 - T_k} = \frac{e^{-N/r} - e^{-N/R}}{e^{-N/R} - e^{-N/kR}}$$

Differentiating:

$$\frac{1}{T_1 - T_k}\, dT = \frac{1}{e^{-N/R} - e^{-N/kR}} \left[e^{-N/r} \, (-N) \left(-\frac{1}{r^2}\right) \cdot \, dr \right]$$

$$\frac{dT}{dr} = (T_1 - T_k) \, \frac{e^{-N/r}}{e^{-N/R} - e^{-N/kR}} \cdot (-N)\left(-\frac{1}{r^2}\right)$$

Evaluating $\frac{dT}{dr}$ at $r = kR$

$$\left.\frac{dT}{dr}\right|_{kR} = (T_1 - T_k) \, \frac{e^{-N/kR}}{e^{-N/R} - e^{-N/kR}} \cdot N \cdot \frac{1}{k^2R^2}$$

$$= (T_1 - T_k) \cdot \frac{N}{k^2R^2} \cdot \frac{e^{-N/kR}}{e^{-N/R} - e^{-N/kR}}$$

$$= (T_1 - T_k) \cdot \frac{N}{k^2R^2} \cdot \frac{1}{\dfrac{e^{-N/R}}{e^{-N/kR}} - 1}$$

$$= (T_1 - T_k) \cdot \frac{N}{k^2R^2} \cdot \frac{1}{e^{-N/R + N/kR} - 1}$$

$$\left.\frac{dT}{dr}\right|_{kR} = (T_1 - T_k) \cdot \frac{N}{k^2R^2} \cdot \frac{1}{e^{(N/kR)(1-k)} - 1}$$

Now

$$Q = -\, 4\pi K \, k^2R^2 \left.\frac{dT}{dr}\right|_{r=kR}$$

Substituting the value of $\left.\frac{dT}{dr}\right|_{r=kR}$

$$Q = +\, 4\pi K \cdot k^2R^2 \cdot (T_1 - T_k) \cdot \frac{N}{k^2R^2} \cdot \frac{1}{e^{(N/kR)(1-k)} - 1}$$

$$Q = \frac{4\pi KN(T_1 - T_k)}{(e^{N/kR(1-k)} - 1)}$$

Note that $N = \frac{w_r C_p}{4\pi k}$

DRAG FORCE AND DRAG COEFFICIENT

• PROBLEM 6-15

Calculate the drag force acting on a 0.75 ft x 7 ft smooth plate when it is pulled along its length on a still water surface at a velocity of 25 ft/s.

For water $\rho = 62.4 \text{ lb/ft}^3$, $\nu = 1.08 \times 10^{-5} \text{ ft}^2/\text{s}$.

Solution: Assume that the laminar boundary layer region ends at a Reynolds number of 5×10^5. The maximum value of the Reynolds number for a laminar boundary layer is 5×10^5. To find the length of the laminar boundary layer region, substitute into the following equation for Re_x.

$$Re_x = \frac{vx}{\nu}$$

or

$$x = \frac{\nu}{v} Re_x$$

$$= \frac{1.08 \times 10^{-5} \times 5 \times 10^5}{25}$$

or

$$x = 0.216 \text{ ft.}$$

This is very small compared to the length of the plate, making it possible to consider the boundary layer as turbulent over the total length. The drag force is given by:

$$F = C_f A \left(\frac{\rho v^2}{2g_c}\right) \tag{1}$$

where

C_f = shear stress coefficient

A = area of the plate

ρ = density of water

v = velocity of the plate

The shear stress coefficient is given by:

$$C_f = \frac{0.072}{(Re)^{1/5}}$$

$$= 0.072 \times \left(\frac{25 \times 7}{1.08 \times 10^{-5}}\right)^{-1/5}$$

$$= 0.0026$$

Substituting into equation (1) for the drag force yields:

$$F = 0.0026 \times \frac{(0.75 \times 7) \times 62.4 \times (25)^2}{2 \times 32.2}$$

$$= 8.27 \text{ lb}_f$$

• PROBLEM 6-16

Calculate the drag force acting on a 3 ft wide by 4 ft. long plane surface when water flows over it at a free-stream velocity of 5 ft/s. The laminar boundary layer region ends at a Reynolds number of 1×10^5.

Solution: The Reynolds number at the end of the plane surface is given by:

$$Re_x = \frac{vx}{\nu}$$

where

v = velocity of flow

x = distance from the leading edge

ν = kinematic viscosity = 1.08×10^{-5} ft^2 per sec

$$Re_x = \frac{5 \times 4}{1.08 \times 10^{-5}}$$

$$= 1.85 \times 10^6$$

The mean value of the term $\frac{R}{\rho v^2}$ is given by,

$$\frac{R}{\rho v^2} = \frac{0.037}{(Re_x)^{0.2}} + \frac{1}{(Re_x)}\left(0.646(Re_c)^{0.5} - 0.037(Re_c)^{0.8}\right)$$

where

Re_x = Reynolds number at the end of the surface

Re_c = maximum value of Reynolds number for a laminar boundary layer = 1×10^5.

Substituting yields:

$$\frac{R}{\rho v^2} = \frac{0.037}{(1.85 \times 10^6)^{0.2}} + \frac{1}{(1.85 \times 10^6)}\left(0.646 \times (10^5)^{0.5} - 0.037(10^5)^{0.8}\right)$$

$$= 0.00197$$

The total drag force acting on the plane surface is given by:

$$F = \frac{R}{\rho v^2} \times \frac{\rho v^2}{g_c} \times A.$$

where

A = area of the surface

Substituting gives:

$$F = 0.00197 \times \frac{62.4 \times (5)^2}{32.2} \times (3 \times 4)$$

$$= 1.15 \text{ lb}_f.$$

• PROBLEM 6-17

> Determine the drag force acting on a 10 ft x 100 ft smooth flat plate when it is pulled lengthwise on a still water surface with a velocity of 20 ft/s. Also calculate the drag force on the first 10 ft length of the plate.
>
> For water $\rho = 62.4 \text{ lb/ft}^3$; $\nu = 1.08 \times 10^{-5} \text{ ft}^2/\text{s}$.

Solution: Assume that the laminar boundary layer region ends at a Reynolds number of 5×10^5. The maximum value of the Reynolds number for a laminar boundary layer is 5×10^5. To find the length of the laminar boundary layer region, substitute the values into the following equation for Re_x.

$$Re_x = \frac{vx}{\nu}$$

or

$$x = \frac{\nu}{v} Re_x$$

or,

$$x = \frac{1.08 \times 10^{-5}}{20} \times 5 \times 10^5$$

$$= 0.27 \text{ ft}$$

This is very small compared to the length of the plate, making it possible to consider the boundary layer as turbulent over the total length. The drag force is given by:

$$F = C_D b l \rho \frac{v^2}{2g_c} \tag{1}$$

where

C_D = coefficient of drag

b = width of the plate

l = length of plate

ρ = density of water

v = velocity of the plate

The Reynolds number at the end of the plate (x = 100 ft) is

$$Re_x = \frac{20 \times 100}{1.08 \times 10^{-5}} = 1.85 \times 10^8$$

For this value of the Reynolds number,

$$C_D = \frac{0.455}{(\log Re_x)^{2.58}} \qquad 10^6 < Re_x < 10^9$$

Therefore,

$$C_D = \frac{0.455}{\left[\log(1.85 \times 10^8)\right]^{2.58}}$$

$$= 0.00196$$

Therefore, the drag force acting on the plate is

$$F = 0.00196 \times (10 \times 100) \times \frac{62.4 \times (20)^2}{2 \times 32.2}$$

$$= 760 \text{ lb}_f$$

To find the drag force on the first 10 ft of the plate, the Reynolds number at the end of this length is needed in order to obtain the relationship for C_D.

Therefore, $$Re_x = \frac{vx}{\nu}$$

$$= \frac{20 \times 10}{1.08 \times 10^{-5}} = 1.85 \times 10^7$$

For this value of the Reynolds number,

$$C_D = \frac{0.455}{(\log Re_x)^{2.58}} \qquad 10^6 < Re_x < 10^9$$

Thus, $$C_D = \frac{0.455}{\left[\log(1.85 \times 10^7)\right]^{2.58}}$$

$$= 0.00273$$

Substituting into equation (1) gives the drag force acting on the first 10 ft of the plate.

$$F = 0.00273 \times (10 \times 10) \times \frac{62.4 \times (20)^2}{2 \times 32.2}$$

$$= 106 \text{ lb}_f$$

• **PROBLEM 6-18**

In an experiment conducted on a 5 m smooth model of a ship being pulled through water at a speed of 3 m/s, the total drag force measured is 70 N. If the wetted surface area of the model is 3.15 m^2, determine:

a) the skin-friction drag force

b) the wave-drag force.

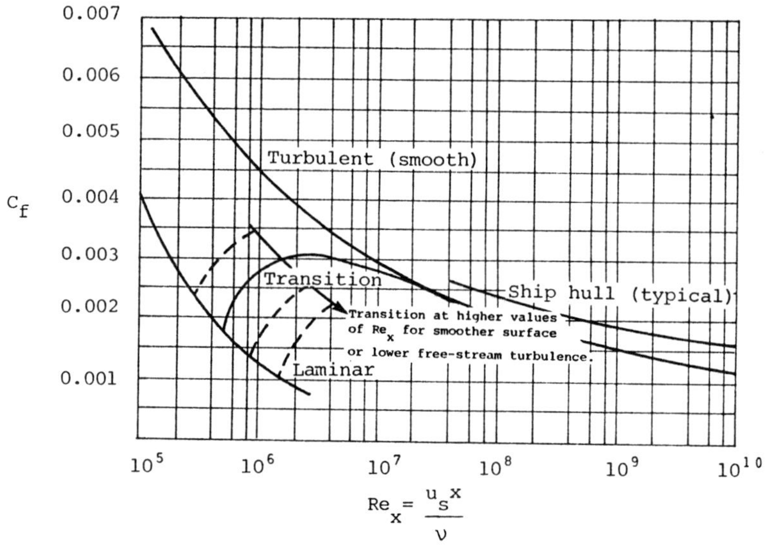

Fig. 1. Drag coefficients for plane surfaces parallel to flow.

Solution:

a) By considering the wetted surface area of the model as equivalent to a flat surface area, the model can be taken as a flat plate of length 5 m and surface area 3.15 m^2.

The Reynolds number at the far end of the model is given by:

$$Re_x = \frac{vx}{\nu}$$

where

v = velocity

x = distance from the leading edge

ν = kinematic viscosity of water

= 1.1×10^{-6} m^2/sec.

Substituting

$$Re_x = \frac{3 \times 5}{1.1 \times 10^{-6}}$$

$$= 1.4 \times 10^7$$

Extrapolating from figure (1) provides a drag coefficient of

$$C_f = 0.0029$$

The skin-friction drag force is given by:

$$F = C_f \cdot A \frac{\rho v^2}{2}$$

Substituting:

$$= \frac{0.0029 \times (3.15)(1000) \times (3)^2}{2}$$

$$F = 41.1 \text{ N}$$

b) The wave drag force is given by the difference between the total drag force and the skin friction drag force.

$$\text{The wave drag force} = 70 - 41.1$$

$$= 28.9 \text{ N.}$$

• PROBLEM 6-19

A fluid flows past a smooth flat plate at a velocity of 2.5 m/s. The length of the plate is 0.3 m and is parallel to the flow. The width is 1 m. Determine the drag force on one side of the plate and the thicknesses δ, δ^*, θ at the trailing edge of the plate if the flowing fluid is:

a) air, $\rho = 1.22 \text{ kg/m}^3$, $\nu = 1.45 \times 10^{-5} \text{ m}^2/\text{s}$

b) water, $\rho = 1000 \text{ kg/m}^3$, $\nu = 1.02 \times 10^{-6} \text{ m}^2/\text{s}$

Solution: The Reynolds number at the trailing edge is required to obtain the equation for the coefficient of discharge C_D, and also to determine the thicknesses δ, δ^* and θ.

The Reynolds number is given by

$$Re_x = \frac{vx}{\nu}$$

where

v = velocity of flowing fluid

x = distance from the leading edge

ν = kinematic viscosity of the fluid

a) when the fluid is air,

$$Re_x = \frac{2.5 \times 0.3}{1.45 \times 10^{-5}} = 51724$$

This indicates that the boundary layer is laminar.

Then, the coefficient of drag is given by:

$$C_D = \frac{1.328}{(Re_x)^{\frac{1}{2}}}$$

$$= \frac{1.328}{(51724)^{\frac{1}{2}}}$$

$$C_D = 0.00584$$

The drag force acting on the plate is given by:

$$F = \tfrac{1}{2} C_D \rho v^2 \times (A)$$

where

ρ = density of the fluid

v = velocity of fluid

A = area of the plate

Substituting yields:

$$F = \tfrac{1}{2} \times 0.00584 \times 1.22 \times (2.5)^2 \times (0.3 \times 1)$$

$$= 0.00668 \text{ N.}$$

The boundary layer thickness at the trailing edge of the plate is given by:

$$\frac{\delta}{x} = \frac{5}{(Re_x)^{\frac{1}{2}}}$$

Therefore

$$\delta = \frac{5 \times 0.3}{(51724)^{\frac{1}{2}}}$$

$$= 0.0066 \text{ m.}$$

The displacement thickness δ^* is given by the ratio:

$$\delta^* = \frac{1.721}{5.0} \times \delta$$

Therefore $$\delta^* = \frac{1.721}{5} \times 0.0066$$

$$\delta^* = 0.0023 \text{ m.}$$

The momentum thickness θ is given by:

$$\theta = \frac{\delta^*}{2.59}$$

Therefore

$$\theta = \frac{0.0023}{2.59}$$

$$\theta = 0.00089 \text{ m.}$$

b) When the fluid is water, the Reynolds number is:

$$Re_x = \frac{2.5 \times 0.3}{1.02 \times 10^{-6}}$$

$$= 735294$$

This indicates that the boundary layer is laminar. Then, the coefficient of drag is given by:

$$C_D = \frac{1.328}{(Re_x)^{\frac{1}{2}}}$$

$$= \frac{1.328}{(735294)^{\frac{1}{2}}}$$

$$C_D = 0.00155$$

The drag force acting on the plate is:

$$F = \tfrac{1}{2}\, C_D \rho v^2 (A)$$

$$= \tfrac{1}{2} \times 0.00155 \times 1000 \times (2.5)^2 \times (0.3 \times 1)$$

$$F = 1.45 \text{ N}$$

The drag force for water is approximately 217 times greater than that for air. This is obvious from the relationship $F \alpha \rho \cdot (\nu)^{\frac{1}{2}}$ which indicates that the drag force is proportional to the density and the square root of the viscosity when other variables remain constant.

The boundary layer thickness at the trailing edge is

$$\delta = \frac{5x}{(Re_x)^{\frac{1}{2}}}$$

Substituting, $$\delta = \frac{5 \times 0.3}{(735294)^{\frac{1}{2}}}$$

$$\delta = 0.00175 \text{ m}$$

The displacement thickness is:

$$\delta^* = \frac{1.721}{5}\,\delta$$

$$= \frac{1.721}{5} \times 0.00175$$

$$\delta^* = 6.02 \times 10^{-4} \text{ m.}$$

The momentum thickness, θ, is given by:

$$\theta = \frac{\delta^*}{2.59}$$

$$= \frac{6.02 \times 10^{-4}}{2.59}$$

$$\theta = 2.32 \times 10^{-4} \text{ m}$$

• **PROBLEM 6-20**

A flat plate 1.5 ft long and 5 ft wide is placed in a stream of water flowing at a velocity of 45 ft/s, such that the flow of water is parallel to the 1.5 ft. side of the plate. Calculate:

a) the boundary layer thickness at the trailing edge.

b) the drag force acting on the plate if the laminar boundary layer region ends at Re = 5×10^5.

c) the drag force acting on the plate for turbulent smooth-wall flow from the leading edge.

d) the drag force acting on the plate for turbulent rough-wall flow. The surface roughness of the plate is $\varepsilon = 0.00035$ ft.

Solution: The Reynolds number at the trailing edge of the plate is required because the boundary layer thickness and the drag force are given by relations involving Re_x.

The Reynolds number at the trailing edge is given by:

$$Re_x = \frac{vx}{\nu} \qquad (1)$$

where

v = velocity of flow

x = distance from the leading edge

ν = kinematic viscosity of water.

From tables for water,

$\rho = 62.4 \text{ lb/ft}^3$, $\nu = 1.08 \times 10^{-5} \text{ ft}^2/\text{s}$

Substituting in equation (1) gives:

$$Re_x = \frac{45 \times 1.5}{1.08 \times 10^{-5}}$$

$$= 6.25 \times 10^6$$

The Reynolds number indicates that the flow at the trailing edge is turbulent.

a) The boundary layer thickness at the trailing edge for turbulent flow is given by:

$$\frac{\delta}{x} = \frac{0.16}{(Re_x)^{1/7}}$$

or, $$\delta = \frac{0.16x}{(Re_x)^{1/7}}$$

Substituting,

$$\delta = \frac{0.16 \times 1.5}{(6.25 \times 10^6)^{1/7}}$$

$$\delta = 0.0257 \text{ ft}$$

b) The coefficient of drag, when the laminar boundary layer region ends at $Re = 5 \times 10^5$, is given by:

$$C_D = \frac{0.031}{(Re_x)^{1/7}} - \frac{1700}{(Re_x)}$$

$$= \frac{0.031}{(6.25 \times 10^6)^{1/7}} - \frac{1700}{6.25 \times 10^6}$$

$$= 3.315 \times 10^{-3} - 2.72 \times 10^{-4} = 3.043 \times 10^{-3}$$

The drag force acting on the plate (considering both sides of the plate) is given by:

$$F = 2\left(\tfrac{1}{2}C_D \rho \frac{v^2 A}{g_c}\right)$$

where

C_D = coefficient of drag

ρ = density of water

v = velocity of water

A = surface area of the plate (one side)

Substituting,

$$F = 2 \times \tfrac{1}{2} \times 3.043 \times 10^{-3} \times 62.4 \times (45)^2 \times (1.5 \times 5) \times \frac{1}{32.2}$$

$$= 89.56 \text{ lb}_f$$

c) The coefficient of drag for a smooth wall flow is given by:

$$C_D = \frac{0.031}{(Re_x)^{1/7}}$$

Substituting,

$$C_D = \frac{0.031}{(6.25 \times 10^6)^{1/7}}$$

$$= 3.315 \times 10^{-3}$$

$$C_D = 0.0033$$

Therefore, the drag force acting on the plate is:

$$F = 2 \times \tfrac{1}{2} C_D \rho \frac{v^2 A}{g_c}$$

$$F = 2 \times \tfrac{1}{2} \times 0.0033 \times 62.4 \times \frac{(45)^2 \times (1.5 \times 5)}{32.2}$$

$$F = 97.1 \text{ lb}_f.$$

d) The coefficient of drag for turbulent rough wall flow is given by:

$$C_D = (1.89 + 1.62 \log \frac{L}{\varepsilon})^{-2.5}$$

where

$\frac{L}{\varepsilon}$ is the ratio of the length to the roughness of the plate.

Substituting

$$C_D = (1.89 + 1.62 \log \frac{1.5}{0.00035})^{-2.5}$$

$$C_D = 0.0059$$

Therefore the drag force is:

$$F = 2 \times \tfrac{1}{2} \times C_D \rho \frac{v^2 A}{g_c}$$

Substituting

$$F = 2 \times \tfrac{1}{2} \times 0.0059 \times 62.4 \times \frac{(45)^2 \times (1.5 \times 5)}{32.2}$$

$$= 173.7 \text{ lb}_f$$

• PROBLEM 6-21

Determine the drag force acting on a vertical pipe 25 m high and 25 cm in diameter, which is located on top of a hill where the wind velocity is 120 km/hr. Take the pressure on the hill as atmospheric pressure and the temperature as 15 °C.

Solution: From the properties table of air, the kinematic viscosity of air corresponding to 15 °C is

$$\nu = 1.46 \times 10^{-5} \text{ m}^2/\text{s}$$

and the density is $\rho = 1.226 \text{ kg/m}^3$

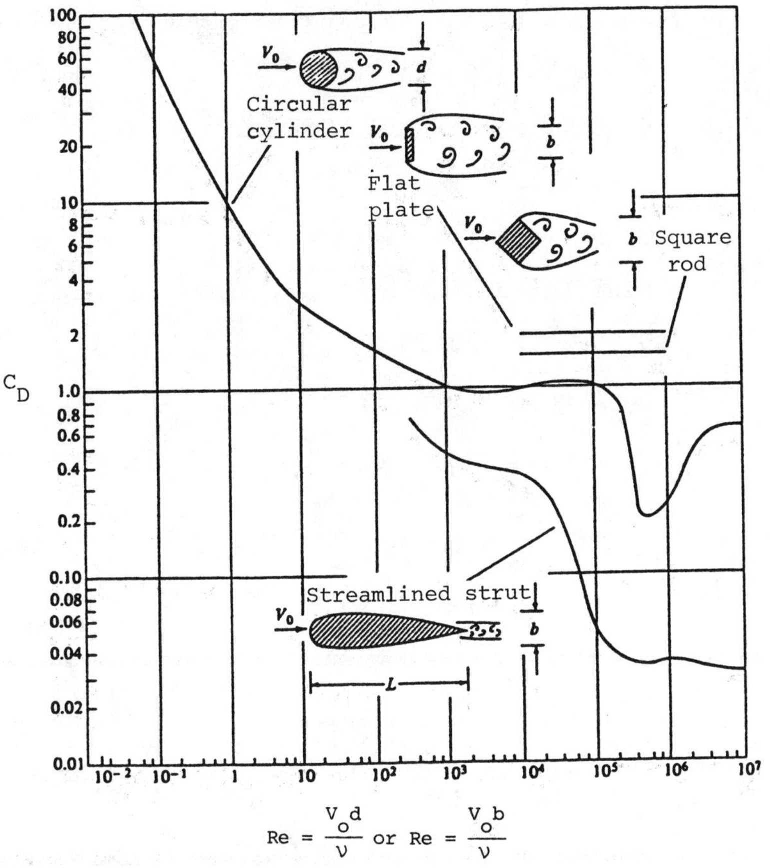

Fig. 1. Drag coefficient vs. Reynolds number for two-dimensional bodies.

The Reynolds number is given by:

$$Re = \frac{vd}{\nu}$$

where

v = wind velocity

d = diameter of the pipe

ν = kinematic viscosity of air

Substituting the values,

$$Re = \left(\frac{120 \times 1000}{60 \times 60}\right) \times \left(\frac{25}{100}\right) \times \frac{1}{1.46 \times 10^{-5}}$$

$$= 5.7 \times 10^{5}$$

From the graph in figure (1) (coefficient of drag, C_D, vs. Reynolds number for two dimensional bodies),

the value of C_D for a circular cylinder is $C_D = 0.2$.

The drag force acting on the pipe is given by:

$$F = \frac{1}{2}C_D \rho v^2 A$$

where

ρ = density of air = 1.226 kg/m^3

v = wind velocity

A = projected area of the pipe

= diameter x length of the pipe

= 0.25 x 25 = 6.25 m^2.

Substituting gives the drag force:

$$F = \frac{1}{2} \times 0.2 \times 1.226 \times \left(\frac{120 \times 1000}{60 \times 60}\right)^2 \times 6.25$$

$$= 851.4 \text{ N}.$$

• PROBLEM 6-22

An infinitely long cylinder is placed in a uniform stream of an incompressible fluid such that the axis of the cylinder is perpendicular to the flow as shown in figure (1). If the force due to friction (shear forces) is neglected, show that the drag force acting on the cylinder is zero.

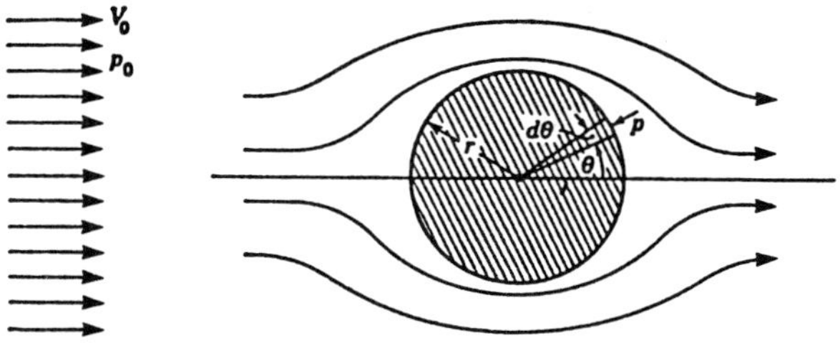

Fig. 1.

Solution: The free-stream velocity and pressure (at a location far from the cylinder) are V_0 and p_0 respectively. The drag force is the component of the total force acting on the cylinder which is parallel to the free stream velocity V_0.

If the shear forces are to be ignored, then the force acting on the cylinder is only due to the pressure on its surface.

Consider a unit length of the cylinder and a strip rdθ on the surface of the cylinder at an angle θ to the free stream velocity V_0. Since the force acting on the cylinder is due to the pressure, the force acting on this elemental strip is radially inwards. The force is given by the product of the pressure and the area:

$$df = p(r d\theta)$$

The drag on this strip is df cosθ or pr cosθ dθ.

Therefore, the drag force on the total circumferential area is given by integrating between the limits 0 and 2π.

$$\text{Drag force/unit length} = \int_0^{2\pi} pr \cos\theta \, d\theta \qquad (1)$$

The pressure p acting on the cylinder is not constant, but a function of the angle θ.

Therefore p must be written in terms of θ and substituted in the integral of equation (1) to evaluate the drag force.

From two dimensional, incompressible, nonviscous theory, the fluid velocity at the surface of the cylinder is:

$$V = 2\, V_0 \sin\theta.$$

Applying Bernoulli's energy equation between a point on the cylinder and a point at the free stream conditions (a far off point) and neglecting the potential energy terms, the energy equation becomes:

$$\frac{V_0^{\,2}}{2} + \frac{p_0}{\rho} = \frac{v^2}{2} + \frac{p}{\rho} \qquad (2)$$

where

ρ = density of the fluid

p = pressure

v = velocity

The subscript 0 indicates the free stream conditions and the variables without subscripts are for a point on the surface of the cylinder.

Substituting the value of v into equation (2) and solving for p,

$$\frac{V_0^{\,2}}{2} + \frac{p_0}{\rho} = \frac{(2V_0 \sin\theta)^2}{2} + \frac{p}{\rho}$$

Therefore,

$$p = p_0 + \frac{\rho V_0^{\,2}}{2} (1 - 4 \sin^2 \theta)$$

Substituting this value of p into equation (1) for the drag force gives:

$$\text{Drag force} = \int_0^{2\pi} \left[p_0 + \frac{\rho V_0^2}{2} (1 - 4 \sin^2\theta) \right] r\cos\theta \, d\theta$$

$$= p_0 r \int_0^{2\pi} \cos\theta \, d\theta + \frac{\rho V_o^2 r}{2} \int_0^{2\pi} \cos\theta \, d\theta - 2\rho V_0^2 r \int_0^{2\pi} \sin^2\theta \cos\theta \, d\theta$$

$$= \left(p_0 r + \frac{\rho V_0^2 r}{2} \right) \int_0^{2\pi} \cos\theta \, d\theta - 2\rho V_0^2 r \int_0^{2\pi} \sin^2\theta \cos\theta \, d\theta$$

$$= \left(p_0 r + \frac{\rho V_0^2 r}{2} \right) \left[\sin 2\pi - \sin 0 \right] - 2\rho V_0^2 r \left[\frac{\sin^3(2\pi) - \sin^3(0)}{3} \right]$$

$$= 0$$

Thus, in the absence of shear forces, the drag force acting on the cylinder is zero.

• PROBLEM 6-23

A 3 mm. diameter glass sphere is falling through water at room temperature. If the specific gravity of the glass is 2.7, determine the settling velocity and the drag force acting on the sphere (see figure (1)).

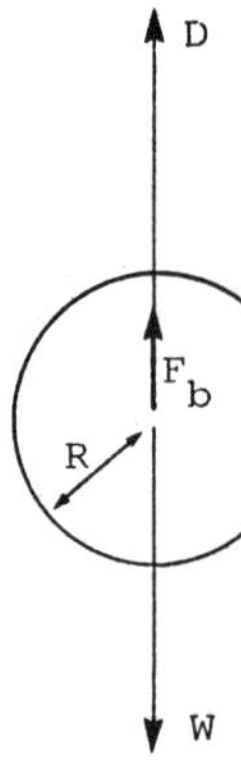

Fig. 1.

Solution: Consider the forces acting on the sphere as it falls through water. F_b is the buoyant force which is equal to the weight of water displaced by the sphere $\left(\rho_w \frac{g}{g_c} V_s\right)$, D is the fluid drag force $(D = C_D \frac{1}{2g_c} \rho v^2 A)$, and w is the weight of sphere $\left(\rho_s \frac{g}{g_c} V_s\right)$. Note that v indicates the velocity of the sphere, while V_s indicates the volume of the sphere. Newton's second law of motion applied to the sphere gives:

$$w - (F_b + D) = m\frac{dv}{dt}$$

As the sphere accelerates from rest, the drag force increases as the square of the velocity. After a very short time of acceleration, the acceleration drops to zero $(\frac{dv}{dt} = 0)$ and $D = w - F_b$. The sphere now falls at a constant velocity called the terminal or settling velocity. Substituting

$$D = w - F_b$$

$$\frac{1}{2} C_D \rho_w \frac{v^2 \pi R^2}{g_c} = \frac{g}{g_c} \frac{4}{3} \pi R^3 \rho_s - \frac{4}{3} \pi R^3 \rho_w \frac{g}{g_c}$$

$$\frac{1}{2} C_D \rho_w \frac{v^2 \pi R^2}{g_c} = \frac{4}{3} \pi R^3 \frac{g}{g_c} (\rho_s - \rho_w)$$

$$C_D = \frac{8}{3} \frac{Rg}{v^2} \left(\frac{\rho_s}{\rho_w} - 1\right) \qquad (1)$$

where

R = radius of the sphere

v = terminal velocity

The coefficient of drag, C_D, depends on whether the flow over the sphere is laminar or turbulent.

Assuming that the flow is in the turbulent Newton's law region, calculate the terminal velocity using $C_D = 0.44$ and then calculate the Reynolds number with the terminal velocity obtained to check whether the assumption is valid.

Substituting $C_D = 0.44$ into equation (1),

$$0.44 = \frac{8}{3} \times \left(\frac{3}{2} \times \frac{1}{25.4} \times \frac{1}{12}\right) \times \frac{1}{v^2} (2.7 - 1) \times 32.2$$

Therefore,

$$v^2 = \frac{8}{3} \times \left(\frac{3}{2} \times \frac{1}{25.4} \times \frac{1}{12}\right) \times \frac{1.7}{0.44} \times 32.2$$

$$= 1.633$$

or $$v = 1.278 \text{ ft/s}$$

Substituting this value of v into the Reynolds number equation:

$$Re = \frac{vd}{\nu}$$

$$= 1.278 \times \left(\frac{3}{2.54 \times 12}\right) \times \frac{1}{1.08 \times 10^{-5}}$$

$$= 1165$$

The Reynolds number indicates that the flow is in the turbulent Newton's law region, since the Reynolds number lies between 1000 and 200,000. Hence the original assumption is correct.

Therefore, the settling velocity of the sphere is:

$$v = 1.278 \text{ ft/s}$$

The drag force acting on the sphere is:

$$D = \tfrac{1}{2} C_D \rho \frac{v^2 A}{g_c}$$

where

A = projected area

Substituting,

$$D = \tfrac{1}{2} \times 0.44 \times \frac{62.4 \times (1.278)^2}{32.2} \times \frac{\pi}{4} \left(\frac{3}{25.4 \times 12}\right)^2$$

$$= 5.3 \times 10^{-5} \text{ lb}_f$$

CHAPTER 7

COMPRESSIBLE FLOW, NON-NEWTONIAN FLOW AND DIMENSIONAL ANALYSIS

PRESSURE DROP, FRICTION FACTOR, VELOCITY AND SHEAR STRESS DISTRIBUTIONS IN NON-NEWTONIAN FLUIDS

• PROBLEM 7-1

A non-newtonian fluid is flowing through a pipe. Obtain a relationship between the velocity and the radial position for steady state laminar flow. The stress rate of shear is given by:

$$\tau = \frac{K}{g_c}\left(\frac{-du}{dr}\right)^n$$

Solution: The shear stress for a non-newtonian fluid is given by:

$$\tau = -\frac{\Delta p}{2L} r$$

where τ = shear stress

Δp = pressure drop across the length of the pipe

L = length of the pipe

r = radius of the pipe

But it is given that

$$\tau = \frac{K}{g_c}\left(\frac{-du}{dr}\right)^n$$

Therefore equating these two equations gives:

$$- \frac{\Delta p g_c}{2KL} r = \left(\frac{-du}{dr}\right)^n$$

Raising both sides to 1/nth power and integrating

$$\left(\frac{-\Delta p g_c}{2KL}\right)^{1/n} \int_{r_i}^{r} r^{1/n} dr = - \int_{u}^{0} du$$

$$\left(\frac{-\Delta p g_c}{2KL}\right)^{1/n} \left[\frac{\gamma^{1/n+1}}{\frac{1}{n} + 1}\right]_{r_i}^{r} = u$$

$$\frac{n}{n+1}\left(\frac{-\Delta p g_c}{2KL}\right)^{1/n} \left[r^{\left(\frac{n+1}{n}\right)} - r_i^{\left(\frac{n+1}{n}\right)}\right] = u$$

$$u = \left(\frac{-\Delta p g_c}{2KL}\right)^{1/n} \left(\frac{n}{n+1}\right) r_i^{\frac{n+1}{n}} \left[1 - \left(\frac{r}{r_i}\right)^{\frac{n+1}{n}}\right]$$

At $r = 0$, $u = u_{max}$

$$u_{max} = \left(\frac{-\Delta p g_c}{2KL}\right)^{1/n} \left(\frac{n}{n+1}\right) r_i^{\left(\frac{n+1}{n}\right)}$$

At $r = r_i$, $u = 0$

Therefore

$$u = u_{max}\left[1 - \left(\frac{r}{r_i}\right)^{\frac{n+1}{n}}\right]$$

• PROBLEM 7-2

A pseudoplastic-non-newtonian fluid is flowing through a schedule 40 standard steel pipe of 1¼ in. dia. at a rate of 15 gal/hr. Determine the pressure drop per foot of pipe.

Properties of the fluid:

density (ρ) = 60 lbm/ft^3; viscosity (μ_{ap}) = 22500 poise.

Solution: The pressure loss in this case is only due to friction. The pressure loss due to friction in a straight pipe is given by:

$$\Delta p = \frac{2fL\rho v^2}{g_c D}$$

where

Δp = pressure loss

f = friction coefficient

L = length of the pipe

v = mean velocity of flow

D = diameter of the pipe

The mean velocity of flow is obtained from the equation:

$$v = \frac{q}{A}$$

where

q = volumetric flow rate

A = cross-sectional area

Substituting and solving for v,

$$v = \left(\frac{15}{7.48} \times \frac{1}{3600}\right) \times \frac{1}{\frac{\pi}{4}\left(\frac{1.38}{12}\right)^2}$$

where 1.38 in. is the ID of the pipe.

$$v = 0.05363 \text{ ft/s}$$

To determine the value of the friction coefficient, f, used in equation (1), it is necessary to obtain the value of the Reynolds number.

The Reynolds number is given by:

$$Re = \frac{\rho VD}{\mu}$$

$$Re = \frac{(60)(0.05363)(1.38/12)}{(22500 \times 6.72 \times 10^{-2})}$$

$$= 2.45 \times 10^{-4}$$

For this value of the Reynolds number (laminar flow) the friction coefficient is given by:

$$f = \frac{16}{2.45 \times 10^{-4}}$$

$$\simeq 65306.$$

Substituting into equation (1)

$$\frac{\Delta p}{L} = \frac{2f\rho v^2}{g_c D}$$

the pressure loss per foot of length is

$$\frac{\Delta p}{L} = \frac{2(65306)(0.05363)^2(12)(60)}{(1.38)(32.2)}$$

$$\simeq 6087 \frac{lb_f/ft^2}{ft}$$

$$\frac{\Delta p}{L} \simeq 42.3 \text{ psi/ft}$$

• PROBLEM 7-3

Estimate the pressure drop and friction loss for a power law fluid which is flowing through a tube of length 15.2 m and an inside diameter of 0.0524 m. The fluid has a mean velocity of 0.0846 m/s. The fluid flow properties are $K' = 14.95\ N\cdot s^{n'}/m^2$, $n' = 0.5$ and density $1060\ kg/m^3$. Calculate the generalized Reynolds number to determine if the flow is laminar.

Repeat the calculations using the friction factor method.

Solution: The pressure drop for a power law fluid is given by:

$$\Delta p = \frac{K'4L}{D}\left(\frac{8V}{D}\right)^{n'} \qquad (1)$$

where

D = Diameter, L = Length, V = Velocity

ρ = density and K', n' are fluid flow properties

The given data is:

$D = 0.0524m$, $V = 0.0846\ m/s$, $L = 15.2m$

$\rho = 1060\ kg/m^3$, $K' = 14.95$, $n' = 0.5$

Substituting in equation (1) gives:

$$\Delta p = \frac{14.95 \times 4 \times 15.2}{0.0524} \times \left(\frac{8 \times 0.0846}{0.0524}\right)^{0.5}$$

$$\Delta p = 62342\ N/m^2$$

The friction loss is given by:

$$F = \frac{\Delta p}{\rho} = \frac{62342}{1060} = 58.81\ J/kg$$

The generalized Reynolds number is

$$Re_{(gen)} = \frac{D^{n'} \cdot V^{2-n'} \cdot \rho}{K'\ 8^{n'-1}}$$

Substituting the values

$$Re_{(gen)} = \frac{(0.0524)^{0.5}(0.0846)^{1.5} \times 1060}{(14.95)(8^{-0.5})}$$

$$\simeq 1.13$$

Therefore the flow is laminar.

The friction factor is

$$f = \frac{16}{Re_{(gen)}}$$

$$f = \frac{16}{1.130} \simeq 14.16$$

The pressure drop is calculated by substituting this value of 'f' in the following expression.

$$\Delta p = 4f\rho \frac{L}{D} \frac{V^2}{2}$$

$$= 4 \times 14.16 \times 1060 \times \frac{15.2}{0.0524} \times \frac{(0.0846)^2}{2}$$

$$\Delta p \simeq 62324 \text{ N/m}^2.$$

• PROBLEM 7-4

A Bingham plastic is flowing between two vertical coaxial cylinders. The outer cylinder is rotating with an angular velocity ω. Consider it to be tangential laminar incompressible fluid flow. If a torque T is applied to the outer cylinder, then determine the velocity and the shear stress distributions for the flow as a function of the torque. Assume the end effects are negligible.

Solution: The velocity components in the r and z directions are zero. $v_r = v_z = 0$.

The velocity component in the θ direction is only a function of r. $v_\theta = v_\theta(r)$. $\tau_{r\theta}$ is the only non-vanishing component of τ. Applying the steady state equation of motion:

$$\frac{1}{r^2}\frac{d}{dr}(r^2\tau_{r\theta}) = 0$$

$$\frac{d}{dr}(r^2\tau_{r\theta}) = 0$$

$$r^2\tau_{r\theta} = C_1$$

$$\tau_{r\theta} = \frac{C_1}{r^2}$$

Since T is the torque at the outer cylinder,

$$T = \left[-\tau_{r\theta} \Big|_{r=R} \right] \cdot 2\pi RL \cdot R$$

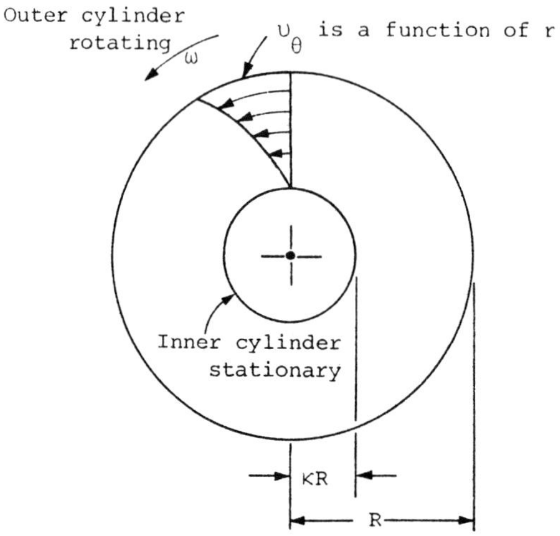

FLOW OF A BINGHAM PLASTIC BETWEEN TWO COAXIAL CYLINDERS, A TORQUE T BEING APPLIED TO THE OUTER CYLINDER.

Figure (1)

The θ momentum flux acts in the negative r-direction, therefore the negative sign is introduced.

$$\tau_{r\theta} = \frac{C_1}{R^2}$$

$$-\frac{T}{2\pi LR^2} = \frac{C_1}{R^2}$$

$$C_1 = -\frac{T}{2\pi L}$$

Therefore, $$\tau_{r\theta} = -\frac{T}{2\pi Lr^2}$$

For Bingham model:

$$\tau = -\left\{ \mu_0 + \frac{\tau_0}{\left| \sqrt{\tfrac{1}{2}(\Delta:\Delta)} \right|} \right\} \Delta \qquad \text{when } \tfrac{1}{2}(\tau:\tau) > \tau_0^2$$

$$\Delta = 0 \qquad \text{when } \tfrac{1}{2}(\tau:\tau) < \tau_0^2$$

Also note

$$\frac{1}{2}(\tau:\tau) = \frac{1}{2} \sum_i \sum_j \tau_{ij}^2$$

For this case $$\frac{1}{2}(\tau:\tau) = \tau_{r\theta}^2$$

Since $\tau_{r\theta} = -\dfrac{T}{2\pi L r^2}$, define a quantity r_0 such that $|\tau_{r\theta}| = \tau_0$.

Hence,
$$r_0 = \sqrt{\frac{T}{2\pi\tau_0 L}}$$

The regions of different flow are identified as $r_0 \geq \kappa R$, $R > r_0 \geq \kappa R$ and $r_0 \geq R$.

Now:

$$\frac{1}{2}(\Delta:\Delta) = \left[r\frac{d}{dr}\left(\frac{v_\theta}{r}\right)\right]^2$$

$$\tau = -\left\{\mu_0 + \frac{\tau_0}{\left|\sqrt{\frac{1}{2}(\Delta:\Delta)}\right|}\right\}\Delta$$

That is

$$\tau_{r\theta} = -\left\{\mu_0 + \frac{\tau_0}{r\frac{d}{dr}\left[\frac{v_\theta}{r}\right]}\right\} r\frac{d}{dr}\left(\frac{v_\theta}{r}\right)$$

$$\tau_{r\theta} = -\left\{r\mu_0\frac{d}{dr}\left(\frac{v_\theta}{r}\right) + \tau_0\right\}$$

$$\tau_{r\theta} = -\tau_0 - \mu_0 r\frac{d}{dr}\left(\frac{v_\theta}{r}\right)$$

But
$$\tau_{r\theta} = -\frac{T}{2\pi L r^2}$$

Therefore,

$$-\tau_0 - \mu_0 r\frac{d}{dr}\left(\frac{v_\theta}{r}\right) = -\frac{T}{2\pi L r^2}$$

$$-\mu_0 r\frac{d}{dr}\frac{v_\theta}{v} = \frac{-T}{2\pi L r^2} + \tau_0$$

$$-\mu_0 r\frac{d}{dr}\left(\frac{v_\theta}{r}\right) = +\frac{T}{2\pi L\mu_0 r^2} - \frac{\tau_0}{\mu_0 r}$$

Integrating

$$\frac{v_\theta}{r} = -\frac{T}{4\pi L\mu_0 r^2} - \frac{\tau_0}{\mu_0}\ln r + C_1$$

The constant C_1 is evaluated by using the boundary condition that describes the flow in the region $\kappa R \leq r \leq R$.

That is $\dfrac{v_\theta}{r} = \omega; \quad r = R$

$$\omega = \frac{-T}{4\pi L\mu_0 R^2} - \frac{\tau_0}{\mu_0}\ln R + C_1$$

$$C_1 = \omega + \frac{T}{4\pi L\mu_0 R^2} + \frac{\tau_0}{\mu_0} \ln R$$

Therefore,

$$\frac{v_\theta}{r} = \frac{-T}{4\pi L\mu_0 r^2} - \frac{\tau_0}{\mu_0} \ln r + \omega + \frac{T}{4\pi L\mu_0 R^2} + \frac{\tau_0}{\mu_0} \ln R$$

$$\frac{v_\theta}{r} = \omega + \frac{T}{4\pi L\mu_0 R^2}\left[1 - \frac{R^2}{r^2}\right] - \frac{\tau_0}{\mu_0} \ln r/R$$

Again, at $r = \kappa R$; $v_\theta = 0$

Hence,

$$0 = \omega + \frac{T}{4\pi L\mu_0 R^2}\left[1 - \frac{R^2}{\kappa^2 R^2}\right] - \frac{\tau_0}{\mu_0} \ln\left(\frac{\kappa R}{R}\right)$$

Rearranging

$$\omega = \frac{T}{4\pi L\mu_0 R^2}\left[\frac{1}{\kappa^2} - 1\right] + \frac{\tau_0}{\mu_0} \ln \kappa$$

$$\frac{v_\theta}{r} = -\frac{T}{4\pi L\mu_0 r^2} - \frac{\tau_0}{\mu_0} \ln r + C_2$$

The integration constant is evaluated by using the boundary condition that describes the flow in the region $\kappa R \leq r \leq r_0$.

That is $\frac{v_\theta}{r} = \omega; \quad r = r_0$

Substituting the boundary condition,

$$\omega = -\frac{T}{4\pi L\mu_0 r_0^2} - \frac{\tau_0}{\mu_0} \ln r_0 + C_2$$

$$C_2 = \omega + \frac{T}{4\pi L\mu_0 r_0^2} + \frac{\tau_0}{\mu_0} \ln r_0$$

$$\frac{v_\theta}{r} = -\frac{T}{4\pi L\mu_0 r^2} - \frac{\tau_0}{\mu_0} \ln r + \omega + \frac{T}{4\pi L\mu_0 r_0^2} + \frac{\tau_0}{\mu_0} \ln r_0$$

$$\frac{v_\theta}{r} = \omega + \frac{T}{4\pi L\mu_0 r_0^2}\left[1 - \frac{r_0^2}{r^2}\right] - \frac{\tau_0}{\mu_0} \ln r/r_0$$

Again $r = r_0$

Then $\frac{v_\theta}{r} = \omega$

This is valid for the region $r_0 \leq r \leq R$.

• **PROBLEM 7-5**

Develop a relation between the volumetric flow rate q and the combined pressure and gravitational forces when a Bingham model fluid is flowing through a vertical pipe of radius R and length L.

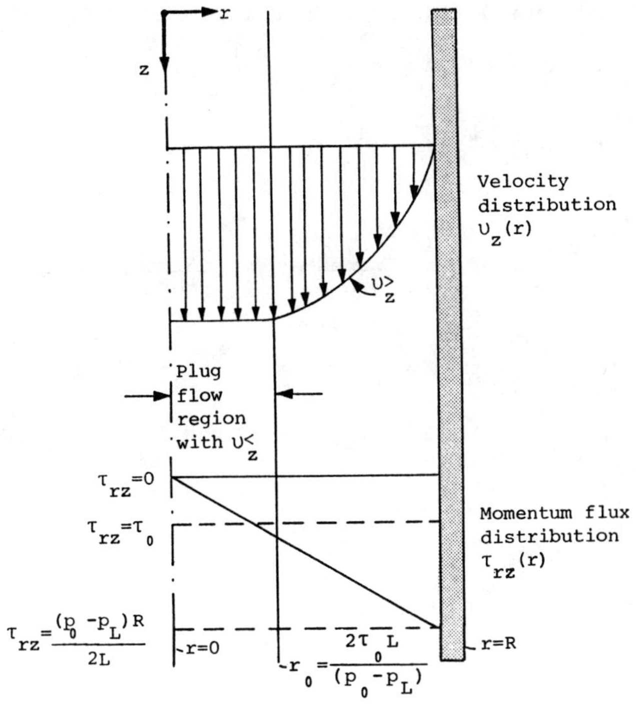

FLOW OF A BINGHAM FLUID IN A CIRCULAR TUBE

<u>Solution</u>: The momentum flux distribution in a pipe is given by:

$$\tau_{rz} = \frac{(P_0-P_L)}{2L} r$$

where $$P = P - \rho gz$$

But for Bingham model

$$\tau_{yx} = -\mu_0 \frac{dv_x}{dy} \pm \tau_0 \qquad \text{if } |\tau_{yx}| > \tau_0$$

and in cylindrical coordinates

$$\tau_{rz} = \tau_0 - \mu_0 \frac{dv_z}{dr}$$

Substituting this into equation (1):

$$\tau_0 - \mu_0 \frac{dv_z}{dr} = \frac{(P_0-P_L)}{2L} r$$

or

$$\frac{dv_z}{dr} = \frac{\tau_0}{\mu_0} - \frac{(P_0-P_L)}{2L\mu_0} r$$

Integrating

$$v_z = \frac{\tau_0}{\mu_0} r - \frac{(P_0-P_L)}{4L\mu_0} r^2 + C_1$$

Employing the boundary condition:

At $r = R; \quad v_z = 0$

$$C_1 = \frac{P_0-P_L}{4L\mu_0} R^2 - \frac{\tau_0}{\mu_0} R$$

Therefore

$$v_z = \frac{\tau_0}{\mu_0} r - \frac{(P_0-P_L)}{4L\mu_0} r^2 + \frac{(P_0-P_L)}{4L\mu_0} R^2 - \frac{\tau_0}{\mu_0} R$$

$$v_z^> = \frac{(P_0-P_L)}{4L\mu_0} R^2 \left[1 - \left(\frac{r}{R}\right)^2\right] - \frac{\tau_0}{\mu_0} R \left[1 - \left(\frac{r}{R}\right)\right]$$

This velocity profile is valid when $r \geq r_0$. But when $r \leq r_0$ the flow is defined by

$$\tau_0 = \frac{(P_0-P_L)}{2L} r_0$$

and is plug flow. To obtain the velocity profile within this region, $r = r_0$ is substituted in the above equation. That is

$$v_z^< = \frac{(P_0-P_L)}{4L\mu_0} R^2 \left[1 - \left(\frac{r_0}{R}\right)^2\right] - \frac{(P_0-P_L)}{2L\mu_0} r_0 R \left[1 - \frac{r_0}{R}\right]$$

$$v_z^< = \frac{(P_0-P_L)}{4\mu_0 L} R^2 \left[1 - \left(\frac{r_0}{R}\right)^2 - \frac{2r_0}{R} + 2\frac{r_0{}^2}{R^2}\right]$$

$$= \frac{(P_0-P_L)}{4\mu_0 L} R^2 \left[1 - 2\frac{r_0}{R} + \left(\frac{r_0}{R}\right)^2\right]$$

$$v_z^< = \frac{P_0-P_L}{4\mu_0 L} R^2 \left[1 - \frac{r_0}{R}\right]^2$$

The volumetric flow rate is given by

$$Q = \int_0^{2\pi}\int_0^R v_z r\,dr\,d\Theta$$

Integrating by parts

$$Q = 2\pi\left[\frac{1}{2} r^2 v_z\Big|_0^R - \frac{1}{2}\int_0^R \left(\frac{dv_z}{dr}\right) r^2\,dr\right]$$

when $r = 0; \quad v_z = v_z$ and when $r = R; \quad v_z = 0$

Therefore the quantity $r^2 v_z$ is zero at $r = 0$ and $r = R$. The lower limit of the integral can be changed to r_0 since

$\frac{dv_z}{dr} = 0$ at $r \leq r_0$.

If $\tau_R > \tau_0$ then

$$Q = \pi \int_{r_0}^{R} \left(\frac{-dv_z^>}{dr}\right) r^2 \, dr$$

$$v_z^> = \frac{P_0-P_L}{4\mu_0 L} R^2 \left[1 - \left(\frac{r}{R}\right)^2\right] - \frac{\tau_0}{\mu_0} R \left[1 - \frac{r}{R}\right]$$

$$\frac{dv_z^>}{dr} = -\frac{(P_0-P_L)}{4\mu_0 L} R^2 \cdot \frac{L}{R^2} \cdot 2r - \frac{\tau_0}{\mu_0} R \left(-\frac{1}{R}\right)$$

$$= -\frac{(P_0-P_L)}{2\mu_0 L} r + \frac{\tau_0}{\mu_0}$$

Therefore

$$Q = \pi \int_{r_0}^{R} \left[\frac{(P_0-P_L)}{2\mu_0 L} r - \frac{\tau_0}{\mu_0}\right] r^2 dr$$

$$= \pi \int_{r_0}^{R} \left[\frac{(P_0-P_L)}{2\mu_0 L} r^3 - \frac{\tau_0}{\mu_0} r^2\right] dr$$

$$= \pi \left[\frac{P_0-P_L}{2\mu_0 L} \frac{r^4}{4} - \frac{\tau_0}{\mu_0} \frac{r^3}{3}\right]_{r_0}^{R}$$

$$= \pi \left[\frac{P_0-P_L}{2\mu_0 L} \frac{R^4}{4} - \frac{\tau_0}{\mu_0} \frac{R^3}{3} - \frac{P_0-P_L}{2\mu_0 L} \frac{r_0^4}{4} + \frac{\tau_0}{\mu_0} \frac{r_0^3}{3}\right]$$

$$Q = \pi \frac{P_0-P_L}{8\mu_0 L} R^4 \left[1 - \frac{\tau_0}{R} \cdot \frac{1}{3} \cdot \frac{8L}{(P_0-P_L)} - \frac{r_0^4}{R^4} + \frac{\tau_0}{3} \frac{r_0^3}{R^4} \frac{8L}{(P_0-P_L)}\right]$$

The momentum flux at the wall is

$$\tau_R = \frac{(P_0-P_L)}{2L} R$$

Then,

$$Q = \pi \frac{(P_0-P_L)}{8\mu_0 L} R^4 \left[1 - \frac{4}{3} \frac{\tau_0}{\tau_R} - \frac{r_0^4}{R^4} \frac{\left(\frac{P_0-P_L}{2L}\right)^4}{\left(\frac{P_0-P_L}{2L}\right)^4} + \frac{\tau_0}{3} \frac{r_0^3 \left(\frac{P_0-P_L}{2L}\right)^3}{R^4 \left(\frac{P_0-P_L}{2L}\right)\left(\frac{P_0-P_L}{2L}\right)^3} \cdot 4\right]$$

$$= \pi \frac{(P_0-P_L)}{8\mu_0 L} R^4 \left[1 - \frac{4}{3}\frac{\tau_0}{\tau_R} - \frac{\tau_0^{\,4}}{\tau_R^{\,4}} + \frac{\tau_0}{3}\frac{\tau_0^{\,3}}{\tau_R^{\,4}} \cdot 4\right]$$

$$= \pi \frac{(P_0-P_L)}{8\mu_0 L} R^4 \left[1 - \frac{4}{3}\frac{\tau_0}{\tau_R} - \frac{\tau_0^{\,4}}{\tau_R^{\,4}} + \frac{4}{3}\frac{\tau_0^{\,4}}{\tau_R^{\,4}}\right]$$

$$= \pi \frac{(P_0-P_L)}{8\mu_0 L} R^4 \left[1 - \frac{4}{3}\frac{\tau_0}{\tau_R} + \frac{1}{3}\frac{\tau_0^{\,4}}{\tau_R^{\,4}}\right]$$

DIMENSIONAL ANALYSIS OF FLUID DRAG, HEAT TRANSFER AND MASS TRANSFER PHENOMENA

• PROBLEM 7-6

Using the Buckingham pi method, develop an expression for the drag on a body when the significant variables are density ρ, viscosity μ, velocity v, length L, and cross-sectional area A.

Solution: In the Buckingham pi method the important variables are first listed. Then the number of dimensionless parameters into which the variables may be combined is determined by the Buckingham pi theorem.

The Buckingham pi theorem states that the functional relationships among q quantities or variables whose units may be given in terms of u fundamental units or dimensions may be written as (q - u) independent dimensionless groups, often called Π's.

The total number of variables is q = 6. The fundamental number of units is u = 3. They are Force F, Length L and time T. The units of the variables are as follows: F_D in F, A in L^2, V in LT^{-1}, ρ in FT^2L^{-4}, μ in FTL^{-2}, L in L. Thus the number of dimensionless groups or Π's are q - u, or 6 - 3 = 3. Therefore,

$$\Pi_1 = f(\Pi_2, \Pi_3)$$

The core group of u (or 3) variables which appear in each Π group and which also contain all the fundamental units among them is selected. Again the selected variables should not contain the same dimensions.

By choosing A, V, ρ as the core variables common to all three groups, then the dimensionless groups are:

$$\Pi_1 = f_1(F_D, A, V, \rho)$$

$$\Pi_2 = f_2(L, A, V, \rho)$$

$$\Pi_3 = f_3(\mu, A, V, \rho)$$

In product form

$$\Pi_1 = F_0{}^1 A^a V^b \rho^c$$

$$F^0L^0T^0 = (F)^1(L^2)^a(LT^{-1})^b(FT^2L^{-4})^c$$

Equating the exponents of F, L and T on both sides of this equation,

F: $0 = 1 + c$

$c = -1$

T: $0 = -b + 2c$

$0 = -b - 2$

$b = -2$

L: $0 = 2a + b - 4c$

$0 = 2a - 2 + 4$

$a = -1$

Therefore, $\Pi_1 = F_0{}^1(A)^{-1}(V)^{-2}(\rho)^{-1}$

$$\Pi_1 = \frac{F_0}{Av^2P}$$

Similarly,

$$\Pi_2 = L^1A^aV^b\rho^c$$

$$F^0L^0T^0 = (L)^1(L^2)^a(LT^{-1})^b(FT^2L^{-4})^c$$

F: $0 = c$

T: $0 = -b + 2c$

$b = 0$

L: $0 = 1 + 2a + b - 4c$

$a = -\frac{1}{2}$

Therefore

$$\Pi_2 = L^1(A)^{-\frac{1}{2}}(V)^0(\rho)^0$$

$$\Pi_2 = \frac{L}{A^{\frac{1}{2}}}$$

Similarly,

$$\Pi_3 = (\mu)^{-1}A^aV^b\rho^c$$

$$F^0L^0T^0 = (FTL^{-2})^{-1}(L^2)^a(LT^{-1})^b(FT^2L^{-4})^c$$

F: $0 = -1 + c$

$$c = +1$$

T: $0 = -1 - b + 2c$

$$b = +1$$

L: $0 = 2 + 2a + b - 4c$

$$= 2 + 2a + 1 - 4$$

$$a = +\frac{1}{2}$$

Therefore, $\Pi_3 = (\mu)^{-1}(A)^{\frac{1}{2}}(V)^1(\rho)^1$

$$\Pi_3 = \frac{A^{\frac{1}{2}}V\rho}{\mu}$$

Substituting the values of Π_1, Π_2, Π_3 in

$$\Pi_1 = f(\Pi_2, \Pi_3)$$

$$\frac{F_D}{AV^2\rho} = f\left(\frac{L}{A^{\frac{1}{2}}}, \frac{A^{\frac{1}{2}}V\rho}{\mu}\right)$$

The drag coefficient c_D is $F_D/A\rho V^2$

Hence,
$$C_D = f\left(\frac{L}{A^{\frac{1}{2}}}, \frac{A^{\frac{1}{2}}V\rho}{\mu}\right)$$

• PROBLEM 7-7

Using the method of dimensional analysis, deduce a relationship between the bubble diameter and the properties of water when bubbles are formed by a gas ejecting out from a small orifice underneath the water surface.

Solution: The problem is to find the dimensionless groups relating the bubble diameter D to the significant variables d, ρ, g_c, σ, μ and g. The total number of variables is q = 7. The fundamental units or dimensions are u = 4. They are mass M, length L, time T and force F. The variables in terms of these fundamental dimensions are as follows:

$$D = L; \quad d = L; \quad \rho = \frac{M}{L^3}; \quad g_c = \frac{ML}{FT^2}; \quad g = \frac{L}{T^2}$$

$$\sigma = \frac{F}{L} \quad \text{and} \quad \mu = \frac{M}{LT}$$

Where D is the bubble diameter, d is the diameter of the orifice, and σ is the surface tension. The number of dimensionless groups or Π's are q-u = 7-4 = 3.

Hence, $\Pi_1 = f(\Pi_2, \Pi_3)$

Let's select d, ρ, g, g_c as the four variables common to all the dimensionless groups. Then the three dimensionless groups are:

$$\Pi_1 = d^a \rho^b g_c^{\,c} g^d D^e$$

$$M^0 L^0 T^0 F^0 = (L^a)\left(\frac{M}{L^3}\right)^b \left(\frac{ML}{FT^2}\right)^c \left(\frac{L}{T^2}\right)^d (L)^e$$

Equating the exponents of M, L, F and T on both sides of this equation,

L: $0 = a - 3b + c + d + e$

M: $0 = b + c$

T: $0 = -2c - 2d$

F: $0 = -c$

From the above equations it is clear that $c = 0$; $d = 0$; $b = 0$.

Let's assume $e = 1$ then $a = -1$.

Therefore

$$\Pi_1 = d^{-1} D'$$

$$\Pi_1 = D/d$$

Similarly

$$\Pi_2 = d^a \rho^b g_c^{\,c} g^d \sigma^e$$

$$M^0 L^0 T^0 F^0 = (L^a)\left(\frac{M}{L^3}\right)^b \left(\frac{ML}{FT^2}\right)^c \left(\frac{L}{T^2}\right)^d \left(\frac{F}{L}\right)^e$$

L: $0 = a - 3b + c + d - e$

M: $0 = b + c$

T: $0 = -2c - 2d$

F: $0 = -c + e$

Solving these equations simultaneously,

$e = 1$; $c = 1$; $b = -1$; $d = -1$; and $a = -2$

Therefore

$$\Pi_2 = d^{-2} \rho^{-1} g_c^1 g^{-1} \sigma^1$$

$$\Pi_2 = \frac{g_c \sigma}{g \rho d^2}$$

Similarly

$$\Pi_3 = d^a \rho^b g_c{}^c g^d \mu^e$$

$$M^0L^0T^0F^0 = (L^a)\left(\frac{M}{L^3}\right)^b \left(\frac{ML}{FT^2}\right)^c \left(\frac{L}{T^2}\right)^d \left(\frac{M}{LT}\right)^e$$

L: $\quad 0 = a - 3b + c + d - e$

M: $\quad 0 = b + c + e$

T: $\quad 0 = -2c - 2d - e$

F: $\quad 0 = -c$

Assuming e = 2 for simplicity, and solving simultaneously,

$$a = -3; \quad d = -1; \quad b = -2; \quad c = 0$$

Therefore

$$\Pi_3 = d^{-3}\rho^{-2}g^{-1}\mu^2$$

$$\Pi_3 = \frac{\mu^2}{d^3\rho^2 g}$$

Substituting the values of Π_1, Π_2 and Π_3 in

$$\Pi_1 = f(\Pi_2, \Pi_3)$$

$$\frac{D}{d} = f\left(\frac{g_c\sigma}{g\rho d^2}, \frac{\mu^2}{g\rho^2 d^3}\right)$$

• PROBLEM 7-8

Obtain the following dimensionless groups N_{Re}, N_{Fr}, N_{Sh}, N_{Sc} and N_{Gr} if the significant variables are D, μ, ρ, K, D_{AB}, g, v and $\Delta\rho_A$.

Solution: The total number of variables is q = 8. The three (u=3) fundamental units are mass M, length L and time T. The variables in terms of these fundamental units are as follows:

$$D = L, \quad \mu = \frac{M}{LT}, \quad \rho = \frac{M}{L^3}, \quad v = \frac{L}{T}, \quad g = \frac{L}{T^2},$$

$$k = \frac{L}{T}, \quad D_{AB} = \frac{L^2}{T}, \quad \Delta\rho_A = \frac{M}{L^3}.$$

Then the number of dimensionless groups or Π's can be assumed to be q - u = 8 - 3 = 5.

Lets select D, μ and ρ as the three variables common to all the dimensionless groups.

Hence,
$$\Pi_1 = D^a \mu^b \rho^c K$$
$$\Pi_1 = (L)^a \left(\frac{M}{LT}\right)^b \left(\frac{M}{L^3}\right)^c \frac{L}{T}$$
$$M^0L^0T^0 = (L^a) \frac{M}{LT}^b \frac{M}{L^3}^c \frac{L}{T}$$

Equating the exponents of M, L and T on both sides of this equation,

$$L: \quad 0 = a - b - 3c + 1 = 0$$
$$M: \quad 0 = b + c$$
$$T: \quad 0 = -b - 1$$

Solving these equations,

$$a = 1, \quad b = -1 \quad \text{and} \quad c = 1$$

Therefore,
$$\Pi_1 = (D)^1(\mu)^{-1}(\rho)^1 K$$
$$\Pi_1 = \frac{D\rho K}{\mu}$$

Similarly
$$\Pi_2 = D^a \mu^b \rho^c D_{AB}$$
$$M^0L^0T^0 = (L^a) \left(\frac{M}{LT}\right)^b \left(\frac{M}{L^3}\right)^c \frac{L^2}{T}$$
$$L: \quad a - b - 3c + 2 = 0$$
$$M: \quad b + c = 0$$
$$T: \quad -b - 1 = 0$$

Solving these equations simultaneously,

$$a = 0; \quad b = -1; \quad c = 1$$
$$\Pi_2 = (D)^0(\mu)^{-1}(\rho)^1 D_{AB}$$
$$\Pi_2 = \frac{\rho D_{AB}}{\mu}$$

Similarly,
$$\Pi_3 = D^a \mu^b \rho^c v$$
$$M^0L^0T^0 = (L^a) \left(\frac{M}{LT}\right)^b \left(\frac{M}{L^3}\right)^c \frac{L}{T}$$

Equating the exponents of M, L and T on both sides of the equation and solving simultaneously,

$$a = +1, \quad b = -1, \quad c = 1$$

Therefore
$$\Pi_3 = \frac{Dv\rho}{\mu}$$

Similarly

$$\Pi_4 = D^a \mu^b \rho^c g$$

$$M^0 L^0 T^0 = L^a \left(\frac{M}{LT}\right)^b \left(\frac{M}{L^3}\right)^c \frac{L}{T^2}$$

Equating the exponents of M, L and T on both sides and solving simultaneously,

$$a = 3, \quad b = -2, \quad c = 2$$

Hence,

$$\Pi_4 = \frac{D^3 \rho^2}{\mu^2} g$$

Similarly,

$$\Pi_5 = D^a \mu^b \rho^c \Delta\rho_A$$

$$= (L^a) \left(\frac{M}{LT}\right)^b \left(\frac{M}{L^3}\right)^c \frac{M}{L^3}$$

Equating the exponents of M, L and T on both sides of the equation and solving simultaneously,

$$a = 0, \quad b = 0, \quad c = -1$$

Therefore,

$$\Pi_5 = \frac{\Delta\rho_A}{\rho}$$

The required dimensionless groups are obtained as follows:

$$\frac{\Pi_1}{\Pi_2} = \frac{D\rho K}{\mu} \frac{\mu}{\rho D_{AB}} = \frac{KD}{D_{AB}} = N_{Sh}$$

$$\frac{1}{\Pi_2} = \frac{\mu}{D_{AB}\rho} = \frac{\nu}{D_{AB}} = N_{Sc}$$

$$\Pi_3 = \frac{Dv\rho}{\mu} = N_{Re}$$

$$\frac{\Pi_3{}^2}{\Pi_4} = \frac{\mu^2}{D^3 \rho^2 g} \cdot \frac{D^2 v^2 \rho^2}{\mu^2} = \frac{v^2}{Dg} = N_{Fr}$$

$$\Pi_4 \Pi_5 = \frac{D^2 \rho^2 g}{\mu^2} \cdot \frac{\Delta\rho_A}{\rho} = \frac{D^3 \rho g}{\mu^2} \Delta\rho_A = N_{Gr}$$

where

N_{Sh} = Sherwood number

N_{Sc} = Schmidt number

N_{Re} = Reynolds number

N_{Fr} = Froude number

N_{Gr} = Grashoff number

FLOW THROUGH A NOZZLE, AIR LIFT PUMP AND A REVERSE POLYTROPIC PROCESS

• PROBLEM 7-9

A pipe of diameter 1.1 ft narrows to a diameter of 0.8 ft. Air moves through it at a mass flowrate of 6.1 slugs/sec. If at the larger diameter a pressure of 110 psig and a temperature of 75 °F exist, calculate the pressure, velocity, density, and temperature in the smaller section.

Solution: The properties at the section of diameter 1.1 ft. will bear a subscript of 1, while those at a diameter of 0.8 ft. will have a subscript of 2.

The pressure and temperature at position 1 are:

$$P_1 = 110 + 14.7 = 124.7 \text{ psia}$$

$$T_1 = 75 + 460 = 535 \text{ R}$$

From the ideal gas law,

$$\rho_1 = \frac{P_1}{gRT_1} \tag{1}$$

where R is the ideal gas constant equal to $53.3 \frac{\text{lbf ft}}{\text{lb}\,^0\text{R}}$ and $g = 32.2$.

Substituting:

$$\rho_1 = \frac{(124.7)(144)}{(32.2)(53.3)(535)} = 0.0196 \frac{\text{slugs}}{\text{ft}^3}$$

The velocity is given by:

$$V_1 = \frac{\mathring{m}}{\rho_1 A_1} \tag{2}$$

where $\mathring{m}$ is the mass flowrate of air.

$$V_1 = \frac{6.1}{(0.0196)(0.950)} = 328 \text{ ft/sec}$$

The velocity of sound is:

$$c_1 = \sqrt{kgRT_1} \tag{3}$$

where k is a ratio of heat capacities (c_p/c_v) equal to 1.4 for air.

Therefore

$$C_1 = \sqrt{(1.4)(32.2)(53.3)(535)}$$

$$= 1134 \text{ ft/sec.}$$

The Mach number is:

$$Ma_1 = \frac{V_1}{C_1} = \frac{328}{1134} = 0.289$$

From the equation of continuity

$$\mathring{m} = 6.1 = \rho_2 V_2 A_2$$

$$6.1 = \rho_2 V_2 (0.503) \qquad (4)$$

Now substituting known values into the following equation

$$\frac{V_1^2}{2} + \frac{k}{k-1}\frac{P_1}{\rho_1} = \frac{V_2^2}{2} + \frac{k}{k-1}\frac{P_2}{\rho_2} \qquad (5)$$

$$\frac{(328)^2}{2} + \frac{1.4(124.7)(144)}{(1.4-1)(0.0196)} = \frac{V_2^2}{2} + \frac{1.4}{(1.4-1)}\frac{P_2}{\rho_2} \qquad (5)$$

Also substitute into the following equation

$$\frac{P_1}{(g\rho_1)^k} = \frac{P_2}{(g\rho_2)^k} \qquad (6)$$

$$\frac{(124.7)(144)}{[(32.2)(0.0196)]^{1.4}} = \frac{P_2}{[(32.2)\rho_2]^{1.4}} \qquad (6)$$

Solving equations (4), (5), and (6) simultaneously yields:

$$\rho_2 = 0.0165$$

$$V_2 = 735 \text{ ft/sec}$$

$$P_2 = 98.0 \text{ psia}$$

Now the temperature at the reduced section can be obtained from the equation

$$T_2 = \frac{P_2}{\rho_2 g R} \qquad (7)$$

$$T_2 = \frac{(98.0)(144)}{(0.0165)(32.2)(53.3)}$$

$$\simeq 498 \text{ R}$$

$$= 38^0\text{F}$$

• PROBLEM 7-10

Air is in a reservoir at 710 kPa abs and 45°C. It leaves the reservoir through a converging nozzle which has an exit area of $5.1 \times 10^{-4} m^2$. If the air enters at a pressure of 525 kPa abs, determine the exit pressure, exit temperature and flowrate.

Solution: The conditions in the reservoir will be identified with a subscript of zero. The exit conditions of the nozzle will bear the subscript one, and the receiver will have a subscript of two.

The critical pressure, P_c, is given by:

$$P_c = P_1 \left(\frac{2}{k+1}\right)^{k/(k-1)}$$

$$= 710 \left(\frac{2}{1.4+1}\right)^{1.4/(1.4-1)} = 375 \text{ kPa abs}$$

where $k = c_p/c_v$ = ratio of heat capacities = 1.4 for air.

The flow is subsonic at the exit of the nozzle because the receiver pressure is greater than the critical pressure. The exit temperature, T_1 is given by

$$T_1 = T_0 \left(\frac{P_1}{P_0}\right)^{(k-1)/k} \tag{1}$$

$$= 318 \left(\frac{525}{710}\right)^{(1.4-1)/1.4} = 291.7^\circ K$$

The mass flowrate of air, $\dot{m}$, is given by:

$$\dot{m} = V_1 A_1 \rho_1 \tag{2}$$

where V_1 is the exit velocity of air, A_1 is the exit area of the nozzle, and ρ_1 is the density at the exit. The exit velocity of the air can be determined from

$$V_1 = \sqrt{2C_p(T_0 - T_1)} \tag{3}$$

where C_p is the heat capacity of air = 1005 J/kg°K.

$$V_1 = \sqrt{2(1005)(26.3)} = 230 \text{ m/sec}$$

The exit density is available from the ideal gas law:

$$\rho_1 = \frac{P_1}{RT_1}$$

where R is the gas constant = 287.1 J/kg·K for air.

Therefore:

$$\rho_1 = \frac{5.25 \times 10^5}{(287.1)(291.7)} = 6.27 \text{ kg/m}^3$$

Substitution in equation (2) provides the mass flowrate:

$$\dot{m} = (230)(5.1 \times 10^{-4})(6.27) = 0.735 \text{ kg/sec}$$

• PROBLEM 7-11

A convergent-divergent nozzle has a throat area which is 55% that of the discharge of the divergent section. This nozzle is connected to a tank where air is maintained at a pressure of 22 atm. and 1100 ^{0}R.

(I) Using a Mach number of 0.82 determine the values of the pressure, temperature, linear velocity, density, and mass velocity at the throat.

(II) Determine the pressure, temperature, linear velocity and mass velocity for the conditions in the tank.

(III) If a supersonic nozzle is employed, determine the maximum Mach number at the exit of the divergent section.

The following figure illustrates the situation:

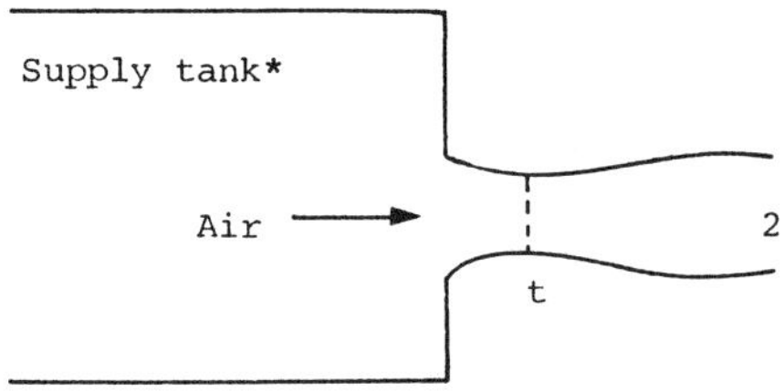

Figure (1)

Solution: The apparatus involved in this problem can be divided into three sections: the supply tank whose properties would be denoted with an asterisk superscript, for the throat they would be represented by t subscript, and for the discharge at the divergent section would be represented by subscript of 2 (see Figure 1).

(I) The throat pressure, P_t, can be obtained from

$$\frac{P_t}{P_o} = \frac{1}{\{1 + [(k-1)/2]M_a{}^2\}^{1/(1-1/k)}} \qquad (1)$$

where P_o is the tank pressure = 22 atm

k is a ratio of heat capacities = 1.4 for air

and M_a is the Mach number = 0.82

Substituting the values

$$P_t = \frac{22}{\{1 + [(1.4-1)/2](.82)^2\}^{3.5}} = 14.15 \text{ atm}$$

The density in the tank can be obtained by using the ideal gas equation:

$$\rho_0 = \frac{P_0 M}{R T_0}$$

where T_0 - tank temperature = 1100 °R

M - molecular weight of air = 29 lbm/lb mol.

R - gas constant = 1545 ft lbf/lb mol-°R

and P_0 - pressure = 22 atm.

Substituting the values

$$\rho_0 = \frac{(22 \times 144 \times 14.7)(29)}{(1545)(1100)} = 0.795 \text{ lb/ft}^3$$

The velocity at the throat, U_t, is provided by equation

$$U_t^2 = \frac{2kg_c RT_o}{M(k-1)} \left[1 - \left(\frac{P_t}{P_o}\right)^{1-1/k}\right] \quad (2)$$

where g_c = 32.2 lbm ft/lbf sec^2

Substituting the values yields:

$$U_t^2 = \frac{2(1.4)(32.2)(1545)(1100)}{29(1.4-1)} \left[1 - \left(\frac{14.15}{22}\right)^{1-1/1.4}\right]$$

$U_t \simeq 1252$ ft/sec

The throat density is obtained from

$$\rho_t = \rho_0 \left(\frac{P_t}{P_o}\right)^{1/k} \quad (3)$$

$$\rho_t = 0.795 \left(\frac{14.15}{22}\right)^{1/1.4} = 0.58 \text{ lb/ft}^3$$

The mass velocity can now be easily obtained:

$G_t = U_t \rho_t = (1252)(0.58) = 726.2$ lb/ft^2·sec

The throat temperature, T_t, is given by equation

$$T_t = T_o \left(\frac{P_t}{P_o}\right)^{1-1/k} \qquad (4)$$

$$T_t = 1100\left(\frac{14.15}{22}\right)^{1-1/1.4} = 969.6^0R$$

(II) The pressure in the tank (P*) can be obtained by substituting P* for P_t and Ma = 1 in equation (1). Therefore eq.(1) after simplifying is

$$\frac{P^*}{P_o} = \left(\frac{2}{k+1}\right)^{1/(1-1/k)} \qquad (5)$$

$$P^* = 22\left(\frac{2}{1.4+1}\right)^{3.5} = 11.62 \text{ atm.}$$

The temperature in the tank is given by combining equations (4) and (5):

$$T^* = T_o\left(\frac{2}{k+1}\right)^{1-1/k} \qquad (6)$$

$$= 1100\left(\frac{2}{1.4+1}\right)^{1-1/1.4}$$

$$= 1044^0R$$

The following equation yields the density of air in the tank, ρ^*.

$$\frac{P_o}{P^*} = \left(\frac{\rho_o}{\rho^*}\right)^k \qquad (7)$$

$$\frac{22}{11.62} = \left(\frac{0.795}{\rho^*}\right)^{1.4}$$

$$\rho^* = 0.504 \text{ lb/ft}^3$$

The tank mass velocity, G*, is given by

$$G^* = \left(\frac{2kg_c\rho_oP_o}{k-1}\right)^{\frac{1}{2}}\left(\frac{P}{P_o}\right)^{1/k}\left[1 - \left(\frac{P}{P_o}\right)^{1-1/k}\right]^{\frac{1}{2}} \qquad (8)$$

Substituting the values

$$G^* = \left[\frac{(2)(1.4)(32.2)(0.795)(22\times144\times14.7)}{(1.4-1)}\right]^{\frac{1}{2}} \times \left[\frac{11.62}{22}\right]^{1/1.4}$$

$$\times \left[1 - \left(\frac{11.62}{22}\right)^{0.286}\right]^{\frac{1}{2}}$$

$$G^* \simeq 748 \text{ lb/ft}^2\cdot\text{sec.}$$

The linear velocity in the tank, U*, can now be obtained

$$U^* = \frac{G^*}{\rho^*} = \frac{748}{0.504} = 1484 \text{ ft/sec.}$$

(III) Properties at the discharge of the divergent section will bear a subscript of 2. The mass velocity at the discharge is:

$$G_r = 0.55\, G^* = 0.55(748) = 411.4 \text{ lb/ft}^2\cdot\text{sec}$$

$\frac{P_2}{P_0}$ can be obtained from the relation

$$G_2 = \left(\frac{2kg_c\rho_0 P_0}{k-1}\right)^{\frac{1}{2}} \left(\frac{P_2}{P_0}\right)^{1/k} \left[1 - \left(\frac{P_2}{P_0}\right)^{1-1/k}\right]^{\frac{1}{2}} \qquad (9)$$

Substituting the values

$$411.4 = \left[\frac{2(1.4)(32.2)(0.795)(22\times 144\times 14.7)}{(1.4-1)}\right]^{\frac{1}{2}} \times \left[1 - \left(\frac{P_2}{P_0}\right)^{0.286}\right]^{\frac{1}{2}} \times \left[\frac{P_2}{P_0}\right]^{1/1.4}$$

$$\left(\frac{P_2}{P_0}\right)^{0.714} \sqrt{1 - \left(\frac{P_2}{P_0}\right)^{0.286}} \simeq 0.1424$$

Solving:

$$\frac{P_2}{P_0} = 0.1113$$

The Mach number is given by:

$$Ma_2 = \sqrt{\frac{2}{k-1}\left[\left(\frac{P_0}{P_2}\right)^{1-1/k} - 1\right]}$$

$$= \sqrt{\frac{2}{1.4-1}\left[\left(\frac{1}{0.1113}\right)^{0.286} - 1\right]}$$

$$= 2.09$$

• PROBLEM 7-12

The upstream conditions for a group of nozzles are

P_0 = pressure = 11 atm., T_0 = temperature = 3200 °R,

and u_0 = velocity = 0.

The stream is composed of air. The nozzle is connected to a large container at 1.1 atm.

(I) For a converging nozzle with a throat diameter of 2.1 in., calculate the mass flowrate ($\mathring{m}$) and the discharge velocity.

(II) Calculate the mass flow rate ($\dot{m}$) and the discharge velocity for a converging-diverging nozzle with no shock inside the nozzle and a throat diameter of 2.1 in.

(III) For the nozzle in part (II), determine the outlet area of the nozzle if the container is maintained at 9 atm. This causes a transverse shock at P = 4.5 atm.

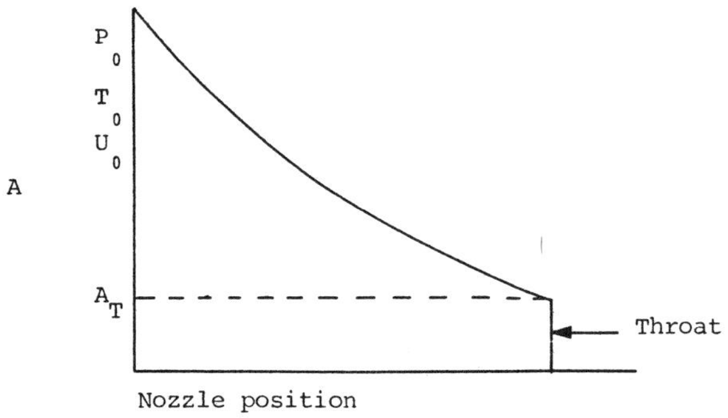

Figure (1)

Solution: (I) A schematic figure of the converging nozzle is shown in Figure 1,

where A is the nozzle area and A_T is the throat area. The critical pressure of the nozzle is given by:

$$P_c = P_o\left(\frac{2}{k+1}\right)^{k/(k-1)} \tag{1}$$

where $k = C_p/C_v$ = ratio of heat capacities = 1.4 for air. Substituting:

$$P_c = 11\left(\frac{2}{1.4+1}\right)^{1.4/0.4} = 5.81 \text{ atm.}$$

For sonic flow, the throat temperature is:

$$T_t = T_o\left(\frac{P_t}{P_o}\right)^{(k-1)/k} \tag{2}$$

$$= 3200\left(\frac{5.81}{11}\right)^{0.286} = 2666R$$

The velocity at the throat is given by:

$$u_t = \frac{kg_c RT}{M} \tag{3}$$

where g_c is a constant equal to 32.2 lbm·ft/lbf·sec^2, R is the gas constant = 1544 ft·lbf/lb mol^{0}R, and M is the molecular weight of air = 29 lb/lb mol. Substituting:

$$u_t = \sqrt{\frac{(1.4)(32.2)(1544)(2666)}{29}}$$

$$\simeq 2530 \text{ ft/sec}$$

A throat diameter of 2.1 inches gives $A_t \simeq 0.0241$ ft^2. The throat density is obtained from the ideal gas law:

$$\rho_t = \frac{pM}{RT} = \frac{(5.81\times 2116.8)(29)}{(1544)(2666)} \simeq 0.0866 \text{ lb/ft}^3$$

The mass flow rate at the throat is:

$$\dot{m} = U_t \rho_t A_t = (2530)(0.0866)(0.0241)$$

$$\dot{m} = 5.28 \text{ lb/sec}$$

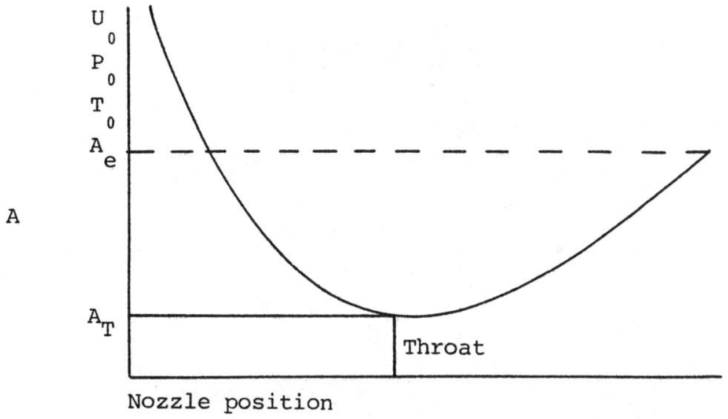

Figure (2)

(II) A schematic of the converging-diverging nozzle is shown in Figure 2, where A_e is the area at the exit of the nozzle. The exit pressure was given as 1.1 atm. The exit velocity U_e is obtained from

$$U_e^2 = \frac{2kg_c RT_o}{(k-1)M}\left[1 - \left(\frac{P_e}{P_o}\right)^{(k-1)/k}\right] \tag{4}$$

Substituting the values

$$U_e^2 = \frac{2(1.4)(32.2)(1544)(3200)}{(1.4-1)(29)}\left[1 - \left(\frac{1.1}{11}\right)^{0.286}\right]$$

$U_e = 4304$ ft/sec

The exit temperature, (T_e), is given by equation (2):

$$T_e = T_o \left(\frac{P_e}{P_o}\right)^{(k-1)/k} = 3200 \left(\frac{1.1}{11}\right)^{0.286} \qquad (2)$$

$T_e = 1656\,^0R$

The density at the exit is calculated using the ideal gas law.

$$\rho_e = \frac{(1.1\times 2116.8)(29)}{(1544)(1656)} = 0.0264 \text{ lb/ft}^3$$

The ratio of the area at the exit to the area at the throat is given by:

$$\frac{A_e}{A_t} = \frac{U_t \rho_t}{U_e \rho_e} \qquad (5)$$

The values at the throat can be obtained from part (I) since the throat diameters and initial conditions are identical. Substituting in equation (5) gives

$$\frac{A_e}{A_t} = \frac{(2350)(0.0866)}{(4304)(0.0264)} = 1.79$$

The area at the nozzle exit is:

$$A_e = A_t(1.79) = (0.0241)(1.79)$$

$$= 0.0431 \text{ ft}^2$$

The mass flow rate of the exit is:

$$\mathring{m}_e = U_e \rho_e A_e = (4304)(0.0264)(0.0431)$$

$$= 4.90 \text{ lb/sec}$$

(III) This is a converging-diverging nozzle as in part (II), however, the container pressure has been changed from 1.1 to 9 atm., therefore the new outlet area has to be calculated. The subscript 1 will refer to the conditions just before the shock. The subscript 2 will be used for the downstream side of the shock, and 3 is for the outlet conditions. The velocity just before the shock is given by equation (4):

$$U_1^2 = \frac{2(1.4)(32.2)(1544)(3200)}{(1.4-1)(29)} \left[1 - \left(\frac{4.5}{11}\right)^{0.286}\right]$$

$U_1 = 2943$ ft/sec

Using the same procedure as in part (II):

$$T_1 = 3200\left(\frac{4.5}{11}\right)^{0.286} = 2478\,^0\text{R}$$

$$\rho_1 = \frac{(4.5 \times 2116.8)(29)}{(1544)(2478)} = 0.0722 \text{ lb/ft}^3$$

$$\frac{A_1}{A_t} = \frac{U_t\rho_t}{U_1\rho_1} = \frac{(2350)(0.0866)}{(2943)(0.0722)} = 0.958$$

$$A_1 = 0.958\ A_t = 0.958 \times 0.0241 = 0.0231 \text{ ft}^2$$

and

$$D_1 = 2.06 \text{ in.}$$

This indicates that the shock occurs very near to the throat, which has a diameter of 2.1 in.

U_2 is calculated from:

$$U_1U_2 = U_t^2$$

$$U_2 = \frac{U_t^2}{U_1} = \frac{(2350)^2}{2943} = 1876 \text{ ft/sec.}$$

Writing a mass balance will yield ρ_2:

$$U_2\rho_2 = U_1\rho_1$$

$$\rho_2 = \frac{U_1\rho_1}{U_2} = \frac{(2943)(0.0722)}{1876}$$

$$= 0.1133 \text{ lb/ft}^3$$

P_2 can be obtained from the following equation:

$$\frac{U_1\rho_1}{g_c}(U_2-U_1) = P_1-P_2$$

Substituting:

$$\frac{(2943)(0.0722)}{32.2}(1876 - 2943) = P_1 - P_2$$

or

$$P_2 - P_1 = 7041 \text{ lbf/ft}^2 = 3.326 \text{ atm.}$$

$$P_2 = P_1 + 3.326 = 4.5 + 3.326 \simeq 7.83 \text{ atm.}$$

The ideal gas law is now employed to calculate T_2:

$$T_2 = \frac{PM}{\rho R} = \frac{(7.8 \times 2116.8)(29)}{(0.1133)(1544)}$$

$$= 2737\text{R}$$

Now to calculate U_3:

$$U_3^2 = \frac{2kg_cP_2}{(k-1)\rho_2}\left[1 - \left(\frac{P_3}{P_2}\right)^{(k-1)/k}\right] + U_2^2 \qquad (6)$$

$$= \frac{(2)(1.4)(32.2)(7.8\times 2116.8)}{(0.4)(0.1133)}\left[1 - \left(\frac{9}{7.8}\right)^{0.286}\right] + (1876)^2$$

$U_3 = 1465$ ft/sec

For this situation using equation (2)

$$T_3 = T_2\left(\frac{P_3}{P_2}\right)^{(k-1)/k}$$

Substituting:

$$T_3 = 2737\left(\frac{9}{7.8}\right)^{0.286} = 2851\,^0R$$

From the ideal gas law:

$$\rho_3 = \frac{(9\times 2116.8)(29)}{(1544)(2851)} = 0.1255 \text{ lb/ft}^3$$

The exit area can be obtained from:

$$\frac{A_3}{A_2} = \frac{U_t\rho_t}{U_3\rho_3} = \frac{(2350)(0.0866)}{(1465)(0.1255)} = 1.11$$

$$A_3 = (1.11)A_2 = (1.11)(0.0241)$$

$$= 0.0268 \text{ ft}^2$$

• PROBLEM 7-13

A reservoir contains air at 22 atm and 1100R. It is connected to a long straight pipe by an isentropic nozzle through which the air flows. The Mach number at the entrance of the pipe (position 1) is $Ma_1 = 0.06$.

(I) Determine $\bar{f}L_{max}/r_H$, where L_{max} is the length of the conduit when Ma = 1.0 at the outlet, $\bar{f}$ is the mean value of the Fanning friction factor, and r_H is the hydraulic radius of the conduit.

(II) Calculate the pressure, density, temperature, linear velocity and mass velocity when $L_2 = L_{max}$, where the subscript two refers to the conditions at the exit of the pipe.

(III) Obtain the mass velocity when $\bar{f}L_{max}/r_H = 400$.

Solution: Part (I) can be solved by substituting numerical values in equation (1) and using k = 1.4 for air. Part (II) is solved by using equations (2) through (6). Solving equation (1) again in part (III) by trial and error provides the Mach number, which permits the mass flow rate to be calculated.

(I) Substituting in equation (1).

$$\frac{\bar{f}L_{max}}{r_H} = \frac{1}{k}\left(\frac{1}{Ma_1^2} - 1 - \frac{k+1}{2}\ln\frac{2\{1+[(k-1)/2]Ma_1^2\}}{Ma_1^2(k+1)}\right) \qquad (1)$$

where k is the ratio of heat capacities which is equal to 1.4 for air.

$$\frac{\bar{f}L_{max}}{r_H} = \frac{1}{1.4}\left(\frac{1}{0.06^2} - 1 - \frac{2.4}{2}\ln\frac{2\{1+[0.2]0.06^2\}}{0.06^2(2.4)}\right)$$

$$= 193$$

(II) The pressure at the end of the nozzle, P_1, is given by equation (2).

$$\frac{P_1}{P_0} = \frac{1}{\{1+[(k-1)/2]Ma^2\}^{1/(1-1/k)}} \qquad (2)$$

where P_0 refers to the pressure of the reservoir. Substituting:

$$P_1 = \frac{22}{\{1+[0.2]0.06^2\}^{3.5}} = \frac{22}{1.003} \approx 22 \text{ atm}$$

The acoustical velocity, (a_1), is given by:

$$a_1 = \sqrt{\frac{g_c kTR}{m}} \qquad (3)$$

where g_c is a constant equal to 32.2 lb ft/lbf sec², T is the temperature, R is the ideal gas constant equal to 1545 lbf·ft/lb mol·°R and M is the molecular weight. Substitution yields:

$$a_1 = \sqrt{\frac{(32.2)(1.4)(1100)(1545)}{29}} = 1625 \text{ ft/sec}$$

The velocity at the beginning of the pipe, (U_1), is:

$$U_1 = (Ma_1)(a_1) = (0.06)(1625) = 97.5 \text{ ft/sec}$$

When $L_2 = L_{max}$, $Ma_2 = 1.0$. These conditions will be denoted by an asterisk (superscript). The temperature, (T^*), when $L_2 = L_{max}$ is given by:

$$\frac{T_1}{T^*} = \frac{1+[(k-1)/2]Ma_2^2}{1+[(k-1)/2]Ma_1^2} \qquad (4)$$

$$\frac{1100}{T^*} = \frac{1+[0.2](1.0)^2}{1+[0.2](0.06)^2}$$

$$T^* = 917R$$

To obtain the density, ρ^*, the density ρ_1 at the inlet of the pipe must first be obtained using the ideal gas law.

$$\rho_1 = \frac{P_1 M}{RT} = \frac{(22)(14.7)(144)(29)}{(1545)(1100)}$$

$$\rho_1 = 0.795 \text{ lb/ft}^3$$

Now substitute in equation (5) and solve for ρ^*.

$$\frac{\rho_1}{\rho^*} = \frac{Ma_2}{Ma_1}\sqrt{\frac{1+[(k-1)/2]Ma_1^2}{1+[(k-1)/2]Ma_2^2}} \qquad (5)$$

$$\frac{0.795}{\rho^*} = \frac{1.0}{0.06}\sqrt{\frac{1+(0.2)(0.06)^2}{1+(0.2)(1.0)^2}}$$

$$\rho^* = 0.0522 \text{ lb/ft}^3$$

The pressure, P^*, can be obtained from equation (6).

$$\frac{P_1}{P^*} = \frac{Ma_2}{Ma_1}\sqrt{\frac{1+[(k-1)/2]Ma_2^2}{1+[(k-1)/2]Ma_1^2}} \qquad (6)$$

$$\frac{22}{P^*} = \frac{1.0}{0.06}\sqrt{\frac{1+(0.2)(1.0)^2}{1+(0.2)(0.06)^2}}$$

$$P^* = 1.21 \text{ atm}$$

The mass velocity,(G),in the pipe is given by:

$$G = \rho_1 U_1 = \rho^* U^*$$

$$G = (0.795)(97.5) = (0.0522)U^* = 77.51 \text{ lb/ft}^2\cdot\text{sec}$$

and therefore

$$U^* = 1484 \text{ ft/sec}$$

(III) Substituting into equation (1) using $\overline{f}L_{max}/r_H = 400$ yields:

$$400 = \frac{1}{1.4}\left(\frac{1}{Ma_1^2} - 1 - \frac{1.4+1}{2}\ln\frac{1.2}{(1/Ma_1^2)+0.7}\right)$$

Trial and error gives $Ma_1 = 0.0425$. The velocity is therefore

$$U_1 = \frac{0.0425}{0.06}(97.5) = 69.1 \text{ ft/sec}$$

and the mass flow rate is:

$$G = (U_1)(\rho_1) = (69.1)(0.795) = 54.9 \text{ lb/ft}^2\cdot\text{sec}$$

• PROBLEM 7-14

12 gal/min of a liquid with a specific gravity of 1.3 is to be lifted with an air pump. If air can be obtained at 55 psig, and the liquid is to be raised 75 ft., determine the power needed using isentropic air compression. The pump has an efficiency of 30%.

Solution: First obtain the work performed per minute by the pump. Correct this value to the actual work with the pump efficiency. The volume of the air needed, (V), is obtained from equation (1) where P is the pressure. Now the isentropic work can be calculated with equation (2).

The work is equal to the product of a force times a distance. The force is the weight of the liquid lifted. The liquid has a density of (1.3)(62.4) = 81.1 lb/ft^3. The weight of the liquid is given by:

$$\text{weight} = \text{mass} \cdot \frac{g}{g_c}$$

$$= (12 \text{ gal})(0.13368 \text{ ft}^3/\text{gal})\ 81.1 \text{ lb/ft}^3$$

$$\times \left(\frac{32.2 \text{ ft/sec}^2}{32.2 \text{ lbm ft}/\text{lb}_f \text{ sec}^2}\right)$$

$$= 130.1 \text{ lbf}$$

The work done by the pump in one minute is therefore:

$$(130.1 \text{ lb}_f)(75 \text{ ft}) = 9758 \text{ ft}\cdot\text{lb}_f$$

The expansion work corrected with the efficiency is:

$$\frac{9758 \text{ ft lb}_f}{0.30} = 3.25 \times 10^4 \text{ ft}\cdot\text{lb}_f$$

The volume of air at standard temperature and pressure can be obtained from:

$$W = P_1 V \ln \frac{P_2}{P_1} \tag{1}$$

$$3.25 \times 10^4 = (14.7)(144) V \ln \left(\frac{69.7}{14.7}\right)$$

$$V = 9.87 \text{ ft}^3/\text{min}$$

The work expended in a isentropic compression can be determined from:

$$W = \frac{\gamma P_1 V_1}{\gamma - 1}\left[\left(\frac{P_2}{P_1}\right)^{(\gamma-1)/\gamma} - 1\right] \tag{2}$$

where $\gamma = C_p/C_v$ = ratio of heat capacities

= 1.4 for air

Substituting:

$$W = \frac{(1.4)(14.7)(144)(9.87)}{(1.4-1)}\left[\left(\frac{69.7}{14.7}\right)^{0.4/1.4} - 1\right]$$

$$= 4.09 \times 10^4 \text{ ft}\cdot\text{lb}_f$$

This is the work done in one minute.

The power necessary is:

$$P = (681.7 \text{ ft}\cdot\text{lb}_f/\text{sec})\left(\frac{1 \text{ hp}}{550 \text{ ft}\cdot\text{lb}_f/\text{sec}}\right)$$

$$= 1.2 \text{ hp}$$

• PROBLEM 7-15

A reversible polytropic process occurs with 2.8 slugs of air. The initial pressure is P_1 = 10 psia and the initial temperature is $T_1 = 65^0$F. The final pressure is P_2 = 18 psia, while the final volume is 1025 ft^3. Find:

(I) the relationship which describes the process

(II) the work done

(III) the quantity of heat transferred

(IV) the change in entropy.

Solution: Knowing the initial and final pressures and densities, the exponent n in equation (1) can be obtained. Equation (2), which describes the process, can then be written. The work is given by equation (5), where V_1 is obtained from equation (4). Using the first law of thermodynamics (equation (6)), the heat transferred is determined. The enthalpy change, (ΔS) is calculated from equation (7).

(I) The ideal gas constant is

$$R = 1714.7 \text{ ft}\cdot\text{lb}_f/\text{slug}\cdot{}^\circ\text{R}$$

From the ideal gas law the initial density is calculated:

$$\rho_1 = \frac{P_1}{RT_1} = \frac{(10)(144)}{(1714.7)(525)} = 0.00160 \text{ slug/ft}^3$$

The final density is given by:

$$\rho_2 = \frac{2.8 \text{ slugs}}{1025 \text{ ft}^3} = 0.00273 \text{ slug/ft}^3$$

Using equation (1) to solve for n:

$$\frac{P_1}{\rho_1{}^n} = \frac{P_2}{\rho_2{}^n} \tag{1}$$

Rearranging:

$$n = \frac{\ln(P_2/P_1)}{\ln(\rho_2/\rho_1)}$$

Substituting:

$$n = \frac{\ln(18/10)}{\ln(0.00273/0.00160)} = 1.10$$

Therefore equation (2) describes this process:

$$\frac{P}{\rho^{1.10}} = \text{constant} \tag{2}$$

(II) Expansion work is given by:

$$W = \int_{V_1}^{V_2} PdV \tag{3}$$

and in this problem the following relationship holds:

$$P_1V_1{}^n = P_2V_2{}^n = PV^n \tag{4}$$

Substituting $P = \frac{P_1V_1{}^n}{V^n}$ from equation (4) into equation (3) yields:

$$W_1 = P_1V_1{}^n \int_{V_1}^{V_2} \frac{dV}{V^n} = \frac{P_2V_2 - P_1V_1}{1 - n} \tag{5}$$

The initial volume can be obtained using equation (4):

$$V_1 = V_2\left(\frac{P_2}{P_1}\right)^{1/n} = 1025\left(\frac{18}{10}\right)^{1/1.10}$$

$$= 1749 \text{ ft}^3$$

Substitution in (5) gives the work:

$$W = \frac{(18)(144)(1025) - (10)(144)(1749)}{1 - 1.10}$$

$$W = -1.3824 \times 10^6 \text{ ft}\cdot\text{lb}_f$$

The negative sign indicates that the work was performed on the gas.

(III) The first law of thermodynamics states that:

$$Q - W = \Delta U = c_v m \Delta T \tag{6}$$

where Q is the heat transferred, ΔU is the change in internal energy, c_v is the specific heat of the gas, m is the mass of gas involved, and ΔT is the temperature change. Using the ideal gas law, the final temperature is:

$$T_2 = \frac{P_2}{\rho_2 R} = \frac{(18)(144)}{(0.00273)(1714.7)} = 554^\circ R$$

Substituting in equation (6) with $c_v = 0.171$ Btu/lb·°R air:

$$Q = \frac{-1.3824 \times 10^6 (ft \cdot lbf)}{778 \left(\frac{ft \cdot lbf}{Btu}\right)}$$

$$+ (0.171 Btu/lb \cdot {}^\circ R)(32.17\ lb/slug)(2.8\ slugs)$$

$$\cdot (554 - 525)$$

$$= -1330\ Btu$$

(IV) The entropy change is given by

$$\Delta S = C_v \ln \left[\frac{P_2}{P_1}\left(\frac{\rho_1}{\rho_2}\right)^{k-1}\right] \tag{7}$$

where $k = C_p/C_v = 1.4$ for air

Substituting:

$$\Delta S = 0.171 \ln \left[\frac{18}{10}\left(\frac{0.00160}{0.00273}\right)^{1.4}\right]$$

$$= -0.02740\ Btu/lb \cdot {}^0 R$$

$$= -0.02740\ Btu/lb \cdot {}^\circ R$$

$$= -2.64\ Btu/R$$

FLOW THROUGH PIPES

• PROBLEM 7-16

A 90 mile pipeline with a 35 in. diameter carries nitrogen gas at 3 lbmoles/sec. Isothermal conditions exist at 65°F. If the exit pressure is $P_2 = 26.0$ psia, determine the entrance pressure P_1.

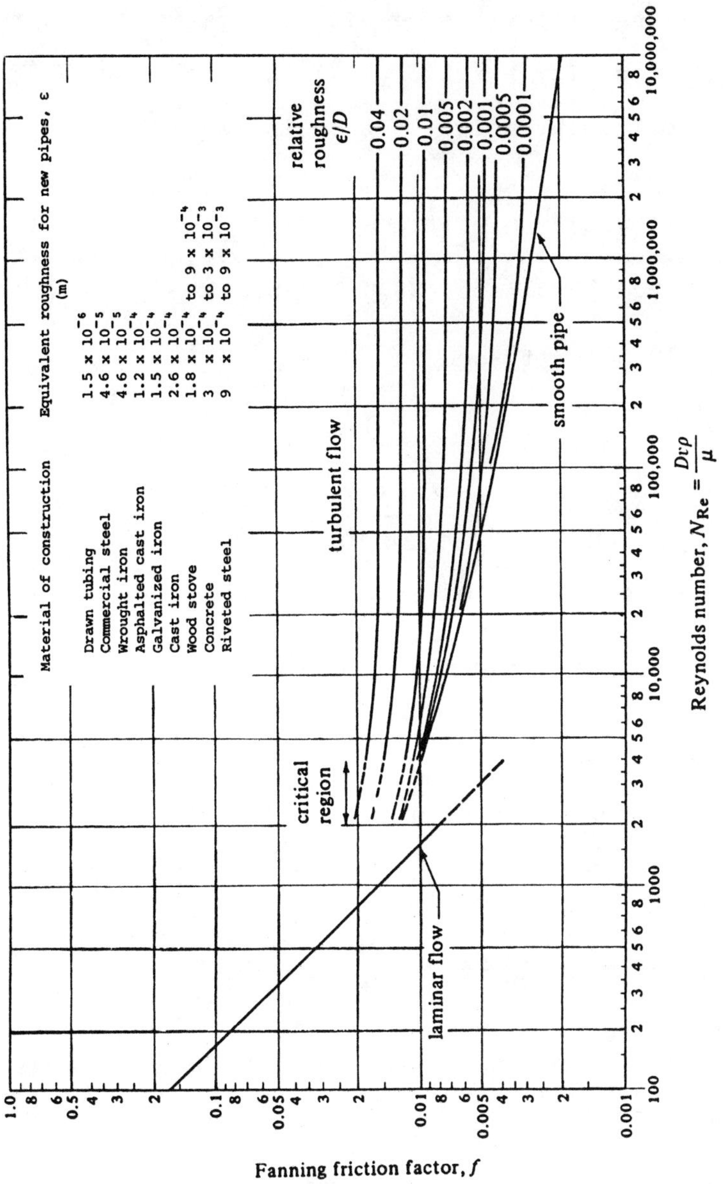

Figure (1) FRICTION FACTORS FOR FLUIDS INSIDE PIPES.

Solution: First calculate the Reynolds number,(Re),based on the pipe diameter,(D), The roughness,(ε), for the pipe is provided at the top of Figure 1. It is now possible to obtain the friction factor,(f), from Figure 1. Use equation (1) with a trial and error procedure to solve for P_1.

The diameter is D = 35/12 = 2.92 ft.

The cross-sectional area for flow is

$$A = \frac{\pi(2.92)^2}{4} = 6.70 \text{ ft}^2$$

The following properties of nitrogen gas are required:

μ = viscosity = 1.173×10^{-5} lb/ft•sec at 65^{0}F

M = molecular weight = 28.0 lb/lbmol

The mass flow rate of nitrogen per unit area is:

$$G = (3.0 \text{ lbmol/sec})(28.0 \text{ lb/lbmol})\left(\frac{1}{6.70 \text{ ft}^2}\right)$$

$$= 12.5 \text{ lb/ft}^2\text{•sec}$$

The Reynolds number is:

$$Re = \frac{DG}{\mu} = \frac{(2.92)(12.5)}{1.173 \times 10^{-5}} = 3,100,000$$

$\varepsilon = 1.5 \times 10^{-4}$ for galvanized iron from Figure 1.

$$\frac{\varepsilon}{D} = \frac{1.5 \times 10^{-4}}{2.92} = 0.000051$$

From Figure 1

$$f = 0.0029$$

Assume P_1 = 85 psia and use equation (1) to solve for $P_1^2 - P_2^2$.

$$P_1^2 - P_2^2 = \frac{4f\Delta LG^2RT}{DM} + \frac{2G^2RT}{M} \ln\left(\frac{P_1}{P_2}\right) \quad (1)$$

where T is the absolute temperature = 525R, ΔL is the length of the pipeline = 475200 ft., and R is the gas constant = 1545.3 ft•lb_f/lbmol•R.

Substituting in equation (1)

$$P_1^2 - P_2^2 = \frac{4(0.0029)(475200)(12.5)^2(1545.3)(525)}{(32.2)(2.92)(28.0)}$$

$$+ \frac{2(12.5)^2(1545.3)(525)}{(28.8) \times 32.2} \ln\left(\frac{85}{26}\right)$$

$$P_1^2 - P_2^2 = 2.654 \times 10^8 + 3.33 \times 10^5$$

where g_c = 32.2 is included to make the English units consistent.

$$P_1^2 - P_2^2 = 2.657 \times 10^8 (lb_f/ft^2)^2$$

Substituting $P_2 = (261b_f/in^2)(144) = 3744\ lb_f/ft^2$

$$P_1^2 = 2.761 \times 10^8 + (3744)^2$$

$$P_1 = 1.672 \times 10^4\ lb_f/ft^2 = 116\ psia$$

Substituting this value of P_1 into equation (1) and solving for $P_1^2 - P_2^2$ again leads to $P_1 = 116$ psia (approx.), which is the final result.

• PROBLEM 7-17

A gaseous mixture with a molecular weight of M = 20 lb/ lbmol moves through a pipeline of 14in. diameter and the Darcy friction factor is f = 0.013. The pressure at the end of the line is 17 psia = P_2 and the temperature of the gas is constant at 65°F. If the pipeline is 17500 ft. long, determine the energy required to move 500 lb/ min. of gas through the line.

Solution: Equation (1) can be employed to solve for P_1, the entrance pressure of the gas in the pipeline. Using the mass flow rate and the mean density of the gas, the average volumetric flow rate, q, can be obtained. The energy expended is then given by:

(pressure drop) × (the average volumetric flow rate).

Equation (1) states that:

$$\frac{P_1^2 - P_2^2}{2RT/M} = \frac{G^2}{g_c} \ln \frac{V_2}{V_1} + \frac{4fLG^2}{2g_cD} \qquad (1)$$

where T is the absolute temperature, R is the ideal gas constant, G is the mass flow rate per unit area, D is the diameter of the pipeline, L is the length of the pipeline, V_2 and V_1 are the final and initial volumes of the gas respectively, and $g_c = 32.2$ lbm ft/lb$_f$ sec^2 is a correction factor employed with English units.

It will be assumed and later verified that the first term on the right side of the equation (1) is negligible.

$$G = \frac{500(lb/min)}{(60\ sec/min)\left(\frac{\pi}{4}\right)(1.17\ ft)^2} = 7.75\ lb/ft^2 sec$$

Separately evaluating the terms of equation (1) for clarity:

$$\frac{4fLG^2}{2g_cD} = \frac{4(0.013)(17500)(7.75)^2}{2(32.2)(1.17)} = 725.4\ lb_f \cdot lb/ft^5$$

$$\frac{R}{M} = \frac{1545.3 \text{ ft}\cdot\text{lbf/lbmol}\cdot{}^0\text{R}}{20 \text{ lb/lbmol}} = 77.3 \text{ ft}\cdot\text{lb}_f/\text{lb}\cdot{}^0\text{R}$$

$$\frac{2RT}{M} = 2(77.3)(525) = 81165 \text{ ft}\cdot\text{lb}_f/\text{lb}$$

$$P_2 = (17)(144) = 2448 \text{ lb}_f/\text{ft}^2$$

Substituting in equation (1)

$$\frac{P_1^2 - (2448)^2}{81165} = 725.4$$

$$P_1 = 8054 \text{ lb}_f/\text{ft}^2 = 55.9 \text{ psia}$$

Enough information is now available to verify that the term neglected in equation is indeed small relative to the other terms.

$$\frac{G^2}{g_c} \ln \frac{V_2}{V_1} = \frac{G^2}{g_c} \ln \frac{P_1}{P_2} = \frac{(7.75)^2}{32.2} \ln \left(\frac{8054}{2448}\right)$$

$$= 2.2$$

The average pressure in the pipeline is:

$$P_{avg} = \frac{P_1 + P_2}{2} = \frac{8054 + 2448}{2} = 5251 \text{ lb}_f/\text{ft}^2$$

The mean density of the gas is:

$$\rho = \frac{(M)(P_{avg})}{RT} = \frac{(20)(5251)}{(1545.3)(525)} = 0.1294 \text{ lb/ft}^3$$

The average volumetric flow rate is:

$$q = \frac{(500 \text{ lb/min})}{(60 \text{ sec/min})(0.1294 \text{ lb/ft}^3)} = 64.40 \text{ ft}^3/\text{sec}$$

The energy expended is equal to

$$(P_1 - P_2)q = (8054 - 2448)64.40$$

$$= 361026 \text{ ft}\cdot\text{lb}_f/\text{sec}$$

$$= 656 \text{ hp}$$

• PROBLEM 7-18

An ideal gas is flowing through a pipe. Refer to Figure 1. The initial pressure is P_1 = 255 psia and the initial density is 1.17 lb/ft^3. The final pressure is P_2 = 32 psia and the final temperature is T_2 = 270^{0}F. The gas has a molecular weight of 40.0 and its ratio of specific heats is k = 1.66.

Determine:

(I) the temperature at the pipe entrance, (T_1),

(II) the density at the end of the pipe, (ρ_2),

(III) the enthalpy change through the pipe, and

(IV) the entropy change through the pipe.

Figure (1)

Solution: Use the given molecular weight to calculate the ideal gas constant, (R). The specific heat, (C_p), can be obtained from equation (1). The ideal gas law now allows the initial temperature, (T_1), and the final density, (ρ_2), to be determined. The enthalpy and entropy changes are given by equations (2) and (3) respectively.

This problem will be solved by using the British system of units. Converting the given values:

$$P_1 = (255)(144) = 36720 \text{ lb}_f/\text{ft}^2$$

$$\rho_1 = \frac{1.17}{32.2} = 0.0363 \text{ slug/ft}^3$$

$$P_2 = (32)(144) = 4608 \text{ lb}_f/\text{ft}^2$$

$$T_2 = 270 + 460 = 730^\circ\text{R}$$

The ideal gas constant is:

$$R = \frac{49720}{40.0} = 1243 \text{ ft}^2/\text{sec}^2\cdot{}^\circ\text{R}$$

The heat capacity is given by:

$$C_p = \frac{kR}{k-1} \tag{1}$$

Substituting:

$$C_p = \frac{1.66(1243)}{1.66-1} = 3126 \text{ ft}^2/\text{sec}^2\cdot{}^\circ\text{R}$$

The ideal gas law is now employed to calculate the initial temperature and final density.

$$T_1 = \frac{P_1}{R\rho_1} = \frac{36720}{(1243)(0.0363)} = 814^\circ\text{R}$$

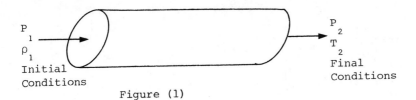

$$\rho_2 = \frac{P_2}{RT_2} = \frac{4608}{(1243)(730)} = 0.0051 \text{ slug/ft}^3$$

Equation (2) gives the enthalpy change, Δh:

$$\Delta h = C_p(T_2 - T_1) \tag{2}$$

Substituting:

$$\Delta h = 3126(730-814) = -263{,}000 \text{ ft}\cdot\text{lb}_f/\text{slug}$$

The entropy change is calculated from:

$$\Delta S = C_p \ln \frac{T_2}{T_1} - R \ln \frac{P_2}{P_1} \tag{3}$$

$$\Delta S = 3126 \ln\left(\frac{730}{814}\right) - 1243 \ln\left(\frac{4608}{36720}\right)$$

$$= 2239 \text{ ft}^2/\text{ Sec}^2\cdot\text{R}$$

• PROBLEM 7-19

A pipeline with a 20 in. diameter is to transport natural gas. The gas is at a constant temperature of 75^0F. A pressure drop of 35 psi is desired. If the initial pressure is P_1 = 60 psi and the mass flow rate of gas is 55000 lb/hr, determine the length of pipe required. The following data is given:

R = ideal gas constant = 96.3 $\text{ft}\cdot\text{lb}_f/\text{lb}\cdot\text{R}$

$k = C_p/C_v$ = ratio of heat capacities = 1.31

μ = viscosity of the gas = 2.34×10^{-7} $\text{lb}_f\cdot\text{sec/ft}^2$

ε = roughness of pipe = 0.00006 ft.

Solution: The subscript 1 will refer to the pipe entrance conditions while 2 will refer to the exit conditions. The Mach number and the Reynolds number can be obtained from equations (1) and (2), respectively. The friction factor, (f), is determined from Figure 1.

Substitution in equation (3) allows the length of pipe, ΔL, to be calculated.

The density at the entrance of the pipeline, ρ_1, can be determined using the ideal gas law:

$$\rho_1 = \frac{P_1}{RT} = \frac{(60)(144)}{(96.3)(535)} = 0.168 \text{ lb/ft}^3$$

The average velocity of the flow is given by:

$$V_1 = \frac{4\dot{m}}{\pi \rho d^2}$$

where $\dot{m}$ is the mass flow rate and d is the diameter of the pipeline. Substituting:

$$V_1 = \frac{4(55000/3600)}{\pi(0.168)(1.7)^2} = 40.1 \text{ ft/sec}$$

The Mach number, (Ma_1) is given by:

$$Ma_1 = \frac{V_1}{(kRg_cT)^{\frac{1}{2}}} \quad (1)$$

where g_c is a constant equal to 32.2 lb ft/$lb_f \cdot sec^2$

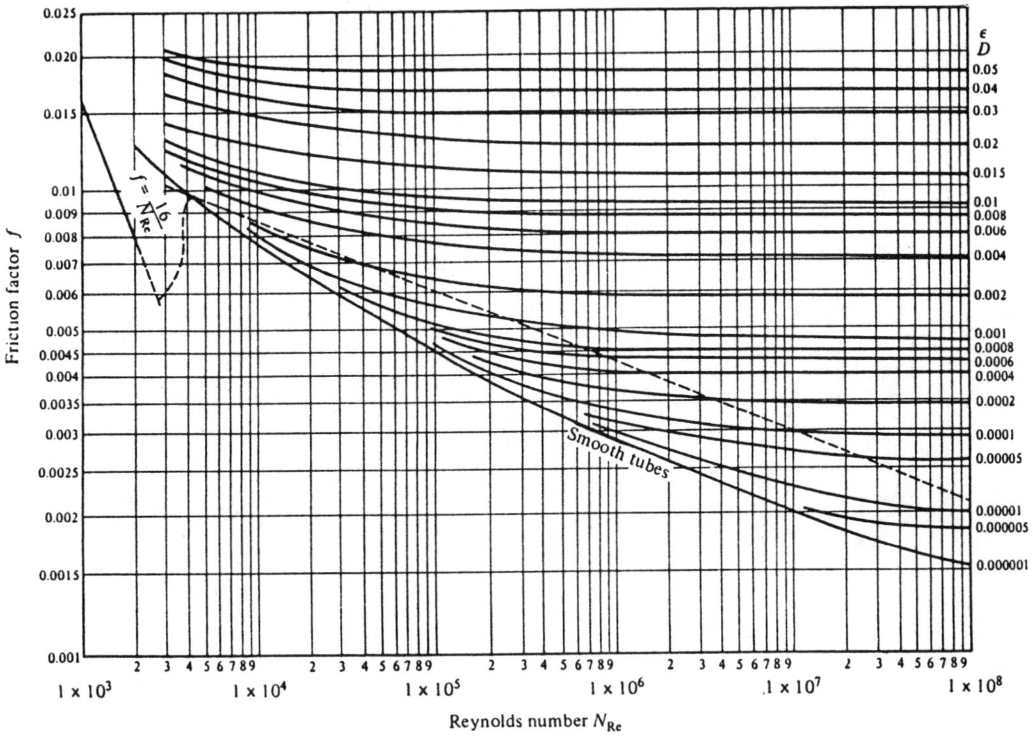

Figure (1)

Substituting in equation (1):

$$Ma_1 = \frac{40.1}{[(1.31)(96.3)(32.2)(535)]^{\frac{1}{2}}}$$

$$= 0.0272$$

The Reynolds number can be obtained from the following equation:

$$Re = \frac{\rho V_1 d}{\mu g_c} \quad (2)$$

Substitution yields:

$$Re = \frac{(0.168)(40.1)(1.7)}{(2.34 \times 10^{-7})(32.2)} = 1.52 \times 10^6$$

Using the Reynolds number and the value $\varepsilon/d = 0.000036$, Figure 1 yields a friction factor of $f = 0.003$.

Equation (3) gives the required pipe length.

$$\frac{1}{kMa_1^2}\left[1 - \left(\frac{P_2}{P_1}\right)^2\right] + \ln\left(\frac{P_2}{P_1}\right)^2 = \frac{f}{d}\Delta L \qquad (3)$$

Substituting:

$$\frac{1}{(1.31)(0.0272)^2}\left[1 - \left(\frac{25}{60}\right)^2\right] + \ln\left(\frac{25}{60}\right)^2 = \frac{0.003\Delta L}{1.7}$$

$$\Delta L = 4.82 \times 10^5 \text{ ft.}$$

CHAPTER 8

ENERGY BALANCE

PUMPS, TURBOMACHINES, BOILERS AND COOLING WATER PLANTS

• PROBLEM 8-1

Oil is to be pumped at a rate of 1) 10 lb/sec, 2) 50 lb/sec through a horizontal pipe of 4 in. dia and 5280 ft length. Calculate the drop in pressure and the theoretical horse-power developed, if the oil density is 59.3 lb/ft^3 and the viscosity is 50 cp. For the case of turbulent flow, assume the Darcy friction factor to be 10 per cent higher than calculated for a smooth pipe.

Solution: (1) For $\mathring{m}$ = 10 lb/sec, to determine the type of flow.

Velocity,

$$v = \frac{\mathring{m}}{\rho A}$$

$$= \frac{10}{59.3 \times \frac{\pi}{4} \times \left(\frac{4}{12}\right)^2}$$

$$= 1.932 \text{ ft/s}$$

Reynolds number,

$$Re = \frac{\rho v D}{\mu}$$

$$= \frac{59.3 \times 1.932 \times \frac{4}{12}}{50 \times 0.000672}$$

$$= 1136.6$$

Since Re is less than 2000, the flow is laminar.

Therefore, the friction factor is given by

$$f = \frac{16}{Re} = \frac{16}{1136.6}$$

The pressure drop is given by

$$\Delta p = \gamma h_f$$

$$= \gamma\ 4f \frac{L}{D} \frac{v^2}{2g}$$

$$= 59.3 \times 4 \times \frac{16}{1136.6} \times \frac{5280}{4/12} \frac{1.932^2}{64.4}$$

$$= 3065.8 \text{ psf}$$

$$= 21.3 \text{ psi}$$

The theoretical horse power is,

$$= \frac{\gamma Q h_f}{550}$$

$$= \frac{\mathring{m}\ h_f}{550} \quad \text{where } h_f = 51.7 \text{ ft.}$$

$$= \frac{(10)(51.7)}{550}$$

$$= 0.95 \text{ hp}$$

(2) For $\mathring{m} = 50$ lb/sec

$$v = 5(1.932)$$

$$= 9.660$$

$$Re = 5(1136.6)$$

$$= 5683$$

Since Re is greater than 3000, the flow is turbulent.

Therefore, the friction factor

$$f = (1.1) \text{ Darcy friction factor (given)}$$

$$= \frac{(1.1)0.079}{Re^{\frac{1}{4}}}$$

$$= \frac{(1.1)(0.079)}{(5683)^{0.25}}$$

or

$$f = 0.01$$

Now,
$$\Delta p = 59.3 \times 4 \times 0.01 \times \frac{5280}{4/12} \times \frac{9.66^2}{64.4}$$

$$= 54,443 \text{ psf}$$

$$= \frac{54,443}{144}$$

$$= 378.1 \text{ psi}$$

The theoretical power required is,

$$= \frac{(50)(918.3)}{550} \qquad (h_f = 918.3 \text{ ft})$$

$$= 83.5 \text{ hp}$$

• PROBLEM 8-2

> A pump at 50% efficiency is employed to pump a fluid, (spgr = 1.2, viscosity = 2.4cp) with a velocity of 6fps, from one storage tank to another through a pipe line. Both tanks are open to atmosphere. The length and diameter of the pipe are 160 ft. and 2.067 in., respectively. If the roughness of the pipe is 0.0018 in., determine the power required to run the pump.

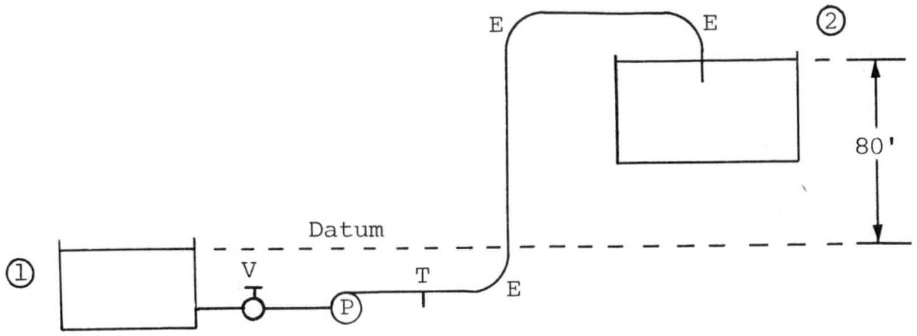

E = 90° std. elbow
T = Tee piece
V = Fully opened globe valves

Solution: Applying Bernoulli's equation between (1) and (2),

$$0 + 0 + Z_1 + W = 0 + 0 + Z_2 + H_f$$

or

$$W = (Z_2 - Z_1) + h_f$$

or

$$W = 80 + h_f \tag{1}$$

where,

$$H_f = \text{Total head loss}$$

$$= h_f + h_{entry} + h_{exit} \tag{2}$$

The entry and exit losses of the piping system are given by,

$$= 0.5 \frac{v^2}{2g} + \frac{v^2}{2g}$$

or

$$h_{entry} + h_{exit} = 1.5 \frac{v^2}{2g}$$

The total frictional loss h_f is given by

$$h_f = f \frac{L}{D} \frac{v^2}{2g}$$

where

f = Moody friction factor, from the Moody diagram

= 0.024

L = pipe length + equivalent length of fittings[from any Std. texts for fluids]

$$= 160 + \left[\underset{\text{(tee)}}{20} + \underset{\text{(Globe valve)}}{340} + \underset{\text{[Elbow]}}{3\times30} \right] \times \left(\frac{2.067}{12} \right)$$

= 237.5 ft

Thus,

$$h_f = (0.024)\left(\frac{237.5}{2.067/12}\right)\left(\frac{v^2}{2g}\right)$$

$$= 33.1 \frac{v^2}{2g}$$

Substituting in (2),

$$H_f = (33.1 + 1.5) \frac{v^2}{2g}$$

$$= 34.6\left(\frac{6^2}{2\times32.2}\right)$$

= 19.34 ft.

Thus,

$$W = 80 + H_f$$

= 80 + 19.34

= 99.4 ft.

= 99.4 ft. (lbf/lb-wt)

$$= 99.4 \text{ ft}\left(\frac{\text{lb}_f}{\text{lbm}}\right)$$

Mass flow rate $= (\gamma A v)$

$$= 62.4 \times 1.2 \times \frac{\pi}{4} \times \left(\frac{2.067}{12}\right)^2 \times 6$$

$$= 10.47 \text{ lbm/sec}$$

$$\text{Power} = \frac{w\mathring{m}}{\eta(550)}$$

$$= \frac{99.34(10.47)}{(550)(0.5)}$$

$$= 3.78 \text{ hp}$$

• PROBLEM 8-3

99 percent sulfuric acid at 70 °F is to be pumped from a tank at atmospheric pressure to a tank 10 ft. higher at 10 psig. The pumping is done through a 1100 ft. 3 in. schedule 40 steel pipe at the rate of 20 gal/min. What is the pressure developed by the pump? Determine the power required by the pump, if the efficiency is 75 percent.

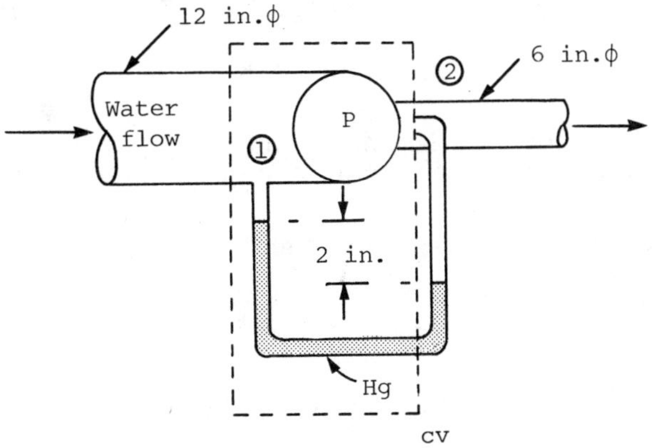

Solution: To determine if equation (1) is applicable, the bulk velocity and the Reynolds number must be calculated.

Friction loss is given by:

$$l_f = \frac{32\mu L U_b}{\rho g_c D^2} \tag{1}$$

For a 3 in., schedule 40 pipe, the cross-sectional area is 0.0513 ft² and the inside diameter is 3.068 in. The bulk velocity is given by:

$$U_b = \frac{W}{A}$$

$$= \frac{20}{60 \times 7.48 \times 0.0513}$$

$$= 0.869 \text{ ft/sec}$$

For 99 percent sulfuric acid,

specific gravity = 1.8342 and

viscosity = μ = 0.0175 lb/ft-sec

The Reynolds number is given by:

$$Re = \frac{\rho U_b D}{\mu} \tag{2}$$

$$Re = \frac{1.8342 \times 62.4 \times 0.869 \times (3.068/12)}{0.0175}$$

$$= 1453$$

This indicates that the flow is laminar, for which equation (1) is applicable.

From equation (1):

$$l_f = \frac{(32)(0.0175)(1100)(0.869)}{(1.8342)(62.4)(32.2)(3.068/12)^2}$$

$$= 2.22 \text{ ft-lb}_f/\text{lb}$$

Since the flow is laminar, the kinetic energy and the expansion and contraction losses can be neglected.

The mechanical energy balance between the tanks gives:

$$\frac{g}{g_c}\Delta z + \frac{\Delta P}{\rho} + l_f + \eta_p W_s = 0 \tag{3}$$

where η_p is the efficiency of the pump.

Substituting known values in equation (3) yields:

$$\frac{32.2}{32.2} \times 10 + \frac{10}{1.8342 \times 62.4} + 2.22 + 0.75\ W_s = 0$$

Therefore,

$$W_s = -16.4 \text{ ft-lb}_f/\text{lb}$$

The required horse power is given by:

$$\text{Power} = \frac{W_s w}{550}$$

where $\quad w$ = flow rate

$$= 20\ \frac{gal}{min}\left(\frac{1\ ft^3}{7.48\ gal}\right)\left(\frac{62.4\times 1.8342\ lb}{ft^3}\right)\left(\frac{1\ min}{60 sec}\right)$$

$$= 5.1\ lb/sec$$

Then,

$$Power = \frac{16.4 \times 5.1}{550}$$

$$= 0.152\ hp$$

The pressure developed by the pump is given by an energy balance around the pump:

$$\frac{\Delta p}{\rho} + \eta_p W_s = 0$$

Then,

$$\Delta p = -\rho\eta_p W_s$$

Substituting the known values gives:

$$\Delta p = -\frac{(1.8342)(62.4)(0.75)(-16.4)}{144}$$

$$= 9.78\ psi.$$

• PROBLEM 8-4

> If the horse power required to pump water through a pipe line is 3HP, find the mass flow rate assuming the flow to be steady and isothermal. Also assume that there is no friction loss in the pipe line.

Solution:

Applying the energy balance,

$$\dot{Q} - \dot{W}_s = \dot{m}\left[\Delta e_{cv} + \Delta e_{cs}\right] \tag{1}$$

where $\quad \Delta e_{cv} = 0$ for steady flow

$$\Delta e_{cs} = \iint_{cs} \left(e + \frac{p}{\rho}\right)$$

$$= \frac{p_2 - p_1}{\rho} + \frac{v_2^2 - v_1^2}{2} + g(y_2 - y_1)$$

for steady isothermal flow.

$$= \frac{p_{o2} - p_1}{\rho} - \frac{v_1^2}{2}$$

where, p_{o2} is the stagnation pressure measured at section (2) as the manometer opening is normal to the flowing fluid stream and p_1 is the static pressure sensed at section (1) because the manometer opening is parallel to the flow direction.

$$\dot{Q} = 0 \quad \text{[no heat transfer across the control volume]}$$

$$\dot{W}_s = 3HP$$
$$= 3(550)$$
$$= 1650 \text{ ft lb}_f/\text{s}$$

$$p_{o2} - p_1 = 2\left[\rho_{Hg} - \rho_{H_2O}\right]$$

$$= \frac{2}{13.6}[13.6 - 1.0] \text{ in. of Hg}$$

$$\dot{m} = \rho AV$$
$$= 62.4 \times \frac{\pi}{4}\left(\frac{12}{12}\right)^2 \times V_1$$
$$= 49V_1$$

Substituting in (1),

$$0 - 1650 = 49V_1\left[0 + \left(\frac{2(12.6)}{13.6 \times 62.4} \times 0.4913 \text{ lb/in}^2 \text{in of Hg} \times 144\right) - \frac{V_1^2}{64.4}\right]$$

Solving the cubic equation for V_1,

$$V_1 = 16.65 \text{ fps}$$

Thus,

$$\dot{m} = \rho AV = 62.4 \times \frac{\pi}{4} \times 16.65$$
$$= 816 \text{ lbm/s}$$

• PROBLEM 8-5

Water is pumped from a large tank into another through a 600 ft. long and 6 in. diameter smooth concrete pipe by means of a 40 hp centrifugal pump having an efficiency of 80%. Calculate the discharge in cfs. Take

$$\mu = 23.83(10^{-6})\text{slug/ft.sec.}$$

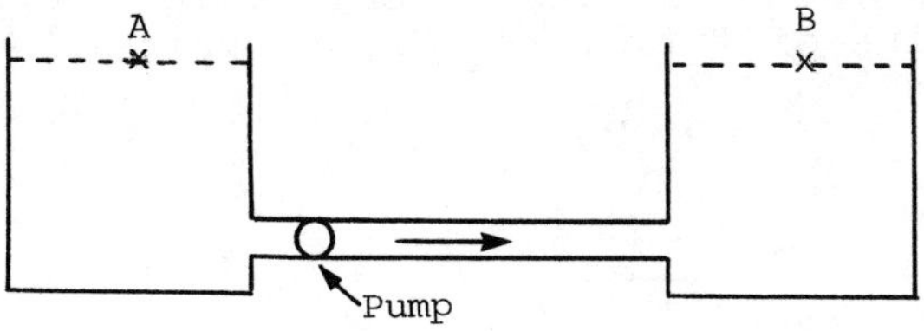

Solution:

Applying Bernoulli's equation,

$$\frac{p_A}{\rho} + \frac{V_A^2}{2} + gz_A + h_a = \frac{p_B}{\rho} + \frac{V_B^2}{2} + gz_B + h_L$$

or

$$0 + 0 + 0 + h_a = 0 + 0 + 0 + h_L$$

or

$$h_a = h_L \qquad (1)$$

where

$$h_a = \text{pump work head}$$

from

$$hp = \frac{\nu q h_a}{\eta \times 550}$$

or

$$h_a = \frac{hp \times \eta \times 550}{\nu AV}$$

$$= \frac{40 \times 0.8 \times 550}{62.4 \times V \times \frac{\pi}{4}\left(\frac{6}{12}\right)^2}$$

$$= \frac{1437}{V}$$

and

$$h_f = \frac{fLV^2}{2gD}$$

$$= \frac{f(600)V^2}{2(32.2)\left(\frac{6}{12}\right)}$$

$$= 18.63 \text{ f } V^2$$

where f = friction factor.

Substituting in (1),

$$\frac{1437}{V} = 18.63 \text{ f } V^2$$

or

$$V^3 = \frac{1437}{18.63f}$$

or

$$V^3 = \frac{77.134}{f} \qquad (2)$$

we have one equation and two unknowns, hence the following method is adopted for finding f.

Assume a value of f, then calculate V and subsequently check the value of f from the Moody chart.

Trial 1 $\quad f = 0.020$

then

$$V^3 = \frac{77.134}{0.020}$$

or

$$V = 15.7 \text{ f/sec.}$$

To check "f", calculate the Reynolds number,

$$Re = \frac{\rho VD}{\mu} = \frac{1.94\left(\frac{6}{12}\right)15.7}{23.83 \times 10^{-6}}$$

$$= 639{,}000$$

For concrete pipe,

$$k/d = \frac{0.012}{6} = 0.002$$

Therefore, from Moody charts,

$$f = 0.024$$

$$\neq f_{assumed}$$

Trial 2 $\quad$ Take $\quad f = 0.024$

$$V^3 = \frac{77.134}{0.024}$$

$$V = 14.3 \text{ fps}$$

Again check for assumed f which, in this case, is equal to the chart value.

Thus,

$$Q = AV = \frac{\pi}{4}\left(\frac{6}{12}\right)^2 (14.3)$$

$$= 2.81 \text{ cfs}$$

• PROBLEM 8-6

Water is steadily pumped between two open reservoirs. The difference in elevation of the two reservoir surfaces is 100 ft. All the piping is 2 in. diameter steel, and its length is 400 ft. If the volume flow rate is 0.2 ft^3/s find the horsepower required to run the pump.

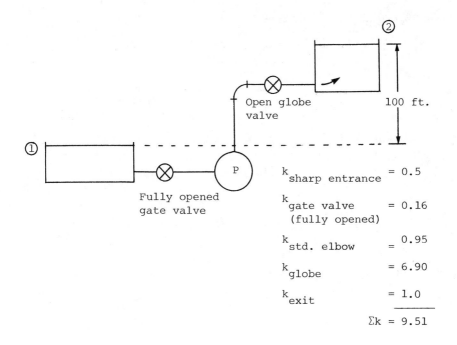

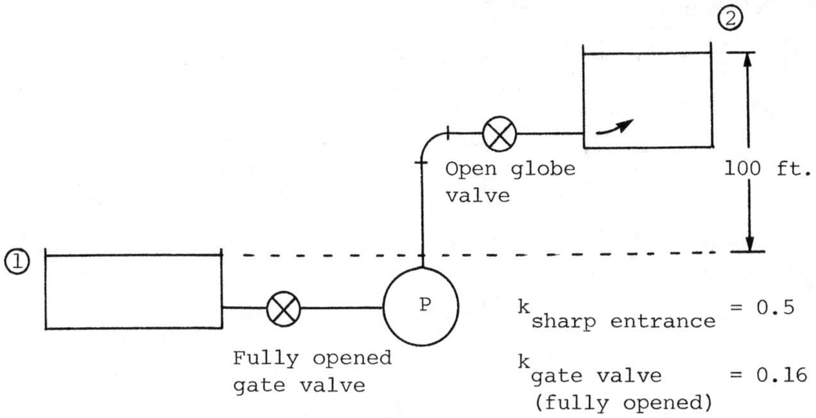

$k_{\text{sharp entrance}} = 0.5$

$k_{\text{gate valve (fully opened)}} = 0.16$

$k_{\text{std. elbow}} = 0.95$

$k_{\text{globe}} = 6.90$

$k_{\text{exit}} = 1.0$

$\Sigma k = 9.51$

Solution: For commercial steel of 2in. diameter pipe, the roughness ratio

$$\frac{\varepsilon}{d} = 0.001.$$

Reynolds number,

$$\begin{aligned} Re &= \frac{Vd}{\nu} \\ &= \frac{0.2}{\frac{\pi}{4}\left(\frac{2}{12}\right)^2} \times \frac{2}{12} \times \frac{1}{0.000011} \\ &= 139{,}000 \end{aligned}$$

From Moody diagram

$$f = 0.0216$$

Head loss through the pipe,

$$\begin{aligned} (h_f)_p = \frac{fLV^2}{2gD} &= \frac{0.0216(400) \times \left(\frac{0.2}{\pi/4(2/12)^2}\right)^2}{(2/12) \times 2 \times 32.2} \\ &= 67.69 \text{ ft.} \end{aligned}$$

Minor losses due to valves, elbows, etc.

$$\begin{aligned} (h_f)_m &= \Sigma k \frac{v^2}{2g} \\ &= (0.5+0.16+0.95+6.9+1.0)\frac{1}{2(32.2)} \times 9.17^2 \\ &= 12.42 \text{ ft.} \end{aligned}$$

Total head loss is

$$(h_f)_T = (h_f)_p + (h_f)_m$$
$$= 67.69 + 12.42$$
$$= 80 \text{ ft.}$$

Applying the Beronulli equation between (1) and (2)

$$\frac{p_1}{\gamma} + \frac{V_1^2}{2g} + Z_1 + h_p = \frac{p_2}{\gamma} + \frac{V_2^2}{2g} + Z_2 + (h_f)_T$$

Since,

$$p_1 = p_2$$

$$V_1 \simeq V_2 \approx 0$$

the Bernoulli equation reduces to

$$h_p = Z_2 - Z_1 + (h_f)_T$$
$$= 100 + 80$$
$$= 180 \text{ ft. pump head.}$$

Horsepower required,

$$HP = \frac{\gamma Q h_p}{550}$$

$$= \frac{62.4 \times 0.2 \times 180}{550} = 4.1 \text{ HP}$$

• PROBLEM 8-7

Determine the work rate of a turbomachine using the data given in figure (1). Water is flowing through the turbomachine at a rate of 20 ft^3/sec. Determine the type of turbomachine (pump or turbine).

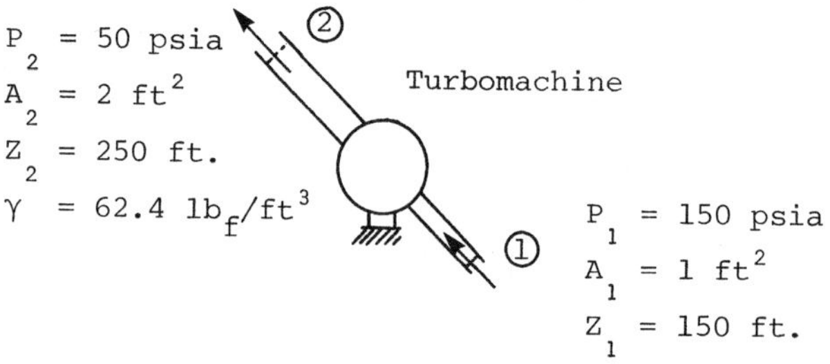

INCOMPRESSIBLE FLOW THROUGH A TURBOMACHINE.

Figure 1.

Solution: Assume the flow from station 1 to station 2 is one-dimensional.

Applying the energy equation for the system:

$$\frac{\delta Q}{\delta t} - \frac{\delta W_{shaft}}{\delta t} = \dot{m}\left[(h_2-h_1) + \frac{V_2^2-V_1^2}{2} + g(z_2-z_1)\right] \qquad (1)$$

Assume the process is adiabatic. Therefore

$$\frac{\delta Q}{\delta t} = 0.$$

Then equation (1) reduces to:

$$\frac{\delta W_{shaft}}{\delta t} = \gamma AV\left[\frac{P_1-P_2}{\gamma} + \frac{V_1^2-V_2^2}{2g} + (z_1-z_2)\right] \qquad (2)$$

There is no change in the internal energy of water. Then

$$VA = 20 \text{ ft}^3/\text{sec}$$

$$V_1 = \frac{20}{A_1} = \frac{20}{1} = 20 \text{ ft/sec}$$

$$V_2 = \frac{20}{A_2} = \frac{20}{2} = 10 \text{ ft/sec}$$

Substituting all the known values in equation (2) yields

$$\frac{\delta W_{shaft}}{\delta t} = 20 \times 62.4\left[\frac{(150-50)\times 144}{62.4} + \frac{(20)^2-(10)^2}{2\times 32.2} + (150-250)\right]$$

$$= 169013.66 \ \frac{\text{ft-lb}_f}{\text{sec}}$$

$$\frac{\delta W_{shaft}}{\delta t} = 169013.66 \times \frac{1}{550}$$

$$= 307.3 \text{ hp.}$$

The work produced by the fluid is positive. Therefore, the turbomachine is a turbine.

• PROBLEM 8-8

Water flows into a turbine which is 90 percent efficient at a rate of 2000 lb/sec from an elevated large tank through a pipe line. The shaft output of the turbine is 1000 hp. The pressure in the pipe at a point 10 ft. below the turbine is 18 psia, and at a point 300 ft. above the turbine is 30 psia. If the entire process is adiabatic, calculate (1) the frictional head loss in the pipe and (2) the temperature rise of the water in flowing through the pipe line and the turbine. Assume constant pipe diameter.

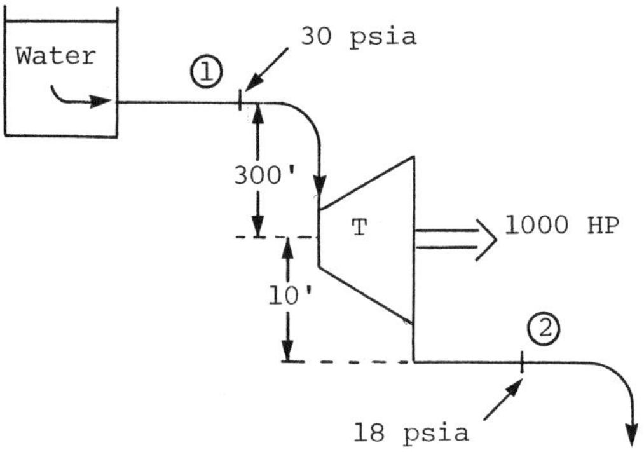

Solution:

Applying the steady state energy equation between (1) and (2), with $V_1 \approx V_2$,

$$\frac{p_1}{\gamma} + Z_1 - h_p = \frac{p_2}{\gamma} + Z_2 + h_f$$

or

$$h_f = \frac{p_1 - p_2}{\gamma} + Z_1 - Z_2 - h_p$$

$$= \frac{(30-18)(144)}{62.4} + \left[300-(-10)\right] - \frac{(1000)(550)}{(2000)(0.9)}$$

$$= 27.7 + 310 - 306$$

or $$h_f = 31.7 \text{ ft. of water.}$$

Writing the over-all energy balance,

$$\Delta Z + \Delta H = -W_s$$

where ΔH = enthalpy change.

$$-310 + \Delta H = -275$$

or $$\Delta H = 35$$

or $$c_p \Delta t + \frac{\Delta p}{\rho} = 35$$

or $$c_p(\Delta t) - 27.7 = 35$$

or $$\Delta t = \frac{35 + 27.7}{(778)(1.0)}$$

or $$\Delta t = 0.0806^0 F.$$

The cooling plant of a big apartment complex is situated on a lake, which is fed by a low stream flow of 7 cfs at 90°F and has only one outflow of 7 cfs near the discharge channel of the cooling plant. The building heat exchanger requires a volumetric flow rate of 14 cfs and increases the temperature of the water by 15°F. Determine the temperature of the recirculated cooling water of the lake if the above conditions exist for a prolonged period. Neglect the heat losses to the ambient air and lake bottom.

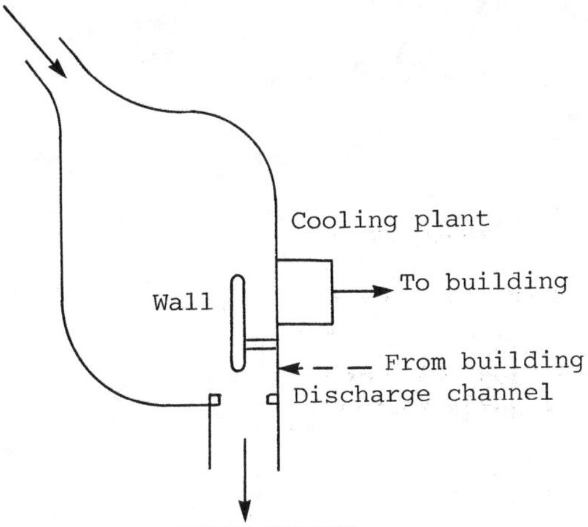

COOLING-WATER SYSTEM

Figure 1.

Solution: The control volume of the system is shown in Fig. 2 with temperature T and volumetric flow rate Q.

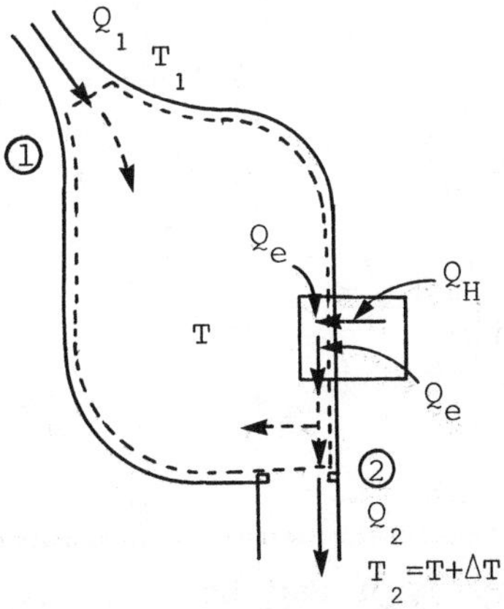

CONTROL VOLUME OF COOLING-WATER SYSTEM

Figure 2.

Applying the energy equation to the control volume in Fig. 2 gives

$$\frac{\delta Q_H}{\delta t} + U_1 P Q_1 = U_2 P Q_2 \qquad (1)$$

where U_1 and U_2 are the internal energies per unit mass at the entrance and exit of the lake respectively. As the pressure and density of the system are constant, the internal energy per unit mass is only a function of temperature. This implies that $U_2 - U_1 = C(T_2 - T_1)$, where C is the heat capacity of water.

Now equation (1) can be written:

$$\frac{\delta Q_H}{\delta t} = C(T_2 - T_1)PQ_1 \qquad (2)$$

since $Q_1 = Q_2$.

The heat gained by the water in the heat exchanger is given by

$$\frac{\delta Q_H}{\delta t} = C\Delta T P Q_e \qquad (3)$$

where Q_e is the volumetric flow rate of the heat exchanger.

Substituting equation (2) in equation (3) gives:

$$C(T_2 - T_1)PQ_1 = C\Delta T P Q_e$$

Solving for T_2

$$T_2 = T_1 + \frac{\Delta T Q_e}{Q_1}$$

Given $\Delta T = 15^0F$, $Q_e = 14$ cfs, $Q_1 = 7$ cfs, $T_1 = 90^0F$

Then,

$$T_2 = 90 + \frac{15 \times 14}{7}$$

$$= 120^0F.$$

As $T_2 = T + \Delta T$,

the lake temperature T is 105^0F.

• PROBLEM 8-10

Determine the heat required by a boiler under steady-state conditions to convert water entering through a 5 in. pipe at 6 psig, 70^0F and a bulk velocity of 4 ft/sec to steam at 650^0F and 350 psig.

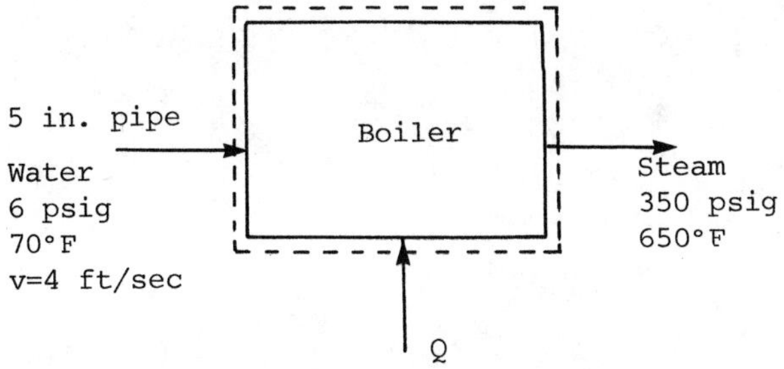

Solution: The normal velocity component exists only at the entrance and exit to the system, therefore the integral over the surface vanishes at all points over the surface, except at the entrance and exit. Given steady-state conditions, the derivative of the volume integral vanishes. There is no shaft work done in the system.

The energy equation to the system is now given by:

$$\int_{A_1} (h_1+\phi_1+k_1)\,\rho_1\,(v\cdot n)dA + \int_{A_2} (h_2+\phi_2+k_2)\rho_2(v\cdot n)dA = Q \quad (1)$$

where
- h - enthalpy per unit mass
- ϕ - potential energy per unit mass
- k - kinetic energy per unit mass
- ρ - density
- v - velocity
- A_1 - area at entrance
- A_2 - area at exit
- Q - heat required

There is no change in elevation and velocity, hence the potential energy and kinetic energy terms can be dropped from equation (1).

Then, $$\int_{A_1} h_1\rho_1(v\cdot n)dA + \int_{A_2} h_2\rho_2(v\cdot n)dA = Q$$

Assume h and ρ are constant across the entrance and exit.

Then, $$h_1\rho_1 \int_{A_1} (v\cdot n)dA + h_2\rho_2 \int_{A_2} (v\cdot n)dA = Q \quad (2)$$

The mass balance is given by

$$\rho_1 \int_{A_1} (v\cdot n)dA + \rho_2 \int_{A_2} (v\cdot n)dA = 0$$

Since

$$\int_{A_1} (v \cdot n)dA = -V_1 A_1$$

then,

$$-\rho_1 V_1 A_1 + \rho_2 \int_{A_2} (v \cdot n)dA = 0 \qquad (3)$$

and equation (2) becomes

$$-h_1 \rho_1 V_1 A_1 + h_2 \rho_2 \int_{A_2} (v \cdot n)dA = Q \qquad (4)$$

Given $V = 4$ ft/sec, $D_1 = 5$ in.

$$A_1 = \frac{\pi D_1^2}{4} = \frac{\pi}{4}\left(\frac{5}{12}\right)^2 = 0.1364 \text{ ft}^2.$$

From the tables of thermodynamic properties, for water at 70^0F, 6 psig, 20.7 psia.

$$h_1 = 38.04 \text{ Btu/lbm}, \quad \rho_1 = 62.27 \text{ lbm/ft}^3$$

for steam at 650^0F, 350 psig, 364.7 psia

$$h_2 = 1337.2 \text{ Btu/lbm}, \quad \rho_2 = 0.5776 \text{ lbm/ft}^3$$

Then,

$$\rho_1 V_1 A_1 = \rho_2 \int_{A_2} (v \cdot n)dA = 62.27 \times 4 \times 0.1364 = 33.97 \text{ lbm/sec}$$

Then substituting in equation (4)

$$Q = -(38.04) \times 33.97 + (1337.2) \times 33.97$$

$$= 44132.5 \text{ Btu/sec}$$

$$= 1.59 \times 10^8 \text{ Btu/hr}$$

• PROBLEM 8-11

The flow rate of water in a frictionless pipe is measured by using a convergent nozzle as shown in the figure. The pipe diameter is 4 in. and throat diameter is 2 in. The maximum manometer reading is 4.0 ft. and the specific gravity of mercury is 13.6. Find the maximum flow rate the manometer can measure.

Solution: Since points M and N of the U tube are at the same elevation and are joined by the same fluid, the pressure acting on these two points will be equal. Thus

$$p_M = p_N$$

or

$$p_1 + \gamma_w(h'+h) = p_2 + \gamma_w h' + \gamma_{Hg} h$$

or

$$p_1 - p_2 = \gamma_{Hg}h - \gamma_w h$$

$$= (\text{Sp.gr.})\gamma_w h - \gamma_w h$$

$$= \gamma_w h(13.6 - 1)$$

or

$$p_1 - p_2 = 12.6(\gamma_w h) \quad (1)$$

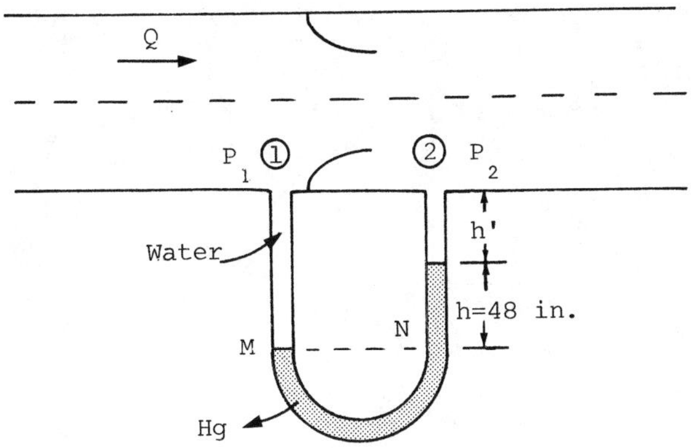

FLOW THROUGH THE PIPE

Applying Bernoulli's equation at 1 and 2

$$\frac{p_1 - p_2}{\gamma_w} = \frac{V_2^2 - V_1^2}{2g}$$

$$= \frac{1}{2g}\left[\frac{Q^2}{A_2^2} - \frac{Q^2}{A_1^2}\right]$$

$$= \frac{Q^2}{2g}\left[\frac{16}{\pi^2 d_2^4} - \frac{16}{\pi^2 d_1^4}\right]$$

or

$$\frac{p_1 - p_2}{\gamma_w} = \frac{8Q^2}{\pi^2 g}\left[\frac{1}{d_2^4} - \frac{1}{d_1^4}\right] \quad (2)$$

Comparing (1) and (2),

$$Q = \left[\frac{\pi^2 g \times 12.6h}{8\left(\frac{1}{d_2^4} - \frac{1}{d_1^4}\right)}\right]^{\frac{1}{2}}$$

Substituting the values of d_1, d_2 and h

$$Q = \left[\frac{\pi^2 g \times 12.6 \times 4}{8\left(\frac{1}{0.16^4} - \frac{1}{0.33^4}\right)}\right]^{\frac{1}{2}}$$

$$= 1.17 \text{ ft}^3/\text{sec}$$

• PROBLEM 8-12

A siphon tube is used to discharge a liquid [$\rho = 1,571$ lbm/ft^3; $\mu = 40\times(10^{-6})$slugs/ft-sec] to a lower tank as shown in the figure. The steel pipe is 2in. diameter and 600 ft. long. It has an effective roughness coefficient of 0.0017. Calculate 1) the flow rate and 2) the height of the fluid below the liquid level in the upper tank that flows full in the pipe.

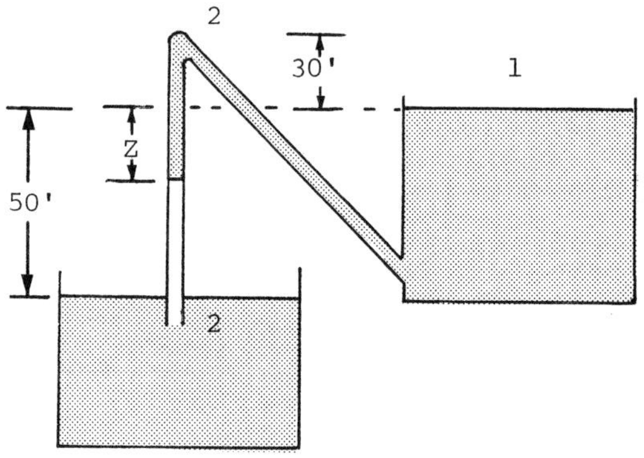

Solution:

The friction factor "f" must first be assumed since the velocity is not known. Applying the Bernoulli equation from point 1 to point 3, with f = 0.019

$$0 = \frac{V_3^2}{2g} + Z_3 + h_f$$

or

$$0 = \frac{V_3^2}{64.4} + \frac{0.019(600)}{1/6}\ \frac{V_2^2}{64.4}$$

or

$$V_3 = 6.63 \text{ fps} = V_2$$

Since f was assumed, it must be checked using

$$\frac{\varepsilon}{d} = \frac{0.0017}{2},$$

and the Reynolds number. From the Moody chart,

$$f = 0.024$$

Again calculating V,

$$V = 6.10 \text{ fps}$$

The new f is:

$$f = 0.0245,$$

which is satisfactory

The minimum allowable pressure head at 2, is equal to the sum of the minimum pressure head and the allowable vapor pressure head. This is given by

$$= \frac{-14.7(144)}{1.571(32.2)} + 0.40$$

or

$$p_3 = -41.4 \text{ ft.}$$

Now, applying the energy equation between (1) and (2),

$$0 = \frac{p_2}{\gamma} + \frac{V_2^2}{2g} + Z_2 + h_f$$

or

$$\frac{p_2}{\gamma} = -\left[30 + \frac{6.11^2}{64.4} + \frac{0.0245(600)6.11^2}{1/6(64.4)}\right]$$

or $\quad p_2 = -81.7$ ft., which is less than the minimum allowable pressure head.

Hence, reapplying the Bernoulli equation with

$$Z_2 = -41.4, \quad V_2 \text{ becomes:}$$

$$V_2 = 2.87 \text{ ft/sec} = V_3$$

Rechecking f,

$$Re = \frac{\rho V d}{\mu}$$

$$= 18,750$$

for which $\quad f = 0.028$

Using the above f,

$$V_2 = 2.69 \text{ ft/s}$$

Again for the above new V_2,

$$f = 0.028$$

Hence, $\quad q = AV$

$$= (2.69)\frac{\pi}{4}\left(\frac{2}{12}\right)^2$$

$$= 0.0587 \text{ cfs}$$

$$= 26.4 \text{ gpm}$$

(2) To find the height z, write the Bernoulli equation between (1) and up to z

$$0 = 0 + \frac{2.69^2}{64.4} - h + 0.028\,\frac{(550+h)}{1/6}\,\frac{2.69^2}{64.4}$$

and

$$h = 10.7 \text{ ft.}$$

CLOSED TANK, FIXED CONTROL VOLUME, MIXING OF TWO LIQUID STREAMS

• PROBLEM 8-13

In an open water reservoir the depth of the exit port from the water surface is h. Prove that the velocity of water coming out of the port is $\sqrt{2gh}$.

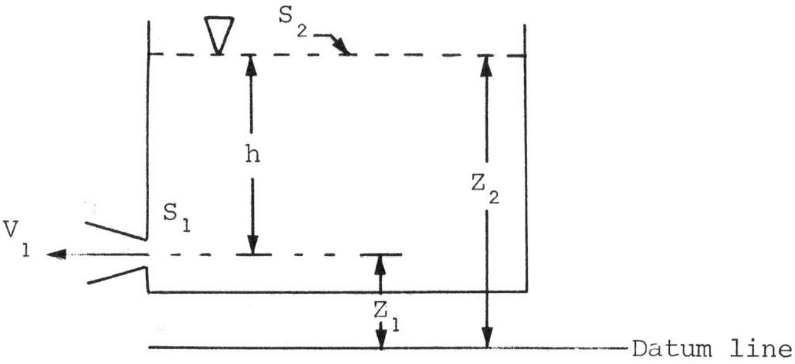

Solution: In this case the energy losses due to friction and the internal energy losses can be neglected.

The pressure of water coming out of the port or orifice is same as atmospheric pressure, because the orifice is exposed to atmospheric conditions. Also, the pressure at the water surface is atmospheric pressure. The Bernoulli's equation can be applied to the two sections S_1 and S_2

$$\frac{P_1}{\rho_1} + \frac{V_1^2}{2g} + Z_1 = \frac{P_2}{\rho_2} + \frac{V_2^2}{2g} + Z_2$$

where P = Pressure

V = Velocity

Z = Height from datum surface

ρ = Density of water

Subscripts 1 and 2 refer to the levels S_1 and S_2.

In this case $P_1 = P_2$ = Atmospheric pressure (P_{atm}). Assuming the rate of discharge as very small compared to the volume of the reservoir and the surface area at section S_2 as very large, the velocity at section S_2 can be considered as negligibly small ($V_2 \approx 0$).

It can be assumed that the density of the water remains unaffected, i.e., $\rho_1 = \rho_2 = \rho$, and $Z_2 - Z_1 = h$

Substituting the values into the equation yields

$$\frac{P_{atm}}{\rho} + \frac{V_1^2}{2g} + Z_1 = \frac{P_{atm}}{\rho} + \frac{(0)^2}{2g} + Z_2$$

Equation reduces to

$$\frac{V_1^2}{2g} = Z_2 - Z_1$$

or

$$\frac{V_1^2}{2g} = h$$

or

$$V_1^2 = 2gh$$

or

$$V_1 = \sqrt{2gh}$$

• PROBLEM 8-14

Determine the rate of change of energy in a system occupying a fixed control volume with three one-dimensional boundary sections, as shown in Fig. 1. Assume steady flow in the control volume. The flow properties are given as

Section	Type	A (ft^2)	V (ft/sec)	ρ (lbm/ft^3)	e (Btu/lbm)
1	Inlet	6.0	15.0	50	6
2	Inlet	9.0	24.0	50	2
3	Outlet	6.0	51.0	50	3

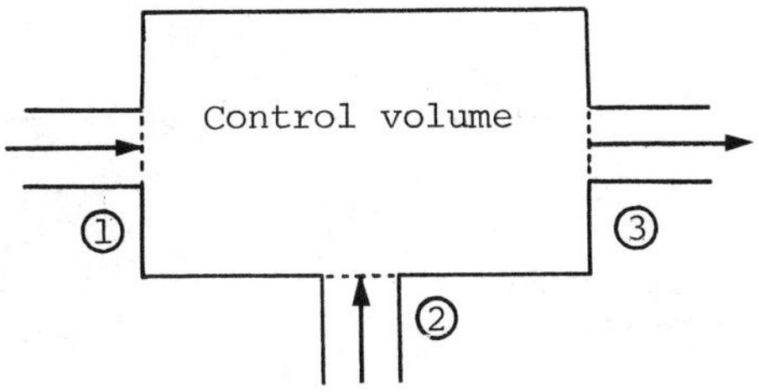

Solution: In this system the control volume is fixed, hence the rate of change of energy is given by

$$\left(\frac{dE}{dt}\right)_{system} = \int_V \frac{\partial}{\partial t}(e\rho)dV + \int_A e\rho(v \cdot n)dA \tag{1}$$

where the energy per unit mass dE/dm = e.

The control volume has steady flow, i.e., $(\partial(e\rho)/\partial t) = 0$. Therefore the volume integral in equation (1) vanishes.

$$\left(\frac{dE}{dt}\right)_{system} = \int_A e\rho(v \cdot n)dA \tag{2}$$

(In Fig. 1 there are two inlet and one outlet sections.)

The normal velocity component exists only at the boundary sections, hence the integral over the surface vanishes everywhere except over the boundary sections. Then,

$$\left(\frac{dE}{dt}\right)_{system} = -e_1\rho_1 A_1 V_1 - e_2\rho_2 A_2 V_2 + e_3\rho_3 A_3 V_3$$

Substituting the known values in the previous equation gives:

$$\left(\frac{dE}{dt}\right)_{system} = -(6)(50)(6)(15) - (2)(50)(9)(24) + (3)(50)(6)(51)$$

$$= -2700 \text{ Btu/sec}$$

This implies that the system is losing energy at the rate of -2700 Btu/sec. All the mass transfer across the boundary is accounted for, therefore by the first law of thermodynamics, it can be concluded that the system must emit heat through the control surface or the system has to do work on the environment through some device not shown in figure (1).

This problem dealt with energy, but examining the mass balance of the system for steady flow in the control volume gives the conservation of mass equation, which reduces to:

$$\left(\frac{dm}{dt}\right)_{system} = \int_A \rho(v\cdot n)dA$$

$$= -\rho_1 A_1 V_1 - \rho_2 A_2 V_2 + \rho_3 A_3 V_3$$

$$= -(50)(6)(15)-(50)(9)(24)+(50)(6)(51)$$

$$= 0 \text{ lbm/sec}$$

This implies that there is no change in the mass of the system, which clearly shows the conservation of mass by this system.

• PROBLEM 8-15

Calculate the viscosity of a fluid when it flows through a narrow tube at a rate of 0.15 ft^3/hr from an open container. Assume negligible minor losses. Take specific weight of the liquid as 58 lb_f/ft^3 and the diameter of the tube as 0.048 in.

Solution:

Area of the tube,

$$A = \frac{\pi}{4} d^2$$

$$= \frac{\pi}{4}\left(\frac{0.048}{12}\right)^2$$

$$= 1.257(10)^{-5}\text{ft}^2$$

velocity, $V = \frac{Q}{A}$

$$= \frac{0.15}{(1.257)(10)^{-5}(3600)}$$

$$= 3.32 \text{ ft/sec}$$

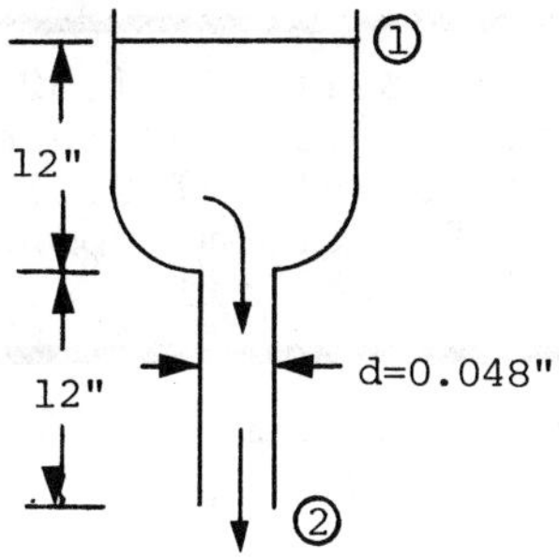

Writing the steady-flow energy equation between (1) and (2),

$$\frac{p_1}{\gamma} + \frac{V_1^2}{2g} + Z_1 = \frac{p_2}{\gamma} + \frac{V_2^2}{2g} + Z_2 + (h_f)_T$$

or
$$(h_f)_T = (Z_1 - Z_2) - \frac{V_2^2}{2g}$$

$$= (h_f)_p + (h_f)_m$$

or
$$(h_f)_T = \frac{24}{12} - \frac{(3.32)^2}{64.4}$$

$$= 1.83 \text{ ft.}$$

First let us assume the type of flow and then check if our assumption is justified. For laminar flow, the head loss is given by,

$$h_f = \frac{32\mu LV}{\rho g d^2}$$

where L is the tube length = 1 ft.

or
$$\mu = \frac{(h_f)\rho g d^2}{32LV}$$

$$= \frac{(1.83)(58)\left(\frac{0.048}{12}\right)^2}{(32)(1)(3.32)}$$

$$= 1.60 \times 10^{-5} \text{ slug/(ft.s)}$$

Determining the type of flow,

$$Re = \frac{\rho Vd}{\mu} = \frac{\frac{58}{32.2} \times 3.32 \times \frac{0.048}{12}}{1.60 \times 10^{-5}}$$

$$= 1500 < 2300$$

Therefore, the flow is laminar which checks with our assumption.

• PROBLEM 8-16

Water of kinematic viscosity $\nu = 1.02 \times 10^{-6} m^2/s$ flows by gravity from a tank (of height h) through a 30m long annulus (steel) pipe at a rate of $0.01 m^3/s$. If the pipe O.D. = 0.1m and its I.D. = 0.06m, compute the height "h" as shown. Neglect entrance effects.

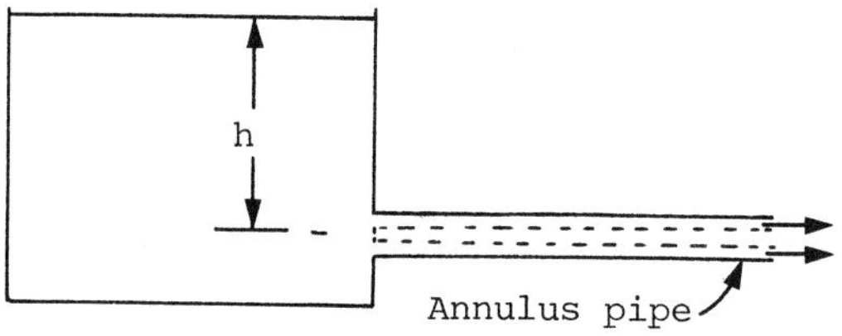

Solution:

Writing the steady-flow energy equation between the free surface of water in the tank and the pipe exit, with $p_1 = p_2 = p_a$ (atmospheric pressure), and $V_1 \approx 0$

$$Z_1 = \frac{V_2^2}{2g} + Z_2 + h_f$$

or

$$h_f = Z_1 - Z_2 - \frac{V^2}{2g}$$

or

$$h_f = h - \frac{V^2}{2g}$$

But V can be computed from

$$V = \frac{Q}{A} = \frac{0.01}{\pi[(0.05)^2-(0.03)^2]}$$

$$= 1.99 \text{ m/s}$$

Thus,

$$h_f = h - \frac{(1.99)^2}{2(9.81)}$$

or

$$h_f = h - 0.20184 \qquad (1)$$

Also,

$$h_f = \frac{fLV^2}{2gD_h} \qquad (2)$$

where D_h is the hydraulic diameter,

$$= 0.01 - 0.06$$

$$= 0.04\text{m}$$

By calculating the Reynolds number we can read the friction factor from the Moody chart for commerical pipe. Therefore,

$$Re = \frac{\rho V D_h}{\mu}$$

$$= \frac{V D_h}{\nu}$$

$$= \frac{(1.99)(0.04)}{1.02 \times 10^{-6}}$$

$$= 78{,}000$$

For commercial steel with diameter 0.04m, the roughness ratio is:

$$\varepsilon/d = 0.00115$$

Thus, $\quad f = 0.0232$

Inserting numerical values in (2) yields

$$h_f = \frac{(0.0232)(30)(1.99)^2}{(2)(9.81)(0.04)}$$

or $\quad h_f = 3.512\text{m}$

Comparing (1) and (2),

$$3.512 = h - 0.2018$$

or $\quad h = 3.71\text{m}$

Better accuracy can be obtained by calculating the exact diameter.

• PROBLEM 8-17

A reservoir discharges water through a galvanised pipe, which is 400 ft. long and 4 in. diameter, into another reservoir at a rate of 0.5 ft^3/sec. If both reservoirs are open to the atmosphere, calculate the difference in height between the water levels in the reservoirs. Assume one-dimensional flow.

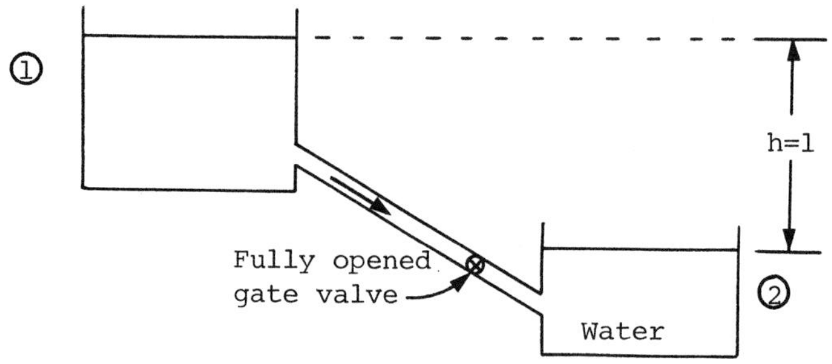

Solution:

The cross-sectional area of the pipe is:

$$A = \frac{\pi d^2}{4}$$

$$= \frac{\pi}{4}\left(\frac{4}{12}\right)^2$$

$$= 0.08727 \text{ ft}^2$$

The flow velocity is:

$$V = \frac{q}{A}$$

$$= \frac{0.5}{0.0873}$$

$$= 5.73 \text{ ft/sec}$$

The roughness ratio is:

$$\frac{\varepsilon}{d} = 0.0015 \quad \text{for galvanised iron pipes.}$$

The Reynolds number is given by,

$$Re = \frac{\rho V d}{\mu}$$

$$= \frac{62.4 \times 5.73 \times \frac{1}{3}}{2.74\times10^{-5}\times32.2} \; \frac{\text{lbf.ft}^{-3}\;\text{ft.sec}^{-1}\text{ft}}{\text{lbf.sec.ft}^{-2}\,\text{lbm.ft.lb}_f\text{.sec}^{-2}}$$

$$= 1.35 \times 10^5$$

From the Moody diagram, the friction factor is:

$$f = 0.0235$$

Now applying the energy equation between (1) and (2),

$$\frac{p_1}{\gamma} + \frac{V_1^2}{2g} + Z_1 = \frac{p_2}{\gamma} + \frac{V_2^2}{2g} + Z_2 + (h_f)_T$$

or $$Z_1 - Z_2 = H = (h_f)_T$$

or $$H = \frac{V^2}{2g}\left[\frac{fL}{d} + K_{gate}\right]$$

$$= \frac{(5.73)^2}{2 \times 32.2}\left[\frac{0.0235}{\frac{4}{12}} \times 400 + 1.7\right]$$

or $$H = 15.3 \text{ ft.}$$

• **PROBLEM 8-18**

A 300 ft. long 9 in. diameter steel pipe carries water from a 16 ft. diameter reservoir as shown. How long will it take for the water surface in the reservoir to drop from $h_1 = 9$ ft. to $h_2 = 1$ ft.?

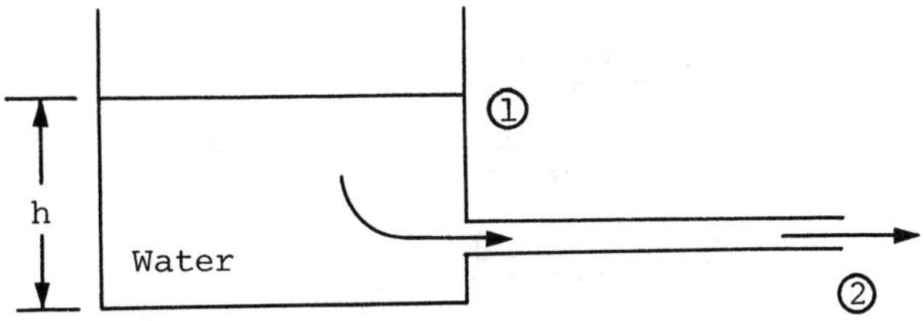

Solution:

Writing the energy equation between 1 and 2

$$\frac{p_1}{\rho} + \frac{V_1^2}{2} + gZ_1 = \frac{p_2}{\rho} + \frac{V_2^2}{2} + gZ_2 + gh_f$$

or $$\frac{V_2^2 - V_1^2}{2} + g(Z_2 - Z_1) + \frac{p_2 - p_1}{\rho} + gh_f = 0$$

Since,

$$p_1 = p_2 = p_{atm}$$

$$\frac{V_1}{V_2} = \frac{A_2}{A_1} = \left(\frac{3/4}{16}\right)^2 = 0.0022$$

$$(Z_2 - Z_1) = -h$$

$$h_f = \frac{fLV^2}{2gd}$$

Therefore $$\frac{V_2^2}{2} - hg + \frac{fLV^2}{2d} = 0$$

or $$V_2 = \sqrt{\frac{2hg}{\left(1 + \frac{fL}{d}\right)}}$$

or

$$V_2 = \sqrt{\frac{\sqrt{2(h)(32.2)}}{\left(1 + f\,\frac{300}{9/12}\right)}} = \frac{8\sqrt{h}}{\sqrt{1 + 400f}}\,.$$

During the time interval dt, let the height of water in the tank change by dh. Then the water discharged is:

$$\frac{\pi}{4}(16)^2(-dh)$$

$$= -64\pi(dh)$$

But this is also equal to:

$$A(\text{height})$$

$$= A(\text{velocity})(\text{time})$$

$$= A(U_2)dt$$

or

$$dt = \frac{-64\pi(dh)}{AU_2}$$

$$= \frac{-64\pi dh}{\frac{\pi}{4}\left(\frac{3}{4}\right)^2 \frac{8\sqrt{h}}{\sqrt{1+400f}}}$$

$$= \frac{-56.9\sqrt{1+400f}}{h^{\frac{1}{2}}}\,dh \text{ sec.}$$

Integrating,

$$t = -\int_9^1 56.9\sqrt{1+400f}\;h^{-\frac{1}{2}}\,dh$$

$$t = 228\sqrt{1+400f} \text{ sec.}$$

By knowing the friction factor from the Moody chart we can calculate the time taken.

Reading from the Moody chart,

$$f = 0.002$$

Thus,

$$t = 228\sqrt{1+400(0.002)}$$

$$= 305 \text{ sec.}$$

Note that some texts define h_f as,

$$= \frac{4fLV^2}{2gd}$$

In that case, $t = 620$ sec.

• PROBLEM 8-19

A closed tank contains a saturated liquid consisting of 60 mole percent water and 40 mole percent alcohol. The tank is heated and the liquid is vaporized until the temperature of the liquid in the tank achieves a final state of 180°F at a pressure of 1 atmosphere. Compute the amount of the original liquid vaporized. Also determine the amount of heat per pount mole required to vaporize the liquid.

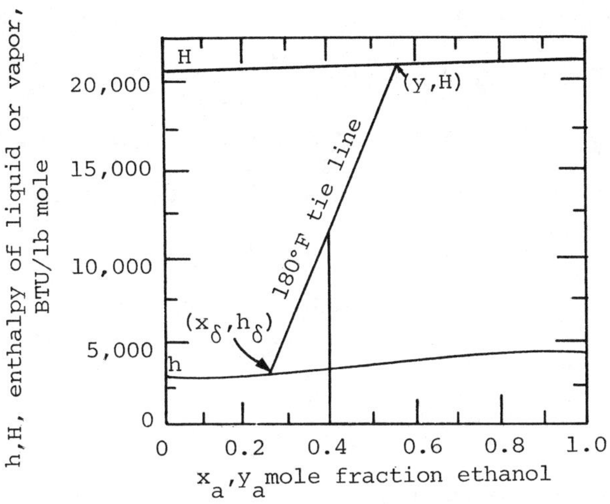

SATURATED LIQUID, VAPOR ENTHALPY CURVE AT 180 °F.

Figure 1.

Solution: From the given conditions it is clear that the system is in equilibrium as liquid vaporization occurs. In a closed tank the vapor formed will always be in contact with the liquid. Thus the liquid is at its bubble point (180°F) and its composition must lie on the saturated liquid enthalpy curve at 180°F. Referring to the graph in Figure 1, the remaining liquid contains 26.5 mole percent alcohol.

Now determine the amount of heat required to vaporize the liquid. From the considerations by which it was concluded that the liquid composition lies on the saturated liquid enthalpy curve. It can also be concluded that the vapor composition must lie on the saturated vapor curve at 180°F. From the graph the mole fraction of alcohol in the vapor is 0.565. Let the amount of the original liquid = 1, the find liquid = δ, and the find vapor = v.

Hence, the following is valid.

$$\delta = 1 - v$$

The application of the inverse lever-arm rule gives the ratio v/l

$$\frac{v}{l} = \frac{\text{length of segment } xx_\delta}{\text{length of segment } yx_\delta}$$

From the graph, $\frac{v}{l} = 0.44$.

Therefore the mole percent of the original liquid vaporized is 44.

Consider l = 1 lb mole of the original liquid. Initial enthalpy at x = 0.4 is lh.

Find enthalpy = $\delta h_\delta + vH$

Let the heat added to the system = q. From the graph

at x = 0.4, saturated liquid, h=3400 Btu/lb mole

at x = 0.265, saturated liquid, h_δ=3100 Btu/lb mole

at y = 0.565, saturated vapor, H=21,000 Btu/lb mole

The principle of enthalpy yields the following simple relationship:

$$lh + q = \delta h_\delta + vH \tag{1}$$

Substituting the known values in equation (1) and simplifying gives:

$$q = (0.56)(3100) + (0.44)(20,800) - (1)(3500)$$

$$= 7388 \text{ Btu/lb mole of original liquid.}$$

• PROBLEM 8-20

Water at 75°F is fed into a cylindrical tank of volume 1100 ft³ at the rate of 30 lbm/min and is heated by a coil. The coil is arranged so that the heat transfer is proportional to the quantity of water in the tank. The tank is fitted with an agitator which has enough power to maintain the water in the tank at a uniform temperature. The coil is of 1 in. outer diameter tubing, 5 ft. diameter, 12 turns and has steam entering at 220°F. The overall heat transfer coefficient is 150 Btu/hr.ft²°F. Assume at t=0 the tank is empty. Determine the temperature of water when the tank is full.

Solution: The following notation is used in solving this problem:

A_o - total area available for heat transfer

$A(t)$ - instantaneous heat transfer area

V_o - volume of liquid in the filled tank

$V(t)$ - instantaneous volume

T - instantaneous temperature of water

T_1 - temperature of inlet water

T_o - temperature of water in the filled tank

T_s - temperature of steam

U_o - overall heat transfer coefficient

t - time measured from start of water flow

$t_o = \rho V_o/w$ - time required to fill the tank

C_p - heat capacity per unit mass

w - mass rate of flow of water into the tank

ρ - density of liquid

The following assumptions are made in formulating this problem:

1. Steam temperature remains constant in coil.
2. The change in density and heat capacity of the water with temperature is negligible.
3. The fluid is incompressible, i.e., $C_p = C_v$.
4. The water in the tank has a uniform temperature throughout.
5. The heat transfer coefficient is constant.
6. The walls of the tank are insulated.

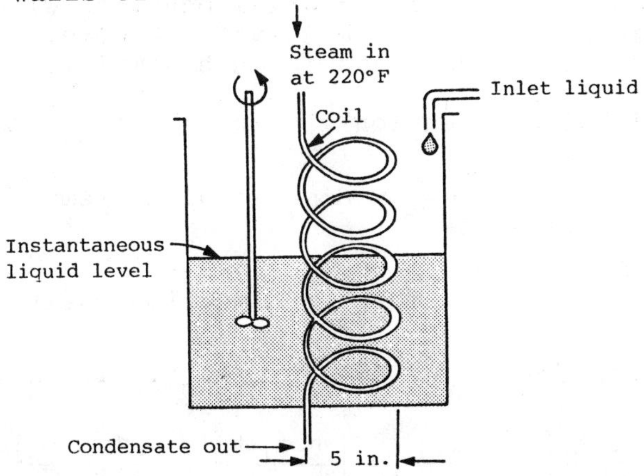

Figure 1. HEATING A LIQUID WITH A VARIABLE LIQUID LEVEL IN A TANK.

The fluid in the tank is chosen as the system. The changes in kinetic and potential energy are negligible. There is no work done in the system. There is no outflow from the system. Therefore the energy balance on the chosen system gives:

$$\frac{d}{dt} U_{tot} = wh_1 + Q \qquad (1)$$

Note that the internal energy of the system is increasing because of heat addition and addition of fluid with enthalpy h_1. Let T_1 be chosen as the thermal datum plane, as U_{tot} and h_1 cannot be obtained absolutely.

This gives $h_1 = 0$ and $U_{tot} = \rho C_p V(T-T_1)$

The heat addition is given by:

$$Q = U_o A(T_s - T) \qquad (2)$$

Substituting equation (2) and other known values in equation (1) gives:

$$\rho C_p \frac{d}{dt}\{V(T-T_1)\} = U_o A(T_s - T) \qquad (3)$$

The instantaneous volume and area are given by;

$$V(t) = \frac{wt}{\rho} \qquad (4)$$

$$A(t) = \frac{wt}{\rho V_o} A_o \qquad (5)$$

Substituting equations (4) and (5) in equation (2) gives:

$$wC_p(T-T_1) + wC_p t\left(\frac{d(T-T_1)}{dt}\right) = U_o A_o \frac{wt}{\rho V_o}(T_s - T) \qquad (6)$$

The initial conditions are $t = 0$, $T = T_1$.

Equation (6) is a differential equation with given initial conditions, which can be solved. However, the dimensionless approach is used and is much simpler.

The following dimensionless variables are defined:

$$\theta = \frac{T-T_1}{T_s-T_1} = \text{dimensionless temperature} \qquad (7)$$

$$\tau = \frac{t}{t_o} = \frac{wt}{\rho V_o} = \text{dimensionless time} \qquad (8)$$

Multiplying equation (6) by $1/wC_p(T_s-T_1)$ gives:

$$\left(\frac{U_o A_o}{wC_p}\right)\left(\frac{wt}{\rho V_o}\right)\left(1 - \frac{T-T_1}{T_s-T_1}\right) = \left(\frac{T-T_1}{T_s-T_1}\right) + t\frac{d}{dt}\left(\frac{T-T_1}{T_s-T_1}\right) \qquad (9)$$

Substituting the dimensionless variables gives:

$$\left(\frac{U_o A_o}{wC_p}\right) \tau(1-\theta) = \theta + \tau \frac{d\theta}{d\tau} \tag{10}$$

Let $N = U_o A_o / wC_p$

Then

$$N\tau(1-\theta) = \theta + \tau \frac{d\theta}{d\tau}$$

or

$$N\tau(1-\theta) = \theta + \frac{N\tau}{N} \frac{d\theta}{d\tau}$$

Let $\eta = N\tau$, then $d\eta = N d\tau$

$$\eta(1-\theta) = \theta + \eta \frac{d\theta}{d\eta} \tag{11}$$

Rewriting equation (11)

$$\frac{d\theta}{d\eta} + \left(1 + \frac{1}{\eta}\right)\theta = 1 \tag{12}$$

The initial conditions now become:

$$\theta = 0 \quad \text{at} \quad \eta = 0 \tag{13}$$

It can be clearly seen from equation (12) that θ is a function of only η. Equation (12) is a first order linear differential equation and the solution is

$$\theta = 1 - \frac{1}{\eta} + \frac{C}{\eta \exp(\eta)} \tag{14}$$

Now multiply equation (14) by η

$$\eta\theta = \frac{C}{\exp(\eta)} + \eta - 1$$

at $\eta = 0$ $\theta = 0$

Therefore, $C = 1$

Then

$$\theta = 1 - \frac{1 - \exp(-\eta)}{\eta} \tag{15}$$

This function is shown graphically in Fig. 2.

When the tank is filled, the temperature of the water in the tank is given by equation (15) when $\tau = 1$ or $3 = N$.

The result, in terms of the previous variables, is:

$$\frac{T_0 - T_1}{T_s - T_1} = 1 - \frac{1 - \exp(-U_0 A_0 / wCp)}{(U_0 A_0 / wCp)} \tag{16}$$

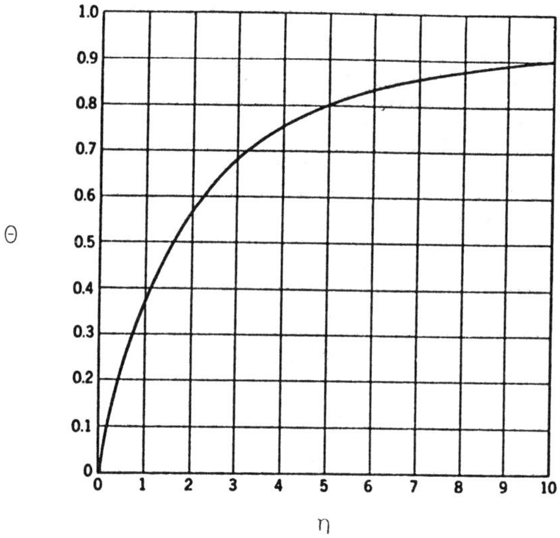

PLOT OF DIMENSIONLESS TEMPERATURE VERSUS $\eta = N_r$ ACCORDING TO (15)

Figure 2.

Given $T_1 = 70^0F$, $T_s = 220^0F$, $U_o = 150$ Btu/hr.ft^2.^{0}F, $w = 30$ lb/min, $C_p = 1$ and $A_o = \pi \times 5 \times 12 \times \left(\pi \times \frac{1}{12}\right) = 49.35$

Substituting in equation (16) yields;

$$\frac{T_0 - 70}{220 - 70} = 1 - \frac{1 - \exp(-(150 \times 49.35)/(30 \times 60 \times 1))}{((150 \times 49.35)/(30 \times 60 \times 1))}$$

Then $\quad T = 184^0F.$

Therefore the temperature of water when tank is filled is 184^0F.

• PROBLEM 8-21

Calculate the diameter of a clean iron pipe of length 10,000 ft., through which oil is flowing at 8.93 cfs. The head loss in the pipe is 75 ft lb/lb.

Assume $\quad v = 0.0001$ ft^2/s and $\varepsilon = 0.00015$ ft.

Solution: The head loss is given by the equation

$$h_f = f \frac{L}{D} \frac{Q^2}{2g\left(\frac{\pi}{4} D^2\right)^2}$$

where

h_f = head loss

f = friction coefficient

L = length of the pipe

D = diameter of the pipe

Q = discharge rate

Rearranging and solving for D, yeilds

$$D = \frac{8LQ^2}{h_f g\pi^2} f$$

Substituting the values in the right-hand side of the equation, yields a relation between D and f.

$$D^5 = \frac{8\times 10,000\times(8.93)^2}{75\times 32.2\times\pi^2}\times f$$

or

$$D^5 = 267 f$$

The value of f is found iteratively from the Moody Diagram, using the Reynolds number and the effective roughness.

The Reynolds number is given by

$$Re = \frac{4Q}{\pi\nu D}$$

where

Re = Reynolds number

Q = Discharge rate

ν = Kinematic viscosity

D = Diameter of the pipe

Taking $f = 0.02$

$$D^5 = 267 \times 0.02$$

or $D = 1.398$ ft.

Calculating Re

$$Re = \frac{4\times 8.93}{\pi\times 0.0001\times 1.398}$$

or $Re = 81,400$

Also, the effective roughness is:

$$\varepsilon/D = 0.00011$$

Using the values of Re and ε/D the friction coefficient, f, comes out to be 0.019 from the Moody chart.

Now, repeating the iterative procedure by using $f = 0.019$ yields

$$D = 1.382 \text{ ft.}$$

$$Re = 82,300$$

$$f = 0.019$$

The f value agrees with the previous value. Therefore the diameter of the pipe is 1.382 ft.

$$\text{or} \quad D = 1.382 \times 12 \text{ in.}$$

$$\text{or} \quad D = 16.6 \text{ in.}$$

• PROBLEM 8-22

Consider a steady and uniform flow of air through a horizontal pipe of 6 in. diameter which is 1,000 ft. long. The inlet conditions are, 70°F, 2200 psf and those of the outlet are T_2°F and 2195 psf. If the flow is adiabatic, compute the outlet temperature, T_2, for both incompressible and compressible flows. Take the flow rate as 0.027 slug/s.

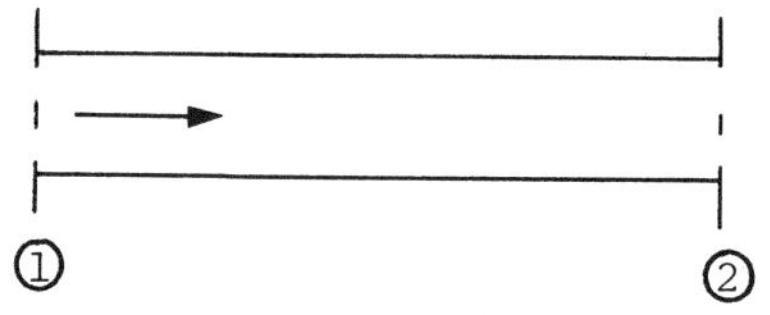

FLOW THROUGH AN INSULATED PIPE

Solution:

The frictional head loss in the pipe causes the temperature rise in the fluid.

First consider the incompressible flow, applying the steady flow energy equation,

$$\frac{p_1}{\gamma} + \frac{V_1^2}{2g} + Z_1 = \frac{p_2}{\gamma} + \frac{V_2^2}{2g} + Z_2 + h_f - h_q + h_s + h_v$$

where

$$Z_1 = Z_2$$

$$V_1 \approx V_2 \text{ (for constant cross-section)}$$

$$h_Q = 0 \text{ (adiabatic flow)}$$

$$h_s = 0 \text{ (no shaft work)}$$

$$h_v = 0 \text{ (no viscous work)}$$

or

$$h_f = \frac{p_1 - p_2}{\gamma}$$

$$= \frac{p_1 - p_2}{\rho g}$$

where

$$\rho = \frac{p_1}{RT_1}$$

$$= \frac{2200}{1715(530)} = 0.00242 \text{ slugs/ft}^3$$

Hence,

$$h_f = \frac{2200 - 2195}{0.00242(32.2)} = 64.2 \text{ ft.}$$

The head loss is reflected in a temperature rise,

$$h_f = \frac{U_2 - U_1}{g}$$

$$= c_v \frac{(T_2 - T_1)}{g}$$

where $c_v = 4290 \text{ ft}^2/\text{s}^2 \cdot {}^0\text{R}$ for air.

Therefore:

$$T_2 = T_1 + \frac{gh_f}{c_v}$$

$$= 70 + \frac{32.2(64.2)}{4290}$$

$$T_2 = 70.48^0\text{F}$$

Finally, consider the flow as compressible.

$$\frac{p_1}{\gamma_1} + \frac{V_1^2}{2g} + Z_1 = \frac{p_2}{\gamma_2} + \frac{V_2^2}{2g} + Z_2 + h_f$$

or

$$\frac{p_1}{\gamma_1} + \frac{V_1^2}{2g} = \frac{p_2}{\gamma_2} + \frac{V_2^2}{2g} + \frac{c_v(T_2 - T_1)}{g}$$

or

$$\frac{p_1}{\rho_1} + \frac{V_1^2}{2} = \frac{p_2}{\rho_2} + \frac{V_2^2}{2} + c_v(T_2 - T_1)$$

where,

$$\rho_2 = \frac{p_2}{RT_2}$$

or

$$\rho_2 = \frac{2195}{1715T_2} = \frac{1.28}{T_2}$$

$$V_2 = \frac{\rho_1}{\rho_2} V_1$$

$$= \frac{0.00242(56.8)T_2}{1.28}$$

or $$V_2 = 0.1074T_2$$

Inserting the numerical values,

$$0.00577T_2^{\,2} + 6005T_2 - 3184000 = 0$$

or $$T_2 = 529.95^0R$$

$$= 69.95^0F$$

In this case there is a slight drop in the temperature. This is due to conversion of pressure work and kinetic energy into internal energy.

CHAPTER 9

CONDUCTION IN VARIOUS SOLID GEOMETRIES

COMPOSITE WALL

• PROBLEM 9-1

A wall of a guest house is constructed as shown in the figure. The inside layer 'a' is ½ in sheetrock (k_a = 0.43 Btu/hr-ft-^oF) and 'b' is an air space of 3½ in. The conductance of the air space is 1.15 Btu/hr-ft^2-^oF. 'c' is a layer of 3/4 in. celotex board (k_c = 0.027 Btu/hr-ft-^oF). The outside layer 'd' is of 4 in. common brick (k_d = 0.40 Btu/hr-ft-^oF). If the inside wall surface temperature is 72^oF and the outside wall surface temperature is 35^oF, determine the rate of heat loss from the wall per square foot area. Also determine the temperature in the wall at a point 4½ in. from the outside wall surface.

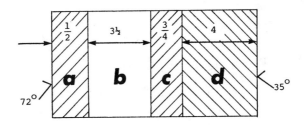

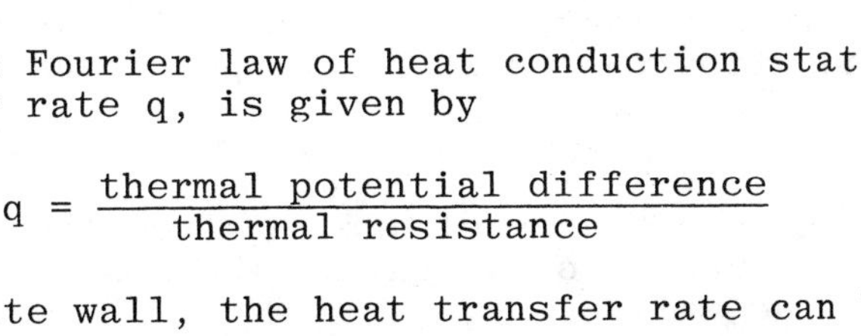

Solution: The Fourier law of heat conduction states that the heat transfer rate q, is given by

$$q = \frac{\text{thermal potential difference}}{\text{thermal resistance}} \qquad (1)$$

For a composite wall, the heat transfer rate can be expressed as

$$q = \frac{\text{overall temperature difference}}{\text{summation of thermal resistances}}$$

i.e., in this case

$$q = \frac{(\Delta T)_{total}}{\frac{\Delta x_a}{k_a A} + \frac{1}{h_b A} + \frac{\Delta x_c}{k_c A} + \frac{\Delta x_d}{k_d A}}$$

or, the heat transfer rate per unit area of the wall

$$\frac{q}{A} = \frac{(\Delta T)_{total}}{\frac{\Delta x_a}{k_a} + \frac{1}{h_b} + \frac{\Delta x_c}{k_c} + \frac{\Delta x_d}{k_d}}$$

where

$(\Delta T)_{total}$ = overall temperature difference

= inside wall temperature - outside wall temperature

Δx = thickness of the layer

k = thermal conductivity of material of the layer

h = conductance

Subscripts a, b, c and d denote the layers.

Substituting the values,

$$\frac{q}{A} = \frac{(72 - 35)}{\frac{1}{2 \times 12 \times 0.43} + \frac{1}{1.15} + \frac{3}{4 \times 12 \times 0.027} + \frac{4}{12 \times 0.4}}$$

$$= \frac{37}{0.0969 + 0.870 + 2.315 + 0.833}$$

$$= \frac{37}{4.115}$$

$$\frac{q}{A} = 8.9915 \text{ Btu/hr-ft}^2$$

Therefore, the rate of heat loss per unit area = 8.991 Btu/hr-ft^2

The temperature at any point in the wall can be found by applying equation (1) between that point and any known temperature point.

The point, at a distance of 4.5 in. from the outside wall surface is in the celotex board. The heat flux is same throughout the wall.

$$\frac{q}{A} = \frac{\Delta T}{\text{thermal resistance}}$$

$$= \frac{T_x - T_{outside\ surface}}{\frac{\Delta x}{k_c} + \frac{\Delta x_d}{k_d}}$$

where

T_x = temperature at the required point

$T_{outside\ surface}$ = outside surface temperature

$\Delta x = (4.5 - 4) = 0.5$ in.

$\Delta x_d = 4$ in.

Substituting the values,

$$8.991 = \frac{T_x - 35}{\frac{0.5}{12 \times 0.027} + \frac{4}{12 \times 0.4}}$$

or, $$8.991 = \frac{T_x - 35}{2.377}$$

Therefore, $T_x = 2.377(8.991) + 35$

$= 56.37^{\circ}F$

Therefore, the temperature at a point 4.5 in. inside from the outside wall surface is $56.37^{\circ}F$.

• PROBLEM 9-2

A plane wall of an oven consists of an inside layer of refractory brick 6 in. thick ($k = 0.08$ Btu/hr-ft-$^{\circ}$F) followed by a 9 in. layer of common brick ($k = 0.8$ Btu/hr-ft-$^{\circ}$F). If the temperature of the inner wall surface is $1800^{\circ}F$ and that of the outer surface is $200^{\circ}F$, determine the rate of heat loss per unit area, through this wall.

Solution: Fourier's simplified law of conduction cannot be used across the given wall, since the thermal conductivity abruptly changes at the interface of the two layers.

So, the thermal resistance offered by each layer is considered separately.

The thermal resistance is defined as $\frac{(\Delta L)}{kA}$

where ΔL = thickness of the layer

k = thermal conductivity

A = area of heat flow

Since the layers are in series, the total resistance of the wall is the sum of the resistances of each layer.

$$\text{Therefore total resistance} = \frac{\Delta L_1}{k_1 A} + \frac{\Delta L_2}{k_2 A}$$

where the subscripts denote layers 1 and 2.

The thermal resistance of a unit area of heat flow is

$$R = \frac{\Delta L_1}{k_1} + \frac{\Delta L_2}{k_2}$$

Substituting the values gives

$$R = \frac{6}{12 \times 0.08} + \frac{9}{12 \times 0.8}$$

$$= 6.25 + 0.9375$$

$$= 7.1875$$

From the principles of conduction, the rate of heat flow is given by the ratio of temperature drop to thermal resistance.

Therefore, the rate of heat loss per unit area is

$$\frac{\text{temperature drop}}{\text{thermal resistance of unit area}}$$

Substituting the values,

$$\text{rate of heat loss/unit area} = \frac{(1800 - 200)}{7.1875}$$

$$= 222.61 \text{ Btu/hr-ft}^2$$

• PROBLEM 9-3

A brick wall consists of $4\frac{1}{2}$ in. thick facing brick (k = 0.8 Btu/hr-ft-$^\circ$F) as the outside layer, 6 in. thick common brick (k = 0.45 Btu/hr-ft-$^\circ$F) as the middle layer and 3/4 in. thick of gypsum plaster (k = 0.24 Btu/hr-ft-$^\circ$F) as the inside layer. The inside and outside heat transfer coefficients are 1.5 Btu/hr-ft^2-$^\circ$F and 5.8 Btu/hr-ft^2-$^\circ$F respectively. If the wall is exposed to air at 70°F on the inside and air at 95°F on the outside, determine the heat gain rate per unit area of the wall and also determine the surface temperature of the wall on the cooler side.

Solution: In this problem heat is transferred both by conduction and convection modes. Convection mode is present between wall surface and surrounding air.

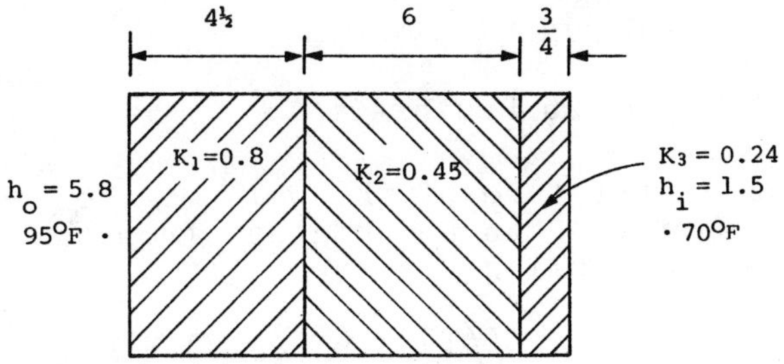

The rate of heat transfer is given by

$$\frac{q}{A} = U(\Delta T)_{overall}$$

where

q = rate of heat transfer

A = area of heat transfer

U = overall heat transfer coefficient

$(\Delta T)_{overall}$ = total temperature differential

The overall heat transfer coefficient U is defined as

$$U = \frac{1}{\frac{1}{h_i} + \frac{\Delta x_1}{k_1} + \frac{\Delta x_2}{k_2} + \frac{\Delta x_3}{k_3} + \frac{1}{h_o}}$$

where

h_i = inside heat transfer coefficient

h_o = outside heat transfer coefficient

Δx = thickness of the layer

k = thermal conductivity of the material of the layer

Subscripts 1, 2 and 3 represent the layers.

Substituting the values into the equation for the overall heat transfer coefficient,

$$U = \frac{1}{\frac{1}{1.5} + \frac{4.5}{12 \times 0.8} + \frac{6}{12 \times 0.45} + \frac{3}{4 \times 12 \times 0.24} + \frac{1}{5.8}}$$

$$= \frac{1}{0.667 + 0.469 + 1.111 + 0.260 + 0.172}$$

$$U \doteq 0.373 \text{ Btu/hr-ft}^2\text{-}^\circ\text{F}$$

Substituting the values in the equation for rate of heat transfer, the heat gain per unit area of the wall (q/A) is,

$$\frac{q}{A} = 0.373 \times (95 - 70)$$

$$= 9.325 \text{ Btu/hr-ft}^2$$

The surface temperature of the wall on the cooler side (i.e., the inside surface) can be obtained from the definition of Newton's law of cooling,

$$q = hA(\Delta T)$$

or,
$$\frac{q}{A} = h(\Delta T)$$

The value of $\frac{q}{A}$ is same as obtained above.

$$h = 1.5 \quad \text{and} \quad \Delta T = (T - 70)^{\circ}\text{F}$$

where T = surface temperature on the inside.

Then, substituting the values gives

$$9.325 = 1.5(T - 70)$$

or,
$$T = \frac{9.325}{1.5} + 70$$

$$T = 76^{\circ}\text{F}$$

Therefore, the temperature of the inside surface of the wall is 76°F.

• PROBLEM 9-4

Consider an oven wall with three layers A, B and C as shown in the figure. The thickness of layers A, B and C are 12 in., 4 in. and 8 in. respectively and their thermal conductivities are 0.78 Btu/hr-ft-$^{\circ}$F, 0.08 Btu/hr-ft-$^{\circ}$F and 0.48 Btu/hr-ft-$^{\circ}$F respectively. Neglecting the thermal resistances of the joints, determine the temperature at the joints, i.e., t_2 and t_3. Given the inner and outer wall surface temperatures as 2000 $^{\circ}$F and 100°F respectively.

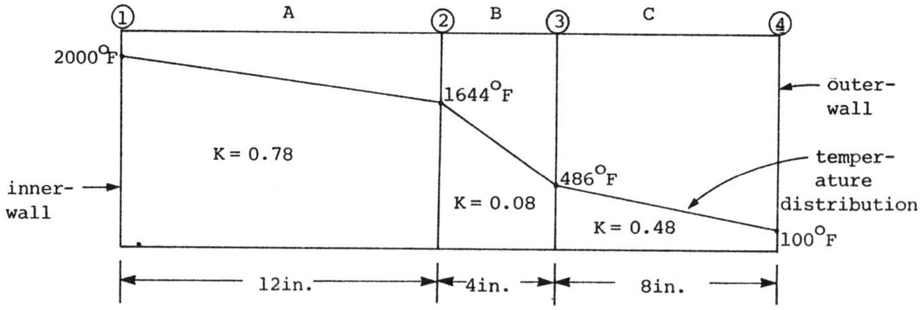

Solution: Temperature at any point inside the wall can be obtained from the heat transfer rate q and one known temperature at any other point.

For a composite wall, the heat transfer rate can be expressed as

$$q = \frac{\text{overall temperature difference}}{\text{summation of thermal resistances}}$$

$$= \frac{(\Delta T)_{overall}}{\frac{\Delta x_a}{k_a A} + \frac{\Delta x_b}{k_b A} + \frac{\Delta x_c}{k_c A}}$$

where $(\Delta T)_{overall}$ = overall temperature differential

Δx = thickness of a layer

k = thermal conductivity

A = area of heat flow

Subscripts a, b, c denote the layers A, B, C respectively.

The heat transfer rate per unit area of flow is

$$\frac{q}{A} = \frac{(\Delta T)_{overall}}{\frac{\Delta x_a}{k_a} + \frac{\Delta x_b}{k_b} + \frac{\Delta x_c}{k_c}}$$

$$= \frac{(2000 - 100)}{\frac{12}{12 \times 0.78} + \frac{4}{12 \times 0.08} + \frac{8}{12 \times 0.48}}$$

or, $$\frac{q}{A} = \frac{1900}{1.28 + 4.17 + 1.39}$$

$$= 277.78 \text{ Btu/hr-ft}^2$$

Since the value of $\frac{q}{A}$ is same through any section, the Fourier's law of conduction can be used to find the temperatures at the joints.

$$\frac{q}{A} = \frac{k\Delta T}{\Delta x}$$

Applying this to the layer A, the rate of heat transfer per unit area $\frac{q}{A}$ is

$$\frac{q}{A} = \frac{0.78 \times (2000 - t_2)}{12/12} = 277.78$$

Therefore

$$(2000 - t_2) = \frac{277.78}{0.78}$$

or, $$t_2 = 2000 - \frac{277.78}{0.78}$$

$$= 1644\,^{\circ}F$$

Similarly, applying the Fourier's law of conduction to layer C,

$$\frac{0.48(t_3 - 100)}{8/12} = 277.78$$

Therefore,

$$t_3 = 277.78 \times \frac{8}{12} \times \frac{1}{0.48} + 100$$

$$= 486^{\circ}F$$

• PROBLEM 9-5

> The top surface of a carbon steel plate, 40 x 70 cm. and 2.5 cm. thick, is maintained at $250^{\circ}C$ by blowing air at $25^{\circ}C$ over it. The convective heat transfer coefficient is 30 W/m^2-K.
>
> a) Find the rate of heat loss from the plate surface
>
> b) If the heat loss due to radiation from the plate is 340 W, in addition to the above mentioned convective heat loss, determine the temperature of the bottom surface.
>
> Thermal conductivity 'K' of the plate is 45 W/m-°K.

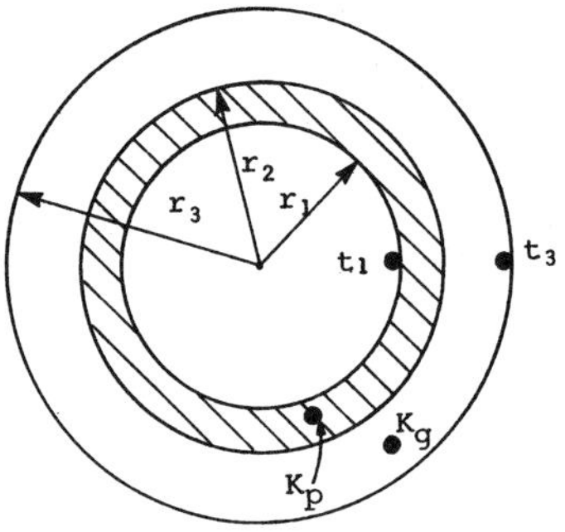

Solution:

a) Heat is lost from the plate surface due to convection.

The rate of heat loss is given by

$$q_c = hA(T_w - T_a)$$

where

q_c = convective heat loss

h = convective heat transfer coefficient

A = plate area

T_w = temperature of the plate surface

T_a = temperature of air

Substituting the values,

$$q_c = 30 \times \frac{40 \times 70}{100 \times 100} \times (250 - 25)$$

$$= 1890 \text{ W.}$$

Therefore, the rate of heat loss by convection is 1890 W.

b) In this case there is an additional heat loss due to radiation, then the total heat loss from the top surface is

$$q = q_c + q_r$$

where

q = total heat loss

q_c = heat loss due to convection

q_r = heat loss due to radiation

The total heat loss from the top surface must be conducted from the bottom surface. Therefore it is obvious that the temperature of the bottom surface of the plate is higher than that of the top surface. From the law of heat conduction, the rate of heat conduction is

$$q = -KA \frac{dT}{dx}$$

where

$\frac{dT}{dx}$ = derivative of temperature w.r.t. length

K = thermal conductivity

or,

$$q = KA \frac{(T - T_w)}{x}$$

where

K = thermal conductivity of the plate

A = area of the plate

T_w = temperature of the top surface

T = temperature of the bottom surface

x = thickness of the plate

Substituting the values,

$$1890 + 340 = 45 \times \frac{40 \times 70}{100 \times 100} \frac{(T - 250)}{2.5} \times 100$$

$$2230 = 504(T - 250)$$

Calculating for T,

$$T = 254.42^{\circ}C$$

Therefore, the temperature of the bottom surface = $254.42^{\circ}C$.

CYLINDRICAL WALL SYSTEMS

• PROBLEM 9-6

A cast iron pipe of 4 in. inside diameter and 4.5 in. outside diameter is insulated with 3/4 in. layer of glass wool. The inside surface of the pipe is at 400 $^{\circ}F$ and the glass wool outer surface is at $90^{\circ}F$. Determine the steady state heat transfer rate per foot length of the pipe.

The thermal conductivity of the material of the pipe is 30 Btu/hr-ft-$^{\circ}F$ and that of the glass wool is 0.032 Btu/hr-ft-$^{\circ}F$.

Solution: For a two layered cylindrical wall, the rate of heat transfer q , is given as

$$q = \frac{2\pi L(\Delta T)}{\frac{1}{k_p} \ln \frac{r_2}{r_1} + \frac{1}{k_g} \ln \frac{r_3}{r_2}}$$

where ΔT = temperature difference between the inside and outside surfaces

r = radius

L = length of the pipe considered

k = thermal conductivity

Subscripts p and g denote pipe and glass wool respectively.

Subscripts 1, 2 and 3 denote the three layers.

Therefore for a foot length of the pipe, the rate of heat transfer is

$$\frac{q}{L} = \frac{2\pi(t_1 - t_3)}{\frac{1}{k_p} \ln \frac{r_2}{r_1} + \frac{1}{k_g} \ln \frac{r_3}{r_2}}$$

Substituting the values,

$$\frac{q}{L} = \frac{2\pi(400 - 90)}{\frac{1}{30} \ln \frac{2.25}{2} + \frac{1}{0.032} \ln \frac{3.0}{2.25}}$$

$$= \frac{2\pi \times 310}{0.00393 + 8.9901}$$

$$\frac{q}{L} = 216.56 \text{ Btu/hr-ft.}$$

• PROBLEM 9-7

A 4 in. schedule 40 wrought iron pipe is covered with 2 in. thick layer of magnesia insulation ($k = 0.041$ Btu/hr-ft-$^{\circ}$F) and $1\frac{1}{4}$ in. thickness of glass wool ($k = 0.032$ Btu/hr-ft-$^{\circ}$F). If the outer surface of the pipe is at 700°F and the outer surface of the glass wool insulation is at 100°F, determine the rate of heat loss per foot length of the pipe.

Solution: This is a composite cylindrical wall conduction problem. This can be solved as a composite plane wall by considering the logarithmic mean radii.

The logarithmic mean radii of the first layer of insulation is given by

$$r_m = \frac{r_2 - r_1}{\ln \frac{r_2}{r_1}}$$

where

r_m = logarithmic mean radii

r_1 and r_2 are the two radii of the layer

logarithmic mean radii of first layer

$$r_{m_1} = \frac{4.25 - 2.25}{\ln \left(\frac{4.25}{2.25}\right)}$$

where 2.25 in. is the outside radii of the pipe.

Therefore $r_{m_1} = 3.145$ in.

Since the thickness of the second layer is very small, the arithmetic mean can be used instead of logarithmic mean.

Arithmetic mean radii of the second layer

$$r_{m_2} = \frac{4.25 + 5.50}{2}$$

$$= 4.875 \text{ in.}$$

The thermal resistance of the first layer, considering as a plane wall layer is given by

$$R = \frac{\Delta x}{kA}$$

where Δx = thickness of the layer

k = thermal conductivity

A = area of heat flow per unit length

Substituting the values, the thermal resistance of the first layer R, is,

$$R_1 = \frac{2/12}{0.041 \times \left(2\pi \times \frac{3.145}{12}\right)}$$

$$= 2.47$$

Similarly the resistance of the second layer, R_2 is

$$R_2 = \frac{1.25/12}{0.032 \times \left(2\pi \times \frac{4.875}{12}\right)}$$

$$= 1.275$$

The total resistance $R = 2.47 + 1.275$

$= 3.745$

The rate of heat flow is given by

$$q = \frac{\Delta T}{R}$$

Substituting the values, the rate of heat loss per foot length of the pipe is:

$$q = \frac{(700 - 100)}{3.745}$$

$$= 160.2 \text{ Btu/(hr)(ft. of pipe)}$$

• **PROBLEM 9-8**

A 3 in. inside diameter and 3.5 in. outside diameter stainless steel pipe (k = 30 Btu/hr-ft-°F) is covered with a 0.5 in. thick asbestos insulation (k = 0.12 Btu/hr-ft-°F). A fluid at 400°F flows inside the pipe. The outside air is at 75°F. The inner and outer surface conductances are 50 Btu/hr-ft²-°F and 5 Btu/hr-ft²-°F. Determine the rate of heat loss per foot length of the pipe.

Solution: In this problem heat is transferred both by conduction and convection modes.

The rate of heat transfer is given by

$$q = \frac{\text{temperature differential}}{\text{thermal resistance}}$$

Thermal resistance is the sum of the individual resistances offered by the layers and the convective films.

The thermal resistance of the convective film is

$$R = \frac{1}{\text{area x conductance}}$$

Hence the total thermal resistance per unit length of pipe

$$= \frac{1}{\pi\left(\frac{3}{12}\right) \times 50} + \frac{\ln \frac{3.5}{3.0}}{2\pi \times 30} + \frac{\ln \frac{4.5}{3.5}}{2\pi \times 0.12} + \frac{1}{\pi\left(\frac{4.5}{12}\right) \times 5}$$

$$= 0.0255 + 0.0008 + 0.3333 + 0.1698$$

$$= 0.5287$$

Therefore, the rate of heat transfer is

$$q = \frac{400 - 75}{0.5287}$$

$$= 615 \text{ Btu/hr-ft (length of pipe)}$$

• **PROBLEM 9-9**

A steam pipe of $1\frac{1}{2}$ in. OD is to be covered with two layers of insulation each of thickness 1 in. The thermal conductivity of one insulation material is 5 times that of the other. Assuming that the inner and outer surface temperatures of composite insulation are fixed, how much will the heat transfer be reduced when the better insulating material is next to the pipe than when it is the outer layer.

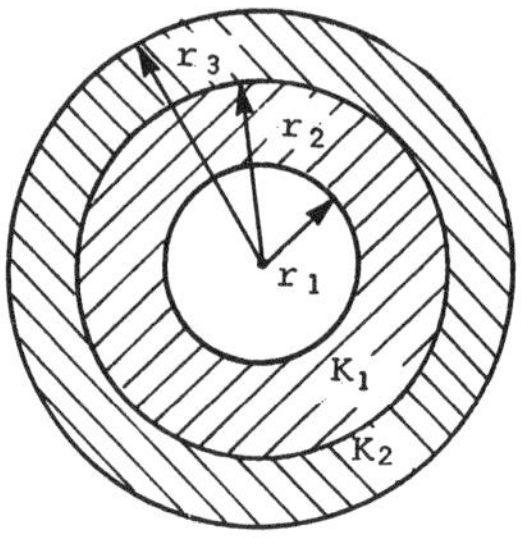

(a)

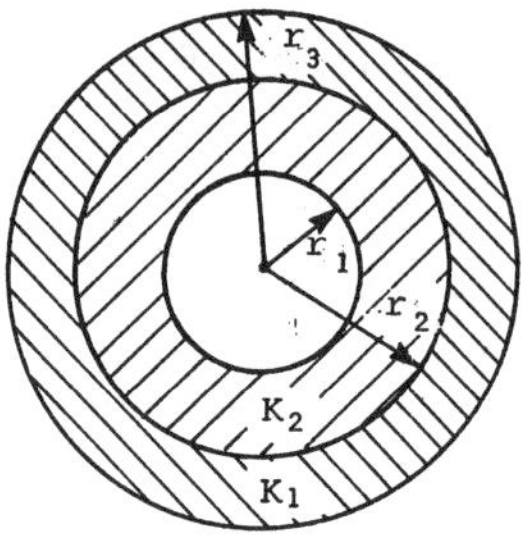

(b)

Solution: Assuming $K_2 = 5K_1$ where material of conductivity K_1 is a better insulator.

T_1 = inside surface temperature of the pipe

T_3 = outside surface temperature of the insulation

r_1 = 0.75 in.

r_2 = 1.75 in.

r_3 = 2.75 in.

When better insulation is inside, figure (a), the rate of heat flow is

$$q_1 = \frac{(T_1 - T_3)2\pi L}{\dfrac{\ln\left(\dfrac{r_2}{r_1}\right)}{K_1} + \dfrac{\ln\left(\dfrac{r_3}{r_2}\right)}{K_2}}$$

where

L = length of the pipe

Substituting the values of r_1, r_2 and r_3 and K_2 in terms of K_1

$$q_1 = \frac{2\pi L(T_1 - T_3)}{\dfrac{\ln\left(\dfrac{1.75}{0.75}\right)}{K_1} + \dfrac{\ln\left(\dfrac{2.75}{1.75}\right)}{5K_1}}$$

$$= \frac{2\pi L(T_1 - T_3)}{\dfrac{0.8473}{K_1} + \dfrac{0.0904}{K_1}} = \frac{2\pi K_1 L(T_1 - T_3)}{0.9377}$$

When better insulation is outside figure (b), the rate of heat flow is

$$q_2 = \frac{(T_1 - T_3)2\pi L}{\dfrac{\ln\left(\dfrac{r_2}{r_1}\right)}{K_2} + \dfrac{\ln\left(\dfrac{r_3}{r_2}\right)}{K_1}}$$

$$= \frac{(T_1 - T_3)2\pi L}{\frac{\ln\left(\frac{1.75}{0.75}\right)}{5K_1} + \frac{\ln\left(\frac{2.75}{1.75}\right)}{K_1}}$$

$$q_2 = \frac{2\pi K_1 L(T_1 - T_3)}{0.6214}$$

Therefore, percentage reduction of heat transfer, when the better insulation is next to pipe, as compared to when it is outside is

$$\frac{q_2 - q_1}{q_2} \times 100\%$$

$$= \frac{\frac{1}{0.6214} - \frac{1}{0.9377}}{\frac{1}{0.6214}} \times 100\%$$

$$= 33.7\%$$

• PROBLEM 9-10

A 12 ft. long 4 in. diameter steel tube is insulated with 1 in. thick layer of an insulating material whose thermal conductivity is 0.05 Btu/hr-ft-°F. If the inner and outer surface temperatures of the insulating layer are 500°F and 100°F respectively, determine the radial rate of heat loss over the total length of the rod.

Solution: This is a cylindrical wall conduction problem. This can be solved as a plane wall by considering the logarithmic mean area.

The logarithmic mean area is defined as

$$A_{lm} = \frac{A_o - A_i}{\ln\left(\frac{A_o}{A_i}\right)}$$

where

A_o = outside surface area

A_i = inside surface area

The outside surface area of the insulation is

$$A_o = \pi \times \frac{6}{12} \times 12$$

$$= 18.85 \text{ ft}^2$$

The inside surface area

$$A_i = \pi \times \frac{4}{12} \times 12$$

$$= 12.57 \text{ ft}^2$$

Therefore, the logarithmic mean surface area of the insulation is

$$A_{lm} = \frac{18.85 - 12.57}{\ln\frac{18.85}{12.57}}$$

$$= 15.5 \text{ ft}^2$$

The rate of heat transfer is given by

$$q = \frac{kA_{lm}\Delta T}{\Delta x}$$

where

Δx = thickness of the insulation

k = thermal conductivity of the insulation

ΔT = temperature differential

A_{lm} = logarithmic mean area

Substituting the values,

$$q = \frac{0.05 \times 15.5(500 - 100)}{(1/12)}$$

$$= 3720 \text{ Btu/hr}$$

• PROBLEM 9-11

Figure shows a composite pipe made up of three different materials a, b and c. A fluid at temperature T_i and surface coefficient of heat transfer h_i flows inside the inner pipe, while another fluid at temperature T_o with a surface coefficient h_o flows over the outside of the composite pipe. Assume that steady state conditions prevail with no generation and radial heat flow only. Develop an expression for the overall heat transfer coefficient based on the inner surface for the composite pipe.

Solution: The rate of heat transfer through each of the layers is same by the law of conservation of energy.

The rate of heat transfer by convection from the inside fluid to the solid surface at r_1 by Newton's cooling law is

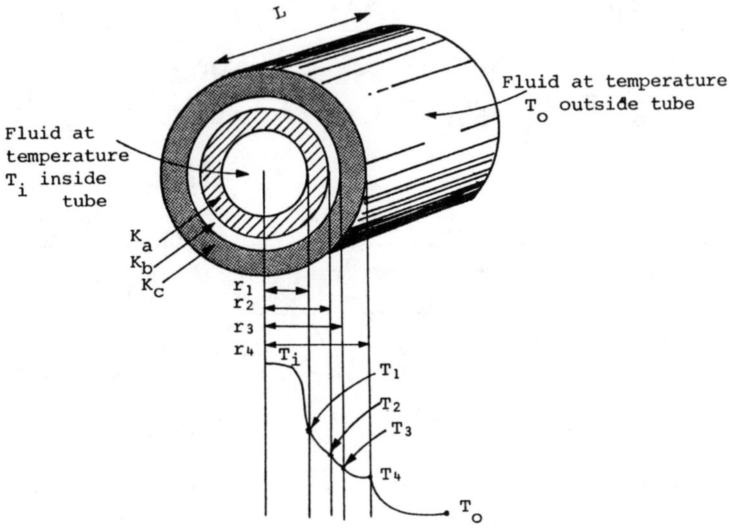

$$q = h_i(2\pi r_1 L)(T_i - T_1)$$

or $$T_i - T_1 = \frac{q}{h_i(2\pi r_1 L)} \qquad (1)$$

The rate of heat transfer by conduction through layer a, is

$$q = 2\pi L k_a \frac{(T_1 - T_2)}{\ln\left(\frac{r_2}{r_1}\right)}$$

or, $$(T_1 - T_2) = q\,\frac{\ln\left(\frac{r_2}{r_1}\right)}{2\pi L k_a} \qquad (2)$$

Similarly for layers b and c,

$$(T_2 - T_3) = q\,\frac{\ln\left(\frac{r_3}{r_2}\right)}{2\pi L k_b} \qquad (3)$$

$$(T_3 - T_4) = q\,\frac{\ln\left(\frac{r_4}{r_3}\right)}{2\pi L k_c} \qquad (4)$$

The rate of heat transfer by convection from r_4 to the outside fluid is

$$q = h_o(2\pi r_4 L)(T_4 - T_o)$$

or, $$(T_4 - T_o) = \frac{q}{h_o 2\pi r_4 L} \qquad (5)$$

Adding equations (1) to (5),

$$(T_i - T_o) = \frac{q}{2\pi L}\left[\frac{1}{h_i r_1} + \frac{\ln \frac{r_2}{r_1}}{k_a} + \frac{\ln \frac{r_3}{r_2}}{k_b} + \frac{\ln \frac{r_4}{r_3}}{k_c} + \frac{1}{h_o r_4}\right]$$

$$\text{or,} \quad q = \frac{2\pi L(T_i - T_o)}{\left[\frac{1}{h_i r_1} + \frac{\left(\frac{1}{k_a}\right)}{\left(\ln \frac{r_2}{r_1}\right)} + \frac{\left(\frac{1}{k_b}\right)}{\left(\ln \frac{r_3}{r_2}\right)} + \frac{\left(\frac{1}{k_c}\right)}{\left(\ln \frac{r_4}{r_3}\right)} + \frac{1}{h_o r_4}\right]} \qquad (6)$$

The overall heat transfer coefficient based on the inner surface is defined as

$$q = (2\pi r_1 L)U(T_i - T_o) \qquad (7)$$

where

U = overall heat transfer coefficient based on inner surface

Comparing equations (6) and (7)

$$r_1 U = \frac{1}{\left[\frac{1}{h_i r_1} + \frac{\left(\frac{1}{k_a}\right)}{\left(\ln \frac{r_2}{r_1}\right)} + \frac{\left(\frac{1}{k_b}\right)}{\left(\ln \frac{r_3}{r_2}\right)} + \frac{\left(\frac{1}{k_c}\right)}{\left(\ln \frac{r_4}{r_3}\right)} + \frac{1}{h_o r_4}\right]}$$

$$\text{or,} \quad U = \frac{1}{\left[\frac{1}{h_i} + \frac{\left(\frac{r_1}{k_a}\right)}{\left(\ln \frac{r_2}{r_1}\right)} + \frac{\left(\frac{r_1}{k_b}\right)}{\left(\ln \frac{r_3}{r_2}\right)} + \frac{\left(\frac{r_1}{k_c}\right)}{\left(\ln \frac{r_4}{r_3}\right)} + \left(\frac{r_1}{h_o r_4}\right)\right]}$$

• PROBLEM 9-12

A 6 in. I.D. and 6.5 O.D. stainless steel (k = 26 Btu/hr-ft-°F) pipe is insulated with a 3.5 in. thick layer of an insulating material (k = 0.04 Btu/hr-ft°F). If the inner surface of the pipe is at 500°F and the outer surface of insulation is at 150°F, determine the rate of heat loss per foot length of the pipe and the temperature at the interface between the pipe and the insulation.

Solution: The thermal resistance of a cylinder is given by

$$\frac{\Delta r}{kA_{1m}}$$

where

Δr = thickness of the cylinder

k = thermal conductivity

A_{1m} = logarithmic mean area

The logarithmic mean area per foot length is given by

$$A_{1m} = \frac{\pi}{12}\left[\frac{d_o - d_i}{\ln \frac{d_o}{d_i}}\right]$$

where

d_o = outside diameter in inches

d_i = inside diameter in inches

The logarithmic mean area of the pipe per unit length

$$A_{1m} = \frac{\pi}{12}\left(\frac{6.5 - 6.0}{\ln \frac{6.5}{6}}\right)$$

$$= 1.635 \text{ ft}^2$$

The logarithmic mean area of the insulation per unit length

$$A_{1m} = \frac{\pi}{12}\left[\frac{13.5 - 6.5}{\ln \frac{13.5}{6.5}}\right]$$

$$= 2.507 \text{ ft}^2$$

Therefore, the thermal resistance of the pipe is

$$R_p = \frac{\Delta r_p}{k_p A_{1m}}$$

$$= \frac{0.5/12}{26 \times 1.635}$$

$$R_p = 0.00098 \text{ hr-}^{\circ}\text{F/Btu}$$

The thermal resistance of the insulation is

$$R_i = \frac{\Delta r_i}{k_i A_{1m}}$$

$$= \frac{3.5/12}{0.04 \times 2.507}$$

$$= 2.909 \text{ hr-}^{o}\text{F/Btu}$$

The total resistance is $R_p + R_i = 2.90998$ hr-^{o}F/Btu

The thermal resistance of the insulation is so large compared to that of the pipe, that the resistance of the pipe can be ignored for general calculations.

The rate of heat loss per foot length of the pipe is

$$q = \frac{(\Delta T)_{overall}}{\text{total resistance}}$$

$$= \frac{500 - 150}{2.90998}$$

$$q = 120.28 \text{ Btu/hr- (ft. length of pipe)}$$

Since the thermal resistance of the pipe is very small, there will be very small temperature drop in the pipe.

The rate of heat transfer

$$q = \frac{\Delta T}{\text{resistance of pipe}}$$

$$120.28 = \frac{500 - T}{0.00098}$$

or $$T = 499.88^{o}\text{F}.$$

• PROBLEM 9-13

An uninsulated metal wire is conducting 900 amps of electricity. The diameter of the wire is 0.50 in. and its thermal conductivity (k) is 10 Btu/hr-ft-^{o}F. The resistance to the flow of electricity is 0.00015 ohms per ft. length. If the heat transfer coefficient at the surface is 6.0 Btu/hr-ft^{2}-^{o}F and the ambient temperature is 65°F, calculate the temperature at the center of the wire.

Solution: The heat transfer rate is provided by equation (1), the expression for power in electrical problems. Dividing by the lateral surface area of a cylindrical wire gives the heat loss per unit area. Substitution in equation (2) yields the surface temperature of the wire, (T_s). Use of equation (3) will provide the temperature at the center of the wire, (T_c).

The rate of heat loss is

$$q = I^2R = (900)^2(0.00015) = 121.5 \frac{W}{ft} \qquad (1)$$

$$= 414.5 \text{ Btu/hr-ft}$$

$$\frac{q}{A} = \frac{414.5}{\pi(0.50/12)} = 3167 \text{ Btu/hr-ft}^2$$

Equation (2) allows, T_s, the surface temperature of the wire to be obtained.

$$h = \frac{q/A}{T_s - T_a} \tag{2}$$

where T_a is the ambient temperature.

Solving for T_s:

$$T_s = T_a + q/Ah$$

$$T_s = 65 + \frac{3167}{6.0} = 592.8^{\circ}F$$

Equation (3) provides T_c, the temperature at the centerline of the wire.

$$T_c = T_s + \frac{q}{A}\frac{r}{2k} \tag{3}$$

where r is the radius of the wire.

$$T_c = 592.8 + \frac{3167(0.25/12)}{2(10)}$$

$$T_c = 596^{\circ}F$$

CONDENSER TUBE WITH INSULATING MATERIAL

• PROBLEM 9-14

A tube of 3.0 in. outside diameter is covered with 2 in. thick layer of an insulating material whose thermal conductivity varies with temperature is given by $k = 0.4 + 8 \times 10^{-4}T$ where T is in $^{\circ}F$. If the inside and outside surface temperatures of the insulating layer are $400^{\circ}F$ and $150^{\circ}F$, determine the rate of heat loss per foot length of the tube.

Solution: For a steady state, radial heat transfer, the rate of heat transfer through the inner surface is same as that through the outer surface.

The rate of heat transfer q through a material whose thermal conductivity varies with temperature is given by

$$q = \frac{-\int_{T_i}^{T_o} k\,dt}{\int_{r_i}^{r_o} \frac{dr}{A}}$$

where

A = area of heat flow

k = thermal conductivity

T = temperature

r = radius

Subscripts 'o' and 'i' denote outside and inside surfaces respectively.

For foot length of the tube the area of heat flow

$$A = 2\pi r$$

Substituting the values,

$$q = \frac{+\int_{150}^{400} (0.4 + 8 \times 10^{-4}T)dT}{\int_{\frac{1.5}{12}}^{\frac{3.5}{12}} \frac{dr}{2\pi r}}$$

Integrating,

$$q = \frac{0.4(400 - 150) + \frac{8 \times 10^{-4}}{2}(400^2 - 150^2)}{\frac{1}{2\pi} \ln\left(\frac{3.5}{1.5}\right)}$$

Simplifying

$$q = \frac{155}{0.135}$$

$= 1148$ Btu/hr per foot length of the tube.

• PROBLEM 9-15

A furnace is lined with a refractory material whose thermal conductivity varies with temperature $k = 0.12 + 5 \times 10^{-5}T$ where T is in $^{\circ}$F. If the thickness of the refractory layer is 5 in. and the inner and outer surface temperatures of it are 2000°F and 200°F, determine the heat flux and the temperature distribution in the refractory material layer.

<u>Solution</u>: The general Fourier's law of conduction is given as

$$q = -k \frac{dT}{dx}$$

where

q = heat flux

k = thermal conductivity

$\frac{dT}{dx}$ = thermal gradient

For a steady state heat transfer through a plane wall, the heat flux q is constant throughout the length of heat flow. Then, for material whose thermal conductivity depends upon temperature

$$q = \frac{-\int_{T_1}^{T_2} k\,dT}{\int_0^L dx} \qquad (1)$$

where

T_1 is the temperature at x = 0

T_2 is the temperature at x = L

For $L = \frac{5}{12}$ ft $\quad T_2 = 200\,^{o}F$

and $T_1 = 2000^{o}F$.

Substituting the values and integrating between the known limits

$$q = \frac{-\int_{2000}^{200} (0.12 + 5 \times 10^{-5}T)dT}{\int_0^{\frac{5}{12}} dx}$$

$$= \frac{0.12(2000 - 200) + \frac{5 \times 10^{-5}}{2}(2000^2 - 200^2)}{\frac{5}{12}}$$

$q = 756$ Btu/hr-ft^2

Therefore the heat flux is 756 $Btu/hr\text{-}ft^2$

To get the temperature distribution in the 5 in. thick layer of the refractory liner, substitute $L = x$ and $T_2 = T$ in the limits of the integrals in equation (1)

i.e.,

$$q = \frac{-\int_{T_1}^{T} k\, dT}{\int_0^x dx}$$

$$\text{or} \qquad \int_0^x dx = \frac{-\int_{T_1}^{T} k\, dT}{q}$$

Substituting the values and integrating

$$x = -\int_{2000}^{T} (0.12 + 5 \times 10^{-5}T)dT \times \frac{1}{756}$$

$$= -\left[0.12(T - 2000) + \frac{5 \times 10^{-5}}{2}(T^2 - 2000^2)\right] \times \frac{1}{756}$$

$$x = -\left[0.12T + 240 - \frac{5 \times 10^{-5}}{2} T^2 + 100\right] \frac{1}{756}$$

$$\text{or} \qquad x = 0.45 - 1.59 \times 10^{-4}T - 3.31 \times 10^{-8}T^2$$

The T^2 term indicates that the temperature profile is not linear.

• PROBLEM 9-16

Cooling water at 60°F flows through a condenser tube of 1 in. O.D. and 0.90 I.D. Steam at 3 in. Hg absolute pressure is condensed on the outer side of the tube. The thermal conductivity of the material of the tube is 70 Btu/hr-ft-°F and the inside and outside convective heat transfer coefficients are 250 $Btu/hr\text{-}ft^2\text{-}^\circ F$ and 1400 $Btu/hr\text{-}ft^2\text{-}^\circ F$ respectively. Determine the rate of condensation of steam per foot length of the tube.

Solution: The cooling water flowing inside the condenser tube is absorbing the latent heat of vaporization of the steam. Hence this is a radial heat transfer problem; heat is being transferred from the outside surface to the inside surface.

From the steam tables, corresponding to 3 in. Hg absolute pressure, the saturation temperature is 115°F, the latent heat of vaporization is 1029 Btu/lb_m.

The rate of heat transfer per foot length of the tube can be obtained from

$$\frac{q}{L} = \frac{2\pi(T_o - T_i)}{\dfrac{1}{r_2 h_o} + \dfrac{\ln(r_2/r_1)}{k} + \dfrac{1}{r_1 h_i}}$$

where

$\frac{q}{L}$ = heat transferred per foot length

T = temperature

r = radius

k = thermal conductivity of the material of the tube

h = film heat transfer coefficient

Subscripts

1 and 2 denote the inside and outside surfaces of the tube.

o and i denote the outside and inside surfaces of the tube.

Substituting the values,

$$\frac{q}{L} = \frac{2\pi(115 - 60)}{\dfrac{1}{\frac{0.5}{12} \times 1400} + \dfrac{\ln \frac{1}{0.9}}{70} + \dfrac{1}{\frac{0.45}{12} \times 250}}$$

Simplifying,

$$\frac{q}{L} = \frac{345.58}{0.0171 + 0.0015 + 0.1067}$$

$$= 2758 \text{ Btu/hr-ft}$$

The rate of condensation of steam per foot length of tube can be obtained by dividing the rate of heat transfer by the latent heat of vaporization.

i.e., $\frac{2758}{1029} = 2.68$ lb_m/hr-ft (length of the tube)

A $1\frac{1}{2}$ in. dia., 12 ft. long, schedule 40, standard steel pipe is used to condense steam on its outer surface, by flowing water through it. The inside and outside film coefficients are 400 Btu/hr-ft^2-$^\circ$F and 1800 Btu/hr-ft^2-$^\circ$F respectively. The overall temperature difference at the inlet, section of the water is 200°F and at the outlet is 90°F. Estimate the amount of heat gained per hour by the water. The I.D. and O.D. of the pipe are 1.610 in. and 1.90 in. respectively. The thermal conductivity of the pipe is 25 Btu/hr-ft-$^\circ$F.

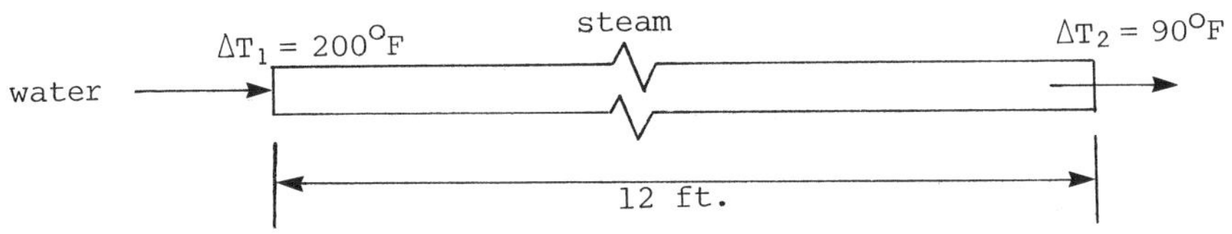

Solution: The cooling water flowing inside the pipe is absorbing the latent heat of vaporization of the steam. Since the temperature difference is not constant along the length of the pipe, the logarithmic mean temperature difference (LMTD) must be used to obtain the rate of heat transfer.

The LMTD is given by

$$\text{LMTD} = \frac{\Delta T_1 - \Delta T_2}{\ln\left(\frac{\Delta T_1}{\Delta T_2}\right)}$$

Substituting the values

$$\text{LMTD} = \frac{200 - 90}{\ln\left(\frac{200}{90}\right)}$$

$$= 137.76^\circ\text{F}$$

The rate of heat transfer is given by

$$q = U.A.(\text{LMTD})$$

where

U = overall heat transfer coefficient based upon the area A

The over-all heat transfer coefficient U_i, based on the inside area is given as

$$\frac{1}{U_i} = \frac{1}{h_i} + \frac{A_i}{h_o A_o} + \frac{A_i x_w}{k_w A_w}$$

where

A = area (circumferential area)

x_w = thickness of the wall

A_w = mean area of the wall (for thin walled pipe)

k_w = thermal conductivity of the wall of the pipe

h = film heat transfer coefficients

Subscripts i and o denote the inside and outside surface of the pipe respectively.

The ratios

$$\frac{A_i}{A_o} = \frac{1.61}{1.90} = 0.8474$$

and $$\frac{A_i}{A_w} = \frac{1.61 \times 2}{1.61 + 1.9} = 0.9174$$

Substituting the values into the equation for the overall heat transfer coefficient gives

$$\frac{1}{U_i} = \frac{1}{400} + \frac{0.8474}{1800} + 0.9174 \frac{(1.9 - 1.61)}{12 \times 2 \times 25}$$

$$= 0.0025 + 0.00047 + 0.00044$$

$$= 0.0034$$

or U_i = 293 Btu/hr-ft $-^{o}F$

The rate of heat transfer

$$q = 293 \times \pi\left(\frac{1.61}{12}\right) \times 12 \times 137.76$$

$$= 204{,}158 \text{ Btu/hr.}$$

• PROBLEM 9-18

Find the critical radius of insulation for a pipe surrounded by asbestos ($k = 0.181$ W/m. ^{o}C) and exposed to air at a temperature of 10°C with $h = 3.5$ W/m^2. ^{o}C. Also, find the heat loss from the pipe at 275°C for the following cases;

a) Pipe with critical radius of insulation
b) Pipe without insulation
c) Pipe with critical radius of insulation + 1.5 cm. thickness insulation
d) Pipe with critical radius of insulation - 1.5 cm. insulation.

Also plot the values of q/L for each case versus radius.

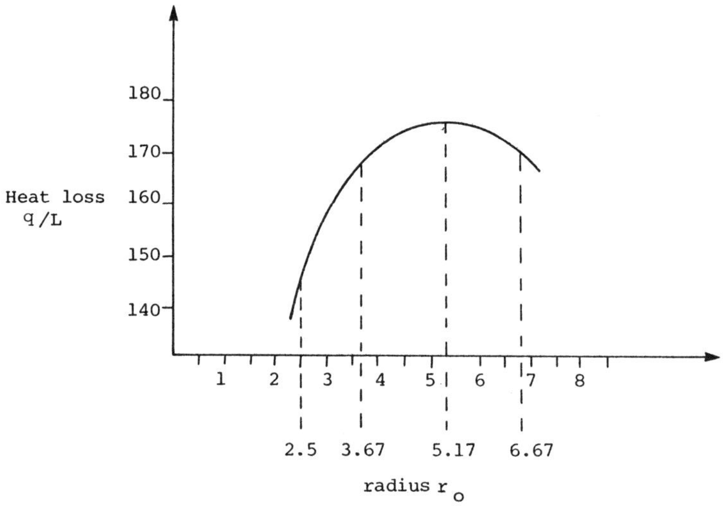

Solution: The critical radius of insulation is given by the equation

$$r_c = \frac{k}{h}$$

$$\therefore \qquad r_c = \frac{0.181}{3.5} = 0.05171 \text{ m} = 5.17 \text{ cm.}$$

a. The outer radius of the pipe is $\frac{5.0}{2}$ = 2.5 cms. The heat transfer is found by calculating the heat conducted through the insulation using the equation

$$q = \frac{2\pi L(T_s - T_\infty)}{\frac{\ln(r_c/r_i)}{k} + \frac{1}{r_c h}}$$

where

T_s = surface temperature of pipe

T_∞ = temperature of surrounding air

r_i = inner radius of insulation

$$\frac{q}{L} = \frac{2\pi(275 - 10)}{\frac{\ln(5.17/2.5)}{0.181} + \frac{1}{(0.0517)(3.5)}} = 174.52 \text{ W/m.}$$

b. Since there is no insulation on the pipe, the heat loss is calculated by finding the heat transfer by convection from the outer surface of the pipe.

$$q = (2\pi rL)h(T_s - T_\infty)$$

$$\frac{q}{L} = (2\pi)(0.025)(3.5)(275 - 10) = 145.69 \text{ W/m}$$

c. In this case the outer radius r_o = 5.17 - 1.5 = 3.67 cm. = 0.0367 m. ∴ using the equation for heat loss per unit length for a cylinder

$$\frac{q}{L} = \frac{2\pi(T_s - T_\infty)}{\frac{\ln(r_o/r_i)}{k} + \frac{1}{r_o h}}$$

$$= \frac{2\pi(275 - 10)}{\frac{\ln(3.67/2.5)}{0.181} + \frac{1}{(0.367)(3.5)}} = 168.08 \text{ W/m}$$

d. Here the outer radius of insulation is $r_o = r_c + 1.5$

$$= 5.17 + 1.5$$
$$= 6.67 \text{ cm.}$$
$$= 0.0667 \text{ m.}$$

Hence heat loss is

$$\frac{q}{L} = \frac{2\pi(275 - 10)}{\frac{\ln(6.67/2.5)}{0.181} + \frac{1}{(0.0667)(3.5)}}$$

$$= 171.56 \text{ W/m.}$$

The values of the heat lost per unit length (q/L) are plotted versus radius in the figure shown.

• PROBLEM 9-19

A copper pipe (1 in. O.D., 0.88 in. I.D. and k = 220 Btu/hr-ft-°F) carries process steam 212°F through a room at 60°F. The heating cost of steam is 0.05 cents/Btu. The pipe is insulated with 85% magnesia (0.57 in. thick and k = 0.038 Btu/hr-ft-°F) at a cost of $3.25 per foot. Estimate the payback period of insulation cost. Assume a constant fluid film resistance (0.95 hr-ft-°F/Btu) and neglect outer surface film resistance.

Solution: The thermal resistance to the heat flow per foot length of the pipe, when the pipe is bare

$$R_1 = \frac{\ln\left(\frac{r_o}{r_i}\right)}{2\pi k} + \text{film resistance}$$

where r_i and r_o denote the inside and outside radii of the pipe.

Substituting the values,

$$R_1 = \frac{\ln\left(\frac{1}{0.88}\right)}{2\pi \times 220} + 0.95$$

$$= 0.95009 \text{ hr-ft-}^{\circ}\text{F/Btu}$$

Therefore, the thermal resistance of the pipe without insulation is $R_1 = 0.95009$ hr-ft-$^{\circ}$F/Btu.

The thermal resistance to the heat flow per foot length of the pipe, when the pipe is insulated, is given by sum of R_1 and the resistance of the insulation.

$$R_2 = R_1 + \text{resistance of insulation}$$

$$= 0.95009 + \frac{\ln\left(\frac{1.57}{1}\right)}{2\pi \times 0.038}$$

$$= 0.95009 + 1.889$$

$$R_2 = 2.839 \text{ hr-ft-}^{\circ}\text{F/Btu}$$

The heat lost from the bare pipe per foot length is given by

$$q_1 = \frac{\Delta T}{R_1}$$

where

ΔT = temperature difference

R_1 = thermal resistance

Substituting the values,

$$q_1 = \frac{212 - 60}{0.95009}$$

$$= 159.98 \text{ Btu/hr.}$$

The heat lost from the insulated pipe per foot length is given by

$$q_2 = \frac{\Delta T}{R_2}$$

Substituting the values,

$$q_2 = \frac{212 - 60}{2.839}$$

$$= 53.54 \text{ Btu/hr.}$$

Net saving of heat per foot length of the pipe by insulating is

$$(q_1 - q_2) = 159.98 - 53.54$$

$$= 106.44 \text{ Btu/hr.}$$

Therefore, amount saved per hour per foot length of the pipe is $\quad 106.44 \times \frac{0.05}{100}$ dollars/hr.

$= 0.05322$ dollars/hr.

Therefore, the time of operation required to recover the insulation cost is

$$\frac{3.25}{0.05322} = 61 \text{ hours.}$$

• **PROBLEM 9-20**

Heat flows through the walls of an annular pipe whose inside and outside radii are R_i and R_0 respectively. The thermal conductivity of the material is directly proportional to the square of temperature.

$$k = aT^2 + b$$

Derive the temperature profile of the wall and compute the heat loss through the walls.

Solution: A heat balance yields,

$$\frac{d}{dr}(rq_r) = 0$$

or $$rq_r = C_1 \qquad \therefore\ q_r = \frac{C_1}{r}$$

Since $\quad q_r = -k\frac{dT}{dr} = -k(aT^2 + b)\frac{dT}{dr} = \frac{C_1}{r}$, we get

$$\left(\frac{aT^3}{3} + bT\right) = -C_1(\ln r) + C_2$$

Boundary conditions: $\quad$ at $r = R_o$, $\quad T = T_o$

$\qquad r = R_i$, $\quad T = T_i$

$$\therefore \quad \frac{aT_o^{\ 3}}{3} + bT_o = -C_1(\ln R_0) + C_2$$

$$\frac{aT_i^{\ 3}}{3} + bT_i = -C_1(\ln R_i) + C_2$$

$$\therefore \quad C_1 = \frac{1}{\ln(R_i/R_o)}\left[\frac{a}{3}(T_o^{\ 3} - T_i^{\ 3}) + b(T_o - T_i)\right]$$

$$\therefore \quad C_2 = \frac{aT_o^{\ 3}}{3} + bT_o + \frac{\ln R_o}{\ln(R_i/R_o)}\left[\frac{a}{3}(T_o^{\ 3} - T_i^{\ 3}) + b(T_o - T_i)\right]$$

$\therefore$ The temperature profile: $\dfrac{aT^3}{3} + bT = -C_1(\ln r) + C_2$

$$\text{or } \frac{aT^3}{3} + bT = \frac{1}{\ln(R_o/R_i)}\left[\frac{a}{3}(T_o^3 - T_i^3) + b(T_o - T_i)\right] \ln r +$$

$$\frac{aT_o^3}{3} + bT_o + \frac{\ln R_o}{\ln(R_i/R_o)}\left[\frac{a}{3}(T_o^3 - T_i^3) + b(T_o - T_i)\right]$$

$$\text{The heat loss through the walls} = q_r \Big|_{r = R_o}^{2\pi R_o L} = 2\pi LC_1$$

$$= \frac{2\pi L}{\ln(R_i/R_o)}\left[\frac{a}{3}(T_o^3 - T_i^3) + b(T_o - T_i)\right]$$

CONVECTION AND INTERNAL HEAT GENERATION

• PROBLEM 9-21

A standard (schedule 40) 1-in.-diameter steel pipe (k = 25 Btu/hr-ft-^oF) has saturated steam at 50 psia flowing through it. The pipe is surrounded with air at 80°F. The inside and outside convective heat transfer coefficients are 1800 Btu/hr-ft^2-^{o}F and 8 Btu/hr-ft^2-^{o}F respectively.

a) Find the rate of heat loss per foot length of pipe

b) If the pipe is insulated with 1 in. thick magnesia insulation (k = 0.04 Btu/hr-ft-^{o}F) determine the percentage reduction of heat loss compared to bare pipe.

Solution:

a) In this case, the rate of heat transfer is radially outwards, and is given by

$$q = \frac{(\Delta T)_{\text{over-all}}}{\frac{1}{h_i A_i} + \frac{\ln(r_o/r_i)}{2\pi kL} + \frac{1}{h_o A_o}} \qquad (1)$$

where

ΔT = temperature differential

h = convective heat transfer

r = radius

A = area of thermal energy flow (circumferential)

L = length of the pipe considered

Subscripts i and o denote inside and outside surfaces of the pipe respectively.

For foot length of the pipe, L = 1 ft.

$$A = 2\pi r$$

The saturation temperature for steam at 50 psia is 281°F

Hence $(\Delta T)_{\text{over-all}} = (281 - 80) = 201^\circ F$

The dimensions of 1 in. std. pipe are 1.049 I.D., 1.315 O.D., thickness = 0.133 in. (obtained from tables)

Substituting the values into equation (1),

$$q = \frac{201}{\left[\frac{1 \times 12}{1800 \times \pi \times 1.049} + \frac{\ln \frac{1.315}{1.049}}{2\pi \times 25} + \frac{1 \times 12}{8 \times \pi \times 1.315}\right]}$$

$$= \frac{201}{0.3668}$$

$$= 548.4 \text{ Btu/hr}$$

Therefore, the rate of heat loss per foot length = 548.4 Btu/hr.

b) In this case, the rate of heat loss is given by

$$q = \frac{(\Delta T)_{\text{over-all}}}{\left[\frac{1}{h_i A_i} + \frac{\ln(r_o/r_i)}{2\pi k_p L} + \frac{\ln(R_o/R_i)}{2\pi k_m L} + \frac{1}{h_o A_o}\right]}$$

where

ΔT = temperature differential

h = convective transfer coefficient

r = radius of the pipe

R = radius of the insulation

k_p = thermal conductivity of the pipe material

k_m = thermal conductivity of the magnesia insulation

L = length of the pipe

A = area of heat flow (circumferential)

Subscripts i and o denote inside and outside surfaces respectively.

Substituting the values,

the rate of heat loss per foot length is

$$q = \frac{201}{\left[\frac{12}{1800 \times \pi \times 1.049} + \frac{\ln \frac{1.315}{1.049}}{2\pi \times 25} + \frac{\ln \frac{3.315}{1.315}}{2\pi \times 0.04} + \frac{12}{8 \times \pi \times 3.315}\right]}$$

= 52.53 Btu/hr.

Therefore, the percentage reduction of heat loss is

$$\frac{548.4 - 52.53}{548.4} \times 100 = 90.4\%$$

• PROBLEM 9-22

A standard (schedule 40) 3/4 in. diameter steel pipe (k = 25 Btu/hr-ft-$^\circ$F) has saturated steam at 40 psia flowing through it. The pipe is covered with 1.25 in. thick of magnesia insulation (k = 0.035 Btu/hr-ft-$^\circ$F). The outside surface of the insulation is exposed to air at 75°F. The inside and outside convective heat transfer coefficients are 800 Btu/hr-ft^2-$^\circ$F and 5 Btu/hr-ft^2-$^\circ$F respectively.

a) Using thermal resistances, determine the rate of heat loss per foot length of the pipe

b) Using the over-all heat transfer coefficient based on the inside area A_i, determine the rate of heat loss per foot length of the pipe.

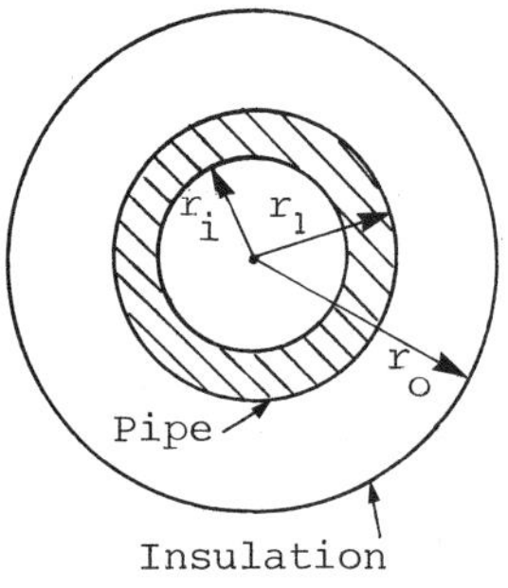

Solution: The dimensions of the standard (schedule 40) 3/4 in. diameter pipe are obtained from the table.

0.824 in. I.D.,   1.05 in. O.D.

thickness of the pipe wall is 0.113 in.

The surface areas of the cylindrical layers of 1 foot length of the pipe are given by

$$A = 2\pi r$$

where

A is the surface area corresponding to the radius r.

Therefore, the inside surface area

$$A_i = 2\pi r_i$$

$$= \pi \times \frac{0.824}{12}$$

or, $A_i = 0.2157 \text{ ft}^2$.

Similarly

$$A_1 = 2\pi r_1$$

$$= \pi \times \frac{1.05}{12}$$

$$A_1 = 0.2749 \text{ ft}^2$$

and $A_o = 2\pi r_o$

$$= \pi \times \frac{3.55}{12}$$

$$A_o = 0.9294 \text{ ft}^2$$

The logarithmic mean area of the pipe surface is

$$A_{p(lm)} = \frac{A_1 - A_i}{\ln(A_1/A_i)}$$

Substituting the values

$$A_{p(lm)} = \frac{0.2749 - 0.2157}{\ln\left(\frac{0.2749}{0.2157}\right)}$$

$$= 0.2441 \text{ ft}^2$$

Similarly the logarithmic mean area of the insulation surface is

$$A_{in(lm)} = \frac{A_o - A_1}{\ln(A_o/A_1)}$$

Substituting the values,

$$A_{in(lm)} = \frac{0.9294 - 0.2749}{\ln\left(\frac{0.9294}{0.2749}\right)}$$

$$= 0.5373 \text{ ft}^2.$$

a) The overall thermal resistance is equal to the sum of the individual thermal resistances in series. The thermal resistance of a convective boundary is given by

$$R = \frac{1}{hA}$$

where

h = convective heat transfer coefficient

A = surface area

Substituting the values for inside and outside surfaces,

For inside surface

$$R_i = \frac{1}{h_i A_i}$$

$$= \frac{1}{800 \times 0.2157}$$

$$R_i = 5.795 \times 10^{-3} \ \frac{1}{Btu/hr\text{-}^{o}F}$$

For outside surface

$$R_o = \frac{1}{h_o A_o}$$

$$= \frac{1}{5 \times 0.9294}$$

$$R_o = 0.2152 \ \frac{1}{Btu/hr\text{-}^{o}F}$$

The thermal resistance of a cylindrical layer is given by

$$R = \frac{r_1 - r_2}{kA_{1m}}$$

where

r_1 and r_2 are the outside and inside radii of the cylindrical layer.

k = thermal conductivity of the material of the layer.

A_{1m} = logarithmic mean area of the cylindrical layer.

Therefore, the thermal resistance of the steel pipe is

$$R_p = \frac{0.113}{25 \times 0.2441} \times \frac{1}{12}$$

$$= 1.543 \times 10^{-3} \ \frac{1}{Btu/hr\text{-}^{o}F}$$

The thermal resistance of the insulation is

$$R_{in} = \frac{1.25}{12 \times 0.035 \times 0.5373}$$

$$= 5.53916 \ \frac{1}{\text{Btu/hr-}^{\circ}\text{F}}$$

Therefore, the over-all thermal resistance is

$$R = R_i + R_o + R_p + R_{in}$$

Substituting the values,

$$R = 5.795 \times 10^{-3} + 0.2152 + 1.543 \times 10^{-3} + 5.53916$$

$$= 5.7617 \ \frac{1}{\text{Btu/hr-}^{\circ}\text{F}}$$

The saturation temperature corresponding to the saturation pressure of 40 psia is 267°F.

The rate of heat transfer is given by

$$q = \frac{\Delta T}{R}$$

where

q = rate of heat transfer

ΔT = temperature potential

R = thermal resistance

Substituting the values,

$$q = \frac{267 - 75}{5.7617} = 33.32 \text{ Btu/hr}$$

b) The overall heat transfer coefficient based on the inside area is

$$U_i = \frac{1}{\frac{1}{h_i} + \frac{(r_1 - r_i)A_i}{k_p A_{p(lm)}} + \frac{(r_o - r_1)A_i}{k_{in} A_{in(lm)}} + \frac{A_i}{h_o A_o}}$$

Substituting the values,

$$U_i = \frac{1}{\frac{1}{800} + \frac{0.113 \times 0.2157}{12 \times 25 \times 0.2441} + \frac{1.25 \times 0.2157}{12 \times 0.035 \times 0.5373} + \frac{0.2157}{5 \times 0.9294}}$$

$$= 0.8046 \text{ Btu/hr-ft}^2\text{-}^{\circ}\text{F}$$

The rate of heat transfer q in terms of U_i is given as

$$q = U_i A_i (\Delta T)$$

$$= 0.8046 \times 0.2157 \ (267 - 75)$$

$$q = 33.32 \text{ Btu/hr.}$$

• PROBLEM 9-23

A spherical shell of cast iron having an inside radius 2.5 in. and outside radius 6 in., contains a solution which liberates heat at the rate of 0.8×10^5 Btu/hr. The outside surface of the shell is held at 120°F. Assuming that the steady state conditions prevail and that the thermal conductivity of the cast iron 45 Btu/hr-ft-$^{\circ}$F reamins constant, determine the temperature distribution in the shell. Find the temperature at r = 5 in.

Solution: For steady state conditions, the rate of flow of thermal energy is constant. The rate of heat flow through a spherical shell is given by

$$q = \frac{T_i - T_o}{\frac{1}{4\pi k}\left(\frac{1}{r_i} - \frac{1}{r_o}\right)} \quad (1)$$

and the temperature distribution is

$$T = T_o + \frac{(T_i - T_o)\left(\frac{1}{r} - \frac{1}{r_o}\right)}{\left(\frac{1}{r_i} - \frac{1}{r_o}\right)} \quad (2)$$

where the subscripts i and o denote the inside and outside surfaces respectively.

The value of $(T_i - T_o)$ can be found out from equation (1) and when substituted into equation (2) gives the required temperature distribution.

Substituting the values into equation (1),

$$0.8 \times 10^5 = \frac{(T_i - T_o)}{\frac{1}{4\pi \times 45}\left(\frac{12}{2.5} - \frac{12}{6}\right)}$$

or, $$(T_i - T_o) = \frac{12}{4\pi \times 45}\left(\frac{1}{2.5} - \frac{1}{6}\right) \times 0.8 \times 10^5$$

$$= 396^{\circ}\text{F}$$

$$T_i = 396 + 120 = 516^{\circ}\text{F}$$

Substituting the values into equation (2)

$$T = 120 + 396 \times \frac{\left(\frac{12}{r} - \frac{12}{6}\right)}{\left(\frac{12}{2.5} - \frac{12}{6}\right)}$$

$$= 120 + \frac{396\left(\frac{1}{r} - \frac{1}{6}\right)}{\left(\frac{1}{2.5} - \frac{1}{6}\right)}$$

$$= 120 + 1697 \times \frac{1}{r} - 283$$

$$T = 1697 \times \frac{1}{r} - 163$$

where r is in inches.

Therefore, the temperature at r = 5 in. is

$$T = \frac{1697}{5} - 163 = 176^{\circ}F$$

• PROBLEM 9-24

> Two large copper plates at temperature of $75^{\circ}F$ are separated by a copper rod ($k = 220$ Btu/hr-ft-$^{\circ}F$) 0.25 in. diameter and 1.2 ft long. The rod is welded to each plate. The space between the plates is filled with insulation which also insulates the lateral faces of the rod. Find the maximum electrical current that the rod may carry if the temperature is not to exceed $300^{\circ}F$ at any point.
>
> The electrical resistivity of the copper rod is 5.3×10^{-8} (ohm)(ft).

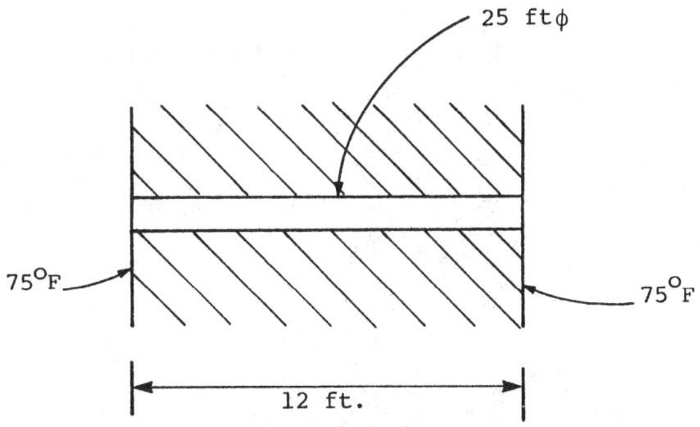

Solution: The electrical resistance of the rod is given by

$$R = \frac{\rho l}{A}$$

where

R = electrical resistance

ρ = electrical resistivity

l = length of the rod

A = cross-sectional area of the rod.

Substituting the values,

$$R = 5.3 \times 10^{-8} \times \frac{1.2}{\frac{\pi}{4}\left(\frac{0.25}{12}\right)^2}$$

$$= 1.87 \times 10^{-4} \text{ ohms.}$$

The insulation of the lateral face of the rod assumes zero radial temperature gradient. Therefore, the temperature field is one dimensional and is axial.

Since both the ends of the rod are at the same temperature ($75^{\circ}F$), the maximum temperature should be at the mid-point of the rod.

The differential equation controlling the heat flow by conduction, when the body is generating heat is

$$\frac{d^2T}{dx^2} + \frac{q'}{k} = 0$$

where

q' = rate of heat generation per unit volume

k = thermal conductivity of the rod = 220 Btu/hr-ft-$^{\circ}F$

The temperature distribution is given by

$$T(x) = T_b + \frac{q'L^2}{8k}\left[1 - \left(\frac{2x}{L}\right)^2\right]$$

where, T_b = temperature at the boundary

L = length of the rod

q' = rate of heat generation per unit volume

At $x = 0$; $T(x) = 300^{\circ}F$

Substituting the values and calculating q',

$$300 = 75 + \frac{q'(1.2)^2}{8 \times 220}(1 - 0)$$

$$q' = 225 \times \frac{8 \times 220}{(1.2)^2}$$

$$= 275{,}000 \text{ Btu/hr-ft}^3$$

But

$$q' = \frac{q}{\text{volume}}$$

where

q = total rate of heat generation

But

$$q = RI^2$$

where

R = resistance in ohm

I = current in amp

Therefore,

$$q' = \frac{RI^2}{\text{volume}}$$

i.e.,
$$275{,}000 = \frac{1.87 \times 10^{-4} \times I^2}{\frac{\pi}{4}\left(\frac{0.25}{12}\right)^2 \times 1.2} \times 3.413$$

Therefore,

$$I = \left[275{,}000 \times \frac{\pi}{4}\left(\frac{0.25}{12}\right)^2 \times \frac{1.2}{3.413} \times \frac{1}{1.87 \times 10^{-4}}\right]^{\frac{1}{2}}$$

$= 420$ amps.

Therefore, the maximum electrical current the rod can carry is 420 amps.

• PROBLEM 9-25

An electrical current flows along a flat plate of carbon steel $\frac{1}{2}$ in. thick, 4 in. wide and 2.5 ft. long, when a potential of 12 volts is applied. Under steady state conditions, if the temperature of the lateral faces is 1500°F, determine the temperature at the center of the plate.

The heat loss from the end surfaces is neglected. Assume that the ohmic heat generated is uniform across the section.

ρ(resistivity of carbon steel) $= 1.25 \times 10^{-4}$ (ohm)(ft)

k(thermal conductivity of carbon steel) = 2.8 Btu/hr-ft-$^{\circ}$F

Solution: Electrical resistance of the plate is given by

$$R = \frac{\rho L}{A}$$

where

R = electrical resistance

ρ = resistivity of carbon steel

L = length of the plate

A = cross-sectional area of the plate

Substituting the values,

$$R = 1.25 \times 10^{-4} \times \frac{2.5}{\frac{1}{2} \times 4} \times 12 \times 12$$

$$= 0.0225 \text{ ohm}$$

The rate of heat generation in the plate is given by I^2R or $\frac{V^2}{R}$.

where

I = amps (current)

V = voltage

R = resistance

Substituting,

the rate of heat generation is

$$= \frac{(12)^2}{0.0225}$$

$$= 6400 \text{ watts}$$

$$= 6400 \times 3.413 \text{ Btu/hr}$$

$$= 21{,}843$$

Therefore, the rate of heat generation per unit volume is

$$\frac{21843}{2.5 \times 4 \times 0.5} \times 12 \times 12$$

$$q' = 629{,}078 \text{ Btu/hr-ft}^3$$

The differential equation controlling the heat flow by conduction, when the body is generating heat is

$$\frac{d^2T}{dx^2} + \frac{q'}{k} = 0 \qquad (1)$$

Integrating,

$$\frac{dT}{dx} + \frac{q'x}{k} = C_1 \qquad (2)$$

where

C_1 is a constant of integration

If the plate is symmetrical

$\frac{dT}{dx}$ at $x = 0$ is

$$\left.\frac{dT}{dx}\right|_{x = 0} = 0$$

Substituting this condition into equation (2) yields $C_1 = 0$

$$\frac{dT}{dx} + \frac{q'x}{k} = 0$$

Integrating again,

$$T + \frac{q'x^2}{2k} = C_2 \qquad (3)$$

But, given $T = 1500$ at $x = \frac{1}{4 \times 12}$ ft.

Substituting the values and calculating for C_2

$$C_2 = 1500 + \frac{629078}{2 \times 2.8 \times (4 \times 12)^2} = 1549$$

Substituting the values into equation (3)

$$T = \frac{-629078}{2 \times 2.8} x^2 + 1549$$

$$\text{or,} \quad T = -112335\, x^2 + 1549 \qquad (4)$$

The temperature at the center of the plate can be obtained by substituting $x = 0$ in equation (4).

$T = 1549^{\circ}F$ is the temperature at the center of the plate.

• PROBLEM 9-26

Heat is produced by nuclear fission within a fuel rod, the rate per unit volume of which is a function of the axial position within the rod,

$$P = P_o\left[1 + b\left(\frac{r}{R_1}\right)^2\right]$$

where R_1 is the radius of the rod. The rod is encapped in an annular layer of cladding cooled by heavy water at temperature T_w. The heat-transfer coefficient at the cladding-heavy water interface is h_L. What is the maximum temperature within the fuel rod.

Solution: For the fuel rod,

$$\frac{d}{dr}(rq_r^f) - P_o\left[1 + b\left(\frac{r}{R_1}\right)^2\right] r = 0$$

$$rq_r^f = P_o\left[\frac{r^2}{2} + \frac{b}{R_1^2}\frac{r^4}{4}\right] + C_1$$

B.C. At $r = 0$, $\frac{dT_f}{dr} = 0$ or $q_r^f = 0$

whence $C_1 = 0$

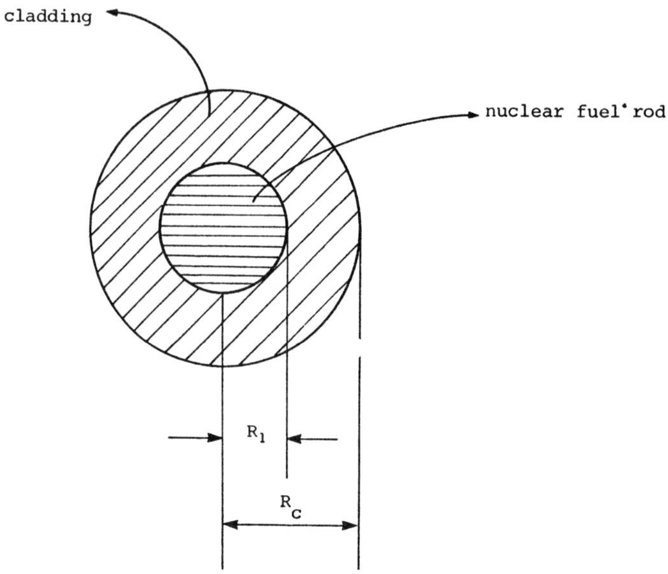

$$\therefore \qquad rq_r^{\ f} = P_o \left[\frac{r^2}{2} + \frac{b}{4R_1^2} r^4\right]$$

But $$q_r^{\ f} = -k_f \frac{dTf}{dr} = P_o \left[\frac{r}{2} + \frac{b}{4R_1^2} r^3\right]$$

$$\therefore \qquad dT_f = -\frac{P_o}{k_f} \left[\frac{r}{2} + \frac{b}{4R_1^2} r^3\right]$$

$$\therefore \qquad T_f = -\frac{P_o}{k_f} \left[\frac{r^2}{4} + \frac{br^4}{16R_1^2}\right] + C_2 \qquad (1)$$

For the cladding, $\frac{d}{dr}(rq_r^{\ c}) = 0$ or $q_r^{\ c} = \frac{C_3}{r}$

Also $$q_r^{\ c} = -k_c \frac{dT_c}{dr} = \frac{C_3}{r} \quad \text{or} \quad T_c = -\frac{C_3}{k_c} \ln r + C_4 \qquad (2)$$

Boundary condition: At $r = R_c$, $q_r^{\ c} = -k \frac{dT_c}{dr} = h_L(T_c - T_L)$

Also at $r = R_1$, $q_r^{\ f} = q_r^{\ c}$

$$\text{or} \qquad P_o \left[\frac{R_1}{2} + \frac{bR_1^3}{4R_1^2}\right] = \frac{C_3}{R_1} \quad \text{or} \quad P_oR_1 \left[\frac{1}{2} + \frac{b}{4}\right] = \frac{C_3}{R_1}$$

$$\text{or} \qquad C_3 = P_oR_1^2 \left[\frac{1}{2} + \frac{b}{4}\right] = \frac{P_oR_1^2}{4} \left[2 + b\right] \qquad (3)$$

Since at $r = R_1$, $T_c = T_f$, we get

$$-\frac{P_o}{k_f} \left[\frac{R_1^2}{4} + \frac{bR_1^4}{16R_1^2}\right] + C_2 = -\frac{C_3}{k_c} \ln R_1 + C_4 \qquad (4)$$

And at $r = R_c$, $q_r^c = h_L(T_c - T_L)$

or $$\frac{C_3}{R_c} = h_L\left[-\frac{C_3 \ln R_c}{k_c} + C_4 - T_L\right]$$

$$\therefore \quad C_4 = C_3\left[\frac{1}{h_L R_c} + \frac{\ln R_c}{k_c}\right] + T_L$$

$$= \left[2 + b\right]\frac{P_o R_1^2}{4}\left[\frac{1}{h_L R_c} + \frac{\ln R_c}{k_c}\right] + T_L \qquad (5)$$

Substituting for C_3 and C_4 in equation (4), we can evaluate C_2 as

$$C_2 = -\frac{P_o R_1^2}{4k_c}\left[2 + b\right]\ln R_1 + (2 + b)\frac{P_o R_1^2}{4}\left[\frac{1}{h_L R_c} + \frac{\ln R_c}{k_c}\right] +$$
$$T_L + \frac{P_o}{k_f}\left[\frac{R_1^2}{4} + \frac{bR_1^4}{16R_1^2}\right]$$

or $$C_2 = -\frac{P_o R_1^2}{4k_c}(2 + b)\ln R_1 + (2 + b)\frac{P_o R_1^2}{4}\left[\frac{1}{h_L R_c} + \frac{\ln R_c}{k_c}\right]$$
$$+ T_L + \frac{P_o}{k_f}\left[\frac{R_1^2}{4} + \frac{bR_1^2}{16}\right]$$

$$\therefore \quad T_f = -\frac{P_o}{k_f}\left[\frac{r^2}{4} + \frac{br^4}{16R_1^2}\right] + C_2$$

or $$T_f - T_L = -\frac{P_o}{k_f}\left[\frac{r^2}{4} + \frac{br^4}{16R_1^2}\right] + C_2 - T_L$$

$(T_f - T_L)$ is maximum when $r = 0$.

$$\therefore (T_f - T_L)_{max} = \frac{(2 + b)P_o R_1^2}{4k_c}\left[\frac{k_L}{h_L R_c} + \ln R_c\right] + \frac{P_o R_1^2}{16k_f}\left[4 + b\right]$$
$$- \frac{P_o R_1^2}{4k_c}(2 + b)\ln R_1$$

$$= \frac{(2 + b)P_o R_1}{4k_c}\left[\ln\frac{R_c}{R_1} + \frac{k_L}{h_L R_c}\right] +$$

$$\frac{P_o R_1^2}{16k_f} (4 + b)$$

ONE, TWO AND MULTIDIMENSIONAL STEADY STATE CONDUCTION

• PROBLEM 9-27

A pipe 4 in. in diameter and 100 ft long carrying the steam is buried in the ground parallel to the ground surface. Assuming the pipe surface temperature to be $300^\circ F$ and ground surface temperature as $60^\circ F$, find the heat loss per hour from the pipe. The ground surface to pipe center distance is 6 ft. Thermal conductivity of soil $k = 0.8$ Btu/hr-ft-$^\circ F$.

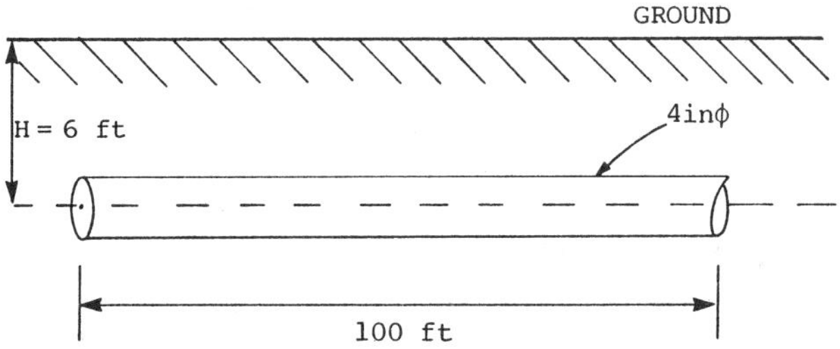

Solution: The rate of heat flow is given by

$$q = kS(T_p - T_s)$$

where

k = thermal conductivity of soil

S = conduction shape factor of the pipe

T_p = temperature of the pipe surface

T_s = temperature of the ground surface

The conduction shape factor for the given case is

$$S = \frac{2\pi L}{\ln\left(\frac{L}{r}\right)\left[1 + \frac{\ln \frac{2H}{L}}{\ln \frac{L}{r}}\right]} = \frac{2\pi L}{\ln \frac{2H}{r}}$$

where

L = length of the pipe

r = radius of the pipe

H = depth at which the pipe is buried

Substituting the values,

$$S = \frac{2\pi \times 100}{\ln\left(\frac{2 \times 6 \times 12}{2}\right)}$$

$$= 146.92$$

Substituting the values into the equation for rate of heat transfer,

$$q = 0.8 \times 146.92(300 - 60)$$

$$= 28,208 \text{ Btu/hr}$$

• PROBLEM 9-28

An oven of 50 cm x 50 cm x 50 cm inside dimensions is made up of firebrick (thermal conductivity 0.75 W/m·K). Each wall of the oven is 15 cm thick. If the inside temperature of the oven is 600°C when the outside air temperature is 35°C, calculate the rate of heat loss from the oven. Neglect the inner and outer convective heat transfer coefficients.

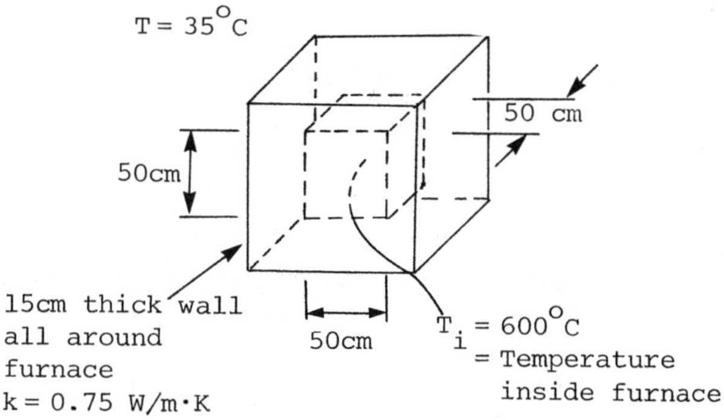

Solution: Neglecting the inner and outer convective heat transfer coefficients, implies that the inner and outer walls of the oven are at the same temperature as the surrounding air.

Therefore, the inner and outer walls of the oven are at 600°C and 35°C respectively.

Two dimensional heat transfer from one surface to another surface is given by

$$q = kS_{total}(\Delta T)$$

where

k = thermal conductivity

S_{total} = overall conduction shape factor

ΔT = temperature difference

S_{total} = sum of the all conduction shape factors

The conduction shape factor for a plane wall S_w is given by

$$S_w = \frac{A}{x}$$

where

A = area of the wall

x = thickness of the wall

$$S_w = \frac{0.5 \times 0.5}{0.15}$$

$$= 1.67$$

The conduction shape factor for an edge is given by

$$S_e = 0.54 \, L_e$$

where

L_e = length of the edge

Substituting, $S_e = 0.54 \times 0.5$

$= 0.27$

The conduction shape factor for a corner is given by

$$S_c = 0.15 \times x$$

where

x = thickness of the wall

substituting,

$$S_c = 0.15 \times 0.15$$

$$= 0.0225$$

The cube shaped oven has six walls, twelve edges and eight corners. So the total shape factor is given by

$$S_{total} = 6S_w + 12S_e + 8S_c$$

$$= 6 \times 1.67 + 12 \times 0.27 + 8 \times 0.0225$$

$$= 13.44$$

Substituting the values into the equation for heat transfer,

$$q = 0.75 \times 13.44 \times (600-35)$$

$$= 5695 \text{ Watts}$$

$$= 5.695 \text{ kW}$$

• PROBLEM 9-29

A steel pipe of 3 in O.D. is placed vertically in the earth as shown in the figure. If saturated steam at 50 psia ($T = 281^{O}F$, $h_{fg} = 923.9$ Btu/lb) is poured into the pipe at the rate of 400 lb_m/hr, determine the depth at which the steam is completely condensed. The temperature of the ground is $60^{O}F$. The thermal conductivity of the earth is 0.8 Btu/hr-ft-^{O}F. Assume that the outside surface temperature of the pipe is equal to the temperature of the steam.

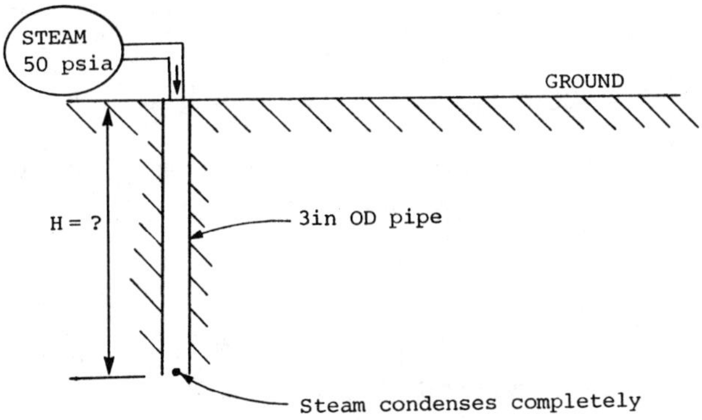

Solution: From the conservation of energy at steady state, the rate of heat loss of the condensing steam is same as the rate of heat transfer to the earth due to the thermal potential.

The rate of heat loss of the condensing steam is given by

$$q_{con} = \dot{m}\, h_{fg}$$

where

$\dot{m}$ = mass flow rate of steam

h_{fg} = evaporation enthalpy of steam

Substituting the values,

$$q_{con} = 400 \times 923.9$$

$$= 369{,}560 \text{ Btu/hr.}$$

The rate of heat transfer to the earth is given by

$$q = kS(T_p - T_s)$$

where

k = thermal conductivity of earth

S = conduction shape factor

T_p = temperature of the pipe surface

T_s = temperature of the ground surface

But,

$$q = q_{con}$$

$$= 369,560 \text{ Btu/hr.}$$

Substituting the values into the heat transfer equation and calculating for S,

$$369,560 = 0.8S(281 - 60)$$

Therefore,

$$S = 2090$$

But the conduction shape factor for the given system is

$$S = \frac{2\pi H}{\ln\left(\frac{2H}{r}\right)}$$

where

H is the required depth

r is the radius of the pipe

Therefore,

$$\frac{2\pi H}{\ln\left(\frac{2H}{r}\right)} = 2090$$

This equation can be solved for H by iterative procedure.

1) let H = 4000 ft.

then $$S = \frac{2\pi \times 4000}{\ln\left(\frac{2 \times 4000 \times 12}{1.5}\right)}$$

$$= 2270$$

2) let H = 3500 ft.

then $$S = \frac{2\pi \times 3500}{\ln\left(\frac{2 \times 3500 \times 12}{1.5}\right)}$$

$$= 2011$$

3) let H = 3650 ft.

then $$S = \frac{2\pi \times 3650}{\ln\left(\frac{2 \times 3650 \times 12}{1.5}\right)}$$

$$= 2090$$

Therefore, the depth at which the steam is completely condensed is 3650 ft.

• PROBLEM 9-30

Determine the temperature distribution in a semi-infinite two dimensional flat plate shown in the figure, if the base temperature is F(x) and the ambient temperature is T_∞.

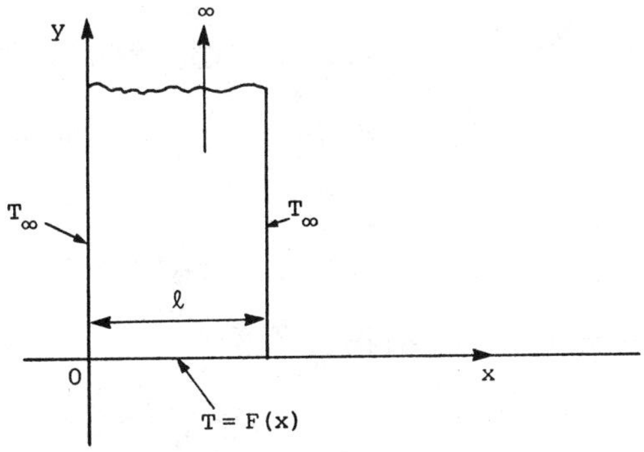

Solution: The controlling differential equation is

$$\frac{\partial^2 T}{\partial x^2} + \frac{\partial^2 T}{\partial y^2} = 0$$

and the given boundary conditions are

$$T(x,\ 0) = F(x)\ ; \quad T(1,\ y) = T_\infty$$

$$T(0,\ y) = T_\infty \quad ; \quad T(x,\ \infty) = T_\infty$$

Since the boundary conditions are non-homogeneous, the differential equation cannot be solved by the method of separation of variables. It requires that the differential equation and three of the boundary conditions to be homogeneous. This can be achieved by a simple transformation

$$\theta = T - T_\infty$$

Writing the differential equation and boundary conditions in terms of θ,

$$\frac{\partial^2\theta}{\partial x^2} + \frac{\partial^2\theta}{\partial y^2} = 0 \qquad (1)$$

$$\theta(x, 0) = F(x) - T_\infty = f(x) \qquad (2)$$

$$\theta(0, y) = 0 \qquad (3)$$

$$\theta(1, y) = 0 \qquad (4)$$

$$\theta(x, \infty) = 0 \qquad (5)$$

The solution to the equation (1) by the method of separation of variables is

$$\theta(x, y) = (A \cos \lambda x + B \sin \lambda x)(Ce^{\lambda y} + De^{-\lambda y})$$

where

A, B, C, D and λ are constants

Using the boundary condition (3)

$$\theta(0, y) = (A + 0)(Ce^{\lambda y} + De^{-\lambda y}) = 0$$

Therefore $A = 0$

So, $\theta(x, y) = B \sin \lambda x(Ce^{\lambda y} + De^{-\lambda y})$

The constant B can be absorbed into the constants C and D.

Therefore,

$$\theta(x, y) = \sin \lambda x \, (Ce^{\lambda y} + De^{-\lambda y})$$

Using the boundary condition (5)

$$\theta(x, \infty) = \sin \lambda x \, (Ce^{\infty} + De^{-\infty}) = 0$$

From the above equation $C = 0$.

Therefore, the differential equation becomes,

$$\theta(x, y) = \sin \lambda x \, (De^{-\lambda y})$$

Now using the boundary condition (4)

$$\theta(1, y) = De^{-\lambda y} \sin \lambda 1 = 0$$

Since $D \neq 0$, $\sin \lambda 1 = 0$

Therefore $\lambda 1 = n\pi \qquad n = 1, \ldots\infty$

$$\text{or} \qquad \lambda = \frac{n\pi}{1} \qquad (6)$$

The solution $\theta(x, y) = De^{-\lambda y} \sin \lambda x$, is a particular solution of the equation (1).

The general solution is obtained by summing all the particular solutions.

Therefore $\theta(x, y) = \sum_{n=1}^{\infty} D_n e^{-\lambda_n y} \cdot \sin \lambda_n x$ is the general solution.

Using the non-homogeneous boundary condition (2)

$$f(x) = \sum_{n=1}^{\infty} D_n \cdot \sin(\lambda_n x)$$

This is a Fourier series. The value of D_n is

$$D_n = \frac{\int_0^1 f(x) \sin(\lambda_n x)\, dx}{\int_0^1 \sin^2(\lambda_n x)\, dx}$$

Simplifying, this reduces to

$$D_n = \frac{2}{1} \int_0^1 f(x) \sin(\lambda_n x)\, dx$$

Substituting the value of D_n into the general solution,

$$\theta(x, y) = \frac{2}{1} \sum_{n=1}^{\infty} \left[\int_0^1 f(\eta) \sin \lambda\, \eta d\eta \right] e^{-\lambda_n y} \sin(\lambda_n x) \qquad (7)$$

where η is a dummy variable

Equation (7) is the required temperature distribution.

• PROBLEM 9-31

> Consider a solid steel block of cylindrical shape 6 in diameter and 3 in long. The two end faces of the cylinder are at 450°F and 150°F respectively. If the cylindrical surface is at 250°F, determine the temperature at the center of the cylinder.

Solution: This problem can be solved by the principle of superposition. If the cylindrical surface temperature 250°F is subtracted from all the temperatures, then the resulting temperatures are:
the cylindrical surface temperature is = 0°F

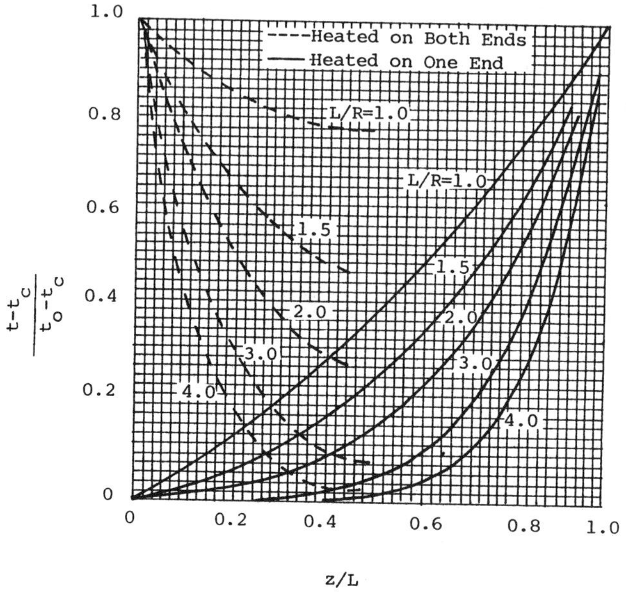

Axial temperature distribution in solid cylinders of finite length.

the end temperatures are 200^{0}F and -100^{0}F respectively.

This system can in turn be considered as equivalent to one cylinder at 0^{0}F on all surfaces and 200^{0}F on one end plus another cylinder at 0^{0}F on all surfaces and -100^{0}F on one end.

For a cylinder with 0^{0}F on the cylindrical surface and 200^{0}F on one end, the temperature at the center of the cylinder may be obtained from the figure.

The coordinate $\frac{z}{L}$ where

z = distance of the point from the end

L = length of the cylinder

for the mid point

$$\frac{z}{L} = 0.5$$

The parameter $\frac{L}{R}$
where

L = length of the cylinder

R = radius of the cylinder

for the mid point

$$\frac{L}{R} = \frac{3}{3} = 1$$

Therefore, from the figure, the corresponding ordinate is 0.385.

Therefore, the temperature at the mid point of the cylinder with $0^{\circ}F$ on the surface and $200^{\circ}F$ on one end is

$$T = 200 \times 0.385$$

$$= 77^{\circ}F$$

Similarly the temperature at the center of the cylinder, with $0^{\circ}F$ on the cylindrical surface and $-100^{\circ}F$ on one end is

$$T = -100 \times 0.385$$

$$= -38.5^{\circ}F$$

Now, superposing these two cylinders and adding $250^{\circ}F$ to all temperatures gives the original cylinder.

Therefore, the temperature at the center of the cylinder is

$$T = 77 - 38.5 + 250$$

$$= 288.5^{\circ}F.$$

HEAT CONDUCTION IN FINS

• PROBLEM 9-32

Consider a plane aluminum ($k = 120$ Btu/hr-ft-$^{\circ}F$) wall at a steady temperature of $650^{\circ}F$. In order to increase the heat dissipation rate to surrounding air at $75^{\circ}F$, three aluminum pin-shaped fins per square inch are attached to the wall. Each fin is of 1/8 in diameter and 1 in long. Determine the percentage increase in the heat dissipation rate, if the coefficient of heat transfer is 28 Btu/hr-ft^2-$^{\circ}F$.

Solution: For a plane aluminum wall, without the fins, the rate of heat dissipation is given by

$$\frac{q}{A} = h(T_s - T_{\infty})$$

where

$\frac{q}{A}$ = rate of heat transfer per unit area

h = coefficient of heat transfer

T_s = temperature of the wall surface

T_∞ = temperature of the surrounding air

Substituting the values,

the rate of heat dissipation per square inch of surface area of the wall, without fins is

$$\frac{q}{A} = \frac{28}{144}(650 - 75)$$

$$= 111.81 \text{ Btu/hr-in}^2$$

Consider a single fin,

the rate of heat dissipation from a single fin is given by

$$q = kA_c m (T_s - T_\infty) \tanh (mL)$$

where

k = thermal conductivity of the fin material

A_c = cross-sectional area of the fin

L = length of the fin

m = parameter of the fin given by $m = \sqrt{\frac{hP}{kA_c}}$

where

h = heat transfer coefficient

P = perimeter of the fin

For a circular cross-section,

$$m = \sqrt{\frac{4h}{kd}} \quad \text{where}$$

d = diameter of the fin.

Therefore,

$$m = \sqrt{\frac{4 \times 28 \times 12}{120 \times 1/8}}$$

$$= 9.466 \text{ ft}^{-1}$$

Substituting the values the equation gives the rate of heat dissipation from a fin

$$q = 120 \times \frac{\pi}{4}\left(\frac{1}{8 \times 12}\right)^2 \times 9.466 \times (650 - 75)\tanh(9.466 \times \frac{1}{12})$$

$$= 55.66 \tanh (0.789)$$

$$= 36.62 \text{ Btu/hr.}$$

Therefore, for three fins, the heat transfer rate is

$$3 \times 36.62 = 109.86 \text{ Btu/hr}$$

The total rate of heat dissipation from the wall with fins is obtained by adding the heat transfer through the fins to the heat transfer through the remaining surface area of the wall.

Thus

$$\left(\frac{q}{A}\right)_{\text{with fins}} = 3 \times 36.62 + \left(\frac{q}{A}\right)_{\text{without fins}} \text{(remaining area of the wall)}$$

$$= 109.86 + 111.81\left[1 - 3 \times \frac{\pi}{4}\left(\frac{1}{8}\right)^2\right]$$

$$= 217.55 \text{ Btu/hr-in}^2$$

Therefore, the percentage increase in the dissipation rate is

$$\frac{217.55 - 111.81}{111.81} \times 100\%$$

$$= 95\%$$

• PROBLEM 9-33

Find the rate of heat transfer through an iron ($k = 25$ Btu/hr-ft-°F) pin fin of ½ in. diameter and 3 in. long. Also determine the temperature at the tip of the fin assuming an atmospheric temperature of 65°F. The surface film coefficient is 1.8 Btu/hr-ft²-°F and the temperature of the hot end of the fin is 250°F.

Solution: Using the approximate solution of fin, the fictitious length of the fin δ can be obtained from

$$\delta = \frac{A_c}{P}$$

where

A_c = cross-section area

P = perimeter of the fin

The effective length L_e is given by

$$L_e = L + \delta$$

where

L = actual length of the fin

Substituting the values,

$$L_e = 3 + \frac{\pi}{4}\left(\frac{1}{2}\right)^2 \times \frac{1}{\pi(1/2)}$$

$$= 3 + \frac{1}{4 \times 2}$$

or, $L_e = 3.125$ in

$L_e = 0.2604$ ft

For this converted fin of length L_e, the boundary conditions are at $x = 0$; $\theta = t_o - t_f$

$$\text{at } x = L_e \text{ ; } \frac{\partial \theta}{\partial x} = 0$$

where θ is the temperature difference with respect to the surrounding air temperature (t_f)

t_o = temperature of the hot end of the fin

The rate of heat transfer for these boundary conditions is

$$q = kmA_c\theta_o \cdot \tanh\ (mL_e)$$

where

m = fin parameter defined as $\sqrt{\frac{4h}{kd}}$ for a circular fin.

k = thermal conductivity of the fin material

θ_o = temperature difference ($t_o - t_f$)

L_e = effective length of the fin

Substituting the values into

$$m = \sqrt{\frac{4h}{kd}}$$

where

h = surface film coefficient

k = thermal conductivity of the fin material

d= diameter of the fin

$$m = \sqrt{\frac{4 \times 1.8 \times 12}{25 \times 0.5}} = 2.629\ \frac{1}{\text{ft}}$$

Substituting the values into the equation

for rate of heat transfer

$$q = 25 \times 2.629 \times \frac{\pi}{4} \left(\frac{0.5}{12}\right)^2 \times (250 - 65) \tanh\ (2.629 \times 0.26)$$

$$= 16.579 \tanh\ (0.6846)$$

$q = 9.81$ Btu/hr.

The temperature at the tip of the fin can be obtained from the temperature distribution equation.

$$\frac{\theta}{\theta_o} = \frac{t - t_f}{t_o - t_f} = \frac{\cosh\left[m(L_e - x)\right]}{\cosh(mL_e)}$$

where

t = temperature at a point x feet from the hot end of the fin

t_o = hot end temperature

t_f = temperature of the surrounding air

For the temperature at the tip,

substitute $x = L_e$ in the above equation.

$$\frac{t_t - t_f}{t_o - t_f} = \frac{1}{\cosh(mL_e)}$$

where

t_t = temperature at the tip

Substituting the values

$$\frac{t_t - 65}{250 - 65} = \frac{1}{\cosh(2.629 \times 0.2604)}$$

$$t_t = 65 + \frac{185}{\cosh(0.6846)}$$

$$= 214^{\circ}\text{F}$$

• PROBLEM 9-34

A small electrical device is having eight pin fins each of 5 mm wide, 0.5 mm thick and 25 mm long, to dissipate the heat generated within it. The thermal conductivity of the fin material is 200 W/m °K and the film heat coefficient is uniform throughout the lengths of the fin at 9 W/m^2 °K. If the device is at 350° K and the ambient air is at 300°K, determine the power dissipated through the fins.

Solution: For ideal fin, (uniform temperature throughout the fin) the rate of heat flow is

$$q_{ideal} = hA(T_f - T_a)$$

where

h = film heat transfer coefficient

A = surface area of the fin

T_f = temperature of the fin

T_a = temperature of the air

Therefore, if the given eight pins were ideal, the total heat dissipation rate is

$$q_{ideal} = hA_t\ (T_f - T_a) \tag{1}$$

where

A_t = total surface area of the fins

A_t = 8 PL

where

P = perimeter

L = length

i.e., $A_t = 8 \times 11 \times 25 \times 10^{-6}$

$= 2.2 \times 10^{-3}\ m^2$

Substituting the values into equation (1)

$$q_{ideal} = 9 \times 2.2 \times 10^{-3}\ (350 - 300)$$

$$= 0.99\ W$$

The effectiveness of the fin, η is given by

$$\eta = \frac{\tanh\ (mL)}{mL} \tag{2}$$

where

$$m = \sqrt{\frac{hP}{kA_c}}$$

where

A_c = cross-sectional area of the fin

P = perimeter of the fin

k = thermal conductivity of fin material

h = film heat transfer coefficient

Substituting the values,

$$m = \sqrt{\frac{9 \times 11 \times 10^{-3}}{200 \times 5 \times 0.5 \times 10^{-6}}}$$

$$= 14.07 \frac{1}{m}$$

Then

$$\eta = \frac{\tanh(14.07 \times 0.025)}{14.07 \times 0.025}$$

$$= \frac{\tanh(0.352)}{0.352}$$

$$\eta = 0.96$$

Since the fins are 96% effective, the actual power dissipation is given by

$$q = \eta q_{ideal}$$

$$= 0.96 \times 0.99$$

or, $q = 0.95$ W

• PROBLEM 9-35

The temperature of hot gas flowing through a pipe is measured by a thermocouple, attached to the bottom of a thermometer pocket which is fitted perpendicularly to the pipe wall. The pocket wall is projected 2.5 in. into the pipe and its thickness is 0.035 in. Find the temperature of the hot gas if the thermocouple reads 375°F when the temperature of the wall is 175°F.

Take the thermal conductivity of the pocket wall = 200 Btu/hr-ft-°F

the film heat transfer coefficient between the gas and thermometer pocket = 24 Btu/hr-ft^2-°F.

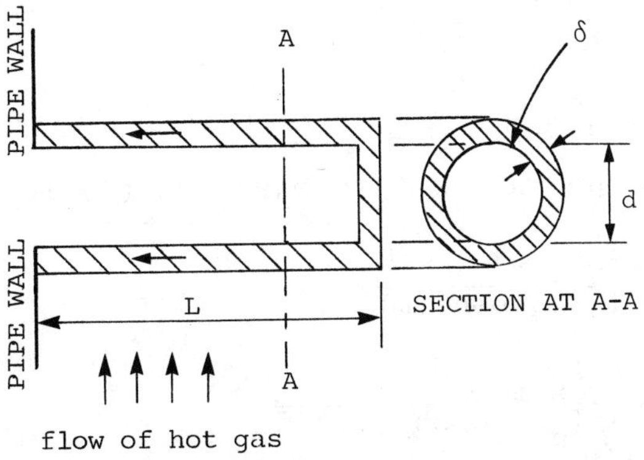

Solution: The arrangement of the thermometer well for measuring the temperature of a flowing gas in a pipe is shown in the figure. The thermometer pocket can be considered as a hollow rod protruding into hot gas at temperature T_g. As the heat flows from the hot gas along the well towards the cooler pipe walls, the thermocouple does not read the true temperature of the hot gas but it reads the temperature at the bottom of the pocket.

This pocket can be considered as a hollow fin as shown in the figure.

Then, the temperature for the fin is given by

$$\frac{\theta}{\theta_o} = \frac{T_x - T_g}{T_o - T_g} = \frac{\cosh [m(L - x)]}{\cosh (mL)} \qquad (1)$$

where

T_o = temperature of the pipe wall

T_g = temperature of the hot gas

T_x = temperature at any distance x measured from the pipe wall

L = length of the pocket

m = parameter of the fin given by

$$m = \sqrt{\frac{hP}{kA_c}} = \sqrt{\frac{h}{k\delta}} \quad \text{for hollow fins.}$$

where

h = film heat transfer coefficient

δ = thickness of the pocket wall

Therefore,

$$m = \sqrt{\frac{25 \times 12}{200 \times 0.035}}$$

$$= 6.55 \text{ ft}^{-1}$$

$$mL = 6.55 \times \frac{2.5}{12}$$

$$= 1.365$$

Substituting the values into equation (1) for x = L

$$\frac{T_L - T_g}{T_o - T_g} = \frac{1}{\cosh (mL)}$$

i.e.,
$$\frac{375 - T_g}{175 - T_g} = \frac{1}{\cosh (1.365)}$$

$$(375 - T_g) = \frac{175 - T_g}{2.08}$$

or, $780 - 2.08\, T_g = 175 - T_g$

or, $T_g = 560^{\circ}F$

Therefore, the corrected temperature of the hot gas is $560^{\circ}F$.

• PROBLEM 9-36

Two cylindrical rods each of diameter 3/4 in. and length 18 in. are heated to a temperature of $275^{\circ}F$ on one end. The coefficient of heat transfer is same all over their surfaces and is equal to 1.5 Btu/hr-ft^2-$^{\circ}F$. The rods are placed in air at temperature $75^{\circ}F$. The thermal conductivities of the rods are $k_1 = 0.65$ Btu/hr-ft-$^{\circ}F$ and $k_2 = 130$ Btu/hr-ft-$^{\circ}F$ respectively.

Find (a) The temperature distribution in the rods and the rate of heat flow from the rods if the heat flux from the rod ends may be neglected.

b) The rate of heat flow from the rods, if the heat flux from the ends is not neglected.

Solution: The rods can be considered as finite length circular fins.

a) The temperature distribution in a finite length fin, neglecting the heat flux from the ends is given by

$$\frac{\theta}{\theta_o} = \frac{t - t_f}{t_o - t_f} = \frac{\cosh m(L - x)}{\cosh mL}$$

where

t_o = temperature of the hot end of the rod

t_f = temperature of the air

L = length of the rod

m = parameter defined by

$$m = \sqrt{\frac{hP}{kA}}$$

where

h = film heat transfer coefficient

P = perimeter of the fin

k = thermal conductivity of the fin material

A = cross-sectional area of the fin

The parameter m for a cylindrical fin is

$$m = \sqrt{\frac{4h}{kd}}$$

where

d = diameter of the fin

Therefore, the parameter m_1 for rod 1 is

$$m_1 = \sqrt{\frac{4 \times 1.5 \times 12}{0.65 \times 0.75}}$$

$$= 12.15 \frac{1}{ft}$$

The parameter m_2 for rod 2 is

$$m_2 = \sqrt{\frac{4 \times 1.5 \times 12}{130 \times 0.75}}$$

$$= 0.86 \frac{1}{ft}$$

Substituting the values in the equation for temperature distribution,

For the rod 1,

$$\frac{t - 75}{275 - 75} = \frac{\cosh\left[12.15(1.5 - x)\right]}{\cosh(12.15 \times 1.5)}$$

or,

$$t = 75 + 200 \frac{\cosh\left[12.15(1.5 - x)\right]}{\cosh(18.225)}$$

For the rod 2,

$$\frac{t - 75}{275 - 75} = \frac{\cosh\left[0.86(1.5 - x)\right]}{\cosh(0.86 \times 1.5)}$$

or,

$$t = 75 + 200 \frac{\cosh\left[0.86(1.5 - x)\right]}{\cosh(1.29)}$$

The rate of heat flow from the fins when the heat flux from the ends is neglected is given by

$$q = kmA\theta_o \tanh(mL)$$

where

$\theta_o = (t_o - t_f)$

A = cross-sectional area of the fin

m = parameter of the fin

L = length of the fin

k = thermal conductivity of the fin material

Substituting the values into the equation for rate of heat flow,

For rod 1,

$$q = 0.65 \times 12.15 \times \frac{\pi}{4}\left(\frac{3}{4 \times 12}\right)^2 \times$$

$$(275 - 75) \tanh (12.15 \times 1.5)$$

$$= 4.985 \tanh (18.225)$$

$$= 4.985 \text{ Btu/hr}$$

For rod 2,

$$q = 130 \times 0.86 \times \frac{\pi}{4}\left(\frac{3}{4 \times 12}\right)^2 (275 - 75) \tanh (0.86 \times 1.5)$$

$$= 68.6 \tanh (1.29)$$

$$= 68.6 \times 0.86$$

$$q = 59 \text{ Btu/hr}$$

b) When the heat flux through the ends is not neglected, the total heat flow rate is given by

$$q = kmA\theta_o \frac{\sinh(mL) + H \cosh(mL)}{\cosh(mL) + H \sinh(mL)}$$

where

$$H = \frac{h}{km}$$

Therefore,

for rod 1

$$H = \frac{1.5}{0.65 \times 12.15} = 0.1899$$

for rod 2,

$$H = \frac{1.5}{130 \times 0.86}$$

$$= 0.0134$$

Substituting the values into the equation for heat flow rate,

for rod 1

$$kmA\theta_o = 0.65 \times 12.15 \times \frac{\pi}{4}\left(\frac{3}{4 \times 12}\right)^2 \times (275 - 75)$$

or $\quad kmA\theta_o = 4.985$

$$mL = 12.15 \times 1.5 = 18.225$$

Therefore,

$$q = 4.985 \times \frac{\sinh (18.225) + 0.1899 \cosh (18.225)}{\cosh (18.225) + 0.1899 \sinh (18.225)}$$

$$= 4.985 \text{ Btu/hr.}$$

For rod 2,

$$kmA\theta_o = 68.6$$

$$mL = 0.86 \times 1.5 = 1.29$$

Therefore,

$$q = 68.6 \frac{\sinh (1.29) + 0.0134 \cosh (1.29)}{\cosh (1.29) + 0.0134 \sinh (1.29)}$$

$$= 59.2 \text{ Btu/hr.}$$

CHAPTER 10

FORCED CONVECTION

TUBES OR PIPES

• PROBLEM 10-1

Water flows through a 1 in. schedule 40 steel pipe at a velocity of 1.6 ft/sec. Find the film coefficient at the inner pipe surface if the water is at 60^0F.

Solution: The film coefficient is determined from the Nusselt number, which is dependent on the Reynolds number. The Reynolds number is given by

$$Re = \frac{D\rho v}{\mu}$$

where

D = inner diameter of pipe

ρ = density of fluid

v = velocity of fluid

μ = viscosity of fluid

From a table of dimensions of standard pipes, the inner diameter of a 1 in. schedule 40 pipe is found to be 1.049 in. The water tables are used to determine the following properties at 60^0F.

Pr = Prandtl number = 7.98

k = thermal conductivity = 0.341 Btu/hr-ft-^{0}F

μ = viscosity = 2.72 lbm/ft-hr

ρ = density = 62.36 lbm/ft^3

Reynolds number may be determined as

$$Re = \frac{(1.049/12)(62.36)(1.6)(3600)}{(2.72)}$$

$$= 11544$$

The flow is turbulent. The Nusselt number correlation is given by

$$Nu = 0.023\ Re^{0.8}Pr^{0.4}$$

$$= 0.023(11544)^{0.8}(7.98)^{0.4}$$

$$= 93.85$$

The film coefficient,

$$h = \frac{Nuk}{D} = \frac{(93.85)(0.341)}{(1.049/12)}$$

$$= 366.1\ \text{Btu/hr-ft}^2\text{-}^0\text{F}$$

• PROBLEM 10-2

A pipe of 2 in. inner diameter is maintained at a constant temperature of 90 ^{0}F. Water flows through the pipe at an average temperature of 80 ^{0}F and an average velocity of 7 ft/sec. Assuming fully developed flow and the surface of the pipe to be smooth, find the rate of heat transfer to the water over a 15 ft. length of pipe.

Solution: In order to calculate the rate of heat transfer to the water, we must first determine the heat transfer coefficient. The properties of water at 80 ^{0}F are

ρ = density = 62.22 lbm/ft^3

k = thermal conductivity = 0.353 Btu/hr-ft-^{0}F

μ = viscosity = 0.000578 lbm/ft-sec

Pr = Prandtl number = 5.89

The Reynolds number is given by

$$Re = \frac{Dv\rho}{\mu}$$

where D = inner diameter of pipe

v = velocity of fluid

ρ = density of fluid

μ = viscosity of fluid

Then

$$Re = \frac{(2/12)(7)(62.22)}{(0.000578)} = 125{,}588$$

Hence the flow is turbulent. Since the temperature difference between the fluid and the wall is only 10^0F, we neglect the effects of change in viscosity with temperature. Then the Nusselt number is given by

$$Nu = hD/K = 0.023\ Re^{0.8}Pr^{0.4}$$

where h = heat transfer coefficient.

Rearranging and solving for h gives

$$h = \frac{(0.023)(125,888)^{0.8}(5.89)^{0.4}(0.353)}{2/12}$$

$$= 1188\ Btu/hr\text{-}ft^2\text{-}{}^0F$$

The rate at which heat is transferred from the wall,

$$Q = (\pi DL)h(T_w - T_m)$$

where L = length of tube

T_w = wall temperature

T_m = average temperature of water

Then $Q = (\pi \times 2/12 \times 15)(1188)(90 - 80)$

$= 93305.3$

• PROBLEM 10-3

Water at $340\,^0$K and a rate of 4 Kg/hr is required for a certain process. Water, available at $300\,^0$K, is to be heated as it passes through a 7mm ID pipe which provides 125 W per meter length of pipe. Determine the length of piping required and the maximum temperature at the exit.

Solution: Use the physical properties of water to verify that the flow is laminar, by calculating the Reynolds number (Re). Then determine q_w, the energy provided to the water per square meter of pipe surface area. Eq.(1) allows the length of pipe to be determined. The maximum temperature at the exit, T_w, can be obtained using eq.(2).

At an average temperature of $320\,^0$K, the properties of water are:

ρ = density ≈ 989 kg/m^3

ν = kinematic viscosity = 0.59×10^{-6} m^2/sec

c_p = specific heat = 4174 J/kg-^{0}K

k = thermal conductivity = 0.614 W/m-^{0}K

D = inside diameter of pipe = 7×10^{-3}m

$\overset{\circ}{m}$ = mass flow rate of water = 1.11×10^{-3}kg/sec

The Reynolds number is:

$$Re = \frac{\rho \bar{u} D}{\mu} = \frac{4\dot{m}}{\pi D \rho \nu}$$

where $\bar{u}$ is the mean velocity of the fluid and μ is the viscosity. Then

$$Re = \frac{4(1.11\times10^{-3})}{\pi(7\times10^{-3})(989)(0.59\times10^{-6})}$$

$$= 346$$

$$q_w = \frac{125 \text{ W/m}}{\pi(7\times10^{-3}\text{m})} = 5684 \text{ W/m}^2$$

Substitution into the equation below provides the length of piping, L.

$$L = \frac{\dot{m}c_p \Delta T}{\pi D q_w} \tag{1}$$

where ΔT is the change in temperature the water undergoes between the entrance and the exit.

$$L = \frac{(1.11\times10^{-3})(4174)(40)}{\pi(7\times10^{-3})(5684)}$$

$$= 1.48\text{m}$$

The maximum temperature at the exit, T_w, is obtained using the equation,

$$T_w = T_b + \frac{11}{48}\frac{q_w D}{k} \tag{2}$$

where T_b is the exiting water temperature required,

$$T_w = 340 + \frac{11(5648)(7\times10^{-3})}{48(0.614)}$$

$$T_w = 354.8^0\text{K}$$

• PROBLEM 10-4

Water at a temperature of 350^0K moves at $2.5 \times 10^{-4}\text{m}^3$/sec through a $\frac{1}{2}$ in. schedule 80 pipe. Calculate the heat transfer coefficient within the pipe.

Solution: Use the physical properties of water to obtain the Reynolds number (Re) and the Prandtl number (Pr). Substitution into the Dittus-Boelter equation gives the Nusselt number (Nu). From the definition of the Nusselt number, the heat transfer coefficient is obtained.

Water at 350^0K has the following properties:

$$\rho = \text{density} = 973.7 \text{ kg/m}^3$$

$$\mu = \text{viscosity} = 3.72 \times 10^{-4} \text{ kg/m-sec}$$

$$k = \text{thermal conductivity} = 0.668 \frac{W}{m-{}^0K}$$

$$Pr = \text{Prandtl number} = 2.33$$

Since volumetric flow rate = $Q = UxA = 2.5\times10^{-4}m^3/sec$,

$$U = \frac{Q}{A} = \frac{2.5 \times 10^{-4}}{A}$$

where u is the fluid velocity and A is the cross-sectional area

$$A = \frac{\pi D^2}{4} = \frac{\pi(1.387 \times 10^{-2}m)^2}{4}$$

$$= 1.51 \times 10^{-4} \text{ m}^2$$

Therefore,

$$u = \frac{2.5 \times 10^{-4}m^3/sec}{1.51 \times 10^{-4} \text{ m}^2} = 1.66 \text{ m/sec}$$

The Reynolds number is:

$$Re = \frac{\rho uD}{\mu} = \frac{(973.7kg/m^3)(1.66m/sec)(1.387\times10^{-2}m)}{(3.72\times10^{-4}kg/m\text{-}sec)}$$

$$= 60,265$$

A turbulent flow regime is indicated. The Dittus-Boelter equation will be employed to obtain the Nusselt number as follows:

$$Nu = 0.023 \; Re^{0.8} \; Pr^{0.33}$$

$$= 0.023(60265)^{0.8}(2.33)^{0.33}$$

$$= 202.8$$

Also,

$$Nu = \frac{hD}{k}$$

where h is the heat transfer coefficient. Solving for h,

$$h = \frac{kNu}{D} = \frac{(0.688 \text{ W/m-}{}^0K)(202.8)}{(1.387\times10^{-2}m)}$$

$$= 10,060 \text{ W/m}^2\text{-}{}^0K$$

A pump will force air at 1 atm. and 100°F (311°K) through a 3 in. I.D. pipe. The flow rate is 60 lbm/hr. A portion of the pipe must be maintained at an inside wall temperature of 230°F (383.3°K), in order to increase the air temperature to 210°F (372.2°K). Determine the heated length L needed to accomplish this.

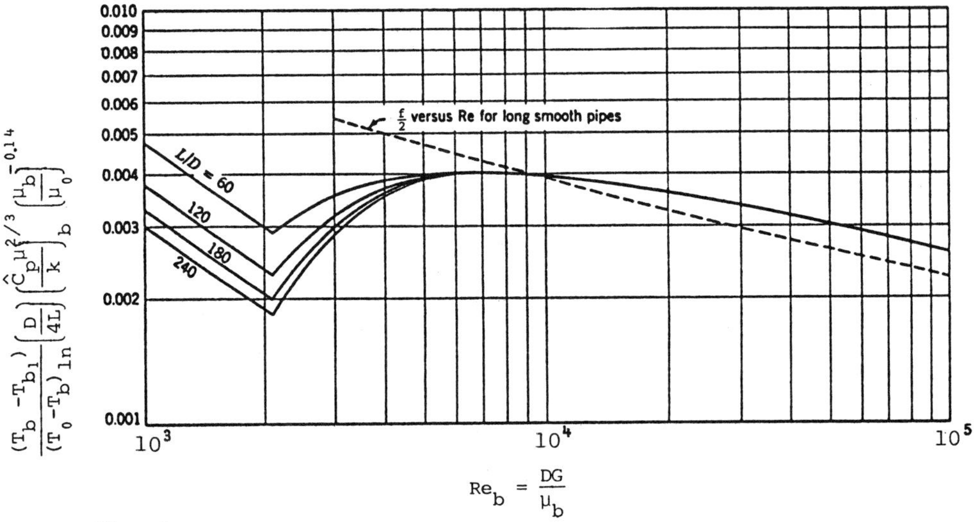

Fig. 1.

Solution: Once the Reynolds number (Re) is obtained, figure (1) can be employed to solve for L/D, thereby allowing L to be determined.

T_{b_1} = bulk temperature of entering air = 311.1°K

T_{b_2} = bulk temperature of exiting air = 372.2°K

T_b = average bulk temperature of air = 341.7°K

T_o = wall temperature of tube = 383.3°K

The physical properties of air are:

μ_b = viscosity = 2.060×10^{-5} kg/m-sec at T_b

μ_o = 2.216×10^{-5} kg/m-sec at T_o

c_p = specific heat = 1.0085 kJ/Kg-°C at T_b

k = thermal conductivity = 0.02940 W/m-°C at T_b

Pr = Prandtl number = $C_p\mu/k$ = 0.707 at T_b

The next step is to evaluate Re at T_b.

$$Re = \frac{D\dot{m}}{A\mu_b} = \frac{4\dot{m}}{\pi D\mu_b}$$

where $\dot{m}$ is the mass flow rate and A is the cross-sectional area of the tube.

$$\dot{m} = 60 \text{ lbm/hr} = 7.57 \times 10^{-3} \text{ kg/sec}$$

$$D = 3 \text{ in} = 0.0762 \text{ m}$$

Sovling for Re,

$$Re = \frac{4(7.57\times10^{-3})}{\pi(0.0762)(2.060\times10^{-5})} = 6140$$

The next step is to use figure (1).

Reading off Re, one obtains

$$\frac{(T_{b_2}-T_{b_1})}{(T_o-T_b)_{\ell n}} \left(\frac{D}{4L}\right) \left(\frac{c_p\mu}{k}\right)_b^{2/3} \left(\frac{\mu_b}{\mu_o}\right)^{-0.14} = 0.004 \qquad (1)$$

where

$$(T_o-T_b)_{\ell n} = \frac{(T_o-T_{b_1})-(T_o-T_{b_2})}{\ln\left[(T_o-T_{b_1})/(T_o-T_{b_2})\right]}$$

$$= \frac{(383.3-311.1)-(383.3-372.2)}{\ln\left[(383.3-311.1)/(383.3-372.2)\right]}$$

$$= 32.63^0\text{K}$$

Solving equation (1) for L/D,

$$\frac{L}{D} = \frac{1}{4(0.004)} \frac{(T_{b_2}-T_{b_1})}{(T_o-T_b)_{\ell n}} \left(\frac{c_p\mu}{k}\right)_b^{2/3} \left(\frac{\mu_b}{\mu_o}\right)^{-0.14}$$

$$= \frac{1}{4(0.004)} \frac{(372.2-311.1)}{32.63} (0.707)^{2/3} \left(\frac{2.060\times10^{-5}}{2.216\times10^{-5}}\right)^{-0.14}$$

$$\frac{L}{D} = 93.8$$

The necessary length is, therefore,

$$L = 93.8\,D = 93.8(0.0762) = 7.15\text{m}$$

A $\frac{1}{5}$ in. I.D. tube is at a constant temperature of 90°F. Water with a mean temperature of 55°F and a mean velocity of 1.5 ft/sec is pumped through this heated tube. Calculate the mean heat transfer coefficient for the first 4 ft. of the tube.

Solution: Use the physical properties of water to determine the Reynolds number (Re) and the Prandtl number (Pr). These values are substituted in equation (1) to solve for the mean Nusselt number (Nu_m). Using the definition of the Nusselt number, the mean heat transfer coefficient can be obtained.

The physical properties of water are:

μ_b = bulk viscosity at 55°F = 2.94 lbm/ft-hr

μ_w = viscosity at wall temperature of 90°F = 1.85 lbm/ft-hr

k = thermal conductivity at 55°F = 0.338 Btu/ft-hr-°F

ρ = density at 55°F = 62.39 lbm/ft³

C_p = specific heat at 55°F = 1.001 Btu/lbm-°F

The Prandtl number is:

$$Pr = \frac{C_p\mu}{k} = \frac{(1.001)(2.94)}{0.338} = 8.7$$

The Reynolds number is:

$$Re = \frac{\rho uD}{\mu} = \frac{(62.39)(1.5)\left(\frac{1/5}{12}\right)(3600)}{2.94}$$

$$= 1910$$

where u is the mean velocity of the water and D is the inside diameter of the tube.

$$\frac{D}{x} = \frac{1}{5 \times 12 \times 4} = \frac{1}{240}$$

where x = the length of the tube

= 4 ft.

Substituting into equation (1),

$$Nu_m = \left[3.66 + \frac{0.0668(D/x)RePr}{1+0.04\left[(D/x)RePr\right]^{2/3}}\right]\left(\frac{\mu_b}{\mu_w}\right)^{0.14} \quad (1)$$

$$\doteq \left[3.66 + \frac{0.0668\left(\frac{1}{240}\right)(1910)(8.7)}{1+0.04\left[\left(\frac{1}{240}\right)(1910)(8.7)\right]^{2/3}}\right]\left(\frac{2.94}{1.85}\right)^{0.14}$$

$$= 6.852$$

Using the definition of the Nusselt number, the heat transfer coefficient is found.

$$Nu_m = \frac{h_m D}{k}$$

$$h_m = \frac{Nu_m k}{D} = \frac{(6.852)(0.338)}{\left(\dfrac{1/5}{12}\right)}$$

$$= 139 \ Btu/hr\text{-}ft^2\text{-}^0F$$

● **PROBLEM** 10-7

Water is travelling inside a ½ in. (0.0127m) I.D. tube, in the hydrodynamically and thermally developed region. The wall temperature is constant. Determine the heat transfer coefficient for laminar flow, given that the thermal conductivity is 0.585 W/m-^{0}C. In addition, calculate the heat transfer between the tube walls and the water for a 30 ft. (9.14m) length of tube, assuming the mean temperature difference between the wall and the water is 80 ^{0}F (44.5 ^{0}C).

Nusselt Number for Laminar Forced Convection in Conduits of Various Cross Sections for Fully Developed Velocity and Temperature Profiles

Shape of Channel Cross Section	$\dfrac{b}{a}$	Nu for Constant Wall Heat Flux	Nu for Constant Wall Temperature
○		4.364	3.66
a□b	1.0	3.63	2.98
a▭b	1.4	3.78	
a▭b	2.0	4.11	3.39
a▭b	4.0	5.35	4.44
a▭b	8.0	6.60	5.95
═══	∞	8.235	7.54
△ 60° 60°		3.00	2.35

Table 1.

Solution: Table (1) gives the Nusselt number for laminar forced convection under conditions of fully developed velocity and temperature profiles, for a constant wall temperature. The Nusselt number (Nu) can be obtained from Table (1). This allows the heat transfer coefficient to be ob-

432

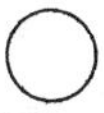

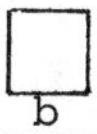

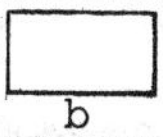

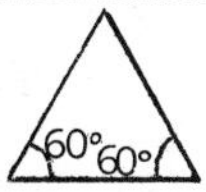

tained and is easily employed to calculate the heat transfer rate.

$$Nu = \frac{hD}{k} \quad \text{where h is the heat transfer coefficient}$$

$$Nu = 3.66$$

Then

$$h = \frac{3.66k}{D} = \frac{3.66(0.585)}{(0.0127)}$$

$$= 168.6 \ W/m^2\text{-}^0C$$

Q, the heat transfer rate between the walls of the tube and the water is given by

$$Q = Ah\Delta T$$

where A is the area available for heat transfer.

$$Q = (\pi DL)(h)\Delta T$$

$$= (\pi)(0.0127)(9.14)(168.6)(44.5)$$

$$= 2736 \ W$$

• PROBLEM 10-8

Each hour, 800 ft^3 of dry air is to be cooled from 110^0F to 70^0F. This is to be accomplished inside a number of copper tubes, 1 in. O.D. and 16-gage. Each of these tubes is inside another copper tube of 1.5 in. O.D. and 14-gage. Water moves through the annulus at 0.9 ft/sec. The water enters at a temperature of 40^0F, and flows countercurrent to the gas. If the air has an inlet velocity of 18 ft/sec, calculate the number of tubes, the length of each required to cool the air.

Solution: Knowing the flow rate of air required and the cross-sectional area of the tubing, the number of tubes may be determined. The heat to be transferred is obtained by using the temperature drop of the air and its heat capacity. An overall heat transfer coefficient can be obtained by calculating a water-side and a gas-side coefficient to be substituted into equation (3). To calculate the length of tubing required, the area for heat transfer, A, must be determined from equation (4).

Calculation of number of tubes:

A 1-in. 16-gage tube has an inside cross-sectional area of 0.00413 ft^2. For an air velocity of 18 ft/sec, each tube has a capacity of:

$$(0.00413 \ ft^2)(18 \ ft/sec)(3600 \ sec/hr) \simeq 268 \ ft^3/hr.$$

A flow rate of 800 ft^3/hr is desired. Therefore, 3 tubes in parallel will satisfy the desired volume of air to be cooled per hour.

Calculation of heat transferred:

One cubic foot of air at 1 atm. and 110°F has a density of

$$\rho_{air} = 0.06969 \text{ lbm/ft}^3$$

The total weight of air to be cooled is

$$(800 \text{ ft}^3/\text{hr})(0.06969 \text{ lbm/ft}^3) \simeq 55.8 \text{ lbm/hr}$$

At a mean temperature of 90°F, the specific heat of air is

$$C_p = 0.24 \text{ Btu/lb-}^0\text{F}$$

Therefore, the heat to be transferred is:

$$(55.8 \text{ lbm/hr})(0.24 \text{ Btu/lbm-}^0\text{F})(110-70)^0\text{F}$$

$$= 535.7 \text{ Btu/hr}$$

Calculation of exit water temperature:

Inside cross-sectional area of 1.5 in tube = 1.398 in^2.

Outside cross-sectional area of 1.0 in tube = 0.7854 in^2.

Annulus cross-sectional area = 0.6126 in^2 or 0.00425 ft^2

However, there are 3 tubes in parallel. Therefore, the cross-sectional area available for the water, which moves through the annulus, is 3(0.00425 ft^2) = 0.01275 ft^2. At a velocity of 0.9 ft/sec, the water flow rate will be:

$$(0.01275 \text{ ft}^2)(0.9 \text{ ft/sec})(3600 \text{ sec/hr})(62.4 \text{ lbm/ft}^3)$$

$$\simeq 2578 \text{ lb water/hr}$$

where a water density of 62.4 lbm/ft^3 has been used. The increase in the water temperature will be:

$$\frac{535.7 \text{ Btu/hr}}{(2578 \text{ lbm/hr})\left(\frac{1.0 \text{ Btu}}{\text{lbm-}^0\text{F}}\right)} = 0.208^0\text{F}$$

where 1.0 Btu/lbm-^{0}F is the specific heat of water. The exit water temperature is, therefore, 40.0 + 0.208 ≃ 40.21°F.

Calculation of mean temperature difference:

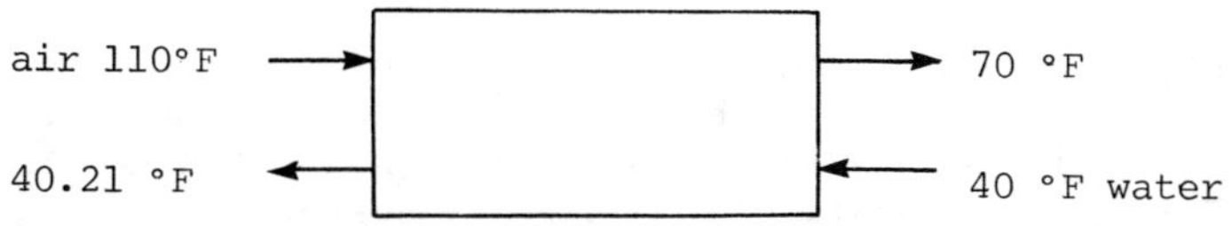

Figure 1.

As shown on figure (1),

$$\Delta t_1 = 110 - 40.21 = 69.79\,^0F$$

$$\Delta t_2 = 70 - 40 = 30\,^0F$$

By definition,

$$\Delta t_{\ell m} = \frac{\Delta t_1 - \Delta t_2}{\ln\left(\frac{\Delta t_1}{\Delta t_2}\right)}$$

Substituting,

$$\Delta t_{\ell m} = \frac{69.79 - 30}{\ln\left(\frac{69.79}{30}\right)} = 47.1\,^0F$$

Calculation of gas-side heat transfer coefficient:

First, calculate the Reynolds number (Re). The properties of air at the mean temperature of 90 °F are:

$$U_m = \text{mass flow rate} = \frac{55.8 \text{ lbm/hr}}{0.01275 \text{ ft}^2} \simeq 4377 \text{ lb/hr-ft}^2$$

$$\mu = \text{viscosity} = 0.0482 \text{ lbm/hr-ft}$$

$$k = 0.01542 \text{ Btu/hr-ft-}^0\text{F}$$

$$D = \text{diameter of tubing} = 0.0725 \text{ ft}$$

$$Re = \frac{U_m D}{\mu} = \frac{(4377 \text{ lbm/hr-ft}^2)(0.0725 \text{ ft})}{0.0482 \text{ lbm/ft-hr}} \simeq 6584$$

$$Pr = \text{Prandtl number} = \frac{C_p \mu}{k} = \frac{(0.2403 \text{ Btu/lbm-}^0\text{F})(0.0482 \text{ lbm/ft-hr})}{0.01542 \text{ Btu/hr-ft-}^0\text{F}}$$

$$= 0.751$$

Since the flow is turbulent,

$$h = 0.023 \frac{k}{D} Re^{0.8}\ Pr^{0.4} \qquad (1)$$

Substituting,

$$h = (0.023)\frac{(0.01542 \text{ Btu/hr-ft-}^0\text{F})}{(0.0725 \text{ ft})}(6584)^{0.8}(0.751)^{0.4}$$

$$h = 4.95 \text{ Btu/hr-ft}^2\text{-}^0\text{F}$$

Calculation of water-side heat transfer coefficient:

When there is flow through a non-circular conduit, four times the shape factor is used in place of the diameter. The shape factor is defined as the cross-sectional area of the channel divided by the perimeter of the heating surface. As previously calculated, the cross-sectional area of the annulus = 0.00425 ft^2. The heated perimeter = $(1\text{in.})(\pi)/12 = 0.2618$ ft.

$$\text{Shape factor} = \frac{0.00425\ \text{ft}^2}{0.2618\ \text{ft}} = 0.01623\ \text{ft}$$

$$\text{Equivalent diameter} = D_E = 4(0.01623) = 0.06492\ \text{ft.}$$

u = water velocity = 0.9 ft/sec

ρ = water density = 62.4 lbm/ft³ at 40°F

μ = water viscosity = 3.749 lbm/ft-hr at 40°F

$$Re = \frac{\rho u D_E}{\mu} = \frac{(62.4)(0.9)(3600)(0.06492)}{(3.749)}$$

$$= 3501$$

Equation (2) will be used with figure (2).

$$\left(\frac{hD}{k}\right)\left(\frac{\mu_s}{\mu}\right)^{0.14}\left(\frac{c_p\mu}{k}\right)^{-0.33} = f\left(\frac{Du\rho}{\mu}\right) \qquad (2)$$

where μ_s is the water viscosity at the temperature of the metal surface. It is safe to assume that the water-side resistance to heat transfer is negligibly small. The greater part of that temperature drop, thus, will occur over the gas film. This means that the average temperature of the metal surface and the average water temperature will be equal. Therefore, the term $(\mu_s/\mu)^{0.14}$ is approximately equal to one.

With a Reynolds number of 3501, figure (2) provides an ordinate of approximately 12. Equation (2) then becomes

$$12 = \left(\frac{hD}{k}\right)\left(\frac{c_p\mu}{k}\right)^{-0.33}$$

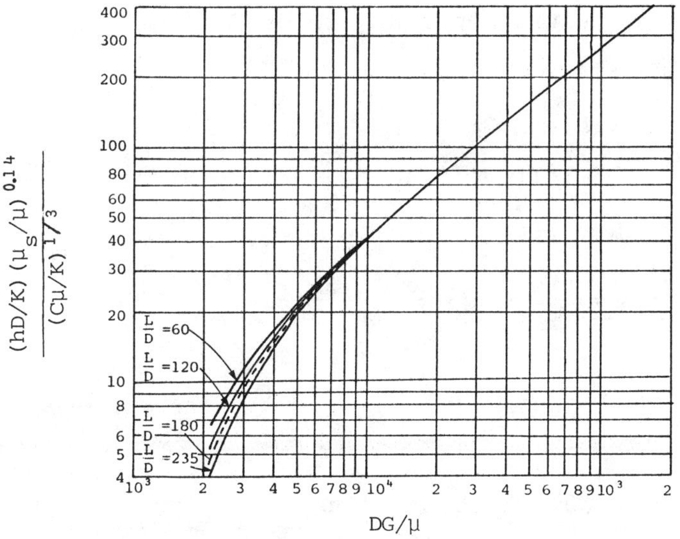

CORRELATION FOR FORCED CONVECTION AT LOW REYNOLDS NUMBERS.

Figure 2.

For water at 40^0F,

$$k = 0.332 \text{ Btu/ft-hr-}^0F$$

$$Pr = 11.35$$

Substituting these additional values into equation (2) yeilds

$$12 = \frac{h(0.06492)}{0.332}(11.35)^{-0.33}$$

or

$$h = 136.8 \text{ Btu/hr-ft}^2\text{-}^0F.$$

<u>Calculation of overall heat transfer coefficient</u>:

Due to the fact that the gas-side coefficient is much smaller than the water-side coefficient, the overall coefficient will approximate the gas-side coefficient, and the inside surface will be employed as a basis for heat transfer, using equation (3).

$$U = \text{overall coefficient} = \frac{1}{\frac{1}{h_1} + \frac{L}{k} + \frac{1}{h_2}} \qquad (3)$$

where L is the thickness of the copper tubing and k is its conductivity.

$$U = \frac{1}{\frac{1}{136.8} + \frac{(0.065/12)}{224} + \frac{1}{4.95}}$$

$$U = 4.78 \text{ Btu/hr-ft}^2\text{-}^0F$$

<u>Calculation of heat transfer area</u>:

Substitution in equation (4),

$$q = UA\,\Delta t_m \qquad (4)$$

where q is the heat transferred, yields

$$(535.7 \text{ Btu/hr}) = (4.78 \text{ Btu/hr-ft}^2\text{-}^0F)A(47.1^0F)$$

or

$$A = 2.38 \text{ ft}^2$$

Each tube has 0.2618 ft^2 of inside surface area per foot of length. There are 3 tubes in parallel. Therefore, the length of each tube is

$$\left(\frac{1 \text{ ft length of pipe}}{0.2618 \text{ ft}^2}\right)\left(\frac{2.38 \text{ ft}^2}{3}\right) = 3.03 \text{ ft.}$$

• PROBLEM 10-9

The bulk temperature of water is to be raised from 50^0F (283.3^0K) to 80^0F (300^0K) by passing it through a 2 in. I.D. (0.0508m) smooth piping, which has a constant wall temperature of 210^0F (372.2^0K). If the average fluid velocity is 10 ft/sec, determine the length of piping needed.

Solution: First calculate the Reynolds number (Re) and the Prandtl number (Pr). Then use in the Sieder-Tate equation to compute h, the heat transfer coefficient. An energy balance can then be made to calculate L.

T_w = wall temperature = 372.2 °K

T_{b_1} = bulk temperature of entering water = 283.3 °K

T_{b_2} = bulk temperature of exiting water = 300 °K

T_b = average bulk temperature = 291.7 °K

c_{pb} = specific heat of water = 4183 J/kg-°C at T_b

k_b = thermal conductivity of water = 0.6 W/m-°C at T_b

μ_b = viscosity of water = 1.05×10^{-3} kg/m-sec at T_b

μ_w = viscosity of water = 2.87×10^{-4} kg/m-sec at T_w

ρ_b = density of water = 998.0 kg/m^3 at T_b

Pr_b = Prandtl number = $c_p\mu/k$ = 7.32 at T_b

$$Re_b = \frac{\rho u d}{\mu}$$

where u is the average fluid velocity. Substituting,

$$Re_b = \frac{(998.0)(3.05)(0.0508)}{1.05 \times 10^{-3}} = 147{,}267$$

For turbulent conditions with a large temperature difference between wall and fluid conditions, the Sieder-Tate equation is recommended.

$$Nu_b = \frac{hD}{k_b} = 0.027\ Re_b^{0.8} Pr_b^{1/3}\left(\frac{\mu_b}{\mu_w}\right)^{0.14}$$

where Nu_b is the Nusselt number evaluated at T_b.

Solving for the heat transfer coefficient,

$$h = \left(\frac{k_b}{D}\right) 0.023\ Re_b^{0.8} Pr_b^{1/3}\left(\frac{\mu_b}{\mu_w}\right)^{0.14}$$

$$= \frac{(0.6)}{(.0508)}(0.023)(147{,}267)^{0.8}(7.32)^{1/3}\left(\frac{1.05\times10^{-3}}{2.87\times10^{-4}}\right)^{0.14}$$

$$= 8621\ \text{W/m}^2\text{-}^0\text{C}$$

It is now possible to write an energy balance:

Heat lost from tube = heat gained by fluid

$$h(\pi DL)(T_w - T_b) = \rho \frac{\pi D^2}{4} uc_{pb}\Delta T_b$$

Solving for L,

$$L = \frac{\rho Duc_{pb}(\Delta T_b)}{4h(T_w - T_b)}$$

$$= \frac{(998.0)(0.0508)(3.05)(4183)(300-283.3)}{4(8621)(372.2-291.7)}$$

$$= 3.89 \text{ m} = 12.76 \text{ ft.}$$

• PROBLEM 10-10

A 1.6 ft long pipe with an inside diameter of 0.03 ft carries water moving at a rate of 18 lbm/hr. Steam condenses on the outside of the pipe, maintaining a constant inside surface temperature of 350 °F. If the water enters at 40 °F, determine the heat transfer coefficient and the outlet temperature of the water, T_{b_2}.

Solution: A trial and error method of solution must be employed as the outlet water temperature is not available. A trial value of $T_{b_2} = 200\,^0F$ is chosen. The Reynolds and Prandtl numbers must be calculated for use in the Sieder-Tate equation (equation (1)), for computing the heat transfer coefficient, $\bar{h}$. Performing an energy balance on the water allows the exit temperature, T_{b_2}, to be obtained. This new outlet temperature will be used to recalculate h_a, until the variation in h_a is not significant.

The properties of water are:

C_{pm} = mean heat capacity = 1.0 Btu/lbm-°F

k_m = mean thermal conductivity = 0.362 Btu/ft-hr-°F

The viscosity of the water will vary with temperature.

Assuming an exit temperature of 200°F,

$$T_{bm} = \text{mean bulk temperature} = \frac{40 + 200}{2} = 120\,^0F$$

μ_b = viscosity of water = 1.36 lbm/ft-hr at 120°F

μ_w = water viscosity at wall temperature of 350°F

= 0.3798 lbm/ft-hr.

The cross-sectional area of the pipe is

$$A = \frac{\pi D^2}{4} = \frac{\pi(0.03)^2}{4} = 7.07 \times 10^{-4} \text{ft}^2$$

The mass flow rate of water per unit area,

$$G = m/A = 18/7.07 \times 10^{-4} = 25460 \text{ lbm/hr-ft}^2$$

The Reynolds number, evaluated at T_{bm},

$$Re = \frac{\rho u D}{\mu} = \frac{DG}{\mu} = \frac{(0.03)(25460)}{(1.36)} = 562$$

where u is the fluid velocity.

The Prandtl number at the bulk mean temperature,

$$Pr = \frac{C_p \mu}{k} = \frac{(1.0)(1.36)}{(0.362)} = 3.76$$

$Re < 2100$ indicates a laminar regime. The flow is also laminar when evaluated at the exit temperature of 200^0F. This indicates that equation (1) can be employed to obtain the average Nusselt number, $\overline{Nu}$.

$$\overline{Nu} = \frac{\bar{h}D}{k} = 1.86\left(RePr\ \frac{D}{L}\right)^{1/3}\left(\frac{\mu_b}{\mu_w}\right)^{0.14} \qquad (1)$$

where L is the length of the piping. Substituting and solving for $\bar{h}$,

$$\frac{\bar{h}(0.03)}{(0.362)} = 1.86\left[(562)(3.76)\left(\frac{0.03}{1.6}\right)\right]^{1/3}\left(\frac{1.36}{0.3798}\right)^{0.14}$$

$$\bar{h} = 91.5 \text{ Btu/hr-ft}^2\text{-}^0\text{F}$$

Now, performing an energy balance on the water,

$$q = \text{heat gained by water} = \dot{m}C_{pm}(T_{b_2} - T_{b_1})$$

$$= 18(1.0)(T_{b_2} - 40) \qquad (2)$$

It is also true that

$$q = \bar{h}A\ \overline{\Delta T} \qquad (3)$$

where $\overline{\Delta T}$ is the average temperature change given by

$$\overline{\Delta T} = \frac{(T_w - T_{b_1}) + (T_w - T_{b_2})}{2}$$

$$= \frac{(350-40)+(350-T_{b_2})}{2} = 330 - 0.5T_{b_2}$$

Setting equations (2) and (3) equal to each other and solving for T_{b_2} gives

$$18(1.\dot{0})(T_{b_2} - 40) = (91.5)[\pi(0.03)(1.6)][330 - T_{b_2}]$$

$$T_{b_2} = 212^0\text{F}$$

This is greater than the value of 200^0F that was used at the start of the problem. Using the new value of T_{b_2}, $T_{bm} = 126^0$F. This corresponds to μ_b = 1.288 lbm/ft-hr. Performing the calculations again shows that the average heat transfer coefficient varies by less than 0.8%. This is not significant, and therefore $T_{b_2} = 212^0$F.

• PROBLEM 10-11

Air entering a tube of diameter 5.08cm (2 in.) is at 1 atm. and 150^0C. It is heated as it moves through the pipe at a velocity of 8m/sec. Determine the heat transfer per unit length of tube, assuming that a constant heat flux exists at the wall, and that the wall temperature is everywhere 20^0C above the air temperature. What is the bulk temperature rise through a 2m length of pipe?

Solution: The first step is to determine if the flow is turbulent or laminar. This can be accomplished by finding the Reynolds number.

Air at 1 atm. and 150^0C has the following properties:

ρ = density = 0.837 kg/m^3

μ = viscosity = 2.38×10^{-5} kg/m-sec

k = thermal conductivity = 0.0352 W/m-^{0}C

C_p = specific heat = 1.017 kJ/kg-^{0}C

Pr = Prandtl number = $C_p\mu/k$ = 0.688

Then

$$Re = \frac{\rho ud}{\mu} = \frac{(0.837)(8)(5.08\times10^{-2})}{2.38\times10^{-5}} = 14,292$$

This indicates turbulent flow.

The following equation, valid for turbulent flow, will allow the heat transfer coefficient to be determined.

$$Nu = \text{Nusselt number} = \frac{hd}{k} = 0.023\ Re^{0.8}Pr^{0.4}$$

where h is the heat transfer coefficient and d is the diameter of the tube. Substituting,

$$Nu = 0.023(14,292)^{0.8}(0.688)^{0.4} = 41.77$$

Then

$$h = \frac{kNu}{d} = \frac{(0.0352)(41.77)}{(0.0508)} = 28.94\ W/m^2\text{-}^0C$$

The heat flow per unit length is obtained from the equation

$$\frac{q}{L} = h\pi d(T_w - T_b) = (28.94)\pi(0.0508)(20) = 92.4 \text{ W/m}$$

where $(T_w - T_b)$ is the difference between the tube wall temperature and the bulk air temperature.

The following equation is employed to determine the bulk temperature rise through a 2m length of pipe:

$$q = \dot{m}C_p\Delta T_b = L\left(\frac{q}{L}\right) \tag{1}$$

where ΔT_b is the bulk temperature rise and $\dot{m}$ is the mass flow rate.

$$\dot{m} = \rho u \frac{\pi d^2}{4} = (0.837)(8)\pi \frac{(0.0508)^2}{4}$$

$$= 1.357 \times 10^{-2} \text{ kg/sec}$$

Substituting into equation (1),

$$(1.357\times10^{-2})(1017)\Delta T_b = (2.0)(92.4)$$

$$\Delta T_b = 13.4^\circ C$$

• PROBLEM 10-12

A 2.5 ft. long copper pipe with a 1.25 in. I.D. carries air at a velocity of 15 ft/min. The entrance temperature of the air is $65^\circ F$. Condensing steam on the exterior of the tube has a heat transfer coefficient of 2000 Btu/hr-ft^2-$^\circ F$. Determine the rate of heat transfer to the air.

Solution: To perform the necessary calculations, the bulk temperature is needed to evaluate the physical properties of the air. To obtain the bulk temperature, the exit temperature of the air is required. However, this is not provided. First, a bulk air temperature must be assumed. Then obtain the heat transfer coefficient for laminar flow, using equation (1). Use this value in equation (2) to obtain the exit temperature. With this exit temperature, calculate the bulk temperature. If it is in agreement with the original assumption, the problem is solved. If they do not agree, repeat the calculations with the new bulk temperature until convergence is achieved. Assume a bulk air temperature of $T_b = 135^\circ F$. The properties of air are:

k = thermal conductivity = 0.0164 Btu/ft-hr-$^\circ F$ at T_b

μ_b = viscosity = 0.0482 lbm/ft-hr at T_b

ρ = density = 0.0666 lbm/ft^3 at T_b

C_p = specific heat = 0.2407 Btu/lbm-^{0}F at T_b

μ_w = viscosity = 0.0525 Btu/lbm-^{0}F at T_w = 210^{0}F

where T_w is the wall temperature. Check if the flow is laminar or turbulent, using the Reynolds number.

$$Re = \frac{\rho u D}{\mu} = \frac{(0.0666)(15)(60)\left(\frac{1.25}{12}\right)}{0.0482}$$

$$= 130$$

The flow is laminar, and the equation below may be used to determine the heat transfer coefficient, h_i.

$$h_i = \left(\frac{k}{D}\right) 1.86 \left(Re \frac{D}{L}\right)^{0.33} \left(\frac{\mu_b}{\mu_w}\right)^{0.14} \qquad (1)$$

where D is the diameter of the tube and L is the length.

$$h_i = \left(\frac{0.0164}{0.1042}\right) 1.86 \left(130 \frac{(0.1042)}{(2.5)}\right)^{0.33} \left(\frac{0.0482}{0.0525}\right)^{0.14}$$

$$h_i = 0.505 \text{ Btu/hr-ft}^2\text{-}^0\text{F}$$

Substitute h_i in equation (2) to solve for T_L, the exit temperature of the air.

$$\ln\left(\frac{T_w - T_L}{T_w - T_o}\right) + 4 \frac{L}{D} \frac{h}{\rho u C_p} = 0 \qquad (2)$$

where T_o is the entrance temperature of the air and u is the velocity of the air. Substituting,

$$0 = \ln \frac{T_w - T_L}{T_w - T_o} + 4 \frac{(2.5)}{(0.1042)} \frac{(0.505)}{(0.0666)(15)(60)(0.2407)}$$

$$\frac{T_w - T_L}{T_w - T_o} = e^{-3.35} = 0.035$$

$$T_L = T_w - 0.035(T_w - T_o)$$

$$= 210 - 0.035(210-65)$$

$$= 205^0\text{F}$$

Then the bulk temperature is

$$T_b = \frac{65 + 205}{2} = 135^0\text{F}$$

This agrees with the original assumption for T_b.

The heat transfer rate is given by

$$q = \rho A u C_p (T_L - T_o)$$

where A is the surface area.

Substituting,

$$q = (0.0666)\left[\frac{\pi}{4}(0.1042)^2\right]\left[15(60)\right](0.2407)(205-65)$$

$$= 17.2 \text{ Btu/hr}$$

• PROBLEM 10-13

Water is moving through a heat exchanger tube with an inside diameter of D = 1.25 in. and a length of L = 9.0 ft. The water enters at 45 °F, with a flow rate of 18 gal/min. The wall temperature is constant at 200 °F. Determine the exit temperature of the water using analogies of Reynolds, Colburn, Prandtl and von Kármán.

Solution: Equation (1) states that an energy balance over a control volume of the tube yields,

$$\ln\left(\frac{T_E - T_w}{T_o - T_w}\right) + St\left(\frac{4L}{D}\right) = 0 \qquad (1)$$

where

T_E = exit temperature

T_o = entrance temperature

T_w = wall temperature

and St = Stanton number; its value depends upon the analogy used.

Solving for T_E,

$$T_E = (T_o - T_w)e^{\left(-St\left(\frac{4L}{D}\right)\right)} + T_w$$

The coefficient of skin friction, C_f, will be needed for use in the four analogies of this problem. This is obtained from the Moody diagram for smooth tubing, corresponding to the Reynolds number, Re.

At an assumed bulk temperature of 70 °F, the kinematic viscosity of water is $\nu = 1.06 \times 10^{-5}$ ft²/sec and the Prandtl number, Pr = 6.78.

$$Re = \frac{Du}{\nu}$$

where u is the fluid velocity:

$$u = \left(18\ \frac{\text{gal}}{\text{min}}\right)\left(\frac{1\ \text{ft}^3}{7.48\ \text{gal}}\right)\left(\frac{1}{0.00852\ \text{ft}^2}\right)\left(\frac{1\ \text{min}}{60\ \text{sec}}\right)$$

$$= 4.7\ \text{ft/sec.}$$

Then the Reynolds number is

$$\text{Re} = \frac{\left(\frac{1.25}{12}\right)\text{ft}\ (4.7\ \text{ft/sec})}{1.06\times10^{-5}\ \text{ft}^2/\text{sec}} = 46{,}187$$

At this Re, $C_f = 0.0053$ from the Moody diagram. Now, find the Stanton number for use in equation (1).

(i) Reynolds analogy:

$$\text{St} = \frac{C_f}{2} = \frac{0.0053}{2} = 0.0027$$

Solving for T_E in equation (1)

$$T_E = (45 - 200)e^{-0.0027\frac{(4)(9)(12)}{1.25}} + 200$$

$$= 139.0^0\text{F}$$

(ii) Colburn analogy:

$$\text{St} = \frac{C_f}{2}(\text{Pr})^{-2/3} = \frac{0.0053}{2}(6.78)^{-2/3}$$

$$= 0.00074$$

Solving for T_E,

$$T_E = 80.0^0\text{F}$$

(iii) Prandtl analogy:

$$\text{St} = \frac{C_f/2}{1 + 5\sqrt{C_f/2}\ (\text{Pr}-1)}$$

$$= \frac{0.0053/2}{1 + 5\sqrt{0.0053/2}\ (6.78-1)}$$

$$= 0.00107$$

and

$$T_E = 92.9^0\text{F}$$

(iiii) von Kármán analogy:

$$\text{St} = \frac{C_f/2}{1 + 5\sqrt{C_f/2}\ \{\text{Pr}-1+\ln[1+\frac{5}{6}(\text{Pr}-1)]\}}$$

$$= \frac{0.0053/2}{1 + 5\sqrt{0.0053/2}\ \{6.78-1+\ln[1+\frac{5}{6}(6.78-1)]\}}$$

$$St = 0.000901$$

and

$$T_E = 86.5^0F$$

• PROBLEM 10-14

A fluid is flowing in a circular pipe of radius R. Heat is being transferred from the walls of the pipe to the fluid at a constant rate q_w per unit area. Derive an expression for the temperature distribution and the local heat transfer coefficient h_x. The flow is laminar and fully developed. Axial conduction is negligible in comparison with radial conduction. Note that at $x = 0$, the bulk mean temperature of the fluid T_{b1} is known.

Solution: The following list of nomenclature will be employed in solving this problem.

C_1, C_2 = constants

C_p = specific heat of fluid

D = diameter of pipe = 2R

$f(x), f'(x)$ = functions of x

$G(r)$ = function of r

k = thermal conductivity of fluid

q_w = constant rate of heat transfer per unit area from the pipe to the fluid

r = radial coordinate

R = radius of pipe

T = temperature

$T_b(x)$ = local bulk mean temperature

T_{b1} = bulk mean temperature at $x = 0$

T_w = wall temperature

u = fluid velocity

U_m = maximum fluid velocity

x = axial coordinate

α = thermal diffusivity

ρ = density of fluid

The partial differential equation which describes the temperature distribution for radial symmetry is

$$\frac{1}{r}\frac{\partial}{\partial r}\left(r\frac{\partial T}{\partial r}\right) + \frac{\partial^2 T}{\partial x^2} = \frac{U}{\alpha}\frac{\partial T}{\partial x} \qquad (1)$$

Because axial conduction is neglected, $\partial^2 T/\partial x^2 = 0$, and equation (1) simplifies to

$$\frac{1}{r}\frac{\partial}{\partial r}\left(r\frac{\partial T}{\partial r}\right) = \frac{U}{\alpha}\frac{\partial T}{\partial x}$$

This differential equation has the following boundary conditions:

(1) Due to radial symmetry, at $r = 0$ for all x, $\partial T/\partial r = 0$.

(2) The heat flux from the wall is a known constant. At $r = R$ for all x, $(\partial T/\partial r)_R = q_w/k$.

(3) At $x = 0$, $T_b = T_{b1}$.

A fully developed temperature profile is described by

$$\frac{\partial T}{\partial x} = \frac{2q_w}{\rho C_p U_m R} = C_1 \qquad (3)$$

where $\partial T/\partial x$ is a constant, C_1, whose value is known.

The velocity profile $u = u(r,x)$ is needed to solve equation (2). For this situation, the velocity profile is

$$u = 2U_m\left(1 - \frac{r^2}{R^2}\right) \qquad (4)$$

Substitution of equations (3) and (4) into equation (2) gives

$$\frac{1}{r}\frac{\partial}{\partial r}\left(r\frac{\partial T}{\partial r}\right) = \frac{2U_m C_1}{\alpha}\left(1 - \frac{r^2}{R^2}\right)$$

Partial integration with respect to r yields

$$r\frac{\partial T}{\partial r} = \frac{2U_m C_1}{\alpha}\left(\frac{r^2}{2} - \frac{r^4}{4R^2}\right) + f(x).$$

Application of the first boundary condition forces $f(x) = 0$. Therefore,

$$\frac{\partial T}{\partial r} = \frac{2U_m C_1}{\alpha}\left(\frac{r}{2} - \frac{r^3}{4R^2}\right) \qquad (5)$$

Equation (5) must fulfill the second boundary condition. Then

$$\left.\frac{\partial T}{\partial r}\right|_R = \frac{U_m C_1 R}{2\alpha}$$

Substituting for C_1 from equation (3) and using $\alpha = k/\rho C_p$, equation (5), evaluated at $r = R$, is

$$\left.\frac{\partial T}{\partial r}\right|_R = \frac{RU_m(2q_w/\rho C_p U_m R)}{2k/\rho C_p} = \frac{q_w}{k}$$

Integrating equation (5) with respect to r again,

$$T = \frac{2U_m C_1}{\alpha}\left[\frac{r^2}{4} - \frac{r^4}{16R^2}\right] + f'(x) \qquad (6)$$

Integration of equation (3) with respect to x will allow the form of f'(x) to be obtained. The result is

$$T = C_1 x + G(r) \qquad (7)$$

Because equations (6) and (7) describe the same temperature distribution, G(r) must equal the function of r in equation (6) within a constant, while C_1x must equal f'(x) within a constant. Therefore equation (6) can be rewritten as

$$T = \frac{2U_m C_1}{\alpha}\left(\frac{r^2}{4} - \frac{r^4}{16R^2}\right) + C_1 x + C_2 \qquad (8)$$

C_2 is a constant which can be obtained from the third boundary condition. The bulk mean temperature is:

$$T_B = \frac{\int_{Ac} uTdA}{\int_{Ac} udA} \qquad (9)$$

For this problem, $dA = 2\pi r dr$. At $x = 0$, substitution of equation (8) for T and equation (4) for u, in equation (9), yields

$$T_{b_1} = \frac{\int_0^R 2U_m\left(1 - \frac{r^2}{R^2}\right)\left[\frac{2U_m C_1}{\alpha}\left(\frac{r^2}{4} - \frac{r^4}{16R^2}\right) + C_1 x + C_2\right] 2\pi r dr}{\int_0^R 2U_m\left(1 - \frac{r^2}{R^2}\right) 2\pi r dr}$$

Integrating and solving for C_2,

$$C_2 = T_{b1} - \frac{14}{96}\frac{C_1 R^2 U_m}{\alpha}$$

Substituting this expression for C_2 into equation (8) yields the temperature distribution as a function of r and x:

$$T(r,x) = \frac{2U_m C_1}{\alpha}\left(\frac{r^2}{4} - \frac{r^4}{16R^2} - \frac{7}{96}R^2\right) + C_1 x + T_{b1} \qquad (10)$$

The local surface coefficient of heat transfer is given by:

$$h_x = \frac{k(\partial T/\partial r)_{r=R}}{T_w - T_b} \qquad (11)$$

The second boundary condition states that $(\partial T/\partial r)_R = q_w/k$. The wall temperature at any x is found from equation (10), setting $r = R$:

$$T_w(x) = \frac{2U_m C_1}{\alpha}\left(\frac{24R^2}{96} - \frac{6R^2}{96} - \frac{7R^2}{96}\right) + C_1 x + T_{b1}$$

$$T_w(x) = \frac{22}{96}\left(\frac{U_m C_1 R^2}{\alpha}\right) + C_1 x + T_{b1} \qquad (12)$$

The local bulk mean temperature, $T_b(x)$, is given by

$$\frac{\partial T_b}{\partial x} = \frac{2q_w}{\rho C_p U_m R} = C_1$$

Integration, with the fact that $T_b = T_{b1}$ at $x = 0$, gives

$$T_b(x) = C_1 x + T_{b1} \qquad (13)$$

Use of the second boundary condition with equations (12) and (13) in equation (11) gives

$$h_x = \frac{k(q_w/k)}{\left(\frac{22}{96}\right)\left(\frac{U_m C_1 R^2}{\alpha}\right)}$$

Substituting for C_1 from equation (3) and setting $\alpha = k/\rho C_p$,

$$h_x = \left(\frac{96}{44}\right)\left(\frac{k}{R}\right)$$

or, in terms of the diameter,

$$h_x = 4.36(k/D)$$

• PROBLEM 10-15

A 19 ft. long tube with a 3/4 in. diameter is designed to heat air from 65^0F to 210^0F. The air flows at 3.0 lbm/hr. Determine the constant heat flux q_w which must be supplied to the air, and also the wall temperature at the end of the tube.

Solution: Using the physical properties of air, calculate the Reynolds number. For laminar flow, equations (1) and (2) can be employed to solve for q_w. Equation (3) can also be used to find the wall temperature at any value of x.

The following nomenclature will be used:

C_1 = a constant

C_p = specific heat of air

D = diameter of tube

k = thermal conductivity of air

q_w = constant rate of heat transfer per unit area from tube to air

r = radial coordinate

R = radius of pipe

Re = Reynolds number

T = temperature

$T_b(x)$ = local bulk mean temperature

$T_w(x)$ = wall temperature

U_m = maximum air velocity

x = axial coordinate

α = thermal diffusivity of air

ρ = density of air

μ = viscosity of air

$\dot{m}$ = mass flow rate of air

At a mean air temperature of $\frac{65 + 210}{2} = 137.5^0F$, air has the following properties:

$k = 0.0166$ Btu/hr-ft-^{0}F

$C_p = 0.2407$ Btu/lbm-^{0}F

$\rho = 0.0663$ lbm/ft^3

$\mu = 0.0494$ lbm/hr-ft

$\dot{m} = \rho\frac{1}{4}\pi D^2 U_m = 3$ lbm/hr

Substituting and solving for U_m,

$$3.0 = (0.0663)(\tfrac{1}{4})\pi\left(\frac{0.75}{12}\right)^2 U_m$$

$$U_m = 14{,}749 \text{ ft/hr}$$

Determine if the air flow is laminar, using the Reynolds number.

$$Re = \frac{\rho U_m D}{\mu} = \frac{(0.0663)U_m\left(\frac{0.75}{12}\right)}{0.0494}$$

$$Re = 0.0839\ U_m$$

Therefore, the Reynolds number

$$Re = 0.0839(14{,}749) = 1237$$

Since the flow is laminar, the following equations can be employed:

$$T_b(x) = C_1 x + T_{b1} \tag{1}$$

where

$$C_1 = \frac{2q_w}{\rho C_p U_m R} \tag{2}$$

In this problem, $T_{b_1} = 65^0F$ at $x = 0$, and at $x = 19$ ft, $T_{b2} = 210^0F$.

Substituting in equation (1) gives

$$210 = C_1(19) + 65$$

or

$$C_1 = 7.63$$

Substituting in equation (2) yields

$$7.63 = \frac{2q_w}{(0.0663)(0.2407)(14749)\left(\frac{0.75}{24}\right)}$$

$$q_w = 28.1 \text{ Btu/hr-ft}^2$$

The wall temperature at the end of the tube can be obtained from

$$T_w(x) = \frac{22}{96}\frac{U_m C_1 R^2}{\alpha} + C_1 x + T_{b1} \tag{3}$$

where

$$\alpha = \frac{k}{\rho C_p} = \frac{0.0166}{(0.0663)(0.2407)}$$

$$= 1.04 \text{ ft}^2\text{/hr.}$$

Then

$$T_w = \frac{22}{96}\frac{(14749)(7.63)\left(\frac{0.75}{24}\right)^2}{1.04} + 7.63(19) + 65$$

$$= 234^0F$$

• PROBLEM 10-16

A cross-flow heat exchanger as shown in figure (1) has 6 tubes in the flow direction and 7 tubes perpendicular to it. The tubes are 3 ft. long and have an outside diameter of 0.75 in. Air will move over this heat exchanger at a rate of 800 ft^3/min, with an entrance temperature of 350^{0}F. The tubes have a surface temperature of 190^{0}F. The longitudinal pitch is $S_L = 1.125$ in. and the transverse pitch is $S_T = 1.5$ in. Using an in-line arrangement of tubes, calculate the convective heat transfer coefficient.

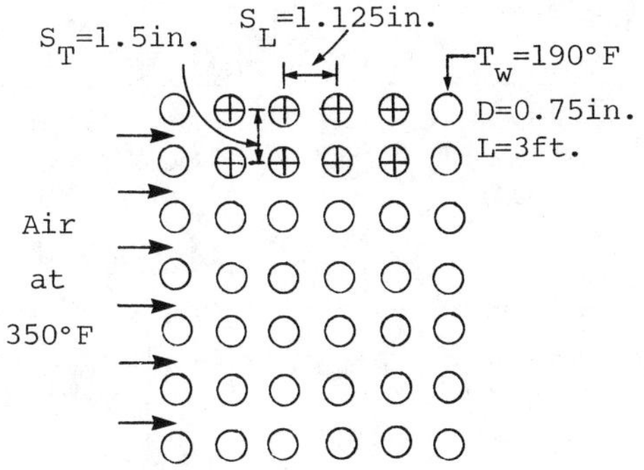

TUBE BANK

Figure 1.

Solution: The first step is to calculate the average Nusselt number (Nu_{avg}) using equation (1), where C and n are tabulated constants available in most heat transfer texts. Re_m is the maximum Reynolds number, given by equation (2). The tables of C and n are only for tube banks of 10 or more rows in the direction of flow. The Nu_{avg} will be calculated for 10 rows, and corrected using the R factor (equation (4)), which is also tabulated, in equation (5) to calculate the average heat transfer coefficient.

For 10 or more tubes in the direction of flow:

$$Nu_{avg} = CRe_m^n \tag{1}$$

The maximum Reynolds number is given by

$$Re_m = \frac{\rho U_m D}{\mu} \tag{2}$$

where U_m is the maximum fluid velocity,

$$U_m = \frac{\text{flow rate}}{\text{minimum area for flow}} \tag{3}$$

At a film temperature of

$$\frac{350 + 190}{2} = 270^0\text{F},$$

air has the following properties:

μ = viscosity = 0.0559 lbm/ft-hr

k = thermal conductivity = 0.0197 Btu/ft-hr-^{0}F

ρ = density = 0.0544 lbm/ft^3

C_p = specific heat = 0.2424 Btu/lbm-^{0}F

Pr = Prandtl number = 0.688

From equation (3),

$$U_m = \frac{\text{flow rate}}{\begin{bmatrix}\text{Area for} \\ \text{forward flow} \\ \text{of air}\end{bmatrix} - \begin{bmatrix}\text{Area of tubes} \\ \text{blocking air} \\ \text{flow}\end{bmatrix}}$$

$$U_m = \frac{\left(800\frac{ft^3}{min}\right)\left(\frac{1\ min}{60\ sec}\right)}{\left[\frac{(1.5in.)(3ft)}{(12in/ft)}\ (7\ tubes)\right] - \left[\frac{(0.75in)(3ft)}{(12in/ft)}(7\ tubes)\right]}$$

$= 10.2$ ft/sec

Substituting into equation (1),

$$Re_m = \frac{(0.0544)(10.2)\left(\frac{0.75}{12}\right)}{0.0559/3600} = 2233$$

The parameters necessary to obtain C and n are

$$\frac{S_T}{D} = \frac{1.5}{0.75} = 2$$

and

$$\frac{S_L}{D} = \frac{1.125}{0.75} = 1.5$$

From the tables

$$C = 0.112 \quad \text{and} \quad n = 0.702$$

for banks with 10 or more tubes in the direction of flow. Substituting into equation (1),

$$Nu_{avg} = 0.112(2233)^{0.702} = 25.13$$

The correction factor, R, for a bank 6 rows deep is

$$R = \frac{Nu_{avg} \text{ for 6 rows deep}}{Nu_{avg} \text{ for 10 rows deep}} \qquad (4)$$

R = 0.94, from a table of R values.

Then

$$Nu_{avg} \text{ for 6 rows deep} = R(Nu_{avg} \text{ for 10 rows deep})$$

$$= 0.94(25.13) = 23.62$$

Finally, the average convective heat transfer coefficient between the air and the tubes is

$$h_{avg} = Nu_{avg}\left(\frac{k}{D}\right) = (23.62)\left(\frac{0.0197}{(0.75/12)}\right) \qquad (5)$$

$$= 7.45\ Btu/hr\text{-}ft^2\text{-}^0F$$

FLOW ACROSS A CYLINDER

• PROBLEM 10-17

Consider a cylinder with its axis perpendicular to the flow of water. The water is at 70°F and has a free-stream velocity, $V_\infty = 6.5$ ft/sec. If a 1 in. schedule 40 pipe whose surface temperature is maintained at 130°F is used, calculate the heat transfer coefficient and the rate of transfer of heat to the water per foot of piping.

Solution: The fluid properties are evaluated at the film temperature, which is the average of the free-stream and wall temperatures. The physical properties of water at the film temperature, (70+130)/2 = 100°F, are

C_p = specific heat = 0.998 Btu/lbm-°F

ν = kinematic viscosity = 0.74×10^{-5} ft²/sec

k = thermal conductivity = 0.363 Btu/hr-ft-°F

Pr = Prandtl number = 4.55

The Reynolds number is given by

$$Re = \frac{Dv_\infty}{\nu}$$

where D = outer diameter of pipe. The outer diameter of a 1 in. schedule 40 pipe is found from the table of dimensions of standard pipes to be 1.315 in. Therefore, the Reynolds number,

$$Re = \frac{Dv_\infty}{\nu} = \frac{(1.315/12)}{0.74 \times 10^{-5}}(6.5) = 96{,}255.6$$

For the given situation, the equation for the heat transfer coefficient is given by

$$\frac{h_m D}{k} = c\, Re^n\, Pr^{1/3}$$

where h_m = heat transfer coefficient.

c,n = constants which depend on Re.

The values of c and n are given for various ranges of the Reynolds number, for flow past a cylinder, in the following table.

Re	c	n
0.4 - 4	0.989	0.330
4 - 40	0.911	0.385
40 - 4000	0.683	0.466
4000 - 40,000	0.193	0.618
40,000 - 400,000	0.0266	0.805

Since Re = 96,255.6, we determine the constants to be c = 0.0266 and n = 0.805. Solving for h_m,

$$h_m = \frac{(0.363)(0.0266)(96,255.6)^{.805}(4.55)^{1/3}}{(1.315/12)}$$

or

$$h_m = 1499.8 \text{ Btu/hr-ft}^2\text{-}^0\text{F}.$$

The rate of heat transfer per foot length of pipe,

$$\frac{Q}{L} = h_m(T_w - T_\infty)(\pi D)$$

where $\frac{Q}{L}$ = heat transfer rate per foot length of pipe

T_w = wall temperature

T_∞ = stream water temperature

Then

$$Q = (1499.8)(130 - 70)(\pi \times 1.315/12)(1 \text{ ft})$$

$$= 30980 \text{ Btu/hr}$$

• PROBLEM 10-18

> Air at 170 °F is transported through a rectangular duct 3 in. high and 6 in. wide. The duct is 18 ft. long, and the walls are maintained at a temperature of 65 °F. Assuming an air flow of 25 lbm/hr, determine the bulk mean temperature of the air as it leaves the duct.

Solution: First, obtain the necessary pnysical properties of air at the mean bulk temperature. Then calculate the hydraulic diameter, D_H. Using D_H in equation (1), solve for the Reynolds number (Re) in terms of U_m, the mean velocity of the air. U_m can be obtained, using the given mass flow rate m. This allows Re to be determined from equation (1). For laminar flow, use table (1) to calculate the forced convection heat transfer coefficient, h_x. An energy balance over the duct will then give the bulk temperature of the exiting air, T_{b_2}.

T_{b_1} = bulk temperature of air entering the duct = 170 °F

Air properties at $T = \frac{170+65}{2} = 117.5\,^0\text{F}$ are

ρ = density = 0.069 lbm/ft³

μ = air viscosity = 0.049 lbm/hr-ft

C_p = specific heat = 0.2405 Btu/lbm-°F

k = thermal conductivity = 0.01607 Btu/ft-hr-°F

a = larger duct dimension = 6 in. = $\frac{1}{2}$ ft.

b = smaller duct dimension = 3 in. = $\frac{1}{4}$ ft.

The hydraulic diameter is defined as:

$$D_H = \frac{4A_c}{P}$$

where A_c is the cross-sectional area and P is the perimeter of the duct.

$$D_H = \frac{4(\frac{1}{4})(\frac{1}{2})}{2(\frac{1}{4})+2(\frac{1}{2})} = \frac{1}{3} \text{ ft.}$$

Now, the Reynolds number is obtained from

$$Re = \frac{\rho U_m D_H}{\mu} = \frac{(0.069)(U_m)\left(\frac{1}{3}\right)}{0.049} \tag{1}$$

$$Re = 0.469\ U_m$$

U_m is obtained using the given mass flow rate:

$$\dot{m} = \rho a b U_m$$

$$25 = (0.069)(\tfrac{1}{2})(\tfrac{1}{4})U_m$$

$$U_m = 2899 \text{ ft/hr}$$

Then equation (1) yields a Reynolds number of

$$Re = 0.469\ U_m = 0.469(2899) = 1360$$

This is a laminar flow.

Local Nusselt numbers, based on the hydraulic diameter D_H, for steady laminar, low speed, constant property, fully-developed (both thermally and hydrodynamically) flow within ducts when axial conduction is neglible. Constant wall flux solutions are for a constant axial flux q''_w, but with perimeter of any cross section having constant temperature.

Table 1

Description of duct Cross-sectional shape	Cross section Hydraulic diameter D_H	Local Nusselt number $=\frac{h_x D_H}{k}$	
		Constant flux q''_w	Constant wall temperature T_w
Case 1 Circular tube of diameter D	D	4.36	3.66
Case 2 Rectangle of width a and height b: a=b	a	3.63	2.98
Case 3 Rectangle of width a and height b: a=2b	$\frac{2}{3}a$	4.11	3.39
Case 4 Rectangle of width a and height b: a=4b	$\frac{2}{5}a$	5.35	4.44
Case 5 Parallel plates spaced a distance b apart	2b	8.22	7.54
Case 6 Equilateral triangle of side length b	$\frac{2}{3}b$	3.00	

Using table (1),

$$\frac{h_x D_H}{k} = 3.39$$

$$\frac{h_x\left(\frac{1}{3}\right)}{0.01607} = 3.39$$

or

$$h_x = 0.163 \text{ Btu/hr-ft}^2\text{-}^0\text{F}$$

A heat balance over a differential section of the duct dL in length, yields

$$h(T-T_W)2\pi r\ dL = -\dot{m}C_p\ dT$$

where T is the air temperature and r is the hydraulic radius of the duct

or

$$\frac{dT}{T-T_W} = \frac{2\pi rhdL}{\dot{m}C_p}$$

Integrating,

$$\ln\left(\frac{T_{b_2}-T_W}{T_{b_1}-T_W}\right) = \frac{2\pi rhL}{\dot{m}C_p}$$

In this case $T_W = 65^0\text{F}$, $T_{b_1} = 170^0\text{F}$, $r = \frac{1}{6}$ ft.

$$h = 0.163 \frac{\text{Btu}}{\text{hr-ft}^2\text{-}^0\text{F}}$$

$$L = 18 \text{ ft}$$

$$\dot{m} = 25 \text{ lbm/hr}$$

$$C_p = 0.2405 \frac{\text{Btu}}{\text{lbm-hr-}^0\text{F}}$$

Solving for T_{b_2}, we get $T_{b_2} = 128^0\text{F}$

• PROBLEM 10-19

A fluid is flowing between two parallel plates (see figure (1)). The flow is laminar and fully developed. Both surfaces are heated and axial conduction is negligible. The bulk mean temperature at x = 0 is T_{b_1} (a known value). Determine the temperature distribution as a function of x and y, the local surface coefficient of heat transfer, and the local Nusselt number.

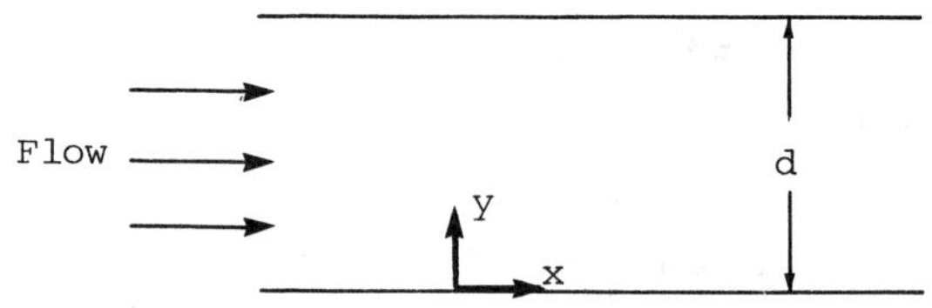

Figure 1.

Solution: The following list of nomenclature will be employed in solving this problem:

$A = A_c$ = cross-sectional area

C_1, C_2 = constants

C_p = specific heat

d = distance between the plates

D_H = hydraulic diameter

$f(x), f'(x)$ = functions of x

h_x = local surface coefficient of heat transfer

k = thermal conductivity of fluid

Nu_x = local Nusselt number

P = wetted perimeter

q_w = the constant heat flux into the fluid at both surfaces

T = temperature

T_b = local bulk temperature

T_{b_1} = bulk temperature at x = 0

T_w = wall temperature

u = fluid velocity

U_m = maximum fluid velocity

x, y } see figure (1)

α = thermal diffusivity

ρ = fluid density

The partial differential equation describing the temperature distribution is:

$$\frac{\partial^2 T}{\partial y^2} = \frac{u}{\alpha}\frac{\partial T}{\partial x} \tag{1}$$

For a fully developed flow, $\partial T/\partial x$ is a constant, as

$$\frac{\partial T}{\partial x} = \frac{\partial T_b}{\partial x} = \frac{2q_w}{\rho U_m C_p d} = C_1 \tag{2}$$

The velocity profile is

$$u = 6U_m\left(\frac{y}{d} - \frac{y^2}{d^2}\right) \tag{3}$$

Substituting equations (3) and (2) into equation (1) yields

$$\frac{\partial^2 T}{\partial y^2} = \frac{6U_m C_1}{\alpha}\left(\frac{y}{d} - \frac{y^2}{d^2}\right) \tag{4}$$

The boundary conditions are:

(1) At $y = d/2$, $\partial T/\partial y = 0$

(2) At $y = 0$, $q_w = -k(\partial T/\partial y)_y = 0$

(3) At $x = 0$, $T_b = T_{b1}$

Integration of equation (4) with respect to y gives

$$\frac{\partial T}{\partial y} = \frac{6U_m C_1}{\alpha}\left(\frac{y^2}{2d} - \frac{y^3}{3d^2}\right) + f(x) \tag{5}$$

Employing the first boundary condition to solve for f(x),

$$0 = \frac{6U_m C_1}{\alpha}\left(\frac{d}{8} - \frac{d}{24}\right) + f(x)$$

Therefore,

$$f(x) = \frac{-6U_m C_1}{\alpha}\left(\frac{d}{12}\right) \tag{6}$$

Substituting for f(x) in equation (5),

$$\frac{\partial T}{\partial y} = \frac{6U_m C_1}{\alpha}\left(\frac{y^2}{2d} - \frac{y^3}{3d^2} - \frac{d}{12}\right) \tag{7}$$

Integrating equation (7) with respect to y,

$$T = \frac{6U_m C_1}{\alpha}\left(\frac{y^3}{6d} - \frac{y^4}{12d^2} - \frac{dy}{12}\right) + f'(x) \tag{8}$$

Now, taking the derivative of equation (8) with respect to x, and setting $\partial T/\partial x$ equal to C_1 by equation (2),

$$\frac{df'(x)}{dx} = C_1$$

Integration gives

$$f'(x) = C_1 x + C_2 \tag{9}$$

Substituting equation (9) for f'(x) into equation (8),

$$T = \frac{6U_m C_1}{\alpha}\left(\frac{y^2}{6d} - \frac{y^4}{12d^2} - \frac{dy}{12}\right) + C_1 x + C_2 \tag{10}$$

The general relationship for T_b is

$$T_b = \frac{\int_{A_c} uT\,dA}{\int_{A_c} u\,dA} \tag{11}$$

Substituting equation (10) for T, equation (3) for u, and dy for dA in equation (11),

$$T_b = \frac{\int_0^d 6U_m\left(\frac{y}{d} - \frac{y^2}{d^2}\right)\left[\frac{6U_mC_1}{\alpha}\left(\frac{y^3}{6d} - \frac{y^4}{12d^2} - \frac{dy}{12}\right) + C_1x + C_2\right]dy}{\int_0^b 6U_m\left(\frac{y}{d} - \frac{y^2}{d^2}\right)dy}$$

Integrating,

$$T_b = C_1x + C_2 - \frac{17}{140}\frac{U_mC_1d^2}{\alpha} \qquad (12)$$

The third boundary condition states that at $x = 0$, $T_b = T_{b1}$. Substituting this into equation (12) and solving for C_2,

$$C_2 = \frac{17}{140}\frac{U_mC_1d^2}{\alpha} + T_{b1} \qquad (13)$$

Equation (12) is now

$$T_b = C_1x + T_{b1} \qquad (14)$$

Substituting equation (13) into equation (10) yields the temperature distribution:

$$T = \frac{6U_mC_1}{\alpha}\left(\frac{y^3}{6d} - \frac{y^4}{12d^2} - \frac{dy}{12}\right) + C_1x + \frac{17}{140}\frac{U_mC_1d^2}{\alpha} + T_{b1} \qquad (15)$$

The local surface coefficient of heat transfer is given by

$$h_x = \frac{-k\left(\frac{\partial T}{\partial y}\right)_{y=0}}{T_w - T_b} \qquad (16)$$

The second boundary condition states that

$$q_w = -k\left(\frac{\partial T}{\partial y}\right)_{y=0} \qquad (17)$$

where q_w is a known constant.

The local wall temperature is provided by equation (15) with $y = 0$:

$$T_w = C_1x + \frac{17}{140}\frac{U_mC_1d^2}{\alpha} + T_{b1}$$

Also, T_b is given by equation (14).

Therefore,

$$T_w - T_b = \frac{17}{140}\frac{U_mC_1d^2}{\alpha}$$

Substituting in $\alpha = k/\rho C_p$, and equation (2) for C_1,

$$T_w - T_b = \frac{17}{140} U_m \frac{2q_w d^2}{\rho U_m C_p d \left(\frac{k}{\rho C_p}\right)}$$

$$= \frac{17}{70} \frac{dq_w}{k} \qquad (18)$$

Substituting equations (18) and (17) in equation (16) yields

$$h_x = \frac{70}{17} \frac{k}{d} = 4.11 \frac{k}{d} \qquad (19)$$

or

$$\frac{h_x d}{k} = 4.11 \qquad (20)$$

Nusselt numbers for duct flow are based on the hydraulic diameter D_H,

$$D_H = \frac{4A}{P}$$

For a one ft. depth of the parallel plates,

$$D_H = \frac{4d}{1+1} = 2d$$

Replacing d in equation (20),

$$Nu_x = \frac{h_x D_H}{k} = 8.22$$

FLOW OVER A FLAT PLATE

• PROBLEM 10-20

Calculate the heat transfer coefficient for water traveling at a velocity of 15 ft/sec in a 3/4 in. 20 BWG tube. Bulk temperatures at the entrance and exit are 65°F and 125°F, respectively. The wall surface temperature is 170°F.

Solution: The first step is to obtain the physical properties necessary to calculate the Reynolds number and the Prandtl number. This will allow calculation of the heat transfer coefficient by three possible correlations: Dittus-Boelter, Colburn, and Sieder-Tate.

The average fluid temperature is

$$\frac{65 + 125}{2} = 95^\circ F$$

At this temperature, the properties of water are:

ρ = density = 62.06 lbm/ft^3

μ = viscosity = 1.75 lbm/hr-ft

c_p = specific heat = 0.998 Btu/lbm-^{0}F

k = thermal conductivity = 0.3605 Btu/hr-ft-^{0}F

Also, at 170^{0}F,

$$\mu_w = 0.9 \text{ lbm/hr-ft}$$

From the standard tubing tables, the inside pipe diameter is

$$D = 0.68 \text{ in.}$$

The Reynolds number is

$$Re = \frac{\rho u D}{\mu} = \frac{(62.06)(15)(3600)(0.68/12)}{1.75}$$

$$= 108,516$$

where u is the fluid velocity.

The Prandtl number is

$$Pr = \frac{c_p \mu}{k} = \frac{(0.998)(1.75)}{0.3605}$$

$$= 4.84$$

Using the Dittus-Boelter relation,

$$h = 0.023 \, Re^{0.8} Pr^{0.4} \left(\frac{k}{D}\right)$$

$$= 0.023(108,516)^{0.8}(4.84)^{0.4}\left(\frac{0.3605}{0.68/12}\right)$$

$$= 2935.2 \text{ Btu/hr-ft}^2\text{-}^0\text{F}$$

Using the Colburn equation,

$$h = 0.023 \, Re^{0.8} Pr^{1/3} \left(\frac{k}{D}\right)$$

$$= 0.023(108,516)^{0.8}(4.84)^{1/3}\left(\frac{0.3605}{0.68/12}\right)$$

$$= 2642.3 \text{ Btu/hr-ft}^2\text{-}^0\text{F}$$

Using the Sieder-Tate correlation,

$$h = 0.023 \, Re^{0.8} Pr^{0.3} \left(\frac{\mu}{\mu_w}\right)^{0.14} \left(\frac{k}{D}\right)$$

$$= 0.023(108,516)^{0.8}(4.84)^{0.3}\left(\frac{1.75}{0.9}\right)^{0.14}\left(\frac{0.3605}{0.68/12}\right)$$

$$= 2751.6 \text{ Btu/hr-ft}^2\text{-}^0\text{F}$$

Water moves through an annulus with a velocity of 9 ft/sec. The space for water flow is bounded by a 3/4 in. O.D. tube and a $1\frac{1}{4}$ in. I.D. tube. The water is initially at 170°F, and is to be cooled. The outer wall of the annulus is insulated, and the inner wall is at 90°F. Calculate the unit thermal convective conductance, $\bar{h}_c$, for the water.

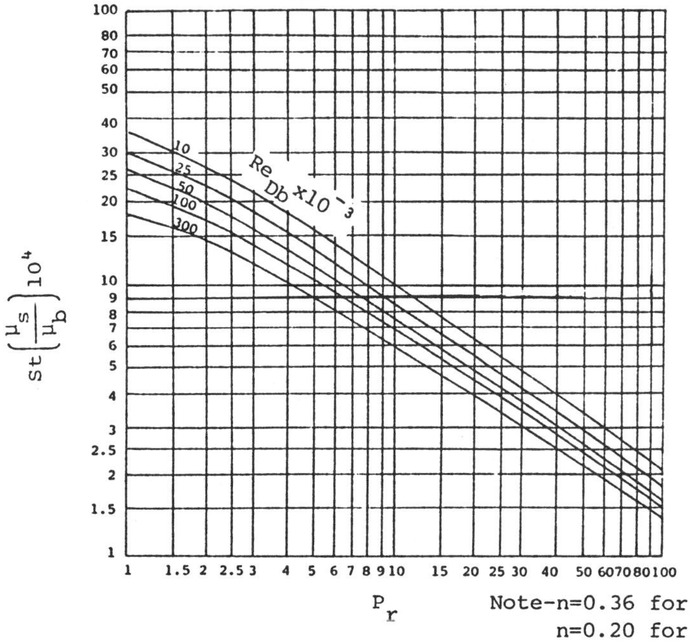

Fig. 1.

Note-n=0.36 for heating
n=0.20 for cooling

VARIATION OF THE STANTON NUMBER WITH PRANDTL NUMBER FOR VARIOUS VALUES OF THE BULK REYNOLDS NUMBER.

Solution: Using the physical properties of water, the Reynolds and Prandtl numbers can be determined at the bulk temperature (T_b = 170°F) and the mean film temperature (T_f = 130°F). The unit convective conductance can be calculated using equation (1), which is based on the properties at the mean film temperature, or equation (2) in conjunction with figure (1), which are based on the bulk properties.

T (°F)	μ(viscosity) (lbm/hr-ft)	k(thermal conductivity) (Btu/hr-ft-°F)
90	1.85	0.360
130	1.24	0.375
170	0.90	0.386

T (°F)	ρ(density) (lbm/ft³)	c_p(specific heat) (Btu/lbm-°F)
90	62.1	0.997
130	61.5	0.998
170	60.8	1.001

The hydraulic diameter, D_H, is employed for non-circular conduits. By definition,

$$D_H = \frac{4A}{P}$$

where A is the cross-sectional area of flow, and P is the wetted perimeter. Since

$$A = \frac{\pi(D_{out}^2 - D_{in}^2)}{4}$$

$$= \frac{\pi}{4}(1.25^2 - 0.75^2) = 0.7854 \text{ in}^2$$

and

$$P = \pi(D_{out} + D_{in})$$

$$= \pi(1.25 + 0.75) = 6.283 \text{ in},$$

$$D_H = \frac{4(0.7854 \text{ in}^2)}{6.283 \text{ in}} = 0.50 \text{ in}$$

Based on the bulk properties,

$$Re_b = \frac{uD_H\rho}{\mu} = \frac{\left(9\ \frac{\text{ft}}{\text{sec}}\right)\left(\frac{3600 \text{ sec}}{\text{hr}}\right)\left(\frac{0.5}{12}\ \text{ft}\right)\left(60.8\ \frac{\text{lbm}}{\text{ft}^3}\right)}{0.90\ \frac{\text{lbm}}{\text{ft-hr}}}$$

$$= 91,200$$

$$Pr_b = \frac{c_p\mu}{k} = \frac{(1.001 \text{ Btu/lbm-}^0\text{F})(0.90 \text{ lbm/hr-ft})}{0.386 \text{ Btu/hr-ft-}^0\text{F}}$$

$$= 2.33$$

Based on the properties at the mean film temperature,

$$Re_f = \frac{(9)(3600)\left(\frac{0.5}{12}\right)(61.5)}{1.24} = 66,956$$

$$Pr_f = \frac{(0.998)(1.24)}{0.375} = 3.30$$

Substituting into the following equation,

$$St = \text{Stanton number} = \frac{\bar{h}_c}{c_p u} = 0.023\ Re_f^{-0.2} Pr_f^{-2/3} \qquad (1)$$

$$\bar{h}_c = \frac{\left(0.998\ \frac{\text{Btu}}{\text{lbm-}^0\text{F}}\right)\left(9\ \frac{\text{ft}}{\text{sec}}\ \ 3600\ \frac{\text{sec}}{\text{hr}}\right)\left(61.5\ \frac{\text{lbm}}{\text{ft}^3}\right)^{0.023}}{(66,956)^{0.2}(3.30)^{2/3}}$$

$$\bar{h}_c = 2236 \text{ Btu/hr-ft}^2\text{-}^0\text{F}$$

From figure (1), $St(\mu_s/\mu_b)^n = 17 \times 10^{-4}$, using $n = 0.2$ for cooling, where μ_s and μ_b are the viscosities at the inner wall temperature (90^0F) and at the bulk temperature respectively. The unit convective conductance can now be determined using the bulk properties:

$$\bar{h}_c = St \frac{k_b}{D_H} Re_b Pr_b \qquad (2)$$

Substituting into equation (2) yields

$$\bar{h}_c = (17 \times 10^{-4}) \frac{\left(0.386 \frac{\text{Btu}}{\text{lbm-}^0\text{F}}\right)}{(0.5/12 \text{ ft})} (91{,}200)(2.33)\left(\frac{1.85}{0.90}\right)^{0.2}$$

$$= 3865 \text{ Btu/hr-ft}^2\text{-}^0\text{F}$$

• PROBLEM 10-22

A wide plate of length 3.5 in. has air at 1 atm. and 180^0F moving parallel to it at a velocity of 190 ft/sec. Determine the average heat flux if the surface of the plate is at a constant temperature of 110^0F.

Solution: First, determine the physical properties of air necessary to calculate the Reynolds and Prandtl numbers. These values will then be employed in equation (1) to determine the heat transfer coefficient, which then allows the average heat flux to be obtained.

The properties of air at a temperautre of $\frac{180+110}{2} = 145^0$F are:

μ = viscosity = 0.0496 lbm/ft-hr

ρ = density = 0.0654 lbm/ft^3

k = thermal conductivity = 0.01674 Btu/hr-ft-^{0}F

c_p = specific heat = 0.2408 Btu/lbm-^{0}F

The Reynolds number is, by definition,

$$Re = \frac{\rho u L}{\mu} = \frac{(0.0654)(190)\left(\frac{3.5}{12}\right)(3600)}{0.0496}$$

$$Re = 263{,}050$$

The Prandtl number is

$$Pr = \frac{c_p \mu}{k} = \frac{(0.2408)(0.0496)}{0.01674} = 0.7135$$

Substituting into equation (1) and solving for h,

$$Nu = \text{Nusselt number} = \frac{hL}{k} = 0.664(Re)^{1/2}(Pr)^{1/3}$$

$$h = \frac{(0.01674)}{\left(\frac{3.5}{12}\right)} (0.664)(263050)^{1/2}(0.7135)^{1/3}$$

$$h = 17.47 \text{ Btu/hr-ft}^2\text{-}^0\text{F}$$

Then

$$\frac{q}{A} = \frac{\text{heat flux}}{\text{area}} = h(\Delta T) = (17.47)(180 - 110)$$

$$= 1223 \text{ Btu/hr-ft}^2$$

• PROBLEM 10-23

A flat plate is maintained at a constant temperature of 225 ^{0}F (107.6 ^{0}C). Air at 1 atm. and a temperature, T_∞, of 140 ^{0}F (60.3 ^{0}C) moves across this plate at a velocity, U_∞, of 2.5 ft/sec (0.762 m/sec). Calculate the local heat transfer coefficient, h_x, at 3 ft (0.91m) from the leading edge of the plate. Also determine the average heat transfer coefficient, $\bar{h}$, from x = 0 to x = 3 ft. Obtain the total heat transfer rate from the plate to the air for the first 3 ft. of the plate per foot (≅0.3m) width of plate.

Solution: Obtain the physical properties of air at 182.5 ^{0}F (84.0 ^{0}C), the average of T_w and T_∞. Use these properties to determine the Reynolds and Prandtl numbers. These values are substituted into equation (1) to solve for the local heat transfer coefficient. The average heat transfer coefficient is obtained by integrating over the plate and employed to calculate the heat transfer rate.

At a temperature of 182.5 ^{0}F,

ν = kinematic viscosity of air = 2.14×10^{-5} m^2/sec

k = thermal conductivity = 0.03054 W/m-^{0}C

α = thermal diffusivity = 3.092×10^{-5} m^2/sec

$Pr = \nu/\alpha = 0.692$

The local Re at x = 0.91m (3 ft.) is:

$$Re_x = \frac{U_\infty x}{\nu} = \frac{(0.762)(0.91)}{2.14\times10^{-5}} = 32{,}403$$

The local Nusselt number (Nu) at x = 0.91m is given by

$$Nu_x = \frac{h_x x}{k} = 0.332\ Re_x^{1/2} Pr^{1/3} \qquad (1)$$

Substituting and solving for h_x,

$$\frac{h_x(0.91)}{0.03054} = 0.332(32,403)^{1/2}(0.692)^{1/3}$$

$$h_x = 1.77 \text{ W/m}^2\text{-sec}$$

The average heat transfer coefficient is obtained by integrating over the length of the plate, as

$$\bar{h} = \frac{\int_0^L h_x dx}{\int_0^L dx} = 2h_{x=L}$$

Therefore,

$$\bar{h} = 2h_x \quad \text{at } x = 3$$

$$= 3.54 \text{ W/m}^2\text{-sec}$$

The heat transfer rate is given by

$$Q = A\, h_m(T_w - T_\infty)$$

$$= (0.3)(0.91)(3.54)(107.6 - 60.3)$$

$$= 45.7 \text{ W} \quad \simeq 156 \text{ Btu/hr}$$

• PROBLEM 10-24

Water at a temperature of $T_\infty = 50^0$F moves at 9 ft/sec across a flat plate of length L = 4 ft, which is at a uniform temperature of 130^0F. Considering that the transition to turbulence occurs at a Reynolds number of 5×10^5, determine the average heat transfer coefficient.

Solution: Using the physical properties of water, calculate the Reynolds number based on the length of the plate. For a turbulent boundary layer, equation (1) can be employed to solve for the average heat transfer coefficient.

T_s = surface temperature of plate = 130^0F

$$T_f = \text{film temperature} = \frac{T_\infty + T_s}{2} = \frac{50 + 130}{2}$$

$$= 90^0\text{F}$$

The physical properties of water at the film temperature are:

k = thermal conductivity = 0.36 Btu/hr-ft-^{0}F

μ = viscosity = 5.14×10^{-4} lbm/ft-sec

ρ = density = 62.11 lbm/ft^3

Pr = Prandtl number = 5.12

The Reynolds number is

$$Re_L = \frac{\rho u L}{\mu}$$

where u is the velocity of the water.

Then

$$Re_L = \frac{(62.11)(9)(4)}{5.14 \times 10^{-4}} = 4.35 \times 10^6$$

Since the transition to turbulence has occurred, equation (1) can now be employed.

$$\overline{Nu} = \text{average Nusselt number} = \frac{hL}{k}$$

$$= 0.036(Pr)^{1/3}\left[Re^{0.8} - 23,200\right] \quad (1)$$

Substituting,

$$\frac{hL}{k} = 0.036(5.12)^{1/3}\left[(4.35\times10^6)^{0.8} - 23,200\right]$$

$$= 11252$$

Then the heat transfer coefficient is

$$h = \frac{11252(0.36)}{4}$$

$$h = 1012.7 \text{ Btu/hr-ft}^2\text{-}^0\text{F}$$

• PROBLEM 10-25

Air at one atm. and 90^{0}F moves at 140 ft/sec across a flat plate of length 3 ft. The temperature at the surface of the plate is 450^{0}F. For a 1 ft. width, determine the heat loss from the entire plate, and also the heat loss from the laminar and turbulent sections of the boundary layer. Then, assuming that the boundary layer is completely turbulent, calculate the heat loss.

Solution: Calculate the Reynolds number for the entire plate. Using this in equation (1), the Nusselt number for the plate may be obtained. From the definition of the Nusselt number, the average film coefficient can be obtained. Equation (2) permits the evaluation of the total heat loss to the air.

Assume a transition from a laminar to a turbulent boundary layer at a critical Reynolds number of $Re_c = 4 \times 10^5$. This permits calculation of the point of transition. Using this information, determine the heat transferred from the laminar and turbulent sections, using equation (3).

Next, assume a turbulent boundary layer for the whole plate, and calculate the heat transfer coefficient with equation (4).

At an average film temperature of $\frac{90 + 450}{2} = 270^0$F, air has the following properties:

k = thermal conductivity = 0.0197 Btu/hr-ft-^{0}F

ν = kinematic viscosity = 1.017 ft^2/hr

Pr = Prandtl number = 0.688

The Re for the whole plate is

$$Re_L = \frac{uL}{D} = \frac{(140)(3600)(3)}{1.017} = 1.49 \times 10^6$$

Substitution in equation (1) yields the Nusselt number:

$$Nu_L = 0.036\ Pr^{1/3}\left[Re^{0.8} - 18,700\right] \qquad (1)$$

$$= 0.036(0.688)^{1/3}\left[(1.49\times10^6)^{0.8} - 18,700\right]$$

$$Nu_L = 2165$$

And since

$$Nu_L = \frac{hL}{k},$$

$$h = \frac{kNu_L}{L} = \frac{(0.0197)(2165)}{3} = 14.2 \text{ Btu/hr-ft}^2\text{-}^0\text{F}$$

Substituting this value into equation (2), the total heat loss yielded is

$$q = Ah(T_s - T_\infty) \qquad (2)$$

where A is the area available for heat transfer, T_s is the surface temperature of the plate, and T_∞ is the air temperature.

$$q = (1)(3)(14.2)(450 - 90)$$

$$= 15,336 \text{ Btu/hr}$$

The point of transition from laminar to turbulent, X_{cr}, can be obtained from the definition of the Reynolds number:

$$Re_{cr} = \frac{X_{cr}U}{\nu}$$

Solving for X_{cr} and substituting,

$$X_{cr} = Re_{cr} \frac{\nu}{u} = (4 \times 10^5) \frac{(1.017)}{140(3600)}$$

$$= 0.807 \text{ ft.}$$

A laminar boundary layer thus exists from the leading edge of the plate to a distance of 0.807 ft. down the plate. The Nusselt number is obtained from equation (3) as

$$Nu_L = 0.664\ Re_L^{1/2}\ Pr^{1/3} \quad (3)$$

$$= 0.664(4 \times 10^5)^{1/2}(0.688)^{1/3}$$

$$= 371$$

Now,

$$Nu_L = \frac{hL}{k}$$

Solving for h, which is the laminar heat transfer coefficient h_{lam}, and substituting gives

$$h_{lam} = \frac{Nu_L k}{L} = \frac{(371)(0.0197)}{(0.807)}$$

$$= 9.06 \text{ Btu/hr-ft}^2\text{-}^0\text{F}$$

The heat transferred in the laminar section is, then

$$q_{lam} = Ah_{lam}(T_s - T_\infty)$$

$$= (1)(0.807)(9.06)(450 - 90)$$

$$= 2632 \text{ Btu/hr}$$

The heat loss from the turbulent section is

$$q_{tur} = q_{tot} - q_{lam} = 15{,}336 - 2632$$

$$= 12{,}704 \text{ Btu/hr}$$

Equation (4) can be used on the assumption that a turbulent boundary layer exists over the entire plate.

$$Nu = \frac{hL}{k} = 0.036\ Re_L^{0.8}\ Pr^{1/3} \quad (4)$$

$$= 0.036(1.49 \times 10^6)^{0.8}(0.688)^{1/3}$$

$$= 2579$$

Then

$$h = \frac{Nuk}{L} = \frac{2579(0.0197)}{3}$$

$$h = 16.9 \text{ Btu/hr-ft}^2\text{-}^0\text{F}$$

The heat loss, assuming complete turbulence, is

$$q = Ah(T_s - T_\infty)$$

$$= (1)(3)(16.9)(450 - 90)$$

$$= 18{,}252 \text{ Btu/hr}$$

• PROBLEM 10-26

In an experiment to study heat transfer, a metal box 35 in. long, 10 in. wide, and 3 in. deep, is propelled at a velocity of 73.3 ft/sec. The box has a surface temperature of $T_s = 145\,^0F$ while the ambient air temperature is $T_\infty = 35\,^0F$. Assume a turbulent boundary layer, and employ the same convective heat transfer coefficient for all sides of the box. Note that the bottom of the box is not exposed to air, and therefore will not lose heat. Calculate the rate of heat flow from the box.

Solution: Use the physical properties of air at the mean temperature of $90\,^0F$ to determine the Prandtl and Reynolds numbers, based on the length of the box, L. Use these values to calculate the average Nusselt number from equation (1).

Equation (2) allows the average convective heat transfer coefficient to be obtained.

Substitution in equation (3) will provide the rate of heat loss from the box.

The physical properties of air at $90\,^0F$ are:

ρ = density = 0.0668 lbm/ft^3

μ = viscosity = 1.34×10^{-5} lbm/ft-sec

Pr = 0.707

$$Re_L = \frac{u\rho L}{\mu} = \frac{(73.3)(0.0668)(35/12)}{1.34\ 10^{-5}} = 1.07 \times 10^6$$

Substituting into equation (1),

$$\overline{Nu}_L = 0.036\ Pr^{1/3} Re^{0.8} \tag{1}$$

$$= (0.036)(0.707)^{1/3}(1.07 \times 10^6)^{0.8}$$

$$= 2136$$

The thermal conductivity of air at $90\,^0F$ =

$$k = 0.01542 \text{ Btu/ft-hr-}^0F$$

Substituting in equation (2) yields $\bar{h}_c$, the average convective heat transfer coefficient.

$$\bar{h}_c = \overline{Nu}_L \frac{k}{L} = (2136) \frac{(0.01542)}{(35/12)} \qquad (2)$$

$$= 11.29 \text{ Btu/hr-ft}^2\text{-}^0\text{F}$$

The total area available for heat transfer is:

$$A = \frac{(35\times10) + 2(3\times10) + 2(3\times35)}{144}$$

$$= 4.31 \text{ ft}^2$$

Substitution into equation (3) yields q, the rate of heat loss from the box, as

$$q = \bar{h}_c A(T_s - T_\infty) \qquad (3)$$

$$= (11.29)(4.31)(145 - 35)$$

$$= 5353 \text{ Btu/hr}$$

CHAPTER 11

FREE CONVECTION

FLOW IN HORIZONTAL PIPES AND TUBES

• PROBLEM 11-1

A horizontal pipe has a 12 in. outside diameter. The temperature of the outer surface is 110°F and the air around it is at 1 atm. and 90°F. Approximate the rate of heat loss by free convection from a unit length of this pipe.

Solution: Air at 1 atm. and a film temperature of 100°F (560 °R) has the following properties.

$$\mu = 0.0467\ lb_m/ft\text{-}hr$$

$$\rho = 0.0710\ lb_m/ft^3$$

$$\hat{C}_p = 0.241\ Btu/lb_m\text{-}^\circ R$$

$$k = 0.0156\ Btu/ft\text{-}hr\text{-}^\circ R$$

$$\beta = 1/T_f = \frac{1}{560}\ ^\circ R^{-1}$$

Other necessary data are:

$$D = 1.0\ ft$$

$$\Delta T = 20^\circ R$$

$$g = 4.17 \times 10^8\ ft/hr^2$$

Substitute into the following eq. :

$$N_{Gr}N_{Pr} = \left(\frac{L^3\rho^2 g\beta\Delta T}{\mu^2}\right)\left(\frac{\hat{C}_p\mu}{k}\right) = \left(\frac{L^3\rho^2 g\beta\Delta T}{\mu}\right)\left(\frac{\hat{C}_p}{k}\right)$$

$$= \left[\frac{(1.0)(0.0710)^2(4.17 \times 10^8)\left(\frac{20}{560}\right)}{0.0467}\right]\left(\frac{0.241}{0.0156}\right)$$

$$= 2.5 \times 10^7$$

From the equation $N_{Num} = 0.525\ (N_{Gr}N_{Pr})^{\frac{1}{4}}$, $N_{Num} = 37.1$

$$h_m = N_{Num}\frac{k}{D} = \frac{(37.1)(0.0156)}{(1.0)} = 0.58\ \frac{\text{Btu}}{\text{hr ft}^{2\,\circ}\text{F}}$$

The amount of heat lost per unit length of pipe is:

$$\frac{Q}{L} = h_m A\frac{\Delta T}{L} = h_m \pi D\Delta T$$

$$= (0.58)\pi(1.0)(20) = 36\ \frac{\text{Btu}}{\text{hr-ft}}$$

This value takes into account heat losses due to convection only.

• PROBLEM 11-2

Determine the heat loss per foot length from an uninsulated pipe (5-in., schedule 40) passing through a hall maintained at a temperature of 80°F. The surface temperature of the uninsulated pipe is 900°F.

Solution: In a system of this type, heat transfer occurs by free convection.

The outer diameter of a 5-in. schedule 40 pipe is 5.563 in. = 0.464 ft.

The heat loss per foot length of pipe is given by

$$\frac{q}{L} = (A/L)h(T_s - T_a) \qquad (1)$$

h can be obtained from the Nusselt number.

The Nusselt number is given by

$$Nu_D = C(Gr_D Pr)^m \qquad (2)$$

The Grashof number is given by

$$Gr_D = \frac{g\beta(T_1 - T_2)d^3\rho^3}{\mu^2} \tag{3}$$

The mean film temperature is the arithmetic mean of surface temperature of pipe and the air temperature in the hall.

Hence, the mean film temperature = (900 + 80)/2 = 490°F.

From air tables, for air at 490°F we have

$\rho = 0.0418\ lb_m/ft^3$ $\qquad$ $\mu = 0.0672\ lb_m/ft\text{-}hr$

$k = 0.0244\ Btu/hr\text{-}ft\text{-}^{\circ}F$ $\qquad$ $Pr = 0.679$

Air at atmospheric pressure can be considered as an ideal gas.

β is the reciprocal of absolute temperature.

Hence, $\beta = \dfrac{1}{80 + 460} = \dfrac{1}{540}$.

From equation (3)

$$Gr_D = \frac{(32.2)(3600)^2(900 - 80)(0.0464)^3(0.0418)^2}{540 \times (0.0672)^2}$$

$$= 2.45 \times 10^7$$

$$Gr_D Pr = 2.45 \times 10^7 \times 0.679$$

$$= 1.66 \times 10^7$$

For $10^4 < (Gr_D Pr) < 10^9$

$$C = 0.525, \ m = 1/4$$

From equation (2)

$$Nu_D = 0.525\ (1.66 \times 10^7)^{1/4}$$

$$= 33.51$$

Thus, $\qquad h = 33.51 \times \dfrac{0.0244}{0.464}$

$$= 1.762\ Btu/hr\text{-}ft^2\text{-}^{\circ}F.$$

From equation (1)

Heat loss per foot length is given by

$$\frac{q}{L} = \pi \times 0.464 \times 1.762\ (900 - 80)$$

$$= 2106.14\ Btu/hr\text{-}ft.$$

Wet steam at 10 psig moves through a pipe 0.5 in. in O.D. Depending on weather conditions the outside of the pipe is in contact with either air or water. Determine the rate of heat loss from the steam to the air and the water, assuming that both are at 40°F.

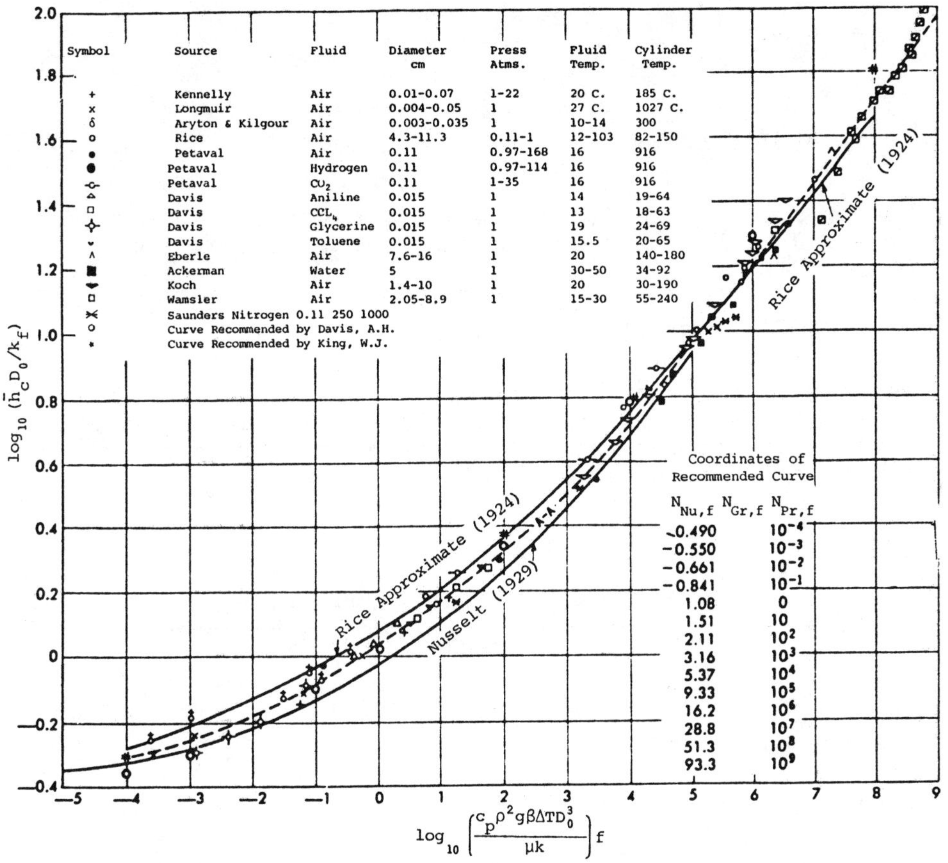

Correlation of data for free-convection heat transfer from horizontal cylinders in gases and liquids.

Fig. 1

Solution: Using the physical properties of air and water, the products of the Grashof and Prandtl numbers are obtained. Using these values in figure (1) allows the Nusselt numbers, Nu, to be determined. The Nusselt numbers permit calculation of the heat transfer coefficients, h_c. Equation (1) then allows the rate of heat loss to be calculated.

Using steam tables, it is determined that the temperature of steam at 10 psig is 238.5°F. The mean film temperature is therefore

$$\frac{40 + 238.5}{2} = 139.25^\circ\text{F}.$$

The properties of air and water at the mean film temperature are:

	Air	Water
C_p = heat capacity Btu/lb-^oF	0.2407	0.9981
ρ = density lb/ft^3	0.0661	61.38
μ = viscosity lb/ft-hr	0.0494	1.139
k = thermal conductivity Btu/ft-hr-^oF	0.0166	0.3779

The product of the Grashof number (based on the outside diameter, D_o of the pipe) and the Prandtl number is:

$$GrPr = \frac{(C_p)(\rho^2)(g)(\beta)(\Delta T)(D_o{}^3)}{(\mu)(k)}$$

where g is the acceleration due to gravity (32.2 ft/sec^2), β is the inverse of the mean film temperature, and ΔT is the difference between the wall temperature (238.5^oF) and the air or water temperature (40^oF).

For air:

$$GrPr = \frac{(0.2407)(0.0661)^2(32.2)(3600)^2\left(\frac{1}{139.25}\right)(198.5)\left(\frac{0.5}{12}\right)^3}{(0.0494)(0.0166)}$$

$$= 5.5 \times 10^4$$

log (GrPr) = 4.7

From figure (1) Nu = 7.76

For water:

$$GrPr = \frac{(0.9981)(61.38)^2(32.2)(3600)^2\left(\frac{1}{139.25}\right)(198.5)\left(\frac{0.5}{12}\right)^3}{(1.139)(0.3779)}$$

$$= 3.8 \times 10^8$$

log (GrPr) = 8.6

From figure (1) Nu = 70.8

The heat transfer coefficients are:

$$h_c = Nu\,\frac{k}{D}$$

For air:

$$h_c = 7.76 \frac{(0.0166)}{(0.5/12)} = 3.09 \text{ Btu/hr-ft}^2\text{-}^{\circ}\text{F}$$

For water:

$$h_c = 70.8 \frac{(0.3779)}{(0.5112)} = 642 \text{ Btu/hr-ft}^2\text{-}^{\circ}\text{F}$$

The heat loss due to convection is given by equation (1)

$$q_c = h_c A(\Delta T) \tag{1}$$

where A is the area available for heat transfer.

For air:

$$q_c = (3.09)\pi\left(\frac{0.5}{12}\right)(1)(198.5) = 80.3 \frac{\text{Btu}}{\text{hr-ft}}$$

For water:

$$q_c = (642)\pi\left(\frac{0.5}{12}\right)(1)(198.5) = 16{,}681 \frac{\text{Btu}}{\text{hr-ft}}$$

The heat lost due to radiation is small enough to be neglected in the case of water. However for air, it must be determined. The heat loss due to radiation is given by:

$$q_r = GA\varepsilon(T_2^4 - T_1^4)$$

where G = the Stefan-Boltzmann constant

$$= 0.1714 \times 10^{-8} \frac{\text{Btu}}{\text{hr-ft}^2\text{-}^{\circ}\text{R}^4},$$

and ε is the emissivity of the pipe (assume 0.9).

$$q_r = (0.1714 \times 10^{-8})(0.9)\pi\left(\frac{0.5}{12}\right)(1)\left[(698.5)^4 - (500)^4\right]$$

$$= 35.4 \text{ Btu/hr-ft}$$

Total heat loss to air = 80.3 + 35.4 = 115.7 Btu/hr-ft

Total heat loss to water = 16,681 Btu/hr-ft

FLOW PAST VERTICAL/HORIZONTAL PLATES

• PROBLEM 11-4

A vertical wall 2.0 ft. (0.610 m) high has a surface temperature of 500°F (533.3 K). It is in contact with air at 120°F (322.2 K). Determine the heat transfer/ft width of wall. Neglect heat transfer due to radiation. Work the problem in English and SI units.

Solution: The Grashof number is the ratio of the buoyancy forces to the viscous forces in free convection, and is analogous to the Reynolds number in forced convection.

The film temperature is:

$$T_f = \frac{T_w + T_b}{2} = \frac{500 + 120}{2} = 310^\circ F$$

$$= 427.8 \text{ K}$$

Air at 310°F has the following properties:

$$k = 0.0205 \text{ Btu/hr}\cdot\text{ft}\cdot{}^\circ\text{F}, \left(0.0356 \text{ W/m}\cdot\text{K}\right)$$

$$\rho = 0.0516 \text{ lb}_m/\text{ft}^3, \left(0.8274 \text{ kg/m}^3\right)$$

$$\mu = 0.0552 \text{ lb}_m/\text{ft}\cdot\text{hr}, \left(2.28 \times 10^{-5} \text{ Pa}\cdot\text{s}\right)$$

$$\beta = \frac{1}{(460 + 310)} = 1.30 \times 10^{-3}\,{}^\circ\text{R}^{-1}, \quad \beta = \frac{1}{427.8}$$

$$= 2.34 \times 10^{-3} \text{ K}^{-1}$$

$$\Delta T = T_w - T_b = 500 - 120 = 380^\circ F, \quad \Delta T = 211.1 \text{ K}$$

$$C_p = 0.2431 \text{ Btu/lb}_m\cdot{}^\circ\text{R}$$

$$N_{Pr} = \frac{C_p \mu}{k} = 0.655$$

The formula for the Grashof number is:

$$N_{Gr} = \frac{L^3 \rho^2 g \beta \Delta T}{\mu^2}$$

In English units

$$N_{Gr} = \frac{(2.0)^3 (0.0516)^2 (32.174)(3600)^2 (1.30 \times 10^{-3})(380)}{(0.0552)^2}$$

$$= 1.45 \times 10^9$$

In S.I. units

$$N_{Gr} = \frac{(0.610)^3(0.8274)^2(9.806)(2.34 \times 10^{-3})(211.1)}{(2.28 \times 10^{-5})^2}$$

$$= 1.45 \times 10^9$$

$$N_{Gr}N_{Pr} = (1.45 \times 10^9)(0.655) = 9.498 \times 10^8$$

From the table below:

Physical Geometry	$(N_{Gr}N_{Pr})$	a	m
Vertical planes and cylinders (verical height L<1 m (3ft))			
	$<10^4$	1.36	1/5
	10^4-10^9	0.59	1/4
	$>10^9$	0.13	1/3
Horizontal cylinders (diameter D used for L and D<0.20 m (0.66 ft))			
	$<10^{-5}$	0.49	0
	10^{-5}-10^{-3}	0.71	1/25
	10^{-3}-1	1.09	1/10
	1-10^4	1.09	1/5
	10^4-10^9	0.53	1/4
	$>10^9$	0.13	1/3
Horizontal plates			
Upper surface of heated	10^5-2×10^7	0.54	1/4
plates of lower surface of cooled plates	2×10^7-3×10^{10}	0.14	1/3
Lower surface of heated plates of upper surface of cooled plates	10^5- 10^{11}	0.58	1/5

the constants a and m can be obtained for use in the equation:

$$N_{Nu} = \frac{hL}{k} = a\left(\frac{L^3\rho^2 g\beta\Delta T}{\mu^2}\right)\frac{C_p\mu}{k}^m = a(N_{Gr}N_{Pr})^m$$

$$a = 0.59 \qquad m = 1/4$$

Solving for h and substituting:

$$h = \frac{k}{L}\, a(N_{Gr}N_{Pr})^m = \left(\frac{0.0205}{2.0}\right)(0.59)(9.498 \times 10^8)^{1/4}$$

$$h = 1.06 \text{ Btu/hr}\cdot\text{ft}^2$$

$$h = \left(\frac{0.0356}{0.610}\right)(0.59)(9.498 \times 10^8)^{1/4} = 6.04 \text{ W/m}^2\cdot\text{K}$$

For a 1 ft. width of wall

$$\text{Area} = (1.0)(1.0) = (1.0) \text{ ft}^2$$

or $(0.305)(0.305) = 0.093 \text{ m}^2$

$$q = hA(T_w - T_b) = (1.06)(1.0)(500 - 120) = 403 \frac{\text{Btu}}{\text{hr}}$$

$$q = 6.04(0.093)(211.1) = 119 \text{ W}$$

• PROBLEM 11-5

Determine the initial rate of heat transfer from a vertically hung 2-ft high flat copper plate to the air at 70°F, 14.7 psia. The copper plate was taken out of an annealing furnace at a temperature of 220 $^{\circ}$F.

Solution: In this system, the heat transfer occurs by natural convection.

The heat transfer rate is given by

$$\frac{q}{A} = h(T_0 - T_\infty) \tag{1}$$

We have to determine h, before determining the heat transfer rate.

The Nusselt number is given by

$$\frac{Nu_D}{\sqrt[4]{\frac{Gr_D}{4}}} = \frac{0.902(Pr)^{1/2}}{(0.861 + Pr)^{1/4}} \tag{2}$$

The Grashof number is given by

$$Gr_D = \frac{g\beta(T_0 - T_\infty)d^3\rho^2}{\mu^2} \tag{3}$$

From air tables, for air

$\mu = 0.048 \text{ lb}_m/\text{hr.ft.}$ $\qquad k = 0.017 \text{ Btu/hr.ft.}^{\circ}\text{F}$

$C_p = 0.241 \text{ Btu/lb.}^{\circ}\text{F}$ $\qquad \rho = \frac{p}{RT} = 0.075 \text{ lb/ft}^3$

The mean film temperature $= (220 + 70)/2 = 145^{\circ}\text{F} = 605^{\circ}\text{R}$.

$$\beta = \frac{1}{T_R} = \frac{1}{605} = 0.00165 \ 1/^{\circ}\text{R}$$

Thus,

$$Gr_D = \frac{(32.2)(3600)^2(0.00165)(220 - 70)(2)^3(0.075)^2}{(0.048)^2}$$

$$= 2.02 \times 10^9$$

$$Pr = \frac{C_p \mu}{k} = \frac{0.241 \times 0.048}{0.017}$$

$$= 0.680.$$

Hence,

$$Nu_D = \frac{0.902(0.680)^{1/2}}{(0.861 + 0.680)^{1/4}} \times \sqrt[4]{\frac{2.02 \times 10^9}{4}}$$

$$= 100.08$$

Thus,

$$h = 100.08 \times \frac{0.017}{2}$$

$$= 0.85 \text{ Btu/hr.ft}^2.{}^\circ F$$

Thus, the heat transfer rate is given by

$$\frac{q}{A} = 0.85\ (220 - 70)$$

$$= 127.5 \text{ Btu/hr-ft}^2.$$

• PROBLEM 11-6

> Compute the heat gained by the room at 80°F from a vertical plate 3 ft. wide and 4 ft. high maintained at 115 °F.

Solution: In this system the heat transfer occurs by natural convection. We have to determine the type of flow, in order to use the appropriate empirical correlation to determine the convective heat transfer coefficient.

The heat gain by the room is given by

$$q = hA(T_1 - T_2) \tag{1}$$

The Nusselt number is given by

$$Nu_D = C(Gr_D Pr)^m \tag{2}$$

where constants C and m depend on the type of flow.

The Grashof number is given by

$$Gr_D = \frac{g\beta(T_1 - T_2)d^3\rho^2}{\mu^2} \tag{3}$$

The mean film temperature $T_f = (115 + 80)/2 = 97.5^{\circ}F$. From air tables, physical properties of air at $97.5^{\circ}F$ are:

$C_p = 0.24\ Btu/lb_m \cdot {}^{\circ}F$ $\qquad$ $k = 0.0155\ Btu/hr\text{-}ft^2\text{-}{}^{\circ}F$

$\mu = 0.0457\ lb_m/ft\text{-}hr$ $\qquad$ $\rho = 0.0714\ lb_m/ft^3$

$\beta = 1.80 \times 10^{-3}\ {}^{\circ}F^{-1}$ $\qquad$ $Pr = 0.705$

Substituting the known values in equation (3)

$$Gr_D = \frac{(32.2)(3600)^2(1.80 \times 10^{-3})(115 - 80)(4)^3(0.0714)^2}{(0.0457)^2}$$

$$= 4.11 \times 10^9$$

Then,

$$Gr_D Pr = 4.11 \times 10^9 \times 0.705$$

$$= 2.9 \times 10^9.$$

Since the flow is turbulent and

for $\quad 10^9 < (Gr_D Pr) < 10^{12}$,

$C = 0.129$ $\qquad$ $m = 1/3$.

equation (2) becomes

$$Nu_D = 0.129(2.9 \times 10^9)^{1/3}$$

$$= 183.96$$

Then, convective heat transfer coefficient is given by

$$h = 183.96 \times \frac{0.0155}{4}$$

$$= 0.71\ Btu/hr\text{-}ft^2\text{-}{}^{\circ}F.$$

Then, the heat gain is given by

$$q = 0.71 \times (4 \times 3 \times 2)(115 - 80)$$

$$= 596.4\ Btu/hr.$$

• PROBLEM 11-7

Find the surface heat transfer coefficient of a 2 ft. high flat plate at $220^{\circ}F$, when immersed in water at $70^{\circ}F$.

Solution: The equation below gives the Nusselt number

$$Nu_D = C(Gr_D Pr)^m \qquad (1)$$

The Grashof number is given by

$$Gr_D = \frac{g\beta(T_1 - T_2)d^3\rho^2}{\mu^2} \qquad (2)$$

The mean film temperature = (220 + 70)/2 = 145°F.

From the liquid water tables, for water at 145°F we have

$\rho = 61.38\ lb_m/ft^3$ $\qquad \mu = 1.105\ lb_m/ft\text{-}hr$

$k = 0.381\ Btu/hr\text{-}ft\text{-}^\circ F$ $\qquad Pr = 2.90$

At a water temperature of 70°F, from standard tables,

$$\beta = 1.05 \times 10^{-4}\ 1/^\circ R$$

Thus, from equation (2)

$$Gr_D = \frac{(32.2)(3600)^2(1.05 \times 10^{-4})(220 - 70)(2)^3(61.38)^2}{(1.105)^2}$$

$$= 1.62 \times 10^{11}$$

$$Gr_D Pr = 1.62 \times 10^{11} \times 2.90$$

$$= 4.70 \times 10^{11}$$

For $\quad 10^9 < (Gr_D Pr) < 10^{12}$

$C = 0.129, \qquad m = 1/3$

Thus, from equation (1)

$$Nu_D = 0.129(4.70 \times 10^{11})^{1/3}$$

$$= 1003.$$

Thus, the surface heat transfer coefficient is given by

$$h = 1003 \times \frac{0.381}{2}$$

$$= 191.1\ Btu/hr\text{-}ft^2\text{-}^\circ F.$$

• PROBLEM 11-8

Determine the maximum rate of heat loss from an electrically heated vertical flat plate, 7 in. high and 3 in. wide, to ambient air at 60°F. At the center of the plate, the maximum allowable surface temperature is

280°F. Consider the unit-surface conductance for radiation as 2 Btu/hr-ft²-°F at the maximum possible surface temperature.

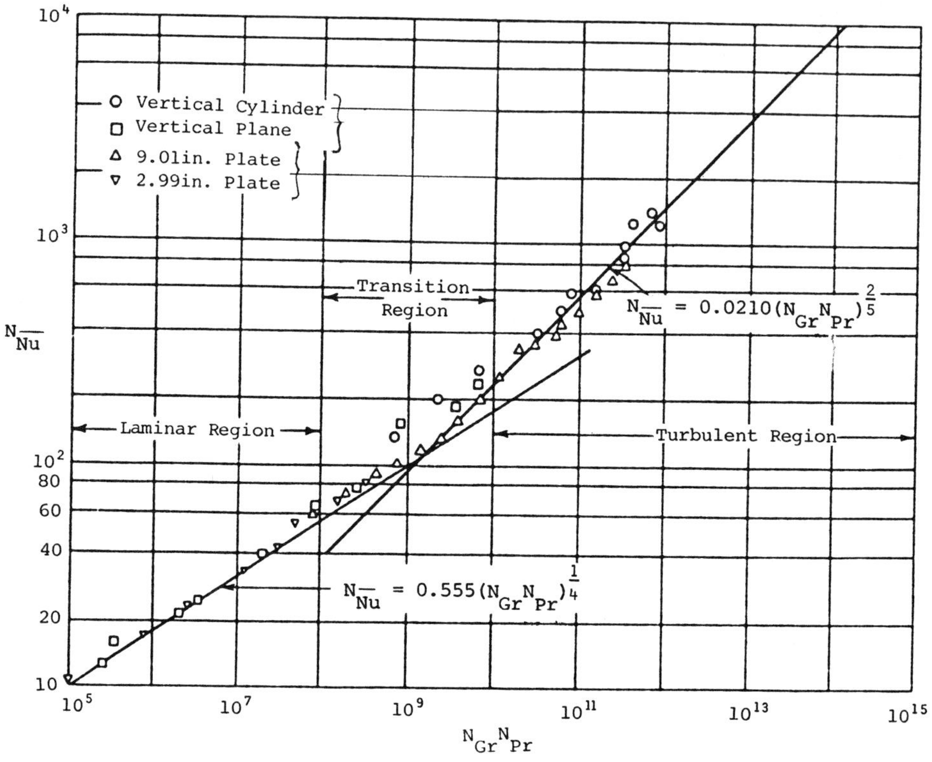

Correlation of data for free-convection heat transfer from vertical plates and cylinders.

Solution: In this system, heat transfer occurs both by natural convection and radiation. The maximum rate of heat loss is given by

$$q = A(h_c + h_r)(T_s - T_\infty) \qquad (1)$$

where A = heat transfer surface area

h_c = convective heat transfer coefficient

h_r = radiation heat transfer coefficient

T_s = surface temperature

T_∞ = ambient temperature

The Grashof number is given by

$$Gr_D = \frac{g\beta\rho^2 d^3(T_s - T_\infty)}{\mu^2}$$

The film temperature = (280 + 60)/2 = 170°F.

From air tables, for air at 170°F

$$\frac{g\beta\rho^2}{\mu^2} = 1.068 \times 10^6 \ 1/^{o}\text{R-ft}^3 \qquad Pr = 0.699$$

$$k = 0.0173$$

Then, the Grashof number is given by

$$Gr_D = 1.068 \times 10^6 \ d^3(T_s - T_\infty)$$

$$= 1.068 \times 10^6 \times \left(\frac{7}{12}\right)^3 \times (280 - 60)$$

$$= 4.66 \times 10^7$$

Hence, flow is laminar.

Then,

$$Gr_D Pr = 4.66 \times 10^7 \times 0.699$$

$$= 3.26 \times 10^7$$

From the figure above, for $Gr_D Pr = 3.26 \times 10^7$ and laminar region, the Nusselt number is 40. Therefore the convective heat transfer coefficient is given by

$$h_c = 40 \times \frac{0.0173}{(7/12)}$$

$$= 1.19 \text{ Btu/hr-ft}^2\text{-}^{o}\text{F}.$$

Then, the maximum rate of heat loss is given by

$$q = \frac{2 \times 7 \times 3}{144} \times (1.19 + 2) \times (280 - 60)$$

$$= 204.7 \text{ Btu/hr}.$$

Thus, almost two-thirds of the total loss is through radiation.

• PROBLEM 11-9

A plate 1 ft. high and 2 ft. wide is welded inside a reservoir to heat the water at 70° F. Determine the required surface temperature of the plate, such that the heat transfer rate from the plate to water is 6000 Btu/hr.

Solution: The heat transfer occurs by natural convection. To determine the surface temperature one needs to know the heat transfer coefficient, which depends on film temperature. But film temperature is the arithmetic mean of surface temperature and water temperature. By Newton's law of cooling

$$q = hA(T_s - T_w)$$

where
- h - heat transfer coefficient
- A - surface area
- T_s - surface temperature
- T_w - water temperature

$$6000 = h(1 \times 2)(T_s - 70)$$

$$3000 = h(T_s - 70) \qquad (1)$$

Assume the conditions of the problem to justify the use of the equation below.

For $10^9 < Ra < 10^{12}$

$$\frac{hL}{k} = Nu_D = 0.13(Ra)^{1/3} \qquad (2)$$

Then, $$h = \left(\frac{k}{L}\right)(0.13\ Ra^{1/3})$$

The Rayleigh number is given by

$$Ra = aL^3(T_s - T_w)$$

where L - characteristic length.

Then,

$$h = 0.13(k/L)(aL^3)^{1/3}(T_s - T_w)^{1/3}$$

$$= 0.13\ ka^{1/3}(T_s - 70)^{1/3}$$

Substituting h in eq. (1),

$$3000 = 0.13\ ka^{1/3}(T_s - 70)^{4/3}$$

$$T_s - 70 = \left[\frac{23077}{ka^{1/3}}\right]^{3/4} \qquad (3)$$

Assume T_s to calculate the film temperature, then obtain properties a and k from water tables; then find T_s from eq. (3) and compare with assumed value. If they are close, the computed value of T_s is the required surface temperature or else take T_s found from eq. (3) as the new assumed value and repeat the procedure.

Assume $T_s = 96^\circ F$

then $T_f = (96 + 70)/2 = 83^\circ F.$

From water tables, for water at $83^\circ F$

$$a = 57.1 \times 10^6 \qquad k = 0.354$$

$$a^{1/3} = (57.1 \times 10^6)^{1/3} = 385.1$$

$$T_s - 70 = \left(\frac{23077}{0.354(385.1)} \right)^{3/4}$$

$$T_s = 117^\circ F$$

Repeating, with $T_s = 117^\circ F$, $T_f = 93.5^\circ F$, $a = 87.9 \times 10^6$, $k = 0.360$ and $a^{1/3} = 444.63$.

$$T_s - 70 = \left(\frac{23077}{0.360(444.63)} \right)^{3/4}$$

$$T_s = 112^\circ F$$

With $T_s = 112^\circ F$, $T_f = 91^\circ F$, $a = 80.6 \times 10^6$, $k = 0.358$ and $a^{1/3} = 432$.

$$T_s - 70 = \left(\frac{23077}{0.358(432)} \right)^{3/4}$$

$$T_s = 112.7^\circ F$$

They are close, so then $112.7^\circ F$ can be considered as the required surface temperature, if it justifies the eq. (2) used.

The Rayleigh number at the film temperature is

$$Ra = aL^3(T_s - T_w) = 80.6 \times 10^6 \times (1)^3(112.7 - 70)$$

$$= 3.44 \times 10^9$$

$Ra > 10^9$ justifies the use of eq. (2). Hence the required surface temperature of the plate is $112.7^\circ F$.

A hot plate at temperature T_0 is suspended in a large body of fluid at temperature T_1. The buoyancy force in the neighborhood of the plate causes the fluid to rise. Develop the dependence of the heat loss on the system variables using the equations of change. Consider the physical properties of fluid as constant. Use the free convection form of the equation of motion.

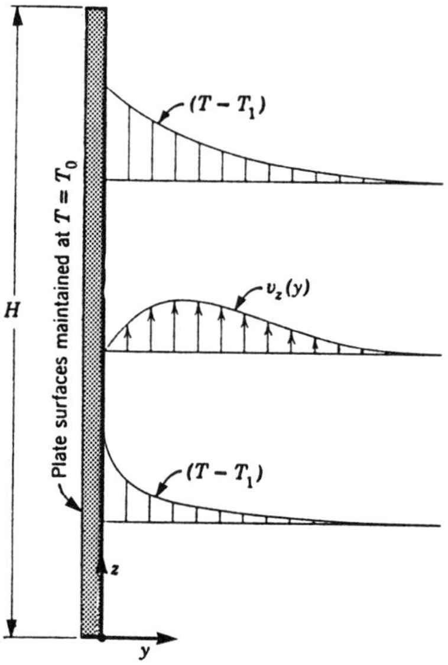

Temperature and velocity profiles in the neighborhood of a heated vertical plate.

Solution: Assume height = H.

x = ∞ implies that velocity components in y and z are functions of only y and z.

Also, assume v_y is very small, in which case the fluid moves almost dierectly upward.

Then, the y-component of the equation of motion can be excluded.

The equations of change are given as:

$$\frac{\partial v_y}{\partial y} + \frac{\partial v_z}{\partial z} = 0 \tag{1}$$

$$\rho\left(v_y \frac{\partial}{\partial y} + v_z \frac{\partial}{\partial z}\right)v_z = \mu\left(\frac{\partial^2 v_z}{\partial y^2} + \frac{\partial^2 v_z}{\partial z^2}\right) + \rho g \beta (T - T_1) \tag{2}$$

$$\rho C_p\left(v_y \frac{\partial}{\partial y} + v_z \frac{\partial}{\partial z}\right)(T - T_1) = k\left(\frac{\partial^2}{\partial y^2} + \frac{\partial^2}{\partial z^2}\right)(T - T_1) \tag{3}$$

The boundary conditions are

(a) at $y = 0$ $v_y = v_z = 0$ $T = T_0$

(b) at $y = \infty$ $v_z = 0$ $T = T_1$

(c) at $y = -\infty$ $v_y = v_z = 0$ $T = T_1$

Equations (2) and (3) are coupled with velocity distribution and temperature rise. It is difficult to find the analytic solutions of such coupled nonlinear differential equations, so they are solved using dimensional analysis.

The following dimensionless variables are defined for convenience:

$$\text{dimensionless temperature} = \theta = (T - T_1)/(T_0 - T_1) \tag{4}$$

$$\text{dimensionless vertical distance} = \zeta = z/H \tag{5}$$

$$\text{dimensionless horizontal distance} = \eta = \left(\frac{B}{\mu\alpha H}\right)^{1/4} y \tag{6}$$

$$\text{dimensionless vertical velocity} = \phi_z = \left(\frac{\mu}{B\alpha H}\right)^{1/2} v_z \tag{7}$$

$$\text{dimensionless horizontal velocity} = \phi_y = \left(\frac{\mu H}{\alpha^3 B}\right)^{1/4} v_y \tag{8}$$

where $\alpha = k/\rho C_p$ and $B = \rho g \beta (T_0 - T_1)$.

The equations of change in terms of the above dimensionless variables can be written as follows:

$$\frac{\partial \phi_y}{\partial \eta} + \frac{\partial \phi_z}{\partial \zeta} = 0 \tag{9}$$

$$\frac{1}{Pr}\left(\phi_y \frac{\partial}{\partial \eta} + \phi_z \frac{\partial}{\partial \zeta}\right)\phi_z = \frac{\partial^2 \phi_z}{\partial \eta^2} + \theta \tag{10}$$

$$\phi_y \frac{\partial \theta}{\partial \eta} + \phi_z \frac{\partial \theta}{\partial \zeta} = \frac{\partial^2 \theta}{\partial \eta^2} \tag{11}$$

As the momentum and energy transport by molecular process in the z-direction is small compared to the convective terms, the terms $\partial^2 v_z/\partial z^2$ in eq. (2) and $\partial^2/\partial z^2$ in eq. (3) are omitted in writing the dimensionless form of the equations of change.

The boundary conditions will change as follows:

(a) at $\eta = 0$ $\phi_y = \phi_z = 0$ $\theta = 1$

(b) at $\eta = \infty$ $\phi_y = \phi_z = 0$ $\theta = 0$

(c) at $\eta = -\infty$ $\phi_y = \phi_z = 0$ $\theta = 0$

It is clear from equations (9) to (11) and boundary conditions that the dimensionless velocity components ϕ_y and ϕ_z and the dimensionless temperature θ will depend on η, ζ, and the Prandtl number Pr. The dependence on the Prandtl number is less because of very slow flow in free convection.

The average heat flux is given by

$$q_{avg} = + \frac{k}{H} \int_0^H - \left.\frac{\partial T}{\partial y}\right|_{y=0} dz \qquad (12)$$

This can be written in terms of dimensionless variables as

$$q_{avg} = + k(T_0 - T_1)\left(\frac{B}{\mu\alpha H}\right)^{1/4} \int_0^1 - \left.\frac{\partial\theta}{\partial\eta}\right|_{\eta=0} d\zeta$$

$$= + k(T_0 - T_1)\left(\frac{B}{\mu\alpha H}\right)^{1/4} \cdot C$$

$$= C \cdot \frac{k}{H}(T_0 - T_1)(GrPr)^{1/4} \qquad (13)$$

$\left.\partial\theta/\partial\eta\right|_{\eta=0}$ depends only on ζ and Pr, because θ is a function of η, ζ, and Pr. The definite integral over ζ will then be a dimensionless function of Pr. With the above remarks, it can be concluded that this function (C) is nearly a constant. This is a weak function of the Prandtl number.

• **PROBLEM 11-11**

The emissivity of inner and outer surfaces of vertical air space in a 6 in. thick and 9 ft. high wall is 0.90. The inner and outer wall surfaces are at 95^0F and 125^0F respectively. Determine the total heat transfer rate across the air space.

Solution: The heat transfer across the air space occurs both by natural convection and radiation.

The total heat transfer rate per unit area is given by

$$q = q_c + q_r \tag{1}$$

By Newton's law of cooling, the convective heat transfer rate across the air space per square foot of surface is given by

$$q_c = h(T_1 - T_2) \tag{2}$$

Air space height L = 9 ft. and thickness b = $\frac{6}{12}$ ft.

Then, L/b = 9/(6/12)

Since L/b > 3, the empirical relation to be used relating the Nusselt and Grashof numbers, depends on the Grashof number.

The mean film temperature $T_f = \frac{1}{2}(125 + 95) = 110^{\circ}F$.

From air tables for air at $110^{\circ}F$

$a = 1.65 \times 10^6\ 1/^{\circ}R\text{-ft}^3$ $k = 0.0159$ Btu/hr-ft-$^{\circ}F$ $Pr = 0.704$

The Rayleigh number is given by,

$$Ra = Gr_L Pr = aL^3(T_1 - T_2)$$

$$\therefore \qquad Gr_L = \frac{aL^3(T_1 - T_2)}{Pr}$$

$$= \frac{1.65 \times 10^6 \times (6/12)^3(125 - 95)}{0.704}$$

$$= 8.79 \times 10^6$$

For $2 \times 10^5 < Gr_L < 10^7$

$$Nu = \frac{0.065(Gr_L)^{1/3}}{(L/b)^{1/9}}$$

$$= \frac{0.065(8.79 \times 10^6)^{1/3}}{(18)^{1/9}}$$

$$= 9.73$$

Hence,

$$h = 9.73 \times \frac{0.0159}{(6/12)}$$

$$= 0.309 \text{ Btu/hr-ft}^2\text{-}^{\circ}F$$

From eq. (2)

$$q_c = 0.309 \times (125 - 95)$$

$$= 9.27 \text{ Btu/hr-ft}^2$$

The radiation heat transfer rate across the air space per square foot of surface is given by

$$q_r = \frac{\sigma(T_1^4 - T_2^4)}{1/\varepsilon_1 + (1/\varepsilon_2 - 1)} \tag{3}$$

where σ = Stefan Boltzman constant

$= 0.1714 \times 10^{-8}$ Btu/hr-ft^2-$^\circ$R^4

T_1 = absolute temperature of outer surface

$= 125 + 460 = 585^\circ$R

T_2 = absolute temperature of inner surface

$= 95 + 460 = 555^\circ$R

ε_1 = emissivity of outer surface

$= 0.90$

ε_2 = emissivity of inner surface

$= 0.90$

Then,

$$q_r = \frac{0.1714 \times 10^{-8}\left[(585)^4 - (555)^4\right]}{\frac{1}{0.90} + \left(\frac{1}{0.90} - 1\right)}$$

$= 31.19$ Btu/hr-ft^2

Then total heat transfer rate per unit area is given by

$$q = 9.27 + 31.19$$

$= 40.46$ Btu/hr-ft^2

• PROBLEM 11-12

A square plate 5 ft. x 5 ft. is heated to 200°F and exposed to ambient air at 70°F. Determine the total heat loss from the plate if, (a) the plate is in a vertical position, and (b) the plate is in a horizontal position. Evaluate the percentage change in heat loss with the change in position of the plate.

Solution: In this system the heat is lost from both the surfaces of plate by natural convection.

The mean film temperature $T_f = (200 + 70)/2 = 135^\circ$F.

From air tables, for air at 135°F

$\rho = 0.0699\ lb_m/ft^3$ $\qquad C_p = 0.241\ Btu/lb_m{}^\circ F$

$\mu = 0.0481\ lb_m/ft\text{-}hr$ $\qquad k = 0.0165\ Btu/hr\text{-}ft\text{-}^\circ F$

$Pr = 0.703$ $\qquad \beta = 1.685 \times 10^{-3}\ 1/^\circ R$

The Grashof number is given by

$$Gr = \frac{g\beta(T_1 - T_2)L^3\rho^2}{\mu^2}$$

$$= \frac{32.2 \times (3600)^2 \times 1.685 \times 10^{-3} \times (200 - 70) \times (5)^3 \times (0.0699)^2}{(0.0481)^2}$$

$$= 2.41 \times 10^{10}$$

(a) If the plate is in a vertical postion

$$GrPr = 2.41 \times 10^{10} \times 0.703$$

$$= 1.69 \times 10^{10}$$

Then, for $\quad 10^9 < GrPr < 10^{12}$

$$Nu = 0.13 \times (GrPr)^{1/3}$$

$$= 0.13 \times (1.69 \times 10^{10})^{1/3} = 333.61$$

Therefore

$$h = 333.61 \times \frac{0.0165}{5}$$

$$= 1.10\ Btu/hr\text{-}ft^2\text{-}^\circ F$$

The heat loss is given by

$$q = 2hA(T_1 - T_2)$$

$$= 2 \times 1.1 \times (5 \times 5) \times (200 - 70)$$

$$= 7150\ Btu/hr$$

(b) The plate is kept in a horizontal plane.

For the upper surface, if $10^9 < GrPr < 10^{12}$

$$Nu = 0.71 \times (GrPr)^{1/4}$$

$$Nu = 0.71 \times (1.69 \times 10^{10})^{1/4}$$

$$= 256.0$$

Therefore,

$$h_{upper} = 256 \times \frac{0.0165}{5}$$

$$= 0.845 \text{ Btu/hr-ft}^2\text{-}^0\text{F}$$

For the lower surface, if $10^9 < GrPr < 10^{12}$

$$Nu = 0.35 \times (GrPr)^{1/4}$$

$$= 0.35 \times (1.69 \times 10^{10})^{1/4}$$

$$= 126.2$$

Therefore,

$$h_{lower} = 126.2 \times \frac{0.0165}{5}$$

$$= 0.416 \quad \text{Btu/hr-ft}^2\text{-}^0\text{F}$$

Then, the total heat loss is given by

$$q = (h_{upper} + h_{lower})A(T_1 - T_2)$$

$$= (0.845 + 0.416) \times (5 \times 5) \times (200 - 70)$$

$$= 4098.25 \text{ Btu/hr}$$

The percentage of extra heat lost, if the plate is in a vertical plane instead of a horizontal plane is given by

$$\% \text{ Error} = \frac{7150 - 4098.25}{4098.25} \times 100$$

$$= 74.5\%$$

FLOW PAST VERTICAL/HORIZONTAL CYLINDERS

• PROBLEM 11-13

A vertical rod, 0.002 in. in diameter and 1 ft. long and at a temperature fo 140^0F, is left in atmospheric air at 80^0F. Calculate the heat transfer rate.

Solution: In the given system the heat transfer occurs by natural convection.

The heat transfer rate is given by

$$q = hA(T_s - T_\infty) \qquad (1)$$

where h - natural convection coefficient

A - surface area

T_s - surface temperature

T_∞ - atmospheric temperature

The Grashof number based on the rod diameter is given by

$$Gr_D = \frac{g\beta\rho^2}{\mu^2} D^3(T_s - T_\infty) \qquad (2)$$

The mean film temperature $T_f = (140 + 80)/2 = 110^\circ F$.

From air tables, for air at $110^\circ F$

$C_p = 0.24\ Btu/lb_m{}^\circ F$ $\qquad k = 0.0159\ Btu/hr\text{-}ft\text{-}^\circ F$

$Pr = 0.705$ $\qquad \frac{g\beta\rho^2}{\mu^2} = 1.65 \times 10^6\ 1/^\circ R\text{-}ft^3$

Then, from eq. (2)

$$Gr_D = 1.65 \times 10^6 \times \left(\frac{0.002}{12}\right)^3 \times (140 - 80)$$
$$= 4.58 \times 10^{-4}$$

Then,

$$Gr_D Pr \frac{D}{L} = 4.58 \times 10^{-4} \times 0.705 \times \frac{0.002}{12 \times 1}$$
$$= 5.38 \times 10^{-8}$$

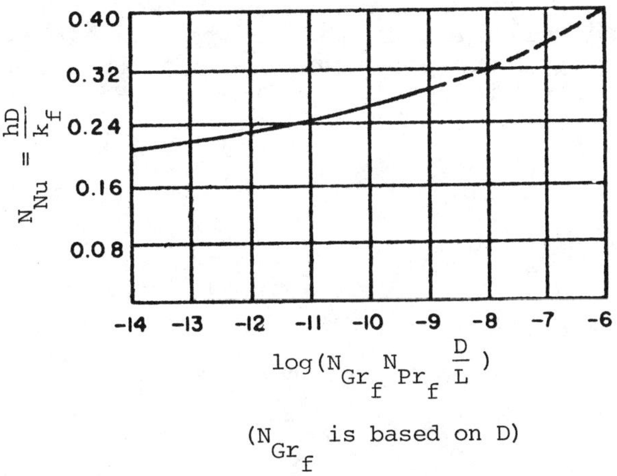

Free-convective heat transfer from small vertical cylinders.

From the figure, at $\log(5.38 \times 10^{-8}) = -7.269$

$$Nu_D = 0.34$$

Then,

$$h = \frac{0.34 \times 0.0159}{(0.002/12)}$$

$$= 32.44 \text{ Btu/hr-ft}^2\text{-}^\circ\text{F}$$

Then, from eq. (1)

$$q = 32.44 \times \left(\frac{0.002 \times \pi \times 1}{12}\right) \times (140 - 80)$$

$$= 1.02 \text{ Btu/hr.}$$

The heat transfer rate = 1.02 Btu/hr.

• PROBLEM 11-14

It is required to reduce the net radiant loss of the horizontal, cylindrical electric heater 2 in. in diameter and 5 ft. long to zero, by keeping it in an oven whose walls are maintained at the surface temperature of the heater. The air in the oven is at 80°F and the heater dissipates energy at the rate of 150 watts. Determine the temperature at which the walls of the oven are to be maintained.

Solution: The net radiant loss from the heater is zero when the oven walls, seen by the heater, are at the same temperature as the heater surface. Since the net radiant loss is zero, the temperature of the heater surface is calculated by applying the conservation of the energy equation. Then, the heat loss is only by natural convection. This implies that the rate of dissipation of energy must be equal to the rate of loss through natural convection.

By Newton's cooling law

$$q = hA(T_s - T_a) \qquad (1)$$

where q = energy dissipated

$= 150$ watts $= 511.95$ Btu/hr

$A = (\pi DL)$=surface area

$$= \pi \times \frac{2}{12} \times 5 = 2.618 \text{ ft}^2$$

T_s = surface temperature

T_a = oven air temperature

$= 80°F$

Then, $511.95 = 2.618\ h(T_s - 80)$

The Rayleigh number is given by

$$Ra = aD^3(T_s - T_a) \qquad (2)$$

Assume the unknown Rayleigh number lies in the range 10^3 to 10^9.

Then, for $10^3 < Ra < 10^9$

$$Nu = 0.53(Ra)^{1/4} \qquad (3)$$

Substituting eq. (2) in eq. (3) gives

$$Nu = 0.53\ a^{1/4} \cdot D^{3/4}\ (T_s - T_a)^{1/4}$$

Then,

$$h = \frac{0.53\ k}{D^{1/4}}\ a^{1/4}\ (T_s - T_a)^{1/4}$$

Substituting $D = \frac{2}{12}$ ft. and $T_a = 80^{\circ}F$ gives,

$$h = 0.83\ ka^{1/4}\ (T_s - 80)^{1/4} \qquad (4)$$

Substituting eq. (4) in eq. (1) gives,

$$511.95 = 2.618 \times 0.83 \times ka^{1/4}\ (T_s - 80)^{5/4}$$

$$235.6 = ka^{1/4}\ (T_s - 80)^{5/4}$$

$$T_s - 80 = \left(\frac{235.6}{ka^{1/4}}\right)^{4/5} \qquad (5)$$

Here iteration is involved, as properties k and a, depend on film temperature which is the average of surface and air temperatures. So assuming T_s, calculate the film temperature. Substitute the properties at film temperature in eq. (5) and calculate T_s. If the calculated value is not in close agreement with the assumed value, take the calculated value as the new assumed value and repeat the procedure until the two successive values of T_s are in close agreement.

Hence, assume $T_s = 150^{\circ}F$.

Then, $T_f = 115^{\circ}F$: from air tables, for air at $115^{\circ}F$

$k = 0.0160$ Btu/hr-ft-$^{\circ}F$ $\quad a = 1.6 \times 10^6$, thus $a^{1/4} = 35.6$

From eq. (5)

$$T_s - 80 = \left(\frac{235.6}{0.0160(35.6)}\right)^{4/5}$$

$$T_s = 203.96^{\circ}F \simeq 204^{\circ}F$$

Now $T_s = 204^{\circ}F$, $T_f = 142^{\circ}F$, from air tables for air at $142^{\circ}F$ $k = 0.0167$, $a = 1.31 \times 10^6$.

Thus $a^{1/4} = 33.8$.

$$\text{Then,} \quad T_s - 80 = \left(\frac{235.6}{0.0167(33.8)} \right)^{4/5}$$

$$T_s = 204.86^{\circ}F \simeq 205^{\circ}F$$

The T_s values 204 and 205 are sufficiently close. Now the Rayleigh number should be checked to make sure that the assumption made is valid. Substituting values in eq. (2) gives

$$Ra = 1.31 \times 10^6 \times \left(\frac{2}{12}\right)^3 \times (205 - 80)$$

$$= 7.6 \times 10^5$$

i.e., the use of eq. (3) is justified.

Thus, the walls of the oven are to be maintained at $205^{\circ}F$.

• PROBLEM 11-15

A cylindrical container 3 ft. in diameter and 5 ft. high has oil. A transformer is immersed in the oil. Determine the surface temperature of the container if the loss of energy is 2.0 kW. Assume the bottom of the container to be insulated and that the loss is only by natural convection to the ambient air at $80^{\circ}F$.

TABLE

Geometry	Range of application	C	n	L
Vertical planes and cylinders	$10^4 < N_{Gr_L} N_{Pr} < 10^9$	0.29	1/4	height
	$10^9 < N_{Gr_L} N_{Pr} < 10^{12}$	0.19	1/3	1
Horizontal cylinders	$10^3 < N_{Gr_L} N_{Pr} < 10^9$	0.27	1/4	diameter
	$10^9 < N_{Gr_L} N_{Pr} < 10^{12}$	0.18	1/3	1
Horizontal plates - heated plates facing up or cooled plates facing down	$10^5 < N_{Gr_L} N_{Pr} < 2 \times 10^7$	0.27	1/4	length of side
	$2 \times 10^7 < N_{Gr_L} N_{Pr} < 3 \times 10^{10}$	0.22	1/3	1
Cooled plates facing up or heated plates facing down	$3 \times 10^5 < N_{Gr_L} N_{Pr} < 3 \times 10^{10}$	0.12	1/4	length of side

Solution: As the bottom of the container is insulated, the loss of energy will only be from sides and top.

Therefore the total energy loss is given by

$$q = q_{top} + q_{sides} \qquad (1)$$

By Newton's law of cooling

$$q = hA(T_s - T_a)$$

Then,

$$q_{top} = h_{top} \times \frac{\pi}{4}(3)^2 \times (T_s - 80)$$

$$= 7.07 \times (h_{top}) \times (T_s - 80) \qquad (2)$$

$$q_{sides} = h_{side} \times \pi(3)(5) \times (T_s - 80)$$

$$= 47.12 \times (h_{side}) \times (T_s - 80) \qquad (3)$$

h in natural convection is given by

$$h = C\left(\frac{T_s - T_a}{L}\right)^n$$

Assume a turbulent boundary layer.

Then, from table (1), in vertical planes for $10^9 < GrPr < 10^{12}$

$C = 0.19 \qquad n = 1/3$

Therefore

$$h_{side} = 0.19\left(\frac{T_s - 80}{5}\right)^{1/3} \qquad (4)$$

Again, from table (1), in horizontal cylinders for $10^9 < GrPr < 10^{12}$

$C = 0.18 \qquad n = 1/3$

Therefore

$$h_{top} = 0.18\left(\frac{T_s - 80}{3}\right)^{1/3} \qquad (5)$$

Substituting eq. (5) in eq. (2),

$$q_{top} = 7.07 \times 0.18 \times \left(\frac{T_s - 80}{3}\right)^{1/3} \times (T_s - 80)$$

$$= 0.88 \times (T_s - 80)^{4/3} \qquad (6)$$

Substituting eq. (4) in eq. (3),

$$q_{side} = 47.12 \times 0.19 \times \left(\frac{T_s - 80}{5}\right)^{1/3} (T_s - 80)$$

$$= 5.24 \times (T_s - 80)^{4/3} \qquad (7)$$

Substituting eqs. (6) and (7) in (1) gives

$$q = 0.88 \times (T_s - 80)^{4/3} + 5.24 \times (T_s - 80)^{4/3}$$

But $\quad q = 2.0 \text{ kW} = 2 \times 3413 = 6826 \text{ Btu/hr}$

Then $\quad 6826 = (0.88 + 5.24)(T_s - 80)^{4/3}$

$$T_s = 273^{\circ}F$$

Verification has to be done to check whether the assumption made is indeed true.

The mean film temperature $T_f = (273 + 80)/2 = 176.5^{\circ}F$

For air at $176.5^{\circ}F$ $\qquad a = 1.02 \times 10^6 \ 1/^{\circ}R\text{-ft}^3$

The Rayleigh number is given by

$$Ra = GrPr = aL^3(T_s - T_a)$$

$$= 1.02 \times 10^6 \times (3)^3(273 - 80)$$

$$= 5.31 \times 10^9$$

Hence, the assumption is correct for the top surface.

For the side

$$Ra = GrPr = 1.02 \times 10^6 \times (5)^3 \times (273 - 80)$$

$$= 2.46 \times 10^{10}$$

Hence, the assumption made and the constants and exponents used for evaluating h are correct.

• PROBLEM 11-16

A fluid is flowing upward over a thin flat vertical plate under steady state laminar conditions. The temperature of the plate is higher than the external fluid temperature. In this case, note that both free and forced convection exist. Develop the criteria which can show when free, forced, or mixed convection will prevail over the situation.

Solution: In order to develop a relation to show free and forced convection effects, one has to compare the relations of pure free convection and pure forced convection.

The average Nusselt number of pure free convection of a laminar flow over a flat plate is given by

$$Nu_{free} = 0.59(Gr)^{0.25}(Pr)^{0.25} \tag{1}$$

The average Nusselt number for pure forced convection of a constant property, laminar, steady flow over a flat plate is given by

$$Nu_{forced} = 0.664\ (Re)^{0.5}\ (Pr)^{1/3} \tag{2}$$

Divide eq. (1) by eq. (2)

$$\frac{Nu_{free}}{Nu_{forced}} = \frac{0.889}{Pr^{0.083}} \times \frac{Gr^{0.25}}{Re^{0.5}}$$

In order to find the relative importance of free and forced convection qualitatively, it can be assumed that the factor $0.889/(Pr)^{0.083}$ is equal to unity. This is a valid assumption except for extreme values of Prandtl number.

Therefore

$$\frac{Nu_{free}}{Nu_{forced}} \simeq \frac{Gr^{0.25}}{Re^{0.5}} \tag{3}$$

The free convection effects dominate when the above ratio is greater than unity.

Then,

$$\frac{Gr^{0.25}}{Re^{0.5}} > 1$$

$$\text{or} \qquad \frac{Gr}{Re^2} > 1$$

The forced convection effects dominate when the ratio in eq. (3) is smaller than unity. This gives

$$\frac{Gr^{0.25}}{Re^{0.5}} < 1$$

$$\text{or} \qquad \frac{Gr}{Re^2} < 1$$

If the ratio in eq. (3) is in the order of unity, both free and forced convection effects are important, i.e., the mixed convection occurs if

$$\frac{Gr^{0.25}}{Re^{0.5}} \simeq 1$$

or $$\frac{Gr}{Re^2} \simeq 1$$

• PROBLEM 11-17

> Water at an average temperature of 110°F in a vertical pipe 4 in. in diameter and 18 in. high, is freely convecting. The wall temperature of the pipe is 220°F. Determine the Reynolds number of forced convection, when it just begins to cause mixed convection.

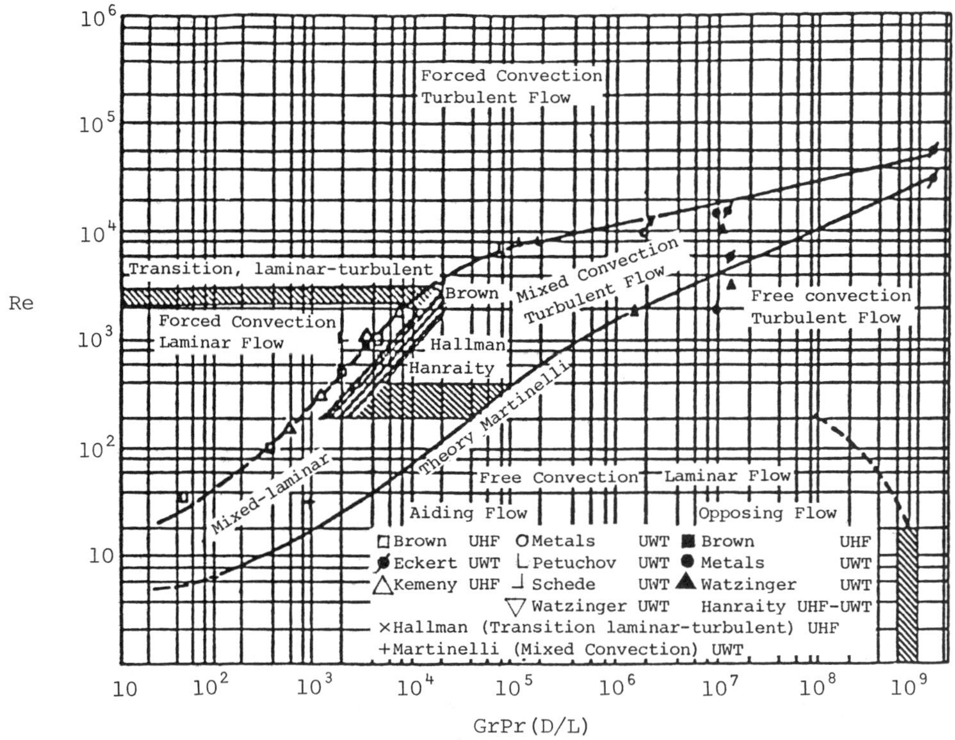

Fig. Regimes of free, forced, and mixed convection for flow through vertical tubes

Solution: The mean film temperature is the arithmetic mean of the wall temperature of the pipe and the average temperature of water.

Then, the mean film temperature $T_f = \frac{220 + 110}{2} = 165°F$.

From water tables, for water at 165°F

$$a = 585.1 \times 10^6 \ 1/°R\text{-}ft^3 \qquad Pr = 2.48$$

The Rayleigh number is given by

$$Ra = GrPr = aL^3(T_1 - T_2)$$

$$= 585.1 \times 10^6 \times \left(\frac{4}{12}\right)^3 \times (220 - 110)$$

$$= 2.38 \times 10^9$$

Then,

$$GrPr(D/L) = 2.38 \times 10^9 \times \left(\frac{4}{18}\right)$$

$$= 5.29 \times 10^8$$

From the figure, for $GrPr(D/L) = 5.29 \times 10^8$ and for tne curve between free and mixed convection, the Reynolds number is

$$Re = 3 \times 10^4 = 30{,}000$$

CHAPTER 12

RADIATION

PARALLEL PLANES AND SPHERES

• PROBLEM 12-1

The emissivities of two parallel plates, P_1 and P_2, are 0.75 and 0.38, respectively. They are maintained at steady temperatures of 117°F and 63°F respectively.

An aluminum shield of emissivity 0.046 is employed. See Figure 1. Calculate the radiative heat flux per unit area:

1) without the radiation shield;
2) with the radiation shield;

The Stefan-Boltzmann constant is

$$0.1714 \times 10^{-8} \text{ Btu/hr-ft}^2\text{-}^0\text{R} .$$

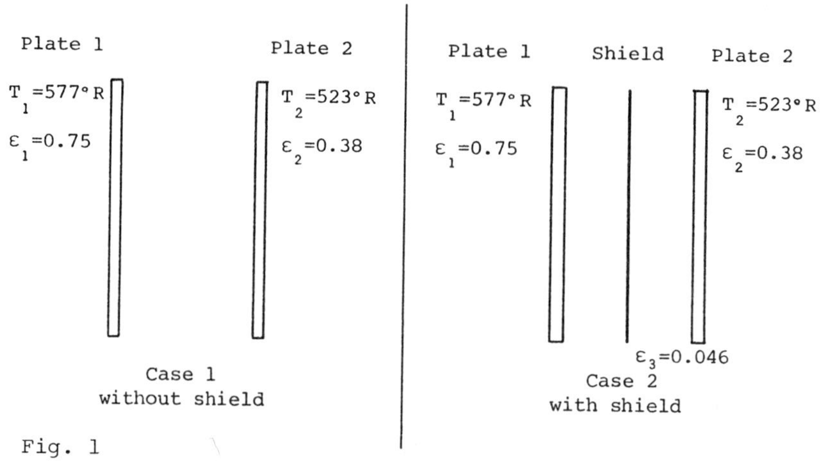

Fig. 1

Solution: Shielding reduces the rate of heat transfer by radiation from one plate to the other.

The radiative heat transfer rate is given by:

$$q = \frac{A_1\sigma[T_1^4 - T_2^4]}{\frac{1-\varepsilon_1}{\varepsilon_1} + \frac{1}{F_{1-2}} + \frac{1-\varepsilon_2}{\varepsilon_2} * \frac{A_1}{A_2}} \tag{1}$$

where q = radiative heat transfer rate

A_1 = surface area of plate 1

A_2 = surface area of plate 2

ε = emissivity

F_{1-2} = shape factor for the two plates 1 and 2.

Since the plates are large and parallel $A_1 = A_2$ and $F_{1-2} = 1$. Substituting in equation (1) and simplifying:

$$\frac{q}{A} = \frac{\sigma[T_1^4 - T_2^4]}{\frac{1}{\varepsilon_1} + \frac{1}{\varepsilon_2} - 1} \tag{2}$$

Assume steady state heat transfer with no heat loss.

For Case 1 Using equation (2)

where $T_1 = 117^0c + 460 = 577^0R$

$T_2 = 63^0c + 460 = 523^0R$

$\varepsilon_1 = 0.75$

$\varepsilon_2 = 0.38$

and $\sigma = 0.1714 \times 10^{-8}$ Btu/hr-ft^2-$^0R^4$

$$\frac{q}{A} = \frac{0.1714\times10^{-8}[(577)^4-(523)^4]}{\frac{1}{0.75} + \frac{1}{0.38} - 1}$$

$$= 20.825 \text{ Btu/hr-ft}^2$$

For Case 2

The rate of heat transfer between plate 1 and the shield is:

$$\frac{q}{A} = \frac{\sigma[T_1^4 - T_3^4]}{\frac{1}{\varepsilon_1} + \frac{1}{\varepsilon_3} - 1} \tag{3}$$

The rate of heat transfer between plate 2 and the shield

is:

$$\frac{q}{A} = \frac{\sigma[T_3^4 - T_2^4]}{\frac{1}{\varepsilon_2} + \frac{1}{\varepsilon_3} - 1} \tag{4}$$

The radiative heat transfer rate between plate 1 and the shield is equal to the radiative heat transfer rate between plate 2 and the shield.

Equating equations (3) and (4) yields:

$$\frac{[T_1^4 - T_3^4]}{\frac{1}{\varepsilon_1} + \frac{1}{\varepsilon_3} - 1} = \frac{[T_3^4 - T_2^4]}{\frac{1}{\varepsilon_2} + \frac{1}{\varepsilon_3} - 1}$$

Substituting the values of T_1, T_2, ε_1, ε_2 and ε_3 gives:

$$\frac{(577)^4 - T_3^4}{\frac{1}{0.75} + \frac{1}{0.046} - 1} = \frac{T_3^4 - (523)^4}{\frac{1}{0.38} + \frac{1}{0.046} - 1}$$

$$T_3^4 = 0.933 \times 10^{11}$$

Substituting in equation (3)

$$\frac{q}{A} = \frac{\sigma[T_1^4 - T_3^4]}{\frac{1}{\varepsilon_1} + \frac{1}{\varepsilon_3} - 1}$$

$$= \frac{0.1714\times10^{-8}\,[(577)^4 - (0.933\times10^{11})]}{\frac{1}{0.75} + \frac{1}{0.046} - 1}$$

$$= 1.362 \text{ Btu/hr-ft}^2$$

Answers: Case 1. rate of radiative heat transfer per unit area without the shield = 20.825 Btu/hr-ft^2

Case 2. rate of radiative heat transfer per unit area with the shield = 1.362 Btu/hr-ft^2

• PROBLEM 12-2

The annular space between two concentric aluminium spheres is evacuated to provide insulation to the system. The radii of the inner and outer spheres are 0.75 ft and 1.0 ft, respectively. The inner sphere contains liquified oxygen and the outer sphere is maintained at 45^{0}F. The boiling temperature of oxygen is -297^{0}F and the emissivity of aluminium is $\varepsilon = 0.03$. Determine the rate of heat flow to the oxygen by radiation.

Solution: The rate of heat loss from the outer sphere to the inner sphere due to radiation is given by:

$$q_1 = \frac{A_1\sigma(T_1^4 - T_2^4)}{\frac{1}{\varepsilon_1} + \frac{A_1}{A_2}\left(\frac{1}{\varepsilon_2} - 1\right)}$$

where A_1 = area of the outer sphere

A_2 = area of the inner sphere

$\varepsilon_1 = \varepsilon_2$ = emissivity of aluminium

T_1 = temperature of the outer sphere

T_2 = temperature of the inner sphere

R_1 = radius of the outer sphere

R_2 = radius of the inner sphere

$$A_1 = 4\pi R_1^2 = 4 \times \frac{22}{7} \times (1.0)^2 = 12.57 \text{ ft}^2$$

$$A_2 = 4\pi R_2^2 = 4 \times \frac{22}{7} \times (0.75)^2 = 7.07 \text{ ft}^2$$

$$\varepsilon_1 = \varepsilon_2 = 0.03$$

The temperature of oxygen will remain unchanged due to phase change.

$$T_2 = 460 - 297 = 163^0\text{R}$$

$$T_1 = 460 + 45 = 505^0\text{R}$$

Substituting the numerical values and calculating

$$q_1 = \frac{12.57 \times 0.1714 \times 10^{-8}\left[(505)^4 - (163)^4\right]}{\frac{1}{0.03} + \frac{12.57}{7.07}\left(\frac{1}{0.03} - 1\right)}$$

$$= \frac{1386.02}{33.33 + 57.48}$$

$$= \frac{1386.02}{90.81}$$

$$q_1 = 15.26 \text{ Btu/hr}$$

The rate of heat loss from the outer sphere to the oxygen by radiation is 15.26 Btu/hr.

A 10-in diameter spherical meat loaf, initially at 80 °F, is wrapped in aluminium foil and placed in a cubical oven of side 4 ft, for cooking. The oven is perfectly insulated and is maintained at 500 °F. Estimate the total initial radiant heat flux to the meat loaf assuming the emissivity of oven-wall and aluminum foil as 0.8 and 0.1 respectively. Figure 1 is an electrical analog which applies to this problem.

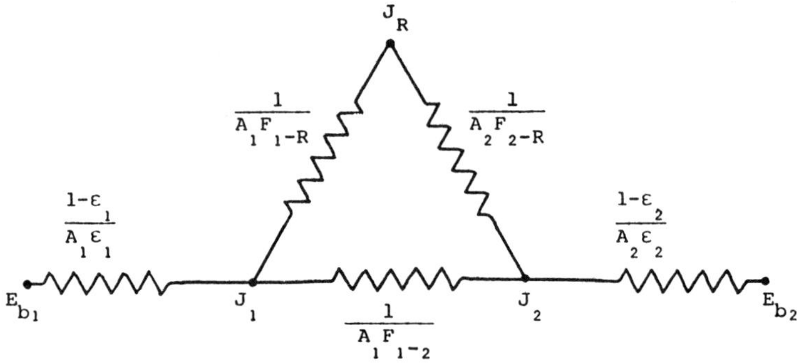

ELECTRICAL ANALOG FOR A TWO-GRAY-SURFACE SYSTEM ENCLOSED BY RERADIATING WALLS.

Solution: The radiant heat flux to the meat loaf is given by:

$$q_{12} = \frac{A_1\sigma(T_1{}^4 - T_2{}^4)}{\dfrac{1-\varepsilon_1}{\varepsilon_1} + \dfrac{1}{F_{12} + 1/\dfrac{1}{F_{1-R}} + \dfrac{A_1}{A_2}F_{2-R}} + \dfrac{1-\varepsilon_2}{\varepsilon_2}\dfrac{A_1}{A_2}} \qquad (1)$$

where the subscripts 1, 2 and R refer to the bottom of oven, the meat loaf, and the other five walls of the oven, respectively.

The given data is as follows:

$$T_1 = 500 + 460 = 960\,^0R$$

$$T_2 = 80 + 460 = 540\,^0R$$

$$T_R = 960\,^0R$$

$$\varepsilon_1 = 0.8$$

$$\varepsilon_2 = 0.1$$

$$\varepsilon_R = 0.8$$

The configuration factor F_{2-1} is given by $\frac{1.0}{6}$ since all radiant energy from the roast impinges equally on all the walls of the oven.

Then from the reciprocity theorem:

$$A_2F_{2-1} = A_1F_{1-2}$$

$$F_{1-2} = \frac{A_2}{A_1} F_{2-1} = \frac{\frac{4}{4}\left(\frac{10}{12}\right)^2 \pi}{4 \times 4} \frac{1.0}{6}$$

$$= 0.023$$

The view factor F_{1-R} is given by $\sum_{i=1}^{n} F_{1-i} = 1.0.$

$$F_{1-R} = 1.0 - F_{1-2} = 1.0 - 0.023$$

$$= 0.977$$

and

$$F_{2-R} = \frac{5}{6}(1.0) = \frac{5}{6}$$

Substituting the numerical values into equation (1) and calculating:

$$q_{1-2} = \frac{A_1\sigma(T_1^4 - T_2^4)}{\frac{1-\varepsilon_1}{\varepsilon_1} + \frac{1}{F_{1-2} + 1/\left(1/F_{1-R} + \frac{A_1}{A_2} F_{2-R}\right)} + \frac{1-\varepsilon_2}{\varepsilon_2} \frac{A_1}{A_2}}$$

$$= \frac{16 \times 0.1714 \times 10^{-8}\left((960)^4 - (540)^4\right)}{\frac{1-0.8}{0.8} + \frac{1}{0.023 + 1/\left[\frac{1}{0.977} + \frac{16}{100\pi} \times 144 \times 5/6\right]} + \frac{1-0.1}{0.1} \cdot \frac{16 \times 144}{100\pi}}$$

$$= \frac{2.096 \times 10^4}{0.25 + \frac{1}{0.023 + 0.140} + 66}$$

$$= \frac{2.096 \times 10^4}{0.25 + 6.135 + 66} = \frac{2.096 \times 10^4}{72.39}$$

$$q_{1-2} = 290 \text{ Btu/hr}$$

• PROBLEM 12-4

> The temperature of a tungsten filament of a light bulb is 6000°R. Calculate the energy emitted by the bulb in the visible wavelength spectrum from 0.4μm to 0.7μm, considering it as a grey body.

Solution: The given data is as follows:

$$\lambda_1 = 0.4 \ \mu m$$

$$\lambda_2 = 0.7 \ \mu m$$

$$T = 6000^0 R$$

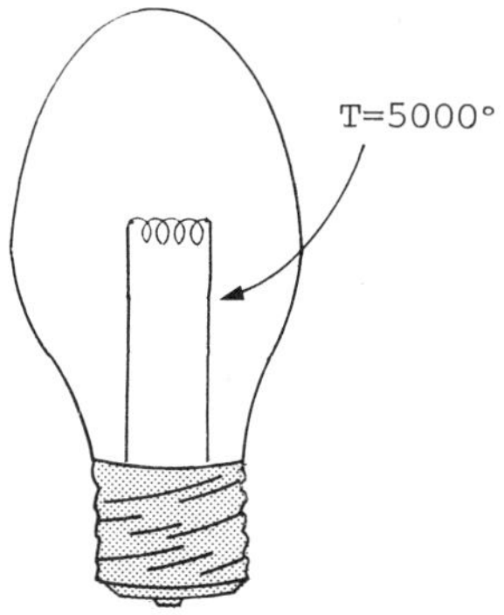

Therefore

$$\lambda_1 T = 0.4 \times 6000 = 2400 \ \mu m^0 R$$

$$\lambda_2 T = 0.7 \times 6000 = 4200 \ \mu m^0 R$$

From tabulated values of λT and $E_b(0 \to \lambda T)/\sigma T^4$ it can be determined that:

For $\lambda_1 T = 2400 \ \mu m^0 R$ $\qquad \dfrac{E_{b(0-2400)}}{\sigma T^4} = 0.0053$

$\lambda_2 T = 4200 \ \mu m^0 R$ $\qquad \dfrac{E_{b(0-4200)}}{\sigma T^4} = 0.1269$

Therefore the energy emitted in the visible wavelength range is:

$$0.1269 - 0.0053 = 0.1216$$

or 12.16% of the energy is released as visible light.

• PROBLEM 12-5

Calculate the solar energy transmitted through a glass plate in the wavelength range 0.3 μm - 4 μm. Assume the surface temperature of the sun to be 10,000°R.

Solution: The given data is as follows:

$$\lambda_1 = 0.3 \ \mu m$$

$$\lambda_2 = 4 \ \mu m$$

Therefore

$$\lambda_1 T = 0.3 \times 10{,}000 = 3{,}000 \ \mu m^0 R$$

$$\lambda_2 T = 4 \times 10{,}000 = 40{,}000 \ \mu m^0 R$$

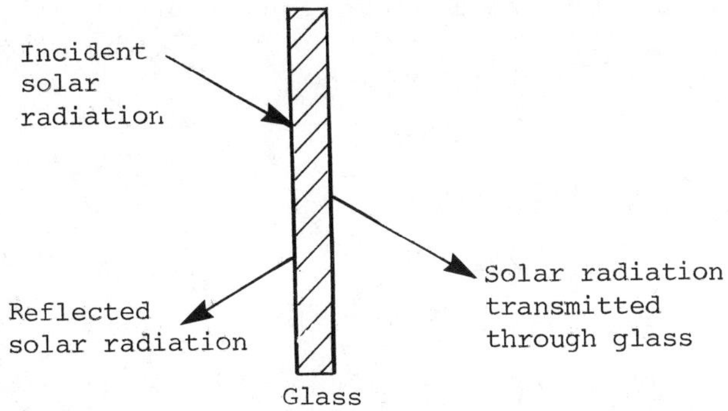

From tabulated values of λT and $E_b(0 - \lambda T)/\sigma T^4$ it can be determined that

For $\lambda_1 T = 3{,}000\ \mu m^0 R$ $\qquad \dfrac{E_{b(0-\lambda)}}{\sigma T^4} = 0.0254$

$\lambda_2 T = 40{,}000\ \mu m^0 R$ $\qquad \dfrac{E_{b(0-\lambda)}}{\sigma T^4} = 0.9891$

Therefore the energy transmitted in the given range is

$$0.9891 - 0.0254 = 0.9637 \text{ or } 96.37\%$$

BLACK BODIES

• PROBLEM 12-6

A gas containing 0.05 mass fraction of CO flows into a container at a rate of 250 lb/hr, where it is mixed with preheated air to oxidize the CO to CO_2. The container radiates 65% of the heat liberated due to combustion. Determine the radiation area required if the container attains a temperature of 1500^0F. The temperature of the surroundings is 150^0F and the heat of combustion of CO to CO_2 is 4350 Btu/lb CO. Assume the contained and the surroundings to be black bodies.

Solution: The overall heat released is given by:

$$Q = m_1 m_2 \Delta h$$

where

m_1 = mass fraction of CO

m_2 = mass flow rate of gas

Δh = heat of combustion

$$Q = 0.05 \times 250 \times 4350$$

$$= 54375 \text{ Btu/hr}$$

The net flux is given by:

$$q = q_1 - q_2$$

$$= \sigma T_1^4 - \sigma T_2^4$$

$$= 0.1714 \times 10^{-8} \times 1960^4 - 0.1714 \times 10^{-8} \times 610^4$$

$$= 25058 \text{ Btu/hr-ft}^2$$

The radiating area is given by:

$$Q_r = qA$$

where Q_r is the radiated away.

$$A = \frac{Q_r}{q}$$

$$= \frac{54357}{25058} \times 0.65$$

$$= 1.41 \text{ ft}^2$$

• PROBLEM 12-7

A spherical automobile component of 6 in diameter, initially at 80°F, is placed in a cubical oven of side 5 ft which is at a temperature of 560°F. Considering both of them as black bodies, calculate the net heat transfered from the oven to the component.

Solution: The net radiative flux from the oven to the component is:

$$q_{12} = A_1 F_{12} \sigma(T_1^4 - T_2^4)$$

where A_1 = area of the oven

F_{12} = view factor from the oven to the component

σ = Stefan Boltzman constant

T_1 = temperature of the oven

T_2 = temperature of the component

It is complicated to calculate F_{12} geometrically. Since F_{21} is known, F_{12} can be calculated by using the relationship between F_{12} and F_{21}. F_{21} is the view factor from the component to the oven, and it is equal to one since all radiation leaving the component falls on the walls of the oven.

Therefore

$$F_{12} = \frac{A_2}{A_1} F_{2-1}$$

$$= \frac{4\pi(3/12)^2}{6[5 \times 5]} (1) = 5.24 \times 10^{-3}.$$

$$q_{12} = A_1 F_{12} \sigma (T_1^4 - T_2^4)$$

$$= 6[5 \times 5] \times 5.24 \times 10^{-3} \times 0.1714 \times 10^{-8} \left[(1020)^4 - (540)^4\right]$$

$$= 1.344 \times 10^3$$

$$q_{12} = 1344 \text{ Btu/hr}$$

• PROBLEM 12-8

Determine the geometric shape factor for radiant heat transfer between a very small disc of area dA_1 and a large parallel disc of area A_2. The large disc is placed directly above the smaller disc. The radius of the larger disc is R and the perpendicular distance between the two discs is L. See Figure 1.

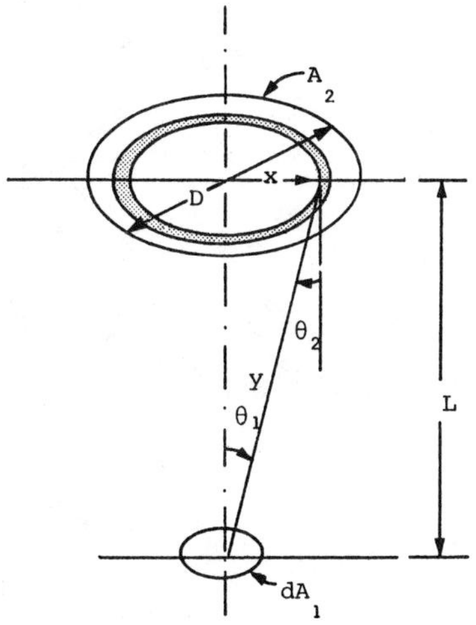

Solution: The geometric shape factor is given by:

$$F_{12} = \frac{1}{dA_1} \int_{A_1} \int_{A_2} \frac{\cos\theta_1 \cos\theta_2}{\pi y^2} dA_1 dA_2 \qquad (1)$$

But $\theta_1 = \theta_2$ since they are alternate angles. Consider a differential area of raidus x and thickness δx. Refer to Figure 1.

Then, $\quad dA_2 = 2\pi x \, dx$

Therefore equation (1) simplifies to

$$F_{12} = \int_{A_2} \frac{\cos^2\theta \cdot 2\pi x}{\pi y^2} dx \qquad (2)$$

From the geometry it is clearly seen that

$y^2 = x^2 + L^2$, using the Pythagorean theorem

$$y = \sqrt{x^2 + L^2}$$

Also,

$$\cos\theta = \frac{\text{adjacent}}{\text{hypotenuse}}$$

$$\cos\theta = \frac{L}{y}$$

but

$$y = \sqrt{x^2 + L^2}$$

Therefore,

$$\cos\theta = \frac{L}{\sqrt{x^2 + L^2}}$$

Substituting the values of $\cos\theta$ and y into equation (2) reduces it to:

$$F_{12} = \int_0^R \frac{L^2}{x^2 + L^2} \cdot \frac{2\pi x}{\pi(x^2 + L^2)} dx$$

The limits of integration are so taken since x varies from 0 to R.

$$F_{12} = \int_0^R \frac{2xL^2}{(x^2 + L^2)^2} dx$$

In order to integrate use the substitution technique.

That is, let $x^2 + L^2 = Z$

Differentiating

$$2xdx = dz$$

Therefore

$$F_{12} = \int_0^R \frac{L^2}{Z^2} dz$$

$$F_{12} = L^2 \left[-\frac{1}{Z} \right]_0^R$$

Substituting back the expression for Z,

$$F_{12} = -L^2 \left[\frac{1}{x^2 + L^2} \right]_0^R$$

Evaluating the limits,

$$F_{12} = -L^2 \left[\frac{1}{R^2 + L^2} - \frac{1}{L^2} \right]$$

$$F_{12} = 1 - \frac{L^2}{R^2 + L^2}$$

$$F_{12} = \frac{R^2}{R^2 + L^2}$$

• PROBLEM 12-9

A room is to be heated by using the floor as a radiating heating source at 120°F. A window in the room has the dimensions shown in Figure 1. If it is assumed that the window and the walls, including the ceiling, act as a black surface at 45°F and 85°F respectively. Find the net heat given out by the floor and also the net heat exchange between the floor and the window.

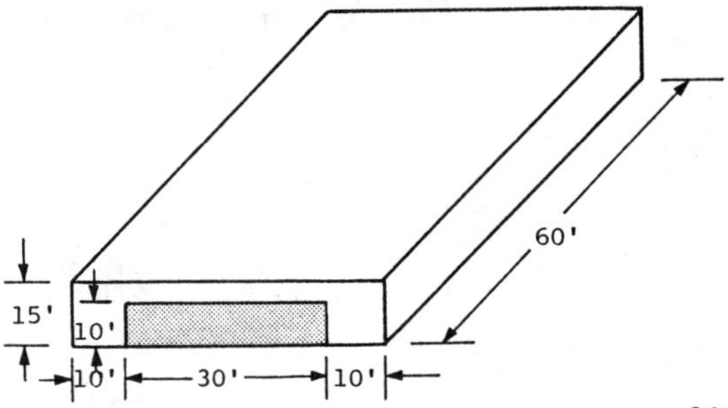

Fig. 1

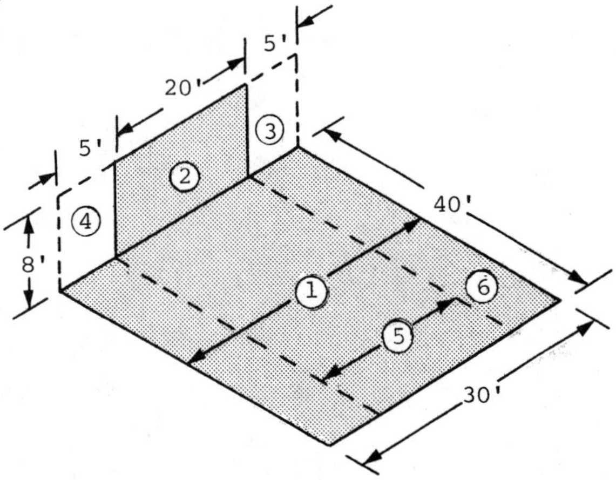

Figure 2

Fig. 3

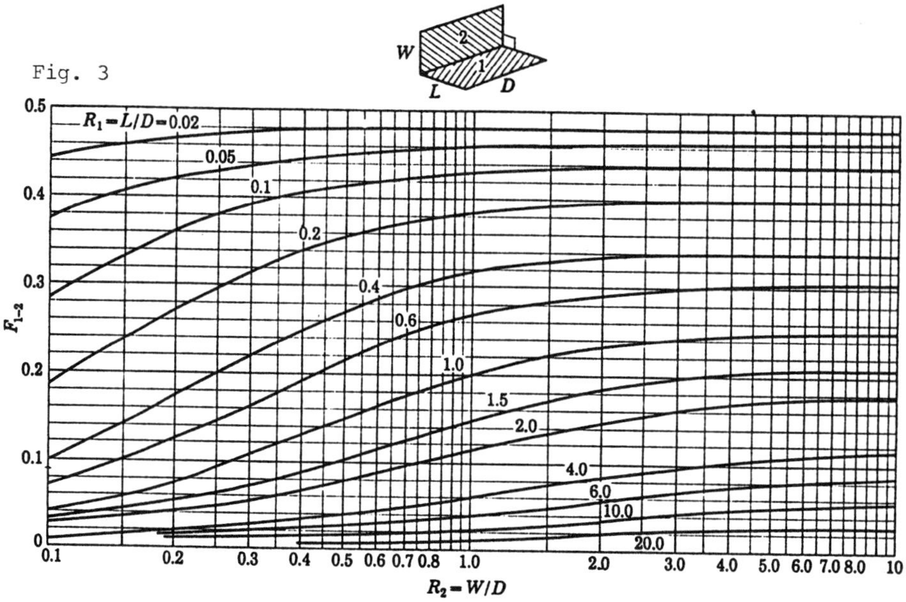

THE RADIATION VIEW FACTOR FOR PERPENDICULAR RECTANGLES WITH A COMMON EDGE.

Solution: Let the subscripts 1 and 2 refer to floor and the window, respectively. Subscripts 3 through 6 refer to divisions shown in the figures provided. Using shape factor algebra, it is known that:

$$A_1F_{1-2} = A_5F_{5-2} + 2A_6F_{6-2}$$

$$= A_5F_{5-2} + \left[A_{(5,6)}F_{(5,6)-(2,3)} - A_5F_{5-2} - A_6F_{6-3}\right]$$

To find $F_{(5,6)-(2,3)}$

$$\frac{L}{D} = \frac{60}{40} = 1.5$$

$$\frac{W}{D} = \frac{10}{40} = 0.25$$

From these values, and using Figure 3

$$F_{(5,6)-(2,3)} = 0.06$$

Also $F_{6-3} = 0.04$

Therefore

$$F_{1-2} = \frac{1}{A_1}\left[A_{(5,6)}F_{(5,6)-(2,3)} - A_6F_{6-3}\right]$$

$$= \frac{1}{50 \times 60}\left[40 \times 60 \times 0.06 - 10 \times 60 \times 0.04\right]$$

$$= \frac{1}{3000}\left[144 - 24\right]$$

$$= 0.04$$

If F_{1-w} represents the view factor between the floor and all the walls, including the ceiling, with the exception of the window, then

$$F_{1-w} = 1 - 0.04$$
$$= 0.96$$

The heat exchange rate between the floor and the window is:

$$q_{12} = A_1 F_{1-2} \sigma (T_1^4 - T_2^4)$$

where

q_{12} = heat exchange rate between 1 and 2

A_1 = area of the floor

F_{1-2} = view factor from 1 to 2

T_1 = temperature of the floor

T_2 = temperature of the window

σ = Stefan-Boltzman constant

$$q_{12} = 50 \times 60 \times 0.04 \times 0.1714 \times 10^{-8} \left[(580)^4 - (505)^4 \right]$$
$$= 9899 \text{ Btu/hr}$$

The net rate of heat given out by the floor is:

$$q_1 = A_1 \sigma \left[T_1^4 - (F_{1-2} T_2^4 + F_{1-w} T_w^4) \right]$$
$$= 50 \times 60 \times 0.1714 \times 10^{-8} \left[(580)^4 - 0.04(505)^4 - 0.96(545)^4 \right]$$
$$= 133020 \text{ Btu/hr}$$

• PROBLEM 12-10

Find the increase in heat exchange between two infinite black parallel plates initally at 100^0F and 200^0F respectively, when the temperature difference is increased by raising the temperature of the second plate to 400^0F. Assume

$$\sigma = 0.1714 \times 10^{-8} \text{ Btu/hr-ft}^2\text{-}^0\text{R}^4.$$

Solution: The heat exchange rate per unit area is given by:

$$\frac{q_{12}}{A} = \varepsilon \sigma (T_1^4 - T_2^4) \qquad (1)$$

where

ε = emissivity = 1 for black bodies

σ = Stefan-Boltzman constant

$= 0.1714 \times 10^{-8}$ Btu/hr-ft^2-^{0}R^4

T_1 = temperature of the first plate

$= 100^0F = (100 + 460) = 560^0R$

T_2 = temperature of the second plate

$= 200^0F = (200 + 460) = 660^0R$

A = area of the plates

q_{12} = heat exchange from plate one to two

T_2' = temperature of the second plate after increasing the temperature

$= 400^0F = (400 + 460) = 860^0R$

Substituting in equation (1) gives:

$$\frac{q_{12}}{A} = 1 \times 0.1714 \times 10^{-8} \left[(560)^4 - (660)^4\right]$$

$$= -157 \text{ Btu/hr-ft}^2$$

The negative sign indicates that heat is taken in.

$$\frac{q_{12}}{A} = 157 \text{ Btu/hr-ft}^2$$

The heat exchange rate per unit area after the temperature of the second plate is raised is:

$$\frac{q_{12}}{A} = \varepsilon\sigma(T_1^4 - T_2'^4)$$

$$= 1 \times 0.1714 \times 10^{-8}(560^4 - 860^4)$$

$$\frac{q_{12}}{A} = 769 \text{ Btu/hr-ft}^2$$

The increase in heat exchange is:

$$769 - 157 = 612 \text{ Btu/hr-ft}^2$$

GREY BODIES

• PROBLEM 12-11

If a thin high thermal conductivity grey plate is introduced parallely between two infinite parallel grey plates of equal area, obtain an equation which provides the reduction in radiant heat transfer between the plates.

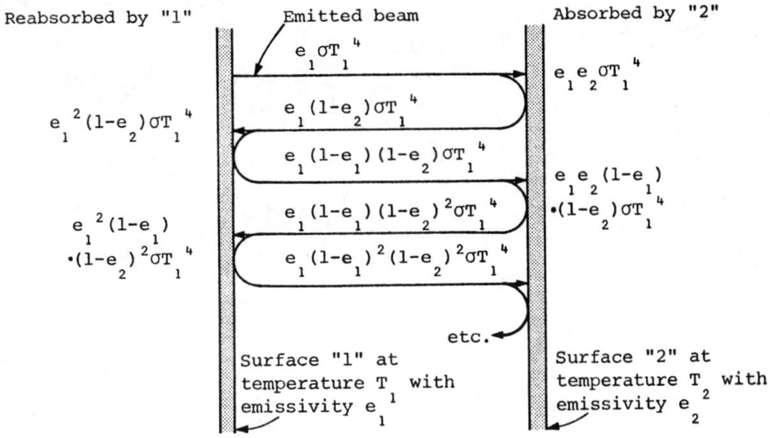

SCHEMATIC DIAGRAM SHOWING WHAT HAPPENS TO RADIATION EMITTED FROM SURFACE "1".

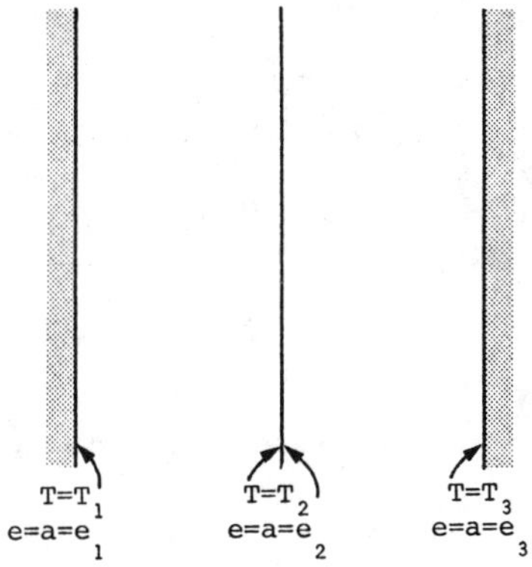

RADIATION SHIELD

Fig. 1

Solution: The total energy absorbed by the second plate can be obtained by summing up energies absorbed from any beam on repeated reflection. (Refer to Figure 1)

$$Q_{\underset{12}{\rightarrow}} = A\sigma T_1^4 \left[e_1e_2 + e_1e_2(1-e_1)(1-e_2) + \ldots\right]$$

where e is the emissivity.

Similarly the total energy absorbed by first plate is:

$$Q_{\underset{21}{\rightarrow}} = A\sigma T_2^4 \left[e_1e_2 + e_1e_2(1-e_1)(1-e_2) + . . .\right]$$

The net total energy transfer is:

$$Q_{12} = A\sigma(T_1^4 - T_2^4)\left[e_1e_2 + e_1e_2(1-e_1)(1-e_2) + . . .\right]$$

which can be simplified to

$$Q_{12} = A\sigma e_1e_2(T_1^4 - T_2^4) \sum_{i=0}^{\infty} \left[(1-e_1)(1-e_2)\right]^i \qquad (1)$$

It is known that

$$\sum_{n=0}^{\infty} x^n = \frac{1}{1-x}$$

Therefore:

$$\sum_{i=0}^{\infty} \left[(1-e_1)(1-e_2)\right]^i = \frac{1}{1-(1-e_1)(1-e_2)}$$

$$= \frac{1}{1-(1-e_2-e_1+e_1e_2)}$$

$$= \frac{1}{1-1+e_2+e_1-e_1e_2}$$

$$= \frac{1}{e_1e_2\left(\frac{1}{e_1}+\frac{1}{e_2}-1\right)}$$

Substituting in equation (1) yields:

$$Q_{12} = A\sigma e_1e_2(T_1^4-T_2^4)\ \frac{1}{e_1e_2\left(\frac{1}{e_1}+\frac{1}{e_2}-1\right)}$$

$$= \frac{A\sigma(T_1^4-T_2^4)}{\frac{1}{e_1}+\frac{1}{e_2}-1}$$

Analagously,

$$Q_{23} = \frac{A\sigma(T_2^4-T_3^4)}{\left(\frac{1}{e_2}+\frac{1}{e_3}-1\right)}$$

To obtain the solution, T_2 must be written in terms of T_1 and T_3.

At steady state:

$$Q_{12} = Q_{23}$$

$$\frac{A\sigma(T_1^4 - T_2^4)}{\left(\frac{1}{e_1}+\frac{1}{e_2}-1\right)} = \frac{A\sigma(T_2^4 - T_3^4)}{\left(\frac{1}{e_2}+\frac{1}{e_3}-1\right)}$$

$$\frac{T_1^4}{\frac{1}{e_1}+\frac{1}{e_2}-1} - \frac{T_2^4}{\frac{1}{e_1}+\frac{1}{e_2}-1} = \frac{T_2^4}{\frac{1}{e_2}+\frac{1}{e_3}-1} - \frac{T_3^4}{\frac{1}{e_2}+\frac{1}{e_3}-1}$$

$$T_2^4\left[\frac{1}{\frac{1}{e_2}+\frac{1}{e_3}-1} + \frac{1}{\frac{1}{e_1}+\frac{1}{e_2}-1}\right] = \frac{T_1^4}{\frac{1}{e_1}+\frac{1}{e_2}-1} + \frac{T_3^4}{\frac{1}{e_2}+\frac{1}{e_3}-1}$$

$$T_2^4\left[\frac{\left(\frac{1}{e_1}+\frac{1}{e_2}-1\right)+\left(\frac{1}{e_2}+\frac{1}{e_3}-1\right)}{\left(\frac{1}{e_2}+\frac{1}{e_3}-1\right)\left(\frac{1}{e_1}+\frac{1}{e_2}-1\right)}\right] = \frac{T_1^4}{\frac{1}{e_1}+\frac{1}{e_2}-1} + \frac{T_3^4}{\frac{1}{e_2}+\frac{1}{e_3}-1}$$

$$T_2^4 = \frac{\left[T_1^4\left(\frac{1}{e_2}+\frac{1}{e_3}-1\right) + T_3^4\left(\frac{1}{e_1}+\frac{1}{e_2}-1\right)\right]}{\left(\frac{1}{e_1}+\frac{1}{e_2}-1\right)+\left(\frac{1}{e_2}+\frac{1}{e_3}-1\right)}$$

Recall that:

$$Q_{12} = \frac{A\sigma(T_1^4 - T_2^4)}{\left(\frac{1}{e_1}+\frac{1}{e_2}-1\right)}$$

Substituting the value of T_2:

$$Q_{12} = \frac{A\sigma\left[T_1^4 - \frac{T_1^4\left(\frac{1}{e_2}+\frac{1}{e_3}-1\right) + T_3^4\left(\frac{1}{e_1}+\frac{1}{e_2}-1\right)}{\left(\frac{1}{e_1}+\frac{1}{e_2}-1\right)+\left(\frac{1}{e_2}+\frac{1}{e_3}-1\right)}\right]}{\left(\frac{1}{e_1}+\frac{1}{e_2}-1\right)}$$

$$Q_{12} = \frac{A\sigma}{\left(\frac{1}{e_1}+\frac{1}{e_2}-1\right)}\left[\frac{T_1^4\left(\frac{1}{e_1}+\frac{1}{e_2}-1\right) - T_3^4\left(\frac{1}{e_1}+\frac{1}{e_2}-1\right)}{\left(\frac{1}{e_1}+\frac{1}{e_2}-1\right)+\left(\frac{1}{e_2}+\frac{1}{e_3}-1\right)}\right]$$

$$Q_{12} = \frac{A\sigma(T_1^4 - T_3^4)}{\left(\frac{1}{e_1}+\frac{1}{e_2}-1\right)+\left(\frac{1}{e_2}+\frac{1}{e_3}-1\right)}$$

The ratio of radiant energy transfer with a middle plate to that without one is:

$$\frac{Q_{12}}{Q_{13}} + \frac{\left(\frac{1}{e_1} + \frac{1}{e_3} - 1\right)}{\left(\frac{1}{e_1} + \frac{1}{e_2} - 1\right) + \left(\frac{1}{e_2} + \frac{1}{e_3} - 1\right)}$$

• PROBLEM 12-12

Determine the geometric shape factor between a small area dA_1 in a vertical plane and a rectangular surface (a × b) in a horizontal plane. The area dA_1 is directly below one corner of the rectangle and the distance between them is H.

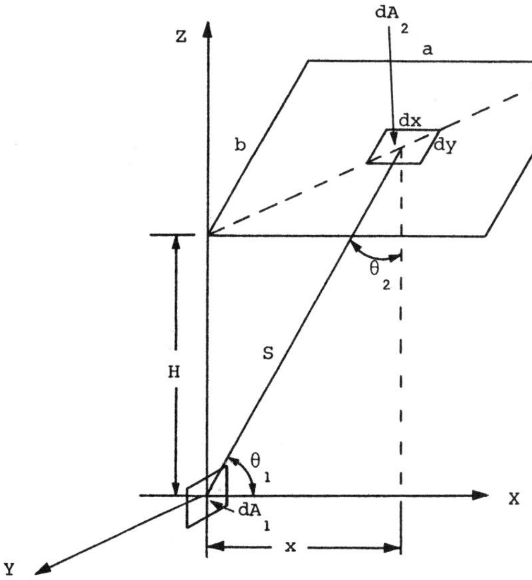

Solution: From the figure

$$\cos\theta_1 = \frac{x}{S}$$

$$\cos\theta_2 = \frac{H}{S}$$

$$S^2 = x^2 + y^2 + H^2$$

$$dA_2 = dx\ dy$$

The limits of x and y are 0 to a and 0 to b, respectively.

From the definition of the shape factor:

$$F_{12} = \int_{A_2} \frac{\cos\theta_1 \cos\theta_2}{\pi S^2}\, dA_2$$

$$F_{12} = \int_{A_2} \frac{\frac{x}{s} \cdot \frac{H}{s}}{\pi s^2} \, dA_2$$

$$= \int_0^a \int_0^b \frac{xH}{\pi s^4} \, dx \, dy$$

$$= \int_0^a \int_0^b \frac{xH}{\pi (x^2+y^2+H^2)^2} dx \, dy$$

$$= \frac{H}{\pi} \int_0^b \left[\int_0^a \frac{x}{(x^2+y^2+H^2)^2} \, dx \right] dy$$

Let $x^2 + y^2 + H^2 = z$

$2xdx = dz$

Substituting,

$$= \frac{H}{\pi} \int_0^b \left[\frac{1}{2} \int_0^a \frac{2x}{(x^2+y^2+H^2)^2} \, dx \right] dy$$

$$= \frac{H}{\pi} \int_0^b \left[\frac{1}{2} \int_0^a \frac{dz}{z^2} \right] dy$$

$$= \frac{H}{\pi} \int_0^b \left[-\frac{1}{2} \cdot \frac{1}{z} \right]_0^a dy$$

$$= \frac{H}{\pi} \int_0^b \left[-\frac{1}{2(x^2+y^2+H^2)} \right]_0^a dy$$

$$= \frac{H}{\pi} \int_0^b \left[\frac{1}{2} \left(\frac{1}{y^2+H^2} - \frac{1}{a^2+y^2+H^2} \right) \right] dy$$

$$= \frac{H}{2\pi} \int_0^b \left(\frac{1}{y^2+H^2} - \frac{1}{y^2+a^2+H^2} \right) dy$$

This is of the form:

$$\int \frac{dx}{x^2+a^2} = \frac{1}{a} \tan^{-1} \frac{x}{a}$$

Therefore

$$F_{12} = \frac{H}{2\pi}\left[\frac{1}{H}\tan^{-1}\left(\frac{y}{H}\right) - \frac{1}{\sqrt{a^2+H^2}}\tan^{-1}\left(\frac{y}{\sqrt{a^2+H^2}}\right)\right]_0^b$$

$$F_{12} = \frac{H}{2\pi}\left[\frac{1}{H}\tan^{-1}\left(\frac{b}{H}\right) - \frac{1}{\sqrt{a^2+H^2}}\tan^{-1}\left(\frac{b}{\sqrt{a^2+H^2}}\right)\right]$$

$$F_{12} = \frac{1}{2\pi}\left[\tan^{-1}\left(\frac{b}{H}\right) - \frac{H}{\sqrt{a^2+H^2}}\tan^{-1}\left(\frac{b}{\sqrt{a^2+H^2}}\right)\right]$$

• PROBLEM 12-13

The products of a combustion reaction in a 2 ft diameter infinite cylinder are at a temperature of 1000°C, a pressure of 1 atm, and contain 25% by volume of both CO_2 and H_2O. If the cylinder walls are maintained at 600°C, then calculate the net radiant energy exchanged between the gases and the cylinder walls.

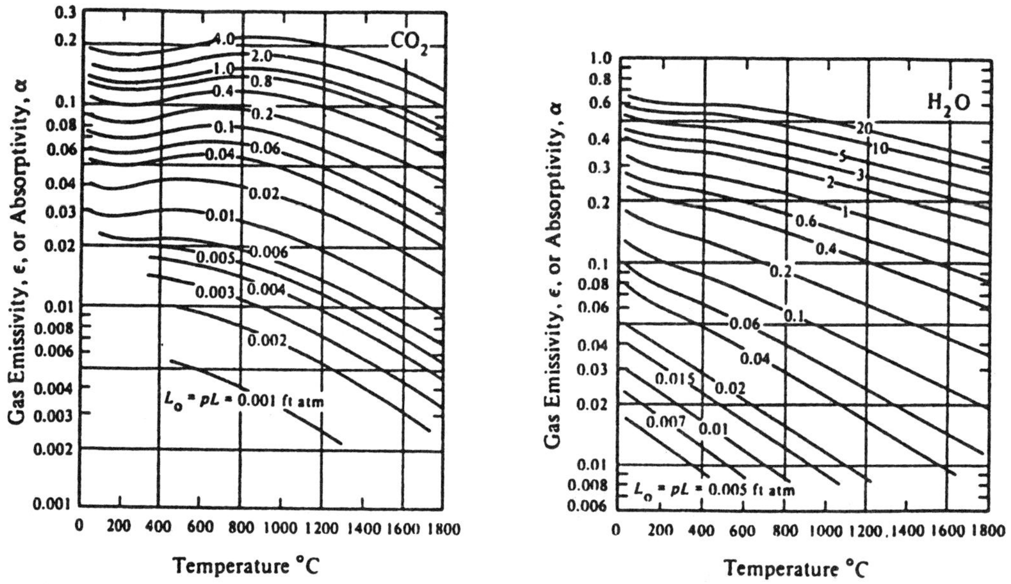

Fig. 1 (a) (b)

EMISSIVITIES OF (a) CARBON DIOXIDE AND (b) WATER VAPOR

Solution: The partial pressure of a gas in a mixture is equal to the product of the total pressure of the mixture and the volume fraction of the gas.

Therefore $P_{H_2O} = 0.25 \times 1 = 0.25$ atm

$P_{CO_2} = 0.25 \times 1 = 0.25$ atm

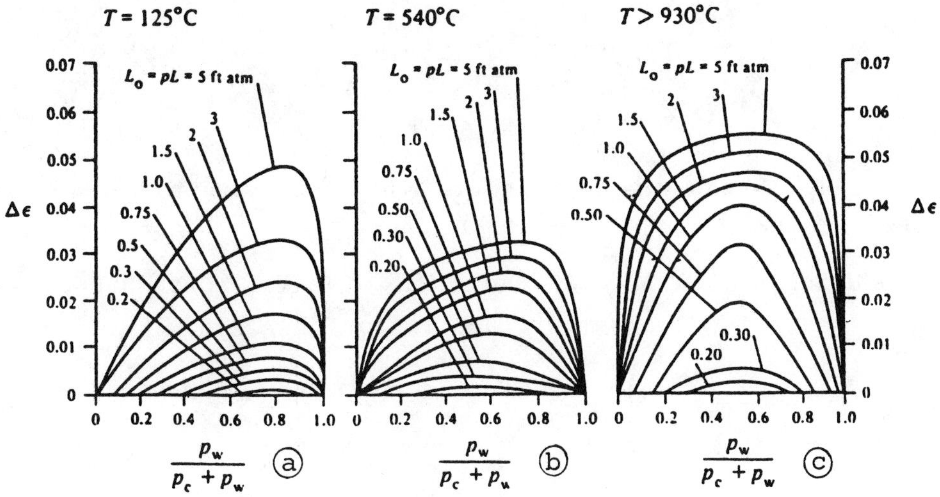

Fig. 2

CORRECTION FOR MUTUAL ABSORPTIVITY OF WATER VAPOR AND CARBON DIOXIDE

The length of an infinite cylinder of diameter D is

$$L = D = 2 \text{ ft}$$

$$L_o = P_{H_2O}L = 0.25 \times 2 = 0.5$$

Using Figure 1b

$$\varepsilon_{H_2O} = 0.13$$

where ε = emissivity.

$$L_o = P_{CO_2}L = 0.25 \times 2 = 0.5$$

Using Figure 1a

$$\varepsilon_{CO_2} = 0.12$$

$$P_{CO_2}L + P_{H_2O}L = 0.25 \times 2 + 0.25 \times 2$$

$$= 1 \text{ ft atm}$$

$$\frac{P_{H_2O}}{P_{H_2O} + P_{CO_2}} = \frac{0.25}{0.25 + 0.25} = 0.5$$

Using Figure 2c

$$\Delta\varepsilon = 0.018$$

$$\varepsilon g = \varepsilon_{CO_2} + \varepsilon_{H_2O} - \Delta\varepsilon$$

$$= 0.12 + 0.13 - 0.018$$

$$= 0.232$$

$$P_{CO_2}L\left(\frac{T_s}{T_g}\right) = 0.25 \times 2 \times \left(\frac{873^0K}{1273^0K}\right)$$

$$= 0.343 \text{ ft atm}$$

where T_g is the gas temperature and T_s is the wall temperature of the cylinder.

Using Figure 1a with the value of $P_{CO_2}L$ which has been adjusted using the temperature factor (T_s/T_g):

$$\varepsilon_{CO_2} = 0.11$$

Therefore

$$\alpha_{CO_2} = \varepsilon_{CO_2}\left(\frac{T_g}{T_s}\right)^{0.65}$$

$$= 0.11\left(\frac{1273}{873}\right)^{0.65}$$

$$= 0.14$$

Similarly

$$P_{H_2O}L\left(\frac{T_s}{T_g}\right) = 0.25 \times 2\left(\frac{873^0K}{1273^0K}\right)$$

$$= 0.343$$

Using Figure 1b

$$\varepsilon_{H_2O} = 0.12$$

and

$$\alpha_{H_2O} = \varepsilon_{H_2O}\left(\frac{T_g}{T_s}\right)^{0.45}$$

$$= 0.12\left(\frac{1273}{873}\right)^{0.45}$$

$$= 0.142$$

And, also

$$\Delta\alpha_g = 0$$

Hence,

$$\alpha_g = \alpha_{CO_2} + \alpha_{H_2O} - \Delta\alpha_g$$

$$= 0.14 + 0.142 - 0$$

$$= 0.282$$

Now,

$$\frac{Q_g}{A_s} = \varepsilon g \sigma T_g^4 = 0.232 \times 0.1714 \times 10^{-8}(2292)^4$$

where $\varepsilon = 0.1714 \times 10^{-8}$ Btu/hr-ft^2-^{0}R^4.

$$\frac{Q_g}{A_s} = 10974 \text{ Btu/hr-ft}^2$$

$$\frac{Q_s}{A_s} = \alpha_g \sigma T_s^4$$

$$= 0.282 \times 0.1714 \times 10^{-8}(1572)^4$$

$$= 2952 \text{ Btu/hr-ft}^2$$

$$\frac{Q_g}{A_s} - \frac{Q_s}{A_s} = 10974 - 2952$$

$$= 8022 \text{ Btu/hr-ft}^2$$

Therefore the net radiant energy exchanged between the gases and the cylinder walls is 8022 Btu/hr-ft^2.

• PROBLEM 12-14

A $1\frac{1}{2}$ in sch. 40 steam pipe is laid in the atmosphere where the temperature is 50^{0}F. The steam inside it is saturated at 100 psia. Consider the pipe to be a grey body and uninsulated. The coefficient of heat transfer by natural convection from the outside surface is 2.0 Btu/hr sq ft R. Calculate the amount of steam condensed per hour per unit length of pipe.

Solution: The total heat loss due to radiation and convection is given by

$$q = q_r + q_c$$

or

$$q = \sigma\varepsilon A(T_p^4 - T_a^4) + h_c A(T_p - T_a) \tag{1}$$

where

q = total rate of loss of thermal energy, Btu/hr

ε = surface emissivity of pipe

A = area of outside surface of pipe

T_p = temperature of pipe surface

T_a = surrounding atmospheric temperature

σ = Stefan-Boltzmann constant

The given data is

$$\sigma = 0.1714 \times 10^{-8} \text{ Btu/hr ft}^2 {}^0\text{R}^4$$

$$\varepsilon = 0.95$$

The outside surface area for $1\frac{1}{2}$ in 40 sch. pipe for unit length is taken from pipe tables

$$= 0.497 \text{ ft}^2/\text{ft}$$

$$T_a = 50 + 460 = 510^0\text{R}$$

$$T_p = 328 + 460 = 788^0\text{R}$$

since the pipe surface temperature is equal to the condensing steam temperature of 328°F, which is obtained from steam tables.

Therefore, substitution in equation (1) yields:

$$q = 0.1714 \times 10^{-8} \times 0.497 \times 0.95 \left[(788)^4 - (510)^4\right] + 2.0 \times 0.497 \times (788 - 510)$$

$$q = 257 + 276$$

$$= 533 \text{ Btu/hr ft of pipe}$$

The rate of condensation = $q/\Delta H$ where ΔH = 888.8 Btu/lb from steam tables

$$= \frac{533}{888.8} = 0.60 \text{ lb of steam/hr-ft of pipe}$$

• PROBLEM 12-15

Solar radiant energy falls on a rectangular black body, 10m x 25m x 0.005m, at a rate of 800 W/m^2. The body is provided with two layers of insulation of 30mm and 10mm thickness, respectively. The thermal conductivities of the body and the insulations are 50 W/m K, 0.05 W/m K (30mm), 0.15 W/m K (10mm) respectively. The inside air temperature is 20°C and the inside convective heat transfer coefficient is 10 W/m^{2}K. The outside air temperature is -1°C and the outside convective heat transfer coefficient is 35 W/m^{2}K. The temperature of space is -20°C. Determine the heat transfer rate through the body. See Figure 1.

Solution: The total incoming heat is due to conduction, convection and radiation.

Therefore

$$Q_{in} = Q_{cond} + Q_{conv} + Q_{radi}$$

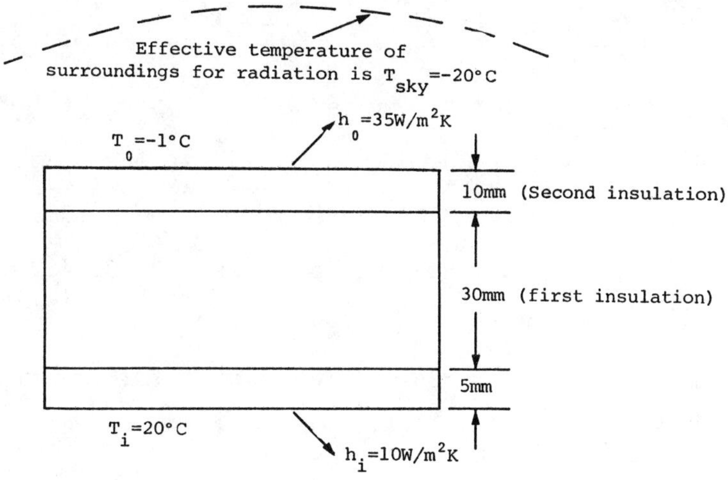

Fig. 1

Incoming heat is also given by,

$$Q_{in} = q_{rad}A_{body}$$

$$= 800 \times (10 \times 25) = 200{,}000 \text{ W}$$

$$Q_{conv} = h_o A_{body}(T_s - T_o)$$

where, Q_{conv} = convective loss to the outside air

h_o = outside convective heat transfer coefficient = 35 W/m²K

A = area of the body = 250m²

T_s = surface temperature of the body

T_o = outside air temperature = -1°C

$$Q_{conv} = 35 \times 250 \times (T_s + 1)$$

$$Q_{conv} = 8750(T_s + 1)$$

The conductive term is:

$$Q_{cond} = \frac{T_s - T_i}{\Sigma R}$$

where Q_{cond} = conduction loss through the body

T_s = body surface temperature

T_i = inside air temperature = 20°C

ΣR = total resistance (conductive and convective) between the outside surface of the body and the inside ambient air

$$\Sigma R = \frac{L}{KA_{body}} + \frac{L_1}{K_1 A} + \frac{L_2}{K_2 A} + \frac{1}{h_i A}$$

where L = thickness of the body = 0.005m

L_1 = thickness of first insulation = 0.03m

L_2 = thickness of second insulation = 0.01m

k = thermal conductivity of the body
= 50 W/m k

k_1 = thermal conductivity of first insulation
= 0.05 W/m k

k_2 = thermal conductivity of second insulation
= 0.15 W/mk

h_i = inside convective heat transfer coefficient = 10 W/m^2k

A = area of the body

$$\Sigma R = \frac{0.005}{50 \times 250} + \frac{0.03}{0.05 \times 250} + \frac{0.01}{0.15 \times 250} + \frac{1}{10 \times 250}$$

$$= 4 \times 10^{-7} + 2.4 \times 10^{-3} + 2.6 \times 10^{-4} + 4 \times 10^{-4}$$

$$\Sigma R = 3.06 \times 10^{-3} \text{ K/W}$$

$$Q_{cond} = \frac{T_s - 20}{3.06 \times 10^{-3}} \text{ W}$$

$$Q_{rad} = A_{body}\varepsilon(e_{bs} - e_{bsky})$$

σ = Stefan-Boltzmann constant
= 5.668×10^{-8} W/m^2k^4

$$e_{bs} = \sigma(T_s + 273)^4 = 5.668 \times 10^{-8}(T_s + 273)^4$$

$$e_{bsky} = \sigma(-20 + 273)^4 = 5.668 \times 10^{-8}(253)^4$$

$$Q_{rad} = 250 \times 1 \times 5.668 \times 10^{-8}\left[(T_s+273)^4-(253)^4\right]$$

Substitution of the various quantities into the following equation,

$$Q_{in} = Q_{cond} + Q_{conv} + Q_{rad}$$

$$2 \times 10^5 = 8750T_s + 8750 + \frac{T_s - 20}{3.06 \times 10^{-3}}$$

$$+ 1.417 \times 10^{-5}\left[(T_s+273)^4-(253)^4\right]$$

$$2 \times 10^5 - 8750 + 5.8 \times 10^4 = 8750T_s + \frac{T_s - 20}{3.06 \times 10^{-3}}$$

$$+ 1.417 \times 10^{-5}(T_s+273)^4$$

$$762.7 = 26.77T_s + T_s - 20 + 4.33 \times 10^{-8}(T_s+273)^4$$

$$782.7 = 27.77T_s + 4.33 \times 10^{-8}(T_s+273)^4$$

T_s has to be obtained by iteration. That is, guess a value for T_s and check if the above equation is satisfied.

By trial and error $T_s = 17^0C$.

The rate of heat transfer through the body is,

$$Q_{cond} = \frac{T_s - 20}{\Sigma R}$$

$$= \frac{17.0 - 20}{3.06 \times 10^{-3}}$$

$$= -980 \text{ W}$$

The negative sign indicates that the heat flows from the inside to the outside of the body.

• PROBLEM 12-16

If a body is cooled below ambient temperature by a system, it can then be used to freeze water. Calculate the maximum air temperature for which freezing takes place.

Solution: The maximum air temperature at the surface of the water is $T_1 = 492^0R$ (32^0F). The rate of heat loss due to radiation is,

$$Q_{rad} = e_1 A_1 \sigma T_1{}^4$$

$$= 0.95 \times 0.1714 \times 10^{-8} \times (492)^4 \times L^2$$

$$= 95L^2 \text{ Btu/m}^{-1} \text{ ft}^2 \qquad (1)$$

where . $e_1 = 0.95$ and $A = L^2$.

The heat gained by convection is:

$$Q_{conv} = hL^2(T_{air} - T_{water})$$

where h is given by,

$$h = 0.2(T_{air} - T_{water})^{\frac{1}{4}}$$

Therefore

$$Q_{conv} = 0.2L^2(T_{air} - T_{water})^{\frac{5}{4}} \qquad (2)$$

Equating equations (1) and (2) yields:

$$0.2L^2(T_{air} - T_{water})^{5/4} = 95L^2$$

$$T_{air} - T_{water} = 138.47$$

$$T_{air} = T_w + 138.47$$

$$= 492 + 138.47$$

$$T_{air} = 630^0R$$

$$= 170^0F$$

CHAPTER 13

UNSTEADY STATE HEAT TRANSFER

SEMI-INFINITE SOLID

• **PROBLEM 13-1**

Calculate the minimum depth at which water pipes have to be positioned below the ground surface to avoid freezing in a geographical area with a mean winter temperature of $7^{\circ}C$ and if the temperature of ambient air suddenly drops to $-8^{\circ}C$ and remains there for a maximum period of 60 hrs.

Solution: In this system, the minimum depth should be calculated for the most severe conditions, i.e., when temperature drops to $-8^{\circ}C$.

The complementary error function is given by:

$$\text{erfc}\ (x) = \frac{T - T_o}{T_s - T_o}$$

$$\text{erfc}\ (x) = \frac{0 - 7}{-8 - 7} = \frac{7}{15}$$

$$= 0.467$$

From the complementary error function tables, for erfc (x) = 0.467, x = 0.515. For dry soil assume $\alpha = 0.52/(2040)(1850)$ $= 1.38 \times 10^{-7}\ \frac{m^2}{sec}$

The minimum depth is calculated by:

$$x = \frac{y}{(4\alpha t)^{\frac{1}{2}}}$$

Therefore, $\quad y = x(4\alpha t)^{\frac{1}{2}}$

$$= 0.515 \left[4(1.38 \times 10^{-7})(60)(3600)\right]^{\frac{1}{2}}$$

$$= 0.178 \text{ m.} = 17.8 \text{ cm.} = 7.0 \text{ in.}$$

Hence, to avoid freezing, the top of the water pipes should be at least 17.8 cm. below the ground surface.

• PROBLEM 13-2

Consider the ground which is near the earth's surface to be maintained at a uniform temperature of 50°F. The ambient air temperature at night quickly drops to 15°F. Find the depth of penetration of 40°F temperature into the ground in 7 hours. The following are the physcial properties of the ground:

$h = 2$ Btu/hr.ft^2.°F $\qquad k = 0.3$ Btu/hr.ft.°F

$\alpha = 0.04$ ft^2/hr.

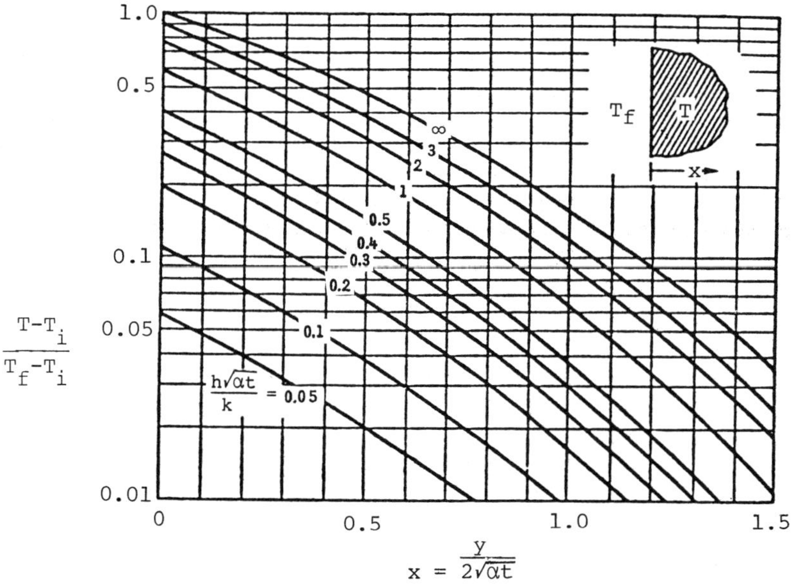

TEMPERATURE HISTORY IN A SEMI-INFINITE SOLID INITIALLY AT A UNIFORM TEMPERATURE AND SUDDENLY EXPOSED AT ITS SURFACE TO A FLUID AT CONSTANT TEMPERATURE.

Figure (1)

Solution: To use fig. (1), assume that there is a sudden change in the ambient air temperature from 50°F to 15°F. This assumption is more severe than what actually occurs, but the solution obtained is safe because the predicted depth of penetration is greater than what will actually occur.

Then,

$$\frac{h}{k}\sqrt{\alpha t} = \frac{2}{0.3}\sqrt{(0.04)(7)}$$

$$= 3.53$$

and

$$\frac{T_i - T}{T_i - T_f} = \frac{50 - 40}{50 - 15}$$

$$= 0.286$$

From fig. (1),

for $\frac{h}{k}\sqrt{\alpha t} = 3.53$ and $\frac{T_i - T}{T_i - T_f} = 0.286$

$$X = \frac{y}{2\sqrt{\alpha t}} = 0.685$$

Then

$$y = (0.685)(2)\sqrt{(0.04)(7)}$$

$$= 0.725 \text{ ft.}$$

Then, the depth of penetration of $40^{\circ}F$ temperature is 0.725 ft.

• PROBLEM 13-3

A semi-infinite solid is initially at a temperature T_0. If the temperature of the surface is instantaneously changed to T_∞, determine the unsteady temperature in the semi-infinite solid. See figure (1).

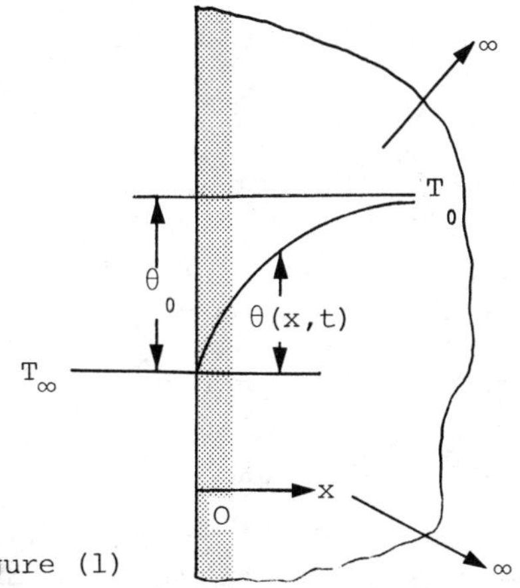

Figure (1)

Solution: The governing differential equation is given as:

$$\frac{\partial \theta}{\partial t} = \alpha \frac{\partial^2 \theta}{\partial x^2} \tag{1}$$

where $\theta = T - T_\infty$

The initial condition is:

$$\theta(x, 0) = T_o - T_\infty = \theta_o \tag{2}$$

The boundary conditions are:

$$\theta(0, t) = 0 \tag{3}$$

$$\theta(\infty, t) = \theta_o \tag{4}$$

The governing differential equation can be solved by both the Laplace transform method and the Fourier series method. Here the solutions are shown using both methods.

(a) Laplace transform method:

The standard Laplace transforms are:

$$L\left\{\frac{df(t)}{dt}\right\} = s\bar{f}(s) - f(0) \tag{5}$$

$$L\left\{\frac{\partial^n f(x, t)}{\partial x^n}\right\} = \frac{d^n \bar{f}(x, s)}{dx^n} \tag{6}$$

Using equations (5) and (6), the transform of equation (1) is written as:

$$L\left\{\frac{\partial \theta}{\partial t}\right\} = L\left\{\alpha \frac{\partial^2 \theta}{\partial x^2}\right\}$$

$$\frac{d^2\bar{\theta}}{dx^2} - \frac{s}{\alpha}\bar{\theta} = \frac{\theta_o}{\alpha} \tag{7}$$

The boundary conditions transform to:

$$\bar{\theta}(0, s) = 0 \tag{8}$$

$$\bar{\theta}(\infty, s) = \frac{\theta_o}{s} \tag{9}$$

The general solution of equation (7) is given by:

$$\bar{\theta}(x, s) = \frac{\theta_o}{s} + A e^{-\frac{s}{\alpha}x} + B e^{\frac{s}{\alpha}x} \tag{10}$$

Applying equation (9) to equation (10),

$$\bar{\theta}(\infty, s) = \frac{\theta_o}{s} + A e^{-\frac{s}{\alpha}\infty} + B e^{\frac{s}{\alpha}\infty} = \frac{\theta_o}{s}$$

This gives $B = 0$.

Now, equation (10) reduces to:

$$\bar{\theta}(x, s) = \frac{\theta_o}{s} + A\, e^{-\frac{s}{\alpha}x} \tag{11}$$

Applying equation (8) to equation (11),

$$\bar{\theta}(0, s) = \frac{\theta_o}{s} + A\, e^{-\frac{s}{\alpha}(0)} = 0$$

Therefore $A = -\dfrac{\theta_o}{s}$

Substituting for the integration constant A in equation (11) gives:

$$\bar{\theta}(x, s) = \frac{\theta_o}{s} - \frac{\theta_o}{s}\, e^{-\frac{s}{\alpha}x}$$

$$\frac{\bar{\theta}(x, s)}{\theta_o} = \frac{1}{s} - \frac{1}{s}\, e^{-\frac{s}{\alpha}x} \tag{12}$$

Applying the inverse Laplace transform to equation (12) gives:

$$\frac{\theta(x, t)}{\theta_o} = \operatorname{erf}\left[\frac{x}{2(\alpha t)^{\frac{1}{2}}}\right] \tag{13}$$

Hence, the unsteady temperature of the solid is:

$$\frac{T(x, t) - T_\infty}{T_o - T_\infty} = \operatorname{erf}\left[\frac{x}{2(\alpha t)^{\frac{1}{2}}}\right] \tag{14}$$

(b) Fourier series method:

The product solution of equation (1) satisfying equation (3) is:

$$\Theta_\lambda(x, t) = b(\lambda)e^{-\alpha\lambda^2 t} \sin \lambda x$$

where λ is the separation parameter.

As the space interval extends to infinity, the integral solution involving all positive values of λ is:

$$\theta(x, t) = \int_0^\infty b(\lambda)e^{-\alpha\lambda^2 t} \sin \lambda x \, d\lambda \qquad x > 0 \tag{15}$$

Applying the initial condition on equation (15) gives:

$$\theta(x, 0) = \int_0^\infty b(\lambda) \sin \lambda x \, d\lambda = \theta_o$$

This is the Fourier sine integral representation of θ_o.

Now $b(\lambda)$ can be evaluated by using the following equation:

$$b(\lambda) = \frac{2}{\pi} \int_0^\infty f(\xi) \sin \lambda\xi \, d\xi$$

here $f(\xi) = \theta_o$

Then

$$b(\lambda) = \frac{2}{\pi} \int_0^\infty \theta_o \sin \lambda\xi \, d\xi$$

but θ_o is constant, therefore:

$$b(\lambda) = 2 \frac{\theta_o}{\pi} \int_0^\infty \sin \lambda\xi \, d\xi \tag{16}$$

Substituting equation (16) in equation (15) gives:

$$\frac{\theta(x, t)}{\theta_o} = \frac{2}{\pi} \int_0^\infty \int_0^\infty e^{-\alpha\lambda^2 t} \sin \lambda x \sin \lambda\xi \, d\lambda \, d\xi \tag{17}$$

Using the trigonometric relationship:

$$\sin A \sin B = \tfrac{1}{2} \left[\cos (A - B) - \cos (A + B)\right]$$

equation (17) can be rewritten as:

$$\frac{\theta(x, t)}{\theta_o} = \frac{1}{\pi} \int_0^\infty \int_0^\infty e^{-\alpha\lambda^2 t} \left[\cos \lambda(x - \xi) - \cos \lambda(x + \xi)\right] d\lambda \, d\xi \tag{18}$$

Using the standard integral,

$$\int_0^\infty e^{-\alpha\lambda^2 t} \cos \lambda x \, d\lambda = \frac{1}{2} \left(\frac{\pi}{\alpha t}\right)^{\frac{1}{2}} e^{-x^2/4\alpha t}$$

equation (18) can be written as,

$$\frac{\theta(x, t)}{\theta_o} = \frac{1}{2(\pi\alpha t)^{\frac{1}{2}}} \int_0^\infty \left[e^{-(x-\xi)^2/4\alpha t} - e^{-(x+\xi)^2/4\alpha t}\right] d\xi \tag{19}$$

Substituting $\eta^2 = (x - \xi)^2/4\alpha t$ in the first integral of equation (19) and $\eta^2 = (x + \xi)^2/4\alpha t$ in the second integral yields:

$$\frac{\theta(x, t)}{\theta_o} = \frac{1}{\pi^{\frac{1}{2}}}\left[\int_{-x/2(\alpha t)^{\frac{1}{2}}}^{\infty} e^{-\eta^2} d\eta - \int_{x/2(\alpha t)^{\frac{1}{2}}}^{\infty} e^{-\eta^2} d\eta\right]$$

or

$$\frac{\theta(x, t)}{\theta_o} = \frac{2}{\pi^{\frac{1}{2}}}\int_0^{x/2(\alpha t)^{\frac{1}{2}}} e^{-\eta^2} d\eta$$

or

$$\frac{\theta(x, t)}{\theta_o} = \text{erf}\left[\frac{x}{2(\alpha t)^{\frac{1}{2}}}\right] \tag{20}$$

Hence, the unsteady temperature of the solid is:

$$\frac{T(x, t) - T_\infty}{T_o - T_\infty} = \text{erf}\left[\frac{x}{2(\alpha t)^{\frac{1}{2}}}\right] \tag{21}$$

Eq. (14) and (21) are identical. This indicates that any one of the two methods can be used to solve this type of problem.

• PROBLEM 13-4

Consider a fall day on which the temperature of the earth soil is constant at 70°F over a depth of several yards. Then suddenly a cold wave drops the ambient air temperature from 70°F to 5°F. The convective heat transfer coefficient above the soil surface is 3 Btu/hr.ft^2.$^\circ$F. Neglect the latent heat effects and assume the physical properties of the soil as $\alpha = 0.02$ ft^2/hr. and k = 0.6 Btu/hr.ft.$^\circ$F. Determine the surface temperature of the soil after 5 hours. Find the depth of penetration of the freezing temperature 32°F into the soil in 5 hours.

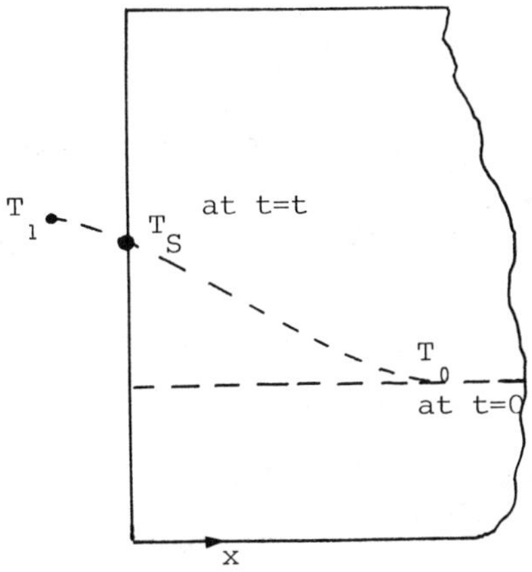

Fig. 1. UNSTEADY-STATE CONDUCTION IN A SEMI-INFINITE SOLID.

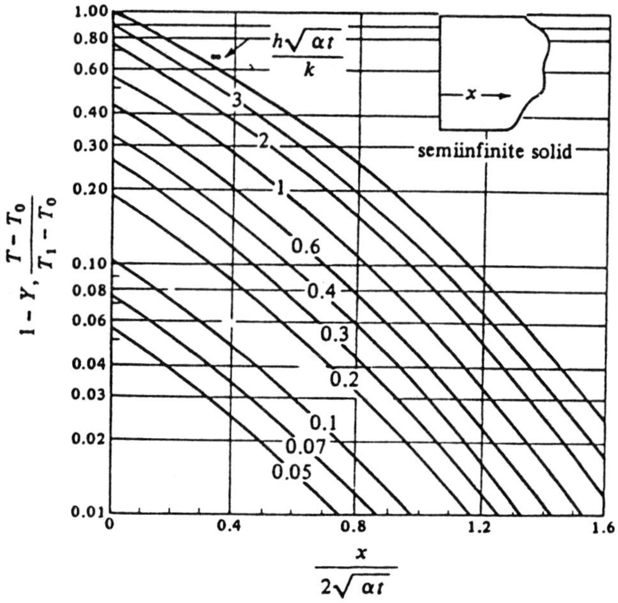

Fig. 2. UNSTEADY-STATE HEAT CONDUCTED IN A SEMIINFINITE SOLID WITH SURFACE CONVECTION.

Solution: In this system the heat transfer is by unsteady-state heat conduction. This is a case of unsteady-state conduction in a semi-infinite solid.

The differential equation governing the given system is:

$$\frac{\partial T}{\partial t} = \frac{k}{\rho C_p} \cdot \frac{\partial^2 T}{\partial x^2}$$

or

$$\frac{\partial T}{\partial t} = \alpha \frac{\partial^2 T}{\partial x^2} \qquad (1)$$

For the conditions given in the problem, the solution of equation (1) is given by:

$$\frac{T - T_0}{T_1 - T_0} = 1 - y = \operatorname{erfc}\left(\frac{x}{2\sqrt{\alpha t}}\right) - \exp\left[\frac{h\sqrt{\alpha t}}{k}\left(\frac{x}{\sqrt{\alpha t}} + \frac{h\sqrt{\alpha t}}{k}\right)\right]\operatorname{erfc}\left(\frac{x}{2\sqrt{\alpha t}} + \frac{h}{k}\sqrt{\alpha t}\right)$$

To obtain the surface temperature, $(T - T_0)/(T_1 - T_0)$ should be calculated.

The value of $(T - T_0)(T_1 - T_0)$ can be determined from fig. 2 if $x/(2\sqrt{\alpha t})$ and $h\sqrt{\alpha t}/k$ are known.

At the surface x = 0 ft.

Then $\frac{x}{2\sqrt{\alpha t}} = 0$

and $\frac{h\sqrt{\alpha t}}{k} = \frac{(3)(\sqrt{(0.02)(5)})}{0.6}$

$= 1.58$

From fig. 2 for $x/(2\sqrt{\alpha t}) = 0$ and $h\sqrt{\alpha t}/k = 1.58$

$$\frac{T - T_0}{T_1 - T_0} = 0.66$$

Given $T_0 = 70^\circ F$ and $T_1 = 5^\circ F$

Then, $\frac{T - 70}{5 - 70} = 0.66$

Therefore, $T = 27.1^\circ F$.

Then, the surface temperature of the soil after 5 hours is $27.1^\circ F$.

In order to find the depth of penetration of the freezing temperature, the value of $x/(2\sqrt{\alpha t})$ must be obtained. The value of $x/(2\sqrt{\alpha t})$ can be determined from fig. 2 if $(T - T_0)/(T_1 - T_0)$ and $h\sqrt{\alpha t}/k$ are known.

Given $T = 32^\circ F$

Then, $\frac{T - T_0}{T_1 - T_0} = \frac{32 - 70}{5 - 70}$

$= 0.585$

and from previous calculations $\frac{h\sqrt{\alpha t}}{k} = 1.58$.

From fig. 2 for $(T - T_0)/(T_1 - T_0) = 0.585$ and $h\sqrt{\alpha t}/k = 1.58$, $x/(2\sqrt{\alpha t}) = 0.1$.

Then, $x = (0.1)(2\sqrt{\alpha t})$

$= (0.1)(2\sqrt{(0.02)(5)})$

$= 0.063$ ft.

Therefore, the depth of penetration of the freezing temperature ($32^\circ F$) into the soil in 5 hours is 0.063 ft.

INFINITE SLAB

• PROBLEM 13-5

A 50 cm. thick brick wall having a thermal diffusivity of 0.005 cm^2/sec is initially at a constant temperature of $25^\circ C$. The temperature of the near face is instantaneously raised and held at $650^\circ C$. If heat flow occurs only perpendicular to the faces of the wall, determine the time required for the perfectly insulated far face of the brick wall to rise from 25°C to 110°C. See figure (1).

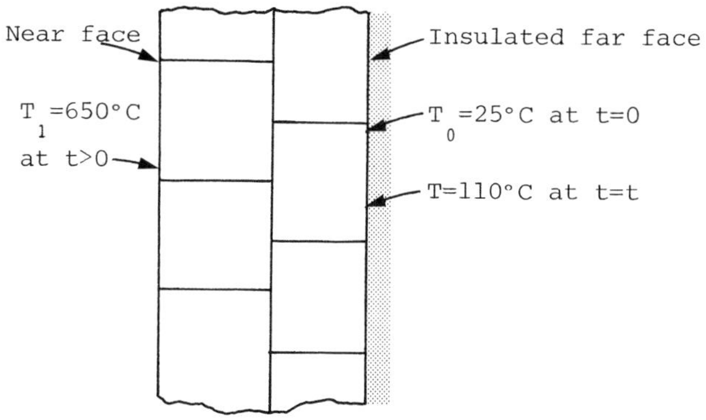

Figure (1)

Solution: In the system given, the heat transfer is by unsteady state conduction. The temperature at any time t and at a distance x away from the near face is given in terms of the complementary error function as:

$$\theta = \sum_{N=0}^{\infty} (-1)^N \cdot \theta' \left[\operatorname{erfc}\left(\frac{2lN + x}{2\sqrt{\alpha t}}\right) + \operatorname{erfc}\left(\frac{2(N+1)l - x}{2\sqrt{\alpha t}}\right)\right] \quad (1)$$

At the far face x = l equation (1) reduces to

$$\theta = \sum_{N=0}^{\infty} (-1)^N \theta' \cdot 2 \cdot \operatorname{erfc}\left[\frac{(2N+1)l}{2\sqrt{\alpha t}}\right] \quad (2)$$

As θ' is constant, equation (2) can be rewritten as:

$$\frac{\theta}{2\theta'} = \sum_{N=0}^{\infty} (-1)^N \cdot \operatorname{erfc}\left[\frac{(2N+1)l}{2\sqrt{\alpha t}}\right] \quad (3)$$

Given $T = 110^\circ C$, $T_0 = 25^\circ C$, $T_1 = 650^\circ C$, $\alpha = 0.005\ cm^2/sec$
$l = 50$ cm.

Substituting the values in equation (3) gives:

$$\frac{110 - 25}{(2)(650 - 25)} = \sum_{N=0}^{\infty} (-1)^N \cdot \operatorname{erfc}\left[\frac{(2N+1)(50)}{2\sqrt{(0.005)t}}\right]$$

where a temperature scale has been employed which causes the initial temperature to be zero.

$$0.068 = \sum_{N=0}^{\infty} (-1)^N \cdot \operatorname{erfc}\left[\frac{(353.6)(2N+1)}{\sqrt{t}}\right]$$

Expanding gives,

$$0.068 = \text{erfc}\left(\frac{353.6}{\sqrt{t}}\right) - \text{erfc}\left(\frac{1060.8}{\sqrt{t}}\right) + \text{erfc}\left(\frac{1768}{\sqrt{t}}\right)$$

The second and higher terms on the right hand side are negligible compared to the first term.

Therefore the equation reduces to:

$$0.068 = \text{erfc}\left(\frac{353.6}{\sqrt{t}}\right)$$

From complementary error function tables for erfc(η) = 0.068, η = 1.3.

$$\text{i.e.,}\quad \frac{353.6}{\sqrt{t}} = 1.3$$

$$(1.3)\ \sqrt{t} = (353.6)$$

$$\sqrt{t} = 272$$

$$t = 73984 \text{ sec.}$$

$$= 20.55 \text{ hr.}$$

Then, the time required for the insulated far face of the brick wall to go from 25°C to 110°C is 20.55 hr.

• PROBLEM 13-6

> The combustion chamber of a rocket-motor has a 7/24 in. thick wall with an initial uniform wall temperature of 90°F. The chamber wall is of alloy steel whose physical properties are k = 25 Btu/hr.ft.°F, ρ = 490 lb/ft^3, c = 0.25 Btu/lb°F and h = heat transfer coefficient = 1100 Btu/hr.ft^2.°F on the flame side. If the combustion gases begin to flow with a temperature of 4600°F after light-off, determine the time the chamber can operate with a temperature less than 2100°F taking the light-off time as t = 0.

Solution: In this system the heat transfer is by unsteady state conduction.

The combustion chamber can be considered as an infinite long flat plate because the wall thickness is very small compared to the diameter. Assume the outer surface of the chamber is well insulated which will give a shorter time and therefore a safer answer than considering the surface as exposed to ambient air. In the transient period the inner surface is the hottest place in the wall.

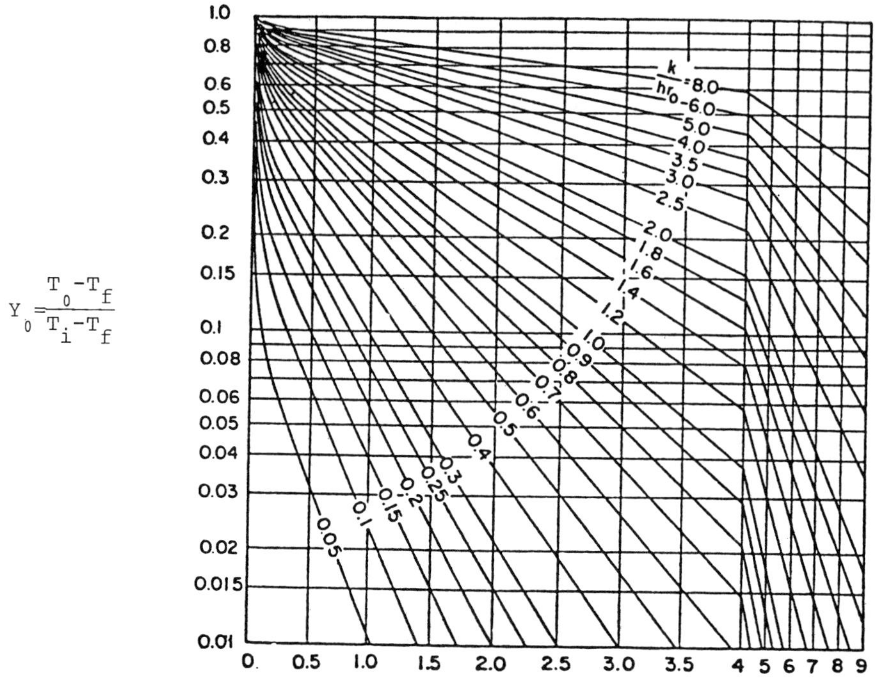

Figure (1) $x = \frac{\alpha t}{r_0^2}$

TEMPERATURE HISTORY AT THE SURFACE OF AN INFINITE SLAB

Figure (1) represents the solution at $x/r_0 = 1$.

Given $r_0 = \frac{7}{24}$ in. = 0.024 ft.

Then,

$$\alpha = \frac{k}{\rho C_p} = \frac{25}{490 \times 0.25}$$

$$= 0.2 \text{ ft}^2/\text{hr}.$$

and

$$\frac{k}{hr_0} = \frac{25}{(1100)(0.024)}$$

$$= 0.947$$

also

$$y = \frac{T_o - T_f}{T_i - T_f}$$

$$= \frac{4600 - 2100}{4600 - 90}$$

$$= 0.554$$

From fig. (1) for y = 0.554 and k/hr_0 = 0.947

$$x = \frac{\alpha t}{r_0^2} = 0.3$$

$$t = (0.3)(0.024)^2/(0.2)$$

$$= 8.64 \times 10^{-4} \text{ hr.}$$

$$= 3.11 \text{ secs.}$$

The chamber can operate for 3.11 secs before the temperature exceeds 2100°F.

• PROBLEM 13-7

Consider an ordinary brick wall which is 12 in. thick, and is initially at 190°F. Suddenly a substance at 70°F is brought in contact with it. The film coefficient is 5 Btu/hr.ft^2.°F. Determine the temperature after 12 hours at a depth of 1 in. Also determine the average temperature of the wall at the end of 12 hours and the heat lost from the wall during 12 hours.

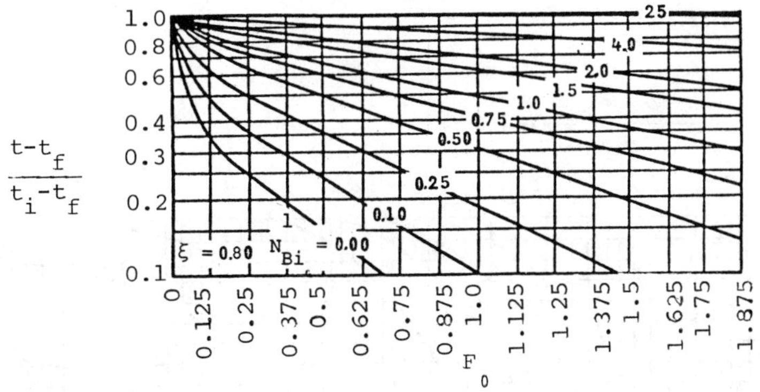

TEMPERATURE-TIME HISTORY IN AN INFINITE SLAB INITIALLY AT TEMPERATURE t_i AND PLACED IN A MEDIUM AT t_f, for ξ=0.8.

Figure (1)

Solution: In this system the heat is transferred from both sides of the wall to the substance.

The physical properties of common brick are

ρ = 110 lb_m/ft^2 $\quad$ C_p = 0.21 Btu/lb_m °F

α = 0.03 ft^2/hr. $\quad$ k = 0.625 Btu/hr.ft.°F

L = 12/2 = 6 in. $\quad$ τ = 12 hours

The Fourier number is given by:

$$F_0 = \frac{\alpha\tau}{L^2}$$

$$= \frac{0.03 \times 12}{(6/12)^2}$$

$$= 1.44$$

The Biot number is given by:

$$B_i = \frac{hL}{k}$$

$$B_i = \frac{(5)(6/12)}{0.625}$$

$$= 4.0$$

$$\xi = \frac{x}{L}$$

$$= \frac{5}{6}$$

$$= 0.833 \simeq 0.8$$

From fig. (1) for $B_i = 4.0$, $\xi = 0.8$, and $F_0 = 1.44$:

$$\frac{t - t_f}{t_i - t_f} = 0.10$$

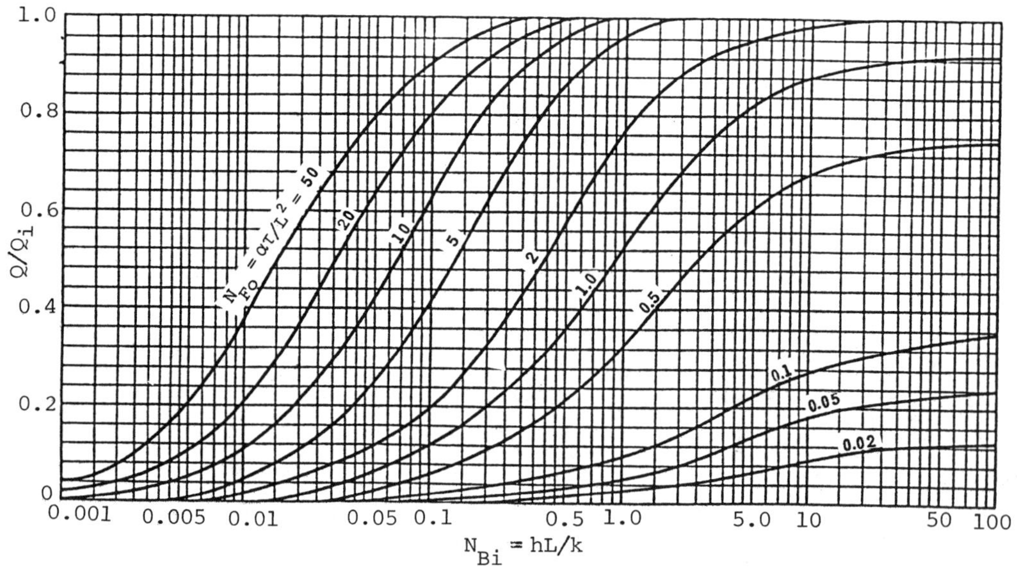

FIG. 2. THE HEAT FLOW FROM AN INFINITE SLAB AS A FUNCTION OF TIME AND THERMAL RESISTANCE. THE SLAB IS INITIALLY AT A UNIFORM TEMPERATURE AND IS PLACED IN A MEDIUM AT CONSTANT TEMPERATURE.

From fig. (2) for $B_i = 4.0$ and $F_0 = 1.44$

$$\frac{Q}{Q_i} = 0.88$$

The heat per unit area stored is given by:

$$\frac{Q_i}{A} = \frac{(12/2)}{12}(110)(0.21)(190 - 70)$$

$$= 1386 \text{ Btu/ft}^2.$$

Then, the temperature at 1 in. depth is given by

$$t = (0.10)(t_i - t_f) + t_f$$

$$= (0.10)(190 - 70) + 70$$

$$= 82^\circ F$$

and

$$\frac{Q}{A} = 0.88 \times 1386$$

$$= 1219.68 \text{ Btu/ft}^2 \text{ from one side.}$$

$$= 2439.4 \text{ Btu/ft}^2 \text{ from both sides.}$$

The heat lost from both sides of the wall during the 12 hours is 2439.4 Btu/ft^2.

The average temperature at the end of 12 hours is given by:

$$t_{av} = (1 - 0.88)(T_i - t_f) + t_f$$

$$= (1 - 0.88)(190 - 70) + 70$$

$$= 84.4^\circ F$$

• PROBLEM 13-8

A ½ in. thick rubber sheet at 80°F has to be cured at 300°F for 60 min. by applying heat from both surfaces. Assume the surfaces are brought to 300°F immediately after the curing is started and maintained there throughout the process. The thermal diffusivity, (α), of rubber is 0.0031 ft^2/hr. Calculate the time required for the center of the sheet to reach 297°F.

Solution: One dimensional unsteady state heat conduction can be represented by the following differential equation.

$$\frac{\partial t}{\partial \theta} = \frac{k}{\rho C_p}\frac{\partial^2 t}{\partial x^2} \tag{1}$$

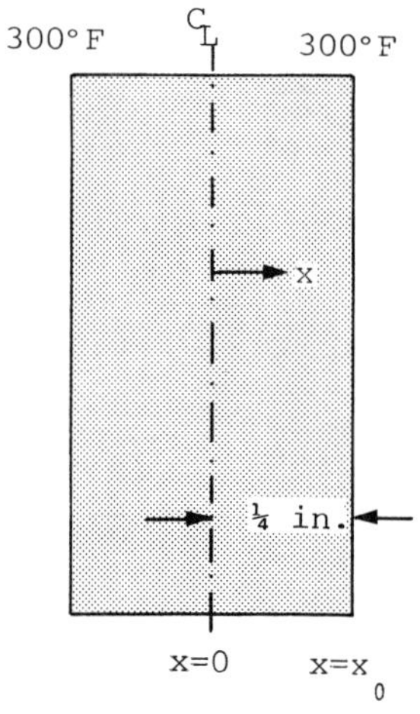

UNSTEADY-STATE HEAT CONDUCTION IN A RUBBER SHEET.

Figure (1)

The center of the sheet is chosen as the origin of the coordinate system.

It is convenient to define dimensionless variables to solve the partial differential equation (1). Let:

$$Y = \frac{300 - t}{300 - 80} \qquad \text{dimensionless temperature}$$

$$\eta = \frac{x}{x_0} \qquad \text{dimensionless distance}$$

$$\tau = \frac{k\theta}{C_p \rho x_0^2} \qquad \text{dimensionless time}$$

where x is the distance from the center of the sheet.

x_0 is half the thickness of the sheet.

Equation (1) in terms of the dimensionless variables can be written as:

$$\frac{\partial Y}{\partial \tau} = \frac{\partial^2 Y}{\partial \eta^2} \tag{2}$$

The solution for equation (2) is a product of two terms, therefore:

$$Y = \tau' N \tag{3}$$

where τ' is a function of only τ and N is a function of only η.

Differentiating equation (3) and substituting in equation (2) gives:

$$N \frac{\partial \tau'}{\partial \tau} = \tau' \frac{\partial^2 N}{\partial \eta^2} \tag{4}$$

Separating variables in eq. (4) gives

$$\frac{1}{\tau} \frac{\partial \tau'}{\partial \tau} = \frac{1}{N} \frac{\partial^2 N}{\partial \eta^2} \tag{5}$$

In eq. (5) the left hand side term is only a function of time and the right hand side term is only a function of distance, hence each term must be equal to a constant. Let the constant be $-a^2$. Then eq. (5) can be written as two ordinary differential equations.

$$\frac{d\tau'}{d\tau} + a^2\tau' = 0 \tag{6}$$

and

$$\frac{d^2 N}{d\eta^2} + a^2 N = 0 \tag{7}$$

The solution of eq. (6) is

$$\tau' = C_1 e^{-a^2 \tau} \tag{8}$$

The solution for the second order, ordinary differential equation (7) can be written as:

$$N = C_2 \sin a\eta + C_3 \cos a\eta \tag{9}$$

Then, the general solution for the partial differential eq. (2) is given by

$$Y = C_1 e^{-a^2 \tau} (C_2 \sin a\eta + C_3 \cos a\eta) \tag{10}$$

$$Y = e^{-a^2 \tau} (A \sin a\eta + B \cos a\eta) \tag{11}$$

where $A = C_1 C_2$ and $B = C_1 C_3$

In equation (11) there are 3 constants A, B and a, which means that three boundary conditions are required to have a complete solution. The boundary conditions are

B.C. (1): There is no heat transfer across the center line of the sheet, because the heat is applied from both the surfaces equally. Therefore $\partial Y/\partial \eta = 0$ at $\eta = 0$.

B.C. (2): The surfaces are maintained at a constant temperature of 300°F at all times. Therefore, $Y = 0$ at $\eta = 1$.

B.C. (3): At $\theta = 0$ the entire sheet is at 80°F. Therefore, $Y = 1$ at $\tau = 0$.

Differentiating eq.(11) partially with respect to η gives

$$\frac{\partial Y}{\partial \eta} = e^{-a^2 \tau} (Aa \cos a\eta - Ba \sin a\eta) \tag{12}$$

Applying B.C. (1) to eq. (12) gives:

$$\left.\frac{\partial Y}{\partial \eta}\right|_{\eta=0} = e^{-a^2\tau}\ (Aa \cos (a \times 0) - Ba \sin (a \times 0)) = 0$$

Therefore,

$$Ae^{-a^2\tau}\ a = 0$$

and $a \neq 0$, because if $a = 0, \sin a\eta = 0$ and $\cos a\eta = 1$ for any η.

Therefore $\quad A = 0$

Now, eq. (11) reduces to

$$Y = Be^{-a^2\tau} \cos a\eta \tag{13}$$

Applying B.C. (2) to eq. (13) gives:

$$Y\Big|_{\eta=1} = Be^{-a^2\tau} \cos a = 0$$

B cannot be zero, because if $B = 0$, $Y = 0$, which is a trivial solution. Therefore $\cos a = 0$.

Therefore $\quad a = (2\eta - 1)\frac{\pi}{2} \quad$ for $\eta = 1, 2, 3, 4 \ldots\ldots$

Therefore the general solution now reduces to

$$Y = \sum_{\eta=0}^{\infty} B_\eta e^{-\left\{(2\eta - 1)\frac{\pi}{2}\right\}^2 \tau} \cos \left\{(2\eta - 1)\frac{\pi}{2}\right\}\eta \tag{14}$$

where η is an integer.

Applying B.C. (3) to eq. (14) gives

$$Y\Big|_{\tau=0} = \sum_{\eta=0}^{\infty} B_\eta e^{-\left\{(2\eta - 1)\frac{\pi}{2}\right\}^2 \times 0}$$

$$\cdot \cos \left\{(2\eta - 1)\frac{\pi}{2}\right\}\eta = 1$$

$$\text{Therefore,}\quad \sum_{\eta=0}^{\infty} B_\eta \cos \left\{(2\eta - 1)\frac{\pi}{2}\right\}\eta = 1 \tag{15}$$

Multiply eq. (15) by $\cos \left[(2i - 1)/2\right]\pi\eta\, d\eta$ and integrate from 0 to 1.

$$\int_0^1 \cos \left[(2i - 1)/2\right]\pi\eta \sum_{\eta=0}^{\infty} B_\eta \cos \left[(2\eta - 1)\frac{\pi}{2}\right]\eta\, d\eta =$$

$$\int_0^1 \cos\left[(2i-1)/2\right]\pi\eta \, d\eta \qquad (16)$$

The first term on the left-hand side can be evaluated using the standard integrals.

$$\int_0^1 B_1 \cos\left(\frac{\pi}{2}\right)\eta \cos\left[(2i-1)/2\right]\pi\eta d\eta = B_1\left[\frac{\sin(i-1)\pi\eta}{(2i-2)\pi} + \frac{\sin i\pi\eta}{2i\pi}\right]_0^1$$

$$= B_1\left[\frac{\sin(i-1)\pi}{(2i-2)\pi} + \frac{\sin i\pi}{2i\pi}\right]$$

$$= 0$$

The above integral is zero for all values of i except 1. All the succeeding terms on the left-hand side vanish in the same way except the ith term. The ith term becomes:

$$\int_0^1 B_i \cos^2\left(\frac{2i-1}{2}\right)\pi\eta \, d\eta = B_i \frac{2}{2i-1}\frac{1}{\pi}\left[\frac{\pi}{2}\frac{2i-1}{2}\eta + \frac{1}{4}\sin(2\pi)\frac{2i-1}{2}\eta\right]_0^1$$

$$= B_i \frac{2}{2i-1}\frac{1}{\pi}\left[\frac{\pi}{2}\frac{2i-1}{2} + 0 - 0 - 0\right]$$

$$= \frac{B_i}{2}$$

The right-hand side of eq. (16) becomes:

$$\int_0^1 \cos\left(\frac{2i-1}{2}\right)\pi\eta \, d\eta = \frac{2}{2i-1}\frac{1}{\pi}\left[\sin\left(\frac{2i-1}{2}\right)\pi\eta\right]_0^1$$

$$= -\frac{2}{2i-1}\frac{1}{\pi}(-1)^i$$

Then, eq. (15) reduces to:

$$\frac{B_i}{2} = -\frac{2}{2i-1}\frac{1}{\pi}(-1)^i$$

Therefore

$$B_i = \frac{-4(-1)^i}{(2i-1)\pi}$$

The general solution is therefore:

$$Y = \sum_{i=1}^{\infty} \frac{-2(-1)^i}{\left[(2i-1)/2\right]\pi} e^{-\left[(2i-1)\frac{\pi}{2}\right]^2\tau} \cos\left[(2i-1)\frac{\pi}{2}\right]\eta \qquad (17)$$

Now eq. (17) can be applied to a specific problem.

$$Y = \frac{300 - 297}{300 - 80} = 0.014$$

$\eta = 0$ at the center

Therefore,

$$0.014 = \frac{4}{\pi} e^{-(\pi/2)^2\tau} - \frac{4}{3\pi} e^{-(3\pi/2)^2\tau} + \frac{4}{5\pi} e^{-(5\pi/2)^2\tau} \ldots .$$

The τ must be obtained by trial and error. As an approximation only the first term on the right hand side will be considered.

Then,

$$\tau = -\left(\frac{2}{\pi}\right)^2 \ln\left(\frac{(\pi)(0.014)}{4}\right)$$

$$= 1.83$$

$$\Theta = \frac{C_p\rho}{k} x_0^{\,2}\tau$$

$$= \frac{1.83}{(0.0031)(48)^2}$$

$$= 0.256 \text{ hr.}$$

$$= 15.36 \text{ min.}$$

To prove the validity of the approximation, check the relative magnitude of the terms in the series solution to see that all the other terms are negligible.

At $\tau = 1.83$,

$$Y = \frac{4}{\pi} e^{-4.51} - \frac{4}{3\pi} e^{-40.64} + \frac{4}{5\pi} e^{-112.9} \ldots .$$

$$= (0.014) - (9.5 \times 10^{-19}) + (2.37 \times 10^{-50}) \ldots$$

A visual inspection of the series indicates that the series is converging rapidly.

The time required for the center of the sheet to reach 297°F is thus 0.256 hr. Eq. (17) can be used to calculate the temperature at any point and time in the rubber sheet by substituting appropriate η and τ.

SHORT CYLINDERS AND SPHERES

• PROBLEM 13-9

An 8.0 cm. outer diameter and 12 cm. long short cylinder is initially at a uniform temperature of 270°C. At time zero the cylinder is placed in a convective environment at $50^{\circ}C$ with $h = 410\ W/m^2.K$. The physical properties of the cylinder are:

$\alpha = 0.048\ m^2/hr$ and $k = 39\ W/m^{\circ}K$

Determine the temperature at the center of the cylinder after 5 minutes.

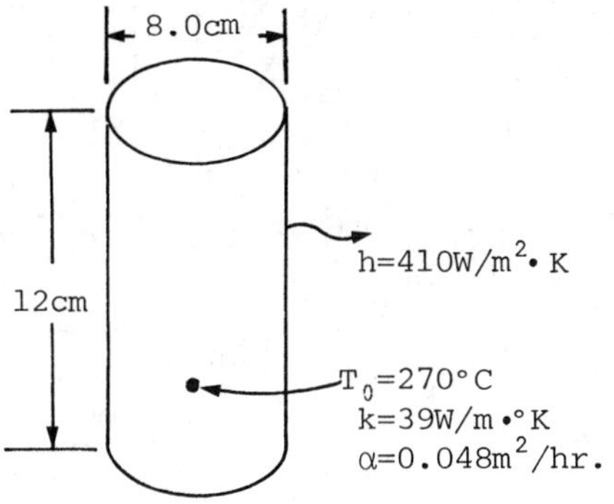

Figure (1)

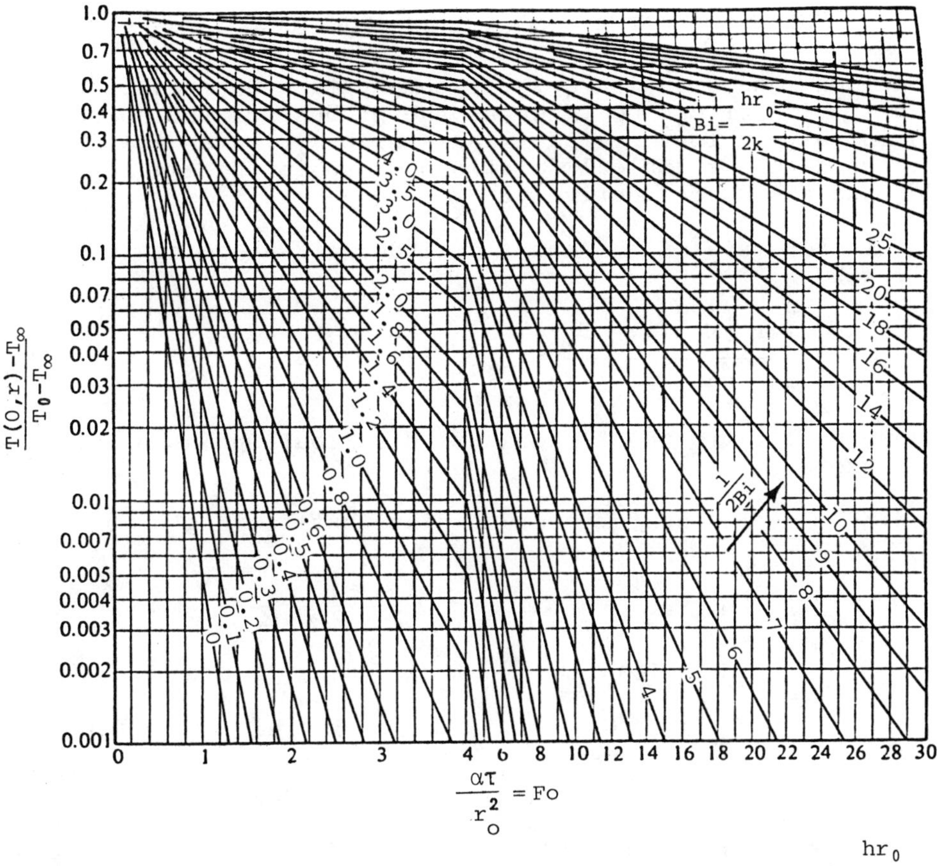

Fig. 2. AXIS TEMPERATURE FOR A LONG CYLINDER OF RADIUS, r_0, $Bi = \frac{hr_0}{2k}$

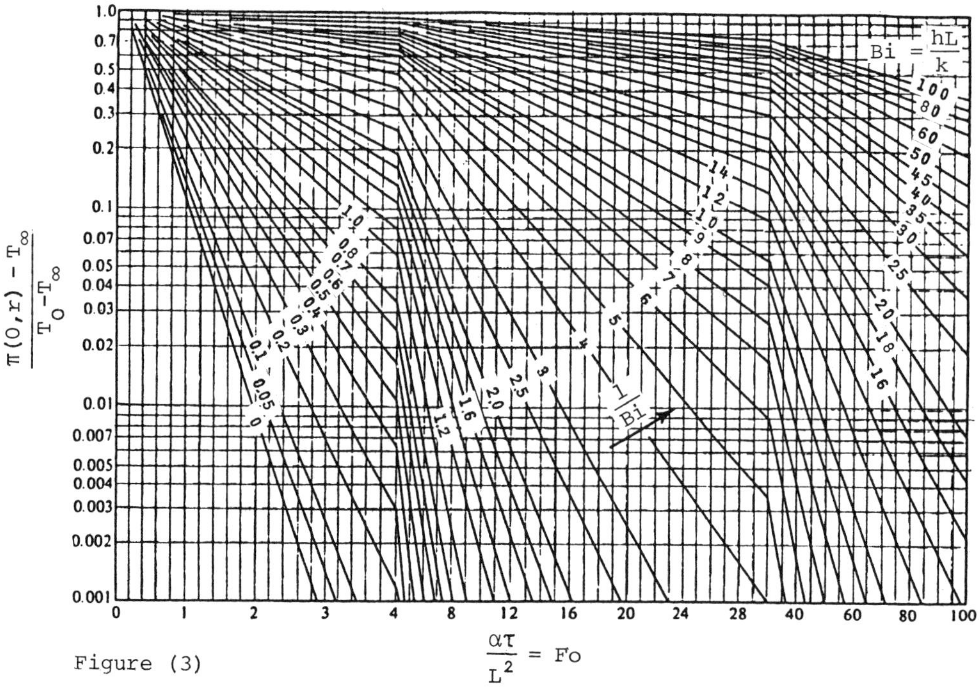

Figure (3)

CENTERLINE TEMPERATURE FOR A SLAB OF THICKNESS, 2L, $Bi=\frac{hL}{k}$

<u>Solution</u>: The solution for the temperature distribution in the short cylinder can be taken as the product of the solutions of an infinitely long cylinder and a slab. Figures (2) and (3) represent the graphical solutions of an infinitely long cylinder and a slab respectively.

The temperature of the short cylinder at any point and time is given by

$$\frac{T(r,\ x,\ \tau) - T_\infty}{T_0 - T_\infty} = C(r,\ \tau)S(x,\ \tau) \tag{1}$$

where $C(r, \tau)$ is the temperature distribution in an infinite cylinder.

and $S(x, \tau)$ is the temperature distribution in a slab.

Given: $L = \frac{12}{2} = 6$ cm. $\qquad r_0 = \frac{D}{2} = \frac{8.0}{2} = 4$ cm.

$h = 410\ W/m^2.{}^\circ K \qquad T_0 = 270^\circ C$

$T_\infty = 50^\circ C \qquad \tau = 5$ min. $= \frac{5}{60} = 0.0833$ hr.

$\alpha = 0.048\ m^2/hr. \qquad k = 39\ W/m.{}^\circ K$

For an infinitely long cylinder:

The Biot number is given by,

$$B_i = \frac{hr_0}{2k}$$

$$= \frac{(410)(0.04)}{2(39)}$$

$$= 0.21$$

$$\frac{1}{2B_i} = \frac{1}{2(0.21)} = 2.38$$

The Fourier number is given by

$$F_0 = \frac{\alpha\tau}{r_0^2}$$

$$= \frac{(0.048)(0.0833)}{(0.04)^2}$$

$$= 2.5$$

From figure (2),

for $d\tau/r_0^2 = 2.5$ and $\frac{1}{2B_i} = 2.38$

$$C(0,\tau) = \frac{T(0,\tau) - T_\infty}{T_0 - T_\infty} = 0.145 \qquad (2)$$

For an infinitely long slab:

The Biot number is given by

$$B_i = \frac{hL}{k}$$

$$= \frac{(410)(0.06)}{39}$$

$$= 0.631$$

$$\frac{1}{B_i} = \frac{1}{0.631}$$

$$= 1.585$$

The Fourier number is given by,

$$F_o = \frac{\alpha\tau}{L^2}$$

$$= \frac{(0.048)(0.0833)}{(0.06)^2}$$

$$= 1.11$$

From figure (3),

for $\alpha\tau/L^2 = 1.11$ and $\frac{1}{B_i} = 1.585$

$$S(0,\tau) = \frac{T(0,\tau) - T_\infty}{T_0 - T_\infty} = 0.61 \tag{3}$$

The temperature at the center of the short cylinder is given by

$$\frac{T(0,0,\tau) - T_\infty}{T_0 - T_\infty} = C(0,\tau)S(0,\tau) \tag{4}$$

Substituting eqs. (2) and (3) in eq. (4) gives:

$$\frac{T(0,0,\tau) - T_\infty}{T_0 - T_\infty} = (0.145)(0.61)$$

$$= 0.088$$

Therefore,

$$T(0,0,5 \text{ min}) = 0.088\ (T_0 - T_\infty) + T_\infty$$

$$= 0.088\ (270 - 50) + 50$$

$$= 69.36^\circ C$$

Then, the temperature at the center of the short cylinder is $69.36^\circ C$ after 5 minutes.

• PROBLEM 13-10

> Determine the time required to reach $550^\circ F$ at the center of a cylindrical stainless steel (18% Cr, 8% Ni) bar which is 10 in. in diameter, if it is heated to $1850^\circ F$ and then quenched in an oil tank at $105^\circ F$ with a film coefficient of 110 Btu/hr.ft^2.$^\circ F$.

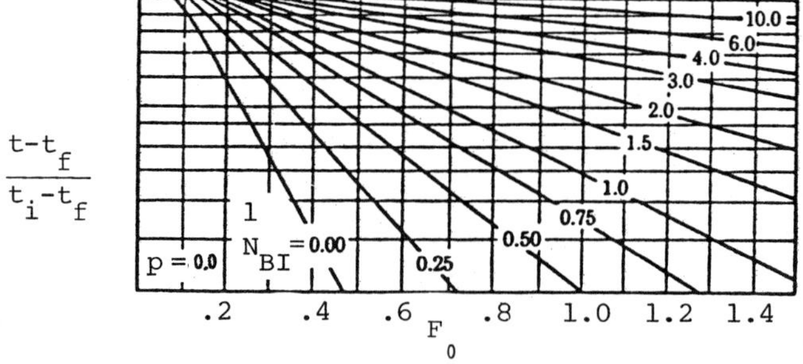

Fig. 1. TEMPERATURE-TIME HISTORY IN A SOLID CYLINDER INITIALLY AT TEMPERATURE t_i, AND PLACED IN A MEDIUM AT t_f, for ρ=0.0, 0.2, AND 0.4.

Solution: In this system the heat transfer is by convection.

The physical properties of stainless steel (18% Cr, 8% Ni) are:

$$\rho = 489 \text{ lb/ft}^3 \qquad \alpha = 0.175 \text{ ft}^2\text{/hr.}$$

$$k = 9.5 \text{ Btu/hr.ft.}^\circ\text{F}$$

The Biot number is given by:

$$B_i = \frac{hR}{k}$$

$$= \frac{(110)(5/12)}{(9.5)}$$

$$= 4.82$$

$$\frac{1}{B_i} = \frac{1}{4.82} = 0.207$$

and $$\frac{t - t_f}{t_i - t_f} = \frac{550 - 105}{1850 - 105}$$

$$= 0.255$$

From figure (1),

for $$\frac{1}{B_i} = 0.207 \qquad \text{and} \qquad \frac{t - t_f}{t_i - t_f} = 0.255$$

$$F_0 = 0.43$$

The Fourier number is given by:

$$F_0 = \frac{\alpha\tau}{R^2}$$

$$0.43 = \frac{(0.175)\tau}{(5/12)^2}$$

Therefore, $\tau = 0.427$ hr.

Then, the time required to reach 550°F at the center of the bar is 0.427 hr.

• PROBLEM 13-11

A 2 in. radius pure copper sphere and a pure copper cube of side 2 in. are heated to 1250°F and then exposed to air at 210°F. The surface film coefficient is 12 Btu/hr.ft^2.$^\circ$F. Determine the temperature of both the sphere and the cube after a period of 10 minutes.

Solution: In this system the heat transfer is by unsteady state convection.

The physical properties of pure copper are:

$$\rho = 560\ lb_m/ft^3 \qquad C_p = 0.0916\ Btu/lb_m\,^{\circ}F$$

For the sphere:

$$\text{Volume,} \quad V = \frac{4}{3}\pi r^3$$

$$\text{Area,} \quad A = 4\pi r^2$$

Therefore,
$$\frac{V}{A} = \frac{(4/3)\pi r^3}{4\pi r^2}$$

$$= \frac{r}{3}$$

$$= \frac{2}{3}\ \text{in.}$$

The time constant is given by,

$$\theta = \frac{\rho C_p V}{hA}$$

$$= \frac{(560)(0.0916)(2)}{(12)(3)(12)}$$

$$= 0.237\ \text{hr.}$$

At $\tau = 10$ min.

$$\frac{\tau}{\phi} = \frac{(10/60)}{0.237} = 0.703$$

The temperature of the sphere after 10 min. is given by:

$$\frac{t - t_i}{t_s - t_i} = e^{-(\tau/\phi)}$$

$$\frac{t - 210}{1250 - 210} = e^{-0.703} = 0.495$$

Therefore, $t = 725^{\circ}F$.

For the cube:

$$\text{Volume,} \quad V = d^3$$

$$\text{Area,} \quad A = 6d^2$$

$$\text{Therefore,} \quad \frac{V}{A} = \frac{d^3}{6d^2}$$

$$= \frac{d}{6}$$

$$= \frac{2}{6} = \frac{1}{3} \text{ in.}$$

The time constant is given by,

$$\phi = \frac{\rho C_p V}{hA}$$

$$= \frac{(560)(0.0916)}{(12)(3)(12)}$$

$$= 0.119 \text{ hr.}$$

$$\text{At } \tau = 10 \text{ min.}$$

$$\frac{\tau}{\phi} = \frac{(10/60)}{0.119}$$

$$= 1.40$$

The temperature of the cube after 10 min. is given by:

$$\frac{t-t_i}{t_s-t_i} = e^{-(\tau/\phi)}$$

$$\frac{t-210}{1250-210} = e^{-1.40}$$

$$\frac{t-210}{1250-210} = 0.247$$

Therefore, $t = 467^\circ F$.

• PROBLEM 13-12

A solid sphere of radius R initially at a uniform temperature T_0 is suddenly placed in a bath at a temperature T_∞. Determine the unsteady temperature of the sphere if the heat transfer coefficient is (a) large and (b) moderate.

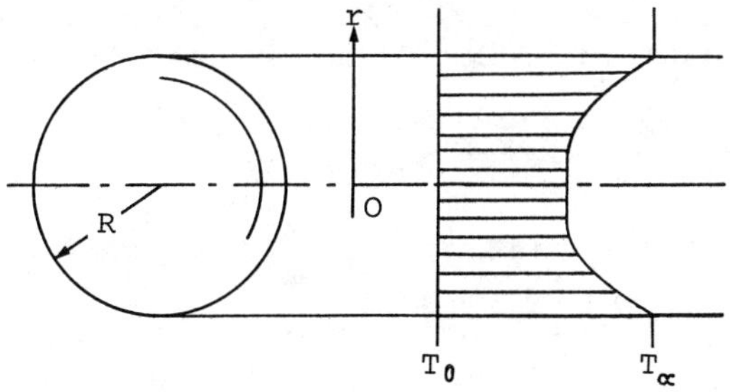

Solution: Define $\theta = T - T_\infty$

The governing differential equation in spherical coordinates is,

$$\frac{\partial\theta}{\partial t} = \frac{a}{r^2}\frac{\partial}{\partial r}\left(r^2 \frac{\partial\theta}{\partial r}\right) \tag{1}$$

The initial condition is,

$$\theta(r,0) = \theta_0$$

The following transformation is used to reduce the spherical Laplacian form of eq. (1) to the cartesian Laplacian form.

$$\theta(r,t) = \psi(r,t)/r$$

Now, eq. (1) reduces to:

$$\frac{\partial\psi}{\partial t} = a\frac{\partial^2\psi}{\partial r^2} \tag{2}$$

The initial condition becomes,

$$\psi(r,0) = r\theta_0$$

(a) For a large heat transfer coefficient:

The boundary conditions are,

1. $\psi(0,t) = 0$

2. $\psi(R,t) = 0$

Assume the solution of eq. (2) is the product of two simple solutions.

$$\psi(r,t) = R(r)\tau(t) \tag{3}$$

Differentiating eq. (3) and substituting in eq. (2) gives,

$$R(r)\frac{d\tau}{dt} = a\ \tau(t)\frac{d^2R}{dr^2}$$

Separating variables,

$$\frac{1}{\tau(t)}\frac{d\tau}{dt} = \frac{a}{R(r)}\frac{d^2R}{dr^2} \tag{4}$$

The left term of eq. (4) is only a function of t and the right term is only a function of r. The equality holds only if both are equal to a constant. Let the constant be $-a\lambda^2$. Therefore

$$\frac{1}{\tau(t)}\frac{d\tau}{dt} = \frac{a}{R(r)}\frac{d^2R}{dr^2} = -a\lambda^2$$

Then, the two ordinary differential eqs. can be written as,

$$\frac{d^2R}{dr^2} + \lambda^2R = 0 \tag{5}$$

$$\frac{d\tau}{dt} + a\lambda^2\tau = 0 \qquad (6)$$

The boundary conditions for eq. (5) are,

$$R(0) = 0 \quad \text{and} \quad R(R) = 0$$

The boundary condition for eq. (6) is,

$$\tau(0) = r\theta_0$$

The solution of eq. (5) is,

$$R_n(r) = A_n\phi_n(r)$$

$$\phi_n(r) = \sin \lambda_n r \qquad \text{characteristic functions}$$

$$\lambda_n R = n\pi \quad n = 1, 2, 3 \qquad \text{characteristic values}$$

The solution of eq. (6) is,

$$\tau_n(t) = C_n e^{-a\lambda_n^2 t}$$

Substituting in eq. (3) gives,

$$\psi(r,t) = \sum_{n=1}^{\infty} a_n e^{-a\lambda_n^2 t} \sin \lambda_n r$$

Applying the initial condition,

$$\psi(r,0) = \sum_{n=1}^{\infty} a_n e^{-a\lambda_n^2 (0)} \sin \lambda_n r = r\theta_0$$

$$r\theta_0 = \sum_{n=1}^{\infty} a_n \sin \lambda_n r$$

The coefficient a_n can be evaluated using a Fourier series as

$$a_n = (-1)^{n+1} \frac{2\theta_0}{\lambda_n}$$

Now the general solution becomes

$$\psi(r,t) = 2 \sum_{n=1}^{\infty} (-1)^{n+1} e^{-a\lambda_n^2 t} \frac{\sin \lambda_n r}{\lambda_n r}$$

Now, the unsteady temperature of the sphere is:

$$\frac{T(r,t) - T_\infty}{T_0 - T_\infty} = 2 \sum_{n=1}^{\infty} (-1)^{n+1} e^{-a\lambda_n^2 t} \frac{\sin \lambda_n r}{\lambda_n r}$$

(b) For a moderate heat transfer coefficient:

The boundary conditions are,

1. $\psi(r,0) = r\theta_0$

2. $-k \frac{\partial\psi(R,t)}{\partial r} = (h - \frac{k}{R})\psi(R,t)$

Assumption of a product solution gives two ordinary differential equations as in the previous case.

$$\frac{d^2 R}{dr} + \lambda^2 R = 0 \tag{7}$$

$$\frac{dT}{dt} + a\lambda^2 R = 0 \tag{8}$$

The boundary conditions for eq. (7) are,

$$R(0) = 0 \quad \text{and} \quad \frac{dR(R)}{dr} + \left(\frac{h}{k} - \frac{1}{R}\right) R(R) = 0$$

The solution for eq. (7) is,

$$R_n(r) = A_n \sin \lambda_n r$$

where $\sin \lambda_n r$ are characteristic functions.

and $(\lambda_n R)\cos \lambda_n R = (1 - B_i) \sin \lambda_n R$

where $B_i = hR/k$ are characteristic values.

The solution for eq. (8) is given as,

$$\tau(t) = C_n e^{-a\lambda_n^2 t}$$

Now the solution for eq. (2) is,

$$\psi(r,t) = \sum_{n=1}^{\infty} a_n e^{-a\lambda_n^2 t} \sin \lambda_n r$$

Applying the initial condition,

$$\psi(r,0) = \sum_{n=1}^{\infty} a_n \sin \lambda_n r = r\theta_0$$

Then, the coefficient a_n is given by,

$$a_n = \frac{2\theta_0(\sin \lambda_n R - \lambda_n R \cos \lambda_n R)}{\lambda_n(\lambda_n R - \sin \lambda_n R \cos \lambda_n R)}$$

The general solution of eq. (2) is,

$$\psi(r,t) = 2 \sum_{n=1}^{\infty} \left(\frac{\sin \lambda_n R - \lambda_n R \cos \lambda_n R}{\lambda_n R - \sin \lambda_n R \cos \lambda_n R} \right) e^{-a\lambda_n^2 t} \cdot \frac{\sin \lambda_n r}{\lambda_n}$$

Hence, the unsteady temperature is given by,

$$\frac{T(r,t) - T_\infty}{T_0 - T_\infty} = 2 \sum_{n=1}^{\infty} \left(\frac{\sin \lambda_n R - \lambda_n R \cos \lambda_n R}{\lambda_n R - \sin \lambda_n R \cos \lambda_n R} \right) e^{-a\lambda_n^2 t} \cdot \frac{\sin \lambda_n r}{\lambda_n r}$$

• PROBLEM 13-13

Deduce the differential energy balance equation in spherical coordinates for heating a sphere, if the temperature variation in angular position is zero.

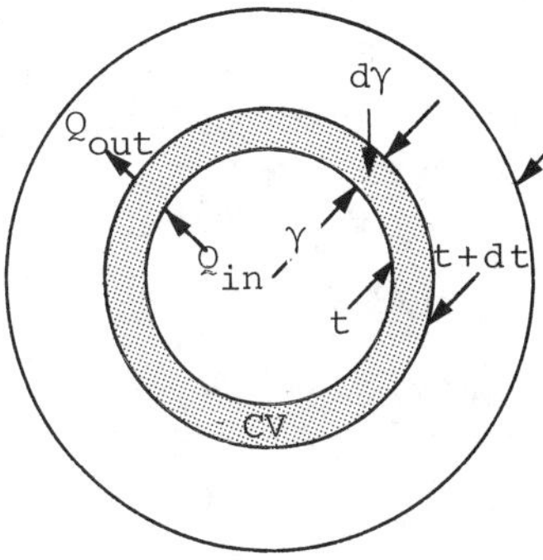

Figure (1)

Solution: As the variation of temperature in angular position is zero, the only possible variation of temperature is in the radial direction.

Let the origin of the coordinate system be the center of the sphere.

The spherical surface at a radial distance r from the center is at a uniform temperature t.

The spherical surface at a radial distance r + dr from the center is at a uniform temperature t + dt.

Consider the control volume with the above two spherical surfaces as boundaries.

The heat flow entering the control volume is given by,

$$Q_{in} = -k(4\pi r^2) \frac{\partial t}{\partial r} \qquad (1)$$

The heat flowing out of the control volume is given by,

$$Q_{out} = -k4\pi(r + dr)^2 \frac{\partial(t + dt)}{\partial r} \tag{2}$$

The net heat gained by the control volume can be obtained by subtracting eq. (2) from eq. (1).

$$Q_{net} = 4\pi k \left[r^2 \frac{\partial^2 t}{\partial r^2} dr + 2rdr \left(\frac{\partial t}{\partial r} + \frac{\partial^2 t}{\partial r^2} dr\right) + dr^2\left(\frac{\partial t}{\partial r} + \frac{\partial^2 t}{\partial r^2} dr\right)\right] \tag{3}$$

The second and third order differentials in eq. (3) can be neglected, therefore:

$$Q_{net} = 4\pi k \left[r^2 \frac{\partial^2 t}{\partial r^2} dr + 2rdr \frac{\partial t}{\partial r}\right] \tag{4}$$

The rate of energy accumulation in the control volume is given by,

$$E = (4\pi r^2 dr)\rho C_p \frac{\partial t}{\partial \theta} \tag{5}$$

But, the energy accumulated has to be equal to the heat gained by the control volume, therefore:

$$4\pi k \left[r^2 \frac{\partial^2 t}{\partial r^2} dr + 2rdr \frac{\partial t}{\partial r}\right] = (4\pi r^2 dr)\rho C_p \frac{\partial t}{\partial \theta} \tag{6}$$

Dividing eq. (6) by $(4\pi r^2 dr)$ gives,

$$\frac{k}{r^2}\left[r^2 \frac{\partial^2 t}{\partial r^2} + 2r \frac{\partial t}{\partial r}\right] = \rho C_p \frac{\partial t}{\partial \theta} \tag{7}$$

Again dividing throughout by ρC_p gives the differential energy equation for unsteady conduction as:

$$\frac{\partial t}{\partial \theta} = \frac{k}{\rho C_p}\left[\frac{\partial^2 t}{\partial r^2} + \frac{2}{r}\frac{\partial t}{\partial r}\right]$$

• PROBLEM 13-14

Water, while being filled in a cylindrical tank from time $t = 0$, is heated by means of a coil carrying heating oil. The tank has a stirrer which maintains the temperature uniform. The area available for heat transfer is proportional to the volume of water in the tank. Estimate the water temperature when the tank is filled.

Solution: Let A_t = total area available

A = instantaneous heat-transfer area

V_t = total volume of tank

V = instantaneous volume of water in tank

T = instantaneous temperature

T_i = temperature of water at inlet

T_2 = temperature of water in filled tank

T_o = temperature of heating oil

θ_o = time required to fill the tank

$\dot{m}$ = mass flow rate of water

$$\therefore \quad \theta_o = \frac{\rho V_o}{\dot{m}}$$

Taking the water inside the tank as the system, and the inlet temperature as the datum,

$$\rho C_p \frac{d}{d\theta}\left[V(T - T_i)\right] = uA(T_o - T) \qquad (1)$$

where u is the overall heat transfer coefficient

since $V = \frac{\dot{m}\theta}{\rho}$ and $A = \frac{\dot{m}\theta}{\rho V_t} A_t$, (1) can be written as

$$\rho C_p \left[(T - T_i)\frac{\dot{m}}{\rho} + \frac{\dot{m}\theta}{\rho}\frac{d(T - T_i)}{d\theta}\right] = \frac{u\dot{m}\theta}{\rho V_t} A_t (T_o - T) \qquad (2)$$

$$\text{or} \quad \dot{m}C_p(T - T_i) + \dot{m}C_p\theta \frac{d(T - T_i)}{d\theta} = \frac{u\dot{m}\theta A_t}{\rho V_t}(T_o - T) \qquad (3)$$

Initial condition: at $\theta = 0$, $T = T_i$

$$\text{Defining} \quad \phi = \frac{T - T_i}{T_o - T_i}, \quad \frac{d(T - T_i)}{d\theta} = (T_o - T_i)\frac{d\phi}{d\theta}$$

and

$$\tau = \frac{\theta}{\theta_o} = \frac{\dot{m}\theta}{\rho V_o}, \quad d\theta = \frac{\rho V_o}{\dot{m}} d\tau$$

$$\frac{d(T - T_i)}{d\theta} = (T_o - T_i)\frac{d\phi}{d\theta} = \dot{m}\frac{(T_o - T_i)}{\rho V_o}\frac{d\phi}{d\tau}$$

$$(T - T_i) = \phi(T_o - T_i)$$

$\therefore$ Equation (3) becomes

$$\dot{m}C_p(T_o - T_i)\phi + \dot{m}C_p\theta \cdot \frac{\dot{m}(T_o - T_i)}{\rho V_o}\frac{d\phi}{d\tau} = \frac{u\dot{m}\theta A_t}{\rho V_t}(T_o - T_i)(1 - \phi)$$

$$\therefore \quad \phi + \frac{\theta \dot{m}}{\rho V_o} \cdot \frac{d\phi}{d\tau} = \frac{uA_t}{C_p \rho V_t}(1 - \phi)$$

$$\text{or} \quad \phi + \tau \frac{d\phi}{d\tau} = C_1(1 - \phi) \tag{4}$$

Redefining $\tau' = C_1\tau$, eq. (4) reduces to

$$\phi + \tau' \frac{d\phi}{d\tau'} = (1 - \phi)$$

$$\text{or} \quad \frac{d\phi}{d\tau'} + \left(1 + \frac{1}{\tau'}\right)\phi = 1 \tag{5}$$

Initial condition: at $\tau' = 0$, $\phi = 0$

(5) is a I-order differential equation whose solution is

$$\phi = 1 - \frac{1}{\tau'} + \frac{C_2}{\tau' \exp \tau'}$$

Using the I.C., we get $C_2 = 1$

$$\therefore \quad \phi = 1 - \frac{1 - \exp(-\tau')}{\tau'} \tag{6}$$

$$\therefore \quad \frac{T - T_i}{T_o - T_i} = 1 - \frac{1 - \exp\left(-\frac{uA_t}{C_p \rho V_t} \cdot \frac{\dot{m}\theta}{\rho V_o}\right)}{\frac{uA_t}{C_p \rho V_t} \cdot \frac{\dot{m}\theta}{\rho V_o}} \tag{7}$$

This gives the temperature of the water at any time θ.

To find the temperature, T_f when the tank is full, i.e., $\tau = 1$ or $\tau' = C_1$

$$\therefore \quad \frac{T_f - T_i}{T_o - T_i} = 1 - \frac{1 - \exp\left(-\frac{uA_t}{C_p \rho V_t}\right)}{\frac{uA_t}{C_p \rho V_t}}$$

• PROBLEM 13-15

Hot oil passing inside a coil of tubes inside a well-stirred tank heats the contents from an entering temperature of T_{in}. Assume the stirring is so efficient that the exit temperature is the same as that inside the tank. If the temperature of the outer surface of the heating coil is T_o, derive expression for the temperature profile as a function of time. What is the temperature for $t = \infty$?

Solution: Take the exit temperature as the datum.

Energy into the system (contents of the tank) = $\dot{m}(T_{in} - T)C_p + uA(T_o - T)$

$$\therefore \quad V_t C_p \rho \frac{dT}{dt} = \dot{m}(T_{in} - T)C_p + uA(T_o - T)$$

Initial condition: At $t = 0$, $T = T_{in}$

Defining $\phi = \dfrac{T - T_{in}}{T_o - T_{in}}$, and $\theta = \dfrac{\dot{m}t}{\rho V_t}$, we get

$$\frac{dT}{dt} = \frac{\dot{m}}{V_t \rho}(T_{in} - T) + \frac{uA}{V_t C_p \rho}(T_o - T)$$

$$\frac{\dot{m}(T_o - T_{in})}{\rho V_t}\frac{d\phi}{d\theta} = \left[-\frac{\dot{m}}{V_t \rho}\phi + \frac{uA}{V_t C_p \rho}(1 - \phi)\right](T_o - T_{in})$$

or
$$\frac{\dot{m}}{\rho V_t}\frac{d\phi}{d\theta} = \left[-\frac{\dot{m}}{V_t \rho}\phi + \frac{uA}{V_t C_p \rho}(1 - \phi)\right]$$

Denoting $\dfrac{\dot{m}}{\rho V_t} = C_1$ and $\dfrac{uA}{V_t C_p \rho} = C_2$, we get

$$C_1 \frac{d\phi}{d\theta} = -C_1\phi + C_2(1 - \phi)$$

$$= -\phi\left[C_1 + C_2\right] + C_2$$

or
$$\frac{d\phi}{d\theta} = -\frac{(C_1 + C_2)}{C_1}\phi + \frac{C_2}{C_1}$$

$$\therefore \quad \frac{d\phi}{-\dfrac{(C_1 + C_2)\phi}{C_1} + \dfrac{C_2}{C_1}} = d\theta$$

$$\therefore \quad \frac{-C_1}{C_1 + C_2}\ln\left(\frac{C_2}{C_1} - \frac{C_1 + C_2}{C_1}\phi\right) = \theta + C_3$$

at $t = 0$, $\theta = 0$, $T = T_{in}$, $\phi = 0$

$$\therefore \quad C_3 = -\frac{C_1}{C_1 + C_2}\ln\frac{C_2}{C_1}$$

$$\therefore \quad \theta = \frac{C_1}{C_1 + C_2}\left[\ln\frac{C_2}{C_1} - \ln\left(\frac{C_2}{C_1} - \frac{C_1 + C_2}{C_1}\phi\right)\right]$$

$$= \frac{C_1}{C_1 + C_2} \cdot \ln\left(\frac{C_2}{C_2 - (C_1 + C_2)\phi}\right)$$

$$\frac{C_1}{C_1 + C_2} \ln\left(\frac{C_2 - (C_1 + C_2)\phi}{C_2}\right) = -\theta$$

As $\theta \to \infty, \quad \frac{C_2 - (C_1 + C_2)\phi}{C_2} \to 0$

or $\phi \to \frac{C_2}{C_1 + C_2} \to \frac{uA/V_t C_p \rho}{\frac{uA}{V_t C_p \rho} + \frac{\dot{m}}{\rho V_t}} = \frac{uA/C_p}{\frac{uA}{C_p} + \dot{m}}$

or $\frac{T - T_{in}}{T_o - T_{in}} = \frac{uA/C_p}{\frac{uA}{C_p} + \dot{m}}$

WIRE, INFINITE SLAB AND LARGE SLAB

• PROBLEM 13-16

A 1/32 in. diameter copper wire is heated to 350°F and then is suddenly immersed in (a) water at 110°F and h = 20 Btu/hr.ft^2.°F and (b) air at 110°F and h = 3 Btu/hr.ft^2.°F. Determine the temperature response in both cases.

Solution: In both cases the heat transfer is by unsteady state convection.

The physical properties of copper are:

$k = 217$ Btu/hr.ft.°F $\qquad C = 0.092$ Btu/lb°F

$\rho = 560$ lb/ft^3

The surface area of wire per inch of length is:

$$A_s = \pi D = \frac{1}{12}\pi \times \frac{1}{32 \times 12} = 6.82 \times 10^{-4} \text{ ft}^2$$

The volume of wire per inch of length is:

$$V = \pi D^2/4$$

$$= \frac{\pi}{4} \times \left(\frac{1}{32 \times 12}\right)^2$$

$$= 5.33 \times 10^{-6}\ ft^3$$

(a) When immersed in water:

The Biot number is given by,

$$Bi = \frac{hD}{4k}$$

$$= \frac{(20) \times \left(\frac{1}{32 \times 12}\right)}{(4)(217)} \ll 0.1$$

Therefore, the internal resistance can be neglected, and the following eq. can be used to determine the temperature response.

$$\frac{T - T_\infty}{T_o - T_\infty} = e^{-(hA/\rho CV)t}$$

$$T(t) = T_\infty + (T_o - T_\infty)\, e^{-(hA/\rho CV)t}$$

Substituting the known values,

$$T(t) = 110 + (350 - 110)\, e^{-\left(\frac{20 \times 6.82 \times 10^{-4}}{560 \times 0.092 \times 5.33 \times 10^{-6}}\right)t}$$

$$T(t) = 110 + 240\, e^{-(49.67)t} \qquad (1)$$

Equation (1) represents the temperature response when immersed in water.

(b) When exposed to air:

$$Bi = \frac{(3)\left[\frac{1}{(32)(12)}\right]}{(4)(217)}$$

$$\ll 0.1$$

Therefore the temperature response is given by,

$$T(t) = 110 + (350 - 110)\, e^{-\left(\frac{3 \times 6.82 \times 10^{-4}}{560 \times 0.092 \times 5.33 \times 10^{-6}}\right)t}$$

$$T(t) = 110 + 240\, e^{-(7.45)t}$$

From the temperature response eqs. in the two cases, it can be concluded that the cooling in water is much faster than in air.

Calculate the time required to raise the temperature of the insulated face of a concrete wall 1.5 ft. thick from 110°F to 1150°F. The wall was initially at a uniform temperature of 110°F and when one side was suddenly exposed to hot gases at 1650°F. The other side is insulated. The hot side heat transfer coefficient is 6 Btu/hr. ft^2.°F.

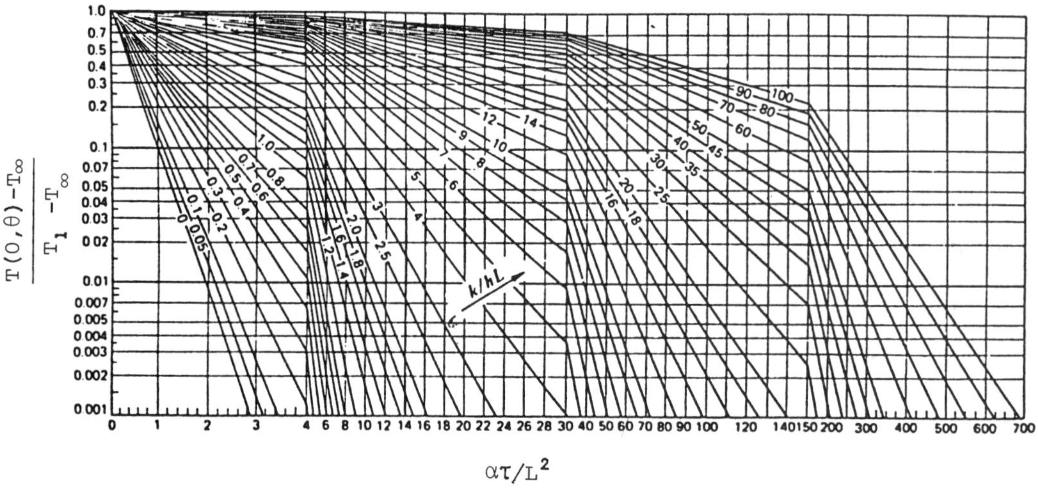

MIDPLANE TEMPERATURE FOR AN INFINITE PLATE OF THICKNESS 2L.

Figure (1)

Solution: In this system the heat transfer is by unsteady state conduction in the concrete wall.

The physical properties of concrete are

$k = 0.55$ Btu/hr.ft.°F $C = 0.21$ Btu/lb°F

$\rho = 145$ lb/ft^3 $\alpha = 0.0188$ ft^2/hr.

This problem can be solved by using fig. (1), which gives the midplane temperature for an infinite plate of thickness 2L.

It can be assumed that the insulated face is the center plane of a slab of thickness 2L. Then at $x = 0$, $\partial T/\partial x = 0$.

Therefore the temperature ratio at the insulated face is:

$$\left.\frac{T - T_\infty}{T_i - T_\infty}\right|_{x=0} = \frac{1150 - 1650}{110 - 1650}$$

$$= 0.325$$

The Biot number is given by,

$$Bi = \frac{hL}{k}$$

$$= \frac{6 \times 1.5}{0.55}$$

$$= 16.36$$

Then,

$$\frac{1}{Bi} = \frac{k}{hL}$$

$$= \frac{1}{16.36}$$

$$= 0.061$$

From fig. (1),

for $(T - T_\infty)/(T_i - T_\infty) = 0.325$ and $k/hL = 0.061$

$$\frac{\alpha t}{L^2} = 0.60$$

$$t = (0.6)\frac{L^2}{\alpha}$$

$$= \frac{(0.60)(1.5)^2}{0.0188}$$

$$= 71.8 \text{ hr.}$$

Therefore, the time required to raise the temperature from $110^\circ F$ to $1150^\circ F$ is 71.8 hr.

• PROBLEM 13-18

Determine the time required to raise the average temperature of a flat plastic slab which is 2.0 in. thick from $85^\circ F$ to $220^\circ F$. The slab is initially at $85^\circ F$ and is then placed between two steel slabs at $260^\circ F$. The physical properties of the plastic are $\rho = 56.5$ lb/ft^3. $k = 0.078$ Btu/hr.ft.$^\circ F$ and $C_p = 0.041$ Btu/lb$^\circ F$

Also determine the amount of heat transferred per square foot of surface area to the plastic as the average temperature of the slab goes from $80^\circ F$ to $220^\circ F$.

Solution: In this system heat transfer is by unsteady state conduction.

Figure (1) can be used to compute the time required to raise the average temperature to the desired amount.

Given quantities are:

$\rho = 56.5\ lb/ft^3$ $\qquad$ $k = 0.078\ Btu/hr.ft.^{o}F$

$C_p = 0.41\ Btu/lb^{o}F$ $\qquad$ $L = \frac{1.0}{12} = 0.0833\ ft.$

$T_s = 260^{o}F$ $\qquad$ $T_a = 85^{o}F$ $\qquad$ $\bar{T}_b = 220^{o}F$

Then, the temperature difference ratio is

$$\frac{T_s - \bar{T}_b}{T_s - T_a} = \frac{260 - 220}{260 - 85}$$

$$= 0.229$$

Figure (1)

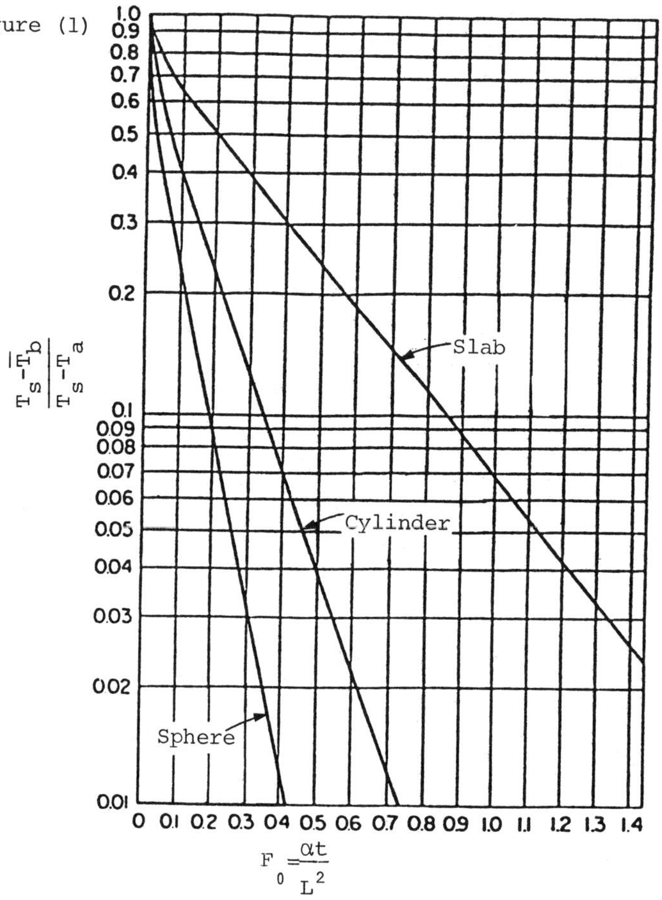

AVERAGE TEMPERATURES DURING UNSTEADY-STATE HEATING OR COOLING OF A LARGE SLAB, AN INFINITELY LONG CYLINDER, OR A SPHERE.

From fig. (1) for a slab,

$$F_o = 0.5$$

The thermal diffusivity is given by,

$$\alpha = \frac{k}{\rho C_p}$$

$$\alpha = \frac{0.078}{(56.5)(0.41)}$$

$$= 3.37 \times 10^{-3} \text{ ft}^2/\text{hr}.$$

The Fourier number is given by,

$$F_o = \frac{\alpha t}{L^2}$$

Then, the time required is,

$$t = \frac{F_o L^2}{\alpha}$$

$$= \frac{(0.5)(0.0833)^2}{3.37 \times 10^{-3}}$$

$$= 1.03 \text{ hr}.$$

The amount of heat transferred per unit surface area is given by,

$$\frac{Q_T}{A} = 2L\rho C_p(\bar{T}_b - T_a)$$

Substituting the known values gives,

$$\frac{Q_T}{A} = (2)(0.0833)(56.5)(0.41)(220 - 85)$$

$$= 521.0 \text{ Btu/ft}^2$$

• PROBLEM 13-19

A metallic slab which is 1.5 ft thick is initially at a uniform temperature at 110°F. The front face of the slab is suddenly exposed to a constant ambient temperature of 0°F. The rear face is insulated. The convective heat transfer coefficient is infinite and the thermal diffusivity is $\alpha = 0.25$ ft^2/hr. Determine the temperature profile of the slab at $t = 0.900$ hr using the Schmidt numerical method with $M = 2.0$. Divide the slab into five discrete slices, each 0.30 ft thick.

Solution: The time increment can be obtained using equation (1).

$$M = \frac{(\Delta x)^2}{\alpha(\Delta t)} \tag{1}$$

Then, $$\Delta t = \frac{(\Delta x)^2}{\alpha M}$$

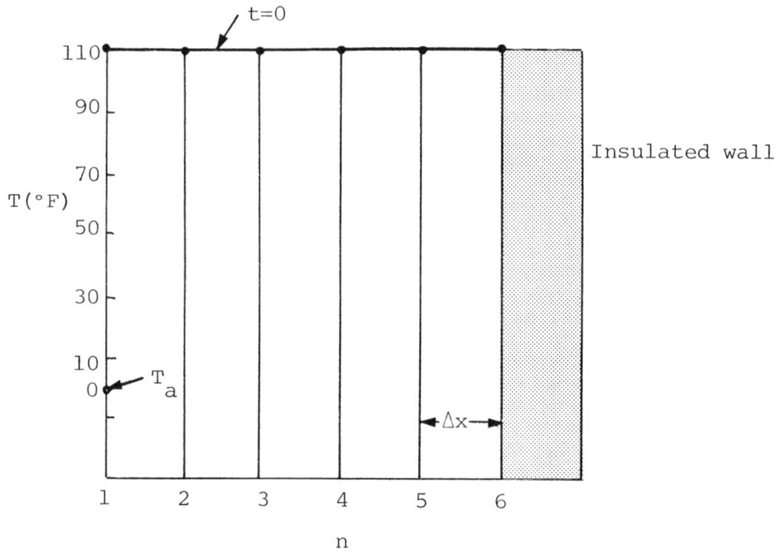

INITIAL TEMPERATURE PROFILE OF SLAB

Figure (1)

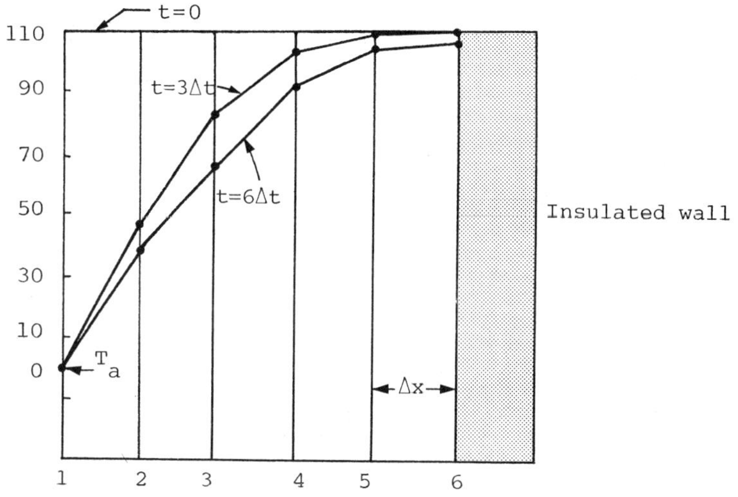

TEMPERATURE PROFILES FOR 3Δt INCREMENTS AND THE FINAL TIME OF 5Δt INCREMENTS.

Figure (2)

Substituting the known values,

$$\Delta t = \frac{(0.3)^2}{(0.25)(2.0)}$$

$$= 0.1800 \text{ hr.}$$

To reach 0.900 hr, 5 time increments of 0.1800 hr are required.

Figure (1) shows the temperature profile at t = 0 with an ambient temperature of $0^{\circ}F$.

The temperature of the insulated face, n = 6, in all time increments can be calculated by:

$$\left(t + \Delta t\right)T_n = \frac{(M - 2)\,{}_tT_n + 2\,{}_tT_{n-1}}{2} \tag{2}$$

for M = 2 and n = 6,

$$\left(t + \Delta t\right)T_6 = \frac{(2 - 2)\,{}_tT_6 + 2\,{}_tT_5}{2}$$

$$= {}_tT_5 \tag{3}$$

The temperature of the front face for the first time increment is,

$${}_1T_a = \frac{T_a + {}_oT_1}{2} = {}_1T_1 \tag{4}$$

and for the remaining time increments,

$$T_1 = T_a \tag{5}$$

The temperatures at n = 2, 3, 4, 5 in all time increments are given by:

$$\left(t + \Delta t\right)T_n = \frac{{}_tT_{n-1} + {}_tT_{n+1}}{2} \tag{6}$$

For the first time increment $(t + \Delta t)$:

at n = 1

$$\left(t + \Delta t\right)T_1 = \frac{T_a + {}_oT_1}{2}$$

$$= \frac{0 + 110}{2}$$

$$= 55^{\circ}F$$

at n = 2

$$\left(t + \Delta t\right)T_2 = \frac{{}_tT_1 + {}_tT_3}{2}$$

$$= \frac{55 + 110}{2} = 82.5^{\circ}F$$

at n = 3

$$\left(t + \Delta t\right)T_3 = \frac{{}_tT_2 + {}_tT_4}{2}$$

$$= \frac{110 + 110}{2} = 110^{\circ}F$$

at n = 4

$$\left(t + \Delta t\right)^{T_4} = \frac{t^{T_3} + t^{T_5}}{2}$$

$$= \frac{110 + 110}{2} = 110^{\circ}F$$

at n = 5

$$\left(t + \Delta t\right)^{T_5} = \frac{t^{T_4} + t^{T_6}}{2}$$

$$= \frac{110 + 110}{2} = 110^{\circ}F$$

From eq. (3) at n = 6

$$\left(t + \Delta t\right)^{T_6} = t^{T_5} = 110^{\circ}F$$

For the second time increment (t + 2Δt):

From eq. (5) at n = 1

$$\left(t + 2\Delta t\right)^{T_1} = T_a = 0^{\circ}F$$

at n = 2

$$\left(t + 2\Delta t\right)^{T_2} = \frac{0 + 110}{2} = 55^{\circ}F$$

at n = 3

$$\left(t + 2\Delta t\right)^{T_3} = \frac{82.5 + 110}{2} = 96.25^{\circ}F$$

at n = 4

$$\left(t + 2\Delta t\right)^{T_4} = \frac{110 + 110}{2} = 110^{\circ}F$$

at n = 5

$$\left(t + 2\Delta t\right)^{T_5} = \frac{110 + 110}{2} = 110^{\circ}F$$

at n = 6

$$T_6 = 110^{\circ}F$$

For the third time increment (t + 3Δt):

$$\left(t + 3\Delta t\right)^{T_1} = 0$$

$$\left(t + 3\Delta t\right)T_2 = \frac{0 + 96.25}{2} = 48.125^\circ F$$

$$\left(t + 3\Delta t\right)T_3 = \frac{55 + 110}{2} = 82.5^\circ F$$

$$\left(t + 3\Delta t\right)T_4 = \frac{96.25 + 110}{2} = 103.125^\circ F$$

$$\left(t + 3\Delta t\right)T_5 = \frac{110 + 110}{2} = 110^\circ F$$

$$\left(t + 3_\Delta t\right)T_6 = 110^\circ F$$

For the fourth time increment $(t + 4\Delta t)$:

$$\left(t + 4\Delta t\right)T_1 = 0$$

$$\left(t + 4\Delta t\right)T_2 = \frac{0 + 82.5}{2} = 41.25^\circ F$$

$$\left(t + 4\Delta t\right)T_3 = \frac{48.125 + 103.125}{2} = 75.625^\circ F$$

$$\left(t + 4\Delta t\right)T_4 = \frac{82.5 + 110}{2} = 96.25^\circ F$$

$$\left(t + 4\Delta t\right)T_5 = \frac{103.125 + 110}{2} = 106.56^\circ F$$

$$\left(t + 4\Delta t\right)T_6 = 110^\circ F$$

For the fifth time increment $(t + 5\Delta t)$:

$$\left(t + 5\Delta t\right)T_1 = 0$$

$$\left(t + 5\Delta t\right)T_2 = \frac{0 + 75.625}{2} = 37.81^\circ F$$

$$\left(t + 5\Delta t\right)T_3 = \frac{41.25 + 96.25}{2} = 68.75^\circ F$$

$$\left(t + 5\Delta t\right)T_4 = \frac{75.625 + 106.56}{2} = 91.1^\circ F$$

$$\left(t + 5\Delta t\right)T_5 = \frac{96.25 + 110}{2} = 103.125^\circ F$$

$$\left(t + 5\Delta t\right)T_6 = 106.56^\circ F$$

The temperature profiles for $3\Delta t$ and the final time of $5\Delta t$ increments are plotted in fig. (2). The accuracy can be increased by taking more slab slices and more time increments.

CHAPTER 14

HEAT EXCHANGES, STIRRED TANKS, CONDENSATION AND BOILING

SHELL AND TUBE HEAT EXCHANGER

• PROBLEM 14-1

In a heat exchanger, an oil is to be cooled from 240°F to 178°F. Water is used as the cooling medium, with a flow rate of 0.3 kg/s and an initial temperature of 46°F. Given the specific heats of oil and water to be 1880J/kg-°K and 4177 J/kg-°K, respectively, and the overall heat transfer coefficient to be 275 W/m^2-°K, calculate the required heat transfer surface area for counter and parallel flow.

Solution: In a parallel flow heat exchanger, the hot and the cold fluid travel in the same direction. In a counter flow heat exchanger, the hot and the cold fluid travel in opposite directions. The rate of heat exchange in counter flow would be greater, implying that less surface area is required.

The temperatures are, in degrees Kelvin,

$$240^\circ F = 388.88^\circ K$$

$$178^\circ F = 354.44^\circ K$$

$$46^\circ F = 281.11^\circ K$$

Equating the heat lost by the oil to the heat gained by water,

$$q = m_w C_{pw} \Delta T_w = m_0 C_{p0} \Delta T_0$$

where $m_w \rightarrow$ mass flow rate of water = 0.3 kg/s

$C_{pw} \rightarrow$ specific heat of water = 4177 J/kg-°K

ΔT_w → temperature difference = $T_{w1} - T_{w2}$

T_{w1} → temperature of water at inlet = 281.11^0K

T_{w2} → temperature of water at outlet

m_0 → mass flow rate of oil = 0.6 kg/s

C_{p0} → specific heat of oil = 1880 J/kg-^0K

ΔT_0 → temperature difference = $T_{01} - T_{02}$

T_{01} → temperature of oil at inlet = 388.88^0K

T_{02} → temperature of oil at outlet = 354.44^0K

Substituting the values,

$$q = m_0 C_{p0} \Delta T_0 = (0.6)(1880)(388.88 - 354.44)$$

$$= 38848.32 \text{ W}$$

$$m_w C_{pw} \Delta T_w = 38848.32$$

$$(0.3)(4177)(T_w - 281.11) = 38848.32$$

or

$$T_w = 312.11^0K = 102^0F$$

a) For counterflow, the log mean temperature difference is given by

$$\Delta T_m = \frac{\Delta T_1 - \Delta T_2}{\ln \frac{\Delta T_1}{\Delta T_2}}$$

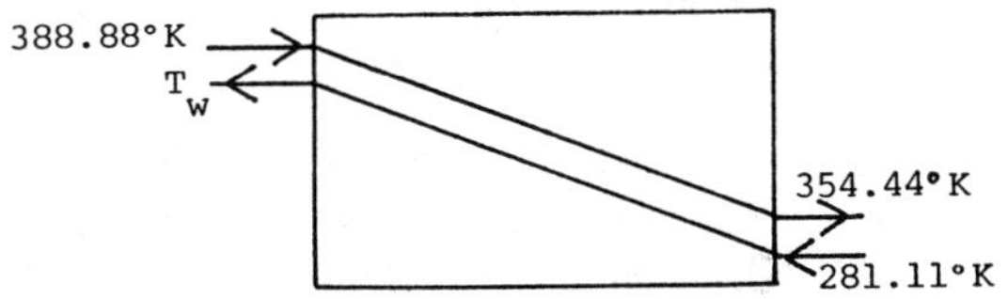

a) COUNTER FLOW

where ΔT_1 → temperature difference at one side of heat exchanger

ΔT_2 → temperature difference at second side of heat exchanger

$$\Delta T_1 = 388.88 - 312.11 = 76.77^0K$$

$$\Delta T_2 = 354.44 - 281.11 = 73.33^0K$$

Substituting the values,

$$\Delta T_m = \frac{76.77 - 73.33}{\ln\left(\frac{76.77}{73.33}\right)} = 75^0K$$

The surface area required for energy transfer is given by

$$A = \frac{q}{U\Delta T_m}$$

where $q \rightarrow$ heat exchanged = 38848.32 W

$U \rightarrow$ overall heat transfer coefficient

$= 275\ W/m^2\text{-}^0K$

and $\Delta T_m \rightarrow$ log mean temperature difference = 75^0K

Substituting the values,

$$A = \frac{38848.32}{(275)(75)} = 1.8835\ m^2 = 20.27\ ft^2$$

b) For parallel flow, the log mean temperature difference is

$$\Delta T_m = \frac{\Delta T_1 - \Delta T_2}{\ln \frac{\Delta T_1}{\Delta T_2}}$$

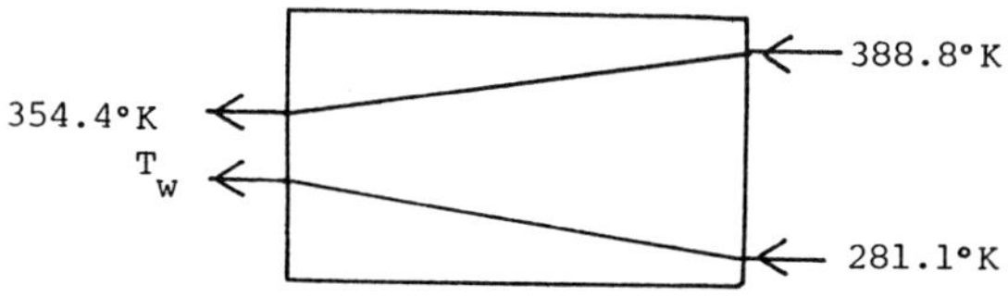

b) PARALLEL FLOW

where $\Delta T_1 \rightarrow$ temperature difference at inlets

$= 388.88 - 281.11 = 107.77$

$\Delta T_2 \rightarrow$ temperature difference at outlets

$= 354.44 - 312.11 = 42.33$

Substituting the values,

$$\Delta T_m = \frac{107.77 - 42.33}{\ln\left(\frac{107.77}{42.33}\right)} = 70.03^0K$$

Since the surface area required for energy transfer is

$$A = \frac{q}{U\Delta T_m}$$

the area is

$$A = \frac{38848.32}{(275)(70.03)} = 2.02m^2 = 21.74\ ft^2$$

• **PROBLEM 14-2**

A counterflow shell-and-tube heat exchanger, (illustrated below) is to be used to heat air from 40°F to 180°F, flowing at the rate of 48,000 lb/hr. Heating action is to be provided by the condensation of steam at 210°F in the shell. The internal diameter of the steel tubes is 2.5 in.

Find a) the size of the heat exchanger, assuming a mass velocity of 8000 lb/hr-ft^2,

and b) the air-side pressure drop.

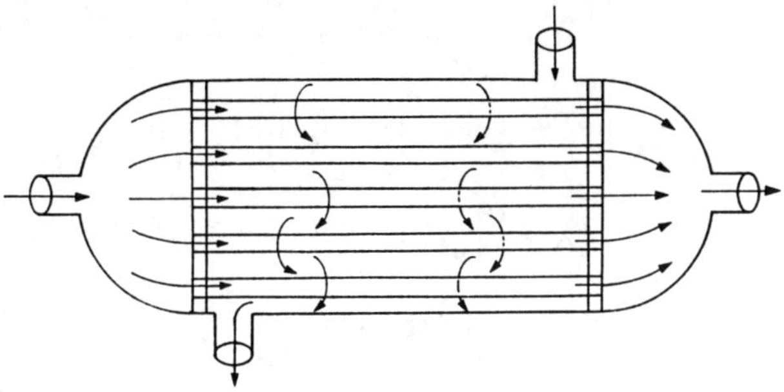

Solution: The mean air temperature is

$$\frac{40 + 180}{2} = 110\,^{\circ}\text{F}.$$

At this temperature, the air tables list

$Pr = 0.71$ $\qquad$ $C_p = 0.24$ Btu/lbm-°F

$\mu = 0.047$ lbm/ft-hr $\qquad$ $k = 0.016$ Btu/hr-ft-°F

The required number of tubes may be found from the relation

$$n\,\frac{\pi D^2}{4} = \frac{\omega_a}{G_a} \tag{1}$$

where $\quad n \rightarrow$ number of tubes

$D \rightarrow$ diameter of the tube

$= \frac{2.5}{12} = 0.208$ ft

$\omega_a \rightarrow$ flow rate of air = 48000 lb/hr

and $\quad G_a \rightarrow$ mass velocity = 8000 lb/hr-ft^2

Substituting the values,

$$n\,\frac{\pi(0.208)^2}{4} = \frac{48000}{8000}$$

or

$$n \cong 177.$$

The Reynolds number Re is

$$Re = \frac{GD}{\mu} \tag{2}$$

Substituting the values,

$$Re = \frac{(8000)(0.208)}{0.047} = 35,404$$

consider the relation

$$\frac{hD}{k} = 0.023\ Re^{0.8}\ Pr^{0.4} \tag{3}$$

Substituting the values in eq.(3), the coefficient of heat transfer is

$$h = \left(\frac{0.016}{0.208}\right)(0.023)(35404)^{0.8}(0.71)^{0.4}$$

$$= 6.72\ Btu/hr\text{-}ft^2\text{-}{}^0F$$

We may take $U \cong h$, as all other resistances are negligible compared to $(1/h)$.

The log mean temperature difference is given by

$$\Delta T_m = \frac{\Delta T_1 - \Delta T_2}{\ln\left(\frac{\Delta T_1}{\Delta T_2}\right)} \tag{4}$$

where $\Delta T_1 = (210 - 60) = 150\,{}^0F$

and $\Delta T_2 = (210 - 180) = 30\,{}^0F$

Substituting the values,

$$\Delta T_m = \frac{150 - 30}{\ln\left(\frac{150}{30}\right)} = 74.56\,{}^0F$$

The surface area required for energy transfer is given by

$$A = \frac{q}{U\Delta T_m} = \frac{\omega C_p \Delta T}{U\Delta T_m} \tag{5}$$

$$\Delta T = 180 - 40 = 140$$

Substituting,

$$A = \frac{(48000)(0.24)(140)}{(6.72)(74.56)} = 3219\ ft^2$$

The surface area is

$$A = \pi DLn \tag{6}$$

where $L \rightarrow$ length of tube

Substituting the values,

$$\pi(0.208)(L)(177) = 3219$$

or $$L = 27.83 \text{ ft}$$

b) The friction factor (f) is expressed as

$$f = 0.046/Re^{0.2} \tag{7}$$

Since $Re = 35,404$,

$$f = \frac{0.046}{(35404)^{0.2}} = 0.0056 \text{ (for an ideal gas)}$$

From the air tables,

$$\rho_1 \text{ at } 40^0F = 0.077 \text{ lbm/ft}^3$$

$$\rho_2 \text{ at } 180^0F = 0.06 \text{ lbm/ft}^3$$

$$\text{mean density } \rho_m = \frac{\rho_1+\rho_2}{2} = \frac{0.077+0.06}{2}$$

$$= 0.0685 \text{ lbm/ft}^3$$

The pressure drop equation is given by

$$P_1 - P_2 = \frac{G^2}{\alpha}\left(\frac{1}{\rho_2} - \frac{1}{\rho_1}\right) + 4f\,\frac{L}{D} \times \frac{G^2}{2\rho_m} + g\rho_m(z_2 - z_1) \tag{8}$$

For horizontal tube, $\alpha = 1$ and $z_2 = z_1$. Then

$$P_1 - P_2 = G^2\left(\frac{1}{\rho_2} - \frac{1}{\rho_1}\right) + 4f\,\frac{L}{D} \times \frac{G^2}{2\rho_m} \tag{9}$$

where $$G = \frac{8000}{3600} = 2.22$$

Substituting,

$$P_1 - P_2 = \frac{(2.22)^2}{32.2}\left[\left(\frac{1}{0.06} - \frac{1}{0.077}\right) + \frac{4(0.0056)}{2(0.0685)} \times \left(\frac{27.83}{0.208}\right)\right]$$

$$P_1 - P_2 = 3.91 \text{ lb/ft}^2 \tag{a}$$

Assuming that the area of the header is twice the flow area of the tubes,

$$\frac{A_1}{A_0} = \frac{A_2}{A_3} = 0.5$$

Finding velocities

$$V_1 = \frac{8000}{(3600)(0.077)} = 28.86 \text{ ft/sec.}$$

$$V_2 = 37.04 \text{ ft/sec}$$

$$V_0 = \frac{V_1}{2} = 14.43 \text{ ft/sec}$$

and $$V_3 = \frac{V_2}{2} = 18.52 \text{ ft/sec}$$

Also, $$K_e = 0.21 \text{ and } K_c = 0.31$$

Applying equations

$$\frac{P_0 - P_1}{\rho_1} + \frac{V_0^2 - V_1^2}{2} = K_c \frac{V_1^2}{2} \tag{10}$$

$$\frac{P_2 - P_3}{\rho_2} + \frac{V_2^2 - V_3^2}{2} = K_e \frac{V_2^2}{2} \tag{11}$$

and rearranging,

$$P_0 - P_1 = \frac{0.077}{2(32.2)}\left[0.31(28.86)^2 + (28.86)^2 - (14.43)^2\right]$$

$$= 1.06 \text{ lb/ft}^2 \tag{b}$$

and

$$P_2 - P_3 = \frac{0.060}{2(32.2)}\left[0.21(37.04)^2 + (18.2)^2 - (37.04)^2\right]$$

$$= 0.07 \text{ lb/ft}^2 \tag{c}$$

Adding equations (a), (b) and (c) gives

$$P_0 - P_3 = (P_1 - P_2) + (P_0 - P_1) + (P_2 - P_3)$$

$$= 3.91 + 1.06 + (-0.07) = 4.9 \text{ lb/ft}^2$$

$$P_0 - P_3 = 4.9 \text{ lb/ft}^2$$

• PROBLEM 14-3

A 95 percent ethyl alcohol solution, Cp = 0.91 Btu/lbm-°F, is to be cooled at the rate of 58,000 lbm/hr from 140°F to 100°F. Water is provided at the rate of 52,000 lbm/hr at 45°F. Given 80 tubes of 2 in. outside diameter with an overall coefficient of heat transfer as 120 Btu/hr-ft^2-°F, calculate the individual tube length for

a) a parallel flow tube-and-shell heat exchanger,

b) a counterflow tube-and-shell heat exchanger,

c) water flows through tubes and alcohol through the

shell, using a reversed-current heat exchanger (2-shell-pass, 80-tube-pass), and

d) a crossflow heat exchanger (one-tube-pass, one-shell-pass).

Solution: The outlet temperature of the water for all of the cases is calculated by equating the heat loss of the alcohol solution to the heat gained by the water, assuming no heat losses to the atmosphere.

$$q = \dot{m}_a C_{pa}(T_{a(in)} - T_{a(out)}) = \dot{m}_w C_{pw}(T_{w(out)} - T_{w(in)})$$

where

$\dot{m}_a$ → flow rate of alcohol = 58,000 lbm/hr

C_{pa} → specific heat of alcohol = 0.91 Btu/lbm-°F

$T_{a(in)}$ → temperature of alcohol at inlet = 140°F

$T_{a(out)}$ → temperature of alcohol at outlet = 100°F

$\dot{m}_w$ → flow rate of water = 52,000 lbm/hr

C_{pw} → specific heat of water = 1.0 Btu/lbm-°F

$T_{w(in)}$ → temperature of water at inlet = 45°F

and $T_{w(out)}$ → temperature of water at outlet.

Substituting the values,

$$58000(0.91)(140 - 100) = 52000(1.0)(T_{w(out)} - 45)$$

$$T_{w(out)} = 85.6°F$$

The rate of heat exchange between the alcohol and the water is

$$q = \dot{m}_a C_{pa}(T_{a(in)} - T_{a(out)})$$

$$= 58000(0.91)(140 - 100)$$

$$= 2,111,200 \text{ Btu/hr}$$

a) The log mean temperature difference for parallel flow is given by

$$\Delta T_m = \frac{\Delta T_1 - \Delta T_2}{\ln\left(\frac{\Delta T_1}{\Delta T_2}\right)}$$

where $\Delta T_1 = 140 - 45 = 95°F$

and $\Delta T_2 = 100 - 85.6 = 14.4°F$

Then

$$\Delta T_m = \frac{95 - 14.4}{\ln\left(\frac{95}{14.4}\right)} = 42.72\,^0F$$

The heat transfer surface area is given by

$$A = \frac{q}{U\Delta T_m}$$

$$A = \frac{2111200}{(120)(42.72)} = 411.83 \text{ ft}^2.$$

For the length of the tube, the relation is

$$A = \pi DLn$$

where $D \rightarrow$ diameter of the tube $= \frac{2}{12}$ ft $= 0.166$ ft

$n \rightarrow$ number of tubes $= 80$

$$411.83 = \pi L(0.166)(80)$$

or $$L = 9.87 \text{ ft}.$$

b) In counterflow, since $\dot{m}_a C_{pa} = \dot{m}_w C_{pw}$, the log mean temperature difference would be

$$\Delta T_m = (T_{a(in)} - T_{w(out)}) = (140-85.6) = 54.4\,^0F$$

Then the required surface area for heat transfer,

$$A = \frac{q}{(U)\Delta T_m}$$

$$= \frac{2111200}{(120)(54.4)} = 323.41 \text{ ft}^2.$$

Now, for the length of the tube,

$$A = \pi DLn$$

Substituting,

$$323.41 = \pi L(0.166)(80)$$

which gives $$L = 7.75 \text{ ft}.$$

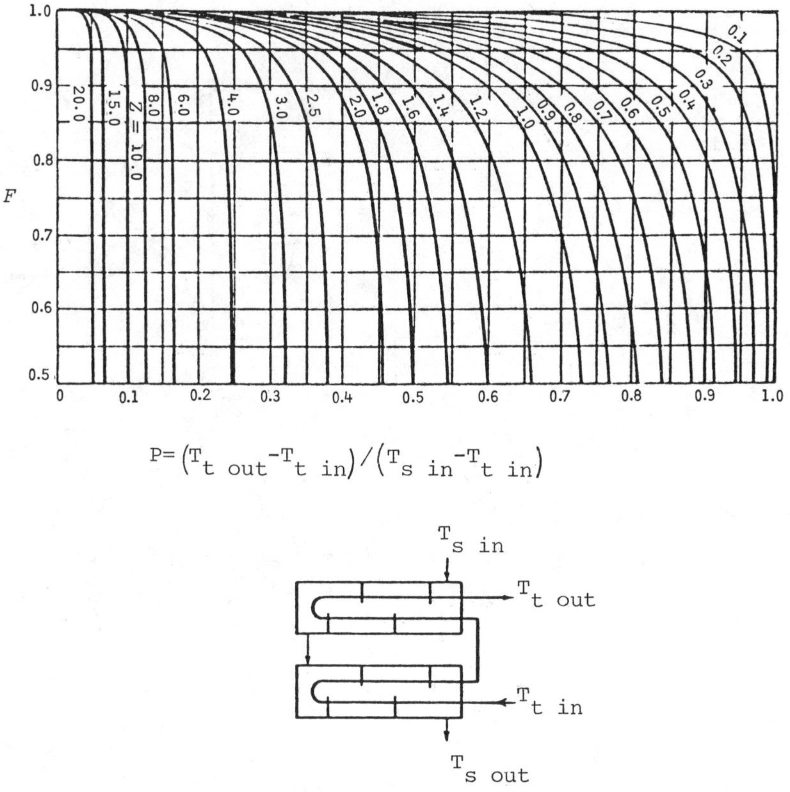

Fig. 1 CORRECTION FACTOR TO COUNTERFLOW 'LMTD' FOR HEAT EXCHANGER WITH TWO SHELL PASSES AND A MULTIPLE OF TWO TUBE PASSES.

c) For a reversed-current heat exchanger, the log mean temperature difference can be found by applying the correction factor from Fig. 1 to the mean temperature for counterflow. Calculating

$$P = \frac{T_{w(out)} - T_{w(in)}}{T_{a(in)} - T_{a(out)}} = \frac{85.6 - 45}{140 - 45} = 0.43$$

and

$$\text{heat capacity ratio/hour-Z} = \frac{\dot{m}_w C_{pw}}{\dot{m}_a C_{pa}} = 1,$$

from the chart (Fig. 1), F = 0.95.

Then the surface area $A = \dfrac{323.41}{0.95} = 340.4 \text{ ft}^2$.

For the length of tube,

$$A = \pi DLn$$

Substituting,

$$340.4 = \pi L(0.166)(80)$$

or $$L = 8.16 \text{ ft.}$$

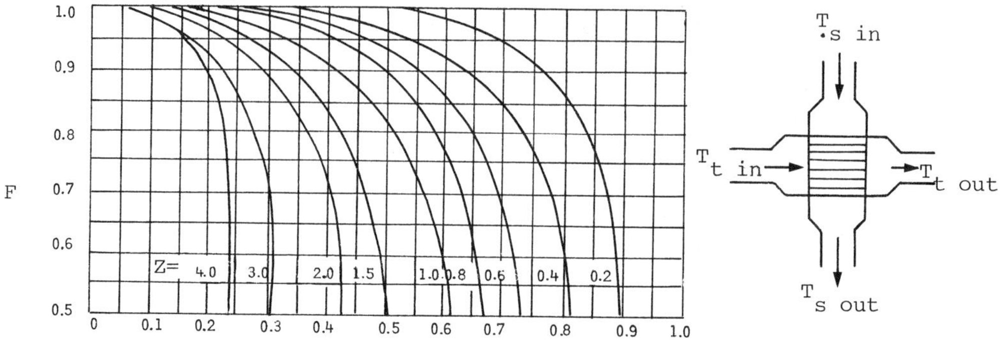

$$\frac{T_{t\ out} - T_{t\ in}}{T_{s\ in} - T_{t\ in}}$$

Fig. 2

CORRECTION FACTOR TO COUNTERFLOW 'LMTD' FOR CROSSFLOW HEAT EXCHANGERS, FLUID ON SHELL SIDE MIXED, OTHER FLUID UNMIXED, ONE TUBE PASS.

d) For a crossflow heat exchanger, the correction factor is found from Fig. 2 as F = 0.9. Then the surface area is

$$A = \frac{323.41}{0.9} = 359.34 \text{ ft}^2.$$

For the length of the tube,

$$359.34 = \pi L(0.166)(80)$$

or $$L = 8.61 \text{ ft.}$$

• PROBLEM 14-4

In the manufacture of rubber, aniline is heated from 70 °F to 110 °F as it flows at the rate of 80 lbm/min. A shell-and-tube exchanger is used, heating oil with inlet and outlet temperatures of 190 °F and 130 °F, respectively. The oil is to make one shell pass while the aniline is to make two tube passes.

Given the overall heat transfer coefficient as 60 Btu/hr-ft^2-°F, calculate the surface area required for the heat exchange. ($C_{p\ aniline}$ = 0.485 Btu/lbm-°F)

Solution: The log mean temperature difference is given by

$$\Delta T_m = \frac{\Delta T_a - \Delta T_b}{\ln\left(\frac{\Delta T_a}{\Delta T_b}\right)}$$

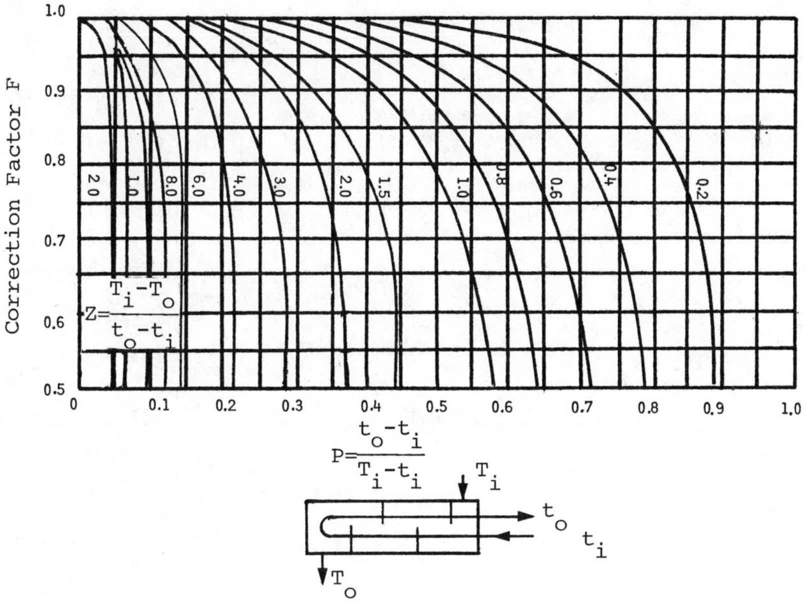

CORRECTION FACTORS FOR HEAT EXCHANGERS WITH ONE SHELL PASS AND TWO (OR MULTIPLES OF TWO) TUBE PASSES.

where $\Delta T_a = T_1 - T_4$

and $\Delta T_b = T_2 - T_3$

Since the temperatures are defined as

$T_1 \rightarrow$ temperature of oil at inlet = $190\,^0F$

$T_2 \rightarrow$ temperature of oil at outlet = $130\,^0F$

$T_3 \rightarrow$ temperature of aniline at inlet = $70\,^0F$

$T_4 \rightarrow$ temperature of aniline at outlet = $110\,^0F$,

we have

$$\Delta T_a = 190 - 110 = 80\,^0F$$

and

$$\Delta T_b = 130 - 70 = 60\,^0F$$

Substituting,

$$\Delta T_m = \frac{80 - 60}{\ln\left(\frac{80}{60}\right)} = 69.52\,^0F$$

The correction factor must be found. Calculating

$$P = \frac{110 - 70}{190 - 70} = 0.333$$

and

$$Z = \frac{190 - 130}{110 - 70} = 1.5,$$

the graph yields F = 0.95.

The heat exchange is given by

$$q = \dot{m}_a C_{pa}(T_4 - T_3)$$

where $\dot{m}_a \rightarrow$ mass flow rate of aniline = 80 lbm/min.

The specific heat of aniline is provided, and the temperatures are known.

$$q = (80)(60)(0.485)(110 - 70)$$

$$= 93120 \text{ Btu/hr}$$

The surface area for heat transfer is given by

$$A = \frac{q}{U \times F \times \Delta T_m}$$

All values are known.

$$A = \frac{93120}{(60)(0.95)(69.52)}$$

$$A = 23.5 \text{ ft}^2$$

• PROBLEM 14-5

A lubricating oil flows at a rate of 10,000 lbm/hr, with a temperature of 180 ^{0}F. It is to be cooled to 100 ^{0}F. Water is used as the cooling agent, flowing at a rate of 8000 lbm/hr with an inlet temperature of 50 ^{0}F.

Calculate the required surface area for heat transfer by using the effectiveness method for

a) a single-shell-pass heat exchanger, and

b) a two-shell-pass heat exchanger.

The overall heat-transfer coefficient is 150 Btu/hr-ft^2-^{0}F.

Solution: Calculating $\dot{m}C_p$ for oil and water,

For oil: $C_0 = \dot{m}_0 \times C_{p0}$

where $\dot{m}_0 \rightarrow$ mass flow rate of oil = 10000 lbm/hr

$C_{p0} \rightarrow$ specific heat of oil = 0.5 Btu/lbm

$C_0 = (10{,}000)(0.5) = 5000$ Btu/hr

Similarly, for water:

$$C_w = \dot{m}_w C_{pw}$$

where $\dot{m}_w = 7000$ lbm/hr and $C_{pw} = 1$ Btu/lbm

$$C_w = (7000)(1) = 7000 \text{ Btu/hr}$$

$$\frac{C_0}{C_w} = \frac{C_{min}}{C_{max}} = \frac{5000}{7000} = 0.714$$

The effectiveness ε is given by

$$\varepsilon = \frac{T_{0(in)} - T_{0(out)}}{T_{0(in)} - T_{w(in)}}$$

Substituting the values,

$$\varepsilon = \frac{180 - 100}{180 - 50} = 0.62$$

a) For a single-shell-pass, referring to Fig. 1,

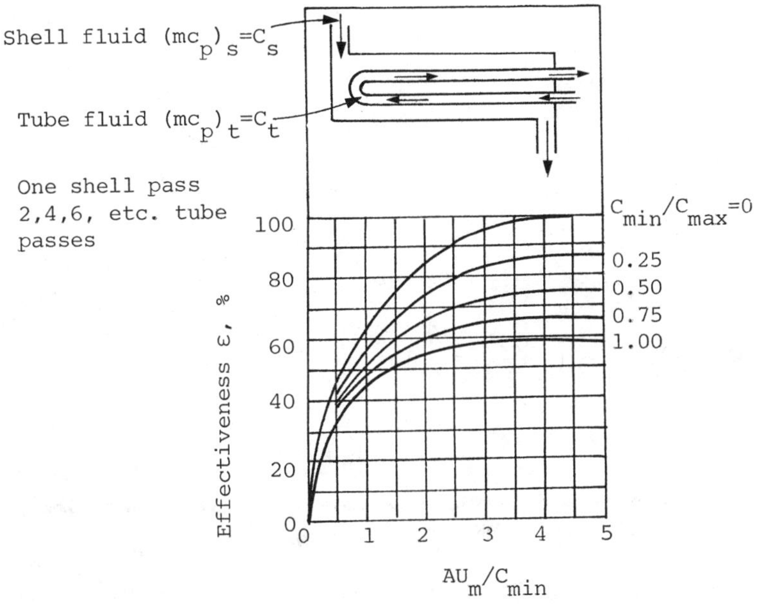

Fig. 1
EFFECTIVENESS FOR A SINGLE-SHELL PASS HEAT EXCHANGER WITH 2,4,6, ETC. TUBE PASSES.

$$\frac{AU}{C_{min}} = 1.7$$

where U → overall heat transfer coefficient

$= 150$ Btu/hr-ft^2- ^{0}F

and $C_{min} = 5000$ Btu/hr

$$\therefore \ A = \frac{(1.7)(5000)}{150} = 56.66 \text{ ft}^2.$$

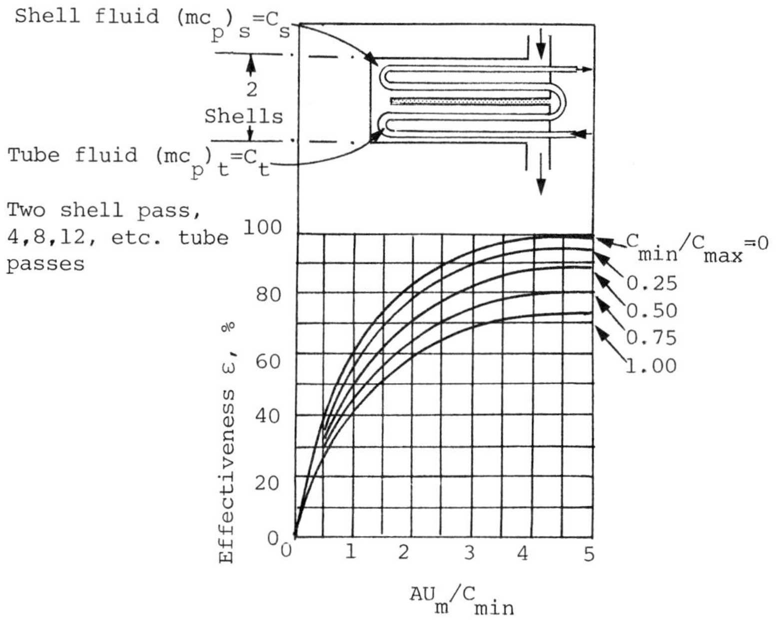

EFFECTIVENESS OF A TWO-SHELL PASS HEAT EXCHANGER WITH 4, 8, 12, ETC. TUBE PASSES

b) For a two-shell-pass arrangement, referring to Fig. 2,

$$\frac{AU}{C_{min}} = 1.35$$

$$A = \frac{(1.35)(5000)}{150} = 45 \text{ ft}^2$$

• PROBLEM 14-6

Water is entering the shell of a one-shell-pass, two-tube-pass heat exchanger at a rate of 12000 lbm/hr at 620°F. Meanwhile, water is entering the tubes at a rate of 24000 lbm/hr and 90°F. The overall heat transfer coefficient of the heat exchanger is 220 Btu/hr-ft^2-°F, with a surface area of 60 ft^2.

Find the outlet temperatures by using the correction factor and NTU methods. Take $C_{p\,water}$ as 1 Btu/lbm-°F.

Solution: a) The capacity ratio is defined as

$$R = \frac{\dot{m}_c C_{pc}}{\dot{m}_h C_{ph}}$$

where $\dot{m}_c \rightarrow$ mass flow rate of cold water = 24,000 lbm/hr

$\dot{m}_h \rightarrow$ mass flow rate of hot water = 12,000 lbm/hr

$C_{ph} = C_{ph} \rightarrow$ specific heat of water = 1 Btu/lbm-°F

Substituting,

$$R = \frac{(24000)(1)}{(12000)(1)} = 2.0$$

Assuming a value of $T_{h(out)}$ as 300°F, $T_{c(out)}$ can be found from the heat balance

$$\dot{m}_c C_{pc}(T_{c(out)} - T_{c(in)}) = \dot{m}_h C_{ph}(T_{h(in)} - T_{h(out)})$$

Substituting the values,

$$(24000)(1)(T_{c(out)} - 90) = (12000)(1)(620 - 300)$$

which gives

$$T_{c(out)} = 250°F$$

The log mean temperature difference is given by

$$\Delta' T_m = \frac{(T_{h(in)} - T_{c(out)}) - (T_{h(out)} - T_{c(in)})}{\ln\left[\frac{T_{h(in)} - T_{c(out)}}{T_{h(out)} - T_{c(in)}}\right]}$$

$$= \frac{[620-250]-[300-90]}{\ln\left(\frac{620-250}{300-90}\right)} = 282°F$$

To determine the effectiveness, P must be found.

$$P = \frac{\left[T_{c(out)} - T_{c(in)}\right]}{\left[T_{h(in)} - T_{c(in)}\right]}$$

$$= \frac{250 - 90}{620 - 90} = 0.3$$

For P = 0.3 and R = 2, the correction factor is F = 0.88. Then the effective ΔT_m is $\Delta' T_m \times F = 282(0.88) = 248$.

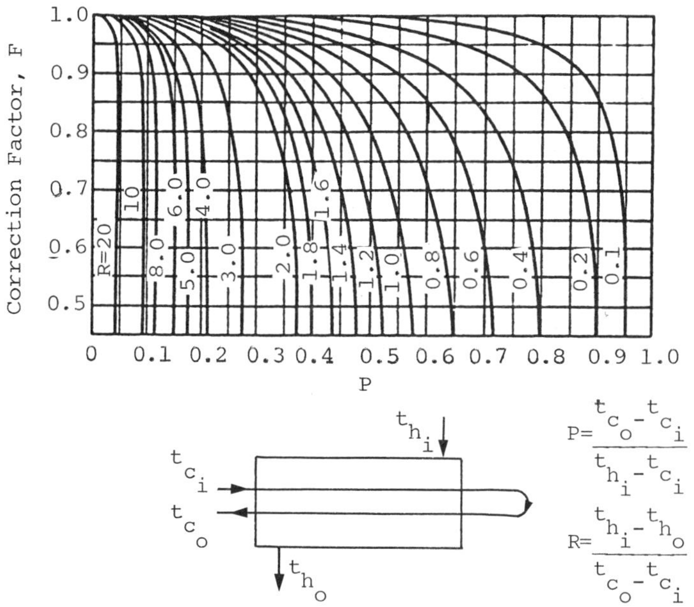

Fig. 1

CORRECTION FACTOR 'F' FOR A ONE-SHELL PASS, TWO-TUBE-PASS HEAT EXCHANGER.

The hot water outlet temperature can be calculated from

$$UA\Delta T_m = \dot{m}_h C_{ph}\left[T_{h(in)} - T_{h(out)}\right]$$

Substituting and solving for $T_{h(out)}$,

$$(220)(60)(248) = (12000)(1)\left[620 - T_{h(out)}\right]$$

$$T_{h(out)} = 347^0F$$

As this value is more than the assumed temperature, a new assumption must be made and calculated similarly. A final value is obtained after some iterations.

ii) If $T_{h(out)} = 325^0F$ is assumed from

$$\dot{m}_c C_{pc}(T_{c(out)} - T_{c(in)}) = \dot{m}_h C_{ph}(T_{h(in)} - T_{h(out)})$$

$$(2400)(1)\left[T_{c(out)} - 90\right] = (12000)(1) \times (620-325)$$

$$T_{c(out)} = 237.5^0F$$

Then

$$P = \frac{\left[T_{c(out)} - T_{c(in)}\right]}{\left[T_{h(in)} - T_{c(in)}\right]}$$

$$= \left[\frac{237.5 - 90}{620 - 90}\right] = 0.28$$

$$\Delta' T_m = \frac{\left[T_{h(in)} - T_{c(out)}\right] - \left[T_{h(out)} - T_{c(in)}\right]}{\ln\left[\frac{T_{h(in)} - T_{c(out)}}{T_{h(out)} - T_{c(in)}}\right]}$$

$$= \frac{(620 - 237.5) - (325 - 90)}{\ln\left(\frac{620 - 237.5}{325 - 90}\right)}$$

$$= 302.79^{\circ}F$$

For P = 0.28 and R = 2, the correction factor F = 0.9.

$$\Delta T_m = \Delta' T_m \times F = 302.79(0.9) = 272.5$$

Substituting into

$$UA\Delta T_m = \dot{m}_h C_{ph}\left[T_{h(in)} - T_{h(out)}\right]$$

gives

$$(220)(60)(272.5) = (12000)(1)\left[620 - T_{h(out)}\right]$$

or

$$T_{h(out)} = 320.25^{\circ}F$$

b) Now the NTU method will be employed.

$$C_{min} = \dot{m}_h \times C_{ph} = 12{,}000 \text{ Btu/hr}^{\circ}F$$

$$C_{max} = \dot{m}_c \times C_{pc} = 24{,}000 \text{ Btu/hr}^{\circ}F$$

$$C_R = \frac{C_{min}}{C_{max}} = 0.5$$

$$\therefore \text{ NTU} = \frac{UA}{C_{min}} = \frac{(220)(60)}{12000} = 1.1$$

For $C_R = 0.5$ and NTU = 1.1, from the graph in Fig. 2, the effectiveness $\varepsilon = 0.58$.

Since

$$\frac{\left[T_{h(in)} - T_{h(out)}\right]}{\left[T_{h(in)} - T_{c(in)}\right]} = \varepsilon$$

the value of $T_{h(out)}$ may be found as

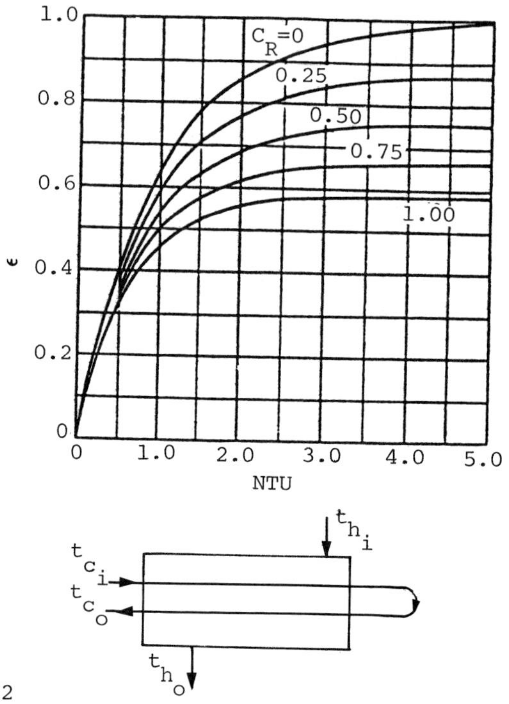

Fig. 2

THE EFFECTIVENESS-NTU RELATIONSHIP FOR A ONE-SHELL PASS, TWO-TUBE-PASS HEAT EXCHANGER.

$$0.58 = \frac{620 - T_{h(out)}}{620 - 90}$$

which gives

$$T_{h(out)} = 312.6°F.$$

The outlet temperature of cold water can be found from the capacity ratio.

$$C_R = \frac{C_{min}}{C_{max}} = \frac{\left[T_{c(out)} - T_{c(in)}\right]}{\left[T_{h(in)} - T_{h(out)}\right]}$$

$$0.5 = \frac{T_{c(out)} - 90}{620 - 312.6}$$

or $$T_{c(out)} = 243.7°F.$$

DOUBLE PIPE HEAT EXCHANGER

• PROBLEM 14-7

Compressed air flowing at the rate of 70 lbm/min is required to be cooled from 130°F to 90°F. A double pipe heat exchanger is provided with a water supply having temperatures at the inlet and outlet as 50°F and 75°F, respectively. The overall heat transfer coefficient is 50 Btu/hr-ft^2-°F.

Calculate the heat exchange surface area required for parallel and counterflow. [$C_{p\ air}$ = 0.24 Btu/lbm-°F]

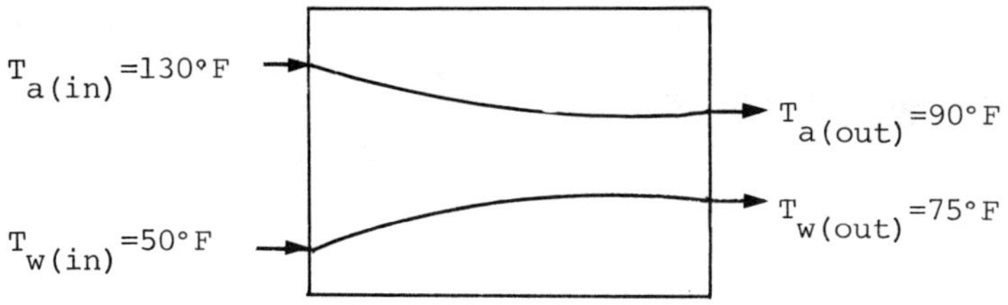

a) Parallel flow

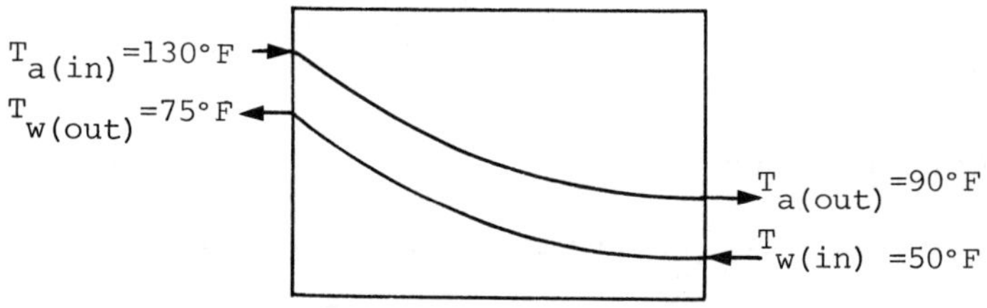

b) Counter flow

TEMPERATURE PLOTS FOR HEAT EXCHANGERS

Solution:

Heat transfer from the air is given by

$$q = \dot{m}_a C_{pa}(T_{a(in)} - T_{a(out)})$$

where $\dot{m}_a$ → mass flowrate = 70 lbm/min

C_{pa} → specific heat of air = 0.24 Btu/lbm-°F

$T_{a(in)}$ → temperature of air at inlet = 130°F

$T_{a(out)}$ → temperature of air at outlet = 90°F

$$q = (70)(60)(0.24)(130 - 90)$$

$$= 40320 \text{ Btu/hr}$$

a) For parallel flow:

The log mean temperature difference is given by

$$\Delta T_m = \frac{\left[T_{a(out)} - T_{w(out)}\right] - \left[T_{a(in)} - T_{w(in)}\right]}{\ln \frac{\left[T_{a(out)} - T_{w(out)}\right]}{\left[T_{a(in)} - T_{w(in)}\right]}}$$

$$\Delta T_m = \frac{[90 - 75] - [130 - 50]}{\ln \frac{(90 - 75)}{(130 - 50)}} = 38.8^0 F$$

The surface area is

$$A = \frac{q}{U\Delta T_m}$$

This becomes

$$A = \frac{40320}{50(38.8)} = 20.78 \text{ ft}^2$$

b) Counterflow:

The log mean temperature difference is given by

$$\Delta T_m = \frac{\left[T_{a(out)} - T_{w(in)}\right] - \left[T_{a(in)} - T_{w(out)}\right]}{\ln \frac{\left[T_{a(out)} - T_{w(in)}\right]}{\left[T_{a(in)} - T_{w(out)}\right]}}$$

Substituting the values,

$$\Delta T_m = \frac{(90 - 50) - (130 - 75)}{\ln\left(\frac{90 - 50}{130 - 75}\right)} = 47.1^0 F$$

For surface area,

$$A = \frac{q}{U\Delta T_m}$$

$$= \frac{40320}{50(47.1)} = 17.12 \text{ ft}^2$$

• PROBLEM 14-8

Water with a flow rate of 60 lbm/min is to be heated from 70^0F to 130^0F. A parallel flow double pipe heat exchanger, U = 320 Btu/hr-ft^2-^{0}F, is supplied with water at a rate of 120 lbm/min, at 200^0F. Estimate the surface area required for the heat exchanger.

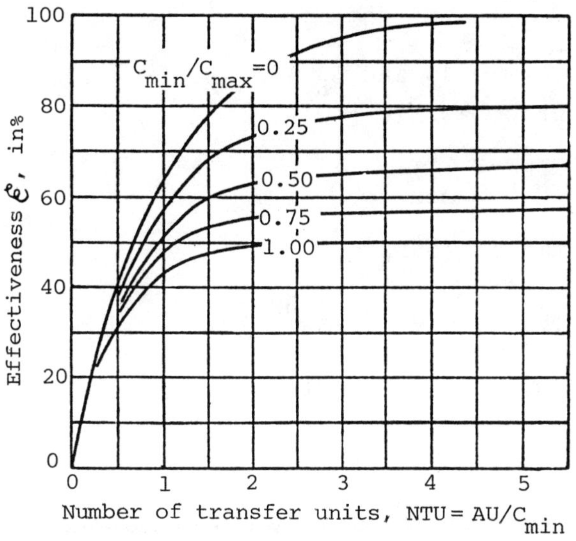

Solution: Calculating $C_c = \dot{m}_c C_{pc}$ and $C_h = \dot{m}_h C_{ph}$,

where $\dot{m}_c$ → mass flowrate of cold water = 60 lbm/hr

$\dot{m}_h$ → mass flowrate of hot water = 120 lbm/hr

C_{pc} → specific heat capacity of cold water

= 0.99 Btu/lbm^{0}F

C_{ph} → specific heat capacity of hot water

= 1.01 Btu/lbm^{0}F

C_c = 60(0.99) = 59.4 Btu/min-^{0}F

and C_h = 120(1.01) = 121.2 Btu/min-^{0}F

Here, $C_{min} = C_c$ = 59.4 Btu/min^{0}F

and $C_{max} = C_h$ = 121.2 Btu/min^{0}F

Now, the.ratio C_R is

$$\frac{C_{min}}{C_{max}} = \frac{59.4}{121.2} = 0.49$$

The effectiveness is given by

$$\varepsilon = \frac{T_{c(out)} - T_{c(in)}}{T_{h(in)} - T_{c(in)}}$$

Substituting,

$$\varepsilon = \frac{130 - 70}{200 - 70} = 0.46$$

Using $\varepsilon = 0.46$ and $C_R = 0.49$, the value of NTU is found from the graph as NTU = 0.8.

From $NTU = \frac{AU}{C_{min}}$

the area may be found as

$$0.8 = \frac{A(320)}{(59.4)(60)}$$

$$A = 8.91 \text{ ft}^2$$

• PROBLEM 14-9

In a counterflow double pipe heat exchanger, water flows at a rate of 70 kg/min and is to be heated from 40°C to 85°C. An oil, specific heat 1.7 kJ/kg°C, is used as the heating agent, with inlet and outlet temperatures of 120°C and 85°C, respectively.

The overall heat transfer coefficient is 400 W/m². Determine

a) the required heat exchanger surface area;

b) the outlet water temperature, taking the same fluid inlet temperatures but with a water flow rate of 50 kg/min. Also estimate the required heat exchanger surface area.

<u>Solution</u>: a) The total energy absorbed by water is given by

$$q = \dot{m}_w C_{pw} \Delta T_w$$

where $\dot{m}_w$ → flow rate of water = 70 kg/min

C_{pw} → specific heat of water = 4.183 kJ/kg-°K

and $\Delta T_w = T_{w2} - T_{w1}$

T_{w2} → temperature of water at outlet = 85°C

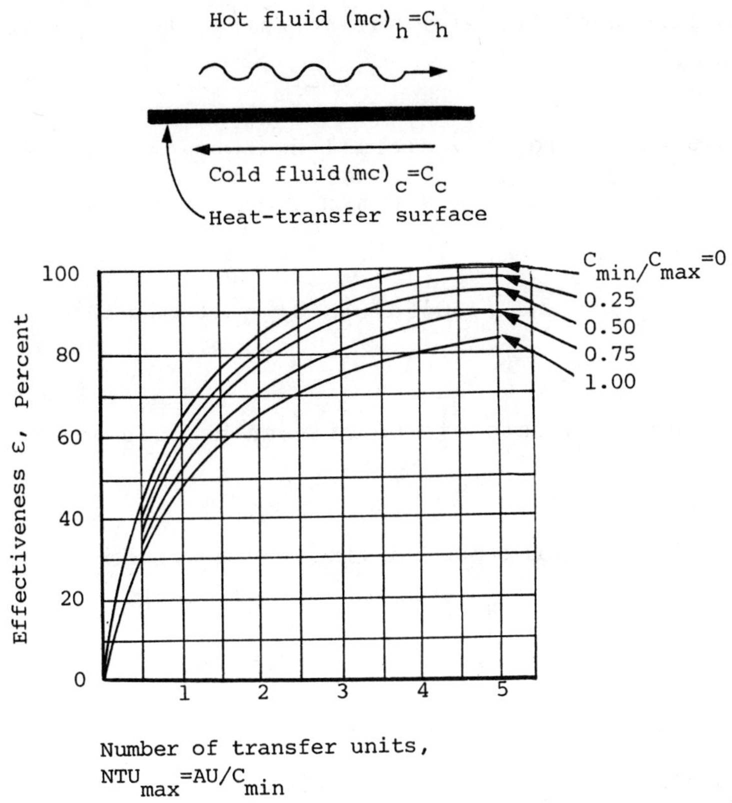

EFFECTIVENESS FOR COUNTERFLOW EXCHANGER PERFORMANCE

T_{W1} → temperature of water at inlet = 40°C

Substituting,

$$q = (70)(4.183)(85 - 40) = 13176 \text{ kJ/min} = 219.6 \text{ kW}$$

The log mean temperature difference is

$$\Delta T_m = \frac{(T_{01} - T_{W2}) - (T_{02} - T_{W1})}{\ln\left(\dfrac{T_{01} - T_{W2}}{T_{02} - T_{W1}}\right)}$$

where T_{01} → temperature of oil at inlet = 120°C

T_{02} → temperature of oil at outlet = 85°C

and $T_{W1} = 40°C \quad T_{W2} = 85°C$

$$\Delta T_m = \frac{(120 - 85) - (85 - 40)}{\ln\left[\dfrac{120 - 85}{85 - 40}\right]} = 39.8°C$$

To find heat transfer surface area, the expression

$$q = UA\Delta T_m$$

is used, where $U \rightarrow$ overall heat transfer coefficient

$$= 400\ W/m^2$$

Substituting,

$$(400)(A)(39.8) = 219.6 \times 10^3$$

or $$A = 13.8\ m^2$$

b) The flow rate of the oil can be calculated from

$$\dot{m}_o C_{po}\, \Delta T_o = \dot{m}_w C_{pw}\, \Delta T_w$$

Substituting and solving for $\dot{m}_o$ gives

$$\dot{m}_o(1.7)(35) = (50)(4.183)(45)$$

or $$\dot{m}_o = 158\ kg/min$$

Calculating the capacity rates,

For water: $C_w = \dot{m}_w C_{pw} = \left(\frac{50}{60}\right)(4183) = 3486\ W/{}^0C$

For oil: $C_o = \dot{m}_o C_{po} = \left(\frac{158}{60}\right)(1700) = 4477\ W/{}^0C$

Here, $C_{min} = 3486\ W/{}^0C$ and $C_{max} = 4477\ W/{}^0C$. Then

$$C_R = \frac{C_{min}}{C_{max}} = \frac{3486}{4477} = 0.778$$

Knowing that $NTU_{max} = \frac{UA}{C_{min}}$, the value of the NTU may be found as

$$NTU = \frac{(400)(13.8)}{3486} = 1.58$$

From the graph, the effectiveness $\varepsilon = 0.66$. Since

$$\varepsilon = \frac{\Delta T_{min}}{\Delta T_{max}} = 0.66,$$

where $\Delta T_{min} = T_{w2} - T_{w1} = T_{w2} - 40$

and $\Delta T_{max} = T_{o1} - T_{w1} = 120 - 40 = 80^0C$

the exit water temperature may be found.

$$T_{w2} - 40 = 80(0.66)$$

or $$T_{w2} = 92.8^{0}C$$

The heat transfer for the above condition is given by

$$q = \dot{m}_w C_{pw} \Delta T_w$$

where $$\dot{m}_w = 50 \text{ kg/min}, \quad C_{pw} = 4.183 \text{ kJ/kg-}^{0}K$$

and $$\Delta T_w = T_{w2} - T_{w1} = 92.8 - 40 = 52.8^{0}C$$

$$q = \left(\frac{50}{60}\right)(4.183)(52.8) = 184 \text{ kW.}$$

The log mean temperature difference is given by

$$\Delta T_m = \frac{\Delta T_1 - \Delta T_2}{\ln \frac{\Delta T_1}{\Delta T_2}}$$

where $$\Delta T_1 = T_{o1} - T_{w2} = 120 - 92.8 = 27.2^{0}C$$

and $$\Delta T_2 = T_{o2} - T_{w1} = 85 - 40 = 45^{0}C$$

Substituting the values,

$$\Delta T_m = \frac{27.2 - 45}{\ln\left(\frac{27.2}{45}\right)} = 35.36$$

Now,

$$q = UA\Delta T_m$$

Substituting and solving for the area yields

$$400(A)(35.36) = 184 \times 10^{3}$$

$$A = 13 \text{ m}^2$$

TURBULENT PIPE FLOW, CONDENSOR AND STIRRED TANKS

• PROBLEM 14-10

A dry saturated steam is condensed at the rate of 740,000 lbm/hr in a single pass steam condenser, with 1.09 in Hg inlet pressure. The inlet and outlet temperatures of the cooling water are 65^0F and 75^0F, respectively.

The temperature of the hot-well is 85^0F. The outside diameter of the tube is 1.5 in, with inside diameter as 1.35 in. The average velocity of the water is 8 ft/sec in each tube. Thermal conductivity for the tube material is 70 Btu/hr-ft-^{0}F, and the steam side film coefficient is 800 Btu/hr-ft^2-^{0}F.

Determine the outside surface area of the tube required for the heat exchange.

Solution: From the given variables,

$$\text{inside diameter of tube} \rightarrow D = \frac{1.35}{12} = 0.1125 \text{ ft.}$$

$$\text{and velocity of water} \rightarrow v = 8\text{ft/sec} = 8(3600) = 28800 \text{ ft/hr}$$

The physical properties of water, from tables, at the mean temperature 70^0F are:

$$\text{density } (\rho) = \frac{62.25}{32.2} = 1.93 \text{ slug/ft}^3$$

$$\text{viscosity } (\mu) = 2.41 \text{ lbm/ft-hr} = \frac{2.41}{32.2}$$

$$= 0.075 \text{ slug/ft-hr}$$

$$\text{specific heat } (C_p) = 0.99 \text{ Btu/lb-}^0\text{F} = 31.88 \text{ Btu/slug-}^0\text{F}$$

$$\text{and thermal conductivity } (k) = 0.346 \text{ Btu/hr-ft-}^0\text{F}$$

The Reynolds number is

$$Re = \frac{vD\rho}{\mu}$$

$$Re = \frac{(28800)(0.1125)(1.93)}{0.075} = 83376$$

The Prandtl number is

$$Pr = \frac{\mu C_p}{k}$$

$$Pr = \frac{(0.075)(31.88)}{0.346} = 6.91$$

Also, the Nusselt number is

$$Nu = \frac{hD}{k}$$

Since

$$Nu = 0.023(Re)^{0.8}(Pr)^{0.4} = \frac{hD}{k},$$

The water-side film coefficient h_w may be calculated as

$$h_w = \left(\frac{k}{D}\right) 0.023(Re)^{0.8}(Pr)^{0.4}$$

Substituting the values,

$$h_w = \left(\frac{0.346}{0.1125}\right)(0.023)(83376)^{0.8}(6.91)^{0.4}$$

$$= 1325 \text{ Btu/hr-ft-}^0\text{F}$$

The overall heat transfer coefficient is defined as

$$U = \frac{1}{\frac{r_o}{h_w r_i} + \frac{r_o \ln(r_o/r_i)}{k} + \frac{1}{h_s}}$$

where $r_o \rightarrow$ outside radius of tube $= \frac{1.5}{2(12)}$ ft $= 0.0625$ ft

$r_i \rightarrow$ inside radius of tube $= \frac{0.1125}{2}$ ft

$= 0.05625$ ft

All the values are known. Substituting,

$$U = \frac{1}{\frac{0.0625}{(1325)(0.05625)} + \frac{0.0625 \ln\left(\frac{0.0625}{0.05625}\right)}{70} + \frac{1}{800}}$$

$$= 458 \text{ Btu/hr-ft}^2\text{-}^0\text{F}$$

Now, the log mean temperature difference is given by

$$\Delta T_m = \frac{(T_s - T_{w1}) - (T_s - T_{w2})}{\ln \frac{(T_s - T_{w1})}{(T_s - T_{w2})}}$$

Substituting the given temperatures,

$$\Delta T_m = \frac{(85 - 65) - (85 - 75)}{\ln\left(\frac{85 - 65}{85 - 75}\right)} = 14.43^0 F$$

The rate of energy required for the condensation of steam at 1.09 in Hg and 85^0F is given by

q = (change in enthalpy at 85^0F) × (Mass rate of condensation of steam)

or

$$q = h_{fg(85^0F)} \times \dot{m}_c$$

where h_{fg} = latent heat of vaporization = $h_g - h_f$

Substituting $h_{fg} = 1045.5$ Btu/lbm

and $\dot{m}_c = 740{,}000$ lbm/hr,

$$q = (1045.5)(740{,}000) = 7.7367 \times 10^{+8} \text{ Btu/hr}$$

Surface area for the heat exchange is given by

$$A = \frac{q}{U\Delta T_m}$$

With all the known variables, the surface area is found to be

$$A = \frac{7.7367 \times 10^8}{(458)(14.43)} = 117064 \text{ ft}^2$$

• PROBLEM 14-11

A standard jacketed tank of 7 ft. dia. is fitted with a 3 ft. dia. 6 blade flat blade turbine impeller. This is a driver at 150 rpm, and is used to heat 1300 U.S. gal. of liquid from 80 to 180^0F. The tank is clean, and is heated with saturated steam. Determine the time required to heat the liquid. The wall thickness of the tank is 1/8 in., and the thermal conductivity of the material is 9.2 Btu/hr-ft-^0F. The steam side heat transfer coefficient (h_s) is 1010 Btu/hr-ft^2-^0F. Neglecting any system heat losses, determine the overall heat transfer coefficient at two different temperatures: 80 and 180^0F.

The liquid has the following properties:

specific heat → Cp = 0.6 Btu/lbm-^0F

thermal conductivity → k = 0.11 Btu/hr-ft-^0F

density → ρ = 59 lbm/ft^3.

Solution: As the tank conforms to the standard, the liquid height equals the tank diameter.

The Reynolds number is given by

$$Re = \frac{\rho N D_i^{\,2}}{\mu} \tag{1}$$

The diameter of the turbine impeller is 3.0 ft.

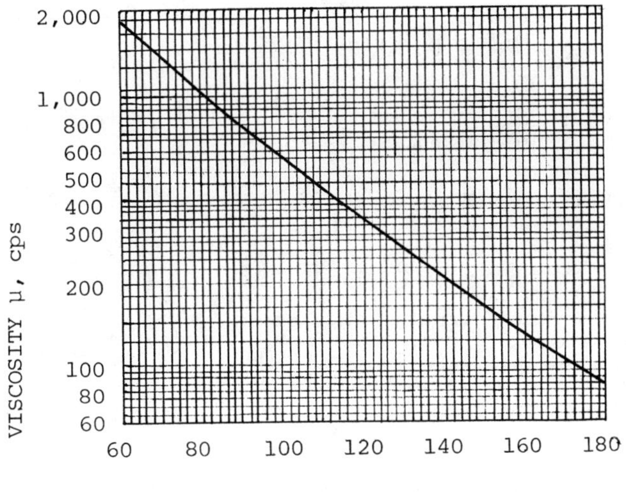

Fig. 1

VISCOSITY-TEMPERATURE PLOT FOR A SPECIFIC LIQUID

From the figure above, the absolute viscosities at 80 and 180°F are:

$\mu_{80°F}$ = 2419.1 lbm/ft-hr $\quad \mu_{180°F}$ = 203.2 lbm/ft-hr

Then from eq.(1), at 80°F

$$Re = \frac{59(150)(60)(3.0)^2}{(2419.1)^2}$$

$$= 1975.53$$

and at 180°F,

$$Re = \frac{59(150)(60)(3.0)^2}{203.2}$$

$$= 23518.7$$

The Prandtl number is given by

$$Pr = \frac{C_p \mu}{k}$$

At 80°F,

$$Pr = \frac{0.6(2419.1)}{0.11}$$

$$= 13195.1$$

while at 180^0F,

$$Pr = \frac{0.6(203.2)}{0.11}$$

$$= 1108.4$$

The Nusselt number is given by

$$Nu = 0.73\ Re^{0.65}\ Pr^{0.33}\ (\mu_w/\mu_b)^{-0.24} \tag{2}$$

Neglecting the viscosity ratio to compute approximate values of h_i, the relation becomes

$$Nu = 0.73\ Re^{0.65}\ Pr^{0.33}$$

Therefore,

$$h_i = 0.73\ Re^{0.65}\ Pr^{0.33} \left(\frac{k}{D_T}\right)$$

At 80^0F,

$$h_i = 0.73(1975.53)^{0.65}\ (13195.1)^{0.33} \left(\frac{0.11}{7}\right)$$

$$= 36.44\ \text{Btu/hr-ft}^2\text{-}^0\text{F}$$

At 180^0F,

$$h_i = 0.73(23518.7)^{0.65}\ (1108.4)^{0.33} \left(\frac{0.11}{7}\right)$$

$$= 80.5\ \text{Btu/hr-ft}^2\text{-}^0\text{F}$$

The wall temperature is given by

$$T_w = T_s - \left[\frac{T_s - T_b}{1 + (h_s/h_i)}\right]$$

The ratio of areas may be neglected, as the difference is negligible.

At $T_b = 80^0$F,

$$T_w = 212 - \left[\frac{212 - 80}{1 + \frac{1010}{36.44}}\right]$$

$$= 207.4^0\text{F}$$

At $T_b = 180^0$F,

$$T_w = 212 - \left[\frac{212 - 180}{1 + \frac{1010}{80.5}}\right]$$

$$T_w = 209.6^0\text{F}$$

Now, the exact values of h_i must be found, using eq.(2).

Then at $T_b = 80^0F$, $T_w = 207.4^0F$.

$\mu_w = 118.5$ lbm/ft-hr $\qquad \mu_b = 2419.1$ lbm/ft-hr

$$h_i = 0.73(1975.53)^{0.65}(13195.1)^{0.33}\left(\frac{0.11}{7}\right)\left(\frac{118.5}{2419.1}\right)^{-0.24}$$

$$= 75.2 \text{ Btu/hr-ft}^2\text{-}^0F$$

At $T_b = 180^0F$, $T_w = 209.6^0F$.

$\mu_w = 113.7$ lbm/ft-hr $\qquad \mu_b = 203.2$ lbm/ft-hr

$$h_i = 0.73(23518.7)^{0.65}(1108.4)^{0.33}\left(\frac{0.11}{7}\right)\left(\frac{113.7}{203.2}\right)^{-0.24}$$

$$= 92.5^0F.$$

The overall heat transfer coefficient U_i, based on the inside area, is given by

$$\frac{1}{U_i} = \frac{1}{h_i} + \frac{A_{wi}x}{A_m K} + \frac{A_{wi}}{A_{wo}h_s}$$

For thin-walled vessels, $A_i \cong A_o \cong A_m$.

Therefore,

$$\frac{1}{U_i} = \frac{1}{h_i} + \frac{x}{K} + \frac{1}{h_s}$$

At 80^0F,

$$\frac{1}{U_i} = \frac{1}{75.2} + \frac{0.0104}{9.2} + \frac{1}{1010}$$

$$= 0.0154$$

or $\qquad U_i = 64.94 \text{ Btu/hr-ft}^2\text{-}^0F$

At 180^0F,

$$\frac{1}{U_i} = \frac{1}{92.5} + \frac{0.0104}{9.2} + \frac{1}{1010}$$

$$= 0.0129$$

$$U_i = 77.52 \text{ Btu/hr-ft}^2\text{-}^0F$$

A curve of U_i as a function of temperature in ^0F is plotted.

The temperature range 80^0F - 180^0F is divided into five increments. The overall heat transfer coefficient U_i at the midpoint of each 20^0F temperature increment is taken. The

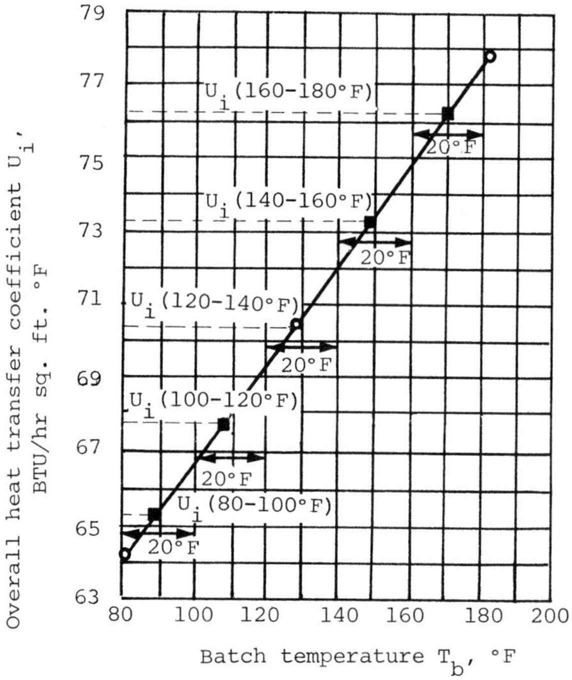

OVERALL HEAT TRANSFER COEFFICIENT AS A FUNCTION OF TEMPERATURE.

time required to heat the liquid over each temperature increment is given by

$$\Delta t = \frac{\dot{m}Cp}{U_i A_i} \ln \frac{T_s - T_{bi}}{T_s - T_{bR}} \qquad (3)$$

where T_{bi} and T_{bR} mark the beginning and end of the time interval Δt.

The liquid mass is given by

$$\dot{m} = \pi(D_T^2/4)H_1 P$$

$$= \pi(7^2/4)(7.0)(59)$$

$$= 15894 \text{ lbm}$$

The time required for a temperature increment is evaluated using eq.(3).

For $80^0F - 100^0F$,

$$\Delta t = \left[\frac{(15894)(0.6)}{(66)(154)}\right] \ln\left(\frac{212 - 80}{212 - 100}\right)$$

$$= 0.154 \text{ hr}$$

For $100^0F - 120^0F$,

$$\Delta t = \left[\frac{(15894)(0.6)}{(68.6)(154)}\right] \ln\left(\frac{212 - 100}{212 - 120}\right)$$

$$= 0.178 \text{ hr}$$

For 120°F - 140°F,

$$\Delta t = \left[\frac{(15894)(0.6)}{(71)(154)}\right] \ln\left(\frac{212 - 120}{212 - 140}\right)$$

$$= 0.214 \text{ hr}$$

For 140°F - 160°F,

$$\Delta t = \left[\frac{(15894)(0.6)}{(73.8)(154)}\right] \ln\left(\frac{212 - 140}{212 - 160}\right)$$

$$= 0.273 \text{ hr}$$

For 160°F - 180°F,

$$\Delta t = \left[\frac{(15894)(0.6)}{(76.4)(154)}\right] \ln\left(\frac{212 - 160}{212 - 180}\right)$$

$$= 0.394 \text{ hr}$$

The total time required to heat the liquid from 80°F to 180°F is given by

$$\Delta t = 0.154 + 0.178 + 0.214 + 0.273 + 0.394$$

$$= 1.213 \text{ hr}$$

• PROBLEM 14-12

The velocity of water flowing through a 2.5 in schedule 40 steel pipe, is 6.5 ft/sec. The mean temperature of the water is 150°F.

a) Is the flow laminar or turbulent?

b) Estimate the water-film coefficients of heat transfer for

i) a turbulent flow regime,
ii) ordinary temperatures.

Solution: a) The type of flow is indicated by the Reynolds number (Re). A value above 2100 indicates a turbulent flow regime, while a value below 2100 denotes a laminar flow. The Reynolds number is defined as

$$Re = \frac{DV\rho}{\mu} \tag{1}$$

where D → inside diameter of pipe $D = \frac{2.469}{12} = 0.20575$ft

V → velocity of water in pipe V = 6.5 ft/sec

ρ → density of water at 150^0F

$$\rho = 61.3 \text{ lbm/ft}^3$$

and μ → viscosity of water at 150^0F

$$\mu = 0.29 \times 10^{-3} \text{ lbm/ft}^2$$

Substituting the values into eq.(1),

$$Re = \frac{(0.20575)(6.5)(61.3)}{0.29 \times 10^{-3}}$$

$$= 282,693$$

As the number is above 21,00, the flow is turbulent.

b) i) For a turbulent water flow, heat transfer coefficient is given by

$$h = 0.023 \frac{k}{D} Re^{0.8} Pr^{0.4} \qquad (2)$$

where $Pr = \frac{\mu Cp}{k}$

The variables are thermal conductivity - k - at 150^0F

$$k = 0.383 \text{ Btu/hr-ft-}^0\text{F}$$

inside diameter of pipe, $D = \frac{2.469}{12} = 0.20575$ ft

velocity of water - V = 6.5 ft/sec

density of water - ρ - at 150^0F, $\rho = 61.3$ lbm/ft^3

viscosity of water - μ - at 150^0F

$$\mu = 0.29 \times 10^{-3} \text{ lbm/ft-s}$$

and specific heat at 150^0F → $C_p = 1.0$ Btu/lbm-^{0}F

Substituting the values in eq.(2),

$$h = 0.023\left(\frac{0.383}{0.20575}\right)(282,693)^{0.8} \times \left[\frac{(1.0)(0.29 \times 10^{-3})(3600)}{0.383}\right]^{0.4}$$

$$h = 1468 \text{ Btu/hr-ft}^2\text{-}^0\text{F}$$

b) ii) To calculate the heat transfer coefficient at ordinary temperatures, the formula is

$$h = 150(1 + 0.011t)\frac{(V)^{0.8}}{(D)^{0.2}} \qquad (3)$$

where mean temperature of water → $t = 150^0F$

velocity of water → $V = 6.5$ ft/sec

inside diameter of pipe → $D = 2.469$ in

Substituting the values in eq.(3) gives

$$h = 150\left[1 + (0.011)(150)\right]\frac{(6.5)^{0.8}}{(2.469)^{0.2}}$$

gives $h = 1483$ Btu/hr-ft^2-^{0}F

• PROBLEM 14-13

Estimate the overall heat transfer coefficient, based on the outside surface area, for hot water flowing with a velocity of 30 cm/sec through a standard 1.5 in. schedule 80 steel pipe. The temperature is 22^{0}C. Take the thermal conductivity of steel as 60 W/m-^{0}C.

Solution: For a 1.5 in. schedule 80 tube, the dimensions are:

$$d \to \text{inside diameter} = 1.5 \text{ in} = \frac{1.5(2.54)}{100} = 0.038 \text{ m}$$

$$D \to \text{outside diameter} = 1.9 \text{ in} = \frac{1.9(2.54)}{100} = 0.048 \text{ m}$$

The coefficient of heat transfer for the flow conditions inside the pipe is evaluated at the bulk temperature.

Properties of water at 90^{0}C (from table) are:

ρ → density = 963.2 kg/m^3

μ → viscosity = 3.06×10^{-4} kg/m-s

k → thermal conductivity = 0.678 W/m-^{0}C

Pr → Prandtl number = 1.9

The Reynolds number is given by

$$Re = \frac{\rho v d}{\mu}$$

where v → velocity of water $= \frac{30}{100} = 0.3$ m/s

Substituting the values,

$$Re = \frac{(963.2)(0.3)(0.038)}{3.06 \times 10^{-4}} = 35,884$$

As this is greater than 2100, the flow is turbulent. Then the Nusselt number is defined as

$$Nu = \frac{h_i d}{k} = 0.023\ Re^{0.8} Pr^{0.4}$$

where h_i → coefficient of heat transfer based on inside of pipe.

Solving for h_i and substituting yields

$$h_i = 0.023 \frac{(0.678)}{(0.038)} (35,884)^{0.8} (1.9)^{0.4}$$

$$= 2337\ W/m^2\text{-}^0C$$

The thermal resistance for a unit length of pipe is given by

$$R_s = \frac{\ln(r_o/r_i)}{2\pi k}$$

where r_o → outside radius of pipe $= \frac{0.048}{2} = 0.024$ m

r_i → inside radius of pipe $= \frac{0.038}{2} = 0.019$ m

Substituting the values,

$$R_s = \frac{\ln(0.024/0.019)}{2\pi(60)} = 6.197 \times 10^{-4}$$

The thermal resistance on the inside of the pipe is

$$R_i = \frac{1}{h_i A_i} = \frac{1}{h_i 2\pi r_i}$$

or

$$R_i = \frac{1}{(2337)(2\pi)(0.019)} = 3.584 \times 10^{-3}$$

The thermal resistance for the outer surface is

$$R_o = \frac{1}{h_o A_o} = \frac{1}{h_o 2\pi r_o} \quad \text{(a)}$$

The relation for h_o in laminar flow is given by

$$h_o = 1.32 \left(\frac{\Delta T}{d}\right)^{1/4} = 1.32 \left(\frac{T_o - T_\infty}{d}\right)^{1/4} \quad \text{(b)}$$

where temperature T_o is unknown.

The energy balance equations are:

$$\frac{T_w - T_i}{R_i} = \frac{T_i - T_o}{R_s} = \frac{T_o - T_\infty}{R_o} \tag{c}$$

where T_w → temperature of water

T_i → temperature of inner pipe surface

From eqs.(a) and (b),

$$\frac{T_o - T_\infty}{R_o} = 2\pi r_o \frac{(1.32)}{d^{1/4}} (T_o - T_\infty)^{5/4} \tag{d}$$

This equation may be combined with eq.(c) to give two equations with two unknowns. Solution by iteration is required.

$$\frac{T_w - T_i}{R_i} = \frac{T_i - T_o}{R_s} \tag{e}$$

$$\frac{T_i - T_o}{R_s} = 2\pi r_o \frac{(1.32)}{d^{1/4}} (T_o - T_\infty)^{5/4} \tag{f}$$

where T_w → temperature of water = 90^0C

T_∞ → temperature of surroundings = 22^0C

$R_i = 3.584 \times 10^{-3}$, $R_s = 6.197 \times 10^{-4}$, $2r_o = 0.048$ m,

and $d = 0.038$ m

Substituting the values into the equations,

$$\frac{90 - T_i}{3.584 \times 10^{-3}} = \frac{T_i - T_o}{6.197 \times 10^{-4}}$$

$$\frac{T_i - T_o}{6.197 \times 10^{-4}} = \frac{\pi(0.048)(1.32)(T_o - 22)^{5/4}}{(0.038)^{1/4}}$$

By iteration, $T_o = 89.54^0$C and $T_i = 89.6^0$C. Substituting into eq.(b),

$$h_o = 1.32\left(\frac{89.54 - 22}{0.038}\right)^{1/4} = 8.57 \text{ W/m}^2\text{-}^0\text{C}$$

and substituting this into eq.(a),

$$R_o = \frac{1}{(8.57)(2\pi)(0.024)} = 0.774$$

The overall heat transfer coefficient based on the outer surface area is given by

$$U_o = \frac{1}{R_i \frac{A_o}{A_i} + A_o R_s + R_o}$$

$$= \frac{1}{\frac{(3.54\times10^{-3})\pi(0.048)}{\pi(0.038)} + \pi(0.048)(6.197\times10^{-4}) + 0.774}$$

$$= 1.284 \text{ W/m-}^0\text{C}$$

The outside area per unit length (1m) is

$$A_o = \pi(0.048)(1) = 0.15079 \text{ m}^2\text{/m length}$$

$$U_o = \frac{1.284}{0.15079} = 8.52 \text{ W/m}^2\text{-}^0\text{C}$$

CONDENSATION ON VERTICAL AND HORIZONTAL TUBES

• PROBLEM 14-14

Consider a vertical cylinder which has an outside diameter of 1.0 ft and is 2.0 ft long. Steam is condensing on the outer surface. The temperature of the outer surface is maintained at 85 ^{0}F with cooling water inside the cylinder. Determine

a) the overall heat transfer coefficient,
b) the total rate of heat transfer, and
c) the total rate of condensation.

The saturation temperature is 105 ^{0}F.

Solution: a) The average heat transfer coefficient is given by:

$$h_{avg} = \frac{1}{L}\int_0^L h(x)\, dx$$

or

$$h_{avg} = \int_0^1 h(x)\, d\left(\frac{x}{L}\right) \tag{1}$$

where h(x) is the local heat transfer coefficient.

The local heat transfer coefficient is given by:

$$Nu_x = \frac{h(x)x}{k}$$

$$h(x) = \frac{KNu_x}{x}$$

$$h(x) = \frac{K}{L}\, Nu_x \left(\frac{L}{x}\right) \tag{2}$$

But

$$Nu_x = (Gr_x Pr/4Ja)^{1/4} \tag{3}$$

Substituting eq.(3) in eq.(2) gives:

$$h(x) = \frac{K}{L}\left[Gr_x Pr/4Ja\right]^{1/4} \left(\frac{L}{x}\right) \tag{4}$$

The local Grashof number is given by,

$$Gr_x = \frac{(\Delta\rho/\rho)gx^3}{\nu^2}$$

$$= \frac{(\Delta\rho/\rho)gL^3}{\nu^2}\left(\frac{x}{L}\right)^3$$

$$= Gr_L \left(\frac{x}{L}\right)^3 \tag{5}$$

Substituting eq.(5) in eq.(4) gives,

$$h(x) = \frac{K}{L}\left[Gr_L Pr/4Ja\right]^{1/4} \left(\frac{x}{L}\right)^{3/4} \left(\frac{L}{x}\right)$$

or $$h(x) = \frac{K}{L}\left[Gr_L Pr/4Ja\right]^{1/4} \cdot \frac{x}{L}^{-\frac{1}{4}}$$

But $$\frac{K}{L}\left[Gr_L Pr/4Ja\right]^{\frac{1}{4}} = h_L$$

Therefore, $$h(x) = h_L\left(\frac{x}{L}\right)^{-\frac{1}{4}} \tag{6}$$

Substituting eq.(6) in eq.(1) gives:

$$h_{avg} = h_L \int_0^1 \left(\frac{x}{L}\right)^{-1/4} d\left(\frac{x}{L}\right)$$

Integrating and evaluating the limits,

$$h_{avg} = \frac{4}{3}\, h_L$$

$$= \frac{4}{3}\left(\frac{K}{L}\right)\left[Gr_L Pr/4Ja\right]^{1/4} \tag{7}$$

The mean film temperature $T_f = \frac{85 + 105}{2} = 95^0F$. From liquid water tables, for water at 95^0F:

$\rho = 62.1\ lb/ft^3$ $\qquad$ $Cp = 0.999\ Btu/lb\,^0F$

$\mu = 0.47 \times 10^{-3}\ lb/ft\text{-}sec$ $\qquad$ $\nu = 7.57 \times 10^{-6}\ ft^2/sec$

$K = 0.362\ Btu/hr\text{-}ft\text{-}^0F$ $\qquad$ $Pr = 4.65$

From saturated water tables, for vapor at $105\,^0F$

$h_{fg} = 1034.15\ Btu/lb$ $\qquad$ $\rho_v = \frac{1}{307.55} = 0.00325\ lb/ft^3$

ρ_v is negligible as compared to ρ of water. Substitution of known quantities in the equation for the Grashof number gives:

$$Gr_L = \frac{(62.1/62.1)(32.2)(2)^3}{(7.57 \times 10^{-6})^2}$$

$$= 4.5 \times 10^{12}$$

The Jakob number is given by,

$$Ja = \frac{Cp\Delta T}{h_{fg}}$$

$$= \frac{0.999(105 - 85)}{1034.15}$$

$$= 0.01932$$

Then, from eq.(7):

$$h_{avg} = \frac{4}{3}\left[\frac{0.362}{2}\right]\left[(4.5\times10^{12})(4.65)/4(0.01932)\right]^{1/4}$$

$$= 978.97\ Btu/hr\text{-}ft^2\text{-}^0F$$

The overall heat transfer coefficient is $978.97\ Btu/hr\text{-}ft^2\text{-}^0F$.

b) The total rate of heat transfer is given by:

$$Q = h_{avg}(\pi DL)(T_s - T_{in})$$

$$Q = (978.97)(\pi)(1.0)(2.0)(105\text{-}85)$$

$$= 123{,}021\ Btu/hr.$$

c) The mass rate of condensation is given by:

$$\dot{m} = \frac{Q}{h_{fg}}$$

$$= \frac{123021}{1304.15}$$

$$= 94.3\ lb/hr$$

• PROBLEM 14-15

Consider a horizontal pipe of 2 in. internal diameter which has saturated steam at 2 psia condensing on .its outer surface. The temperature of the outer surface of the pipe is maintained at 100°F. Determine the rate of steam condensation per foot of pipe length.

Solution: The saturation temperature of steam at 2 psia from the steam tables is 126.04°F, and the latent heat is 1022.1 Btu/lb.

The mean film temperature is $T_f = \frac{126.04 + 100}{2} = 113.02°F$. From tables for liquid water at 113.02°F,

$\rho = 62.15 \text{ lb/ft}^3$ $\mu = 1.49 \text{ lb/ft-hr}$

$k = 0.368 \text{ Btu/hr-ft-}^0\text{F}$

The Nusselt number is given by,

$$Nu_D = 0.725 \left[\frac{g\rho^2 h_{fg} D^3}{\mu k \Delta t}\right]^{1/4}$$

$$= 0.725 \left[\frac{(32.2)(3600)^2 (62.15)^2 (1022.1)(2/12)^3}{(1.49)(0.368)(126.04 - 100)}\right]^{1/4}$$

$$= 619.82$$

Then, the heat transfer coefficient given by:

$$h = \frac{Nu_x K}{D}$$

$$h = (619.82)\frac{0.368}{2/12}$$

$$= 1368.6 \text{ Btu/hr-ft}^2\text{-}^0\text{F}$$

The rate of steam condensation per foot of pipe length is given by:

$$\frac{\dot{m}}{L} = \frac{Q}{L}\frac{1}{h_{fg}}$$

$$= \pi D h \frac{\Delta t}{h_{fg}}$$

$$= \pi\left(\frac{2.0}{12}\right)(1368.6)\frac{(126.04 - 100)}{1022.1}$$

$$= 18.26 \text{ lb/hr-ft}$$

• PROBLEM 14-16

Consider a 1 in. outer diameter cylinder which is 6 ft long with an average wall temperature of 140°F. If the cylinder is used for condensing steam at 7 psia, determine the unit-surface conductances of the cylinder in both the horizontal and vertical positions.

Solution: The heat is transferred from the steam to the cylinder. The physical properties are taken at the mean condensate film temperature.

The saturation temperature from steam tables at 7 psia is 176.82°F. Then, the mean condensate film temperature is

$$T_f = \frac{176.82 + 140}{2} = 158.41^{0}F.$$

From tables of liquid water at 158.41°F:

$\rho_1 = 61.1\ lb/ft^3$ $\qquad$ $k = 0.3847\ Btu/hr\text{-}ft\text{-}^{0}F$

$\mu_1 = 0.276 \times 10^{-3}\ lb/ft\text{-}sec = 0.9936\ lb/ft\text{-}hr$

From steam tables, for water vapor at 176.82°F:

latent heat $h_{fg} = 992.1\ Btu/lb$

$\rho_v = 0.0186\ lb/ft^3$

When the cylinder is in the horizontal position, the unit surface conductance is given by:

$$h_c = 0.725\left[\frac{g\rho_1(\rho_1 - \rho_v)h_{fg}k^3}{\mu_1 D(T_{sv} - T_s)}\right]^{1/4}$$

$$= 0.725\left[\frac{61.1(61.1-0.0186)(32.2)(3600)^2(992.1)(0.3847)^3}{(1/12)(0.9936)(176.82-140)}\right]^{1/4}$$

$$= 1680.3\ Btu/hr\text{-}ft^2\text{-}^{0}F$$

When the cylinder is in the vertical position, the unit surface conductance is given by:

$$h_c = 0.943\left[\frac{g\rho_1(\rho_1 - \rho_v)h_{fg}k^3}{\mu_1 L(T_{sv} - T_s)}\right]^{1/4}$$

$$= 0.943\left[\frac{(32.2)(3600)^2(61.1)(61.1-0.0186)(992.1)(0.3847)^3}{(0.9936)(6)(176.82-140)}\right]^{1/4}$$

$$h_c = 750.3\ Btu/hr\text{-}ft^2\text{-}^{0}F$$

The unit surface conductances of the given cylinder in the horizontal and the vertical positions are 1680.3 Btu/hr-ft^2-^{0}F and 750.3 Btu/hr-ft^2-^{0}F, respectively.

• PROBLEM 14-17

> The heat generated through condensation of saturated steam on the outside of a vertical tube goes towards boiling a liquid flowing inside it. The section that is heated by the steam is 10 ft high and 2 inches in outside diameter. Calculate the steam temperature that would supply 92,000 Btu/hr of heat at a tube-surface temperature of 200^{0}F, assuming film condensation.

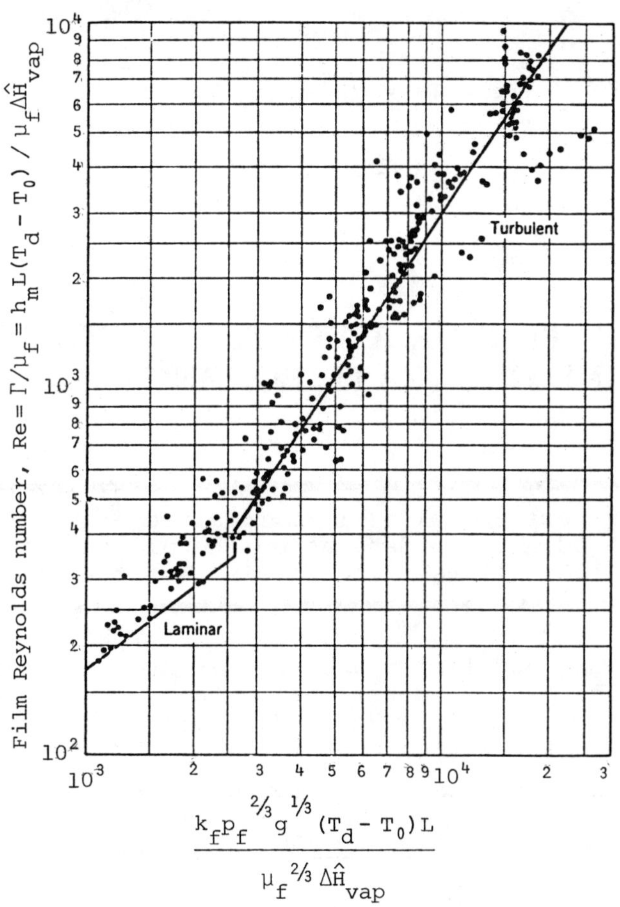

Solution: I Trial: Assume $T_d = 200^0F$

$$\Delta\hat{H}_{vap} = 978 \text{ Btu/lbm}$$

$$k_f = 0.393 \text{ Btu/hr-ft-}^0\text{F}$$

$$\rho_f = 60.1 \text{ lb/ft}^3$$

$$\mu_f = 0.738 \text{ lb/ft-hr}$$

Making an energy balance around the tube, we get

$$Q = W\Delta\hat{H}_{vap} = \pi D\Gamma\ \Delta\hat{H}_{vap}$$

$$Re_{film} = \frac{\Gamma}{\mu} = \frac{Q}{\pi D\mu\Delta\hat{H}_{vap}} = \frac{92,000}{\pi\left(\frac{2}{12}\right)(0.738)978} = 244$$

From the plot, for this ordinate, the flow is seen to be laminar and the abscissa = 1700 or

$$\frac{k_f\rho_f^{2/3}g^{1/3}(T_d - T_o)L}{\mu_f^{5/3}\Delta H_{vap}} = 1700$$

$$T_d - T_o = 22^0F$$

$$T_d = 200 + 22 = 222^0F$$

CONDENSATION ON A VERTICAL CYLINDER / PLATE AND NUCLEATE BOILING PHENOMENA

• PROBLEM 14-18

A 2 ft high vertical plate is maintained at 200°F. If steam at 15 psia is condensing on the plate, determine the average heat transfer coefficient of the plate.

Solution: The physical properties are to be obtained from tables at the mean condensate film temperature. From steam tables the saturation temperature of water at 15 psia is 213.03°F, and the latent heat is h_{fg} = 969.7 Btu/lb. Therefore the mean condensate film temperature is

$$T_f = \frac{213.03 + 200}{2} = 206.52^0F.$$

From tables of water properties at 206.52°F:

$$\rho = 59.94 \text{ lb/ft}^3$$

$$\mu = 0.2 \times 10^{-3} \text{ lb/ft-s} = 0.72 \text{ lb/ft-hr}$$

$$k = 0.3933 \text{ Btu/hr-ft-}^0F$$

The relation from which h will be determined is to be

obtained based on the Reynolds number (Re). Re depends on the amount of steam condensed. Therefore it is necessary to first assume that the film is laminar and then verify the assumption at the end. If the film is laminar, the relation that can be used in determining h is given by:

$$Nu_L = 1.13 \left[\frac{g\rho^2 h_{fg} L^3}{\mu k \Delta t}\right]^{1/4}$$

$$= 1.13 \left[\frac{(32.2)(3600)^2(59.94)^2(969.7)(2)^3}{(0.72)(0.3933)(213.03-200)}\right]^{1/4}$$

$$= 8467.1$$

Therefore, the average heat transfer coefficient is given by:

$$h = \frac{Nu_L k}{L}$$

$$h = \frac{(8467.1)(0.3933)}{2}$$

$$= 1665 \text{ Btu/hr-ft}^2\text{-}^0\text{F}$$

Then, the amount of steam condensed per foot of width is:

$$\Gamma_{max} = 1665 \times \frac{(2)(13.03)}{969.7}$$

$$= 44.7 \text{ lb/ft-hr}$$

Now, the Reynolds number is:

$$Re = \frac{\Gamma_{max}}{\mu}$$

$$= \frac{44.7}{0.72}$$

$$= 62$$

This indicates that the original assumption of a laminar film was valid.

If the film is not laminar, then the following equation should be used.

$$Nu_L = 0.0134 \left[\frac{g\rho^2 L^3}{\mu^2}\right]^{1/3} (Re)^{0.4}$$

This equation can be solved only by iteration, because Re is needed to determine the Nusselt number, by which the heat transfer coefficient is calculated.

The surface of a 5 ft vertical plate is completely covered by a film of condensed steam. The average coefficient of heat transfer is 900 Btu/hr-ft^2-^{0}F, and the partial pressure of the water vapor is 15 psia. Assume the flow is laminar, and determine the surface temperature of the plate.

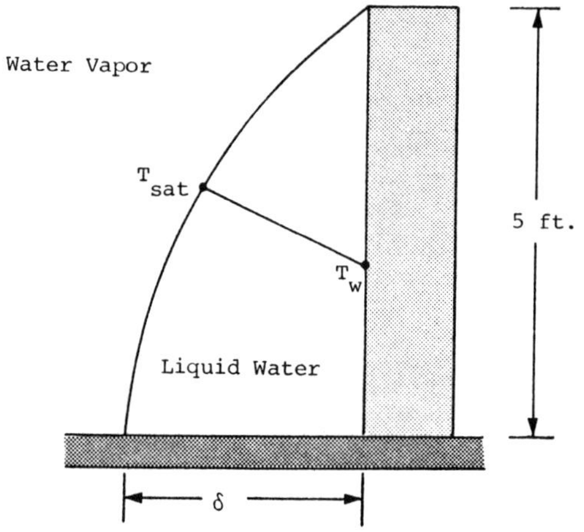

Solution: Assume the conduction effects dominate in heat transfer, and the surface temperature of the vertical plate is uniform.

Then, the relation between the local and average heat transfer coefficient is given by:

$$h_{av} = \frac{4}{3} h_{x=L}$$

$$h_{av} = \frac{4}{3} \left[\frac{k_l^3 \rho_l(\rho_l - \rho_v) g h_{fg}}{4\mu_l(T_{sat} - T_w)L} \right]^{1/4} \tag{1}$$

where h_{av} - average heat transfer coefficient

k_l - thermal conductivity of liquid water

ρ_l - density of liquid water

ρ_v - density of water vapor

h_{fg} - latent heat of vaporization

μ_l - viscosity of liquid water

T_{sat} - saturation temperature

T_w - surface temperature

L - characteristic length

Raising both sides of eq.(1) to the power of 4 gives:

$$h_{av}^4 = \frac{256}{81} \frac{k_1^3 \rho_1(\rho_1-\rho_v)gh_{fg}}{4\mu_1(T_{sat} - T_w)L}$$

$$T_{sat} - T_w = \left(\frac{64}{81}\right) \frac{k_1^3 \rho_1(\rho_1-\rho_v)gh_{fg}}{\mu_1 L\, h_{av}^4}$$

Then,
$$T_w = T_{sat} - \left(\frac{64}{81}\right) \frac{k_1^3 \rho_1(\rho_1-\rho_v)gh_{fg}}{\mu_1 L\, h_{av}^4} \qquad (2)$$

Given $h_{av} = 900\ \text{Btu/hr-ft}^2\text{-}^0\text{F}$

$g = 32.2\ \text{ft/sec}^2 = 4.173 \times 10^8\ \text{ft/hr}^2$

$L = 5$ ft

From steam tables:

saturation temperature at 15 psia is 213.03^0F.

latent heat $h_{fg} = 969.7$ Btu/lb

vapor density $\rho_v = 0.0380\ \text{lb/ft}^3$

liquid density $\rho_1 = 59.81\ \text{lb/ft}^3$

thermal conductivity of liquid $k_1 = 0.3935\ \text{Btu/hr-ft-}^0\text{F}$

viscosity $\mu_1 = 0.194 \times 10^{-3}$ lb/ft-sec = 0.698 lb/ft-hr

Substituting in eq.(2) gives:

$$T_w = 213.03 - \left(\frac{64}{81}\right) \frac{(0.3935)^3(59.81)(59.81-0.0380)(4.123\times10^8)(969.7)}{(0.698)(5)(900)^4}$$

$= 182.6^0$F

The surface temperature of the plate is 182.6^0F.

• PROBLEM 14-20

Consider a copper kettle which has a flat bottom with a 10 in. diameter. Water is boiled at a rate of 50 lbm/hr at atmospheric pressure. Find the burning out heat flux for nucleate boiling.

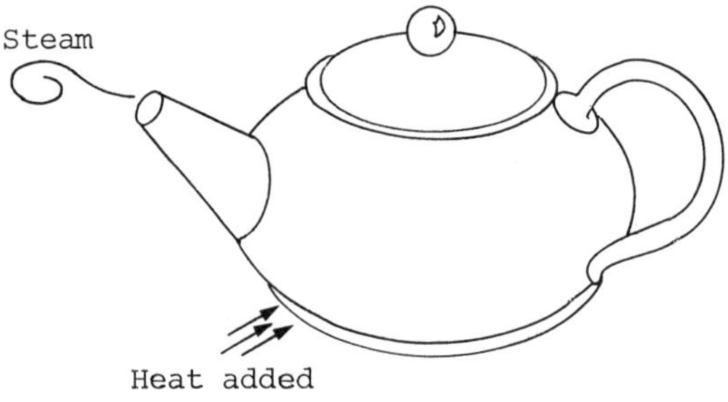

Fig. 1

Solution: Assume that the heat transfer from the surface of the kettle to the surrounding liquid takes place purely by convection until the temperature of the kettle surface is a few degrees above the boiling temperature of the liquid (pool boiling). Also assume that steady state conditions prevail in the system.

From steam tables, at atmospheric pressure:

$T_{sat} = 212^0F$ $\quad\quad$ $h_{fg} = 970$ Btu/lbm

$\sigma = 40 \times 10^{-4}\ lb_f/ft$ $\quad\quad$ $\rho_1 = 60.0\ lbm/ft^3$

$\rho_v = 0.038\ lbm/ft^3$

At the point of maximum heat transfer, we have the following equation:

$$q_b = \frac{Q_b}{A} = \frac{\pi}{24}(h_{fg}\rho_v) \times \left[\frac{\sigma g g_c(\rho_1-\rho_v)}{\rho_v{}^2}\right]^{1/4} \times \left[\frac{\rho_1+\rho_v}{\rho_1}\right]^{-1/2} \quad (1)$$

Q_b can be evaluated using eq.(1) since all the other quantities are known.

$$A = 0.545\ ft^2$$

$$g = 32.2\ ft/sec^2$$

$$g_c = 32.2\ lbm\ ft/lb_f\text{-}sec^2$$

Substituting in eq.(1) gives:

$$Q_b = \frac{\pi}{24}(0.545\times970\times0.038)\left[\frac{(40\times10^{-4})(32.2)(32.2)(60-0.038)}{(0.038)^2}\right]^{1/4} \times \left[\frac{60+0.038}{60}\right]^{-1/2}$$

$= 2.629 \times 20.37 \times 0.99$

$= 53.2$ Btu/sec

$= 1.91 \times 10^5$ Btu/hr

Then, the burning out heat flux for nucleate boiling is 1.91×10^5 Btu/hr.

• PROBLEM 14-21

A polished stainless steel surface is electrically heated from the bottom to boil water at atmospheric pressure. If the surface temperature is $230\,^0$F, calculate the heat flux from the surface to the water and compare this value with the critical heat flux of nucleate boiling.

Solution: The heat transfer from the surface to the water takes place purely by convection until the temperature of the surface is a few degrees above the boiling temperature of water (pool boiling). If the temperature increases further, the energy level of the water adjacent to the surface becomes so high that some of the water molecules transform into vapor nuclei and form vapor bubbles on the surface. The bubbles formed will grow in diameter and are displaced from the surface by buoyant forces. They then rise into the liquid above. The heating takes place by intense convection currents which are induced by the motion of the bubbles. This process of heat transfer is called nucleate boiling.

Assume that at $18\,^0$F excess temperature nucleate boiling exists. Then, the heat flux is given by:

$$\frac{q}{A} = \left(\frac{C_1 \Delta T_x}{C_{sf} h_{fg} Pr_L^{1.7}}\right)^3 \mu_1 h_{fg} \left(\frac{g(\rho_1 - \rho_v)}{g_c \sigma}\right)^{0.5} \qquad (1)$$

where C_1 = specific heat of saturated liquid

q/A = heat flux

h_{fg} = latent heat of vaporization

g_c = conversion factor 32.2 lbm ft/lb_f-sec^2

g = gravitational constant 32.2 ft/sec^2

σ = surface tension of the liquid to vapor interface

ρ_1 = density of the saturated liquid

ρ_v = density of the saturated vapor

Pr_l = Prandtl number of saturated liquid

μ_l = viscosity of the liquid

C_{sf} = emprical constant which depends on the nature of the heating surface-fluid combination

For the given fluid surface combination C_{sf} = 0.0132.

From steam tables, at atmospheric pressure:

h_{fg} = 970 Btu/lbm	ρ_l = 60.04 lb/ft^3
ρ_v = 0.0373 lb/ft^3	σ = 40.3 × 10^{-3} lb$_f$/ft
μ_l = 0.702 lb/ft-hr	C_l = 1.0 Btu/lbm^{0}F
Pr_l = 1.82	ΔT_x = 230 - 212 = 18^{0}F

Substituting ΔT_x in eq.(1) gives:

$$\frac{q}{A} = \left(\frac{1.0(18)}{(0.0132)(970)(1.82)^{1.7}}\right)^3 (0.702)(970)\left[\frac{(32.2)(60.04-0.0373)}{(32.2)(40.3\times10^{-4})}\right]^{0.5}$$

$$= 10883.25 \text{ Btu/hr-ft}^2$$

The burning out heat flux is given by:

$$\frac{q}{A} = 143\rho_v h_{fg}(g/g_c)^{1/4}\left[(\rho_l-\rho_v)/\rho_v\right]^{0.6} \tag{2}$$

Substituting in eq.(2) gives:

$$\frac{q}{A} = 143(0.0373)(970)(32.2/32.2)^{1/4}\left[(60.04-0.0373)/0.0373\right]^{0.6}$$

$$= 434204 \text{ Btu/hr-ft}^2$$

The heat flux is less than the critical heat flux, therefore at 18^{0}F excess temperature nucleate-boiling exists. Then, the underlying assumptions made in the application of eq.(1) are satisfied.

• PROBLEM 14-22

> The emissivity of a hemispherical surface of a 2 in. diameter steel rod is 0.88. The surface temperature of the rod is 1400 °F. The rod is quenched in saturated water at 220 °F. Determine the average heat transfer coefficient between the horizontal bar and the water.

<u>Solution</u>: In this system the boiling is most likely film boiling, because the temperature difference

$$T_w - T_o = 1400 - 220 = 1180\,^0F,$$

is higher than what is usual for nucleate boiling. Assume stable film boiling exists. Then, the surface heat transfer coefficient is given by:

$$h = h_{co} + h_r\left[\frac{3}{4} + \frac{1}{4}\,\frac{h_r}{h_{co}}\left(\frac{1}{2.62 + h_r/h_{co}}\right)\right] \qquad (1)$$

where

$$h_{co} = 0.62\left[\frac{k_v^3\,\rho_v(\rho-\rho_v)g(h_{fg}+0.4C_p\Delta T)}{\mu_v D\Delta T}\right]^{1/4} \qquad (2)$$

$$h_r = \sigma\varepsilon\left(\frac{T_w^4 - T_o^4}{T_w - T_o}\right) \qquad (3)$$

σ = Stefan-Boltzmann constant

0.1714×10^{-8} Btu/hr-ft^2-$^0R^4$

k_v = thermal conductivity of vapor

ρ_v = density of superheated vapor

ρ = density of saturated liquid

h_{fg} = latent heat of vaporization

D = diameter of rod

$\Delta T = T_w - T_o$

The mean film temperature is given by:

$$T_f = \frac{1}{2}(T_w + T_o)$$

$$= \frac{1}{2}(1400 + 220) = 810\,^0F$$

The saturation pressure at 220 °F is 17.19 psia.

From steam tables, for vapor at 17.19 psia and 810^0F:

$\rho_v = 0.0195\ lbm/ft^3$ $\qquad h_{fg} = 965.3\ Btu/lbm$

$\mu_v = 0.0616\ lbm/ft\text{-}hr$ $\qquad Cp = 0.5\ Btu/lbm^0F$

$k_v = 0.0325\ Btu/hr\text{-}ft\text{-}^0F$ $\qquad \rho = 59.63\ lbm/ft^3$

Given: $D = \frac{2}{12} = 0.1667\ ft$

$\Delta T = 1400 - 220 = 1180^0F$

Substituting in eq.(2) gives:

$$h_{co} = 0.62\left[\frac{(0.0325)^3(0.0195)(59.63-0.0195)(4.17\times10^8)\ 965.3+0.4(0.5)(1180)}{(0.0616)(0.1667)(1180)}\right]^{\frac{1}{4}}$$

$= 22.22\ Btu/hr\text{-}ft^2\text{-}^0F$

Substituting in eq.(3) yields:

$$h_r = (0.1714\times10^{-8})(0.88)\left(\frac{1860^4 - 680^4}{1860 - 680}\right)$$

$$= 15.03\ Btu/hr\text{-}ft^2\text{-}^0F$$

Therefore the ratio is,

$$\frac{h_r}{h_{co}} = \frac{15.03}{22.22}$$

$$= 0.676$$

Substituting in eq.(1) gives:

$$h = 22.22 + 15.03\left[\frac{3}{4} + \frac{1}{4}(0.676)\left(\frac{1}{2.62+0.676}\right)\right]$$

$$= 34.26\ Btu/hr\text{-}ft^2\text{-}^0F$$

The average surface heat transfer coefficient is 34.26 $Btu/hr\text{-}ft^2\text{-}^0F$.

CHAPTER 15

DIFFUSION IN GASES AND LIQUIDS

EQUILIBRIUM COMPOSITIONS, DEW POINT, MASS AND MOLAR AVERAGE VELOCITIES

• **PROBLEM 15-1**

A mixture of N_2 and O_2 gases contains equal weight of each gas. The absolute velocities are given as:

$$\vec{v}_{N_2} = -7\,\vec{i} \text{ m/sec}$$

$$\vec{v}_{O_2} = +7\,\vec{i} \text{ m/sec}$$

where $\vec{i}$ is a unit vector in the x direction. Obtain the mass and molar average velocities.

Solution: Basis: 1 gm of the gas mixture

The average mass velocity, $\vec{v}$, can be calculated using equation (1).

$$\vec{v} = \sum_{i=1}^{2} m_i v_i \tag{1}$$

Substituting:

$$\vec{v} = \frac{1}{2}(-7\vec{i}) + \frac{1}{2}(+7\vec{i})$$

$$= 0$$

Equation (2) yields the molar average velocity, $\vec{v}^*$.

$$\vec{v}^* = \sum_{i=1}^{2} x_i \vec{v}_i \qquad (2)$$

The mole fractions, x_i, can be obtained using equation (3).

$$x_i = \frac{m_i/M_i}{\Sigma m_j/M_j} \qquad (3)$$

where M is the molecular weight of the species.

$$x_{N_2} = \frac{\frac{1}{2} \cdot \frac{1}{28}}{\frac{1}{2} \cdot \frac{1}{28} + \frac{1}{2} \cdot \frac{1}{32}} = 0.53$$

$$x_{O_2} = \frac{\frac{1}{2} \cdot \frac{1}{32}}{\frac{1}{2} \cdot \frac{1}{28} + \frac{1}{2} \cdot \frac{1}{32}} = 0.47$$

Substituting in equation (2);

$$\vec{v}^* = 0.53\ (-7\vec{i}) + 0.47(+7\vec{i})$$

$$= -0.42\vec{i}\ \text{m/sec}$$

• PROBLEM 15-2

Determine the dew point of a mixture of benzene and n-pentane gases. The composition is 60 mole percent benzene and 40 mole precent n-pentane. The total pressure is 1 atm.

Solution: Raoult's law may be applied at this pressure. Since the vapor pressures are functions of the temperature, which must be calculated, an iterative approach is required.

For benzene:

$$y_B = \frac{P_B}{760} x_B = 0.60 \qquad x_B = \frac{456}{P_B}$$

For n-pentane:

$$y_P = \frac{P_P}{760} x_P = 0.40 \qquad x_P = \frac{304}{P_P}$$

At the desired temperature:

$$x_B + x_P = 1$$

or:

$$\frac{456}{P_B} + \frac{304}{P_P} = 1 \qquad (1)$$

Assuming a temperature and obtaining vapor pressure data allows the problem to be solved by trial and error.

At T = 100°C

$$P_B = 1350.2 \text{ mm Hg}$$

$$P_P = 4420.4 \text{ mm Hg}$$

and substituting in equation (1):

$$\frac{456}{1350.2} + \frac{304}{4420.4} = 0.406 \neq 1$$

At T = 65°C

$$P_B = 465.8 \text{ mm Hg}$$

$$P_P = 1851.7 \text{ mm Hg}$$

and

$$\frac{456}{465.8} + \frac{304}{1851.7} = 1.14 \neq 1$$

At T = 69°C

$$P_B = 532.9 \text{ mm Hg}$$

$$P_P = 2066.3 \text{ mm Hg}$$

and

$$\frac{456}{532.9} + \frac{304}{2066.3} = 1.00$$

The dew point is 69°C.

• PROBLEM 15-3

Benzene and iso-pentane are mixed at 1.5 atm. and 110°F. Determine the compositions of the liquid and vapor using Raoult's law.

Solution: The vapor pressure data are:

Vapor pressure of benzene at 110°F = 212 mm Hg

Vapor pressure of iso-pentane at 110°F = 1273 mm Hg

The total pressure is 1.5(760) = 1140 mm Hg.

For benzene:

$$y_B = \frac{P_B}{P} x_B = \frac{212}{1140} x_B = 0.186\ x_B \qquad (1)$$

For iso-pentane:

$$y_P = \frac{P_P}{P} x_P = \frac{1273}{1140} x_P = 1.12\ x_P \qquad (2)$$

Since it is a 2 component system, it is clear that:

$$x_B + x_P = 1 \qquad (3)$$

and

$$y_B + y_P = 1 \qquad (4)$$

Solving equations (1) through (4) simultaneously yields:

$x_B = 0.13 \qquad x_P = 0.87$

$y_B = 0.02 \qquad y_P = 0.98$

DIFFUSIVITY CALCULATIONS

• PROBLEM 15-4

Argon has a viscosity of 2.097×10^{-4} g/cm.sec at 273°K and 1 atm. If argon behaves as an ideal gas:

(I) Obtain the equivalent molecular diameter (σ).

(II) Estimate the viscosity of argon at 350°C and 1 atm.

(III) Estimate the diffusivity of argon at 0°C and 1 atm.

(IV) Estimate the thermal conductivity (k) of argon at 0°C and 1 atm.

Employing an experimental value of $\sigma = 3.65 \times 10^{-8}$ cm for argon and using the theory for spherical molecules:

(V) Obtain the viscosity of argon at 0°C and 1 atm.

(VI) Obtain the viscosity of argon at 350°C and 1 atm.

(VII) Obtain the diffusivity of argon at 0°C and 1 atm.

(VIII) Obtain the thermal conductivity of argon at 0°C and 1 atm.

Solution:

(I) The equivalent molecular diameter is given by equation (1):

$$\sigma = \sqrt{\frac{8.28 \times 10^{-20} \quad T^{1.5}\rho}{\mu P m^{1/2}}} \qquad (1)$$

where:

$$\rho = \frac{39.94 \text{ g/gmol}}{22400 \text{ cm}^3\text{/gmol}} = 1.783 \times 10^{-3} \text{ g/cm}^3$$

Therefore:

$$\sigma = \sqrt{\frac{8.28 \times 10^{-20} \; (273)^{1.5}(1.783 \times 10^{-3})}{(2.097 \times 10^{-4})(1)(39.94)^{1/2}}}$$

$$= 2.242 \times 10^{-8} \text{ cm}$$

(II) The absolute viscosity is proportional to $T^{1/2}$. Therefore:

$$\frac{\mu_{623}}{\mu_{273}} = \left(\frac{623}{273}\right)^{1/2}$$

and

$$\mu_{623} = (2.097 \times 10^{-4}) \left(\frac{623}{273}\right)^{1/2}$$

$$= 3.17 \times 10^{-4} \text{ g/cm.sec}$$

(III) The arithmetic mean speed is given by:

$$\bar{c} = \sqrt{\frac{8RT}{M\pi}}$$

$$= \sqrt{\frac{8(8.314 \times 10^7)(273)}{(39.94)\pi}}$$

$$= 3.80 \times 10^4 \text{ cm/sec}$$

where $R = 8.314 \times 10^7$ ergs/g.mol$^\circ$K

The mean free path (l) is defined by:

$$l = \frac{RT}{7.78 \times 10^{29} \times P\pi\sigma^2}$$

Substituting:

$$l = \frac{(8.314 \times 10^7)(273)}{(7.78 \times 10^{29})(1)\pi(2.242 \times 10^{-8})^2}$$

$$= 1.847 \times 10^{-5} \text{ cm}$$

The mass diffusivity is given by:

$$D = \frac{1}{6} l\bar{c}$$

$$= \frac{1}{6} (1.847 \times 10^{-5})(3.80 \times 10^{4})$$

$$= 0.117 \text{ cm}^2/\text{sec}$$

(IV) The thermal conductivity is given by:

$$k = \frac{20.7 \times 10^{-20} \sqrt{T/M}}{\sigma^2}$$

therefore

$$k = \frac{20.7 \times 10^{-20} \sqrt{273/39.94}}{(2.242 \times 10^{-8})^2}$$

$$= 1.077 \times 10^{-3} \frac{\text{ergs}}{\text{sec-cm}^2 \text{ -}^{\circ}\text{C/cm}}$$

$$= 2.57 \times 10^{-11} \frac{\text{cal}}{\text{sec-cm}^2\text{-}^{\circ}\text{C/cm}}$$

(V) The viscosity can be obtained from:

$$\mu = \frac{2.6693 \times 10^{-21} \sqrt{MT}}{\sigma^2}$$

$$= \frac{2.6693 \times 10^{-21} \sqrt{(39.94)(273)}}{(3.65 \times 10^{-8})^2}$$

$$= 2.09 \times 10^{-4} \text{ g/cm-sec}$$

This is very close to the experimental value of the viscosity given in the problem statement.

(VI) The viscosity at 350°C is yielded by the following equation:

$$\mu = \frac{2.6693 \times 10^{-21} \sqrt{MT}}{\sigma^2}$$

$$= \frac{2.6693 \times 10^{-21} \sqrt{(39.94)(623)}}{(3.65 \times 10^{-8})^2}$$

$$= 3.16 \times 10^{-4} \text{ g/cm-sec}$$

(VII) The mass diffusivity can be calculated from:

$$D = \frac{2.628 \times 10^{-19} \sqrt{T^3/M}}{P\sigma^2}$$

$$= \frac{2.628 \times 10^{-19}\sqrt{(273)^3/39.94}}{(1)(3.65 \times 10^{-8})^2}$$

$$D = 0.141 \text{ cm}^2/\text{sec}$$

(VIII) The thermal conductivity is given by:

$$k = \frac{15}{4}\frac{R}{M}\mu$$

$$= \frac{15}{4}\left(\frac{1.987}{39.94}\right)(2.09 \times 10^{-4})$$

$$= 3.90 \times 10^{-5} \frac{\text{cal}}{\text{sec-cm}^2\text{-}^\circ\text{C/cm}}$$

where R = 1.987 cal/gmol-K

• PROBLEM 15-5

Evaluate the diffusion coefficient for CO_2 in air at 1 atm (and 30 °C) using equation (1).

Solution: Equation (1) states that the diffusion coefficient D is given by:

$$D = 435.7 \frac{T^{3/2}}{P(V_A^{1/3} + V_B^{1/3})^2}\sqrt{\frac{1}{M_A} + \frac{1}{M_B}} \qquad (1)$$

where V is the atomic volume of the species and M is the molecular weight.

P is the pressure in N/m^2 and T is the temperature in °K.

$$V_{CO_2} = 34.0$$

$$V_{air} = 29.9$$

$$M_{CO_2} = 44$$

$$M_{air} = 28.9$$

Substitution in (1) yields:

$$D = \frac{(435.7)(303)^{3/2}}{(1.0132 \times 10^5)\left[(34.0)^{1/3} + (29.9)^{1/3}\right]^2}\sqrt{\frac{1}{44} + \frac{1}{28.9}}$$

$$= 0.135 \text{ cm}^2/\text{sec}$$

• PROBLEM 15-6

Calculate and compare the diffusivity of water vapor in air at 25°C and 1 atm with its experimental value, 0.256 cm^2/sec.

Solution: The diffusivity (D) is given by:

$$D = 0.0043 \frac{T^{3/2}}{P(V_A^{1/3} + V_B^{1/3})^2} \sqrt{\frac{1}{M_A} + \frac{1}{M_B}} \qquad (1)$$

where V and M are the molecular volume and molecular weight respectively. P is the pressure in atm and T is the temperature in K.

$$V_{H_2O} = 18.9$$

$$V_{air} = 29.9$$

$$M_{H_2O} = 18$$

$$M_{air} = 29$$

Substitution in (1) yields:

$$D = 0.0043 \frac{(273 + 25)^{3/2}}{1(18.9^{1/3} + 29.9^{1/3})^2} \sqrt{\frac{1}{18} + \frac{1}{29}}$$

$$= 0.201 \text{ cm}^2/\text{sec}$$

• PROBLEM 15-7

Approximate the diffusivity of H_2O in oxygen at 65°F and 0.75 atm absolute.

Solution: Equation (1) will be employed.

$$D = \frac{0.0043\ T^{1.5}}{P(V_a^{1/3} + V_b^{1/3})^2} \sqrt{\frac{1}{M_a} + \frac{1}{M_b}} \qquad (1)$$

where:

D = diffusivity, cm^2/sec

T = temperature, °K

P = absolute pressure, atm

M = molecular weight

V = molecular volume at normal boiling point, $cm^3/gmol$

$V_{H_2O} = 18.9$

$V_{O_2} = 2(7.4) = 14.8$

$M_{H_2O} = 18$

$M_{O_2} = 32$

$T = 65^{\circ}F = 292^{\circ}K$

Substituting in (1):

$$D = \frac{0.0043(292)^{1.5}}{0.75(18.9^{1/3} + 14.8^{1/3})^2} \sqrt{\frac{1}{18} + \frac{1}{32}}$$

$$= 0.322 \ cm^2/sec$$

• PROBLEM 15-8

Approximate the diffusivity of methanol vapor (A) through air (B) at 1 atm and 25°C.

ATOMIC AND MOLECULAR VOLUMES

Atomic volume, $m^3/1000$ atoms x 10^3		Molecular volume, $m^3/kmol$ x 10^3		Atomic volume, $m^3/1000$ atoms x 10^3		Molecular volume, $m^3/kmol$ x 10^3	
Carbon	14.8	H_2	14.3	Oxygen	7.4	NH_3	25.8
Hydrogen	3.7	O_2	25.6	In methyl esters	9.1	H_2O	18.9
Chlorine	24.6	N_2	31.2	In higher esters	11.0	H_2S	32.9
Bromine	27.0	Air	29.9	In acids	12.0	COS	51.5
Iodine	37.0	CO	30.7	In methyl ethers	9.9	Cl_2	48.4
Sulfur	25.6	CO_2	34.0	In higher ethers	11.0	Br_2	53.2
Nitrogen	15.6	SO_2	44.8	Benzene ring: subtract	15	I_2	71.5
In primary amines	10.5	NO	23.6	Naphthalene ring: subtract	30		
In secondary amines	12.0	N_2O	36.4				

Fig. 1.

Solution: Values of the force constants for air can be obtained from standard tables:

$r_B = 0.3711$ nm $\qquad \varepsilon_B/k = 78.6$ K

Those for methanol can be estimated using equations (1) and (2). The term kT/ε_{AB} (k is the Boltzmann constant and ε_{AB} is the energy of molecular attraction) allows the collision function $f(kT/\varepsilon_{AB})$ to be obtained from figure (2). Substitution in equation (3) permits the diffusivity to be calculated.

The molar volume of methanol can be obtained by employing figure (1);

$$V_A = 1(0.0148) + 4(0.0037) + 1(0.0074)$$
$$= 0.037$$

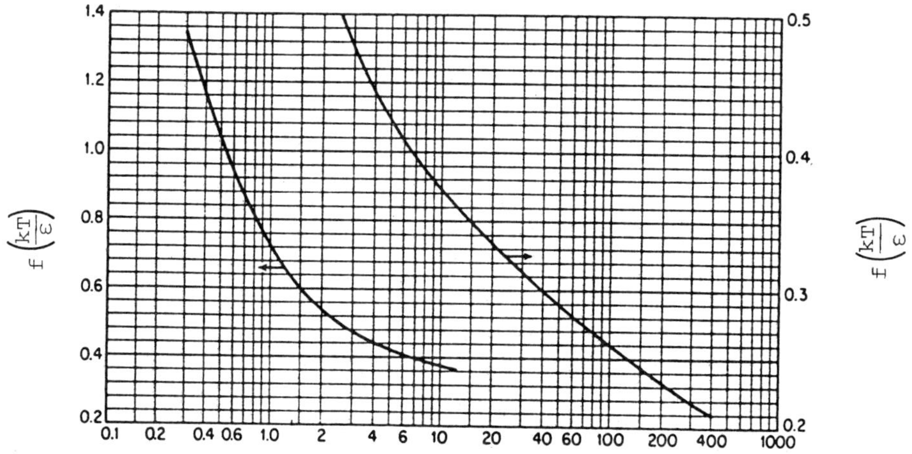

Fig. 2. $\frac{kT}{\varepsilon}$

COLLISION FUNCTION FOR DIFFUSION

The normal boiling point of methanol is $T_{b,A} = 65^{\circ}C$. Substitution into equations (1) and (2) provides the force constants for methanol.

$$r_A = 1.18\ V_A^{1/3} \quad (1)$$
$$= 1.18(0.037)^{1/3} = 0.394 \text{ nm}$$

$$\frac{\varepsilon_A}{k} = 1.21\ T_{b,A} \quad (2)$$

$$\frac{\varepsilon_A}{k} = 1.21(338) = 409 \text{ K}$$

The molecular separation at collision (r_{AB}) is given by:

$$r_{AB} = \frac{r_A + r_B}{2} = \frac{0.394 + 0.3711}{2}$$
$$= 0.3826 \text{ nm}$$

The energy of molecular attraction, ε_{AB}, is given by:

$$\frac{\varepsilon_{AB}}{k} = \sqrt{\left(\frac{\varepsilon_A}{k}\right)\left(\frac{\varepsilon_B}{k}\right)}$$

$$= \sqrt{(409)(78.6)} = 179.3\ K$$

Therefore

$$\frac{kT}{\varepsilon_{AB}} = \frac{298}{179.3} = 1.662$$

From figure (2), the collision function for diffusion is:

$$f\left(\frac{kT}{\varepsilon}\right) = 0.58$$

The diffusivity can be obtained from equation (3)·

$$D_{AB} = \frac{10^{-4}(1.084 - 0.249\sqrt{1/M_A + 1/M_B}\ T^{1.5}\sqrt{1/M_A + 1/M_B}}{P_t(r_{AB})^2 f(kT/\varepsilon_{AB})} \qquad (3)$$

where:

D_{AB} = diffusivity, m^2/sec

T = absolute temperature, ^0K

M = molecular weight, kg/kmol

P_t = absolute pressure, N/m^2

The molecular weight term is:

$$\sqrt{\frac{1}{M_A} + \frac{1}{M_B}} = \sqrt{\frac{1}{32} + \frac{1}{29}} = 0.256$$

Substituting in equation (3);

$$D_{AB} = \frac{10^{-4}(1.084 - 0.249 \times 0.256)(298)^{1.5}(0.256)}{(101.3 \times 10^3)(0.3826)^2(0.58)}$$

$$= 1.56 \times 10^{-5}\ m^2/sec$$

• PROBLEM 15-9

Pure nitrogen is passed over the opening of a long narrow test tube which contains liquid cyclohexane filled to 11 cm below the top. The temperature is 17^0C and the pressure is 1 atm. After 20.2 hr the liquid level drops 0.22 cm. Using this data determine the diffusivity of the binary gas system.

Solution: The density of cyclohexane is 48.6 lb/ft^3 while the vapor pressure is 0.082 atm. These values are at the given conditions of temperature and pressure. This is an example of steady-state diffusion of cyclohexane (A) through nondiffusing nitrogen (B). The molal flux can be obtained from the change in the liquid level using equation (1).

$$N_A = \frac{\rho_{AL}}{M_A}\frac{dx}{dt} = \frac{D}{RTx}\left(\frac{P}{p_{B,lm}}\right)(p_{A1} - p_{A2}) \qquad (1)$$

where x is the diffusion distance and M_A is the molecular weight of A.

Integrating in the limits:

$$0 \leq t \leq t$$

and

$$x_0 \leq x \leq x$$

yields:

$$D = \frac{\rho_{AL} RT p_{B,lm}(x^2 - x_0^2)}{2M_A tP(p_{A1} - p_{A2})} \qquad (2)$$

where

$$p_{B,lm} = \frac{p_{B2} - p_{B1}}{\ln\left(\frac{p_{B2}}{p_{B1}}\right)} = \frac{1 - (1 - 0.082)}{\ln\left(\frac{1}{1 - 0.082}\right)} = 0.958 \text{ atm}$$

Substituting in equation (2)

$$D = \frac{(48.6 \frac{lb}{ft^3})(1.314 \frac{atm\ ft^3}{lb\text{-}mol\text{-}K})(290\ K)(0.958\ atm)}{2(84.16 \frac{lb}{lb\text{-}mol}\ (20.2\ hr)\left(\frac{3600\ sec}{hr}\right)(1\ atm)(0.082\ atm - 0\ atm)}$$

$$\left[(0.368\ ft)^2 - (0.361\ ft)^2\right]$$

$$= 9.02 \times 10^{-5}\ ft^2/sec$$

• PROBLEM 15-10

Winkelmann's method will be employed to obtain the diffusivity of carbon tetrachloride (CCl_4) vapor in air. The liquid carbon tetrachloride is placed in a long thin vertical tube and kept at a constant temperature. Air is blown past the open top of the tube to maintain a carbon tetrachloride concentration of zero at this location. Assuming that only molecular diffusion occurs, determine the diffusivity at 47°C and 1 atm. The following experimental data are available:

Time		CCl_4 level in tube
hr	min	cm
0	0	0.00
0	25	0.26
3	6	1.28
7	35	2.33
22	15	4.38
32	36	5.46
46	52	6.71
55	28	7.36
80	23	9.04
106	26	10.47

The density of liquid CCl_4 is 1.53 g/cm^3 at $47^\circ C$, and its vapor pressure is 284 mm Hg. Use a gram molecular volume of 22.4 liters.

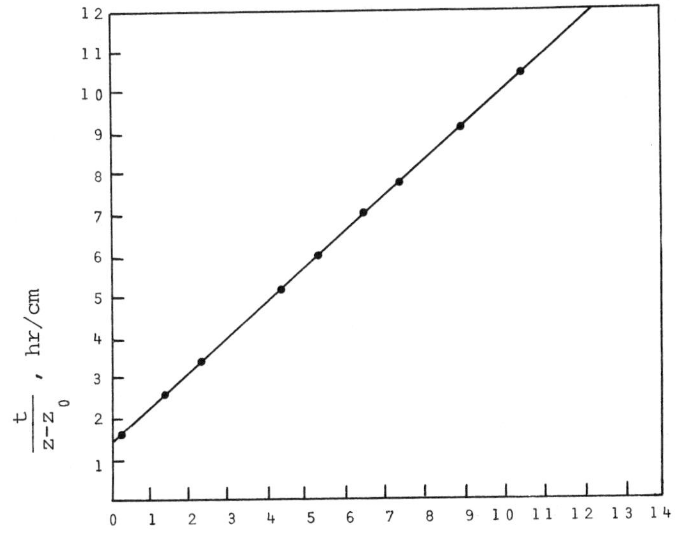

Fig. 1.

$\frac{t}{z-z_0}$ versus $z-z_0$

Solution: The mass transfer rate (N_A), is:

$$N_A = D \frac{C_A}{Z} \frac{C_T}{C_{Bm}} \tag{1}$$

where the subscript A refers to CCl_4, C_A is the saturation concentration at the liquid CCl_4-air interface, and Z is the distance through which mass transfer occurs.

N_A is also given by:

$$N_A = \frac{\rho_L}{M} \cdot \frac{dZ}{dt} \qquad (2)$$

Equating equations (1) and (2) yields:

$$\frac{\rho_L}{m}\frac{dZ}{dt} = D\,\frac{C_A}{Z}\,\frac{C_T}{C_{Bm}} \qquad (3)$$

Performing the integration with $Z = Z_0$ at $t = 0$ gives:

$$Z^2 - Z_0^2 = \frac{2MD}{\rho_L}\,\frac{C_A C_T t}{C_{Bm}} \qquad (4)$$

Values of $Z - Z_0$ are given.

Equation (4) can be written in the following form:

$$(Z - Z_0)(Z - Z_0 + 2Z_0) = \frac{2MD}{\rho_L}\,\frac{C_A C_T t}{C_{B,m}}$$

Therefore:

$$\frac{t}{Z - Z_0} = \frac{\rho_L C_{Bm}}{2MDC_A C_T}(Z - Z_0) + \frac{\rho_L C_{Bm}}{MDC_A C_T} Z_0 \qquad (6)$$

A graph of $\frac{t}{Z - Z_0}$ versus $Z - Z_0$ is shown in figure (1). The slope m is:

$$m = \frac{\rho_L C_{Bm}}{2MDC_A C_T} = 0.844 \text{ hr/cm}^2$$

and

$$D = \frac{\rho_L C_{Bm}}{2MC_A C_T M} \qquad (7)$$

The following are either known or can be obtained:

$$C_T = \frac{1}{22400}\left(\frac{273}{320}\right) = 3.81 \times 10^{-5}\ \frac{\text{gmol}}{\text{cm}^3}$$

$$C_A = \left(\frac{284}{760}\right)\left(\frac{1}{22400}\right)\left(\frac{273}{320}\right) = 1.42 \times 10^{-5}\ \frac{\text{gmol}}{\text{cm}^3}$$

$$\frac{C_{Bm}}{C_T} = \left(\frac{1}{C_T}\right)\frac{C_{B1} - C_{B2}}{\ln\left(\frac{C_{B1}}{C_{B2}}\right)} = \left(\frac{1}{760}\right)\frac{760 - 476}{\ln\left(\frac{760}{476}\right)} = 0.799$$

$m = 154$ g/gmol

$\rho_L = 1.53$ g/cm^3

Substitution in equation (7) yields:

$$D = \frac{(1.53\ g/cm^3)(0.799)}{2(154\ g/gmol)(1.42 \times 10^{-5}\ g\ mol/cm^3)(0.844\ hr/cm^2)}$$

$$= 331.2\ cm^2/hr$$

DIFFUSION RATE

• PROBLEM 15-11

Four gallons of gasoline (A) is poured on a surface area of 20 ft^2. Determine the time necessary for the gasoline to evaporate into still dry air (B). The diffusivity is D_{AB} = 6.5 ft^2/hr. Evaporation occurs through a 6 in. film at 65°F. The gasoline has a vapor pressure of 2 psia.

Solution: Equation (1) will be employed to calculate the mass flux of gasoline, N_A. Knowing the mass to be evaporated, the time can be easily obtained.

The evaporation of gasoline into air is an example of molecular diffusion into a stagnant gas. The evaporation process is described by the equation:

$$N_A = \frac{cD_{AB}}{\delta} \frac{(y_{A1} - y_{A2})}{y_{B,lm}} \qquad (1)$$

where δ is the film thickness and c is the concentration of the mixture. This concentration (c) is roughly equal to the concentration of dry air.

$$c = 0.075\ lb/ft^3$$

The mole fractions of the species can be obtained using the given pressure data:

$$y_{A1} = \frac{2}{14.7} = 0.136 \qquad y_{B1} = 1 - 0.136 = 0.864$$

$$y_{A2} = 0.0 \qquad y_{B2} = 1.0$$

Substituting in equation (1), the mass flux is:

$$N_A = \frac{(0.075\ lb/ft^3)(6.5\ ft^2/hr)}{0.5\ ft}\left[\frac{0.136}{\left(\frac{-0.136}{\ln 0.864}\right)}\right]$$

$$N_A = 0.143\ \frac{lb}{hr\ ft^2}$$

t = time for evaporation

$$t = \frac{4 \text{ gal}}{20 \text{ ft}^2} \frac{6 \text{ lb}}{\text{gal}} \frac{\text{hr-ft}^2}{0.143 \text{ lb}} = 8.39 \text{ hr}$$

where a mean gasoline density of 6 lb/gal has been employed.

• PROBLEM 15-12

Calculate the time needed for a water spill to evaporate into still air at 74°F and 1 atm., with an absolute humidity of 0.0019 lb of water per lb of dry air. The water is 0.039 in. above the ground surface and is at a constant temperature of 74°F. Evaporation occurs by the process of molecular diffusion through a gas film of thickness 0.19 in.

Solution: A basis of 1 ft^2 of surface area will be used. Equation (1) will yield the moles of water evaporated per square foot per unit time.

The volume of the water evaporated is:

$$V = (1 \text{ ft}^2) \frac{0.039 \text{ in}}{12 \text{ in/ft}} = 0.00325 \text{ ft}^3$$

The weight of water evaporated is:

$$W = (0.00325 \text{ ft}^3) \left(7.48 \frac{\text{gal}}{\text{ft}^3}\right) \left(8.34 \frac{\text{lb}}{\text{gal}}\right)$$

$$W = 0.203 \text{ lb}$$

The moles of water evaporated equals

$$\frac{0.203 \text{ lb}}{18 \text{ lb/lb mole}} = 0.0113 \text{ lb mole}$$

The molar concentration of the gas phase (c) is given by the ideal gas law.

$$c = \frac{P}{RT} = \frac{1 \text{ atm}}{(0.73 \text{ atm ft}^3/\text{lb mole R})(534 \text{ R})}$$

$$= 0.00257 \text{ lb mole/ft}^3$$

The diffusivity of water vapor in air is 0.258 cm^2/sec at 538 R and 1 atm. Correcting this value to the desired temperature:

$$D_{AB}/T_2 = D_{AB}/T_1 \left(\frac{T_2}{T_1}\right)^{3/2}$$

Substituting the values,

$$D_{AB} = 0.258 \left(\frac{534}{538}\right)^{3/2} = 0.255 \text{ cm}^2/\text{sec}$$

or

$$D_{AB} = \left(0.255\ \frac{cm^2}{sec}\right)\left(3.87\ \frac{ft^2/hr}{cm^2/sec}\right)$$

$$= 0.987\ ft^2/hr$$

From psychrometric charts, the saturation humidity is 0.0188 lb water/lb dry air at 74°F.

Converting:

$$\left(0.0188\ \frac{\text{lb water}}{\text{lb dry air}}\right)\left(\frac{\text{lb mole water}}{\text{18 lb water}}\right)\left(\frac{\text{29 lb air}}{\text{lb mole air}}\right)$$

$$= 0.0303\ \frac{\text{lbmole } H_2O}{\text{lb mole air}}$$

On a mole fraction basis

$$y_{A1} = 0.0303/1.0303 = 0.0294$$

$$y_{A2} = \left(0.0019\ \frac{\text{lb water}}{\text{lb dry air}}\right)\left(\frac{\text{lb mole water}}{\text{18 lb water}}\right)\left(\frac{\text{29 lb air}}{\text{lb mole air}}\right)$$

$$= 0.00306\ \frac{\text{lb mole water}}{\text{lb mole air}}$$

Converting to mole fractions:

$$y_{A2} = \frac{0.00306}{1.00306} = 0.0031$$

$$y_{A1} - y_{A2} = 0.0263$$

Since there are only two components in the system:

$$y_{B1} = 1 - y_{A1} = 0.9706$$

$$y_{B2} = 1 - y_{A2} = 0.9969$$

Now evaluate $y_{B,lm}$ for use in equation (1):

$$y_{B,lm} = \frac{y_{B2} - y_{B1}}{\ln(y_{B2}/y_{B1})} = \frac{0.9969 - 0.9706}{\ln(0.9969/0.9706)} = 0.984$$

The length of diffusion, $\Delta z = 0.0158$ ft.

Substituting in equation (1);

$$N_A = \frac{cD_{AB}}{\Delta z}\ \frac{y_{A1} - y_{A2}}{y_{B,lm}} \tag{1}$$

$$= \frac{(0.00257\ \text{lb mole/ft}^3)(0.987\ ft^2/hr)}{(0.0158\ ft)}\left(\frac{0.0263}{0.984}\right)$$

$$= 0.00429 \text{ lb mole/ft}^2\text{-hr}$$

For each square foot 0.0113 lb mole must be evaporated. Therefore the time necessary is:

$$t = \frac{0.0113 \text{ lb mole/ft}^2}{0.00429 \text{ lb mole/ft}^2\text{-hr}} = 2.63 \text{ hr.}$$

• PROBLEM 15-13

Approximate the rate at which water diffuses into dry air at 1 atm and 25°C from the bottom of a test tube 12 mm in diameter and 16 cm in length.

Solution: Employ equation (1) to determine the mass flux of water. The saturation pressure at 25°C is taken as the partial pressure of the water at the bottom of the test tube (P_{w1}). The vapor pressure at the top (p_{w2}), is zero because the liquid is diffusing into dry air.

Therefore:

$$p_{A1} = p_{atm} - p_{w1} = 14.7 - 0.459 = 14.24 \text{ psia}$$
$$= 9.819 \times 10^4 \text{ N/m}^2$$

$$p_{A2} = p_{atm} - p_{w2} = 14.7 - 0 = 14.7 \text{ psia}$$
$$= 1.013 \times 10^5 \text{ N/m}^2$$

The diffusivity of water vapor in air at 25°C is:

$$D = 0.258 \text{ cm}^2\text{/sec}$$

Equation (1) states that:

$$\dot{m}_w = \frac{pDM_w A}{RT(\Delta z)} \ln \frac{p_{A2}}{p_{A1}} \quad (1)$$

where M_w is the molecular weight of water and R is the ideal gas constant.

Substituting:

$$\dot{m}_w = \frac{(1.013 \times 10^5)(0.258 \times 10^{-4})(18)\pi(6 \times 10^{-3})^2}{(8316)(298)(0.16)} \ln\left(\frac{1.013}{0.9819}\right)$$

$$= 4.184 \times 10^{-10} \text{ kg/sec}$$

• PROBLEM 15-14

At steady state conditions, Oxygen (A) diffuses through Nitrogen (B). Consider the nitrogen as nondiffusing. The temperature is $0^\circ C$ and the total pressure is 1×10^5 N/m^2. The partial pressure of oxygen at two locations, 2.2 mm apart, is 13500 and 6000 N/m^2. The diffusivity is 1.81×10^{-5} m^2/sec.

(I) Determine the diffusion rate of oxygen.

(II) Determine the diffusion rate of oxygen (A) using as the nondiffusing gas a mixture of nitrogen (B) and carbon dioxide (C) in a volume ratio of 2:1. The diffusivities are $D_{O_2 - N_2} = 1.81 \times 10^{-5}$ m^2/sec,

$D_{O_2 - CO_2} = 1.85 \times 10^{-5}$ m^2/sec.

Solution:

(I) Equation (1) applies for the case of steady state diffusion of A through nondiffusing B.

$$N_A = \frac{D_{AB}p_t}{RT(\Delta z)\bar{p}_{B,lm}} (\bar{p}_{A1} - \bar{p}_{A2}) \tag{1}$$

where N_A is the molar flux of A, $\bar{p}_A$ is the partial pressure of A, and Δz is the length across which A is diffusing. The log mean pressure is given by:

$$\bar{p}_{B,lm} = \frac{\bar{p}_{B2} - \bar{p}_{B1}}{\ln(\bar{p}_{B2}/\bar{p}_{B1})} \tag{2}$$

The following information is known:

$T = 273$ K

$D_{AB} = 1.81 \times 10^{-5}$ m^2/sec

$p_t = 1 \times 10^5$ N/m^2

$\Delta z = 0.0022$ m

$R = 8314$ $N \cdot m/kmol \cdot K$

$\bar{p}_{A1} = 12.5 \times 10^3$ N/m^2

$\bar{p}_{A2} = 6000$ N/m^2

$\bar{p}_{B1} = 10^5 - 12500 = 8.75 \times 10^4$ N/m^2

$\bar{p}_{B2} = 10^5 - 6000 = 9.40 \times 10^4$ N/m^2

Substituting in equation (2):

$$\bar{p}_{B,lm} = \frac{(9.40 \times 10^4) - (8.75 \times 10^4)}{\ln\left(\frac{9.40}{8.75}\right)}$$

$$= 90711 \text{ N/m}^2$$

Substitution in equation (1) yields

$$N_A = \frac{(1.81 \times 10^{-5})(10^5)}{(8314)(273)(0.0022)(90711)} (12500 - 6000)$$

$$= 2.60 \times 10^{-5} \text{ kmol/m}^2\text{-sec}$$

(II) A similar approach will be employed. The mole fractions of B and C independent of the diffusing species A are:

$$y_B = 2/(2 + 1) = 0.667$$

$$y_C = 1 - 0.667 = 0.333$$

Substitution in equation (3) gives the mean diffusivity:

$$D_{A,m} = \frac{1}{y_B/D_{AB} + y_C/D_{AC}} \qquad (3)$$

$$= \frac{1}{\frac{0.667}{1.81 \times 10^{-5}} + \frac{0.333}{1.85 \times 10^{-5}}}$$

$$= 1.82 \times 10^{-5} \text{ m}^2\text{/sec}$$

Now substitute into equation (1):

$$N_A = \frac{(1.82 \times 10^{-5})(12500 - 6000)(1 \times 10^5)}{(8314)(273)(0.0022)(90711)}$$

$$= 2.61 \times 10^{-5} \text{ kmol/m}^2\text{-sec}$$

• PROBLEM 15-15

A porous sintered mass of silica has a void fraction ε of 0.31, a tortuosity of 4.0, and is 2.5 mm thick. The pores contain water at 291 K. On one side of the silica, NaCl is maintained at a concentration of 0.2 kmol/m^3 and water flows by on the other side. Taking into account only the resistance of the silica, determine the steady state diffusion of NaCl.

Solution: Equation (1) will be employed to solve this problem.

$$N_A = \frac{\varepsilon D_{AB}(c_{A1} - c_{A2})}{\tau(z_2 - z_1)} \qquad (1)$$

The diffusivity of NaCl in water at $18^{\circ}C$ is:

$$D_{AB} = 1.21 \times 10^{-9} \ m^2/sec$$

Also:

$$c_{A1} = 0.2 \ kmol/m^3$$

and

$$c_{A2} = 0$$

Substituting in equation.(1):

$$N_A = \frac{(0.31)(1.21 \times 10^{-9})(0.2 - 0)}{(4.0)(0.0025 - 0)}$$

$$= 7.50 \times 10^{-9} \ kmol \ NaCl/m^2\text{-sec}$$

• PROBLEM 15-16

A solid sphere of naphthalene (A) with a radius of 2.5 mm is surrounded by still air (B) at 300 K and 1 atm. Take the surface temperature of the naphthalene as $300^{0}K$ and its vapor pressure at this temperature as 0.104 mm Hg. The diffusivity of napthalene in air at $318^{0}K$ is 6.92×10^{-6} m^2/sec. Determine the rate at which naphthalene evaporates.

Solution: Equation (1) provides the molar flux of naphthalene (A) per unit area.

$$N_A = \frac{D_{AB}P(p_{A1} - p_{A2})}{RTrp_{Bm}} \qquad (1)$$

where:

P is the total pressure = 1.01325×10^5 N/m^2

r = radius of naphthalene sphere = $\frac{2.5}{1000}$ m

R = 8314 $m^3 \cdot Pa/kgmol \cdot K$

$p_{A1} = (0.104/760.0)(1.01325 \times 10^5) = 13.9 \ N/m^2$

$p_{A2} = 0$

The diffusivity must be obtained at the desired temperature:

$$D_{AB}\Big|_{T_2} = D_{AB}\Big|_{T_1} \left(\frac{T_2}{T_1}\right)^{3/2}$$

$$D_{AB}\Big|_{300K} = 6.92 \times 10^{-6} \left(\frac{300}{318}\right)^{3/2}$$

$$= 6.34 \times 10^{-6} \text{ m}^2/\text{sec}$$

The log mean pressure term is given by:

$$p_{B,m} = \frac{p_{B1} + p_{B2}}{2}$$

where:

$$p_{B1} = 1.01325 \times 10^5 - 13.9 = 1.01311 \times 10^5$$

$$p_{B2} = 1.01325 \times 10^5 \text{ N/m}^2$$

Note the logarithmic mean has been replaced by an arithmetic mean since the values of p_{B1} and p_{B2} are very similar.

$$p_{B,m} = 1.01318 \times 10^5 \text{ N/m}^2$$

Substituting in equation (1):

$$N_A = \frac{(6.34 \times 10^{-6})(1.01325 \times 10^5)(13.9 - 0)}{(8314)(300)(2.5/1000)(1.01318 \times 10^5)}$$

$$= 1.41 \times 10^{-8} \text{ kgmol/m}^2\text{-sec}$$

• PROBLEM 15-17

A column is used to absorb ammonia in water from a feed of air and ammonia. The column is at 1 atm and 0°C. Assume the resistance to transfer is completely in the gas phase, in a gas film 1.5 mm thick. The partial pressure of NH_3 is 55 mm Hg at one point in the column. What is the transfer rate per unit area at this location in the column? The diffusivity of ammonia in air is 0.198 cm^2/sec at 0°C.

Solution: The molar rate of transfer of ammonia (A) is given by equation (1).

$$N_A = \frac{D}{y_2 - y_1} \frac{C_T}{C_{Bm}} (c_{A2} - c_{A1}) \qquad (1)$$

The molar concentration of NH_3 in the gas, c_{A2}, equals:

$$c_{A2} = \frac{1}{22400} \times \frac{273}{273} \times \frac{55}{760} = 3.23 \times 10^{-6} \frac{\text{gmoles}}{\text{cm}^3}$$

$$c_{A1} = 0$$

and

$$\frac{C_T}{C_{B,m}} = \frac{760}{(760 - 705)/\ln(760/705)} = 1.038$$

Substituting in equation (1):

$$N_A = \left(\frac{0.198}{0.15}\right)(1.038)(3.23 \times 10^{-6})$$

$$= 4.4 \times 10^{-6} \text{ gmoles/cm}^2\text{-sec}$$

• PROBLEM 15-18

A vessel which contains gases A and B at 1 atm and 40°F is connected to another vessel with a different concentration of the gases at the same conditions of pressure and temperature. The vessels are connected by a 9 in. long tube of inside diameter 1.5 in.

(I) Determine the steady state rate of transport of gas A between the vessels if the concentration of A in one tank is 85 mole percent and that in the other is 7 mole percent. Transfer occurs by molecular diffusion and the diffusivity is $D_{AB} = 1.75$ ft²/hr.

(II) The tanks are now at 5 and 70°F. Obtain the rate of heat transfer by molecular transport. The following properties are given:

ρ = gas density = 0.07 lb/ft³

C_p = heat capacity of gas = 0.30 Btu/lb°F

α = thermal diffusivity = 1.75 ft²/hr

Solution:

(I) Equation (1) can be integrated and solved for the molar flux of gas A, N_A.

$$\frac{N_A}{A} = -\frac{D}{RT}\left(\frac{dp_A}{dx}\right) \qquad (1)$$

This is a case of equimolar counter diffusion of gases A and B. The following hold:

at $x = 0$, $C_A = 0.85\, C_t$, $p_A = 0.85\, P$

and

at $x = 0.75$ ft $p = 0.075\, P$

Integration of equation (1) yields

$$\frac{N_A}{A} = -\frac{D}{RT}\frac{(0.075\ P - 0.85\ P)}{(0.75 - 0)} \quad (2)$$

where:

$P = 1$ atm

$T = 500$ R

$R = 0.7302$ atm ft³/lb mole·R

Substitution in (2) yields:

$$\frac{N_A}{A} = -\frac{(1.75)(0.075 - 0.85)}{(0.7302)(500)(0.75)}$$

$$= 4.95 \times 10^{-3} \text{ lb moles/hr-ft}^2$$

where:

$$A = \frac{\pi(1.5)^2}{4(144)} = 0.01227 \text{ ft}^2$$

Therefore:

$$N_A = 6.07 \times 10^{-5} \text{ lb moles/hr}$$

(II) Equation (3) provides the rate of heat transfer, q, between the two tanks.

$$q = -\alpha\rho C_p \frac{(T - T_1)}{(x_2 - x_1)} A \quad (3)$$

at $x_1 = 0$, $T_1 = 70^\circ F = 530$ R

and

at $x_2 = 0.75$ ft, $T_2 = 5^\circ F = 465$ R

Substituting in equation (3) gives:

$$q = \frac{-(1.75)(0.075)(0.30)(465 - 530)(0.01227)}{(0.75 - 0)}$$

$$= 0.04187 \text{ Btu/hr.}$$

• PROBLEM 15-19

The water surface, in an open cylindrical tank is 25 ft below the top. Dry air is blown over the top of the tank and the entire system is maintained at $65^\circ F$ and 1 atm. If the air in the tank is stagnant, determine the diffusion rate of the water.

Solution: This is an example of water vapor (A) diffusing through stationary air (B). The top of the tank will be designated as 2 and the surface of the water as 1. The diffusivity for water vapor in air is

$$D = 0.97 \text{ ft}^2/\text{hr at } 65^\circ\text{F}$$

The partial pressure of water at point 1 is the saturated vapor pressure of water at 65°F. Thus $p_{A1} = 0.022$ atm. Because the air stream at 2 is dry, $p_{A2} = 0.0$ atm. Equation (1) will be employed to obtain the diffusion rate of water, N_A.

$$\frac{N_A}{A} = -\frac{DP(p_{A2} - p_{A1})}{RTp_{B,lm}(y_2 - y_1)} \qquad (1)$$

where:

$$p_{B,lm} = \frac{p_{B2} - p_{B1}}{\ln(p_{B2}/p_{B1})} \qquad (2)$$

and

$$p_{B1} = 1.0 - 0.022 = 0.978 \text{ atm}$$

$$p_{B2} = 1.0 - 0 = 1.0 \text{ atm}$$

also:

$$y_2 - y_1 = 25 \text{ ft}$$

$$R = 0.730 \text{ ft}^3\text{-atm/lb-mole-R}$$

Substituting in equation (2):

$$p_{B,m} = \frac{1 - 0.978}{\ln\left(\frac{1}{0.978}\right)} = 0.989$$

Equation (1) yields:

$$\frac{N_A}{A} = -\frac{(0.97)(1)(0 - 0.022)}{(0.730)(460 + 65)(0.989)(25 - 0)}$$

$$= 2.25 \times 10^{-6} \text{ lb moles/ft}^2\text{-hr}$$

• PROBLEM 15-20

At the bottom of a cylindrical container is n-butanol. Pure air is passed over the open top of the container. The pressure is 1 atm and the temperature is 70°F. The diffusivity of air-n-butanol is 8.57×10^{-6} m²/sec at the given conditions. If the surface of n-butanol is 6.0 ft below the top of the container, calculate the diffusion rate of n-butanol.

Solution: The n-butanol vapor will diffuse through stagnant air to the top of the container where it is removed by an air stream. This is an example of steady-state unidirectional diffusion of n-butanol (A) through stationary air (B). For this situation, equation (1) can be employed to determine the rate of diffusion of n-butanol.

$$N_A = \frac{Dp}{RT(\Delta x)p_{B,lm}}(p_{A1} - p_{A2}) \qquad (1)$$

where:

$$p_{B,lm} = \frac{p_{B2} - p_{B1}}{\ln(p_{B2}/p_{B1})} \qquad (2)$$

At the given conditions, n-butanol has a vapor pressure of

$$p_{A1} = 0.009 \text{ atm}$$

The following values are known:

$$T = 294.4 \text{ K}$$

$$\Delta x = 6.0 \text{ ft} = 1.829 \text{ m}$$

$$R = 0.08205 \text{ m}^3\text{-atm/kgmol-K}$$

$$P = 1 \text{ atm} \qquad p_{A2} = 0 \text{ atm}$$

$$p_{B1} = 1 - p_{A1} = 0.991 \text{ atm}$$

$$p_{B2} = 1 \text{ atm}$$

Substituting in equation (2):

$$p_{B,lm} = \frac{1 - 0.991}{\ln(1/0.991)} = 0.995 \text{ atm}$$

Equation (1) yields

$$N_A = \frac{(8.57 \times 10^{-6})(1)(0.009 - 0)}{(0.08205)(294.4)(1.829)(0.995)}$$

$$= 1.75 \times 10^{-9} \text{ kgmol/m}^2\text{-sec}$$

• PROBLEM 15-21

The duct shown in figure (1) connects two tanks. One tank holds a mixture of 70 mole percent nitrogen and 30 mole percent oxygen, and the other tank has a mixture of 75 mole percent oxygen and 25 mole percent nitrogen. The pressure is uniform, 1.0 atm, and the temperature is 50.0°F. The diffusivity for nitrogen-oxygen system is 0.728 ft^2/hr. The nitrogen will diffuse through the duct in the direction of decreasing diameter.

(I) Calculate the rate of transfer of nitrogen between the two tanks due to molecular diffusion.

(II) If the duct is replaced by a tube of diameter $(d_1 + d_2)/2$, then determine the rate of transfer of nitrogen.

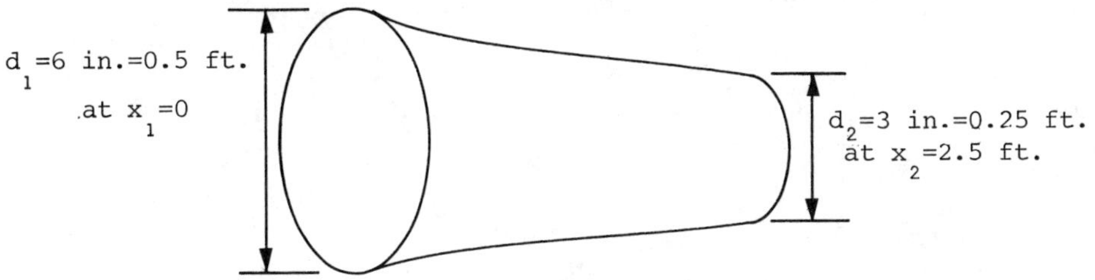

Figure 1.

Solution:

(I) The tanks are assumed to be large enough that steady-state transfer exists. Equimolar counter-diffusion occurs in the duct, where the rate of transfer at any cross section is:

$$N_A = \frac{q_A}{A} = -\frac{D}{RT}\frac{dp_A}{dx} \tag{1}$$

where q_A is the rate of transfer of nitrogen (A) in the x direction in moles per unit time. The cross sectional area at any distance x between x_1 and x_2 is given by:

$$A = \frac{\pi d^2}{4} = \frac{\pi}{4}\left[d_1 - \left(\frac{d_1 - d_2}{x_2 - x_1}\right)x\right]^2 \tag{2}$$

Substituting equation (2) into equation (1) for A, and integrating yields:

$$q_A = \frac{\pi D}{4RT}\left(\frac{d_1 - d_2}{x_2 - x_1}\right)\frac{p_{A1} - p_{A2}}{\left[\dfrac{1}{d_1 - \left(\dfrac{d_1 - d_2}{x_2 - x_1}\right)x_2}\right] - \left[\dfrac{1}{d_1 - \left(\dfrac{d_1 - d_2}{x_2 - x_1}\right)x_1}\right]} \tag{3}$$

where:

$p_{A1} = 0.7(1 \text{ atm}) = 0.7$ atm

$p_{A2} = 0.25(1 \text{ atm}) = 0.25$ atm

$T = 510$ R

$x_1 = 0.0$ ft

$x_2 = 2.5$ ft

and

$$R = 0.7302 \text{ atm-ft}^3/\text{lb-mole-R}$$

Substituting in equation (3) yields

$$q_A = \frac{\pi(0.728)}{4(0.7302)(510)} \left(\frac{0.50 - 0.25}{2.5}\right) \frac{0.7 - 0.25}{\left[0.5 - \left(\frac{0.5 - 0.25}{2.5}\right)2.5\right] - \left[\frac{1}{0.5}\right]}$$

$$= 3.46 \times 10^{-5} \text{ lb-mole/hr.}$$

(II) If equation (3) is employed for this section with $d_1 = d_2 = d$, one obtains: $q_A = 0/0$. Applying L'Hopital's rule to equation (3) yields:

$$q_A = \frac{D(p_{A1} - p_{A2})}{RT(x_2 - x_1)} \frac{\pi d^2}{4} \quad (4)$$

Substituting in (4) with $d = \frac{0.25 + 0.5}{2} = 0.375$ ft gives:

$$q_A = \frac{(0.728)(0.7 - 0.25)}{(0.7302)(510)(2.5)} \frac{\pi(0.375)^2}{4}$$

$$= 3.89 \times 10^{-5} \text{ lb-mole/hr}$$

• PROBLEM 15-22

A gas diffuses through the walls of a pyrex tube whose cross-section is shown in the figure. Derive a relation for the rate of diffusion of the gas through the tube as a function of the diffusivity of the gas in pyrex, its interfacial concentration in the pyrex and the dimensions of the tube.

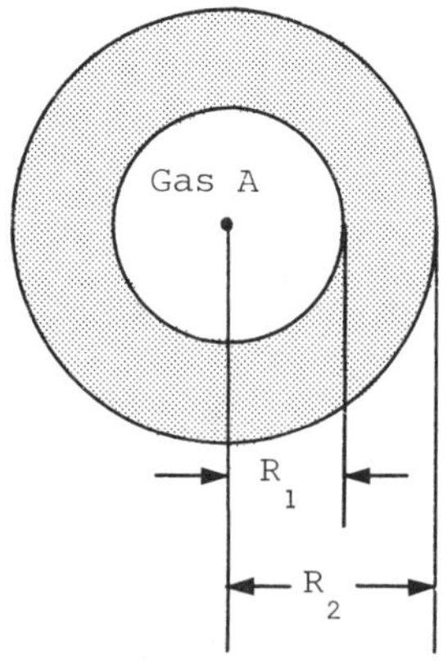

Solution: A shell bal e yields

$$\frac{1}{r}\frac{\partial}{\partial r}\left(r\frac{\partial C_A}{\partial r}\right) = 0$$

or $$r\frac{\partial C_A}{\partial r} = C_1 \quad \text{where } C_1 = \text{constant}$$

Integrating, $C_A = C_1 \ln r + C_2$ where C_2 = constant

Boundary conditions: At $r = R_1$, $C_A = C_{A1}$

$r = R_2$, $C_A = C_{A2}$

$$\therefore \quad C_{A1} = C_1 \ln R_1 + C_2$$

$$C_{A2} = C_1 \ln R_2 + C_2$$

$$\therefore \quad C_1 = \frac{C_{A1} - C_{A2}}{\ln(R_1/R_2)}$$

The rate of diffusion of the gas $= N_A = -D_A \left.\frac{\partial C_A}{\partial r}\right|_{r=R_2}$

Since $$\frac{\partial C_A}{\partial r} = \frac{C_1}{r} = \frac{C_{A1} - C_{A2}}{r\ln(R_1/R_2)}$$

$$N_A = -D_{AB}\frac{C_{A1} - C_{A2}}{R_2 \ln(R_1/R_2)} = \frac{D_{AB}(C_{A1} - C_{A2})}{R_2 \ln(R_2/R_1)}$$

Molar rate of diffusion: $N_A \times \text{area} = N_A \times 2\pi R_2 L$

$$= 2\pi L \frac{D_{AB}(C_{A1} - C_{A2})}{\ln R_2/R_1}$$

• PROBLEM 15-23

A spherical particle, A of radius R_1, is suspended in a gas B. A diffuses through a stagnant gas film of radius R_2. Derive an expression for the rate of diffusion of A.

Solution: A shell balance yields $\frac{\partial}{\partial r}(r^2 N_{Ar}) = 0$

or $r^2 N_{Ar.} = \text{constant} = R_1{}^2 N_{AR_1} = R_2{}^2 N_{AR_2}$

Also since this is a diffusion of A through nondiffusing B, $N_B = 0$.

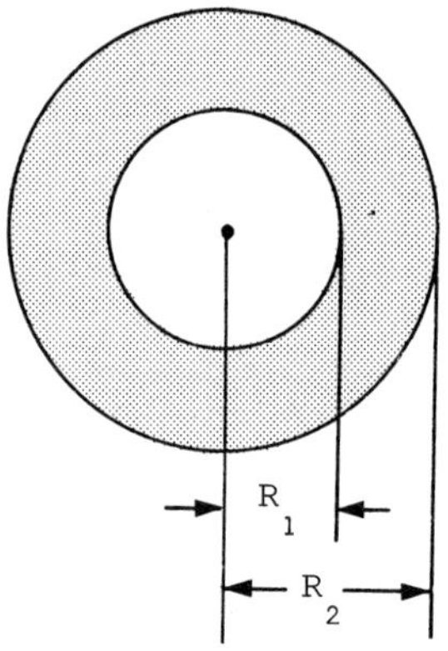

Thus the equation $N_A = -cD_{AB}\frac{\partial x_A}{\partial r} + x_A(N_A + N_B)$ becomes

$$N_A = -cD_{AB}\frac{\partial x_A}{\partial r} + x_A N_A$$

or $N_A = -\frac{cD_{AB}}{1 - x_A}\frac{\partial x_A}{\partial r}$

$$\therefore \quad R_1^2 N_{AR1} = r^2 N_{Ar} = -\frac{cD_{AB}}{1 - x_A} r^2 \frac{\partial x_A}{\partial r}$$

Integrating with the boundary conditions, at $r = R_1;\ x_A = x_{A1}$

$r = R_2;\ x_A = x_{A2}$

we get $(R_1^2 N_{AR1})\left[-\frac{1}{r}\right]_{R_1}^{R_2} = +cD_{AB}\left[\ln(1 - x_A)\right]_{x_{A1}}^{x_{A2}}$

or $$R_1^2 N_{AR1}\left[\frac{1}{R_1} - \frac{1}{R_2}\right] = cD_{AB}\ln\left(\frac{1 - x_{A2}}{1 - x_{A1}}\right)$$

or $$\frac{N_{AR1}R_1(R_2 - R_1)}{R_2} = cD_{AB}\ln\left(\frac{1 - x_{A2}}{1 - x_{A1}}\right)$$

or $$N_{AR1} = \frac{cD_{AB}}{R_2 - R_1}\left(\frac{R_2}{R_1}\right)\ln\left(\frac{1 - x_{A2}}{1 - x_{A1}}\right)$$

Since $1 - x_{A2} = x_{B2}$ and $1 - x_{A1} = x_{B1}$

$$N_{AR1} = \frac{cD_{AB}}{R_2 - R_1}\left(\frac{R_2}{R_1}\right)\ln\left(\frac{x_{B2}}{x_{B1}}\right)$$

• PROBLEM 15-24

What is the effect on the absorption rate due to raising the total pressure from 1 to 3 atm in the following situations:

(I) The absorption of methane from an air-methane mixture which has 15 percent CH_4 by volume. Pure water is used as the solvent. Assume the gas film offers the main resistance to diffusion.

(II) The absorption of CH_4 from an air-CH_4 mixture which has 25 percent CH_4 by volume. A solution of CH_4 in water is employed as the solvent. The vapor pressure of methane over the solution is 0.17 atm.

Solution:

(I) From the Stefan equation the rate of diffusion is:

$$N_A = \frac{Dp}{RTx} \ln \frac{p_{B2}}{p_{B1}} \tag{1}$$

Writing a ratio for the two pressures:

$$\frac{N_A(1\text{ atm})}{N_A(3\text{ atm})} = \frac{\left[\frac{Dp}{RTx}\left(\ln \frac{p_{B2}}{p_{B1}}\right)\right]_{1\text{ atm}}}{\left[\frac{Dp}{RTx}\left(\ln \frac{p_{B2}}{p_{B1}}\right)\right]_{3\text{ atm}}}$$

$$= \frac{\left[\ln \frac{p_{B2}}{p_{B1}}\right]_{1\text{ atm}}}{\left[\ln \frac{p_{B2}}{p_{B1}}\right]_{3\text{ atm}}} \tag{2}$$

Note that the term Dp does not vary with changes in pressure. The following values can be obtained:

For 1 atm

$p_{B1} = 0.85$ atm $\qquad p_{B2} = 1$ atm

For 3 atm

$p_{B1} = 3(0.85) = 2.55$ atm $\qquad p_{B2} = 3$ atm

Substitution in equation (2) yields:

$$\frac{N_A(1\text{ atm})}{N_A(3\text{ atm})} = \frac{\ln\left(\frac{1}{0.85}\right)}{\ln\left(\frac{3}{2.55}\right)} = 1$$

Therefore the pressure change has no effect on the absorption rate.

(II) Equation (1) applies in this situation. The following pressure data is available.

For 1 atm:

$p_{B1} = 0.75$ atm $\qquad\qquad p_{B2} = 1 - 0.17 = 0.83$ atm

For 3 atm:

$p_{B1} = 3(0.75) = 2.25$ atm $\qquad p_{B2} = 3 - 0.17 = 2.83$ atm

Substituting in equation (2) yields:

$$N_A(3\text{ atm}) = \frac{\ln\left(\frac{2.83}{2.25}\right)}{\ln\left(\frac{0.83}{0.75}\right)} N_A(1\text{ atm}) = 2.26\ N_A(1\text{ atm})$$

Therefore the pressure rise causes a 126 percent gain in absorption.

• PROBLEM 15-25

Ammonia, from a mixture of air and ammonia, diffuses into water at a pressure of 0.75 atm. The diffusion occurs in a stagnant gas layer at 65°C. At one location, the gas has 2.9 % ammonia by volume, and the amount of ammonia in the water is small enough so that the partial pressure of ammonia is negligible. The air contains no water vapor. The following data are given:

Diffusivity of ammonia in air = 1.125 cm^2/sec

Diffusivity of water vapor in air = 1.302 cm^2/sec

Diffusivity of water vapor in ammonia = 1.538 cm^2/sec

Vapor pressure of water = 0.247 atm at 65°C

Determine the diffusion rate of ammonia with and without the vaporization of water.

Solution:

A = ammonia

B = water vapor

C = air

When not considering water vaporization, the problem reduces to diffusion of gas A through stagnant gas C. Equation (1) is employed in this situation.

$$N_a = \frac{k}{x} \frac{(p_{a1} - p_{a2})}{p_{cm}} = \frac{D_{ac}P}{RT} \frac{(p_{a1} - p_{a2})}{p_{cm}} \qquad (1)$$

To simplify calculations, the term $z = N_a \times RT$ will be solved for. Substituting in equation (1) yields:

$$N_a = -\frac{(1.125)(0.75)}{RTx} \frac{[(0.75)(0.029) - 0][0.75 - 0.728]}{\ln\left(\frac{0.75}{0.728}\right)}$$

$$N_a \times RT = z = -0.0136$$

With water vaporization, the problem involves the diffusion of gases A and B through stagnant gas C. Equations (2) and (3) apply in this case.

$$r_{ac}N_a + r_{bc}N_b = \frac{1}{x} \ln \frac{p_{c2}}{p_{c1}} \qquad (2)$$

$$N_a + N_b = \frac{D_{ab}P}{RTx} \ln \left[\frac{\left(\frac{r_{ab} - r_{ac}}{r_{ab} - r_{bc}}\right)\frac{N_a + N_b}{N_b} p_{b2} - \frac{N_a + N_b}{N_a} p_{a2} + \left(\frac{r_{ac}-r_{bc}}{r_{ab}-r_{bc}}\right)P}{\left(\frac{r_{ab} - r_{ac}}{r_{ab} - r_{bc}}\right)\frac{N_a + N_b}{N_b} p_{b1} - \frac{N_a + N_b}{N_a} p_{a1} + \left(\frac{r_{ac}-r_{bc}}{r_{ab}-r_{bc}}\right)P} \right]$$

(3)

where:

$$r_{ac} = \frac{1}{k_{ac}} = \frac{RT}{D_{ac}P} = \frac{RT}{(1.125)(0.75)} = 1.185 \text{ RT}$$

$$r_{ab} = \frac{RT}{(1.538)(0.75)} = 0.8669 \text{ RT}$$

$$r_{bc} = \frac{RT}{(1.302)(0.75)} = 1.024 \text{ RT}$$

Therefore:

$$\frac{r_{ab} - r_{ac}}{r_{ab} - r_{bc}} = \frac{0.8669 \text{ RT} - 1.185 \text{ RT}}{0.8669 \text{ RT} - 1.024 \text{ RT}} = 2.02$$

$$\frac{r_{ac} - r_{bc}}{r_{ab} - r_{bc}} = \frac{1.185 \text{ RT} - 1.024 \text{ RT}}{0.8669 \text{ RT} - 1.024 \text{ RT}} = -1.02$$

and at $x = 0$

$$p_{a1} = 0$$

$p_{b1} = 0.247$ atm

$p_{c1} = 0.75 - 0.247 = 0.503$ atm

while at $x = x$

$p_{a2} = (0.75)(0.029) = 0.022$ atm

$p_{b2} = 0.0$ atm

$p_{c2} = 0.75 - 0.022 = 0.728$ atm

Substituting in equation (2) gives

$$(1.185\ RT)N_a + (1.024\ RT)N_b = \frac{1}{x} \ln \left(\frac{0.728}{0.503}\right)$$

$$N_b = \frac{0.361}{RTx} - 1.157\ N_a \qquad (4)$$

Now substitute into equation (3):

$$N_a + N_b = \frac{(1.53)(0.75)}{xRT} \ln \left[\frac{-\dfrac{N_a + N_b}{N_a}(0.022) + (-1.02)(0.75)}{(2.02)\left(\dfrac{N_a + N_b}{N_b}\right)(0.247) + (-1.02)(0.75)}\right]$$

and replace N_b by equation (4). Rearranging and letting $z = N_a \times RT$ yields:

$$0.314 - 0.137\ z = \ln \left[\frac{0.881z^2 - 0.266z - 0.00287}{0.807z^2 - 0.096z}\right]$$

Using the previously calculated value of $z = -0.0136$ as an approximation gives:

$$0.314 - 0.137(-0.0136) = \ln \left[\frac{0.881z^2 - 0.266z - 0.00287}{0.807z^2 - 0.096z}\right]$$

Solving the quadratic equation for z gives the values:

-0.0223

and

-0.5707

The value $z = -0.0223$ is the answer, since it is nearer to the first approximation and makes physical sense. Recalculating using this value of z does not offer a significant improvement in the answer.

Therefore:

$$N_a = -\frac{0.0223}{xRT}$$

or

$$N_a \times RT = -0.0223$$

The previous value was $N_a \times RT = -0.0136$ when the vaporization of water was neglected.

STAGNANT FILM/EQUIMOLAL COUNTER DIFFUSION

• PROBLEM 15-26

> It is desired to remove water from an air-water mixture which contains 35 percent water by volume. The mixture diffuses into a section of still air 0.2 in. in length, after which it is completely removed from the mixture by absorption. At the absorption plane, the water concentration is small enough to be neglected. The system operates at 1 atm and 59.0°C. Determine the rate of water diffusing through the air layer.

Solution: For the case of steady-state diffusion of A (water) through nondiffusing B (air), equation (1) applies.

$$N_A = \frac{D_{AB}P(p_{A1} - p_{A2})}{RTzp_{B,lm}} \quad (1)$$

where:

$$p_{B,lm} = \frac{p_{B2} - p_{B1}}{\ln\left(\frac{p_{B2}}{p_{B1}}\right)} \quad (2)$$

The following values are known:

$p_{A1} = 0.35$ atm $\qquad p_{B1} = 0.65$ atm

$p_{A2} = 0$ atm $\qquad p_{B2} = 1.0$ atm

Substituting in equation (2):

$$p_{B,lm} = \frac{1.0 - 0.65}{\ln\left(\frac{1.0}{0.65}\right)} = 0.81 \text{ atm}$$

For air-water, the diffusivity is $D_{AB} = 1.18$ ft^2/hr. Substitution in equation (1) yields:

$$N_A = \frac{(1.18)(1)(0.35 - 0)}{(0.729)(598)\left(\frac{0.2}{12}\right)(0.81)}$$

$= 0.07$ lb mole/ft^2-hr

where R = 0.729 atm-ft^3/lb mole-R

• PROBLEM 15-27

A cylindrical vessel of diameter 7.0 ft is filled to 2.5 ft below the open top with pure n-butanol. Inside the tank, the air is stationary, but currents above it maintain a small enough concentration of n-butanol there to allow it to be neglected. The system is at 77.0°C and 1 atm. The diffusivity of n-butanol in air at these conditions is 0.438 ft^2/hr. Determine the rate of evaporization of n-butanol from the vessel at steady state conditions.

Solution: Equation (1) describes this situation, where the subscript A refers to the n-butanol and subscript b will refer to the air. Integration of equation (1) provides equation (2), which can be solved for the evaporation rate, N_A. Equation (1) states:

$$\frac{N_A}{A} = -\frac{Dp}{RTp_b z}\frac{dp_A}{dx} \tag{1}$$

where $A = \frac{\pi D^2}{4} = \frac{\pi(7)^2}{4} = 38.5$ ft^2

and $p_b = P - p_A$

Therefore, equation (1) can be rewritten as:

$$\frac{N_A}{38.5} = -\frac{DP}{RTz}\int_{p_{A1}}^{p_{A2}} \frac{dp_A}{P - p_A}$$

Integration yields:

$$\frac{N_A}{38.5} = \frac{DP}{RTz} \ln\left(\frac{P - p_{A2}}{P - p_{A1}}\right) \tag{2}$$

where:

p_{A1} = vapor pressure of n-butanol at 77.0°C

= 144 mm Hg

p_{A2} = 0.0 atm

R = 0.7302 ft^3-atm/lb mole-R

$z = 2.5$ ft

$T = 630$ R

Substituting in equation (2):

$$N_A = \frac{(38.5)(0.438)(1)}{(0.7302)(630)(2.5)} \ln\left(\frac{760 - 0}{760 - 144}\right)$$

$$= 3.08 \times 10^{-3} \text{ lb moles/hr}$$

• PROBLEM 15-28

Two large tanks, each contain a mixture of nitrogen (A) and oxygen (B), but at different concentrations. Tank 1 has 85 mole percent N_2 and 15 mole precent O_2, while tank 2 has 25 mole percent N_2 and 75 mole percent O_2. A tube 1.5 m long with an inside diameter of 0.150 m connects the two tanks. If the pressure is 1 atm and the temperature is 0^oC, calculate the rate of diffusion of N_2 between the tanks assuming steady state transfer.

Solution: The diffusivity of N_2 in O_2 is 1.81×10^{-5} m^2/sec at the given conditions. This problem is an example of equimolar counter diffusion, and the flux of A per unit area is given by equation (1).

$$N_A = \frac{D\ p_{A1} - p_{A2}}{RT(\Delta x)} \qquad (1)$$

Multiplying by the area provides the total rate of A transferred, W_A.

$$W_A = \frac{D\ p_{A1} - p_{A2}}{RT(\Delta x)} \left(\frac{\pi d^2}{4}\right) \qquad (2)$$

The following values are known:

$d = 0.150$ m

$T = 273$ K

$\Delta x = 1.5$ m

$R = 0.08205$ m^3-atm/kgmol-K

$p_{A1} = 0.85(1 \text{ atm}) = 0.85$ atm

$p_{A2} = 0.25(1 \text{ atm}) = 0.25$ atm

Substituting in equation (2) yields:

$$W_A = \frac{(1.81 \times 10^{-5})(0.85 - 0.25)}{(0.08205)(273)(1.5)} \left(\frac{\pi}{4}\right) (0.150)^2$$

$$= 5.71 \times 10^{-9} \text{ kgmol/sec}$$

A carbon particle of diameter $d_c = 0.12$ in. is burned in pure oxygen at $1440^{\circ}F$ and 1 atm; according to the reaction: $C + O_2 \rightarrow CO_2$. Assume that a layer of CO_2 forms around the particle so that at the surface of the carbon particle $p_{CO_2} = 1$ atm and $p_{O_2} = 0$. Far from the particle, $p_{CO_2} = 0$ and $p_{O_2} = 1$ atm. Determine the rate of burning of the carbon.

Solution: This is an example of equimolar counter diffusion. Equation (1), which is expressed in spherical coordinates, describes this situation. The subscript A denotes CO_2. The diffusivity

$$N_A = -(4\pi r^2)\frac{D}{RT}\frac{dp_A}{dr} \qquad (1)$$

is needed and can be obtained from equation (2),

$$D = 0.0069 \frac{T^{3/2}}{p(V_A^{1/3} + V_B^{1/3})^2} \sqrt{\frac{1}{M_A} + \frac{1}{M_b}} \qquad (2)$$

where:

T = absolute temperature = $1900^{\circ}R$

p = total pressure = 1.0 atm

V_A = molecular volume of CO_2 = 29.6

V_B = molecular volume of O_2 = 14.8

M_A = molecular weight of CO_2 = 44 lb/lbmol

M_B = molecular weight of O_2 = 32 lb/lbmol

Substituting in equation (2):

$$D = 0.0069 \frac{(1900)^{3/2}}{(1.0)\left[(29.6)^{1/3} + (14.8)^{1/3}\right]^2} \sqrt{\frac{1}{44} + \frac{1}{32}}$$

$$= 4.3 \text{ ft}^2/\text{hr}$$

Integration of equation (1) between $r = r_c$ and $r = \infty$ yields:

$$p_{AO} - p_{A\infty} = \frac{N_A RT}{4\pi D}\left(\frac{1}{r_c} - \frac{1}{\infty}\right)$$

It is known that $p_{A\infty} = 0$.

Therefore:

$$N_A = N_{CO_2} = \frac{4\pi D p_{AO} r_c}{RT}$$

$$= \frac{4\pi(4.3)(1.0)(14.7)(144)\left(\frac{0.06}{12}\right)}{(1545)(1900)}$$

$$= 1.95 \times 10^{-4} \text{ lb moles/hr}$$

where R = 1545 lb_f-ft/lbmol-R.

Due to the stoichiometry, $N_{CO_2} = N_c$ which leads to a carbon burning rate of:

$$(1.95 \times 10^{-4})(12) = 2.34 \times 10^{-3} \text{ lb/hr.}$$

• PROBLEM 15-30

Gas A diffuses through a stagnant film of gas surrounding a catalyst particle. A undergoes the following reaction

$$3A \rightarrow B$$

at the particle surface, instantaneously, B diffuses back through the stagnant film into the bulk. Assuming isothermal conditions, obtain an expression for the local reaction rate in terms of the effective gas-film thickness and the bulk gas stream compositions, x_{AO} and x_{BO}.

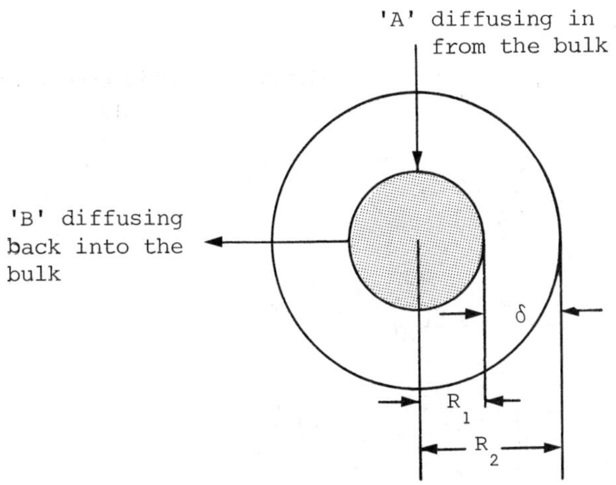

Solution: It can be seen from the following reaction that for every 1 mole of B diffusing back, there are 3 moles of A diffusing into the film towards the catalytic surface.

$$N_B = -\frac{N_A}{3}$$

Since $$N_A = -cD_{AB}\frac{\partial x_A}{\partial r} + x_A(N_A + N_B)$$

$$N_A = -cD_{AB}\frac{\partial x_A}{\partial r} + \frac{2}{3}x_A N_A$$

or $$N_A = -\frac{cD_{AB}}{(1 - \frac{2}{3}x_A)}\frac{\partial x_A}{\partial r}$$

A shell balance yields $\frac{d}{dr}(r^2 N_A) = 0$

or $r^2 N_A = C_1$

or $$\left(\frac{cD_{AB}}{1 - \frac{2}{3}x_A}\right) r^2 \frac{\partial x_A}{\partial r} = C_1$$

or $$\frac{dx_A}{1 - \frac{2}{3}x_A} = \frac{C_1}{cD_{AB}}\frac{dr}{r^2}$$

Integrating $$-\frac{3}{2}\left[\ln\left(1 - \frac{2}{3}x_A\right)\right] = -\frac{C_1}{cD_{AB}}\left[\frac{1}{r}\right] + C_2$$

Boundary conditions:

at $r = R_1$, $x_A = 0$

$r = R_2 = R_1 + \delta$, $x_A = x_{AO}$ where $\delta \rightarrow$ thickness of gas film

$$\therefore \quad -\frac{3}{2}\left(\ln(1)\right) = -\frac{C_1}{cD_{AB}}\frac{1}{R_1} + C_2$$

$$-\frac{3}{2}\left(\ln(1 - \frac{2}{3}x_{AO})\right) = -\frac{C_1}{cD_{AB}}\left(\frac{1}{R_2}\right) + C_2$$

$$\therefore \quad \frac{C_1}{cD_{AB}}\left[\frac{1}{R_2} - \frac{1}{R_1}\right] = \frac{3}{2}\left[\ln\left(\frac{1 - \frac{2}{3}x_{AO}}{1}\right)\right]$$

whereby C_1 can be evaluated.

The local reaction rate = the rate of diffusion at the catalyst surface

$$= - cD_{AB} \left.\frac{\partial x_A}{\partial r}\right|_{r=R_1} = - cD_{AB}\left(\frac{C_1}{cD_{AB}}\right)\left.\left(\frac{1 - \frac{2}{3} x_A}{r^2}\right)\right|_{r=R_1}$$

$$= - cD_{AB} \left(\frac{C_1}{cD_{AB}}\right)\left(\frac{1}{R_1^{\ 2}}\right)$$

$$= - cD_{AB} \frac{3}{2} \left[\frac{\ln\left(1 - \frac{2}{3} x_{AO}\right)}{R_1^{\ 2}}\right] \left(\frac{R_2 R_1}{R_1 - R_2}\right)$$

$$= + cD_{AB}\left(\frac{3}{2}\right) \frac{\ln\left(1 - \frac{2}{3} x_{AO}\right) R_2}{R_1 (R_1 - R_2)}$$

$$= \frac{3}{2} cD_{AB} \left(\frac{R_2}{R_1}\right) \frac{\ln\left(1 - \frac{2}{3} x_{AO}\right)}{(R_1 - R_2)}$$

• PROBLEM 15-31

A rectangular section of a porous solid 0.5 in. thick is submerged in 100 % ethanol. The voids of the solid compose 50 % of its volume. The solid is removed from the ethanol after thorough soaking and placed in an agitated tank of water at 80°F. Only molecular diffusion occurs in the pores, and the diffusivity inside the pores is approximately one tenth of its value outside the solid. What length of time is required for the mass fraction of ethanol at the center of the solid to drop to 0.008? Assume the concentration of ethanol in the water phase is always zero.

Solution: Because the densities of water and ethanol are reasonably similar, it is assumed that ρ is constant. Therefore the following holds true:

$$\frac{\partial \rho_A}{\partial t} = D \frac{\partial^2 \rho_A}{\partial z^2} \qquad (1)$$

or

$$\frac{\partial x_A}{\partial t} = D \frac{\partial^2 x_A}{\partial z^2} \qquad (2)$$

These equations indicate that the diffusivity is constant. An average value of $D = 1.1\ \text{cm}^2/\text{sec}$ will be employed. To simplify the equations, the following substitutions are used:

$$\alpha\cdot = \frac{Dt}{z_0^{\ 2}}$$

$$W = x_A$$

$$m = \frac{z}{z_0}$$

where the distance z is taken perpendicular to the middle of the solid and z_0 is half the width of the solid. Substituting into equation (2) provides:

$$\frac{\partial W}{\partial \alpha} = \frac{\partial^2 W}{\partial m^2} \qquad (3)$$

It is now possible to postulate that the solution to this differential equation exists as the product of two terms:

$$W = \alpha' M \qquad (4)$$

The term α' is a function of α, where time is variable, and M is solely a function of m and therefore only depends on distance. Differentiating equation (4) gives:

$$M \frac{\partial \alpha'}{\partial \alpha} = \alpha' \frac{\partial^2 M}{\partial m^2} \qquad (5)$$

or

$$\frac{1}{\alpha'} \frac{\partial \alpha'}{\partial \alpha} = \frac{1}{M} \frac{\partial^2 M}{\partial m^2} \qquad (6)$$

Time and distance are not dependent on each other. This implies that both sides of the equation equal to a constant, $-b^2$. Therefore:

$$\frac{\partial \alpha'}{\partial \alpha} + b^2 \alpha' = 0 \qquad (7)$$

and

$$\frac{\partial^2 M}{\partial m^2} + b^2 M = 0 \qquad (8)$$

Equation (7) has a solution of:

$$\alpha' = G_1 e^{-b^2 \alpha} \qquad (9)$$

and equation (8) has a solution of:

$$M = G_2 \sin bm + G_3 \cos bm \qquad (10)$$

Therefore:

$$W = \alpha' M = G_1 e^{-b^2 \alpha}(G_2 \sin bm + G_3 \cos bm) \qquad (11)$$

where G_1, G_2, and G_3 are constants. The boundary conditions for $W(m,\alpha)$ necessary to evaluate the constants are:

(I) $\frac{\partial W}{\partial m}(0,\alpha) = 0$

(II) $W(1,\alpha) = 0$

(III) $W(m,0) = 1.0$

Taking the derivative $\partial W/\partial m$ of equation (11) allows the first boundary condition to be applied.

$$\frac{\partial W}{\partial m} = G_1 e^{-b^2\alpha}(G_2 b \cos bm - G_3 b \sin bm) \tag{12}$$

Evaluating at $m = 0$ gives:

$$\frac{\partial W}{\partial m} = bG_1 G_2 e^{-b^2\alpha} \tag{13}$$

For this expression to equal zero, G_2 must be zero. Therefore:

$$W = B\, e^{-b^2} \cos bm \tag{14}$$

where the constant B combines G_1 and G_3. The second boundary condition can now be utilized.

$$B\, e^{-b^2\alpha} \cos b = 0$$

Many values of b satisfy this condition, for example, $\pi/2$, $3\pi/2$, $5\pi/2$... . An infinite series of cosine terms can be written.

$$W = B_1 e^{-(\pi/2)^2\alpha}\cos(\pi/2)m + B_2 e^{-(3\pi/2)^2\alpha}\cos\left(\frac{3\pi}{2}\right)m +$$

$$B_3 e^{-(5\pi/2)^2\alpha} \cos\left(\frac{5\pi}{2}\right) m + \ldots +$$

$$B_i e^{-\left[(2i-1)\pi/2\right]^2\alpha} \cos\left[\frac{(2i-1)\pi}{2}\right] m \tag{15}$$

where i is an integer. With the third boundary condition, equation (15) can be written:

$$1 = B_1 \cos\left(\frac{\pi}{2}\right) m + B_2 \cos\left(\frac{3\pi}{2}\right) m + B_3 \cos\left(\frac{5\pi}{2}\right) m +$$

$$\ldots + B_i \cos\left(\frac{2i-1}{2}\right)\pi m \tag{16}$$

Now multiply each side of this equation by $\cos\left[\frac{(2i-1)}{2}\right]\pi m dm$ and integrate from 0 to 1. The left side is then:

$$\int_0^1 \cos\left(\frac{2i-1}{2}\right)\pi m dm = \frac{2}{(2i-1)\pi}\left[\sin\left(\frac{2i-1}{2}\right)\pi m\right]_0^1$$

$$= -\frac{2}{(2i-1)\pi}(-1)^i \tag{17}$$

Integrating the first term on the right side gives:

$$\int_0^1 B_i \cos\left(\frac{\pi}{2}\right) m \cos\left(\frac{2i-1}{2}\right)\pi m dm$$

$$= B_1 \left[\frac{\sin\ (i - 1)\pi m}{(2i - 2)\pi} + \frac{\sin\ i\pi m}{2i\pi}\right]_0^1$$

$$= B_1 \left[\frac{\sin\ (i - 1)\pi}{(2i - 2)\pi} + \frac{\sin\ i\pi}{2i\pi}\right]$$

$$= 0$$

All terms on the right side are zero except the ith term, which is:

$$B_i \int_0^1 \cos^2\left(\frac{2i - 1}{2}\right)\pi m dm$$

$$= B_i \frac{2}{(2i - 1)\pi} \left[\frac{\pi}{2} \frac{2i - 1}{2} m + \frac{1}{4} \sin\ (2\pi) \frac{2i - 1}{2} m\right]_0^1$$

$$= B_i \frac{2}{(2i - 1)\pi} \left[\frac{\pi}{2} \frac{2i - 1}{2} + 0 - 0 - 0\right]$$

$$= \frac{B_i}{2}$$

Equation (16) can now be written:

$$- \frac{2}{(2i - 1)\pi} (-1)^i = \frac{A_i}{2}$$

which gives

$$A_i = - \frac{4(-1)^i}{(2i - 1)\pi}$$

The general solution is:

$$W = \frac{4}{\pi} e^{-(\pi/2)^2\alpha} \cos\left(\frac{\pi m}{2}\right) - \frac{4e^{-(3\pi/2)^2\alpha}}{3\pi} \cos\left(\frac{3\pi m}{2}\right)$$

$$+ \frac{4e^{-(5\pi/2)^2\alpha}}{5\pi} \cos\left(\frac{5\pi m}{2}\right) \ . \ . \ .$$

This can be written:

$$W = \sum_{i=1}^{i=\infty} - \frac{2(-1)^i}{\left(\frac{2i - 1}{2}\pi\right)} \exp\left[- \frac{(2i - 1)^2\pi^2\alpha}{4}\right] \cos\left(\frac{2i - 1}{2}\right) \pi m$$

Using $m = 0$ and $W = 0.008$

$$\alpha = 2.06$$

Therefore:

$$t = \frac{\alpha z_0^2}{D}$$

$$= \frac{(2.06)(\frac{1}{12} \cdot \frac{1}{4})^2}{\left(\frac{1}{10}\right)(1.1)(3.87)}$$

$$= 2.10 \times 10^{-3} \text{ hr} = 0.126 \text{ min.}$$

CHAPTER 16

CONVECTIVE MASS TRANSFER

EVAPORATION RATES AND SUBLIMATION RATES

• PROBLEM 16-1

What are the compositions of the gas and liquid phases existing under equilibrium? Assume ideality in both phases. i.e., Raoult's law and Dalton's law are valid.

Solution: Let gas be denoted by A and liquid by B.

The Raoult's law states that the partial pressure $\bar{p}$ of a solute gas A equals the product of its vapor pressure p at the same temperature and its mole fraction in the solution x.

Therefore

$$\bar{p}_A = x_A p_A$$

$$\bar{p}_B = x_B p_B$$

According to Dalton's law, the sum of partial pressures is equal to the total pressure.

Then, $$p = \bar{p}_A + \bar{p}_B$$

$$= x_A p_A + x_B p_B$$

$$= (1 - x_B) p_A + x_B p_B$$

Solving for x_B, gives

$$x_B = \frac{p - p_A}{p_B - p_A}$$

This implies that the liquid composition is a linear function of only total pressure, because for a constant temperature the vapor pressures p_A and p_B are fixed. The total pressure varies from $p = p_A$ at $x_B = 0$ to $p = p_B$ at $x_B = 1$.

The vapor composition is given by

$$\bar{p}_B = y_B p = x_B p_B$$

Then,

$$y_B = x_B p_B / p$$

Substituting for x_B gives

$$y_B = \frac{p_B}{p}\left(\frac{p - p_A}{p_B - p_A}\right)$$

The composition of gas is given as

$$y_A = \left[1 - \left(\frac{p - p_A}{p_B - p_A}\right)\right]\frac{p_A}{p}$$

• PROBLEM 16-2

The wet-bulb thermometer reads a temperature of 65°F when air at atmospheric pressure and 95°F blows across the thermometer. Determine the relative humidity of the air stream.

Solution: The concentration of water-vapor in the air stream is given by

$$\rho C_p \left(\frac{\alpha}{D}\right)^{2/3} (T_\infty - T_w) = (C_w - C_\infty) h_{fg} \qquad (1)$$

where ρ = density of air

C_p = specific heat of air

α = thermal diffusivity

D = diffusion coefficient

T_∞ = temperature of air

T_w = wet-bulb temperature

C_w = concentration at wet-bulb temperature

C_∞ = concentration of water vapor

h_{fg} = latent heat of vaporization

From air tables, for air at 1 atm and 95°F.

$$\rho = 0.0717 \text{ lb/ft}^3$$

$$C_p = 0.24 \text{ Btu/lb}^\circ\text{F}$$

$$\frac{\alpha}{D} = \frac{Sc}{Pr} = 0.843$$

$$T_w = 65^\circ\text{F}$$

$$T_\infty = 95^\circ\text{F}$$

$$C_w = 9.785 \times 10^{-4} \text{ lb/ft}^3$$

$$h_{fg} = 1039.8 \text{ Btu/lb}$$

Substituting the known quantities gives

$$(0.0717)(0.24)(0.843)^{2/3}(95 - 65) = (9.785 \times 10^{-4} - C_\infty)(1039.8)$$

$$C_\infty = 5.365 \times 10^{-4} \text{ lb/ft}^3$$

i.e. concentration of vapor is 5.365×10^{-4} lb/ft^3. At 95°F the saturation concentration is read from steam tables as

$$C_g = 2.475 \times 10^{-3} \text{ lb/ft}^3$$

Then, the relative humidity (RH) is the ratio of concentration of vapor to the concentration at saturation conditions for the air stream.

Therefore,

$$RH = \frac{5.365 \times 10^{-4}}{2.475 \times 10^{-3}}$$

$$= 21.7\ \%$$

• PROBLEM 16-3

A volatile fuel when spilled on a large flat surface quickly spreads over a depth 1/4 in. and a length of 7 ft. The fuel is at 60°F with a vapor pressure of 2 psia has the physical properties $\nu = 10^{-5}$ ft/sec, $\rho = 54$ lb$_m$/ft^3 and $D_{AB} = 0.55$ ft^2/hr. The kinematic viscosity of air is 1.62×10^{-4} ft^2/sec. If a breeze at 75°F blows parallel to the fuel surface at 15 mph, determine the evaporation rate.

Solution: Assume the evaporation rate is sufficiently small, so that there is no influence on the hydrodynamic boundary layer.

The Reynolds number is given by

$$Re_L = \frac{V_\infty L}{\nu}$$

$$= \frac{15 \times 1760 \times 3 \times 7}{3600 \times 1.62 \times 10^{-4}}$$

$$= 9.5 \times 10^5$$

At this Reynolds number, both laminar and turbulent flow exist. The Schmidt number of air is given by

$$(Sc)_{air} = \frac{\mu}{\rho D_{AB}}$$

$$(Sc)_{air} = \frac{\nu}{D_{AB}}$$

$$= \frac{1.62 \times 10^{-4} \times 3600}{0.55}$$

$$= 1.06$$

Therefore, the average Sherwood number is given by

$$Sh = \frac{k_c L}{D_{AB}} = 0.0365\ (Re_L)^{4/5} - 840$$

$$= 0.0365\ (9.5 \times 10^5)^{4/5} - 840$$

$$= 1370.4$$

Then

$$k_c = \frac{(0.55)(1370.4)}{7}$$

$$k_c = 107.7 \text{ ft/hr}$$

The mass-transfer rate is given by

$$N_A = \frac{k_c}{R_A T_A} (p_{AS} - p_{A\infty})$$

where N_A = mass flux

R_A = universal gas constant

T_A = film temperature

p_{AS} = vapor pressure of fuel

$p_{A\infty}$ = vapor pressure of air

k_c = mass-transfer coefficient

Substituting the known quantities gives

$$N_A = \frac{107.7}{(76)(460 + 67.5)} (2 - 0)(144)$$

$$N_A = 0.774 \ lb_m/hr\text{-}ft^2$$

Therefore, the evaporation rate is 0.774 $lb_m/hr\text{-}ft^2$. It is small as assumed before.

• PROBLEM 16-4

The transpiration cooling with liquid oxygen as cooling medium is used to protect the combustion chamber walls from being destroyed. The temperature of inside surface of walls should be maintained at 1170°R by adding liquid oxygen at 170°R through the porous walls into the chamber. The temperature of the gas stream is 3100°R and the heat transfer coefficient for the turbulent flow without the addition of oxygen is 250 Btu/hr.ft^2.°F. Find the required rate of addition of oxygen.

Solution: The transpiration cooling is done by making the walls porous and forcing the cooling medium through the walls into the combustion chamber.

The situation present in this case is of transferring A through stagnant B.

Hence, the approximate result is obtained by using the following equation.

$$N_A = \frac{k}{\delta_m C_{pA}} \ln \left[1 + \frac{C_{pA}}{\Delta H_A} (t_o - t_s) \right] \tag{1}$$

Replacing k/δ_m by h^o, eq. (1) reduces to

$$N_A = \frac{h^o}{C_{pA}} \ln \left[1 + \frac{C_{pA}}{\Delta H_A} (t_o - t_s) \right] \tag{2}$$

The mean film temperature between wall and liquid oxygen is

$$T_f = \frac{170 + 1170}{2}$$

$$= 670^oR$$

From oxygen tables, for oxygen at 670°R

$$C_{pA} = 0.223 \ Btu/lb^oF = 7.136 \ Btu/lb\text{-}mole^oF$$

$$h_{fg} = 2928 \ Btu/lb\text{-}mole$$

Then,

$$\Delta H_A = 2928 + 7.136\ (1170 - 170)$$

$$= 10064 \text{ Btu/lb-mole}$$

The mean film temperature between wall and gas stream is given by

$$C_{pA} = 0.265 \text{ Btu/lb}^\circ\text{F} = 8.48 \text{ Btu/lb-mole}^\circ\text{F}$$

Substituting the known quantities in eq. (2) gives

$$N_A = \frac{250}{8.48} \ln\left[1 + \frac{8.48}{10064}(3100 - 1170)\right]$$

$$= 28.5 \text{ lb-moles/hr.ft}^2$$

Hence, the required rate of addition of oxygen is 28.5 lb-moles/hr.ft^2.

The value of h can be obtained by using

$$h^\circ = h\left[1 + \frac{C_{pA}}{\Delta H_A}(t_o - t)\right]_{lm} \qquad (3)$$

where

$$\left[1 + \frac{C_{pA}}{\Delta H_A}(t_o - t)\right]_{lm} = \frac{(C_{pA}/\Delta H_A)(t_o - t_s)}{\ln\left[1 + \frac{C_{pA}}{\Delta H_A}(t_o - t_s)\right]} \qquad (4)$$

Then, substituting known quantities in eq. (4) gives

$$\left[1 + \frac{C_{pA}}{\Delta H_A}(t_o - t)\right]_{lm} = \frac{(8.48/10064)(3100 - 1170)}{\ln\left[1 + \frac{8.48}{10064}(3100 - 1170)\right]}$$

$$= 1.684$$

Then, substituting known quantities in eq. (3) gives

$$h^\circ = h(1.684)$$

$$h = \frac{h^\circ}{1.684}$$

$$= \frac{250}{1.684}$$

$$= 148.46 \text{ Btu/hr.ft}^2.^\circ\text{F}$$

$$h' = h\left[1 + \frac{C_{pA}}{\Delta H_A}(t_o - t_s)\right] \qquad (5)$$

Substituting known quantities in eq. (5) gives

$$h' = 148.46 \left[1 + \frac{8.48}{10064}(3100 - 1170)\right]$$

$$= 389.89 \text{ Btu/hr.ft}^2.^{\circ}\text{F}$$

Looking at the above three coefficients, it can be said that, if there is no mass transfer $h^{o} = 250$ will prevail; if mass transfer is involved h will include the energy carried by the mass transfer of A, so the value is changed to h = 148.46; the conduction heat transfer rate across the fictitious film is h' = 389.89.

• PROBLEM 16-5

Find the sublimation rate of a uranium hexafluoride UF_6 cylinder 7 mm. diameter when exposed to an air stream flowing at a velocity of 3.5 m/s. The bulk air is at 65°C and 1 atm. pressure. The surface temperature of the solid is 40°C at which its vapor pressure is 410 mm. Hg (54.65 kN/m^2).

The average heat transfer coefficient of fluid flowing perpendicular to a circular cylinder for fluid Reynolds number between 1 and 4000 is given by

$$Nu = 0.43 + 0.532\,(Re)^{0.5}(Pr)^{0.31}$$

where Nu and Re are calculated with the cylinder diameter and fluid properties at mean temperature of cylinder and bulk-fluid.

Solution: The mass transfer coefficient is given by

$$Sh_{av} = 0.43 + 0.532(Re)^{0.5}(Sc)^{0.31} \tag{1}$$

The Reynolds number is given by

$$Re = \frac{du\rho}{\mu} \tag{2}$$

The mean film temperature is

$$T_f = \frac{65 + 40}{2} = 52.5^{\circ}C$$

Average partial pressure of UF_6 at 52.5°C is 205 mm. Hg (27.33 kN/m^2).

$$\text{mole fraction of } UF_6 = \frac{27.33}{101.33} = 0.27$$

mole fraction of air = 0.73

From air tables, for air at 52.5°C and 0.73 composition

$$\rho = 4.15 \text{ kg/m}^3$$

$$\mu = 2.75 \times 10^{-5} \text{ kg/m.sec.}$$

diffusivity = 9.06×10^{-6} m^2/sec.

Substituting the known quantities in eq. (2) gives

$$Re = \frac{(7 \times 10^{-3})(3.5)(4.15)}{2.75 \times 10^{-5}}$$

$$= 3697.3$$

The Schmidt number is given by

$$Sc = \frac{\mu}{\rho D_{AB}} \qquad (3)$$

where

D_{AB} = diffusion coefficient

Substituting known quantities in eq. (3) gives

$$Sc = \frac{2.75 \times 10^{-5}}{(4.15)(9.06 \times 10^{-6})}$$

$$= 0.731$$

Substituting known quantities in eq. (1) gives

$$Sh_{av} = 0.43 + 0.532(3697.3)^{0.5}(0.731)^{0.31}$$

$$= 29.78$$

But $Sh_{av} = \dfrac{F_{av} d}{cD_{AB}}$

$$c = \frac{1}{22.41} \frac{273.14}{273.14 + 52.5}$$

$$= 0.0374 \text{ kmol/m}^3$$

Then, the mass transfer coefficient is given by

$$F_{av} = \frac{Sh_{av} cD_{AB}}{d}$$

$$= \frac{(29.78)(0.0374)(9.06 \times 10^{-6})}{7 \times 10^{-3}}$$

$$= 1.442 \times 10^{-3} \text{ kmol/m}^2\text{.sec.}$$

For air $N_B = 0$, then $N_A/(N_A + N_B) = 1.0$

$$\frac{c_A}{c} = \frac{54.65}{101.33} = 0.54$$

The mass flux is given by

$$N_A = \frac{N_A}{N_A + N_B} F_{av} \ln\left[\frac{(N_A/(N_A + N_B)) - c_{A2}/c}{(N_A/(N_A + N_B)) - c_{A1}/c}\right]$$

$$= (1.0)(1.442 \times 10^{-3}) \ln\left(\frac{1 - 0}{1 - 0.54}\right)$$

$$= 1.12 \times 10^{-3} \text{ kmol } UF_6/m^2.s$$

The mass-flux is based on the entire cylinder area.

The N_A obtained above is an instantaneous mass flux. Mass transfer will quickly reduce the cylinder dia, hence the Reynolds number and F_{av} will change with time. The empirical correlation for Nu_{av} and Sh_{av} are no longer valid because the surface will not remain in circular shape and causes the local F to change along the perimeter.

• PROBLEM 16-6

The relative humidity and temperature of an air flowing over a water surface with an average velocity of 5 ft/sec are respectively 42 percent and 75°F. The average temperature of the water surface is 65°F. If the length of the water surface parallel to the direction of the air flow is 7 inches, determine the quantity of water evaporated per hour per square foot of surface area.

Solution: The given system is the case of a steady state diffusion of A through nondiffusing B.

The mean film temperature $T_f = \frac{75 + 65}{2} = 70^\circ$F. From air tables, for air at 70°F and 1 atm. pressure

$$\mu = 0.0183 \text{ centipoise} = 0.0443 \text{ lb/hr.ft}$$

$$\rho = 0.0751 \text{ lb/ft}^3$$

The Reynolds number is given by

$$Re = \frac{\rho VL}{\mu}$$

$$= \frac{(0.0751)(5 \times 3600)(7/12)}{0.0443}$$

$= 17800$

This implies the flow is laminar.

For laminar flow over a flat surface, the heat transfer coefficient is given by

$$Nu = 0.331 \sqrt[3]{Pr} \sqrt{Re} \tag{1}$$

The heat transfer coefficient in eq. (1) is local value, but the average value for the surface between x = 0 and any point on the surface is twice the point value.

Now, based on average heat transfer coefficient eq. (1) becomes

$$Nu = 0.662 \sqrt[3]{Pr} \sqrt{Re} \tag{2}$$

The analogous mass transfer coefficient is given by

$$\frac{h_{Mc} L}{D_{AB}} = 0.662 \sqrt[3]{Sc} \sqrt{Re} \tag{3}$$

From diffusivity table, for air-water system at $70^{\circ}F$

$$D_{AB} = 0.969 \text{ ft}^2/\text{hr}.$$

The Schmidt number is given by

$$Sc = \frac{\mu}{\rho D_{AB}}$$

$$= \frac{0.0443}{(0.0751)(0.969)}$$

$$= 0.609$$

Solving eq. (3) for h_{Mc}

$$h_{Mc} = 0.662 \frac{D_{AB}}{L} \sqrt[3]{Sc} \sqrt{Re}$$

Substituting known quantities gives

$$h_{Mc} = (0.662) \frac{0.969}{(7/12)} \sqrt[3]{0.609} \sqrt{17,800}$$

$$= 124.4 \text{ ft/hr}$$

The case is of water vapor diffusing into a non-diffusing gas, air.

Therefore, the mass transfer is given by

$$N_A = h_{Mc} \left(\frac{p}{RTp_{BM}}\right)(p_{A1} - p_{A2}) \tag{4}$$

From psychrometric chart;

for temperature 75°F, relative humidity 42 percent

$p_v = 0.180$ psia

$p_a = 14.7 - 0.180 = 14.52$ psia

for temperature 65°F, saturated

$p_v = 0.303$ psia

$p_a = 14.7 - 0.303$

$= 14.4$ psia

Substituting the known quantities in eq. (4) gives

$$N_A = \frac{(124.4)(14.7)(144)(0.303 - 0.180)}{1544(460 + 70)\left(\frac{14.52 + 14.4}{2}\right)}$$

$$= 0.00274 \text{ lb mole/hr.ft}^2$$

Therefore, the quantity of water evaporated per hour per square foot is 0.0494 lb/hr. ft^2.

• PROBLEM 16-7

Air at 105°F is flowing over a water surface 2.5 ft long and 2.5 ft wide at 80°F with an average velocity of 7.5 ft/sec. Assume molecular weights of air-vapor mixture and water are 29.0 and 18.0 respectively. Also assume the density and viscosity to be 0.070 lb/ft^3 and 0.049 lb/ft.hr. If the relative humidity of air is 42 percent, determine the quantity of water evaporated per hour per square foot of water surface.

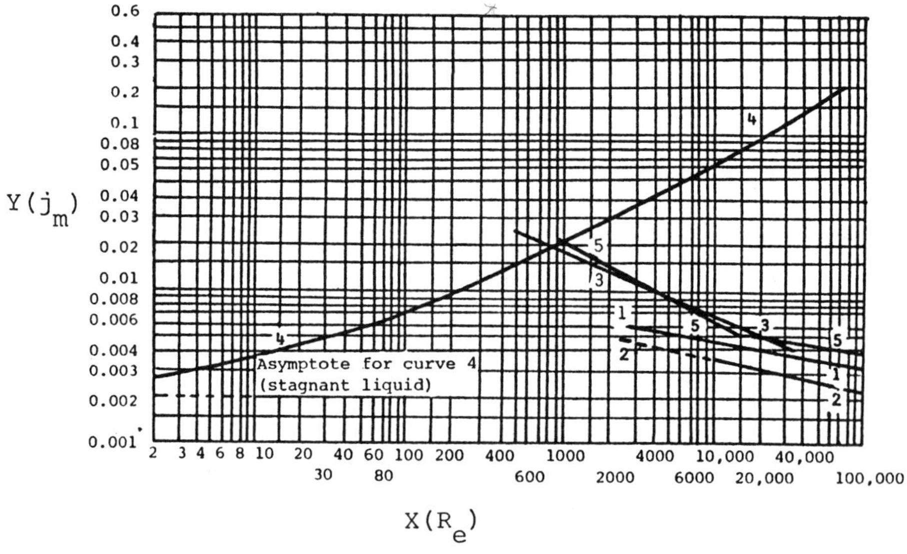

Solution: Assume that the given system can be approximated as a fluid flowing parallel to a flat plate (water surface).

The Reynolds number is given by

$$Re = \frac{v\rho L}{\mu}$$

$$= \frac{(7.5 \times 3600)(0.070)(2.5)}{0.049}$$

$$= 96428.6$$

From the fig. above the value of y for curve 5 and x = 96428.6 is 0.0036.

The equation for j is given by

$$j_M = 0.0036 = \frac{h_{Mp} p_{BM}}{G_M} (Sc)^{2/3} \qquad (1)$$

From the diffusivity table

$$D_{AB} = 0.992 \text{ ft}^2/\text{hr}$$

Neglect the influence of temperature on D_{AB}.

The Schmidt number is given by

$$Sc = \frac{\mu}{\rho D_{AB}} \qquad (2)$$

$$= \frac{0.049}{0.070(0.992)}$$

$$= 0.706$$

G_M is given by

$$G_M = \frac{v\rho}{M}$$

$$= \frac{(7.5 \times 3600)(0.070)}{29}$$

$$= 65.2 \text{ lb-mole/hr.ft}^2$$

From psychrometric charts

for temperature 105°F, relative humidity 40%

$$p_v = 0.46 \text{ psia}$$

$$p_a = 14.7 - 0.46$$

$$= 14.24 \text{ psia}$$

for temperature 80°F, saturated

$$p_v = 0.51 \text{ psia}$$

$$p_a = 14.7 - 0.51 = 14.19 \text{ psia}$$

Hence,

$$p_{BM} = \frac{14.24 + 14.19}{2}$$

$$= 14.215 \text{ psia}$$

$$= 2047 \text{ psf}$$

Then, mass transfer coefficient from eq. (1) is given by

$$h_{Mp} = \frac{j_M G_M}{p_{BM}(Sc)^{2/3}}$$

Substituting the known quantities gives

$$h_{Mp} = \frac{0.0036(65.2)}{2047(0.706)^{2/3}}$$

$$= 0.000145 \text{ lb-mole/ft}^2\text{-hr-psf}$$

$$= 0.3074 \text{ lb-mole/hr-ft}^2\text{-atm}$$

The mass transfer rate of water vapor is given by

$$N_A = h_{Mp}(p_{v1} - p_{v2})$$

$$= 0.000145(0.51 - 0.46)144$$

$$= 0.00105 \text{ lb-mole/hr-ft}^2$$

Then, the quantity of water evaporated per hour from the area of 6.25 sq. ft. is

$$W = (0.00105)(6.25)(18)$$

$$= 0.118 \text{ lb}_m/\text{hr}.$$

• PROBLEM 16-8

Consider a naphthalene pipe 1 in. internal diameter and 7 ft. long through which air at 50°F passes at bulk velocities of (a) 3 ft/sec and (b) 60 ft/sec. The average pressure of air is 1 atm and the change in pressure along the tube is negligible. Determine the sublimation rate of naphthalene in the pipe in pounds per hour, if naphthalene surface is at 50°F.

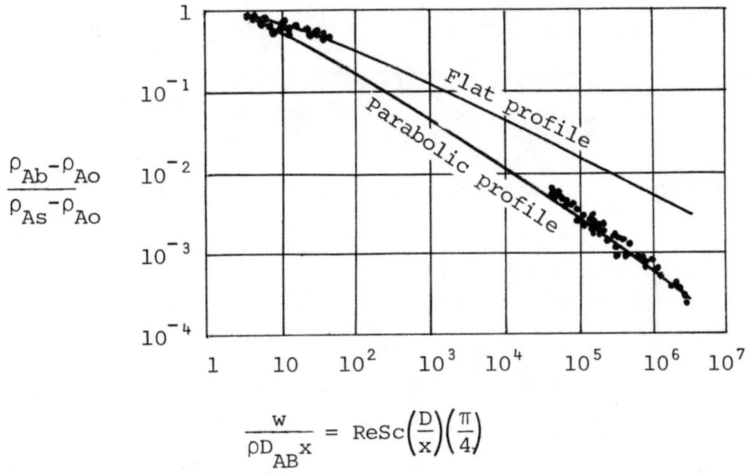

EXIT CONCENTRATION OF SOLUTE FOR LAMINAR FLOW IN A PIPE.

Solution: From air tables for air at $50^{\circ}F$ and 1 atm

$$\rho = 0.078 \text{ lb/ft}^3$$

$$\mu = 1.20 \times 10^{-5} \text{ lb/ft-sec}$$

Properties of naphthalene at $50^{\circ}F$

vapor pressure = 0.0209 mm. Hg

molecular diffusivity in air = 0.200 ft^2/hr

molecular weight = 128.2

(a) Given $U_b = 3$ ft/sec

The Reynolds number is given by

$$Re = \frac{\rho v L}{\mu}$$

$$= \frac{(0.078)(3)(\frac{1}{12})}{1.20 \times 10^{-5}}$$

$$= 1625$$

This implies that the flow is laminar.

The Schmidt number is given by

$$Sc = \frac{\mu}{\rho D_{AB}}$$

$$= \frac{(1.2 \times 10^{-5})3600}{(0.078)(0.200)}$$

$$= 2.77$$

Then,

$$\text{ReSc}\,\frac{D}{x}\,\frac{\pi}{4} = (1625)(2.77)\left(\frac{1}{12 \times 7}\right)\left(\frac{\pi}{4}\right)$$

$$= 42.09$$

From the figure above, for parabolic profile and $\text{ReSc}\,\frac{D}{x}\,\frac{\pi}{4} =$ 42.09

$$\frac{\rho_{Ab} - \rho_{Ao}}{\rho_{As} - \rho_{Ao}} = 0.40$$

At the entrance of the pipe air is free from naphthalene, so $\rho_{Ao} = 0$.

The concentration ρ_{As} of naphthalene at the interface is found from the vapor pressure by the following approximation which is valid for dilute mixtures.

$$\rho_{As} = \frac{(0.0209)(128.2)(0.078)}{760(29)}$$

$$= 9.5 \times 10^{-6}\ \text{lb/ft}^3$$

Hence, the discharge concentration of naphthalene is

$$\rho_{Ab} = (0.40)(9.5 \times 10^{-6})$$

$$= 3.8 \times 10^{-6}\ \text{lb/ft}^3$$

Then, the total sublimation rate is

$$= \frac{\pi}{4}\left(\frac{1}{12}\right)^2 (2)(3.8 \times 10^{-6})(3600)$$

$$= 1.5 \times 10^{-4}\ \text{lb/hr}$$

(b) Given $U_b = 60$ ft/sec.

The Reynolds number is

$$\text{Re} = \frac{\left(\frac{1}{12}\right)(60)(0.078)}{1.20 \times 10^{-5}}$$

$$= 32500$$

This implies the flow is turbulent. Hence, to find the mass-transfer coefficient the following equation is used.

$$\text{Sh} = 0.023\ \text{Re}^{0.8}\ \text{Sc}^{0.33} \qquad (1)$$

$$= 0.023\ (32500)^{0.8}\ (2.77)^{0.33}$$

$$= 131$$

The mole fraction of naphthalene is so low that $(1 - x_A)_{lm} \sim 1$.

Hence $\quad k^0_\rho = k_\rho$

$$k_\rho = \frac{Sh \cdot D}{d} = \frac{(131)(0.200)}{(1/12)}$$

$$= 314.4 \text{ ft/hr.}$$

As the sublimation rate is low, the total volumetric rate of flow can be independent of the distance from the tube inlet.

Writing a naphthalene balance for a differential length of pipe gives

$$\frac{\pi}{4}\left(\frac{1}{12}\right)^2 (60) d\rho_{Ab} = k_\rho \left(\frac{\pi}{12}\right) dx\ (\rho_{As} - \rho_{Ab})$$

$$\int_0^{\rho_{Ab}} \frac{d\rho_{Ab}}{\rho_{As} - \rho_{Ab}} = \frac{48}{60} k_\rho \int_0^7 dx$$

Integrating on both sides gives,

$$- \ln \frac{\rho_{As} - \rho_{Ab}}{\rho_{As}} = \frac{48}{60} k_\rho\ (7)$$

$$- \ln \frac{\rho_{As} - \rho_{Ab}}{\rho_{As}} = \frac{48}{60} \frac{(314.4)(7)}{3600}$$

$$= 0.489$$

Therefore

$$\frac{\rho_{As}}{\rho_{As} - \rho_{Ab}} = 1.631$$

$$\rho_{Ab} = 0.387\ \rho_{As}$$

$$\rho_{Ab} = (0.387)(9.5 \times 10^{-6})$$

$$= 3.68 \times 10^{-6} \text{ lb/ft}^3$$

The discharge mixing up concentration is 3.68×10^{-6} lb/ft^3.

Therefore the total sublimation rate is

$$= \frac{\pi}{4}\left(\frac{1}{12}\right)^2 (60)(3.68 \times 10^{-6})(3600)$$

$$= 4.335 \times 10^{-3} \text{ lb/hr.}$$

• PROBLEM 16-9

Consider a 3 in. diameter and 5 ft. long vertical cylinder of a humidification apparatus on whose outside surface a thin film of water is flowing down. At right angles to the cylinder flows dry air at 110°F and 1 atm with a velocity of 22 ft/sec. The temperature of water is 70°F. The water is restricted from going beyond the bottom of the cylinder. Determine the rate at which water has to be supplied if the entire surface of the cylinder has to be used for the evaporating process.

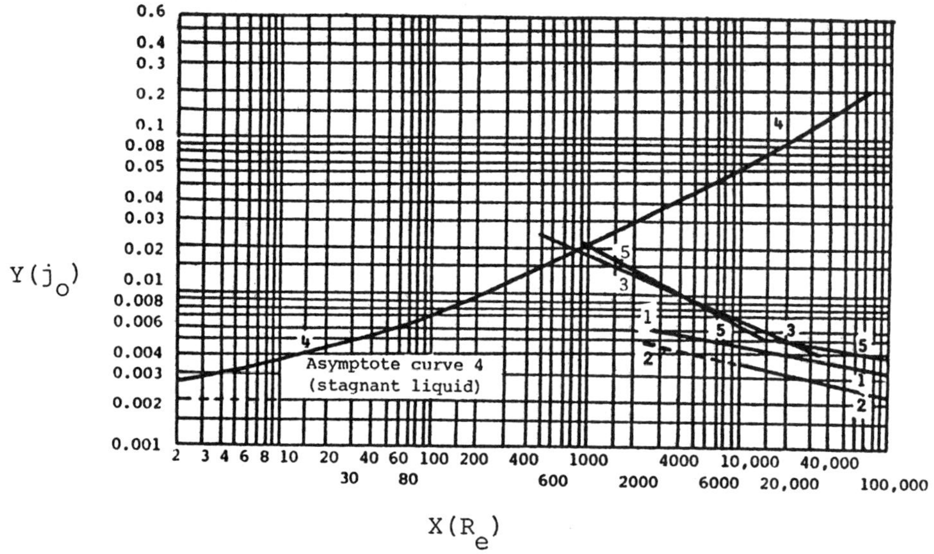

Solution: The mean film temperature is given by

$$T_f = \frac{110 + 70}{2} = 90^\circ F = 550^\circ R$$

From air tables, for air at 90°F

$$\mu = 0.01876 \text{ centipoise}$$

$$= 0.0454 \text{ lb/ft-hr} = 1.26 \times 10^{-5} \text{ lb/ft-sec.}$$

The density of the air at 550°R is given by

$$\rho = \frac{nM_{air}}{V} = \frac{PM_{air}}{RT}$$

$$= \frac{1(29)}{(0.73)(550)}$$

$$= 0.0722 \text{ lb/ft}^3$$

The Reynolds number is given by

$$Re = \frac{\rho VD}{\mu}$$

$$Re = \frac{(0.0722)(22)(3/12)}{1.26 \times 10^{-5}}$$

$$= 31516$$

From the figure above, for Re = 31516 and curve 3, $j_D = 0.0045$

But j_D is also given by

$$j_D = \frac{k_G P_{B,lm}(Sc)^{0.66}}{G_M} = 0.0045 \qquad (1)$$

where k_G = mass transfer coefficient

$P_{B,lm}$ = log mean partial pressure of the nondiffusing air

G_M = molar mass velocity

S_c = Schmidt number

From diffusivity tables, for air-water system at 550^0R

$$D_{AB} = 1.021 \text{ ft}^2/\text{hr}$$

The Schmidt number is given by

$$Sc = \frac{\mu}{\rho D_{AB}}$$

$$= \frac{1.26 \times 10^{-5} \times 3600}{(0.0722)(1.021)}$$

$$= 0.615$$

From steam tables,

vapor pressure of water at 70^0F is 18.79 mm.

Then, the interfacial and bulk concentrations are

at the interface P_{H_2O} = 18.79 mm Hg; P_{air} = 741.21 mm Hg.

in the bulk of gas P_{H_2O} = 0 mm Hg; P_{air} = 760 mm Hg.

Hence, the log mean partial pressure of the nondiffusing air is

$$P_{B,lm} = \frac{760 - 741.21}{\ln\left(\frac{760}{741.21}\right)}$$

$$= 750.57 \text{ mm Hg.}$$

The molar mass velocity of the air flowing normal to the cylinder is given by

$$G_M = \frac{V\rho}{M}$$

$$= \frac{(22)(3600)(0.0722)}{29}$$

$$= 197.2 \text{ lb mole/ft}^2\text{-hr.}$$

From eq. (1) the mass transfer coefficient is given by

$$k_G = \frac{0.0045\ G_M}{P_{B,lm}(Sc)^{0.66}}$$

Substituting the known quantities gives

$$k_G = \frac{(0.0045)(197.2)}{(750.57)(0.615)^{0.66}}$$

$$= 0.00163 \text{ lb mole/hr-ft}^2\text{-mm Hg.}$$

The following equation gives the mass flux

$$N_A = k_G\ (P_{H_2O,i} - P_{H_2O,\infty})$$

$$= 0.00163\ (18.79 - 0)$$

$$= 0.0306 \text{ lb mole/hr-ft}^2.$$

The surface area of cylinder is

$$A_s = \pi DL$$

$$= \pi(0.25)(5)$$

$$= 3.927 \text{ ft}^2.$$

$$\text{Feed rate} = N_A M A_s$$

$$= (0.0306)(18)(3.927)$$

$$= 2.16 \text{ lb/hr.}$$

The rate at which water has to be supplied is 2.16 lb/hr.

MASS TRANSFER COEFFICIENTS AND FILM THICKNESS

• PROBLEM 16-10

The wet surface of a cylinder placed perpendicular to a turbulent air stream flowing with a velocity of 20 ft/sec absorbs ammonia NH_3. For this process mass transfer data is not available, but heat transfer tests conducted with same geometry and air velocity yielded a heat transfer coefficient, h = 12 Btu/hr.ft^2.$^\circ$F. Determine the mass transfer coefficient h_D for the absorption of NH_3.

Solution: This is a case where NH_3 is absorbed by water.

The equation for j_H is given as

$$j_H = \frac{h}{\rho C_p V} (Pr)^{2/3} \tag{1}$$

where j_H = heat transfer dimensionless group

h = heat transfer coefficient

ρ = density of air

C_p = specific heat of air

Pr = Prandtl number

V = velocity of air

The equation for j_D is given as

$$j_D = \frac{h_D}{V} (Sc)^{2/3} \tag{2}$$

where j_D = mass transfer dimensionless group

h_D = mass transfer coefficient

V = velocity of air

Sc = Schmidt number

Assume $j_D = j_H$

Hence, from eqs. (1) and (2)

$$\frac{h_D}{V} (Sc)^{2/3} = \frac{h}{\rho C_p V} (Pr)^{2/3}$$

Then,

$$h_D = \frac{h}{\rho C_p}\left(\frac{Pr}{Sc}\right)^{2/3} \quad (3)$$

For air

$$\rho = 0.075 \text{ lb/ft}^3$$

$$C_p = 0.24 \text{ Btu/lb}^{\circ}\text{F}$$

$$Pr = 0.74$$

For dilute NH_3 - air mixtures

$$p_{bm} = P \quad \text{and} \quad Sc = 0.61$$

Substituting the known quantities in eq. (3) gives

$$h_D = \frac{12}{(0.075)(0.24)}\left(\frac{0.74}{0.61}\right)^{2/3}$$

$$= 758.3 \text{ ft/hr.}$$

Therefore, the mass transfer coefficient for absorption of ammonia is 758.3 ft/hr.

• PROBLEM 16-11

(a) A mixture of air and water vapor is passing over a flat plate 2 ft long at a rate of 210 ft/sec at 1 atm and 75°F. Determine the mass transfer coefficient of water vapor in air if the flow is turbulent and the concentration of water vapor in air is very low (i.e., $p_{bm}/P \simeq 1$).

(b) Find the mass transfer coefficient of water vapor in air when the mixture is passing over a sphere 3 in in diameter. Assume all other conditions to be same as in part (a).

Solution: The given system is a case of diffusion of water vapor in nondiffusing air. From air tables for air at 1 atm and 75°F.

$$\rho = 0.0744 \text{ lb/ft}^3$$

$$\mu = 0.0184 \text{ centipoise} = 0.0045 \text{ lb/ft-hr} = 1.24 \times 10^{-5} \text{ lb/ft-sec}$$

$$\nu = 16.62 \times 10^{-5} \text{ ft}^2\text{/sec}$$

From diffusivity tables, for air-water system

$$D_{AB} = 23.7 \times 10^{-5}\ ft^2/sec$$

The Schmidt number is given by

$$Sc = \frac{\nu}{D_{AB}}$$

where ν = kinematic viscosity

D_{AB} = diffusion coefficient

Substituting the known values gives

$$Sc = \frac{16.62 \times 10^{-5}}{23.7 \times 10^{-5}}$$

$$= 0.7013$$

(a) For flow over a flat plate:

The Reynolds number is given by

$$Re_L = \frac{VL}{\nu}$$

$$= \frac{(210)(2)}{16.62 \times 10^{-5}}$$

$$= 2527075.8$$

This implies the flow is turbulent.

For turbulent flow,

$$j_D = \frac{0.037}{(Re_L)^{0.2}}$$

$$= \frac{0.037}{(2527075.8)^{0.2}}$$

$$= 0.00194$$

but j_D is also given by

$$j_D = \frac{h_D}{V}(Sc)^{2/3}$$

whence

$$h_D = \frac{j_D V}{(Sc)^{2/3}}$$

Substituting the known quantities gives

$$h_D = \frac{(0.00194)(210)}{(0.7013)^{2/3}}$$

$$h_D = 0.516 \text{ ft/sec}$$

Hence, the mass transfer coefficient of water vapor in air is 0.516 ft/sec.

(b) For a flow over a sphere:

The Reynolds number is given by

$$Re_D = \frac{VD}{\nu}$$

$$= \frac{(210)(3/12)}{16.62 \times 10^{-5}}$$

$$= 315884.5$$

This implies the flow is turbulent.

The Sherwood number is given by

$$Sh = \frac{h_D D}{D_{AB}} = 2.0 \left[1 + 0.276 (Re_D)^{\frac{1}{2}} (Sc)^{\frac{1}{2}}\right]$$

Solving for h_D gives

$$h_D = 2.0 \frac{D_{AB}}{D} \left[1 + 0.276 (Re_D)^{\frac{1}{2}} (Sc)^{\frac{1}{2}}\right]$$

$$= (2.0) \frac{(23.7 \times 10^{-5})}{(3/12)} \left[1 + 0.276(315884.5)^{\frac{1}{2}}(0.7013)^{\frac{1}{2}}\right]$$

$$= 0.25 \text{ ft/sec}$$

Hence, the mass transfer coefficient of water vapor in air is 0.25 ft/sec.

• PROBLEM 16-12

Consider a sphere 2 in. in diameter of naphthalene placed in air at 115°F flowing with a velocity of 1.1 ft/sec. The vapor pressure of solid naphthalene is 0.565 mm Hg and the diffusivity of naphthalene in air at 115°F is 7.5×10^{-5} ft^2/sec. Determine the mass transfer coefficient and the mass transfer flux of naphthalene to air at 115°F and 1 atm.

Solution: This is the case of A diffusing through stagnant B.

As the concentration of naphthalene is low, the physical properties of air can be used.

From air tables, for air at 115°F

$\mu = 0.0469$ lb/ft-hr

$\rho = 0.0692$ lb/ft^3

The Schmidt number is given by

$$Sc = \frac{\mu}{\rho D_{AB}} \tag{1}$$

where μ = absolute viscosity of air

ρ = density of air

D_{AB} = diffusion coefficient

Substituting the known quantities in eq. (1) gives

$$Sc = \frac{0.0469}{(0.0692)(7.5 \times 10^{-5})(3600)}$$

$$= 2.51$$

The Reynolds number is given by

$$Re = \frac{\rho V D}{\mu} \tag{2}$$

where V = velocity of air

D = diameter of sphere

Substituting the known values in eq. (2) gives

$$Re = \frac{(0.0692)(1.1)(3600)(2/12)}{0.0469}$$

$$= 973.8$$

For gases with Schmidt number in the range of 0.6 - 2.7 and Reynolds number 1 - 48000, the following equation is used.

$$Sh = 2 + 0.552\,(Re)^{0.53}\,(Sc)^{1/3} \tag{3}$$

Substituting the known quantities gives

$$Sh = 2 + 0.552\,(973.8)^{0.53}\,(2.51)^{1/3}$$

$$= 30.78$$

but Sherwood number is also given by

$$Sh = k'_c \frac{L}{D_{AB}} = k'_c \frac{D}{D_{AB}} \quad (4)$$

Therefore,

$$k'_c = \frac{D_{AB} Sh}{D}$$

Substituting the known values in the above eq. gives

$$k'_c = \frac{(30.78)(7.5 \times 10^{-5})}{(2/12)} = 0.01385 \text{ ft/sec}$$

$$= 49.86 \text{ ft/hr}$$

Converting the mass transfer coefficient

$$k'_c C = k'_c \frac{P}{RT} = k'_G P$$

$$k'_G = \frac{k'_c}{RT}$$

Hence, for $T = 460 + 115 = 575^{\circ}R$

$$k'_G = \frac{49.86}{(0.73)(575)}$$

$$= 0.1188 \text{ lb mol/hr-ft}^2\text{-atm}$$

As the naphthalene concentration is low $y_{BM} \cong 0$ and $k'_G \cong k_G$.

For A diffusing through stagnant B

$$N_A = k_G (P_{A1} - P_{A2})$$

$$P_{A1} = \frac{0.565}{760}$$

$$= 7.43 \times 10^{-4} \text{ atm}$$

$$P_{A2} = 0$$

Then,

$$N_A = 0.1188 (7.43 \times 10^{-4})$$

$$= 8.83 \times 10^{-5} \text{ lb mol/hr.ft}^2$$

The area of the sphere is

$$A = \pi D^2$$

$$= \pi(2/12)^2$$

$$= 8.73 \times 10^{-2} \text{ ft}^2$$

Therefore the total mass evaporated is

$$N_A A = (8.83 \times 10^{-5})(8.73 \times 10^{-2})$$

$$= 7.709 \times 10^{-6} \text{ lb mol/hr}$$

• PROBLEM 16-13

A spherical globule of glucose, 1/8 in. in dia dissolves in water flowing at 0.6 ft/sec. Given that the temperature of water as $25^\circ C$ and the diffusivity of glucose in water at $25^\circ C$ as 4.14×10^{-3} cm^2/sec, calculate the mass transfer coefficient of glucose in water.

Solution: We assume that the concentration of glucose in water is so small that the properties of the solution are the same as that of pure water.

$$\therefore \qquad \mu = 0.9 \ C_p \text{ at } 25^\circ C$$

$$\rho = 62.2 \ lb_m/ft^3$$

$$\therefore \qquad Re = \frac{DV\rho}{\mu} = \frac{\frac{1}{8} \times \frac{1}{12} (0.6)(62.2)}{0.9 \times 6.717 \times 10^{-4}} = 643$$

$$Sc = \frac{\mu}{\rho D_{AB}} = \frac{0.9 \times 6.717 \times 10^{-4}}{62.2 \times 4.14 \times 10^{-3}} \times (30.48)^2$$

$$= 2.181$$

Using Froessling correlation for mass transfer,

$$Sh = 2.0 + 0.6 \ (Sc)^{1/3} \ (Re)^{1/2}$$

$$= 2.0 + 0.6 \ (2.181)^{1/3} \ (643)^{1/2}$$

$$= 21.731$$

Also, $$Sh = \frac{kD}{D_{AB}} = 21.731$$

$$\therefore \qquad k = 21.731 \times \frac{D_{AB}}{D} = 21.731 \times \frac{4.14 \times 10^{-3} \times 1}{\frac{1}{8} \times \frac{1}{12} \times (30.48)^2}$$

$$= 8.56 \times 10^{-3} \text{ ft/sec} = 33.468 \text{ ft/hr}$$

where k is the mass transfer coefficient of glucose in water.

Carbon dioxide from an aqueous solution has to be removed by an air stream flowing at 3.0 ft/sec using 3 in. internal diameter wetted wall column. At one point in the column the CO_2 concentration in air stream is 1 mole percent and in the water is 0.5 mole percent. If the column is operated at 10 atm and $80^{\circ}F$, find the gas-phase mass transfer coefficient and the mass flux at that point in the column.

Solution: The convective mass transfer coefficient of a gas is found by using the following equation

$$\frac{k_c D}{D_{AB}} \frac{p_{B,lm}}{P} = 0.023\ (Re)^{0.83}\ (Sc)^{0.44} \tag{1}$$

where A is the diffusing species

k_c = mass transfer coefficient

D = diameter of the column

D_{AB} = diffusion coefficient

$p_{B,lm}$ = log mean partial pressure of constituent B

P = total pressure

Re = Reynolds number

Sc = Schmidt number

The mass diffusivity and dimensionless parameters are estimated at bulk conditions of the air stream.

The mass diffusivity of CO_2 in air at $492^{\circ}R$ and 1 atm is $1.46 \times 10^{-4}\ ft^2/sec$.

The corrected value for bulk conditions is

$$D_{AB} = 1.46 \times 10^{-4} \times \frac{1}{10} \times \left(\frac{572}{492}\right)^{3/2}$$

$$= 1.83 \times 10^{-5}\ ft^2/sec$$

$$= 0.066\ ft^2/hr$$

Assume viscosity and density of air represent the bulk conditions, since the concentration of CO_2 is low.

From air tables, for air at $80^{\circ}F$

$$\mu = 0.0185\ cp$$

$$= 0.0448\ lb/ft\text{-}hr$$

$$= 1.24 \times 10^{-5}\ lb/ft\text{-}sec$$

Density of air is given by

$$\rho_{air} = \frac{P}{RT} M_{air}$$

$$= \frac{(10)(29)}{(0.73)(540)}$$

$$= 0.736 \text{ lb/ft}^3$$

The Schmidt number is given by

$$Sc = \frac{\mu}{\rho D_{AB}}$$

Substituting the known values gives

$$Sc = \frac{0.0448}{(0.736)(0.066)}$$

$$= 0.922$$

The Reynolds number is given by

$$Re = \frac{\rho VD}{\mu}$$

$$= \frac{(0.736)(3.0)(3/12)}{1.24 \times 10^{-5}}$$

$$= 44516.0$$

The Henry's law constant for CO_2 in water at 80^0F is 1.64 x 10^3 atom/mole fraction CO_2 in solution.

The partial pressure of CO_2 with a concentration of 0.005 mole fraction at the interface is 8.2 atm.

The concentrations in terms of pressure are at the interface:

$$p_A = 8.2 \text{ atm.}$$

$$p_B = 1.8 \text{ atm.}$$

in the bulk gas phase

$$p_A = 0.1 \text{ atm.}$$

$$p_B = 9.9 \text{ atm.}$$

The log mean partial pressure of constituent B is given by

$$p_{B,lm} = \frac{9.9 - 1.8}{\ln(9.9/1.8)}$$

$$= 4.75 \text{ atm.}$$

From eq. (1)

$$k_c = 0.023\,(Re)^{0.83}\,(Sc)^{0.44}\left(\frac{P}{p_{B,lm}}\right)\left(\frac{D_{AB}}{D}\right)$$

Substituting the known quantities in the above equation gives

$$k_c = (0.023)(44516)^{0.83}(0.922)^{0.44}\left(\frac{10}{4.75}\right)\left(\frac{0.066}{3/12}\right)$$

$$= 89 \text{ ft/hr}$$

The mass flux is given by

$$N_A = k_c(C_{A,i} - C_{A,\infty})$$

$$= \frac{k_c}{RT}(P_{A,i} - P_{A,\infty})$$

$$= \frac{89}{(0.73)(540)}(8.2 - 0.1)$$

$$= 1.83 \text{ lb mole/hr.ft}^2.$$

• PROBLEM 16-15

A vertical pipe 60 mm. internal diameter and 1.6 m long has 0.2 mm. thick water film at 293°K running down on the inside wall and air stream containing ammonia is flowing through the pipe. The interfacial mole fraction of ammonia is 0.0372. If the water at inlet is pure, determine the mass rate of removal of ammonia from the air stream.

Solution: The molar absorption rate of ammonia can be computed using the following equation.

$$\dot{M} = 2\pi DC\left[\frac{D_{12}VL}{\pi}\right]^{\frac{1}{2}}\left(x_{1,u} - x_{1,in}\right) \qquad (1)$$

where D = diameter of pipe

C = molar concentration

D_{12} = diffusion coefficient

V = liquid surface velocity

L = length of pipe

$x_{1,u}$ = concentration of ammonia at the interface

$x_{1,in}$ = concentration of ammonia at the inlet

As the concentration of ammonia is low, the influence of ammonia on properties of pure water is negligible.

From steam tables, for water at 293°K

$$\rho = 997.4 \text{ kg/m}^3$$

$$\mu = 1.028 \times 10^{-3} \text{ kg/m.sec.}$$

$$\nu = 1.03 \times 10^{-6} \text{ m}^2\text{/sec.}$$

The molar concentration is given by

$$C = \frac{\rho}{M}$$

$$C = \frac{997.4}{18}$$

$$= 55.41 \text{ k mole/m}^3$$

From diffusivity tables, for NH_3-water system at 293°K is

$$D_{12} = 1.76 \times 10^{-5} \text{ cm}^2\text{/sec.}$$

$$= 1.76 \times 10^{-9} \text{ m}^2\text{/sec.}$$

Since $\Delta\rho = \rho$, the liquid surface velocity is related to the film thickness by

$$V = \frac{g\delta^2}{2\nu}$$

$$= \frac{(9.81)(0.2 \times 10^{-3})^2}{(2)(1.03 \times 10^{-6})}$$

$$= 0.1905 \text{ m/sec.}$$

Substituting all the known quantities in eq. (1) gives

$$\dot{M} = (2)(\pi)(60 \times 10^{-3})(55.41)\left[\frac{(1.76 \times 10^{-9})(0.1905)(1.6)}{\pi}\right]^{\frac{1}{2}} \times$$

$$(0.0372 - 0)(3600)$$

$$= 0.0366 \text{ k mole/hr}$$

Hence the mass rate of removal of ammonia from the air stream is

$$\dot{m} = M_{NH_3}\dot{M}$$

$$= (17)(0.0366)$$

$$= 0.6222 \text{ kg/hr.}$$

Consider the evaporation of liquid ammonia into air at $80^{\circ}F$ and 1 atm. Given the heat transfer coefficient in the same apparatus and at the same liquid and gas flow rates as 810 Btu/hr.ft^2.$^{\circ}F$, estimate the mass transfer coefficient of liquid ammonia vaporizing into air.

Solution: The equation for j_H is

$$j_H = \frac{h_c}{C_p \rho u} Pr^{2/3} \quad (1)$$

The equation for j_D is

$$j_D = \frac{k_G M_{av} p_{B,M}}{\rho u} Sc^{2/3} \quad (2)$$

The heat mass transfer analogy is used to estimate the mass transfer coefficient ($j_D = j_H$).

Therefore,

$$\frac{k_G M_{av} p_{B,M}}{\rho u} Sc^{2/3} = \frac{h_c}{C_p \rho u} Pr^{2/3}$$

Solving for k_G gives

$$k_G = \left(\frac{h_c}{C_p \rho}\right) \left(\frac{\rho}{M_{av} p_{B,M}}\right) \left(\frac{Pr}{Sc}\right)^{2/3}$$

$$k_G = \left(\frac{h_c}{C_p \rho}\right) \left(\frac{P}{RT p_{B,M}}\right) \left(\frac{C_p \mu}{k} \frac{\rho D_{AB}}{\mu}\right)^{0.67} \quad (3)$$

where k_G = mass transfer coefficient

h_c = heat transfer coefficient

C_p = specific heat of air

ρ = density of air

P = pressure of air

T = temperature of air

$p_{B,M}$ = mean partial pressure

μ = viscosity of air

k = thermal conductivity of air

D_{AB} = diffusion coefficient

Assume the concentration of ammonia is low; hence, the influence of ammonia on the physical properties of air is negligible.

From air tables, for air at 80°F and 1 atm.

$$\mu = 0.0185 \text{ cp} = 0.045 \text{ lb/ft.hr.}$$

$$\rho = 0.07372 \text{ lb/ft}^3$$

$$C_p = 0.24 \text{ Btu/lb}^\circ\text{F}$$

$$k = 0.0151 \text{ Btu/hr.ft.}^\circ\text{F}$$

From diffusivity tables, for NH_3-air system at 80°F

$$D_{AB} = 1.1 \text{ ft}^2/\text{hr}$$

For dilute gas $p_{B,M} = P$

Substituting the known quantities in eq. (3) gives

$$k_G = \left(\frac{810}{0.24 \times 0.07372}\right)\left(\frac{1}{(0.73)(540)}\right)\left[\frac{0.24(0.045)}{0.0151} \times \frac{(0.07372)(1.1)}{0.045}\right]^{0.67}$$

$$k_G = 137.66 \text{ lb moles/hr-ft}^2\text{-atm}$$

If the Prandtl and Schmidt numbers are taken to be unity, then eq. (3) reduces to

$$k_G = \frac{h_c}{C_p \rho RT}$$

$$= \frac{810}{(0.24)(0.07372)(0.73)(540)}$$

$$= 116.14 \text{ lb moles/hr-ft}^2\text{-atm.}$$

The percentage difference between two estimated values is 15.6 percent.

• PROBLEM 16-17

Consider a bed at 60°F and packed with 1.5 in. diameter naphthalene spheres. The air passes through the bed at an average velocity of 3 ft/sec. Find the average convective mass transfer coefficient $\bar{k}_c$ for sublimation of naphthalene. Given $D_{na} = 0.21 \text{ ft}^2/\text{hr}$.

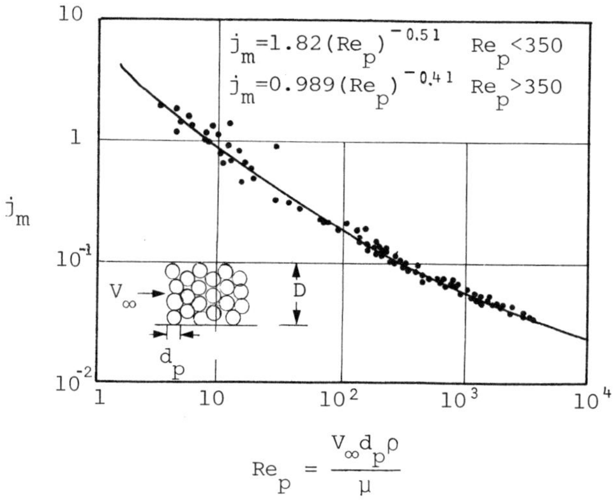

SINGLE-PHASE FLOW IN PACKED BEDS OF SPHERICAL GRANULAR SOLIDS.

Solution: Assume the concentration of naphthalene is low. Hence, the influence of naphthalene on properties of air is negligible.

From air tables,

For air at $60^\circ F$, the physical properties are:

$$\mu = 0.0180 \text{ cp} = 0.0436 \text{ lb}_m/\text{ft-hr}$$

$$= 1.212 \times 10^{-5} \text{ lb}_m/\text{ft-sec}$$

$$\rho = 0.0764 \text{ lb/ft}^3$$

$$\nu = 1.59 \times 10^{-4} \text{ ft}^2/\text{sec}$$

The Reynolds number based on the sphere diameter is given by

$$Re = \frac{VD}{\nu} \tag{1}$$

where V = velocity of air

D = diameter of sphere

ν = kinematic viscosity of air

Substituting the known quantities in eq. (1) gives

$$Re = \frac{(3)(1.5/12)}{1.59 \times 10^{-4}}$$

$$= 2358.5$$

From the fig. above for Re > 350

$$j_M = 0.989\ (Re)^{-0.41}$$

$$= 0.989\ (2358.5)^{-0.41}$$

$$= 0.0414$$

But j_M is also given by

$$j_M = \frac{k_c}{V}\ Sc^{2/3} = 0.0414 \qquad (2)$$

where k_c = mass transfer coefficient

V = velocity of air

Sc = Schmidt number

The Schmidt number is given by

$$Sc = \frac{\mu}{\rho D_{na}} \qquad (3)$$

where μ = viscosity of air

ρ = density of air

D_{na} = diffusion coefficient

Substituting the known quantities in eq. (3) gives

$$Sc = \frac{(1.212 \times 10^{-5})(3600)}{(0.0764)(0.21)}$$

$$= 2.72$$

From eq. (2)

$$k_c = (0.0414)\ \frac{V}{(Sc)^{2/3}} \qquad (4)$$

Substituting the known quantities gives

$$k_c = (0.0414)\ \frac{3}{(2.72)^{2/3}}$$

$$k_c = 0.0637\ \text{ft/sec}$$

which is the convective mass transfer coefficient for the sublimation of naphthalene.

Dry air at 110°F is flowing through a wind tunnel at a velocity of 32 ft/sec. If a 6 in. diameter porous cylinder which is continuously saturated with water is placed normal to the flow in the wind tunnel, determine the convective mass transfer coefficient. $D_{aw} = D_{wa} = 0.91\ ft^2/hr$.

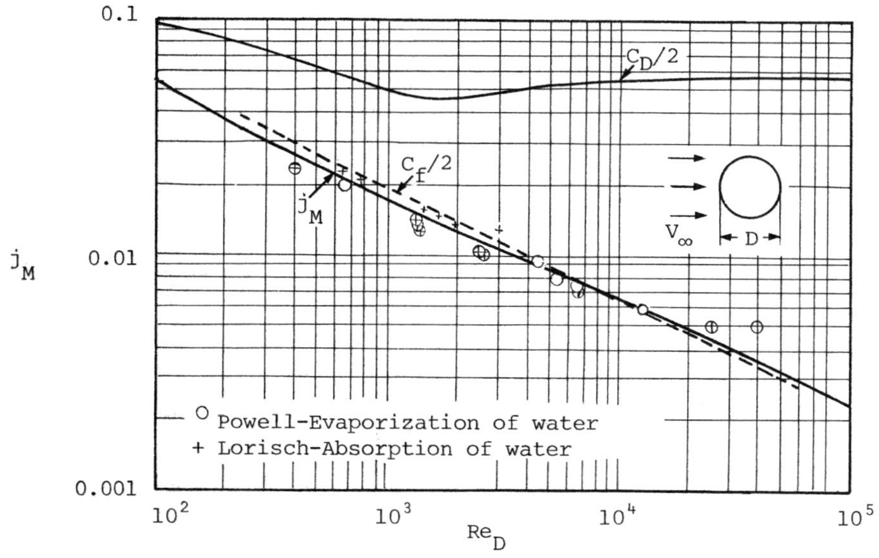

MASS TRANSFER IN FLOW PAST SINGLE CYLINDER.

Solution: Assume the concentration of water in air is low. Hence the influence of water on physical properties of air is negligible.

From air tables,

for air at 110°F, the physical properties are

$$\mu = 0.0192\ cp = 0.0466\ lb_m/ft\text{-}hr$$

$$= 1.294 \times 10^{-5}\ lb_m/ft\text{-}sec$$

$$\rho = 0.0698\ lb/ft^3$$

$$\nu = 1.854 \times 10^{-4}\ ft^2/sec$$

The Reynolds number based on the cylinder diameter is given by

$$Re = \frac{VD}{\nu} \qquad (1)$$

where V = velocity of air

D = diameter of cylinder

ν = kinematic viscosity of air

Substituting the known quantities in eq. (1) gives

$$Re = \frac{(32)(0.5)}{1.854 \times 10^{-4}}$$

$$= 86300$$

From figure above, for Re = 86300 the average j factor for mass transfer is

$$j_M = 0.0025$$

But j_M is also given by

$$j_M = \frac{k_c}{V} (Sc)^{2/3} = 0.0025 \tag{2}$$

where k_c = mass transfer coefficient

V = velocity of air

Sc = Schmidt number

The Schmidt number is given by

$$Sc = \frac{\mu}{\rho D_{aw}} \tag{3}$$

where μ = viscosity of air

ρ = density of air

D_{aw} = diffusion coefficient

Substituting the known quantities in eq. (3),

$$Sc = \frac{(1.294 \times 10^{-5})(3600)}{(0.0698)(0.91)}$$

$$= 0.733$$

Solving the eq. (2) for k_c,

$$k_c = 0.0025 \frac{V}{(Sc)^{2/3}}$$

Substituting the known quantities,

$$k_c = (0.0025) \times \frac{32}{(0.733)^{2/3}}$$

$$= 0.0984 \text{ ft/sec}$$

• PROBLEM 16-19

During an experiment conducted in the laboratory, air-ammonia mixture is blown downward parallel to a falling water film on the inside of a pipe.

(a) Determine the effective thickness x in cm. Compare the result in (a) with the following:

(b) the value obtained from the Gilliland equation.

(c) the effective film thickness for heat transfer to gas flowing in a dry pipe with the same Reynolds number.

(d) the value obtained from friction data using the Colburn theoretical equation.

(e) the value estimated using Arnold theory based on the value obtained in (c) for heat transfer.

The following data is noted during the experiment:

Diameter of gas passage	4.15 cm.
Length of wetted surface	92.0 cm.
Inlet temperature of water	13.5°C
Outlet temperature of water	18.8°C
Average inlet gas velocity	217 cm/sec
Downward velocity of liquid surface	52.0 cm/sec
Inlet temperature of gas	26.0°C
Outlet temperature of gas	24.5°C
p_{AG}, gas inlet	122 mm. Hg
p_{Ai}, gas inlet	0 mm. Hg
p_{Ai}, gas outlet	3.8 mm. Hg
Rate of absorption	7.20 g/min.
Barometric pressure	756 mm. Hg

Solution: The density of air at standard temperature and pressure is

$$\rho = 1.293 \text{ kg/m}^3$$

$$= 4.46 \times 10^{-5} \text{ g.mol/cm}^3$$

The air flow at standard conditions is given by

$$W = \rho VA$$

where ρ = density of air

V = velocity of air

A = cross sectional area of pipe

Substituting the known quantities and making correction for the given conditions

$$W = (4.46 \times 10^{-5})(217)(3600)\,\frac{\pi}{4}\,(4.15)^2\left(\frac{273}{299}\right)\left(\frac{634}{760}\right)$$

$$= 359 \text{ g.mols/hr}$$

Ammonia in inlet gas

$$= 359 \times \frac{122}{634}$$

$$= 69.1 \text{ g.mols/hr}$$

Ammonia absorbed

$$= \frac{7.2 \times 60}{17}$$

$$= 25.4 \text{ g.mols/hr}$$

Ammonia in exit gas = 69.1 - 25.4

$$= 43.7 \text{ g.mols/hr}$$

p_{AG} of exit gas

$$= \frac{43.7}{359 + 43.7}\,(756)$$

$$= 82 \text{ mm.}$$

At top

$$p_{BM} = 756 - \frac{122}{2} = 695 \text{ mm.}$$

At bottom

$$p_{BM} = \frac{(756 - 3.8) + (756 - 82)}{2}$$

$$= 713.1 \text{ mm.}$$

$$\text{Average } p_{BM} = \frac{695 + 713.1}{2}$$

$$= 704.05 \text{ mm.}$$

Wetted surface area = $4.15 \times \pi \times 92.0$

$$= 1199.5 \text{ cm}^2$$

The mass flux is given by

$$N_A = \frac{7.2}{17 \times 60 \times 1199.5}$$

$$= 5.88 \times 10^{-6} \text{ g.mols/cm}^2\text{-sec}$$

Δp at top = 122 mm.

Δp at bottom = 82 - 3.8 = 78.2 mm.

Then the average Δp is given by

$$\Delta p_{av} = \frac{122 - 78.2}{\ln\left(\frac{122}{78.2}\right)}$$

$$= 98.5 \text{ mm.}$$

The diffusion coefficient is given by

$$D_{AB} = 0.0043 \frac{T^{3/2}}{P\left(V_A^{1/3} + V_B^{1/3}\right)^2} \sqrt{\frac{1}{M_A} + \frac{1}{M_B}} \quad (1)$$

$$= 0.0043 \frac{(273 + 20.7)^{3/2}}{\frac{756}{760}\left(26.7^{1/3} + 29.9^{1/3}\right)^2} \sqrt{\frac{1}{17} + \frac{1}{29}}$$

$$= 0.179 \text{ cm}^2/\text{sec}$$

The rate of diffusion is given by

$$N_A = \frac{D_{AB}P}{RTx} \frac{(p_{A1} - p_{A2})}{p_{BM}} \quad (2)$$

Solving for x gives

$$x = \frac{D_{AB}P\Delta p}{N_A RTp_{BM}} \quad (3)$$

Substituting the known quantities gives

$$x = \frac{(0.179)(756/760)(98.5)}{(5.88 \times 10^{-6})(82.07)(293.7)(704.05)}$$

$$= 0.176 \text{ cm}$$

Hence, the effective thickness is 0.176 cm.

(b) The Gilliland equation is

$$\frac{d}{x} = 0.023 \left(\frac{du\rho}{\mu}\right)^{0.83} \left(\frac{\mu}{\rho D_{AB}}\right)^{0.44} \quad (4)$$

$$u\rho = \frac{(359 \times 29) + (69.1 - \frac{25.4}{2}) \times 17}{(3600)\frac{\pi}{4}(4.15)^2}$$

$$= 0.2335 \text{ g/cm}^2\text{-sec}$$

From tables, for air at 20°C

$$\mu = 0.000185 \text{ g/cm.sec.}$$

The Reynolds number is given by

$$Re = \frac{\rho u d}{\mu}$$

$$= \frac{(0.2335)(4.15)}{0.000185}$$

$$= 5238$$

The average molecular weight of gas is

$$= \frac{359 \times 29 + (69.1 - \frac{25.4}{2}) \times 17}{359 + (69.1 - \frac{25.4}{2})}$$

$$= 27.4$$

From tables

$$Sc = \frac{\mu}{\rho D_{AB}} = 0.79$$

Substituting all the known quantities in eq. (4) gives

$$\frac{d}{x} = 0.023\ (5238)^{0.83}\ (0.79)^{0.44}$$

$$= 25.33$$

Then, $x = \frac{4.15}{25.33} = 0.164$ cm.

compared to 0.176 cm obtained from the experimental data.

(c) McAdams equation for heat transfer to fluids flowing in pipes in turbulent flow is

$$\frac{hd}{k_H} = \frac{d}{x} = 0.0225 \left(\frac{du\rho}{\mu}\right)^{0.8} \left(\frac{c\mu}{k_H}\right)^{0.4} \quad (5)$$

For diatomic gases, $\frac{c\mu}{k_H} = 0.74$, approximately.

Substituting the known values in eq. (5) gives

$$\frac{d}{x} = 0.0225\ (5238)^{0.8}\ (0.74)^{0.4}$$

$$= 18.85$$

Therefore, $x = \frac{4.15}{18.85} = 0.220$ cm.

compared to 0.176 cm obtained from experimental data.

(d) The Colburn's equation is

$$k_G = \frac{f\rho u}{2p_{BM}M_M\phi_D} \qquad (6)$$

where k_G = a coefficient of material transfer

f = friction factor in the Fanning equation

ρ = density of the main gas stream

M_M = average molecular weight of the main gas stream

p_{BM} = mean partial pressure of the nondiffusing or inert gas in the laminar layer

$\phi_D = 1 - r + r\left(\frac{\mu_f}{\rho D}\right)$

r = ratio of the fluid velocity at the boundary between laminar and eddy layers, to the average velocity u of the main fluid stream

μ_f = average absolute viscosity of the laminar layer

D = diffusion coefficient of gas A through the inert gas B.

The value of r is approximately given by

$$r = 5.9\sqrt{f}$$

But

$$x = \frac{D_{AB}P\Delta p}{RTp_{BM}N_A} \qquad (7)$$

and

$$N_A = k_G\Delta p \qquad (8)$$

Substituting eq. (6) in eq. (8) give

$$N_A = \frac{f\rho u\Delta p}{2p_{BM}M_M\phi_D} \qquad (9)$$

Substituting eq. (9) in eq. (7) gives

$$x = \frac{D_{AB} P 2 M_M \phi_D}{RT f \rho u} \tag{10}$$

At Re = 5238

$$f = 0.0095 \text{ for smooth pipe}$$

$$r = 5.9 \sqrt{0.0095}$$

$$= 0.5751$$

$$\phi_D = 1 - 0.5751 + 0.5751\ (0.79)$$

$$= 0.879$$

Substituting known values in eq. (10) gives

$$x = \frac{(0.179)(756)2(27.4)(0.879)}{(82.07)(760)(293.7)(0.0095)(0.2335)}$$

$$= 0.160 \text{ cm.}$$

(e) Using the Arnold theory

$$x_D = \frac{(c\mu/k_H)\left[1 - r + r(\mu/\rho D_{AB})\right] x_H}{(\mu/\rho D_{AB})\left[1 - r + r(c\mu/k_H)\right]} \tag{11}$$

From (c)

$$\frac{c\mu}{k_H} = 0.74 \quad \text{and} \quad x_H = 0.220 \text{ cm.}$$

$$\frac{\mu}{\rho D_{AB}} = 0.79$$

Then, from (d)

$$1 - r + r\left(\frac{\mu}{\rho D_{AB}}\right) = 0.879$$

and $r = 0.5751$

Then,

$$1 - r + r\left(\frac{c\mu}{k_H}\right) = 1 - 0.5751 + 0.5751 \times 0.74$$

$$= 0.8505$$

Substituting all the known values in eq. (11) gives

$$x_D = \frac{(0.74)(0.879)(0.220)}{(0.79)(0.8505)}$$

$= 0.213$ cm.

The values of x calculated in the last three methods are close to the value calculated from the experimental data.

• PROBLEM 16-20

Pure air at an average pressure of 1 atm. enters a solid naphthalene pipe 1.2 in. in diameter at a velocity of 2.5 ft/sec. If the temperature of the system is 115°F, determine the length of pipe required for the average concentration of naphthalene vapor in the air to reach a value of $2.24 \times 10^{-5}\ lb_m/ft^3$ (i.e., 10 percent of saturation).

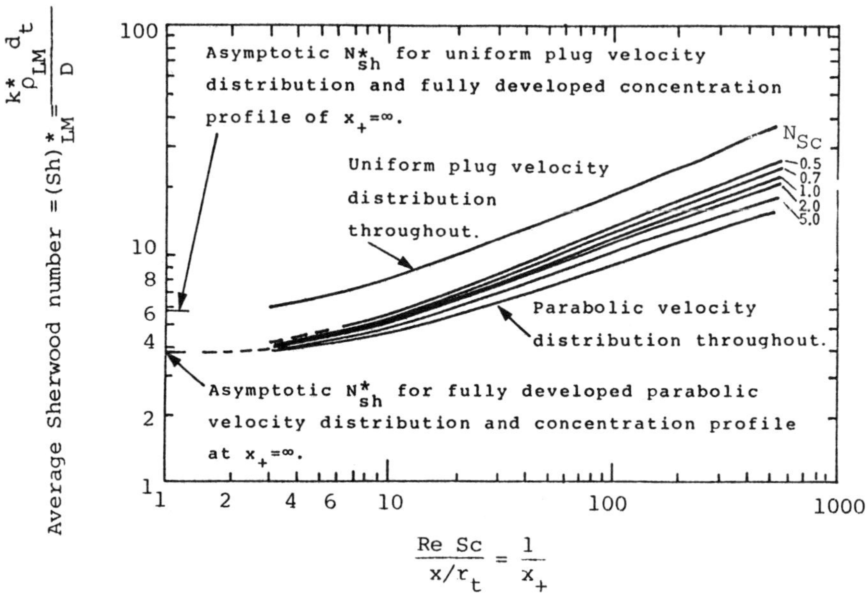

AVERAGE SHERWOOD NUMBERS FOR MASS TRANSFER IN LAMINAR FLOW THROUGH A TUBE WITH UNIFORM WALL CONCENTRATION.

Solution: Assume the concentration of naphthalene is low; hence the influence of naphthalene on the physical properties of air is negligible.

From air tables,

for air at 115°F

$$\rho = 0.0692\ lb/ft^3$$

$$\mu = 0.0469\ lb/ft\text{-}hr$$

$$Sc = 2.485$$

The Reynolds number is given by

$$Re = \frac{\rho VD}{\mu}$$

where ρ = density of air

V = velocity of air

D = diameter of pipe

μ = absolute viscosity of air

Substituting the known quantities gives

$$Re = \frac{(0.0692)(2.5)(3600)(1.2/12)}{0.0469}$$

$$= 1328$$

Therefore the flow is laminar.

Then

$$\frac{ReSc}{x/r} = \frac{(1328)(2.485)(1.2)}{(12 \text{ x } 2\ )x}$$

$$= \frac{165}{x}$$

and
$$\frac{q_{AW}}{A} = \frac{\pi d^2 V \Delta\rho_A}{4\pi dx}$$

$$= \frac{(1.2)(2.5)(3600)(2.24 \text{ x } 10^{-5})}{12(4)x}$$

$$\frac{q_{AW}}{A} = \frac{0.00504}{x}$$

$$\Delta\rho_{Alm} = \frac{(0.000224 - 0) - (0.000224 - 0.0000224)}{2.303 \log [0.000224/(0.000224 - 0.0000224)]}$$

$$= 0.000213 \text{ lb/ft}^3$$

Average Sherwood number,

$$(Sh)_{lm} = \frac{k_{\rho lm} d}{D_{AB}}$$

$$= \frac{q_{AW}}{A\Delta\rho_{Alm}} \frac{d}{D_{AB}}$$

Substituting all the known quantities,

$$(Sh)_{lm} = \frac{0.00504(1.2/12)}{(0.000213)(0.2727)x}$$

$$= \frac{8.68}{x}$$

Then,

$$x = \frac{8.68}{(Sh)_{lm}}$$

and $$\frac{ReSc}{x/r} = \frac{165}{x}$$

x is obtained by trial and error method using the procedure given below.

Assume a value for x and read the corresponding $(Sh)_{lm}$ from the interpolated curve for Sc = 2.485 in the figure above. Then, with read $(Sh)_{lm}$ calculate x and see whether the calculated x is close to the assumed value of x, if it is, the result is the calculated x, otherwise assume the calculated x as the new value for x and repeat the procedure.

The result obtained in this case is

$$x = 0.5 \text{ ft.}$$

$$\frac{ReSc}{x/r} = 330$$

$$(Sh)_{lm} = 17.5$$

Therefore the length of pipe required is 0.5 ft.

• PROBLEM 16-21

Consider an air stream flowing over a smooth solid naphthalene plate with a velocity of 116 ft/sec at points far away from the surface of the plate. The air stream pressure is 1 atm. and the temperature of the system is 115°F. Assume the influence of non-unity Schmidt number is negligible. Assuming turbulent boundary layer from the leading edge, determine the following:

(a) the average coefficient of mass transfer over the first 1.5 ft from the leading edge of the plate.

(b) the average mass transfer rate per unit width over the first 1.5 ft from the leading edge of the plate.

(c) the local coefficient of mass transfer at 1.5 ft from the leading edge of the plate.

(d) the local concentration gradient of naphthalene at the surface at 1.5 ft from the leading edge.

Solution: Assume the concentration of naphthalene is low. Hence the influence of naphthalene on the physical properties of air is negligible. Take the surface temperature of plate to be 115°F.

From air tables, for air at 115°F

$$\rho = 0.0692 \text{ lb/ft}^3$$

$$\mu = 0.0469 \text{ lb/ft-hr}$$

$$Sc = 2.485$$

$$D_{AB} = 0.2727 \text{ ft}^2\text{/hr}$$

$$\rho_{AO} = 0.000224 \text{ lb/ft}^3$$

The Reynolds number is given by

$$Re = \frac{\rho VL}{\mu} \tag{1}$$

where ρ = density of air

V = velocity of air

L = characteristic length

μ = absolute viscosity of air

Substituting the known quantities in eq. (1) gives

$$Re = \frac{(0.0692)(116)(3600)(1.5)}{0.0469}$$

$$= 9.24 \times 10^5$$

(a) Neglect the departure of Sc = 2.485 for this system from Sc = 1.0.

The average Sherwood number is given by

$$(Sh)_m = \frac{k_{\rho m} L}{D_{AB}} = 0.0365\ (Re)^{0.8} \tag{2}$$

Solving for $k_{\rho m}$ gives

$$k_{\rho m} = 0.0365\ \frac{D_{AB}}{L}\ (Re)^{0.8} \tag{3}$$

Substituting the known quantities gives

$$k_{\rho m} = 0.0365 \left(\frac{0.2727}{1.5}\right) (9.24 \times 10^5)^{0.8}$$

$$= 393 \text{ ft/hr}$$

Therefore the average coefficient of mass transfer over first

1.5 ft from leading edge of the plate is 393 ft/hr.

(b) The average mass transfer rate is given by

$$q_{AW} = k_{\rho m}A(\rho_{AO} - \rho_{A\infty}) \tag{4}$$

Substituting the known quantities in equation (4) gives

$$q_{AW} = 393(1.5 \times 1)(0.000224 - 0)$$

$$= 0.132 \text{ lb/hr}$$

(c) The local Sherwood number is given by

$$(Sh)_x = \frac{k_\rho x}{D_{AB}} = 0.0292\ (Re)^{0.8} \tag{5}$$

Solving eq. (5) for k_ρ gives

$$k_\rho = 0.0292 \left(\frac{D_{AB}}{x}\right)(Re)^{0.8} \tag{6}$$

Dividing eq. (6) by eq. (3) and substituting x = L gives

$$\frac{k_\rho}{k_{\rho m}} = \frac{0.0292}{0.0365}$$

Then,

$$k_\rho = \frac{0.0292}{0.0365}\, k_{\rho m} \tag{7}$$

Substituting the value of $k_{\rho m}$ in eq. (7) gives

$$k_\rho = \frac{0.0292}{0.0365}\,(393)$$

$$= 314.4 \text{ ft/hr}$$

Therefore the local coefficient of mass transfer at 1.5 ft from the leading edge is 314.4 ft/hr.

(d) Assume the naphthalene leaves the solid surface by molecular diffusion.

For the differential element of surface area wdx.

$$dq_{AW} = k_\rho wdx(\rho_{AO} - \rho_{A\infty}) = -D_{AB}\ wdx \left(\frac{\partial \rho_A}{\partial y}\right)_{y=0}$$

At 1.5 ft from the leading edge, the local concentration gradient of naphthalene is

$$\left(\frac{\partial \rho_A}{\partial y}\right)_{y=0} = \frac{314.4(0 - 0.000224)}{0.2727}$$

$$= -0.2582 \text{ lb/ft}^4.$$

• PROBLEM 16-22

Pure air at an average pressure of 1 atm. enters a solid naphthalene pipe 1.2 in. in internal diameter at a velocity of 25 ft/sec. If the temperature of the system is $115^{\circ}F$, determine the length of the pipe required for the average concentration of naphthalene vapor in the air to reach a value of 5.6×10^{-5} lb/ft^3 (i.e., 25 percent of saturation value). Neglecting entrance effects, obtain the minimum and maximum lengths required using all the necessary relations.

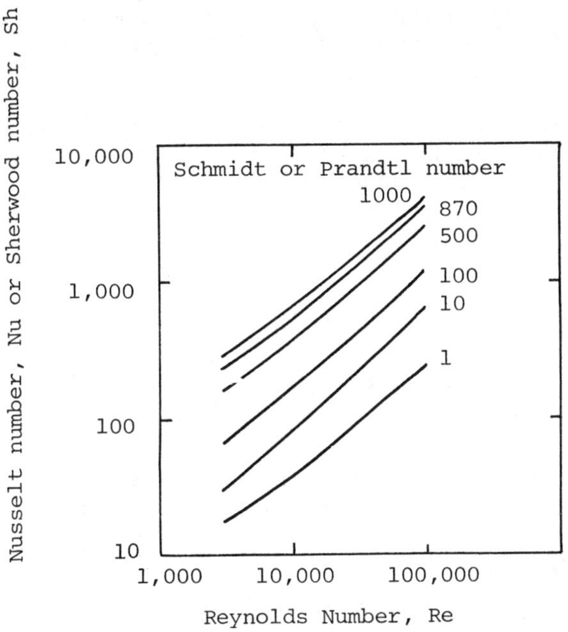

Dependence of the Sherwood (or Nusselt) number upon Re and Sc(or Pr) for turbulent flow in smooth tubes, according to the analogy of Gowariker and Garner.

Solution: Assume the concentration of naphthlene in air is low. Hence the influence of naphthalene on the physical properties of air is negligible.

The surface temperature of naphthalene pipe is to be taken as $115^{\circ}F$.

From air tables, for air at $115^{\circ}F$

$$\rho = 0.0692 \text{ lb/ft}^3$$

$$u = 0.0469 \text{ lb/ft-hr}$$

$$Sc = 2.485$$

$$D_{AB} = 0.2727 \text{ ft}^2\text{/hr}$$

$$\rho_{AO} = 0.000224 \text{ lb/ft}^3$$

The Reynolds number is given by

$$Re = \frac{\rho V d}{\mu}$$

$$= \frac{(0.0692)(25)(3600)(1.2/12)}{0.0469}$$

$$= 13279.3$$

Therefore the flow is turbulent.

The Reynolds analogy between momentum and mass transfer is not applicable because the value of Schmidt number under the prevailing conditions is 2.485.

Therefore the attention is confined to analogies where a laminar sublayer and a turbulent core or a buffer zone in between the two preceeding zones is assumed.

$$\frac{\pi d^2}{4} V d\rho_{AB} = k_\rho \pi d\, (\rho_{AW} - \rho_{AB}) dx$$

Integrating the above eq. gives

$$\ln\frac{\rho_{AW} - \rho_{AB1}}{\rho_{AW} - \rho_{AB2}} = \frac{4L}{Vd}\left(\frac{D_{AB}}{d}\,Sh\right) = \frac{4L}{d}\,\frac{Sh}{ReSc} \qquad (1)$$

For flow in smooth tubes over the Reynolds number range 3000 to 100,000, the friction factor is given by Blasius equation as

$$f = 0.079\ (Re)^{-0.25}$$

$$= 0.079\ (13279.3)^{-0.25}$$

$$= 7.36 \times 10^{-3}$$

The Sherwood number is given by

$$Sh = \frac{k_\rho d}{D_{AB}} = \frac{(f/2)ReSc}{1 + 5\sqrt{f/2}\,(Sc - 1)}$$

$$\frac{Sh}{ReSc} = \frac{f/2}{1 + 5\sqrt{f/2}\,(Sc - 1)} \qquad (2)$$

$$= \frac{(7.36 \times 10^{-3}/2)}{1 + 5\sqrt{7.36 \times 10^{-3}/2}\,(2.485 - 1)}$$

$$= 0.002537$$

$$\ln\frac{\rho_{AW} - \rho_{AB1}}{\rho_{AW} - \rho_{AB2}} = 2.303 \log\left[\frac{(0.000224 - 0)}{(0.000224 - 0.000056)}\right]$$

$$= 0.2876$$

From eq. (1)

$$L = \frac{d}{4}\,\frac{ReSc}{Sh}\,\ln\frac{\rho_{AW} - \rho_{AB1}}{\rho_{AW} - \rho_{AB2}} \qquad (3)$$

$$= \frac{1.2(0.2876)}{12(4)(0.002537)}$$

$$L = 2.83 \text{ ft.}$$

$$\frac{Sh}{ReSc} = \frac{f/2}{1 + 5\sqrt{f/2}\,\{Sc - 1 + \ln\left(1 + \frac{5}{6}(Sc - 1)\right)\}} \qquad (4)$$

$$= \frac{7.36 \times 10^{-3}/2}{1 + 5\sqrt{7.36 \times 10^{-3}/2}\,\{2.485 - 1 + \ln\left(1 + \frac{5}{6}(2.485 - 1)\right)\}}$$

$$= 0.00217$$

Then,

$$L = \left(\frac{0.002537}{0.00217}\right) 2.83$$

$$= 3.31 \text{ ft.}$$

when $(E_D/E_M) = 1.6$

$$\frac{Sh}{ReSc} = \frac{(f/2)E_D/E_M}{1 + 5\sqrt{f/2}\,\{(E_D/E_M)Sc - 1 + \ln\left(1 + \frac{5}{6}\left(\frac{E_D}{E_M}Sc - 1\right)\right)\}}$$

$$= \frac{(7.36 \times 10^{-3}/2)1.6}{1 + 5\sqrt{7.36 \times 10^{-3}/2}\{1.6(2.485) - 1 + \ln\left(1 + \frac{5}{6}(1.6(2.485) - 1)\right)\}}$$

$$= 0.0025814$$

Then,

$$L = 2.83\left(\frac{0.002537}{0.0025814}\right)$$

$$= 2.781 \text{ ft.}$$

From standard figure, when Sc = 2.485

$$\frac{F(\mu/\rho D)}{(\mu/\rho D)^{1/3}} = 1.0061$$

Then,

$$F(\mu/\rho D) = 1.0061(2.485)^{1/3}$$

$$= 1.363$$

and

$$\phi_D = 1 + \sqrt{f/2}\left[\frac{14.5}{3}(Sc)^{2/3}F(\mu/\rho D) + 5\ ln\frac{1 + 5.64(Sc)}{6.64(1 + 0.041(Sc))} - 4.77\right]$$

$$= 1 + \sqrt{\frac{7.36 \times 10^{-3}}{2}}\left[\frac{14.5}{3}(2.485)^{2/3}(1.363) + 5\ ln\frac{1 + 5.64(2.485)}{6.64\ (1 + 0.041(2.485))} - 4.77\right]$$

$$= 1.662$$

$$\frac{Sh}{ReSc} = \frac{1}{\phi_D}\ (f/2)$$

$$= \frac{1}{1.662}\left(\frac{7.36 \times 10^{-3}}{2}\right)$$

$$= 0.002214$$

Then,

$$L = 2.83\left(\frac{0.002537}{0.002214}\right)$$

$$= 3.24\ ft.$$

From the fig. above, for Re = 13279.3 and Sc = 2.485

$$Sh = 69$$

Then,

$$\frac{Sh}{ReSc} = \frac{69}{(13279.3)(2.485)}$$

$$= 0.002091$$

$$L = 2.83\left(\frac{0.002537}{0.002091}\right)$$

$$= 3.43\ ft.$$

$$k_{\rho lm} = 0.023\left(\frac{D_{AB}}{d}\right)(Re)^{0.83}(Sc)^{1/3}$$

$$= 0.023\left(\frac{0.2727}{1.2/12}\right)(13279.3)^{0.83}(2.485)^{1/3}$$

$$= 224.61\ ft/hr.$$

Therefore the naphthalene balance over length L is

$$\frac{\pi}{4}\left(\frac{1.2}{12}\right)^2(25)(3600)(5.6 \times 10^{-5}) = (224.61)\pi\left(\frac{1.2}{12}\right) L \times \frac{5.6 \times 10^{-5}}{2.303\ log\left[22.4 \times 10^{-5}/(22.4 - 5.6) \times 10^{-5}\right]}$$

$$0.039584 = 0.01373 \text{ L}$$
$$\text{L} = 2.88 \text{ ft.}$$

From the six estimates made above

$$2.66 \text{ ft} \leq \text{L} \leq 3.43 \text{ ft}$$

The average length is 3.06 ft.

Therefore the average flux at the wall over 3.06 ft is

$$\frac{\pi d^2 V \Delta\rho_A}{4\pi dx} = \frac{\left(\frac{1.2}{12}\right)(25)(3600)(5.6 \times 10^{-5})}{4(3.06)}$$

$$= 0.0412 \text{ lb/ft}^2\text{-hr.}$$

• PROBLEM 16-23

A 1/2 in. diameter sphere of solid benzoic acid is allowed to fall 11 ft in a stationary column of pure water. Determine the quantity of benzoic acid dissolved during the fall. Find the time required to dissolve the same quantity of benzoic acid if the sphere is suspended in water and completely free from forced convection. In both the cases, the system is at a temperature of 80°F.

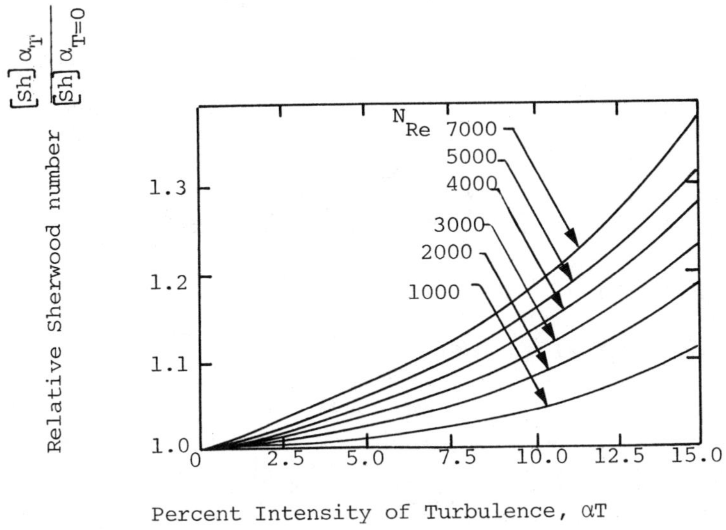

RELATIVE SHERWOOD NUMBER FOR A SPHERE AS A FUNCTION OF THE INTENSITY OF TURBULENCE.

Solution: Assume the concentration of benzoic acid in water is low. Hence the influence of benzoic acid on the physical properties of water is negligible.

From steam tables, for water at $80^\circ F$

$$\rho = 62.2 \text{ lb/ft}^3$$

$$\mu = 0.578 \times 10^{-3} \text{ lb/ft-sec}$$

$$= 2.08 \text{ lb/ft-hr}$$

$$D_{AB} = 4.7 \times 10^{-5} \text{ ft}^2\text{/hr}$$

The density of solid benzoic acid is 79.03 lb/ft^3.

The terminal velocity of sphere calculated from standard equation is 1.08 ft/sec. Neglecting the initial acceleration effects, the sphere falls 11 ft in 10.19 secs. The Reynolds number is given by

$$Re = \frac{\rho V d}{\mu}$$

$$= \frac{(62.2)(1.08)(0.5/12)}{0.578 \times 10^{-3}}$$

$$= 4842.56$$

The density of saturated aqueous solution of benzoic acid is 62.174 lb/ft^3. Hence, the difference in densities of a saturated aqueous solution of benzoic acid and pure water at $80^\circ F$ is 0.026 lb/ft^3.

The Grashof number is given by

$$Gr = \frac{g d^3 \Delta\rho}{\rho} \left(\frac{\rho}{\mu}\right)^2$$

$$= \frac{(4.17 \times 10^8)(0.5/12)^3(0.026)}{62.174} \left(\frac{62.2}{2.08}\right)^2$$

$$= 11280.3$$

The Schmidt number is given by

$$Sc = \frac{\mu}{\rho D_{AB}}$$

$$= \frac{2.08}{(62.2)(4.7 \times 10^{-5})}$$

$$= 711.5$$

Then,

$$0.4(Gr)^{0.5}(Sc)^{-1/6} = 0.4(11280.3)^{0.5}(711.5)^{-1/6}$$

$$= 14.22$$

This implies that natural convection effects are negligible.

The Sherwood number is given by

$$Sh_{\alpha_{T=10}} = 0.692\ (Re)^{0.514}(Sc)^{1/3}$$

$$= 0.692(4842.56)^{0.514}(711.5)^{1/3}$$

$$= 484.13$$

From the above figure, for Re = 4842.56 and α_T = 10 percent.

$$\frac{Sh_{\alpha_{T=10}}}{Sh_{\alpha_{T=0}}} = 1.155$$

$$Sh_{\alpha_{T=0}} = \frac{484.13}{1.155}$$

$$= 419.16$$

The mass flux is given by

$$(n_{AO})_{av} = \frac{D_{AB}}{d} Sh\ (\rho_{AO} - \rho_{A\infty})$$

$$= \frac{4.7 \times 10^{-5}}{(0.5/12)} (419.16)(0.213 - 0)$$

$$= 0.1\ lb/ft^2\text{-hr}$$

Therefore, the quantity of benzoic acid dissolved during the fall of sphere by 11 ft in 10.19 sec is

$$(n_{AO})_{av}\pi d^2\left(\frac{10.19}{3600}\right) = (0.1)\pi\left(\frac{0.5}{12}\right)^2\left(\frac{10.19}{3600}\right)$$

$$= 1.544 \times 10^{-6}\ \text{lb benzoic acid}$$

Hence, the reduction in mass of sphere is only 0.052 percent.

When the sphere is suspended in water free from forced convection, the equation for Sherwood number is

$$Sh = 2 + 0.6(Gr)^{1/4}(Sc)^{1/3}$$

$$= 2 + 0.6(11280.3)^{1/4}(711.5)^{1/3}$$

$$= 57.2$$

The equation of Sherwood number is also given as

$$Sh = 2 + 0.6(Gr)^{1/4}(Sc)^{1/4}$$

$$= 2 + 0.6(11280.3)^{1/4}\ (711.5)^{1/4}$$

$$= 33.94$$

The Sherwood number calculated by the later equation gives a more conservative estimate of time for dissolution, hence

$$t = 10.19 \left(\frac{419.16}{33.94}\right)$$

$$= 125.86 = 2.10 \text{ min.}$$

• PROBLEM 16-24

Consider a 1/4 in. metallic pipe through which pure water flows at an average velocity of 0.06 ft/sec. After 1.5 ft from the entrance, the metallic pipe is replaced by a pipe of same diameter, 4.5 ft long and made of benzoic acid. Determine the average concentration of benzoic acid in the water at the exit of the pipe. The temperature of the system is 80^0F.

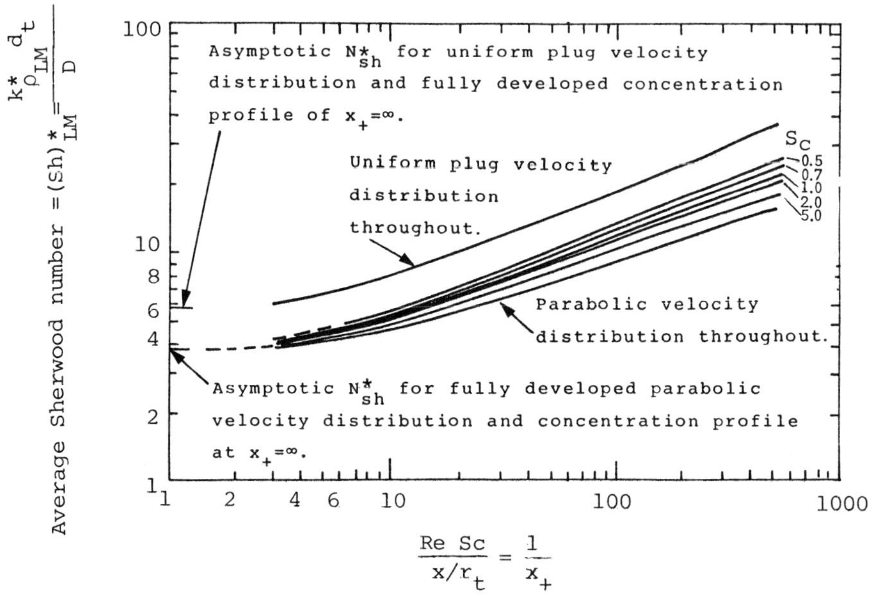

AVERAGE SHERWOOD NUMBERS FOR MASS TRANSFER IN LAMINAR FLOW THROUGH A TUBE WITH UNIFORM WALL CONCENTRATION.

Solution: Assume the concentration of benzoic acid in the water is low. Hence the influence of benzoic acid on the physical properties of pure water is negligible.

From water tables, for water at 80^0F

$$\rho = 62.2 \text{ lb/ft}^3$$

$$\mu = 0.578 \times 10^{-3} \text{ lb/ft-sec}$$

$$= 2.08 \text{ lb/ft-hr}$$

$$D_{AB} = 4.7 \times 10^{-5}\ ft^2/hr$$

Saturation solubility of aqueous solution of benzoic acid is 0.213 lb/ft^3.

The Reynolds number is given by

$$Re = \frac{\rho Vd}{\mu}$$

Substituting the known values gives

$$Re = \frac{(62.2)(0.06)(0.25/12)}{0.578 \times 10^{-3}}$$

$$= 134.5$$

This implies the flow is laminar.

Then,

$$\left(\frac{x}{d}\right)_{dev} = 0.05\ Re$$

$$x_{dev} = 0.05\ (Re)d$$

$$= 0.05\ (134.5)\ \frac{0.25}{12}$$

$$= 0.1401\ ft.$$

This implies that the velocity profile is parabolic at the inlet to the benzoic acid section of the pipe.

The Schmidt number is given by

$$Sc = \frac{\mu}{\rho D_{AB}}$$

$$= \frac{2.08}{(62.2)(4.7 \times 10^{-5})}$$

$$= 711.5$$

Then,

$$\frac{ReSc}{x/r} = \frac{(134.5)(711.5)(0.125)}{(4.5)(12)}$$

$$= 221.5$$

From the above figure, for $\frac{ReSc}{x/r} = 221.5$ and $Sc = 711.5$

$$(Sh)_{LM} = 12.4$$

The Sherwood number is also given by

$$(Sh)_{LM} = 3.66 + \frac{0.0668\left[(d/x)ReSc\right]}{1 + 0.04\left[(d/x)ReSc\right]^{2/3}}$$

Substituting all the known values gives

$$(Sh)_{LM} = 3.66 + \frac{0.0668\ (2(221.5))}{1 + 0.04\left[2(221.5)\right]^{2/3}}$$

$$= 12.56$$

$$(Sh)_{LM} = k_{\rho LM}\frac{d}{D_{AB}}$$

Solving for $k_{\rho LM}$ gives

$$k_{\rho LM} = (Sh)_{LM}\frac{D_{AB}}{d}$$

$$= \frac{12.56\ (4.7 \times 10^{-5})}{0.25/12}$$

$$= 0.0284\ \text{ft/hr.}$$

$$A = \pi dx$$

$$= \pi\left(\frac{0.25}{12}\right)(4.5)$$

$$= 0.295\ \text{ft}^2.$$

$$q_{AW} = k_{\rho LM}A\frac{(\rho_{AO} - \rho_{Ai}) - (\rho_{AO} - \rho_{ABO})}{\ln\left(\frac{\rho_{AO}}{\rho_{AO} - \rho_{ABO}}\right)} = \frac{\pi}{4}d^2V(\rho_{ABO} - \rho_{Ai})$$

$$0.0284(0.295)\frac{(0.213 - 0) - (0.213 - \rho_{ABO})}{2.303\log\left[0.213/(0.213 - \rho_{ABO})\right]} =$$

$$\frac{\pi}{4}\left(\frac{0.25}{12}\right)^2(0.06)3600\rho_{ABO}$$

$$\log\left[\frac{0.213}{0.213 - \rho_{ABO}}\right] = 0.04943$$

$$\rho_{ABO} = 0.023\ \text{lb/ft}^3.$$

Therefore, the average concentration of benzoic acid in water is 0.023 lb/ft^3.

Consider a solid naphthalene plate suspended vertically in pure air at 1 atm and is entirely free from forced convection.

Determine:

(a) the average coefficient of mass transfer over the first 1.5 ft down the plate

(b) the average mass transfer rate over 1.5 ft from the upper edge

(c) the local coefficient of mass transfer at 1.5 ft from the upper edge of the plate

(d) the local concentration gradient at the surface of the plate at 1.5 ft below the upper edge

(e) the local thickness of the momentum and concentration boundary layers at 1.5 ft below the upper edge of the plate

(f) the maximum velocity in the boundary layer at 1.5 ft from the upper edge of the plate

The temperature of the system is 115°F.

Solution: In this case, the boundary layer flow due to natural convection is downward because at a given temperature, naphthalene-air mixture is dense than pure air. The gravity acts in the positive x-direction.

The Grashof number is given by

$$Gr_D = gx^3 \frac{(\rho_0 - \rho_\infty)/\rho_0}{(\mu/\rho)^2} \tag{1}$$

Then, the Sherwood number is given by

$$(Sh)_x = \frac{k_\rho x}{D_{AB}} = \frac{2x}{\delta} = 0.508(Sc)^{\frac{1}{2}}(0.952 + Sc)^{-\frac{1}{4}}(Gr_D)^{\frac{1}{4}} \tag{2}$$

The temperature of the naphthalene surface is taken as 115°F.

(a) From air tables, for air at 115°F and 1 atm

$$\rho_{air} = 0.0692 \text{ lb}_m/\text{ft}^3$$

$$\rho_{A0} = 0.000224 \text{ lb}_m/\text{ft}^3$$

$$\mu_{air} = 0.0194 \text{ cp} = 0.0469 \text{ lb}_m/\text{ft-hr}$$

$$P_A = 1.553 \text{ lb}_f/\text{ft}^2$$

$$D_{AB} = 0.2727 \text{ ft}^2/\text{hr}$$

Then,

$$P_{BO} = 14.7\ (144) - 1.553$$

$$= 2115.247 \quad b_f/\text{ft}^2$$

$$\rho_{BO} = \frac{2115.247\ (29)}{1545\ (575)}$$

$$= 0.06905 \text{ lb}_m/\text{ft}^3$$

$$\rho_0 = \rho_{AO} + \rho_{BO}$$

$$= 0.069274 \text{ lb}_m/\text{ft}^3.$$

Substituting all the known quantities in eq. (1) gives

$$Gr_D = \frac{(4.17 \times 10^8)(1.5)^3(0.069274 - 0.0692)(0.0692)^2}{0.069274(0.0469)^2}$$

$$= 3.273 \times 10^6$$

The Schmidt number is given by

$$Sc = \frac{\mu}{\rho D_{AB}}$$

$$= \frac{0.0469}{(0.0692)(0.2727)}$$

$$= 2.485$$

Then,

$$Gr_D Sc = (3.273 \times 10^6)(2.485)$$

$$= 8.133 \times 10^6$$

This implies the flow in the boundary layer is laminar.

Solving eq. (2) for k_ρ gives

$$k_\rho = 0.508\ \frac{D_{AB}}{x}\ (Sc)^{\frac{1}{2}}\ (0.952 + Sc)^{-\frac{1}{4}}\ Gr_D^{\frac{1}{4}} \qquad (3)$$

Substituting the known values gives

$$k_\rho = 0.508\ \left(\frac{0.2727}{1.5}\right)(2.485)^{\frac{1}{2}}(0.952 + 2.485)^{-\frac{1}{4}}(3.273 \times 10^6)^{\frac{1}{4}}$$

$$= 4.55 \text{ ft/hr}$$

The average coefficient of mass transfer over a length L is

$$k_{\rho m} = \frac{1}{L} \int_0^L k_\rho dx = \frac{4}{3} (k_\rho)_{x=L} \tag{4}$$

$$(k_{\rho m}) = \frac{4}{3} (4.55)$$

$$= 6.067 \text{ ft/hr}$$

Therefore the average coefficient of mass transfer over first 1.5 ft down the plate is 6.067 ft/hr.

(b) For a plate of width 1.5 ft

$$q_{AW} = k_{\rho m} (1.5 \times 1.5)(\rho_{A0} - \rho_{A\infty}) \tag{5}$$

$$= 6.067 (1.5 \times 1.5)(0.000224 - 0)$$

$$= 0.00306 \text{ lb/hr}$$

Then, the average mass transfer rate over 1.5 ft from the upper edge is 0.00306 lb/hr.

(c) From (a) the local coefficient of mass transfer at 1.5 ft from the upper edge of the plate is 4.55 ft/hr.

(d) $$\left(\frac{\partial \rho_A}{\partial y}\right)_{y=0} = \frac{-k_\rho(\rho_{A0} - \rho_{A\infty})}{D_{AB}} \tag{6}$$

$$= \frac{-4.55(0.000224 - 0)}{0.2727}$$

$$= -0.00374 \text{ lb}_m/\text{ft}^4$$

Hence, the local concentration gradient at the surface of the plate at 1.5 ft below the upper edge is $-0.00374 \text{ lb}_m/\text{ft}^4$.

(e) Solving eq. (2) for δ gives

$$\delta = \delta_c = \frac{2D_{AB}}{k_\rho} \tag{7}$$

$$= \frac{2(0.2727)}{4.55}$$

$$= 0.1199 \text{ ft.}$$

Therefore, the local thickness of the momentum and concentration boundary layers at 1.5 ft is 0.1199 ft.

(f) The maximum velocity at any point in the boundary layer is given by

$$u_{max} = 0.766 \frac{\mu}{x\rho} (0.952 + Sc)^{-\frac{1}{2}} (Gr_D)^{\frac{1}{2}} \tag{8}$$

$$= 0.766 \left(\frac{0.0469}{1.5(0.0692)}\right) (0.952 + 2.485)^{-\frac{1}{2}} (3.273 \times 10^6)^{\frac{1}{2}}$$

$$= 337.74 \text{ ft/hr} = 0.0938 \text{ ft/sec}$$

Then, the maximum velocity in the boundary layer at 1.5 ft from the upper edge is 0.0938 ft/sec.

• PROBLEM 16-26

Consider an air stream flowing over a solid naphthalene plate with a velocity of 16 ft/sec at points far away from the surface of the plate. The air stream pressure is 1 atm and the temperature of the system is 115°F. Determine:

(a) the average coefficient of mass transfer over first 1.5 ft from leading edge.

(b) the average mass transfer rate per unit width over first 1.5 ft from leading edge of the plate.

(c) the local coefficient of mass transfer at 1.5 ft from leading edge of the plate.

(d) the local concentration gradient of naphthalene at the surface at 1.5 ft from the leading edge.

(e) the local thicknesses of the momentum and concentration boundary layers at 1.5 ft from the leading edge of the plate.

Solution: The vapor pressure of naphthalene as a function of temperature are given by

$$\log P_A = 12.198 - (6881/T) \tag{1}$$

where P_A in lb_f/ft^2 and T in °R

and $\log P_A^+ = 11.84528 - (3857/T)$ (2)

where P_A^+ in mm Hg and T in °K.

For the vapor pressure of naphthalene the approximate temperature taken is 115°F.

(a) From air tables, for air at 115°F and 1 atm.

$$\rho = \frac{14.7(144)29}{1545(575)}$$

$$= 0.0691 \; lb_m/ft^3$$

$$\mu = 0.0194 \text{ cp}$$

$$= 0.0469 \; lb_m/ft\text{-}hr$$

$$D_{AB} = 0.2727 \text{ ft}^2/\text{hr}$$

The Reynolds number is given by

$$Re = \frac{\rho VL}{\mu}$$

at $$L = 1.5 \text{ ft}$$

$$Re = \frac{(0.0691)(16)(3600)(1.5)}{0.0469}$$

$$= 127297.22$$

This implies the flow in the boundary layer is laminar.

The Schmidt number is given by

$$Sc = \frac{\mu}{\rho D_{AB}}$$

$$= \frac{0.0469}{(0.0691)(0.2727)}$$

$$= 2.489$$

The average mass transfer coefficient is given by

$$k_{\rho m} = 0.646 \left(\frac{D_{AB}}{L}\right) (Re)^{\frac{1}{2}} (Sc)^{1/3} \quad (3)$$

Substituting the known quantities gives

$$k_{\rho m} = 0.646 \left(\frac{0.2727}{1.5}\right)(127297.22)^{\frac{1}{2}}(2.489)^{1/3}$$

$$= 56.8 \text{ ft/hr}$$

Therefore the average coefficient of mass transfer over first 1.5 ft from leading edge is 56.8 ft/hr.

(b) $\rho_{A\infty} = 0$, since the gas stream is of pure air. Then ρ_{AO} is calculated from the ideal gas law using the saturation vapor pressure of naphthalene at 115°F.

From eq. (1)

$$\log P_A = 12.198 - \frac{6881}{575}$$

$$= 0.2310$$

$$P_A = 1.702 \text{ lb}_f/\text{ft}^2$$

$$\rho_{AO} = \frac{P_A M}{RT}$$

$$= \frac{1.702(128.16)}{1545(575)}$$

$$= 0.000246 \ lb_m/ft^3$$

The mass transfer rate is given by

$$q_{AW} = k_{\rho m} \ (1.5 \times 1)(\rho_{AO} - \rho_{A\infty}) \tag{4}$$

$$q_{AW} = 56.8(1.5 \times 1)(0.000246 - 0)$$

$$= 0.0210 \ lb_m/hr$$

(c) For local mass transfer coefficient

$$(Sh)_x = \frac{k_\rho x}{D_{AB}} = 0.323 \ Re^{\frac{1}{2}} \ Sc^{1/3} \tag{5}$$

and for a mean mass transfer coefficient

$$(Sh)_m = \frac{k_{\rho m} L}{D_{AB}} = 0.646 \ Re^{\frac{1}{2}} \ Sc^{1/3} \tag{6}$$

For a given x, dividing eq. (6) by eq. (5) gives

$$\frac{k_{\rho m}}{k_\rho} = 2$$

Therefore

$$k_\rho = \frac{k_{\rho m}}{2}$$

$$= \frac{56.8}{2}$$

$$= 28.4 \ ft/hr$$

Hence the local coefficient of mass transfer at 1.5 ft from leading edge of the plate is 28.4 ft/hr.

(d) The local concentration gradient of naphthalene at the surface is given by

$$\left(\frac{\partial \rho_A}{\partial y}\right)_{y=0} = \frac{k_\rho \ (\rho_{AO} - \rho_{A\infty})}{D_{AB}} \tag{7}$$

Substituting the known quantities in eq. (7) gives

$$\left(\frac{\partial \rho_A}{\partial y}\right)_{y=0} = \frac{28.4(0 - 0.000246)}{0.2727}$$

$$=-0.02562 \ lb/ft^4$$

(e) the local thicknesses of the momentum and concentration boundary layer at 1.5 ft are

$$\delta = \frac{4.64\ L}{Re^{\frac{1}{2}}}$$

$$= \frac{4.64(1.5)}{(127297.22)^{\frac{1}{2}}}$$

$$= 0.01951\ \text{ft}$$

$$\delta_c = 0.0162\ \left(\frac{\mu}{\rho D_{AB}}\right)^{-1/3}$$

$$= 0.0162\ \left(\frac{0.0469}{(0.0691)(0.2727)}\right)^{-1/3}$$

$$= 0.01195\ \text{ft.}$$

• PROBLEM 16-27

1,250 lb of water, in a tank of 3 ft diameter and 4 ft deep is agitated with an 8 in diameter impeller at a stirrer Reynolds number, Re = 100,000. Suddenly, 250 lb of $CuSO_4 \cdot 5H_2O$ crystals 1/4 in. in diameter are dropped into the tank. For the dissolution of the crystals of anhydrous solids into agitated water, the mass transfer coefficient is given by

$$\frac{k'_c\ d_T}{D} = 0.052\ Re_s^{0.833}\ Sc^{0.5}$$

where d_T = diameter of tank

Re_s = stirrer Reynolds number

Sc = Schmidt number

D = diffusivity

Calculate the time required to (i) dissolve all but 10 lb of the crystals and (ii) completely dissolve the crystals. Use the following physical properties. Make relevant assumptions.

$$D = 0.73 \times 10^{-5}\ \text{cm}^2/\text{sec}$$

density of hydrated crystals = 143 lb/ft^3

kinematic viscosity of the solution = 1 cs

solution density = 62.4 lb/ft^3

solubility of $CuSO_4$ in water = 0.0229 mole fraction at 20°C

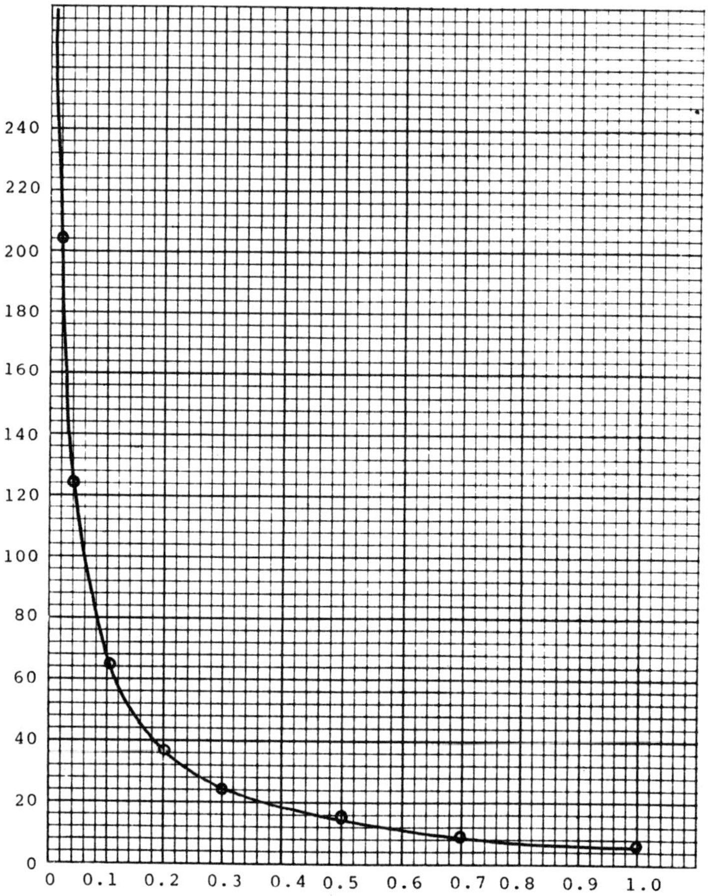

$M_{AS} \rightarrow$

Solution:

Assumptions:

(i) Temperature is constant at 20°C

(ii) Kinematic viscosity of the solution is also constant

(iii) The crystals are spherical in shape and remain so without break-up as they dissolve

(iv) k_c' remains constant for all crystal sizes

Let M_{AS} = moles of hydrated $CuSO_4$ in solid phase

$\dot{m}_{1AS}$ = molar rate of hydrated $CuSO_4$ solid coming into the tank

$\dot{m}_{2AS}$ = molar rate of hydrated $CuSO_4$ solid leaving the tank

$\dot{m}_{mAS}$ = molar rate of transfer from solution phase to solid phase

A mass balance on solid phase gives

$$\frac{dM_{AS}}{dt} = \dot{m}_{1AS} - \dot{m}_{2AS} + \dot{m}m_{AS}$$

Since $\dot{m}_{1AS} = \dot{m}_{2AS} = 0$, $\frac{dM_{AS}}{dt} = \dot{m}_{mAS}$

Also $\dot{m}_{mAS} = - \dot{m}_{mAf}$ = rate of transfer from solid to solution phase

$$\therefore \quad N_{Af} = \dot{m}_{mAf}/A = \frac{k'_c}{\phi}(C_{Ai} - C_A) = \frac{k'_c C_{Tf}}{\phi}(x_{Ai} - x_A)$$

where

$$\phi = \frac{(N_R - x_A) - (N_R - x_{Ai})}{N_R \ln\left(\frac{N_R - x_A}{N_R - x_{Ai}}\right)} = \frac{X_{Ai} - X_A}{N_R \ln\left(\frac{N_R - x_A}{N_R - x_{Ai}}\right)}$$

$$N_R = \frac{N_A}{N_A + N_B} = \frac{1}{6} \quad \text{since in this case} \quad N_B = 5\, N_A$$

$$\therefore \quad \frac{dM_{AS}}{dt} = - Ak'_c\, C_{Tf}\, N_R \ln\left(\frac{N_R - x_A}{N_R - x_{Ai}}\right) \tag{1}$$

Let M_{ASO} = initial moles of solid hydrate

n = no. of crystals

C_{TS} = total concentration of solid hydrate

r = radius of solid crystal at any time t

r_o = initial radius of solid crystal

$$\therefore \; n = \frac{M_{ASO}}{C_{TS}\frac{4}{3}\pi r_o^3} = \frac{M_{AS}}{C_{TS}\frac{4}{3}\pi r^3} \quad \text{or } r = \left(\frac{M_{AS}}{M_{ASO}}\right)^{1/3} r_o$$

$$\therefore \; A = n4\pi r^2 = \frac{3M_{ASO}}{C_{TS} r_o}\left(\frac{M_{AS}}{M_{ASO}}\right)^{2/3} \tag{2}$$

Also

$$x_A = \frac{M_{ASO} - M_{AS}}{M_{Bfo} + 5(M_{ASO} - M_{AS}) + (M_{ASO} - M_{AS})}$$

$$= \frac{M_{ASO} - M_{AS}}{M_{Bfo} + 6(M_{ASO} - M_{AS})}$$

where M_{Bfo} = initial number of moles of water

From the data, $Sc = \dfrac{0.01}{0.73 \times 10^{-5}} = 1370$

$$\therefore \quad k_c' = \frac{0.73 \times 10^{-5}}{91.44} \times 0.052 \times (100{,}000)^{0.833} \times (1370)^{0.5}$$

$$= 2.247 \times 10^{-3} \text{ cm/sec} = 0.2653 \text{ ft/hr}$$

Molecular weight of hydrate = 160 + 90 = 250

$$\therefore \quad M_{AS} = \frac{250}{250} = 1 \text{ lb.mole}$$

$$C_{TS} = \frac{143}{250} \text{ lb.mol/ft}^3$$

$$r_o = \frac{1}{8} \text{ in} = \frac{1}{96} \text{ ft}$$

From equation (2), $A = \dfrac{3\left(M_{ASO}\right)^{1/3}\left(M_{AS}\right)^{2/3}}{C_{TS}r_o}$

$$= \frac{3 \times 1}{\frac{143}{250} \times \frac{1}{96}}\left(M_{AS}\right)^{2/3} = 503.5\left(M_{AS}\right)^{2/3} \text{ ft}^2$$

$$M_{Bfo} = \frac{1250}{18} = 69.44$$

From equation (3), we get

$$x_A = \frac{1 - M_{AS}}{69.44 + 6(1 - M_{AS})} = \frac{1 - M_{AS}}{75.44 - 6M_{AS}} \qquad (5)$$

Assuming very dilute solution,

$$C_{Tf} = \frac{62.4}{18} = 3.467 \text{ lb.mole/ft}^3$$

Using equation (1),

$$\int_0^t dt = \int_{M_{ASO}}^{M_{ASf}} \frac{-dM_{AS}}{503.5\, M_{AS}^{2/3} \times 0.2653 \times 3.4667 \times \frac{1}{6} \times \ln\left(\frac{0.1667 - x_A}{0.1667-0.0229}\right)}$$

(i) When 10 lb. of crystals are left,

$$M_{ASf} = \frac{10}{250} = 0.04$$

$$\therefore\ t_f\Big|_{M_{ASf}=0.04} = 1.2957 \times 10^{-2} \int_{0.04}^{1.0} \frac{dM_{AS}}{(M_{AS})^{2/3} \ln\left(\frac{0.1667 - x_A}{0.1438}\right)} \quad (6)$$

where x_A is obtained from equation (5) as $= \dfrac{1 - M_{AS}}{75.44 - 6M_{AS}}$

Equation (6) is integrated graphically by plotting

$$\left[M_{AS} \ln \frac{0.1667 - x_A}{0.1438}\right]^{-1} \quad \text{against } M_{AS}$$

Thus $\quad t_f\Big|_{M_{ASf}=0.04} = 0.371$ hr

(ii) When $M_{AS} = 0.001$, $x_A = 0.01324$,

$$\frac{0.1667 - x_A}{0.1438} = 1.0671, \quad M_{AS}{}^{2/3} \ln\left(\frac{0.1667 - x_A}{0.1438}\right)^{-1} = 1538.6$$

Making a linear assumption,

$$t_f\Big|_{M_{ASf}=0.001} = 1.2957 \times 10^{-2} \left[28.7 + (0.01 - 0.001) \times 933\right]$$

$$= 0.48 \text{ hr.}$$

This is the time required for 99% dissolution.

• PROBLEM 16-28

A mixture of carbon dioxide and air is moving at 2.5 ft/sec inside a 3-in. wetted wall column. The CO_2 concentration in the air is 0.12 mole fraction at one location in the column. Also at this location, the water in the air-water interface is 0.006 mole fraction. If the column works at 10 atm. and 25°C, determine the mass-transfer coefficient and the mass flux at the given location.

Solution: The diffusivity of CO_2 in air at 1 atm. and 25°C is $D = 0.164$ cm²/sec and the Schmidt number is $Sc = 0.94$. With this information and the data in the problem statement, equation (1) can be employed to evaluate the mass transfer coefficient, k_c. Equation (2) is then applied to determine the mass flux, N_A.

The diffusivity of gases is dependent on pressure according to:

$$D_2 = D_1\left(\frac{P_1}{P_2}\right)$$

Therefore at 10 atm:

$$D_2 = 0.164 \left(\frac{1}{10}\right) = 0.0164 \text{ cm}^2/\text{sec}$$

or $0.0635 \text{ ft}^2/\text{hr}$.

The Schmidt number is independent of the pressure. The partial pressure of CO_2 in the gas phase,

$$\bar{p}_A = \bar{x}_A P = (0.12)(10) = 1.2 \text{ atm}$$

It is given that the concentration of CO_2 in the liquid at the interface is 0.006 mole fraction. The partial pressure of CO_2 in the gas phase at the interface, p_{Ai}, is given by the equilibrium vapor pressure of CO_2 above the liquid.

$$p_{Ai} = H\, x_{Ai}$$

$$= (1640)(0.006) = 9.84 \text{ atm.}$$

Since the concentration of carbon dioxide in air is low, the properties of air will be used as an approximation for the air-CO_2 mixture.

$$\mu_{air} = 0.018 \text{ cp at } 25^\circ\text{C and 10 atm}$$

$$\rho_{air} = 0.0808 \text{ lb/ft}^3 \text{ at STP}$$

$$\rho_{air} = 0.0808 \left(\frac{273}{298}\right)\left(\frac{10}{1}\right) = 0.7402 \frac{\text{lb}}{\text{ft}^3} \text{ at 10 atm and } 25^\circ\text{C}.$$

The Reynolds number,

$$Re = \frac{\rho u d}{\mu} = \frac{(0.7402)(2.5)\left(\frac{3}{12}\right)}{(0.018)(6.72 \times 10^{-4})} = 38200$$

This high Reynolds number indicates that the air flow is turbulent. Since air is almost insoluble in water, this is a case of diffusion through a nondiffusing gas, for which the following equation can be used.

$$\left(\frac{k_c d}{D_{AB}}\right)\left(\frac{c_{B,lm}}{c_t}\right) = 0.023\, (Re)^{0.83}\, (Sc)^{0.33} \qquad (1)$$

where B refers to air, and:

$$\frac{c_{B,lm}}{c_t} = \frac{p_{B,lm}}{p_t}$$

also:

$$p_{B,lm} = \frac{(p_{b1} - \bar{p}_b)}{\ln\left(\frac{p_{b1}}{\bar{p}_b}\right)}$$

$$p_{b1} = p_t - p_{A1} = 10 - 9.84 = 0.16 \text{ atm}$$

$$\bar{p}_b = (p_t - \bar{p}_A) = 10 - 1.2 = 8.8 \text{ atm}$$

Therefore

$$p_{B,lm} = \frac{0.16 - 8.8}{\ln\left(\frac{0.16}{8.8}\right)} = 2.16 \text{ atm}$$

and

$$\frac{p_{B,lm}}{p_t} = \frac{2.16}{10} = 0.216$$

Substituting in equation (1) and solving for k_c:

$$k_c = 0.023 \frac{(0.0635)}{(3/12)}\left(\frac{1}{0.216}\right)(38200)^{0.83} (0.94)^{0.33}$$

$$= 168 \text{ lb moles/ft}^2\text{hr}$$

The mass flux,

$$N_A = -k_c(c_{Ai} - \bar{c}_A) \tag{2}$$

where:

$$c_A = p_A/RT$$

$$R = 0.729 \text{ atm-ft}^3\text{/lbmol-R}$$

$$T = 536.4 \text{ R}$$

Equation (2) can be rewritten as:

$$N_A = -\frac{k_c}{RT}(p_{A1} - \bar{p}_A)$$

Substituting in this form of the equation:

$$N_A = -\frac{168}{(0.729)(536.4)}(9.84 - 1.2)$$

$$= -3.71 \text{ lbmoles/ft}^2\text{hr}$$

The negative sign indicates that the mass flux is from the wall towards the center of the tube.

CHAPTER 17

UNSTEADY STATE MOLECULAR DIFFUSION, MOLECULAR DIFFUSION WITH CHEMICAL REACTION

COMPOSITION, RATE OF DIFFUSION BY NUMERICAL METHODS

• PROBLEM 17-1

Steel, with an initial carbon concentration of 0.30% by weight, is placed in a carburizing atmosphere for 1.5 hr. The surface concentration of carbon, $c_{A,s}$, is 0.75%. The diffusivity of carbon in steel is 1.1×10^{-11} m^2/sec at the existent conditions of pressure and temperature. Obtain the concentration of carbon at 0.015, 0.025, and 0.045 cm under the surface of the steel.

Solution: Due to the low concentration of carbon in the steel, its density is assumed constant. This allows the following equation to be written:

$$\frac{c_{A,s} - c_A}{c_{A,s} - c_{Ao}} = \text{erf}\left(\frac{x}{2\sqrt{Dt}}\right) \tag{1}$$

where:

c_A is the concentration of carbon at a point x

$c_{A,s} = 0.0075$

$c_{A,o} = 0.003$

Substitution in equation (1) yields:

$$\frac{0.0075 - c_A}{0.0075 - 0.003} = \text{erf}\left(\frac{x}{2\sqrt{1.1\times10^{-11}\ \frac{m^2}{sec}(5400sec)}}\right)$$

$$c_A = 0.0075 - 0.0045\,\text{erf}\left(\frac{x}{4.87 \times 10^{-4}}\right)$$

At $x = 0.015$ cm $= 1.5 \times 10^{-4}$m

$$\text{erf}\left(\frac{x}{4.87 \times 10^{-4}}\right) = \text{erf}\left(\frac{1.5 \times 10^{-4}}{4.87 \times 10^{-4}}\right)$$

$$= \text{erf}(0.31) = 0.33888$$

from tables of the error function. Therefore:

$$c_A = 0.0075 - 0.0045(0.33888)$$

$$= 0.0060 = 0.60\% \text{ carbon}$$

At $x = 0.025$ cm $= 2.5 \times 10^{-4}$m

$$\text{erf}\left(\frac{2.5 \times 10^{-4}}{4.87 \times 10^{-4}}\right) = \text{erf}(0.51) = 0.52920$$

and

$$c_A = 0.0075 - 0.0045(0.52920)$$

$$= 0.0051 = 0.51\% \text{ carbon}$$

At $x = 0.045$ cm $= 4.5 \times 10^{-4}$m

$$\text{erf}\left(\frac{4.5 \times 10^{-4}}{4.87 \times 10^{-4}}\right) = \text{erf}(0.92)$$

$$= 0.80677$$

and

$$c_A = 0.0075 - 0.0045(0.80677)$$

$$= 0.0039 = 0.39\% \text{ carbon}$$

• PROBLEM 17-2

A rectangular section of wood is 3 in. thick with a moisture content of $c_i = 28\%$ (based on dry wood). The equilibrium moisture content is $c_e = 7\%$. A coating which does not allow moisture to pass through is applied to the edges and ends. The surface resistance is small enough to neglect ($k/hr_0 = 0$) and the diffusivity of water through wood is 0.00005 ft^2/hr.

Determine the drying time necessary to obtain a center line moisture content of $c_c = 9\%$ (dry basis).

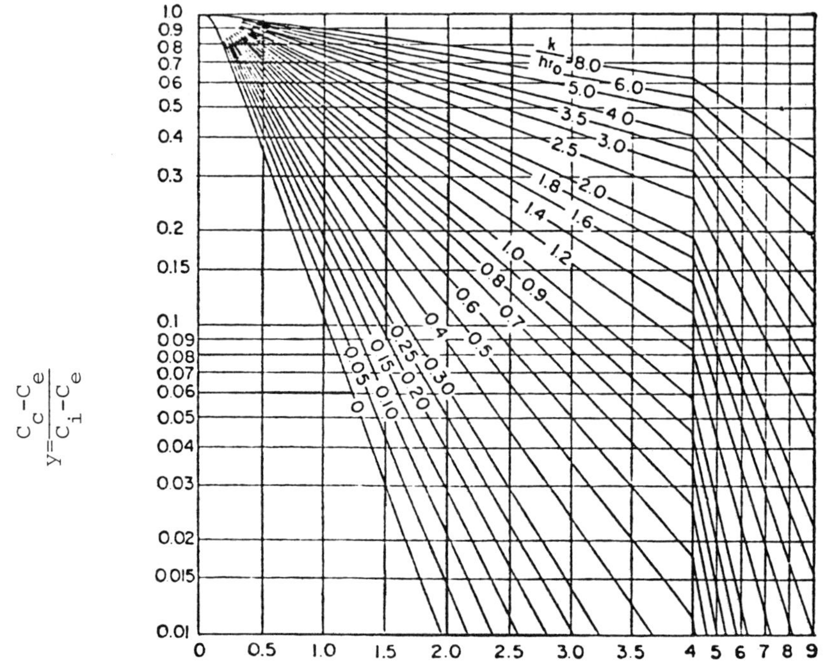

Fig. 1

TEMPERATURE HISTORY AT THE CENTER OF AN INFINITE SLAB.

Solution: First evaluate the term Y for use with Figure 1.

$$Y = \frac{c_c - c_e}{c_i - c_e} = \frac{9 - 7}{28 - 7} = 0.095$$

Now employ Figure 1 with $k/hr_0 = 0$ to obtain:

$$X = 1.1 = \frac{Dt}{r_0^2}$$

Using x = 0 for the center line,

$$r_0 = \left(\frac{1.5}{12}\right) \text{ft.}$$

Solving for the time:

$$t = \frac{Xr_0^2}{D} = \frac{(1.1)\left(\frac{1.5}{12}\right)^2}{0.00005} = 344 \text{ hr.}$$

• PROBLEM 17-3

A hot mild steel rod is placed in a carbonaceous substance. The rod has an initial carbon concentration of $c_i = 0.22\%$ by weight. The concentration of carbon at the surface of the rod is $c_e = 1.4\%$ at equilibrium. Determine the time necessary for a point at 0.15 cm below the surface, to attain a carbon concentration of 0.78%. The diffusivity of carbon in steel is 5.7×10^{-6} cm^2/sec.

Solution: Equation (1) can be employed to obtain the solution.

$$c^* = \text{erfc}\left(\frac{x}{\sqrt{4Dt}}\right) \tag{1}$$

where:

$$c^* = \frac{c - c_i}{c_e - c_i} \tag{2}$$

and c is the concentration at a location x. At x = 0.15 cm c = 0.78%. Substituting in equation (2) yields:

$$c^* = \frac{0.78 - 0.22}{1.4 - 0.22} = 0.475$$

Substitution in equation (1) gives:

$$\frac{x}{\sqrt{4Dt}} = \text{erfc}^{-1}(0.475)$$

From a table of complementary error functions:

$$\frac{x}{\sqrt{4Dt}} = 0.51$$

Solving for the time:

$$t = \left(\frac{x}{0.51}\right)^2 \left(\frac{1}{4D}\right)$$

$$= \left(\frac{0.15}{0.51}\right)^2 \left(\frac{1}{4(5.7 \times 10^{-6})}\right)$$

$$= 3794 \text{ sec}$$

$$= 1.1 \text{ hr}$$

A semiinfinite solid rectangular section contains a solute β at a concentration of $c_0 = 1.2 \times 10^{-2}$ kgmol/m³. One face of the object is then contacted with a moving fluid which contains a concentration of $c_1 = 0.15$ kgmol β/m³. The convective coefficient is $k_c = 2.3 \times 10^{-7}$ m/sec and the equilibrium distribution coefficient is K = 2.1. Determine the amount of β in the solid at the surface (z = 0) and at z = 0.012 m below the surface, at 35000 sec. after contact with the fluid. The diffusivity of β in the solid is

$$D = 4.2 \times 10^{-9} \text{ m}^2/\text{sec}.$$

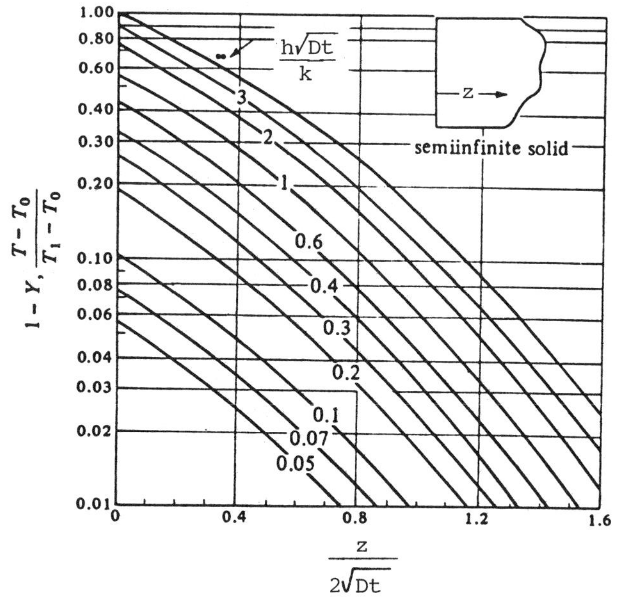

Fig. 1

UNSTEADY-STATE HEAT CONDUCTED IN A SEMIINFINITE SOLID WITH SURFACE CONVENTION.

Solution: Figure 1 will be employed to solve this problem. First evaluate the following term for use on Figure 1.

$$\frac{h\sqrt{Dt}}{k} = \frac{Kk_c}{D}\sqrt{Dt}$$

$$= \frac{(2.1)(2.3\times10^{-7})}{4.2\times10^{-9}}\sqrt{(4.2\times10^{-9})(35000)}$$

$$= 1.394$$

Now, evaluate the abscissa of Figure 1 for z = 0.012 m.

$$\frac{z}{2\sqrt{Dt}} = \frac{0.012}{2\sqrt{4.2 \times 10^{-9}(35000)}} = 0.495$$

From Figure 1, an ordinate of $1 - Y = 0.29$ is obtained.

Equation (2) allows the concentration c to be obtained. The relationship for unsteady state heat transfer is

$$1 - Y = \frac{T - T_0}{T_1 - T_0} .$$

The corresponding expression for unsteady state mass transfer with $K \neq 1.0$ is given by equation (2).

$$1 - Y = \frac{c - c_0}{c_1/K - c_0} \qquad (2)$$

Substituting gives:

$$0.29 = \frac{c - 1.2 \times 10^{-2}}{\frac{0.15}{2.1} - 1.2 \times 10^{-2}}$$

$$c = 2.92 \times 10^{-2} \text{ kgmol}\beta/\text{m}^3$$

at $z = 0.012$m.

At $z = 0$m

$$\frac{z}{2\sqrt{Dt}} = 0$$

Again using Figure 1

$$1 - Y = 0.70 = \frac{c - 1.2 \times 10^{-2}}{\frac{0.15}{2.1} - 1.2 \times 10^{-2}}$$

and

$$c = 5.36 \times 10^{-2} \text{ kgmol}\beta/\text{m}^3$$

• PROBLEM 17-5

An alloy has been formed into porous spheres with 27% voids and radii of r = 6mm. The voids are completely filled with a solution of KCl in water of concentration 0.20 g KCl/cm^3. After exposure to pure flowing water, 85% of the salt is removed from the spheres in 4.65 hrs. The temperature was 26°C and the average diffusivity of KCl in water is 1.83×10^{-9} m^2/sec.

If the spheres had been soaked with a K_2CrO_4 solution of concentration 0.26 g/cm^3, determine the time required for 85% of the salt to leave when the spheres are placed in a moving stream of water which contains 0.03 g K_2CrO_4/cm^3. The average diffusivity of K_2CrO_4 in water is 1.13×10^{-9} m^2/sec at 26°C.

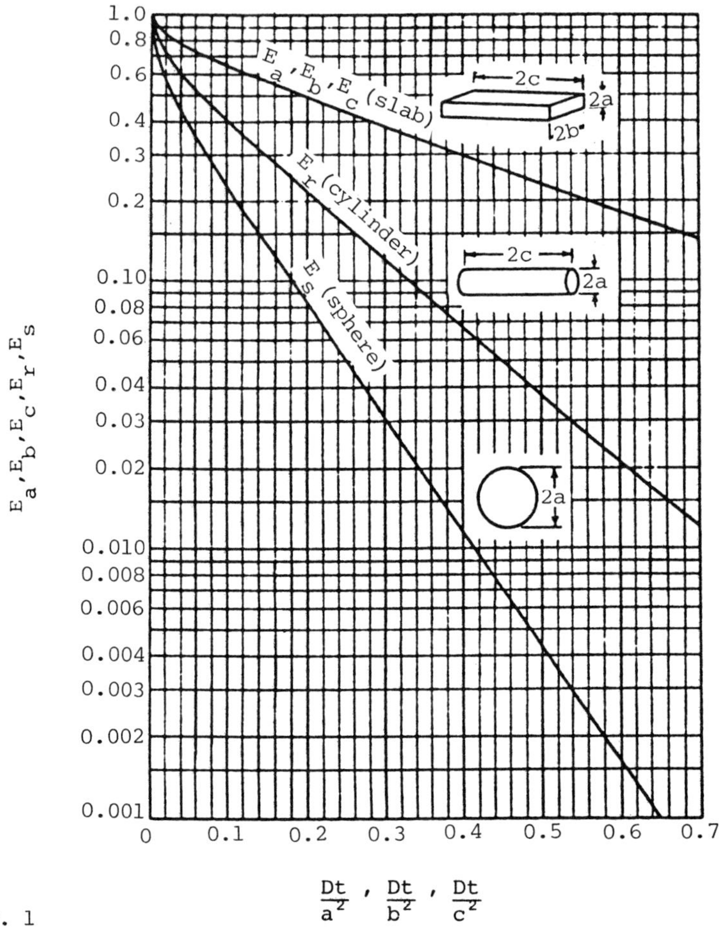

Fig. 1

UNSTEADY-STATE DIFFUSION.

Solution: For the spheres $r = a = 0.006$m, and for the diffusion of KCl $t = 4.65(3600) = 16740$ sec. If the spheres are contained in pure water, the final concentration of the salt will be $c_{S,\infty} = 0$. To remove 85% of the KCl

$$\frac{c_{S,t} - c_{S,\infty}}{c_{So} - c_{S,\infty}} = 0.15 = E_S$$

Using this value of E_S with Figure 1 gives:

$$\frac{D_{eff}t}{a^2} = 0.14$$

where D_{eff} is the effective diffusivity. Solving for D_{eff}:

$$D_{eff} = \frac{0.14a^2}{t} = \frac{0.14(0.006)^2}{16740}$$

$$= 3.01 \times 10^{-10}\ \text{m}^2/\text{sec}$$

and

$$\frac{D}{D_{eff}} = \frac{1.83 \times 10^{-9}}{3.01 \times 10^{-10}} = 6.080$$

For the diffusion of K_2CrO_4:

$$c_{So} = 0.26$$

$$c_{S,\infty} = 0.03$$

$$c_{S,t} = 0.15(0.26) = 0.039 \text{ g/cm}^3$$

and

$$E_S = \frac{c_{S,t} - c_{S,\infty}}{c_{So} - c_{S,\infty}} = \frac{0.039 - 0.03}{0.26 - 0.03} = 0.0391$$

Employing Figure 1 again:

$$D_{eff} \frac{t}{a^2} = 0.279 \qquad (1)$$

From the previous calculations:

$$D_{eff} = \frac{D}{6.080} = \frac{1.13 \times 10^{-9}}{6.080} = 1.859 \times 10^{-10} \text{ m}^2/\text{sec}$$

Substituting for D_{eff} in equation (1) yields:

$$t = \frac{0.279a^2}{D_{eff}} = \frac{(0.279)(0.006)^2}{1.859 \times 10^{-10}}$$

$$= 54000 \text{ sec}$$

$$= 15.0 \text{ hr.}$$

• PROBLEM 17-6

> Dry styrofoam spheres of 2.5 in. diameter are exposed to a shower of pure water for 3.5 hr. If the diffusivity of water in the foam is 0.0007 ft^2/hr, determine the amount of water in the spheres after 3.5 hr.

Solution: A dry styrofoam basis will be employed. It is assumed that $\omega_{A,\infty}$ = 1 lbm water/lbm foam. Since the spheres are initially dry $\omega_{Ai} = 0$. If the surface resistance is assumed to be low enough to neglect, then $k_c \to \infty$ and $D/k_cR \to 0$. Also:

$$\frac{Dt}{R^2} = \frac{(0.0007)(3.5)}{(2.5/24)^2} = 0.226$$

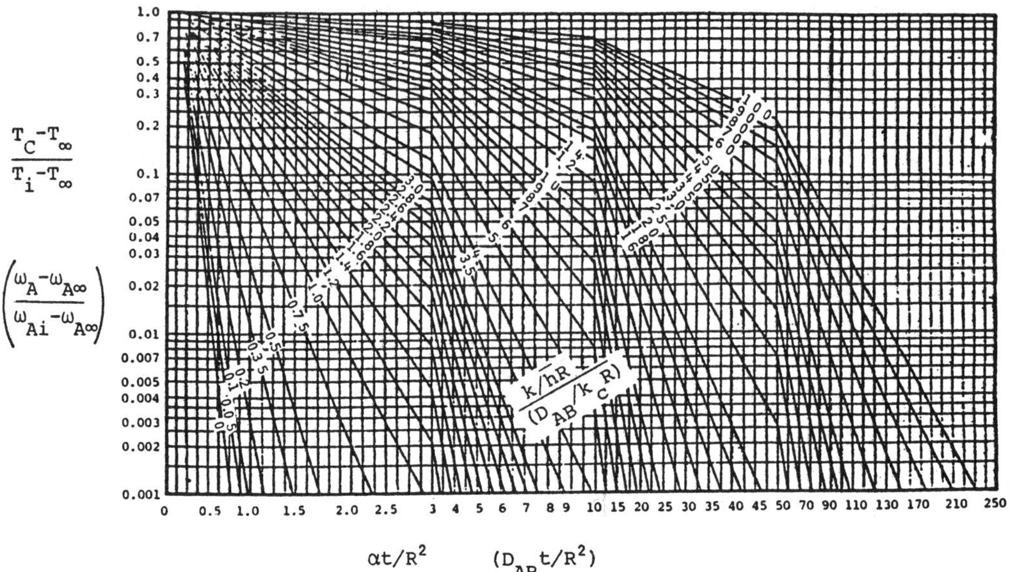

Fig. 1

CENTER TRANSIENT TEMPERATURE (AND MASS CONCENTRATION) FOR A SPHERE OF RADIUS R.

Employing this value with Figure 1 yields:

$$\frac{\omega_A - \omega_{A\infty}}{\omega_{Ai} - \omega_{A\infty}} \simeq 0.21$$

Substituting:

$$\frac{\omega_A - 1}{0 - 1} \simeq 0.21$$

$$\omega_A = \simeq 0.79 \text{ lbm water/lbm foam}$$

• PROBLEM 17-7

A 2.2 ft. long wooden cylinder with a diameter of 1.1 ft, has a moisture content of 36% by weight. A moisture content of 21% by weight is desired. This can be obtained by placing the cylinder in a dryer which is kept at 6% water by weight. What is the drying time when:

(I) the ends of the cylinder are covered to prevent water loss.

(II) the lateral surface area of the cylinder is covered.

(III) none of the surfaces are covered.

Use a diffusivity of

$$D = 0.00041 \text{ ft}^2\text{/hr.}$$

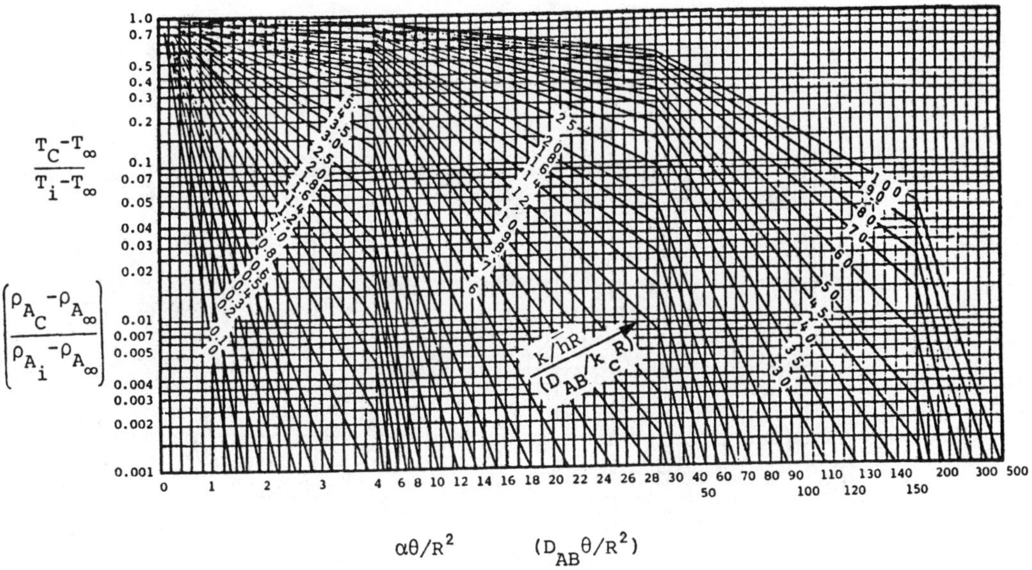

CENTERLINE TRANSIENT TEMPERATURE (AND MASS CONCENTRATION) FOR AN INFINITELY LONG CYLINDER OF RADIUS R.

Solution: Using a dry wood basis ($\rho_{A\infty} = 0$), the concentration gradient is:

$$\frac{\rho_{Ac} - \rho_{A\infty}}{\rho_{Ai} - \rho_{A\infty}} = \frac{0.21 - 0.0}{0.36 - 0.0} = 0.58 \quad (1)$$

where ρ_{Ac} is the moisture content at the center of the cylinder. Assuming the surface resistance is small enough to neglect, implies that:

$$\frac{D}{k_c r} \to 0 \quad \text{and} \quad \frac{D}{k_c L} \to 0$$

(I) Figure 1 applies for the case of a cylinder with both ends sealed.

Employing the concentration gradient obtained from equation (1) yields:

$$\frac{D\theta}{r^2} = 0.19$$

Solving for the time, θ:

$$\theta = \frac{0.19r^2}{D} = \frac{(0.19)\left(\frac{1.1}{2}\right)^2}{0.00041} = 140 \text{ hr.}$$

(II) Figure 2 will be used with this case.

The result is:

$$\frac{D\theta}{L^2} = 0.34 \quad \text{for a cylinder of length } 2L$$

and

$$\theta = \frac{0.34L^2}{D} = \frac{0.34\left(\frac{2.2}{2}\right)^2}{0.00041} = 1003 \text{ hr.}$$

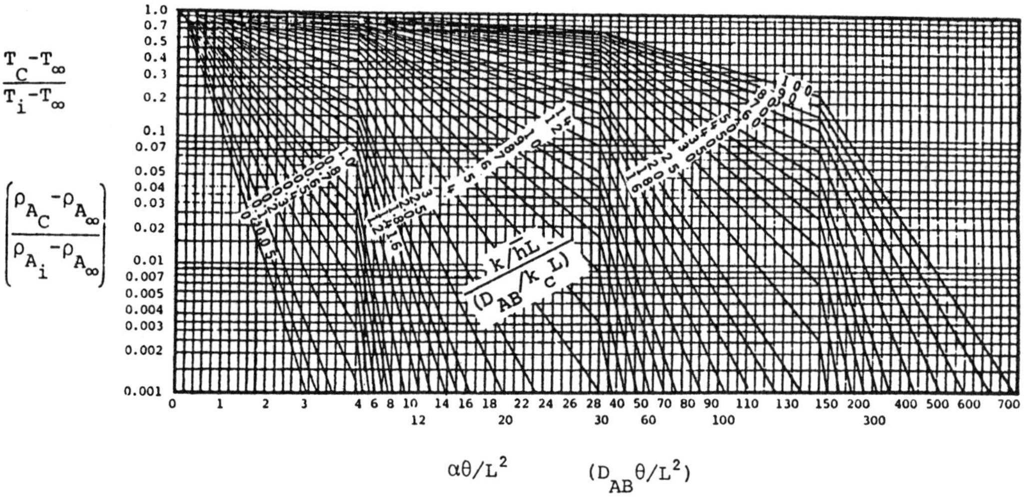

CENTERLINE TRANSIENT TEMPERATURE (AND MASS CONCENTRATION) FOR AN INFINITE PLATE OF THICKNESS 2L.

(III) Using the data from sections (I) and (II), it is calculated that the mass transfer rate at the cylindrical surface is (1003/140) = 7.2 times greater than that at the ends of the cylinder. An estimate of the drying time when all surfaces are exposed is:

$$\theta = 140 - \frac{1}{7.2} 140 = 121 \text{ hr.}$$

This gives:

$$\frac{D\theta}{L^2} = \frac{(0.00041)(121)}{(2.2/2)^2} = 0.041$$

and $$\frac{D\theta}{r^2} = \frac{(0.00041)(121)}{(1.1/2)^2} = 0.164$$

Using these values with Figures 1 and 2 permits the estimated drying time to be verified. From Figure 1:

$$\left(\frac{\rho_{Ac} - \rho_{A\infty}}{\rho_{Ai} - \rho_{A\infty}}\right)_{\substack{\text{inf.}\\ \text{cyl.}}} = 0.72$$

and from Figure 2:

$$\left(\frac{\rho_{Ac} - \rho_{A\infty}}{\rho_{Ai} - \rho_{A\infty}}\right)_{\substack{2L\\ \text{plate}}} = 0.82$$

Now substitute in equation (2):

$$\left(\frac{\rho_{Ac} - \rho_{A\infty}}{\rho_{Ai} - \rho_{A\infty}}\right)_{\substack{\text{short} \\ \text{cyl.}}} = \left(\frac{\rho_{Ac} - \rho_{A\infty}}{\rho_{Ai} - \rho_{A\infty}}\right)_{\substack{2L \\ \text{plate}}} \left(\frac{\rho_{Ac} - \rho_{A\infty}}{\rho_{Ai} - \rho_{A\infty}}\right)_{\substack{\text{inf.} \\ \text{cyl.}}}$$

$$= (0.82)(0.72)$$

$$= 0.59$$

This agrees well with the value of 0.58 calculated with equation(1), thus verifies the estimated drying time.

• PROBLEM 17-8

A rectangular wooden section has dimensions of 11 in. by 11 in. by 1 in. A stream of dry air is passed over the wood to lower its moisture content. Only the two large faces are exposed to the dry air. On the surface a constant moisture content of 6 wt.% exists. When 11 hr. of drying have elapsed the moisture content of the center drops from 16 to 9 wt.%. Assume that the convective mass transfer coefficient is great enough so that the relative resistance m, is negligible.

Determine:

(I) the effective diffusivity.

(II) the moisture content at the center when all faces are exposed to the dry air.

(III) the time required to decrease the moisture content of an 11 in. cube constructed of identical wood from 16 to 9 wt.% using all faces.

Flat plate

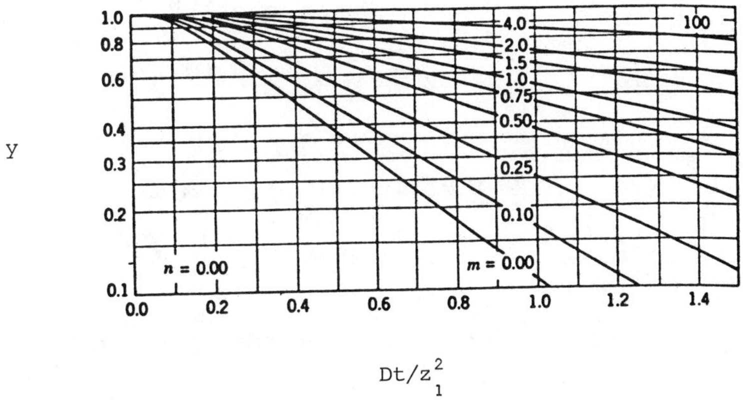

Fig. 1

Solution: (I) The unaccomplished changes for this part are:

$$W_{As} = \frac{0.06}{1-0.06} = 0.064 \text{ lbm water/lbm dry wood}$$

$$W_{Ai} = \frac{0.16}{1-0.16} = 0.190 \text{ lbm water/lbm dry wood}$$

$$W_{A} = \frac{0.09}{1-0.09} = 0.099 \text{ lbm water/lbm dry wood}$$

The unaccomplished concentration ratio is:

$$Y = \frac{W_{As} - W_A}{W_{As} - W_{Ai}} = \frac{0.064 - 0.099}{0.064 - 0.190} = 0.278$$

W_A is the moisture concentration at the center of the slab ($z = 0$). The relative position is $n = z/z_1 = 0$, where $2z_1$ is the thickness of the slab. The relative resistance m, is negligible and will be set equal to zero.

Figure 1 then yields:

$$\frac{Dt}{{z_1}^2} = 0.61.$$

Solving for the diffusivity:

$$D = \frac{0.61{z_1}^2}{t} = \frac{(0.61)\left(\frac{1}{24}\text{ ft}\right)^2}{11 \text{ hr}}$$

$$= 9.63 \times 10^{-5} \text{ ft}^2/\text{hr}$$

(II) The unaccomplished changes must now be determined for the other faces. For both edges:

$$\frac{Dt}{{z_1}^2} = \frac{(9.63 \times 10^{-5})(11)}{\left(\frac{11}{2} \cdot \frac{1}{12}\right)^2}$$

$$= 0.005$$

With n = 0 and m = 0, Figure 1 gives Y = 1.0. Therefore

$$Y_{total} = Y_x Y_y Y_z = (1.0)(1.0)(0.278)$$

$$= 0.278$$

and $W_A = 0.099$ lbm water/lbm dry wood

This indicates that the water lost through the edges is negligible.

(III) The 11 in. cube has an unaccomplished ratio of

$$Y = Y_x Y_y Y_z = Y_z^3$$

$$Y_z = Y^{1/3} = (0.278)^{1/3} = 0.653$$

$$z_1 = \frac{11}{2} \cdot \frac{1}{12} = 0.458 \text{ ft.}$$

$$n = z/z_1 = 0$$

$$m = 0$$

Figure (1) yields:

$$\frac{Dt}{z_1^2} = 0.28$$

Solving for time:

$$t = \frac{(0.28)z_1^2}{D} = \frac{(0.28)(0.458)^2}{9.63 \times 10^{-5}}$$

$$= 610 \text{ hr.}$$

• PROBLEM 17-9

A 6% agar gel has a urea concentration of 6g/100cm³. The gel is in the shape of a cube with 3.5 cm sides. Five faces of the cube are covered, while one is in contact with a moving stream of pure water. The urea diffuses into the water, and after 67 hrs. the urea concentration in the gel has reached an average value of 3.1 g/100 cm³. If the resistance to diffusion exists only in the gel, then determine:

(I) The diffusivity of the urea in the gel.

(II) The time required for the average urea concentration to drop to 1.1 g/cm³.

(III) The time required for the average urea concentration to drop to 1.1 g/cm³, when two opposite sides of the cube are exposed to water.

Solution: (I) The following values are known:

$$a = 3.5/2 = 1.75 \text{ cm} = \frac{1}{2} \text{ length of a cube side}$$

$$c_{A_o} = 6 \text{ g}/100 \text{ cm}^3$$

$$c_{At} = 3.1 \text{ g}/100 \text{ cm}^3$$

$$c_{A,\infty} = 0 \quad \text{for pure water}$$

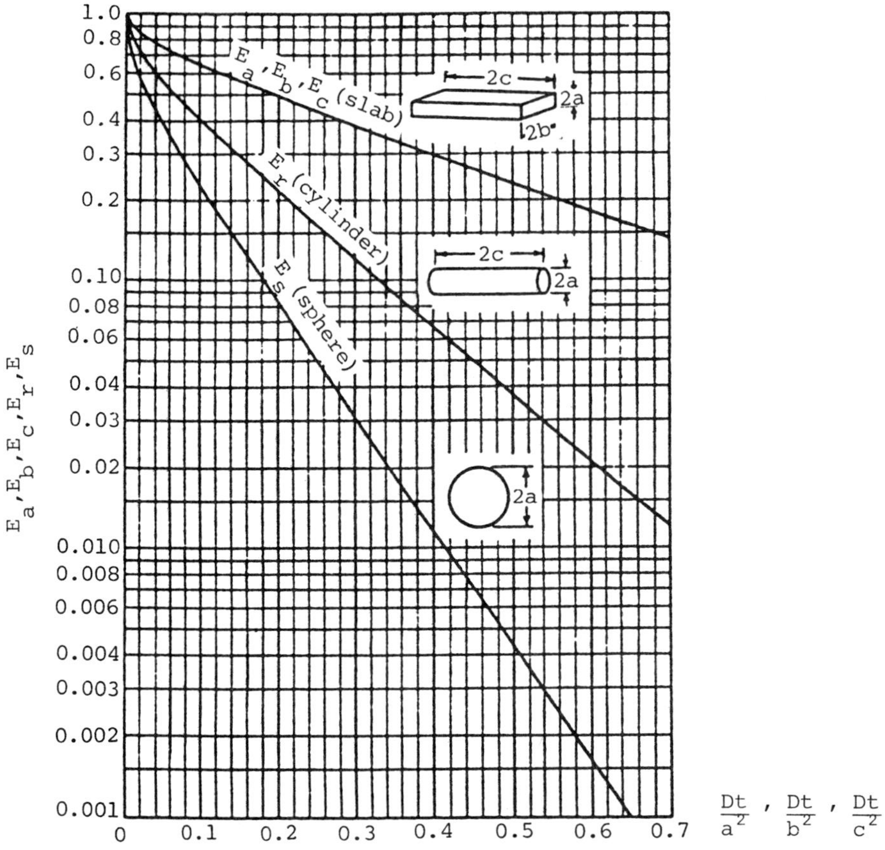

UNSTEADY-STATE DIFFUSION.

Substituting in equation (1):

$$E = \frac{c_{At} - c_{A\infty}}{c_{Ao} - c_{A\infty}} = \frac{3.1 - 0}{6 - 0} = 0.52 \qquad (1)$$

Figure 1 will now provide a value for the term $Dt/4a^2$. The 4 has been added because only 1 face of the cube is exposed.

$$\frac{Dt}{4a^2} = 0.18$$

Solving for D:

$$D = \frac{(0.18)4a^2}{t} = \frac{0.18(4)(1.75)^2}{241200}$$

$$= 9.14 \times 10^{-6}\ \text{cm}^2/\text{sec}$$

(II) Using $c_{At} = 1.1$ g/cm³ in equation (1):

$$E = \frac{1.1 - 0}{6 - 0} = 0.18$$

Figure 1 provides:

$$\frac{Dt}{4a^2} = 0.58$$

Solving for t:

$$t = \frac{(0.58)4a^2}{D} = \frac{(0.58)(4)(1.75)^2}{9.14 \times 10^{-6}}$$

$$= 7.77 \times 10^5 \text{ sec}$$

$$= 216 \text{ hr.}$$

(III) Repeating part (II) with two opposite sides exposed:

$$\frac{Dt}{a^2} = 0.58$$

where the 4 which was added previously has now been removed. Solving for the time:

$$t = \frac{0.58a^2}{D} = \frac{(0.58)(1.75)^2}{9.14 \times 10^{-6}}$$

$$= 1.94 \times 10^5 \text{ sec}$$

$$= 53.9 \text{ hr.}$$

• PROBLEM 17-10

A drop of water with a diameter of 0.12 in. is surrounded by still air at 78^0F. The air has water vapor of partial pressure 0.01037 atm. Determine the time necessary for the drop to evaporate at a pressure of 1 atm.

Solution: The rate of evaporation of the drop is:

$$\frac{-dm_A}{dt} = 4\pi r^2 N_{Ar} = \frac{4\pi DPr_S}{RT} \ln\left(\frac{P - P_{Ab}}{P - P_{As}}\right) \qquad (1)$$

where $-dm_A/dt$ is the instantaneous evaporation rate in lbmole/hr. Also:

$$m_A = \frac{4\pi r_s^3 \rho_A}{3M_A} \quad \text{and} \quad r_S = \left(\frac{3M_A m_A}{4\pi\rho_A}\right)^{1/3}$$

Substituting for r_S and m_A in equation (1) and integrating yields:

$$t = \frac{\rho_A r_s^2 RT}{(2M_A DP)\ln\left[\frac{P - P_{Ab}}{P - P_{As}}\right]} \tag{2}$$

When evaporation occurs the temperature of the drop falls to the wet bulb temperature, T_w, a steady state value. For this situation $T_w = 60^0F$ which corresponds to a vapor pressure of $p_{As} = 0.01742$ atm. A diffusivity of water vapor in air of 1.00 ft^2/hr will be employed. Also:

ρ_A = density of water = 62.4 lb/ft^3

M_A = molecular weight of water = 18 lb/lbmole

R = 0.7302 atm-ft^3/lbmole-R

$T = \text{average temperature} = \frac{78 + 60}{2} = 69^0F$

= 529 R

Substituting in equation (2) yields:

$$t = \frac{(62.4)(0.06/12)^2(0.7302)(529)}{2(18)(1.00)(1)\ln\left[\frac{1 - 0.01037}{1 - 0.01742}\right]}$$

= 2.3 hr

• PROBLEM 17-11

A slab of thickness 0.006m contains a solute A. The concentration gradient of A is given in table (1), where z is the distance from the exposed surface.

table (1)

z(m)	concentration (kgmol A/m^3)	location, n
0.0	2.0×10^{-3}	1(exposed)
0.0015	2.5×10^{-3}	2
0.003	3.0×10^{-3}	3
0.0045	3.5×10^{-3}	4
0.006	4.0×10^{-3}	5(insulated)

The diffusivity of the solute in the slab is $D = 2.5 \times 10^{-9}$ m^2/sec. The top of the slab is brought in contact with a fluid of concentration $c_A = 6.2 \times 10^{-3}$ kg-mol A/m^3. The distribution coefficient is K =

$c_A/c_n = 1.40$. The bottom of the slab is insulated and unsteady state diffusion occurs only in the z direction. Determine the concentration profile when 2250 sec. have elapsed. Assume the convective mass transfer coefficient, k_c, is infinite, and employ $\Delta z = 0.0015$ m with $M = 2.0$.

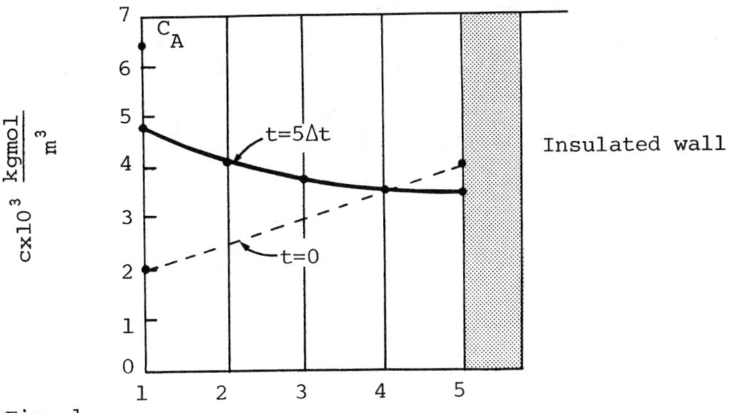

Fig. 1

Solution: A numerical solution will be used to solve this problem. Using the equation given below the time increment, Δt, can be obtained.

$$M = \frac{(\Delta x)^2}{D\Delta t} \tag{1}$$

$$\Delta t = \frac{(\Delta x)^2}{DM} = \frac{(0.0015)^2}{(2.5\times 10^{-9})(2.0)}$$

$$= 450 \text{ sec.}$$

Thus, 2250/450 = 5 time increments are required.

For the top of the slab (n=1), the concentration for the first time increment is

$$_1c_A = \frac{c_A/K + {_0c_1}}{2} = {_1c_1} \qquad (n=1) \tag{2}$$

where $_0c_1$ is the initial concentration at $n = 1$. For the other time increments:

$$c_1 = \frac{c_A}{K} \qquad (n=1) \tag{3}$$

For all time increments

$$n = 2,3,4 \quad \text{with } M = 2$$

$$_{t+\Delta t}c_n = \frac{_tc_{n-1} + {_tc_{n+1}}}{2} \qquad (n=2,3,4) \tag{4}$$

At the insulated face (n=5); substitute f = n = 5 in the equation below:

$$_{t+\Delta t}c_f = \frac{1}{M}\left[(M-2)\,{}_tc_f + 2\,{}_tc_{f-1}\right] \qquad (5)$$

$$= \frac{(2-2)\,{}_tc_5 + 2\,{}_tc_4}{2} = {}_tc_4 \quad (n=5)$$

For Δt or $t + \Delta t$, which is the first time increment, the concentration for n = 1 is given by equation (2):

$$_{t+\Delta t}c_1 = \frac{c_A/K + {}_0c_1}{2} = \frac{6.2 \times 10^{-3}/1.40 + 2.0 \times 10^{-3}}{2}$$

$$= 3.2 \times 10^{-3}$$

Employing equation (4) for n = 2,3, and 4:

$$_{t+\Delta t}c_2 = \frac{{}_tc_{n-1} + {}_tc_{n+1}}{2} = \frac{{}_tc_1 + {}_tc_3}{2} = \frac{3.2 \times 10^{-3} + 3.0 \times 10^{-3}}{2}$$

$$= 3.1 \times 10^{-3}$$

$$_{t+\Delta t}c_3 = \frac{{}_tc_2 + {}_tc_4}{2} = \frac{2.5 \times 10^{-3} + 3.5 \times 10^{-3}}{2} = 3.0 \times 10^{-3}$$

$$_{t+\Delta t}c_4 = \frac{{}_tc_3 + {}_tc_5}{2} = \frac{3.0 \times 10^{-3} + 4.0 \times 10^{-3}}{2} = 3.5 \times 10^{-3}$$

Equation (5) will be used for n = 5:

$$_{t+\Delta t}c_5 = {}_tc_4 = 3.5 \times 10^{-3}$$

With $2\Delta t$ equation (3) will be employed for n = 1, equation (4) for n = 2,3,4, and equation (5) for n = 5.

$$_{t+2\Delta t}c_1 = \frac{c_A}{K} = \frac{6.2 \times 10^{-3}}{1.40} = 4.4 \times 10^{-3} \text{ (remains constant in future)}$$

$$_{t+2\Delta t}c_2 = \frac{{}_{t+\Delta t}c_1 + {}_{t+\Delta t}c_3}{2} = \frac{4.4 \times 10^{-3} + 3.0 \times 10^{-3}}{2}$$

$$= 3.7 \times 10^{-3}$$

$$_{t+2\Delta t}c_3 = \frac{{}_{t+\Delta t}c_2 + {}_{t+\Delta t}c_4}{2} = \frac{3.1 \times 10^{-3} + 3.5 \times 10^{-3}}{2}$$

$$= 3.3 \times 10^{-3}$$

$$_{t+2\Delta t}c_4 = \frac{{}_{t+\Delta t}c_3 + {}_{t+\Delta t}c_5}{2} = \frac{3.0 \times 10^{-3} + 3.5 \times 10^{-3}}{2}$$

$$= 3.25 \times 10^{-3}$$

$${}_{t+2\Delta t}c_5 = {}_{t+\Delta t}c_4 = 3.5 \times 10^{-3}$$

Using $3\Delta t$:

$${}_{t+3\Delta t}c_1 = 4.4 \times 10^{-3}$$

$${}_{t+3\Delta t}c_2 = \frac{4.4 \times 10^{-3} + 3.3 \times 10^{-3}}{2} = 3.85 \times 10^{-3}$$

$${}_{t+3\Delta t}c_3 = \frac{3.7 \times 10^{-3} + 3.25 \times 10^{-3}}{2} = 3.475 \times 10^{-3}$$

$${}_{t+3\Delta t}c_4 = \frac{3.3 \times 10^{-3} + 3.5 \times 10^{-3}}{2} = 3.4 \times 10^{-3}$$

$${}_{t+3\Delta t}c_5 = 3.25 \times 10^{-3}$$

Using $4\Delta t$:

$${}_{t+4\Delta t}c_1 = 4.4 \times 10^{-3}$$

$${}_{t+4\Delta t}c_2 = \frac{4.4 \times 10^{-3} + 3.475 \times 10^{-3}}{2} = 3.938 \times 10^{-3}$$

$${}_{t+4\Delta t}c_3 = \frac{3.85 \times 10^{-3} + 3.4 \times 10^{-3}}{2} = 3.625 \times 10^{-3}$$

$${}_{t+4\Delta t}c_4 = \frac{3.475 \times 10^{-3} + 3.25 \times 10^{-3}}{2} = 3.363 \times 10^{-3}$$

$${}_{t+4\Delta t}c_5 = 3.4 \times 10^{-3}$$

Using $5\Delta t$:

$${}_{t+5\Delta t}c_1 = 4.4 \times 10^{-3}$$

$${}_{t+5\Delta t}c_2 = \frac{4.4 \times 10^{-3} + 3.625 \times 10^{-3}}{2} = 4.013 \times 10^{-3}$$

$${}_{t+5\Delta t}c_3 = \frac{3.938 \times 10^{-3} + 3.363 \times 10^{-3}}{2} = 3.651 \times 10^{-3}$$

$${}_{t+5\Delta t}c_4 = \frac{3.625 \times 10^{-3} + 3.4 \times 10^{-3}}{2} = 3.513 \times 10^{-3}$$

$${}_{t+5\Delta t}c_5 = 3.363 \times 10^{-3}$$

The concentration profile after 2250 sec. is shown in Figure 1.

A clay slab initially has a uniform distribution of 14 mass percent water. The slab is 2.2 in. thick and the edges are covered to prevent mass transfer. Air at 19°C and low humidity is blown over the large faces of the clay. The drying rate is determined by the effectiveness of moisture diffusion in the slab. Calculate the effective diffusivity when the average moisture content drops to 9 mass percent in 360 min. Use an equilibrium moisture content of 1.9 mass percent at these conditions.

Using the same initial moisture content, calculate the average amount of moisture in the following objects constructed of identical clay and dried for 24 hrs. in similar conditions:

1) A solid sphere with a diameter of 5 in.

2) A solid cylinder with both ends covered to prevent mass transfer. The length is 12 in. and the diameter is 10 in.

3) The cylinder of part 2) with only one end covered to stop mass transfer.

4) The cylinder of part 2) with both ends uncovered.

5) A slab of thickness 6 in. and width 10 in. which has both ends covered.

6) A slab of dimensions 6 × 8 × 10 in.

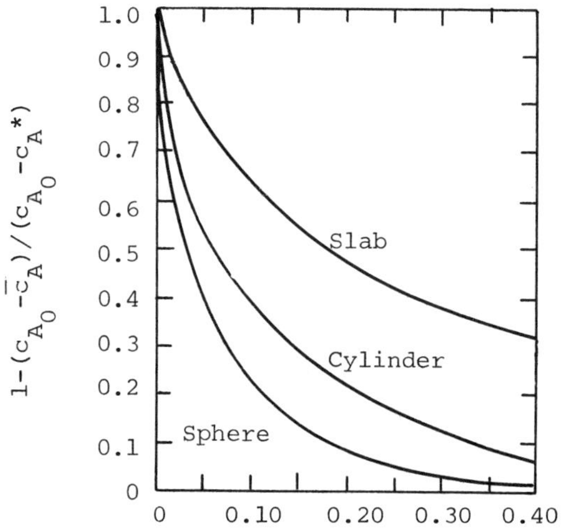

Fig. 1

$\frac{Dt}{r_s^2}$ or $\frac{Dt}{a^2}$

UNSTEADY-STATE MOLECULAR DIFFUSION IN A SPHERE, SLAB, OR CYLINDER.

Solution: Figure 1 will be employed to solve this problem.

The ordinate of this figure is the fraction of solute unremoved, E. Instead of concentrations, the mass of moisture per unit mass of dry solid, X_A, will be employed. Therefore:

$$E = \frac{\bar{c}_A - c_A^*}{c_{A_0} - c_A^*} = \frac{\bar{X}_A - X_A^*}{X_{A_0} - X_A^*} \qquad (1)$$

and

$$X_{A_0} = 14/86 = 0.1628 \text{ lb moisture/lb dry solid}$$

$$\bar{X}_A = 9/91 = 0.0989 \text{ lb moisture/lb dry solid}$$

$$X_A^* = 1.9/98.1 = 0.0194 \text{ lb moisture/lb dry solid}$$

Substituting in equation (1) yields:

$$E = \frac{0.0989 - 0.0194}{0.1628 - 0.0194} = 0.55$$

Figure 1 then provides:

$$\frac{Dt}{a^2} = 0.16$$

for a slab of thickness 2a.

Solving for the diffusivity:

$$D = \frac{0.16a^2}{t} = \frac{0.16\left(\frac{1.1}{12}\right)^2}{360} \; (60)$$

$$D = 2.2 \times 10^{-4} \text{ ft}^2\text{/hr}$$

1) For a sphere:

$$\frac{Dt}{r_s^2} = \frac{(2.2 \times 10^{-4})(24)}{(2.5/12)^2} = 0.122$$

where r_s is the radius of the sphere. From Figure 1:

$$E = 0.19$$

Solving equation (1) for $\bar{X}_A$, the average moisture content:

$$\bar{X}_A = X_A^* + E(X_{A_0} - X_A^*)$$

$$= 0.0194 + 0.19(0.1628 - 0.0194)$$

$$= 0.0466$$

and

$$\frac{0.0466}{1.0466}(100) = 4.45$$ mass percent final average moisture content

2) For a cylinder with both ends covered:

$$\frac{Dt}{a^2} = \frac{5.28 \times 10^{-3}}{(5/12)^2} = 0.030$$

where a is the radius of the cylinder.

Figure 1 gives:

$$E_{cyl} = 0.71$$

and

$$\bar{X}_A = 0.0194 + 0.71(0.1434)$$

$$= 0.1212$$

The final average moisture content is:

$$\frac{0.1212}{1.1212}(100) = 10.8$$ mass percent

3) For a cylinder with one end uncovered:

$$\frac{Dt}{a^2} = \frac{(5.28 \times 10^{-3})}{(5/12)^2} = 0.030$$

$$\frac{Dt}{(2a_1)^2} = \frac{5.28 \times 10^{-3}}{\left[2\left(\frac{6}{12}\right)\right]^2} = 0.00528$$

where a is the radius of the cylinder and $2a_1$ is the length of the cylinder. Note that the 2 is needed only when the opposite face is still covered. Figure 1 yields:

$E_{cyl} = 0.71$ from cylinder curve

$E_{2a_1} = 0.93$ from slab curve

The total fraction of water unremoved is:

$$E = E_{cyl}E_{2a_1} = (0.71)(0.93)$$

$$= 0.660$$

Therefore,

$$\bar{X}_A = 0.0194 + 0.660(0.1434)$$

$$= 0.1140$$

and the final average moisture content is:

$$\frac{0.1140}{1.1140}(100) = 10.2$$ mass percent

4) For a cylinder with two ends uncovered:

$$\frac{Dt}{a^2} = \frac{5.28 \times 10^{-3}}{(5/12)^2} = 0.030$$

$$\frac{Dt}{a_1{}^2} = \frac{5.28 \times 10^{-3}}{(6/12)^2} = 0.021$$

Figure 1 gives:

$$E_{cyl} = 0.71$$

$E_{a_1} = 0.83$ from slab curve

and

$$E = E_{cyl}E_{a_1} = (0.71)(0.83) = 0.589$$

Therefore:

$$\overline{X}_A = 0.0194 + 0.589(0.1434)$$
$$= 0.1039$$

The final average moisture content is:

$$\frac{0.1039}{1.1039}(100) = 9.41 \text{ mass percent}$$

5) For a slab with 2 ends covered:

$$\frac{Dt}{a_1{}^2} = \frac{5.28 \times 10^{-3}}{(3/12)^2} = 0.084$$

$$\frac{Dt}{a_2{}^2} = \frac{5.28 \times 10^{-3}}{(5/12)^2} = 0.030$$

where the thickness is $2a_1$ and the width is $2a_2$.

Figure 1 yields:

$$E_{a_1} = 0.64$$

$$E_{a_2} = 0.80$$

Therefore:

$$E = E_{a_1}E_{a_2} = (0.64)(0.80) = 0.512$$

and

$$\overline{X}_A = 0.0194 + 0.512(0.1434)$$
$$= 0.0928.$$

The final average moisture content is:

$$\frac{0.0928}{1.0928}(100) = 8.49 \text{ mass percent}$$

6) For a slab with all faces uncovered:

$$\frac{Dt}{a_1^2} = \frac{5.28 \times 10^{-3}}{(3/12)^2} = 0.084$$

$$\frac{Dt}{a_2^2} = \frac{5.28 \times 10^{-3}}{(4/12)^2} = 0.048$$

$$\frac{Dt}{a_3^2} = \frac{5.28 \times 10^{-3}}{(5/12)^2} = 0.030$$

where $2a_1$ is the thickness, $2a_2$ is the width, and $2a_3$ is the length. Figure 1 gives:

$$E_{a_1} = 0.64$$

$$E_{a_2} = 0.77$$

$$E_{a_3} = 0.80$$

Therefore

$$E = E_{a_1} E_{a_2} E_{a_3} = (0.64)(0.77)(0.80)$$

$$= 0.394$$

and

$$\overline{X}_A = 0.0194 + 0.394(0.1434)$$

$$= 0.0759.$$

The final average moisture content is:

$$\frac{0.0759}{1.0759}(100) = 7.05 \text{ mass percent}$$

DIFFUSION WITH CHEMICAL REACTION

• PROBLEM 17-13

Consider the reaction $2A \rightarrow A_2$ in a catalytic reactor. The reaction is not instantaneous but the rate at which A disappears at the catalytic surface is proportional to the concentration of A at that surface. Find the molar flux of A.

$$N_{AZ} = k_1'' c_A = ck_1'' x_A$$

where k_1'' is a rate constant.

Solution: It is clear from the figure that A has to diffuse through the gas film which surrounds each catalyst particle

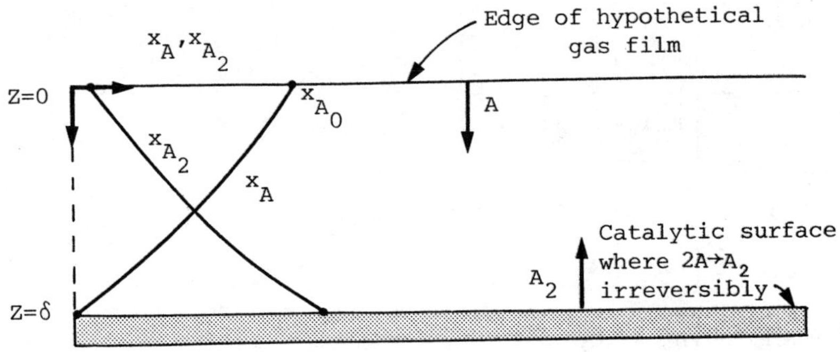

IDEALIZED PICTURE OF THE DIFFUSION PROBLEM NEAR A CATALYST PARTICLE.

before it reaches the catalyst surface. For every two moles of A moving in the positive Z-direction, there is one mole of A_2 moving in the negative Z-direction.

Therefore, at steady state

$$N_{A_2Z} = -\frac{1}{2} N_{AZ}$$

For two component system, it is given that

$$N_{AZ} = -cD_{AB}\frac{\partial X_A}{\partial Z} + x_A(N_{AZ} + N_{BZ})$$

Substitute $N_{BZ} = N_{A_2Z} = -\frac{1}{2} N_{AZ}$

Then,

$$N_{AZ} = -cD_{AA_2}\frac{dX_A}{dZ} + x_A(N_{AZ} - \frac{1}{2} N_{AZ})$$

$$N_{AZ} - \frac{1}{2} N_{AZ}x_A = -cD_{AA_2}\frac{dX_A}{dZ}$$

$$N_{AZ}(1 - \frac{1}{2} x_A) = -cD_{AA_2}\frac{dX_A}{dZ}$$

$$N_{AZ} = \frac{-cD_{AA_2}}{(1 - \frac{1}{2}x_A)}\frac{dX_A}{dZ}$$

By performing a mass balance on species A over a thin slab of the gas film of thickness ΔZ,

$$\frac{dN_{AZ}}{dZ} = 0$$

But $$N_{AZ} = \frac{-cD_{AA_2}}{(1 - \frac{1}{2}x_A)}\frac{dX_A}{dZ}$$

Therefore

$$\frac{d}{dZ}\left[\left(\frac{-cD_{AA_2}}{(1-\frac{1}{2}x_A)}\right)\frac{dX_A}{dZ}\right] = 0$$

$$\frac{d}{dZ}\left(\frac{1}{(1-\frac{1}{2}x_A)}\,\frac{dX_A}{dZ}\right) = 0$$

Integrating once

$$\frac{1}{(1-\frac{1}{2}x_A)}\,\frac{dx_A}{dZ} = c_1$$

Integrating again

$$-2\ln(1-\frac{1}{2}\,x_A) = c_1 z + c_2$$

The integration constants are evaluated by using the boundary conditions.

B.C. (1) At $Z = 0$, $x_A = x_{A_0}$

B.C. (2) At $Z = \delta$, $x_A = \dfrac{N_{AZ}}{cK_1''}$

Substituting the first boundary condition

$$-2\ln(1-\frac{1}{2}\,x_{A_0}) = c_2$$

Substituting the second boundary condition

$$-2\ln\left(1-\frac{1}{2}\,\frac{N_{AZ}}{cK_1''}\right) = c_1\delta + c_2$$

But

$$c_2 = -2\ln(1-\frac{1}{2}\,x_{A_0})$$

Hence

$$-2\ln\left(1-\frac{1}{2}\,\frac{N_{AZ}}{cK_1''}\right) = c_1\delta - 2\ln(1-\frac{1}{2}\,x_{A_0})$$

$$c_1\delta = -2\left\{\ln\left(1-\frac{1}{2}\,\frac{N_{AZ}}{cK_1''}\right)\right\} + 2\ln(1-\frac{1}{2}\,x_{A_0})$$

$$c_1 = \frac{-2}{\delta}\left[\ln\left(\frac{1-\frac{1}{2}\left(\frac{N_{AZ}}{cK_1''}\right)}{1-\frac{1}{2}\,x_{A_0}}\right)\right]$$

Substitute the values of c_1 and c_2 in

$$-2\ln(1-\frac{1}{2}\,x_A) = c_1 z + c_2$$

$$-2\ln\left(1-\frac{1}{2}x_A\right) = \frac{-2}{\delta}\left[\ln\frac{1-\frac{1}{2}\frac{N_{AZ}}{cK_1''}}{1-\frac{1}{2}x_{A_0}}\right]Z \;-2\ln\left(1-\frac{1}{2}x_{A_0}\right)$$

$$\ln\left(1-\frac{1}{2}x_A\right) = \ln\left(\frac{1-\frac{1}{2}\frac{N_{AZ}}{cK_1''}}{1-\frac{1}{2}x_{A_0}}\right)^{z/\delta} + \ln\left(1-\frac{1}{2}x_{A_0}\right)$$

$$\ln\left(1-\frac{1}{2}x_A\right) = \ln\left(\frac{1-\frac{1}{2}\frac{N_{AZ}}{cK_1''}}{1-\frac{1}{2}x_{A_0}}\right)^{z/\delta}\cdot\left(1-\frac{1}{2}x_{A_0}\right)$$

$$\left(1-\frac{1}{2}x_A\right) = \left(\frac{1-\frac{1}{2}\frac{N_{AZ}}{cK_1''}}{1-\frac{1}{2}x_{A_0}}\right)^{z/\delta}\cdot\left(1-\frac{1}{2}x_{A_0}\right)$$

$$\left(1-\frac{1}{2}x_A\right) = \left(1-\frac{1}{2}\frac{N_{AZ}}{cK_1''}\right)^{z/\delta}\left(1-\frac{1}{2}x_{A_0}\right)^{1-z/\delta}$$

which is also equal to

$$\ln\left(1-\frac{1}{2}x_A\right) = \frac{z}{\delta}\ln\left(1-\frac{1}{2}\frac{N_{AZ}}{cK_1''}\right) + (1-z/\delta)\ln\left(1-\frac{1}{2}x_{A_0}\right)$$

Differentiating on both sides to find $\frac{dx_A}{dz}$

$$\left(\frac{1}{1-\frac{1}{2}x_A}\right) - \frac{1}{2}\,dx_A = \left[\frac{1}{\delta}\ln\left(1-\frac{1}{2}\frac{N_{AZ}}{cK_1''}\right) - \frac{1}{\delta}\ln\left(1-\frac{1}{2}x_{A_0}\right)\right]dz$$

$$\left(\frac{1}{1-\frac{1}{2}x_A}\right) - \frac{\delta}{2}\frac{dx_A}{dz} = \ln\left(\frac{1-\frac{1}{2}\frac{N_{AZ}}{cK_1''}}{1-\frac{1}{2}x_{A_0}}\right)$$

$$\frac{dx}{dz} = \frac{-2\left(1-\frac{1}{2}x_A\right)}{\delta}\ln\left(\frac{1-\frac{1}{2}\frac{N_{AZ}}{cK_1''}}{1-\frac{1}{2}x_{A_0}}\right)$$

But

$$N_{AZ} = \frac{-c\,D_{AA_2}}{1-\frac{1}{2}x_A}\frac{dx_A}{dz}$$

Substituting the value of $\frac{dx_A}{dz}$

$$N_{AZ} = \frac{-c\ D_{AA_2}}{(1 - \frac{1}{2}x_A)} \quad \frac{-2(1 - \frac{1}{2}x_A)}{\delta} \quad \ln\left[\frac{1 - \frac{1}{2}\frac{N_{AZ}}{cK_1''}}{1 - \frac{1}{2}x_{A0}}\right]$$

$$N_{AZ} = \frac{2c\ D_{AA_2}}{\delta} \ln\left[\frac{1 - \frac{1}{2}\frac{N_{AZ}}{cK_1''}}{1 - \frac{1}{2}x_{A0}}\right]$$

• PROBLEM 17-14

If the exhaust gases contain 0.22% of NO by weight, calculate

(i) The minimum value of δ allowable if a NO reduction rate of 0.032 lb/ft^2hr is to be achieved.

(ii) The corresponding minimum allowable value of K.

Use the following data.

The gases are at:

$T = 1200^0F$

$P = 18.2$ psia

Average molecular wt. of the gases = 30.0

Effective rate constant K = 760 ft/hr

Diffusion coefficient $D_{1m} = 4.0\ ft^2/hr$

Solution: It is known that

$$j_1 = \frac{\rho m}{\frac{1}{K} + \frac{\delta}{D}}$$

$$\frac{1}{K} + \frac{\delta}{D} = \frac{\rho m}{j_1}$$

$$\frac{\delta}{D} = \frac{\rho m}{j_1} - \frac{1}{K}$$

$$\delta = D\left[\frac{\rho m}{j_1} - \frac{1}{K}\right]$$

But

$$\rho = p/\frac{RT}{M}$$

Therefore

$$\delta = D\left(\frac{\rho m}{\frac{RT}{M} \cdot j_1} - \frac{1}{K}\right)$$

Substituting the given values and calculating

$$\delta = 4.0\left[\frac{18.2 \times 144 \times 30}{1545 \times 1660} \times \frac{0.0022}{0.032} - \frac{1}{760}\right]$$

$$\delta = 0.0032 \text{ ft}$$

$$K = \frac{\rho D}{\delta} = \frac{\rho m}{RT}\frac{D}{\delta}$$

$$= \frac{18.2 \times 144}{1545 \times 1660} \times 30 \times \frac{4.0}{0.0026}$$

$$= 47 \text{ lb/ft}^2\text{hr}$$

• PROBLEM 17-15

Explain the mass transfer process using flat plate model, if 0.3 mole fraction aqueous Hydrochloric acid is pumped into a fractured limestone formation. Assume that the flat plate model is applicable and the velocity in the fractures is 2 ft/sec.

Solution: If the reaction is of the form

$$aA + bB \rightarrow \text{products}$$

the effects of stoichiometry of chemical reaction is included, then the Sherwood number is given by:

$$N_{Sh} = \left(1 + \frac{aC_B}{bC_{AS}}\right) 0.664\, N_{Sc_A}^{1/3}\, R_{e_L}^{1/2}$$

But the actual reaction is

$$CaCO_3 + 2HCl \rightarrow CaCl_2 + H_2O + CO_2$$

Therefore

$$a = 1; \quad b = 2$$

The molar density is related to mole fraction by

$$C_i = x_i C$$

Substituting this into

$$1 + a\frac{C_B}{bC_{As}}$$

we get,

$$1 + \frac{ax_B C}{bx_{As} C}$$

$$1 + \frac{1 \cdot x_B}{2x_{As}}$$

Again,

$$x_B = 0.3$$

and

$$x_{As} = 4 \times 10^{-6} = \text{Solubility of } CaCO_3 \text{ in water}$$

Substituting the numerical values

$$1 + \frac{0.3}{2 \times 4 \times 10^{-6}} = 3.75 \times 10^4$$

The concentration gradient is small due to less solubility. The driving force is still less when the chemical reaction takes place but the gradient is larger since it is applied over a shorter distance.

• PROBLEM 17-16

An instantaneous reaction $C + O_2 \rightarrow CO_2$ occurs at the surface of the particle when the spherical coal particle of 0.05 in. diameter burns in air at 2500 °F. If the coal consists of pure carbon of 85 lbm/ft^3 density and the mass diffusivity of oxygen in the mixture is 8.0 ft^2/hr, then calculate the time required to burn the coal, completely.

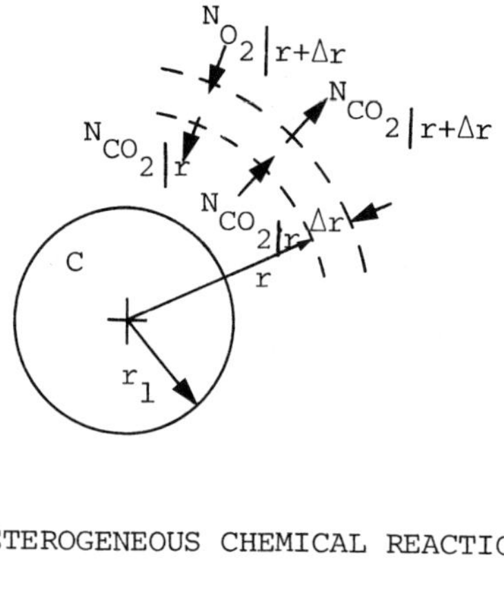

DIFFUSION WITH HETEROGENEOUS CHEMICAL REACTION.

Solution: It is clear from the figure that O_2 has to diffuse through a stagnant film before it reaches the coal particle surface. For one mole of O_2 moving in one direction, there is one mole of CO_2 moving in the other direction. Therefore, at steady state

$$N_{CO_2} = -N_{O_2}$$

For three component system, it is given that

$$N_{O_2} = -\rho D_{O_2\text{-mix}} \, d\frac{\omega_{O_2}}{dr} + \omega_{O_2}(N_{O_2} + N_{CO_2} + N_{N_2})$$

Since there is no motion of Nitrogen $N_{N_2} = 0$.

Also it is known $N_{CO_2} = -N_{O_2}$

Substituting these values in the N_{O_2} equation. That is

$$N_{O_2} = -\rho \, D_{O_2\text{-mix}} \frac{d\omega_{O_2}}{dr}$$

By performing a mass balance on species O_2 over a thin slab of the particle surface

$$\frac{d}{dr}(r^2 N_{O_2}) = 0$$

$$r^2 N_{O_2} = C$$

Let the constant C be $r_1{}^2 N_{O_2}\big|_1$. Therefore,

$$r^2 N_{O_2} = r_1{}^2 N_{O_2}\big|_1 = -r^2 \rho D_{O_2\text{-mix}} \frac{d\omega_{O_2}}{dr}$$

The boundary conditions are

$$r = r_1 \quad ; \quad \omega_{O_2} = 0$$

$$r = \infty \quad ; \quad \omega_{O_2} = 0.21$$

Hence,

$$r_1{}^2 N_{O_2}\big|_1 = -r^2 \rho \, D_{O_2\text{-mix}} \frac{d\omega_{O_2}}{dr}$$

$$r_1{}^2 N_{O_2}\big|_1 \frac{r^2}{dr} = -\rho \, D_{O_2\text{-mix}} \, d\omega_{O_2}$$

Integrating, using the given limits. That is

$$r_1{}^2 N_{O_2}\big|_1 \int_{r_1}^{r\to\infty} \frac{r^2}{dr} = -\rho D_{O_2\text{-mix}} \int_0^{0.21} d\omega_{O_2}$$

$$r_1 N_{O_2}\big|_1 = -\rho D_{O_2\text{-mix}}(0.21)$$

But $$\rho = \frac{P}{RT}$$

Assuming standard conditions, R is calculated

$$R = \frac{PV}{\eta T} = \frac{1 \times 359}{1 \times 492} = 0.73 \ \frac{\text{atm-ft}^3}{\text{lbmolmix}^0\text{R}}$$

$$\rho = \frac{P}{RT} = \frac{1}{0.73 \times (2960)} = 4.62 \times 10^{-4} \ \text{lbmol/ft}^3$$

The rate of burning of coal particle is given by

$$N_{O_2} = \frac{-\rho D_{O_2\text{-mix}}(0.21)}{r_1}$$

$$= \frac{-(4.62 \times 10^{-4}) \times 8 \times 0.21}{0.05/12}$$

$$N_{O_2} = -0.186 \ \text{lbmolO}_2\text{/hr-ft}^2$$

$$N_C = +0.186 \ \text{lbmolC/hr-ft}^2$$

$$\bar{\rho}_c = \frac{\rho_c}{M_c} = \frac{85 \ \text{lbm/ft}^3}{12 \ \text{lbm/lbmol}} = 7.08 \ \text{lbmol/ft}^3$$

Hence,

$$\dot{m} = 4\pi r_1{}^2 N_C$$

$$= 4 \times \pi \times \left(\frac{0.05}{12}\right)^2 \text{ft}^2 \times 0.186 \ \text{lbmol/hr-ft}^2$$

$$= 4.058 \times 10^{-5} \ \text{lbmol/hr}$$

$$\text{Total moles of carbon} = \frac{\text{Volume} \times \text{density}}{\text{Molecular weight}}$$

$$= \frac{\frac{4}{3}\pi \left(\frac{0.025}{12}\right)^3 \times 85}{12.01}$$

$$= 2.68 \times 10^{-7} \ \text{lbmoles}$$

Therefore time required to burn the coal completely

$$= \frac{2.68 \times 10^{-7}}{4.058 \times 10^{-5}} = 6.6 \times 10^{-3} \ \text{hr}$$

$$= 23.77 \ \text{sec}$$

• PROBLEM 17-17

A reaction takes place in presence of air in a fluidized coal reactor at 1200°K, with the limiting factor being the diffusion of oxygen counter to that of carbon monoxide formed at the particle surface. The spherical coal particle of diameter 2.0×10^{-4}m consists of pure carbon of density 1.35×10^3 kg/m³. The diffusivity of oxygen in the mixture is 1.5×10^{-4} m²/s. Assuming steady state process, calculate the time required to reduce the diameter of carbon to 8×10^{-5}m.

Solution: The mass transfer of oxygen to the surface of the coal particle is given by

$$W_{O_2} = 4\pi c\, D_{O_2\text{-air}} R \ln\left(\frac{1}{1.21}\right)$$

From the reaction $2C + O_2 \rightarrow 2CO$, it is clear that for every mole of oxygen, two atoms of carbon will disappear, therefore

$$W_c = 2W_{O_2}$$

The disappearance of the coal can also be defined in terms of the molar density of the coal and the change in its volume with time by

$$W_c = \frac{\rho_{coal}}{M_{coal}} \frac{dv}{dt}$$

$$W_c = \frac{\rho_c}{M_c} 4\pi R^2 \frac{dR}{dt}$$

But $$W_c = 2W_{O_2}$$

Therefore,

$$2W_{O_2} = \frac{\rho_c}{M_c} 4\pi R^2 \frac{dR}{dt}$$

Again $$W_{O_2} = 4\pi c\, D_{O_2\text{-air}} R \ln\left(\frac{1}{1.21}\right)$$

Hence,

$$(2)4\pi c\, D_{O_2\text{-air}} R \ln\left(\frac{1}{1.21}\right) = \frac{\rho_c}{M_c} 4\pi R^2 \frac{dR}{dt}$$

Cancelling the common terms and rearranging, gives

$$dt = \frac{\rho_c}{2M_c c D_{O_2\text{-air}} \ln\left(\frac{1}{1.21}\right)} R\, dR$$

The limits of integration are:

$$t = 0 \quad ; \quad R = R_{initial}$$

$$t = t_{final}; \quad R = R_{final}$$

Integrating the above equation using these limits

$$\int_{t=0}^{t_{final}} dt = \frac{\rho_c}{2M_c cD_{O_2\text{-air}} \ln\left(\frac{1}{1.21}\right)} \int_{R_{initial}}^{R_{final}} RdR$$

$$t_{final} = \frac{\rho_c}{2M_c cD_{O_2\text{-air}} \ln\left(\frac{1}{1.21}\right)} \left.\frac{R^2}{2}\right|_{R_{initial}}^{R_{final}}$$

$$t_{final} = \frac{\rho_c}{2M_c cD_{O_2\text{-air}} \ln\left(\frac{1}{1.21}\right)} \left(\frac{R^2_{final}}{2} - \frac{R^2_{initial}}{2}\right)$$

Given data is as follows:

ρ_c = Density of coal = 1.35×10^3 kg/m^3

= 1.35×10^6 g/m^3

M_c = 12 g/mol

$R_{initial}$ = 1.0×10^{-4}m = Initial radius of the coal particle

R_{final} = 4×10^{-5}m = Final radius of the coal particle

$P = 1.013 \times 10^5$ Pa

$R = 8.314$ Pa•m^3/mol•k

$T = 1200^0$K

$D_{O_2\text{-air}} = 1.5 \times 10^{-4}$m^2/s

$$t_{final} = \frac{\rho_c}{4M_c cD_{O_2\text{-air}} \ln\left(\frac{1}{1.21}\right)} \left(R^2_{final} - R^2_{initial}\right)$$

But

$$c = \frac{P}{RT}$$

Hence,

$$t_{final} = \frac{\rho_c RT}{4M_c PD_{O_2\text{-air}} \ln\left(\frac{1}{1.21}\right)} \left(R^2_{final} - R^2_{initial}\right)$$

Substituting the values and calculating

$$t_{final} = \frac{(1.35\times10^6)(8.314)(1200)((4\times10^{-5})^2-(1.0\times10^{-4})^2)}{4\times12\times(1.013\times10^5)\times(1.5\times10^{-4})\times\ln(1/1.21)}$$

$$t_{final} = \frac{-113.14}{-139.03}$$

$$t_{final} = 0.81 \text{ sec.}$$

• PROBLEM 17-18

Carbon dioxide undergoes the following irreversible reaction with sodium carbonate

$$CO_2 + Na_2CO_3 + H_2O \xrightarrow{k_1} 2NaHCO_3$$

As shown in the figure, CO_2 dissolves in a solution of sodium carbonate in water and diffuses into the bulk phase. As it diffuses, it undergoes the above irreversible reaction. Develop an expression for the concentration profile of CO_2 in the liquid phase and its average concentration.

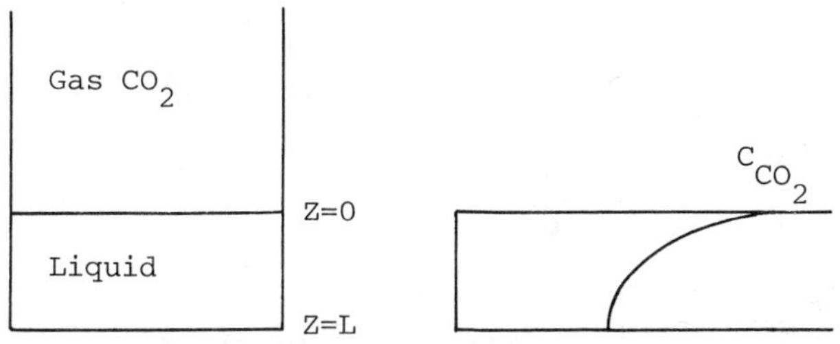

Solution: The material balance over an infinitesimal cross-section of thickness Δz, gives

$$N_{CO_2}\Big|_z s - N_{CO_2}\Big|_{z+\Delta z} s - k_1 c_{CO_2} s\Delta z = 0$$

Dividing throughout by $s\Delta z$, we get

$$\frac{N_{CO_2}\Big|_z - N_{CO_2}\Big|_{z+\Delta z}}{\Delta z} - k_1 c_{CO_2} = 0$$

Taking the limit as $\Delta z \to 0$ yields,

$$\frac{dN_{CO_2}}{dz} + k_1 c_{CO_2} = 0$$

Assuming CO_2 and $NaHCO_3$ concentrations are small,

$$N_{CO_2} = -D \frac{dc_{CO_2}}{dz}$$

$$-D \frac{d^2 c_{CO_2}}{dz^2} + k_1 c_{CO_2} = 0$$

Solving this differential equation with the boundary conditions

$$\text{at } z = 0 \qquad c_{CO_2} = c^*_{CO_2}$$

$$\text{at } z = L \qquad N_{CO_2} = 0$$

where $c^*_{CO_2}$ is the solubility of CO_2 in water, we get

$$\frac{c_{CO_2}}{c^*_{CO_2}} = \frac{\cosh\left[\sqrt{k_1 L^2/D}\left(1 - \frac{z}{L}\right)\right]}{\cosh\sqrt{k_1 L^2/D}}$$

The average concentration of $CO_2 = c^{av}_{CO_2}$

$$= \frac{\int_0^L (c_{CO_2}/c^*_{CO_2})dz}{\int_0^L dz}$$

$$= \frac{\int_0^L \left(\cosh\left[\sqrt{k_1 L^2/D}(1-z/L)\right]/\cosh\sqrt{k_1 L^2/D}\right)dz}{\int_0^L dz}$$

$$= \frac{1}{\sqrt{k_1 L^2/D}} \tanh\sqrt{k_1 L^2/D}$$

• PROBLEM 17-19

Gas A diffuses into a catalyst pellet through its pores and is converted to B through chemical reaction on the catalyst surface. Develop an expression for the concentration profile for species A within the catalyst pellet.

Solution: Let c_{As} be the concentration of A at the catalyst

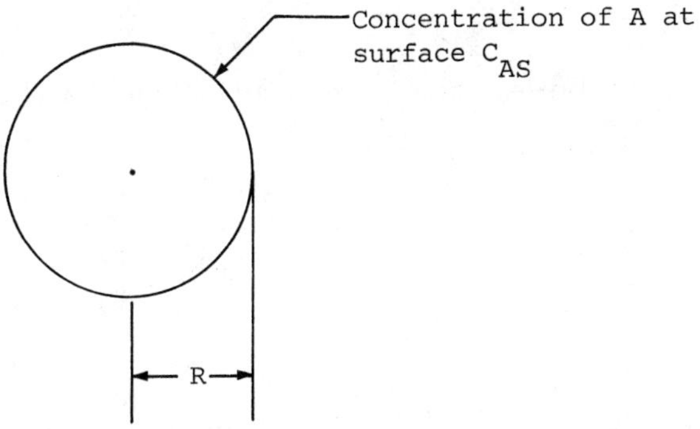

surface.

Making a mass balance on a spherical shell of thickness Δr, gives:

$$\frac{d}{dr}(r^2 N_{Ar}) = r^2 R_A$$

where R_A is the rate of reaction in lb moles/ft^3. But $N_{Ar} = -D_A \frac{dc_A}{dr}$ where D_A is the effective diffusivity of A in the porous catalyst medium.

$$\text{therefore} \quad -D_A \frac{d}{dr}\left(r^2 \frac{dc_A}{dr}\right) = r^2 R_A$$

But $R_A = -k_1' a c_A$ where k_1' is the reaction rate constant and a is surface area per unit pellet volume.

$$\text{therefore} \quad \frac{-D_A}{r^2}\left[r^2 \frac{d^2 c_A}{dr^2} + 2r \frac{dc_A}{dr}\right] = -k_1' a c_A$$

or

$$\frac{d^2 c_A}{dr^2} + \frac{2}{r}\frac{dc_A}{dr} = \frac{+k_1' a c_A}{D_A}$$

The general solution for the above equation is

$$\frac{c_A}{c_{As}} = \frac{c_1}{r}\cosh\left(\sqrt{\frac{k_1' a}{D_A}}\right) r + \frac{c_2}{r}\sinh\left(\sqrt{\frac{k_1' a}{D_A}}\right) r$$

The boundary conditions are

$$\text{at } r = 0, \quad \frac{dc_A}{dr} = 0$$

$$r = R, \quad c_A = c_{As}$$

Using the above boundary conditions yields the concentration profile as

$$\frac{c_A}{c_{As}} = \left(\frac{R}{r}\right) \frac{\sinh(r\sqrt{k_1'a/D_A})}{\sinh(R\sqrt{k_1'a/D_A})}$$

CHAPTER 18

MASS TRANSFER COEFFICIENTS, INTERFACIAL COMPOSITION AND SIMULTANEOUS MOMENTUM, HEAT AND MASS TRANSFER

MASS TRANSFER RATES AND COMPOSITION

• PROBLEM 18-1

A gas containing NH_3 is flowing in a tube absorber the inside of which is wetted with water at a rate of 5000 Kg/hr. The absorber consists of 55 tubes and the average temperature (T) is 30°C. Each tube is of 60mm I.D. and 5m long. Calculate the mass transfer coefficient β for ammonia in the liquid phase.

Solution: The wetted perimeter = 55 × 0.06 × π = 10.36m. Then

$$\Gamma = \frac{5000}{10.36} = 482.6 \text{ Kg/m·hr}$$

$$n = 2.885 \text{ Kg/m·hr}$$

$$N_{Re} = \frac{4\Gamma}{n} = \frac{4 \times 482.6}{2.885} = 670$$

For low concentrations,

$$\theta = 40.41 \times 10^{-6}\text{m (water)}$$

$$\delta = 0.00597 \text{ Kg/m·hr}$$

$$m = \frac{M_A}{M} = \frac{17}{18} = 0.945$$

$$N_{Sh} = \frac{mn}{\delta} = \frac{0.945 \times 2.885}{0.00597} = 457$$

The mass transfer coefficient for ammonia in liquid phase is given by

$$\beta = \frac{\delta}{\theta} c\, N_{Re}^{A} N_{Sh}^{B} \left(\frac{\theta}{L}\right)^{D} \qquad (\text{For } N_{Re} < 2100)$$

$$\beta = \frac{\delta}{(\theta)^{-D+1}} c\, N_{Re}^{A} N_{Sh}^{B} L^{-D}$$

where

$$A = 0.33, \quad B = 0.5, \quad C = 0.725, \quad D = 0.5$$

Substituting the numerical values and calculating

$$\beta = \frac{0.00597 \times 0.725 \times 670^{0.33} \times 457^{0.5} \times 5^{-0.5}}{(40.41 \times 10^{-6})^{0.5}}$$

$$= \frac{0.00597 \times 0.725 \times 8.56 \times 21.37 \times 0.447}{(6.356 \times 10^{-3})}$$

$$\beta = 55.67 \text{ Kg/m}^2 \cdot \text{hr}$$

• PROBLEM 18-2

> The value of the coefficient K_G in a wetted wall column for the absorption of SO_2 in air by water at $70\,^0F$ is 0.068 lbmol/hr•sqft•atm. The resistance of gas and liquid films are equal in the absorption of SO_2. The diffusivities of SO_2 and NH_3 at $49\,^0F$ are 0.115 and 0.168 cm^2/sec, respectively. Find the value of K_G for the absorption of NH_3 in water at $49\,^0F$ when all other conditions are the same.

Solution: The relation between the overall and individual coefficients is given as

$$\frac{1}{K_G} = \frac{1}{k_G} + \frac{1}{Hk_L} = \frac{1}{0.068} = 14.7$$

It is given that the gas and liquid film resistances are equal, therefore,

$$k_G = Hk_L = \frac{1}{7.35} = 0.136$$

Lets assume that k_L for both solutes is the same. The values of H for SO_2 at 70^0 and for NH_3 at 49^0 are roughly 0.14 and 2.5, respectively.

Then,

$$Hk_L \text{ for } NH_3 = 0.136 \times \frac{2.5}{0.14} = 2.428$$

The ratio of diffusion rates for SO_3 and NH_3 in the gas film is given by

$$\frac{N_{SO_2}}{N_{NH_3}} = \frac{\left[k_G(P_G - P_i)\right]_{SO_2}}{\left[k_G(P_G - P_i)\right]_{NH_3}} = \frac{\left[\frac{DP}{RTX} \cdot \frac{P_G - P_i}{P_B}\right]_{SO_2}}{\left[\frac{DP}{RTX} \quad \frac{P_G - P_i}{P_B}\right]_{NH_3}}$$

Lets assume the mean pressure of the inerts are same for both cases, since the mixture is very dilute. Therefore,

$$(k_G)_{NH_3} = (k_G)_{SO_2} \frac{(D/XT)_{NH_3}}{(D/xT)_{SO_2}}$$

The ratio of effective gas film thicknesses is given by

$$\frac{(d/x)_{SO_2}}{(d/x)_{NH_3}} = \frac{\left[0.023(du\rho/\mu)^{0.83}\,(\mu/\rho D)^{0.44}\right]_{SO_2}}{\left[0.023(du\rho/\mu)^{0.83}\,(\mu/\rho D)^{0.44}\right]_{NH_3}}$$

and

$$\frac{x_{NH_3}}{x_{SO_2}} = \left(\frac{D_{NH_3}}{D_{SO_2}}\right)^{0.44}$$

It is clear that

$$(K_G)_{NH_3} = (K_G)_{SO_2} \frac{(D/T)_{NH_3}}{(D/T)_{SO_2}} \frac{x_{SO_2}}{x_{NH_3}}$$

or

$$(K_G)_{NH_3} = (K_G)_{SO_2} \left(\frac{D_{NH_3}}{D_{SO_2}}\right)^{0.56} \frac{T_{SO_2}}{T_{NH_3}}$$

Substituting the numerical values and calculating $(K_G)_{NH_3}$,

$$(K_G)_{NH_3} = 0.136 \times \left(\frac{0.168}{0.115}\right)^{0.56} \times \left(\frac{529}{509}\right)$$

$$(K_G)_{NH_3} = 0.174$$

$$\frac{1}{K_G} = \frac{1}{(K_G)_{NH_3}} + \frac{1}{(HK_L)_{NH_3}}$$

$$= \frac{1}{0.174} + \frac{1}{2.428}$$

$$\frac{1}{K_G} = 6.158$$

$$K_G = 0.16 \text{ lbmol/hr·sqft·atm.}$$

Water is flowing down a vertical wall 1.5m long at a rate of 0.08 Kg/sec per unit width. Calculate the rate of absorption of CO_2 into the water film at 25°C and 1 atm. pressure.

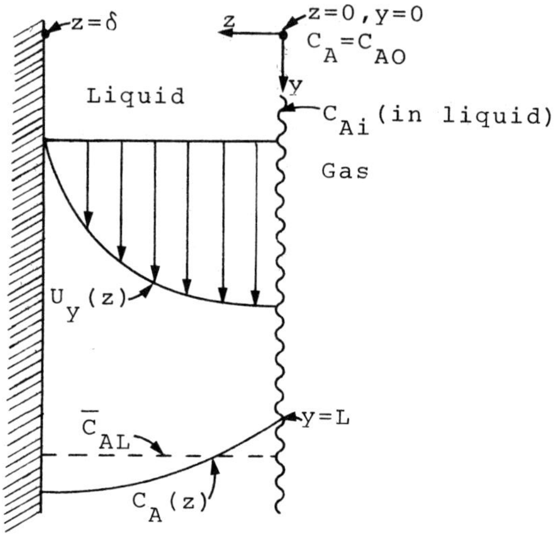

Fig. 1 FALLING LIQUID FILM

Solution: The necessary data is taken from standard tables and is as follows:

The solubility of CO_2 in water at the required condition = 0.0336 Kmol/m³ soln

Diffusion coefficient = $D_{AB} = 1.96 \times 10^{-9} m^2/sec$

Solution density = ρ = 998 Kg/m³

Viscosity = $\mu = 8.94 \times 10^{-4}$ Kg/m·sec

and

$$\Gamma = \rho \delta v_y = 0.05 \text{ Kg/m·sec}$$

The film thickness in terms of mass flow rate is

$$\delta = \sqrt[3]{\frac{3\mu\Gamma}{\rho^2 g}}$$

where

δ = film thickness

Γ = mass flow rate = $(\rho \delta v_y)$

Therefore,

$$\delta = \left[\frac{3 \times 8.94 \times 10^{-4} \times 0.05}{(998)^2 \times 9.8}\right]^{1/3} = 2.415 \times 10^{-4} \text{m}$$

The Reynolds number for this system is given by:

$$N_{Re} = \frac{4\Gamma}{\mu} = \frac{4 \times 0.05}{8.94 \times 10^{-4}} = 223$$

The mass transfer coefficient is given by

$$K_{L,av} = \left(\frac{6D_{AB}\Gamma}{\pi\rho\delta L}\right)^{1/2}$$

$$= \left[\frac{6 \times 1.96 \times 10^{-9} \times 0.05}{\pi \times 998 \times 2.415 \times 10^{-4} \times 1.5}\right]^{1/2}$$

$$K_{L,av} = 2.275 \times 10^{-5} \text{ Kmol/m}^2\cdot\text{sec}$$

$$\Gamma = \rho\delta v_y$$

$$v_y = \frac{\Gamma}{\rho\delta}$$

$$v_y = \frac{0.05}{998 \times 2.415 \times 10^{-4}}$$

$$= 0.207 \text{ m/sec}$$

The rate of absorption is given by

$$N_{Aav} = \frac{v_y\delta}{L}(C_{A,L} - C_{Ao}) = K_{L,av}(C_{Ai} - C_A)_M$$

But $$(C_{Ai} - C_A)_M = \frac{(C_{Ai} - C_{Ao}) - (C_{Ai} - C_{A,L})}{\text{Ln}\left[(C_{Ai} - C_{Ao})/C_{Ai} - C_{AL}\right]}$$

Therefore,

$$\frac{v_y\delta}{L}(C_{A,L} - C_{Ao}) = K_{L,av}\left\{\frac{(C_{Ai} - C_{Ao}) - (C_{Ai} - C_{AL})}{\text{Ln}\left(\frac{C_{Ai} - C_{Ao}}{C_{Ai} - C_{AL}}\right)}\right\}$$

The conc at the top of the wall

$$= C_{A,i} - C_A = C_{A,i} - C_{Ao} = C_{Ai} = 0.0336 \text{ Kmol/m}^3$$

The concentration at the bottom of the wall

$$= C_{A,i} - C_{A,L} = 0.0336 - C_{A,L} \text{ Kmol/m}^3.$$

Substituting the numerical values into the equation

$$\frac{v_y\delta}{L}(C_{AL} - C_{Ao}) = K_{Lav}\left\{\frac{(C_{Ai} - C_{Ao}) - (C_{Ai} - C_{AL})}{Ln\left\{\frac{C_{AL} - C_{Ao}}{C_{Ai} - C_{AL}}\right\}}\right\}$$

$$\frac{0.207 \times 2.415 \times 10^{-4}}{1.5} C_{A,L} = 2.275 \times 10^{-5} \times$$

$$\left\{\frac{0.0336 - (0.0336 - C_{A,L})}{Ln\left(\frac{0.0336}{0.0336 - C_{A,L}}\right)}\right\}$$

$$0.3327 \times 10^{-4} C_{A,L} = \frac{2.275 \times 10^{-5}\ C_{A,L}}{Ln\left(\frac{0.0336}{0.0336 - C_{A,L}}\right)}$$

$$Ln\left(\frac{0.0336}{0.0336 - C_{A,L}}\right) = \frac{2.275 \times 10^{-5}}{0.3327 \times 10^{-4}} = 0.6837$$

$$\frac{0.0336}{0.0336 - C_{A,L}} = 1.981$$

$$0.0336 = 1.981(0.0336 - C_{A,L})$$

$$C_{A,L} = \frac{0.0329}{1.981} = 0.0166\ \text{Kmol/m}^3$$

The rate of absorption:

$$= \delta v_y(C_{A,L} - C_{Ao})$$

$$= 0.207(2.415 \times 10^{-4})(0.0166 - 0)$$

$$= 8.29 \times 10^{-7}\ \text{Kmol/sec per unit width.}$$

• PROBLEM 18-4

A drop of water is allowed to fall into dry still air at 1 atm pressure with a velocity of 225 cm sec^{-1}. The drop is spherical in shape with 0.03cm diameter. The temperature of air is 145°F and the surface temperature of the drop is 70°F. The vapor pressure of water at 70°F is 0.0247 atm.

Assuming pseudo steady state process, calculate the net rate of evaporation from the water drop.

Solution: The solubility of air in water is negligible. Hence

$$W_B = 0 \quad \text{(suffix B represents water)}$$

Rate of evaporation is given by

$$W_A = k_x A(x_{Ao} - x_{A\infty}) + x_{Ao}(W_A + W_B)$$

But $$W_B = 0$$

Therefore $$W_A = k_x A(x_{Ao} - x_{A\infty}) + x_{Ao} W_A$$

$$W_A = \frac{k_x A(x_{Ao} - x_{A\infty})}{(1 - x_{Ao})}$$

where

k_x = mass transfer coefficient

A = surface area of water drop

It is known that

$$k_x = \frac{C_f D_{AB}}{D}\left[2 + 0.6\left(\frac{DV_\infty \rho_f}{\mu_f}\right)^{1/2}\left(\frac{\mu}{\rho D_{AB}}\right)_f^{1/3}\right]$$

where the subscript f denotes that the properties are evaluated at the film temperature (T_f).

$$T_f = \frac{T_o + T_\infty}{2} = \frac{70 + 150}{2} = 110^\circ F$$

The properties of air at this film temperature:

$$\rho_f = 1.08 \times 10^{-3} \text{ g}\cdot\text{cm}^{-3}$$

$$\mu_f = 1.93 \times 10^{-4} \text{ g}\cdot\text{cm}^{-1}\text{sec}^{-1}$$

$$D_{ABf} = 0.284 \text{ cm}^2/\text{sec}$$

$$C_f = \frac{1.08 \times 10^{-3}}{29} = 3.72 \times 10^{-5} \text{ g}\cdot\text{mole/cm}^3$$

Substituting the numerical values and calculating

$$k_x = C_f D_{AB}\left[2 + 0.6\left(\frac{Dv_\infty \rho_f}{\mu_f}\right)^{1/2}\left(\frac{\mu}{\rho D_{AB}}\right)_f^{1/3}\right]$$

$$k_x = \frac{(3.72\times10^{-5})(0.284)}{0.03}\left[2 + 0.6\left(\frac{0.03\times225\times1.08\times10^{-3}}{1.93 \times 10^{-4}}\right)^{1/2}\right.$$

$$\times \left(\frac{1.93 \times 10^{-4}}{0.284 \times 128 \times 10^{-3}}\right)^{1/3}\Bigg]$$

$$K_x = \frac{3.72 \times 10^{-5} \times 0.284}{0.03}\left[2 + 0.6(37.77)^{1/2}(0.629)^{1/3}\right]$$

$$= 1.85 \times 10^{-3} \text{gmol/sec}\cdot\text{cm}^2$$

Substituting the value of K_x in the expression to find the rate of evaporation:

$$W_A = k_x \cdot \pi D^2 \quad \frac{x_{Ao} - x_{A\infty}}{1 - x_{Ao}}$$

It is given that

$$x_{Ao} = 0.0247$$

$$x_{A\infty} = 0$$

In order to evaluate x_{Ao} complete insolubility of air in water, ideal gas behavior and equilibrium at the interface are assumed.

Therefore, the rate of evaporation:

$$W_A = (1.85 \times 10^{-3})(\pi \times 0.03 \times 0.03) \times \left(\frac{0.0247 - 0}{1 - 0.0247}\right)$$

$$W_A = 1.324 \times 10^{-7} \text{ gmole/sec.}$$

• PROBLEM 18-5

The tank shown in Figure 1 has concentrated sulfuric acid moving at a low velocity through the bottom. The air above is at 1 atm. and 19°C with a relative humidity of 49%. If there is negligible resistance to diffusion in the liquid phase and the air above is stationary, determine the amount of water vapor present in the air that is absorbed by the acid.

Solution: The amount of water vapor absorbed by the sulfuric acid is equivalent to the mass of water vapor that diffuses through the air in the tank. The mass rate of diffusion of water vapor (A) is G_A:

$$G_A = \frac{d}{s} A\Delta\pi_A \qquad (1)$$

where d is the dynamic diffusivity of A(0.0563 kg/m·hr), and $\Delta\pi_A$ is the driving modulus.

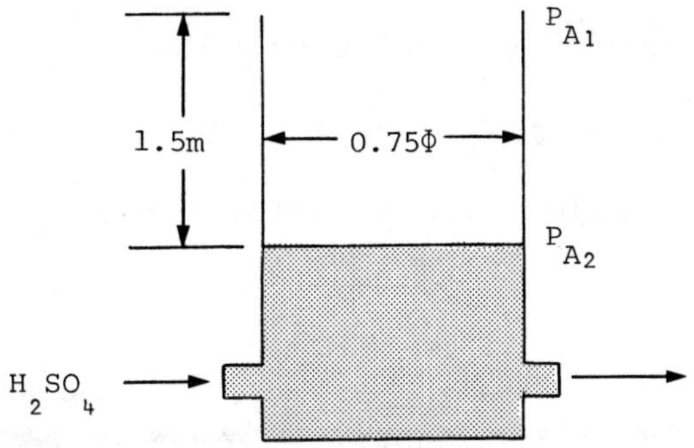

Fig. 1

$$s = \text{diffusion length} = 1.5\text{m}$$

$$A = \frac{(0.75)^2\pi}{4} = 0.442\text{m}^2$$

$$\Delta\pi_A = \frac{\Delta p_A}{\bar{p}_s} \qquad (2)$$

where $\bar{p}_s$ is the average partial pressure of the sulfuric acid.

The following is known:

$$\phi = \text{relative humidity} = \frac{p_{A_1}}{p_A} = 0.49$$

where p_A is the vapor pressure of water at 19°C. p_A = 17.4 mm Hg. Therefore $p_{A_1} = (0.49)(17.4) = 8.53$mm Hg.

p_{A_2} = the vapor pressure of water at the interface. This is considered negligible due to the absorption of water vapor by the acid.

Atmospheric pressure = 736mm Hg at 19°C.

Therefore:

$$p_{s_1} = p - p_{A_1} = 736 - 8.53 = 727.5\text{mm Hg}$$

and

$$p_{s_2} = p - p_{A_2} = 736 - 0 = 736\text{mm Hg}$$

$$\bar{p}_s = \frac{p_{s_1} + p_{s_2}}{2} = 731.8\text{mm Hg}$$

Substituting in equation (2):

$$\Delta\pi_A = \frac{p_{A_1} - p_{A_2}}{\bar{p}_s} = \frac{8.53 - 0}{731.8} = 0.01166$$

Substitution in equation (1) yields:

$$G_A = \frac{0.0563}{1.5}(0.442)(0.01166)$$

$$= 1.93 \times 10^{-4} \text{ Kg/hr}$$

which is the absorption rate of water vapor by the sulfuric acid.

• PROBLEM 18-6

A flue gas stream containing SO_2 is to be stripped by absorbing the SO_2 in a dilute basic solution strip. The process occurs in a tower of diameter D = 4000mm which contains wooden strips shown in Figure 1, where a = 40mm, b = 15mm, and c = 100mm. The gas flowrate is 15500 Kg/hr at 20 °C and 1 atm. Determine the mass transfer coefficient for the gas phase.

Fig. 1

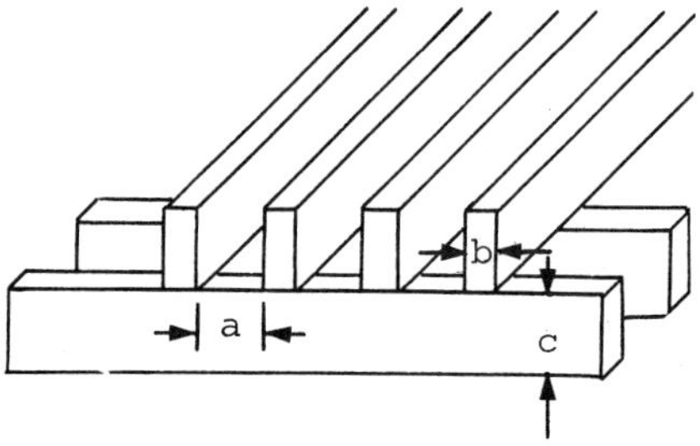

Solution: The mass transfer coefficient for the gas, k_g is given by:

$$k_g = Sh \frac{\delta}{d_e} \tag{1}$$

where $d_e \simeq 2a = 2(0.040) = 0.080$m and δ is the dynamic diffusivity of SO_2 through the flue gases. The value for SO_2 diffusion through air will be employed.

$$\delta = 0.128 \text{ kg/m·hr} \quad \text{at } 25^\circ C.$$

The Sherwood number is given by:

$$Sh = 0.04\psi Re^{0.8} Sc^{0.33} \tag{2}$$

The value of the dynamic diffusivity at 20°C is determined by:

$$\delta_{20} = \delta_{25}\left(\frac{T_{20}}{T_{25}}\right)^{1/2} = 0.128\left(\frac{293}{298}\right)^{1/2}$$

$$= 0.1269$$

From tables of the physical properties of air, the viscosity is:

$$\mu = 0.067 \text{ kg/m·hr} \quad \text{at } 20^\circ\text{C}$$

The Reynolds number can be obtained from equation (3) and the Schmidt number from equation (4):

$$Re = \frac{g_e d_e}{\mu} \tag{3}$$

$$Sc = \frac{m\mu}{\delta} \tag{4}$$

where

$$g_e = \frac{G}{\varepsilon A} \tag{5}$$

and

$$G = \text{gas flowrate} = 15500 \text{ kg/hr}$$

$$A = \frac{\pi D^2}{4} = \frac{\pi(4)^2}{4} = 12.6 \text{ m}^2$$

$$\varepsilon = \frac{a}{a+b} = \frac{40}{40+15} = 0.73$$

Substituting in equation (5) gives:

$$g_e = \frac{15500}{(0.73)(12.6)} = 1685 \text{ kg/m}^2\text{·hr}$$

which is the mass flowrate per unit area.

Also:

$$m = \frac{M_{SO_2}}{M_{Air}} = \frac{64}{29} = 2.21$$

Substituting into equations (3) and (4) yields:

$$Re = \frac{(1685)(0.080)}{0.067} = 2012$$

$$Sc = \frac{(2.21)(0.067)}{0.1269} = 1.17$$

Also:

$$\psi = 0.875 + \left(\frac{4\sqrt{Re}\ b^2}{d_e c}\right)^{0.4}$$

$$= 0.875 + \left(\frac{4\sqrt{2012}\ (0.015)^2}{(0.080)(0.10)}\right)^{0.4} = 2.786$$

Solving for the Sherwood number using equation (2):

$$Sh = 0.04(2.786)(2012)^{0.8}(1.17)^{0.33}$$

$$= 51.6$$

The mass transfer coefficient is given by equation (1):

$$k_g = (51.6)\ \frac{(0.1269)}{0.080}$$

$$= 81.9\ kg/m^2 \cdot hr$$

• PROBLEM 18-7

H_2S is absorbed from air at 2 atm. total pressure and 30^0C in a packed bed. The gas-phase mass transfer coefficient, k_c', has been predicted to be 11 lb•mole/hr-ft^2•(lb•mole/ft^3). At a given location, the mole fraction of H_2S in the liquid at the interface is 2×10^{-5} and the partial pressure of H_2S in the air is 0.05 atm. Given Henry's law constant as

$$600\ \frac{atm}{mole\ fraction}$$

calculate the local rate of absorption of H_2S in the water.

Solution: The local mass transfer rate $= \frac{k_c'}{\phi}\ (C_A - C_{Ai}^*)$ where ϕ = correction factor = 1.

C_A = concentration of H_2S in the gas phase $= \frac{0.05}{2} \times C_T$

C_T = total conc of the gas phase $= \frac{p}{RT} = \frac{2}{82.05 \times 303}$

$$= 8.04\times 10^{-5}\ gmmoles/cm^3$$

$$= 8.04 \times 10^{-5} \times \frac{2.204}{1000} \times (30.48)^3$$

$$= 5.021 \times 10^{-3}\ lb\ moles/ft^3$$

$$C_A = \frac{0.05}{2} \times 5.021 \times 10^{-3} = 1.255 \times 10^{-4}\ lb\ moles/ft^3$$

mole fraction of H_2S in the liquid at the interface = 2×10^{-5}

$\therefore$ conc. of H_2S at the interface $= C_A^* = (H \times x_A)\ \frac{1}{RT}$

$$= 600\times 2\times 10^{-5} \times \frac{1}{82.05\times 303}$$

$$= 4.8267\times 10^{-7}\ \frac{gm\ moles}{ft^3}$$

$$= 3.01237\times 10^{-5}\ \frac{lb\ moles}{ft^3}$$

The local rate of absorption $= \frac{k'_c}{\phi} (C_A - C_A^*)$

$= 11.0 \times (5.021 \times 10^{-3} - 3.01237 \times 10^{-5})$

$= 0.0549$ lb•moles/hr•ft^2

INTERFACIAL COMPOSITION

• PROBLEM 18-8

A pure gas flows through a packed column and absorbs substance A from a liquid. The inlet and exit mole fraction of A in the liquid are 0.005 and 0.002, respectively. It is known that $H_L = 1$ ft. and $H_G = 2$ ft. Also $(L/G)_{actual} = 5.0$. Determine x_{AS} at the location where $y_A = 0.01$. At equilibrium y = 10x.

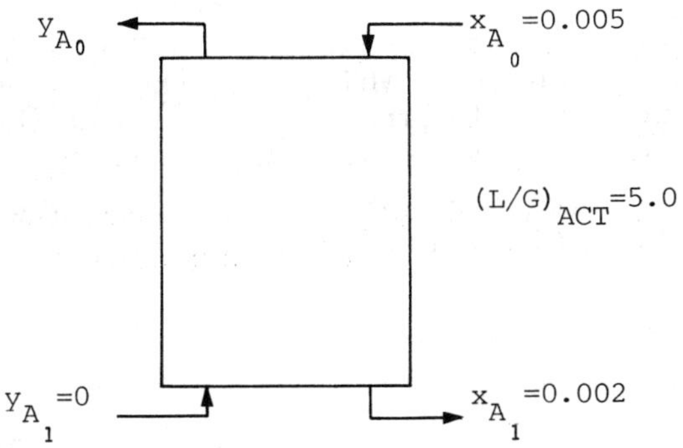

Fig. 1

Solution: A graphical approach will be employed for solving this problem. It is known that the following equations are valid:

$$\frac{-k_x}{k_y} = \frac{y_A - y_{AS}}{x_A - x_{AS}} \tag{1}$$

where

$$\frac{k_x}{k_y} = \frac{H_G}{H_L}\frac{L}{G} = \frac{2}{1}(5.0) = 10 \tag{2}$$

Equation (1) defines a straight line of slope -10 which intersects the equilibrium curve, $y_{AS} - 10x_{AS}$ (3) at the point (x_{AS}, y_{AS}).

The value of x_{AS} is obtained by finding the intersection of lines (1) and (3). To plot equation (3), the point (0,0) and the slope of 10 is sufficient. To plot equation (1), a point on the line is required.

To solve the problem, the equilibrium line and the operating line are plotted.

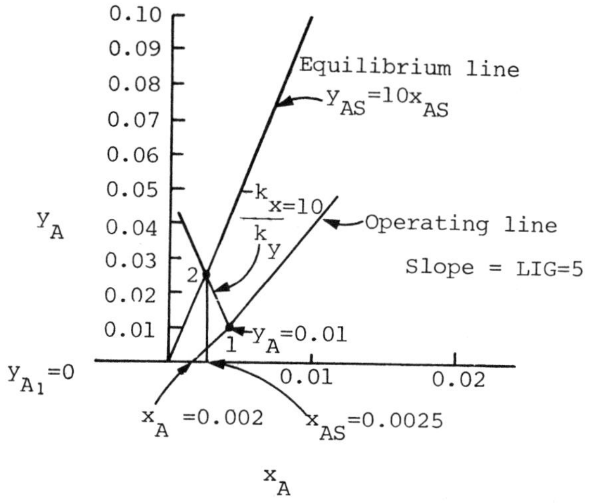

The operating line has a slope of $L/G = 5.0$ and passes through the point (0.002,0), which are the values at the bottom of the tower (see Figure 1). Now find the point on the operating line where $y_A = 0.01$ and plot equation (1) through this point with a slope of -10. The abscissa of the point where equation (1) intersects the equilibrium line is $x_{AS} = 0.0025$.

• PROBLEM 18-9

A toluene-xylene mixture is fractionated in a bubble-cap column. Approximate the gas-phase mass transfer coefficient. The following pertinent data are given:

G_g = vapor flowrate = 23.6 kgmole/hr

G_ℓ = liquid flowrate = 17.84 kgmole/hr

M_g = average molecular weight of gas = 93.2 kg/kgmole

M_ℓ = average molecular weight of liquid = 93.8 kg/kgmole

ρ_ℓ = average density of liquid = 778.4 kg/m^3

t = average column temperature = 113.0 °C

p = average column pressure = 1 atm.

$\omega_{\ell 0}$ = liquid velocity at entrance to column

= 0.10 m/sec

D = inside diameter of column = 680 mm

W = weir height above the plate = 65 mm

H = weir height above the slots = 30 mm

d = outside cap diameter = 85 mm

n = number of caps on the column diameter perpendicular to the direction of liquid flow on the plate = 5

h = liquid head over the weir = 8.1 mm

Solution: The following equation will be employed to solve for the mass transfer coefficient, k_g.

$$St = \frac{k_g V_p}{G_g} = 1.7Sc^{-2/3}\left(\frac{\omega_\ell}{\omega_{\ell 0}}\right)^{1/4} \tag{1}$$

where

St = Stanton number

Sc = Schmidt number

and ω_ℓ = liquid velocity.

Also:

$$V_p = AH = \frac{\pi(0.680)^2}{4}(0.030)$$
$$= 0.0109m^3$$

The Schmidt number is given by,

$$Sc = \frac{\mu_g}{M_g \delta} \tag{2}$$

where

μ_g = gas viscosity = 0.0332 kg/m·hr

and

δ = dynamic diffusivity = 5.18×10^{-4}kgmole/m·hr

Substituting in equation (2):

$$Sc = \frac{0.0332}{(93.2)(5.18 \times 10^{-4})} = 0.688$$

The liquid velocity ω_ℓ can be obtained from,

$$\omega_\ell = \frac{V_\ell}{A_p} \tag{3}$$

where:

$$V_\ell = \frac{G_\ell M_\ell}{\rho_\ell} = \frac{(17.84)(93.8)}{(778.4)(3600)} = 5.97 \times 10^{-4} m^3/sec$$

and

$$A_p = (D - nd)(W + h)$$

$$= (0.680 - 5(0.085))(0.065 + 0.0081)$$

$$= 0.0186 m^2$$

Substituting in equation (3) yields:

$$\omega_\ell = \frac{5.97 \times 10^{-4}}{0.0186} = 0.032 \text{ m/sec}$$

Solving equation (1) for k_g gives:

$$k_g = \left(\frac{G_g}{V_p}\right) 1.7 Sc^{-2/3} \left(\frac{\omega_\ell}{\omega_{\ell 0}}\right)^{1/4}$$

$$= \left(\frac{23.6}{0.0109}\right) 1.7(0.688)^{-2/3} \left(\frac{0.032}{0.10}\right)^{1/4}$$

$$= 3552 \text{ kgmole/m}^3 \cdot \text{hr}$$

• PROBLEM 18-10

Calculate the saturation concentration of oxygen in water exposed to dry air at 1 atm. and 25°C. Given the Henry's constant for dissolved oxygen in water at 25°C

$$= 4.12 \times 10^9 \frac{\text{Pa}}{\text{mole of } O_2/\text{total mole of solution}}$$

Solution: Basis: 1 liter of the solution.

Assuming that the properties of solution remains the same as that of pure water due to the low concentration of dissolved oxygen in it,

$$\text{no. of moles present} = 1 \times \rho_{H_2O} \times \frac{1}{MW_{H_2O}} = \frac{1 \times 1000}{18}$$

$$= 5.556 \times 10 \text{ kgm moles}$$

$$= 55.56 \text{ gm}\cdot\text{moles}$$

The mole fraction of O_2 in air $= x_{O_2} = 0.21$

∴ The partial pressure of O_2 in air $= p_{O_2} = P_T \times x_{O_2}$

$$= (1.013 \times 10^5) \times 0.21 = 2.1273 \times 10^4 \text{Pa}$$

∴ Saturation concentration of dissolved oxygen in water

$$= c_{O_2} = \frac{p_{O_2}}{H}$$

where

$$H = \text{Henry's law constant} = 4.12 \times 10^9 \ \frac{\text{Pa}}{\text{mole } O_2/\text{mole of solution}}$$

$$c_{O_2} = \frac{2.1273 \times 10^4}{4.12 \times 10^9} = 5.1633 \times 10^{-6} \ \frac{\text{mole of } O_2}{\text{mole of solution}}$$

or since no. of moles in 1 liter of solution = 5.556×10^4

$$c_{O_2} = 5.1633 \times 10^{-6} \times 55.56 = 2.869 \times 10^{-4} \ \frac{\text{moles of } O_2}{\text{liter of solution}}$$

$$= 2.869 \times 10^{-4} \times 0.032 = 9.1792 \times 10^{-6} \ \frac{\text{kg of } O_2}{\text{liter of solution}}$$

or

$$c_{O_2} = 9.1792 \times 10^{-3} \ \frac{\text{kg of } O_2}{\text{m}^3 \text{of solution}}$$

$$= 9.1792 \ \frac{\text{mg of } O_2}{\text{liter of solution}}$$

• PROBLEM 18-11

Water is used as the absorbent in an ammonia absorber that is functioning at 1 atm. and 21°C. At one location in the apparatus, the bulk gas has 10.1% ammonia by volume. The ammonia has a partial pressure of 2.27 kpa at the interface. The liquid contains 1.2% NH_3 by weight. An ammonia absorption rate of 0.051 kgmole/hr•m^2 exists at this location.

(I) Determine $X, Y, Y_i, X_i, X^*, Y^*, K_y, K_x, k_y$, and k_x.

(II) Calculate the percentage of the resistance to mass transfer in each phase.

(III) Check the validity of the following equation:

$$\frac{1}{K_y} = \frac{1}{k_y} + \frac{H'}{k_x}$$

Solution: Using the given data:

$$X = \frac{1/M_{NH_3}}{\dfrac{\text{weight \% absorbent}}{M_{\text{absorbent}}}} = \frac{1/17}{\dfrac{98.8}{18}} = 0.0107$$

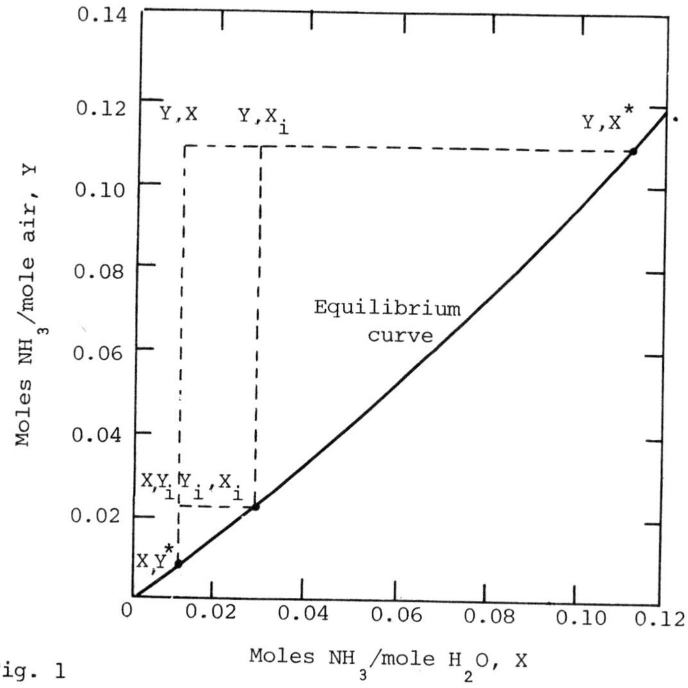

Fig. 1

EQUILIBRIUM CURVE

$$Y = \frac{\text{Volume \% } NH_3 \text{ in gas phase}}{100 - \text{Volume \% } NH_3} = \frac{10.1}{89.9} = 0.112$$

$$Y_i = \frac{p_{NH_3}}{P_t - p_{NH_3}} = \frac{2.27}{101 - 2.27} = 0.0230$$

Using the equilibrium curve given in Figure 1:

$X_i = 0.03$

$X^* = 0.113$

$Y^* = 0.007$

Also:

$K_y(Y - Y^*) = NH_3$ absorption rate $= 0.051$ (1)

$K_x(X^* - X) = 0.051$ (2)

$k_y(Y - Y_i) = 0.051$ (3)

$k_x(X_i - X) = 0.051$ (4)

Substitution in equations (1) through (4) yields:

$K_y = 0.486$ kgmole/hr·m^2·mole-ratio driving force

$K_x = 0.499$ kgmole/hr·m^2·mole-ratio driving force

k_y = 0.573 kgmole/hr·m²·mole-ratio driving force

k_x = 2.64 kgmole/hr·m²·mole-ratio driving force

(II) The percentage of the gas phase resistance in the total mass transfer resistance using the gas-phase and the liquid phase concentrations is given by equations (5) and (6), respectively.

$$100 \frac{[Y - Y_i]}{[Y - Y^*]} = 100 \frac{[0.112 - 0.0230]}{[0.112 - 0.007]} = 84.8\% \tag{5}$$

$$100 \frac{[X^* - X_i]}{[X^* - X]} = 100 \frac{[0.113 - 0.03]}{[0.113 - 0.0107]} = 81.1\% \tag{6}$$

These values would be equal if the equilibrium curve was a straight line.

(III) Let

$$\frac{1}{K_y} = \frac{1}{k_y} + \frac{H'}{k_x} \tag{7}$$

where

$$H' = \frac{Y_i - Y^*}{X_i - X} = \frac{0.0230 - 0.007}{0.03 - 0.0107} = 0.829$$

Substituting into equation (7) gives:

$$\frac{1}{K_y} = \frac{1}{0.573} + \frac{0.829}{2.64}$$

$$K_y = 0.486$$

which checks with the previously calculated value, thereby verifying equation (7).

• PROBLEM 18-12

Derive the continuity equation for the heavy phase considering convective flow, dispersion, interfacial mass transfer and I order chemical reaction in a continuous contactor. Also, state the boundary conditions.

Solution: Let

D_L = dispersion coefficient in the heavy phase

v_L, c_L = velocity and concentration at a distance z in heavy phase

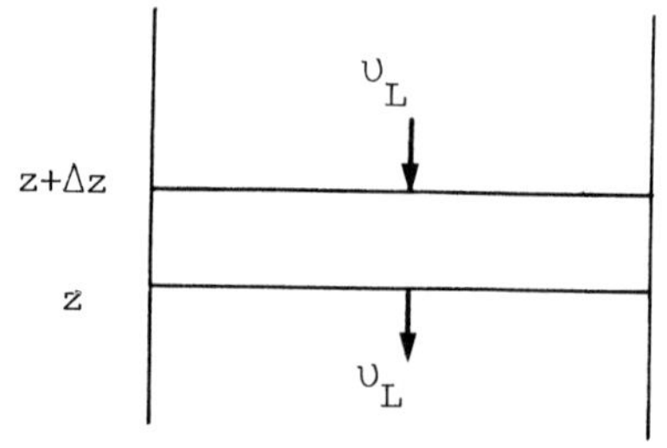

s = total tower cross-section

ε = void fraction in the tower

a = mass transfer per unit packed volume

f_v = fraction of void occupied by light phase

s_L = fraction of tower cross-section covered by heavy phase

$= s\varepsilon\,(1 - f_v)$

Δv_L = volume occupied by heavy phase across which material balance is done $= s_L \Delta z$

K_{vc} = mass transfer coefficient based on light phase

K_{ec} = phase equilibrium constant

k_L = reaction rate constant

A material balance on the volume element:

$$\text{mass in} = \left(-D_L \frac{dc_L}{dz}\right)_z s_L + v_L c_L \Big|_{z+\Delta z} s_L + K_{vc}(c_v - K_{ec} c_L) a s \Delta z$$

dispersion   convection   mass transfer from light phase

$$\text{mass out} = -D_L \frac{dc_L}{dz}\Big|_{z+\Delta z} s_L + v_L c_L \Big|_z S_L + k_L c_L \Delta v_L$$

dispersion   convection   reaction

$$\text{Accumulation} = \frac{d}{dt}(c_L \Delta v_L) = \Delta v_L \frac{dc_L}{dt}$$

Since mass in - mass out = accumulation, we get upon dividing throughout by $\Delta V_L = s\Delta z = \varepsilon(1-f_v)s\Delta z$ and letting $\Delta z \to 0$

$$\frac{dc_L}{dt} = D_L \frac{d^2 c_L}{dz^2} + \frac{d}{dz} v_L c_L + \frac{K_{vc} a}{\varepsilon(1 - f_v)} (c_v - K_{ec} c_L) - k_L c_L$$

Boundary conditions:

$$\text{at } z = 0, \quad \frac{dc_L}{dz} = 0; \quad \text{at } z = L, \quad v_L c_{L_0} = v_L c_L + \left(-D_L \frac{dc_L}{dz}\right)$$

To put it in a dimensionless form, define

$$\hat{z} = \frac{z}{L} ; \qquad \hat{c}_L = \frac{c_L}{c_R} ; \qquad \hat{c}_v = \frac{c_v}{K_{ec} c_R}$$

$$\therefore \frac{D_L c_R}{L^2} \frac{d^2 \hat{c}_L}{d\hat{z}^2} + \frac{v_L c_R}{L} \frac{d\hat{c}_L}{d\hat{z}} + \frac{K_{vc} a}{\varepsilon(1 - f_v)} K_{ec} c_R (\hat{c}_v - \hat{c}_L) - k_L c_R \hat{c}_L$$

$$= c_R \frac{d\hat{c}_L}{dt}$$

At steady state, $\frac{d\hat{c}_L}{dr} = 0$; dividing throughout by $\frac{c_R v_L}{L}$

$$\frac{D_L}{v_L L} \frac{d^2 \hat{c}_L}{d\hat{z}^2} + \frac{d\hat{c}_L}{d\hat{z}} \frac{K_{vc} aL}{\varepsilon(1 - f_v) v_L} K_{ec} (\hat{c}_v - \hat{c}_L) - \frac{k_L L}{v_L} \hat{c}_L = 0$$

Boundary conditions:

$$\text{at } \hat{z} = 0, \quad \frac{d\hat{c}_L}{d\hat{z}} = 0 ;$$

$$\text{at } \hat{z} = 1, \quad \hat{c}_{LO} = \hat{c}_L - \frac{D_L}{L v_L} \frac{d\hat{c}_L}{d\hat{z}}$$

MOMENTUM, HEAT AND MASS TRANSFER

• **PROBLEM 18-13**

A wet bulb thermometer is showing 15.55°C when dry air at atmospheric pressure is blowing across the thermometer. Estimate the dry air temperature.

Solution: The heat required for evaporation of water is taken from air, therefore from the energy balance.

$$hA(T_\infty - T_w) = \dot{m}_w h_{fg}$$

where

A = surface area (evaporating)

h = convective heat transfer coefficient

T_∞ = temperature of the surrounding air

T_w = surface temperature of water

$\dot{m}_w$ = mass of water evaporated

h_{fg} = heat of evaporation for water

But again

$$\dot{m}_w = h_D A(C_w - C_\infty)$$

where C_w is the concentration at the surface.

But

$$\frac{h}{h_D} = \rho C_p \left(\frac{\alpha}{D}\right)^{2/3}$$

Therefore,

$$hA(T_\infty - T_w) = \dot{m}_w h_{fg}$$

$$hA(T_\infty - T_w) = h_D A(C_w - C_\infty)h_{fg}$$

$$\frac{h}{h_D}(T_\infty - T_w) = (C_w - C_\infty)h_{fg}$$

$$(T_\infty - T_w)\rho C_p \left(\frac{\alpha}{D}\right)^{2/3} = (C_w - C_\infty)h_{fg}$$

From steam tables at 15.55°C (60°F)

$$P_g = 0.2561 \text{ lb/in}^2 = 1765 \text{ N/m}^2$$

Then

$$C_w = \frac{P_w}{R_w T_w} = \frac{1765 \times 18}{8315 \times 288.55} = 0.0132 \text{ kg/m}^3$$

$$h_{fg} = 1059.7 \text{ Btu/lbm}$$
$$= 2.464 \times 10^6 \text{ J/kg}$$

$$C_p = 1.005 \text{ kJ/kg}^0\text{C}$$

$$\frac{\alpha}{D} = \frac{Sc}{Pr} = 0.82$$

$C_\infty = 0$ (because the free stream consists of only dry air)

$$\rho = \frac{P}{RT} = \frac{1.0132 \times 10^5}{287 \times 288.55} = 1.223 \text{ Kg/m}^3$$

Substituting the numerical values and calculating

$$(T_\infty - T_w)\rho C_p \left(\frac{\alpha}{D}\right)^{2/3} = (C_w - C_\infty)h_{fg}$$

$$T_\infty - T_w = \frac{(C_w - C_\infty)h_{fg}}{\rho C_p (\alpha/D)^{2/3}}$$

$$= \frac{(0.0132 - 0)2.464 \times 10^6}{1005 \times 1.223 \times (0.82)^{2/3}}$$

$$= \frac{0.0132 \times 2.464 \times 10^6}{1005 \times 1.223 \times 0.876}$$

$$T_\infty - T_w = 30.20^0C$$

$$T_\infty = T_w + 30.20^0C$$

$$= 15.55 + 30.20$$

$$T_\infty = 45.75^0C$$

Accurate temperature T_∞ can be obtained by using the corrected density, that is calculating the density at the mean temperature $\frac{T_\infty + T_w}{2}$ and using this value to find T_∞.

• PROBLEM 18-14

> A drop of water, spherical in shape (5mm diameter) is moving in air ($T_\infty = 25^0C$) with a velocity of 8m/sec.
> Find the steady state temperature of the drop if the relative humidity is $\gamma = 50\%$. Assume negligible radiation and heat loss due to evaporation is equal to the heat gained by convection.

Solution: From the conservation of energy, heat loss by evaporation is equal to the heat gained by convection.

Hence,

$$Q_{convection} + Q_{evaporation} = 0$$

But

$$Q_{convection} = hA(T_s - T_\infty)$$

and

$$Q_{evaporation} = \dot{m}_{H_2O} h_{fg}$$

where

$$\dot{m}_{H_2O} = \text{mass transfer rate of water to air}$$

Again

$$\dot{m}_{H_2O} = h_D A\left[C_{(H_2O)_s} - C_{(H_2O)_\infty}\right]$$

where

$$h_D = \text{mass transfer coefficient of water}$$

$$h_D = h/\rho C_p(Le)^{2/3}$$

Le is the Lewis number which is approximately 1 for all water-air diffusion systems.

$$\frac{h}{h_D} = \rho C_p$$

It is known that

$$C_{(H_2O)s} = \frac{P_{sat}}{RT_s}$$

Now, substituting the above expressions into the equation,

$$Q_{convection} + Q_{evaporation} = 0$$

$$hA(T_s - T_\infty) + h_D A h_{fg}\left(C_{(H_2O)_s} - C_{(H_2O)_\infty}\right) = 0$$

where

A = surface area of the drop

h = convective heat transfer coefficient

T_s = surface temperature of the drop

T_∞ = temperature of the surrounding air

h_{fg} = heat of evaporation for water

$C_{(H_2O)_s}$ = concentration of water at the surface of the drop

ρ = density of air

C_p = specific heat of air.

Assume the initial drop in temperature to be $T_w = 25°C$. Then the corresponding P_{sat} and h_{fg} from the steam tables are

$$P_{sat} = 0.4594 \text{ lb/in}^2 = 3.166 \text{ kN/m}^2$$

$$h_{fg} = 1050.1 \text{ Btu/lbm} = 2442.5 \text{ kJ/kg}$$

The values of C_p and ρ for air at $T_\infty = 25°C$ are

$$\rho = 1.24 \text{ kg/m}^3$$

$$C_p = 1.005 \text{ kJ/kg°K}$$

Hence,

$$C_{(H_2O)_s} = \frac{P_{sat}}{RT_s} = \frac{3.166}{0.437 \times 298} = 0.0243 \text{ kg/m}^3$$

It is given that $\gamma_\infty = 0.6$. But

$$\gamma = \frac{P_v}{P_g} \quad \text{and} \quad P_g = 3.166 \text{ kN/m}^2$$

$$P_v = \gamma P_g = 0.6 \times 3.166 = 1.8996 \text{ kN/m}^2$$

Also

$$C_{(H_2O)_\infty} = \frac{1}{2} C_{(H_2O)_s} = \frac{1}{2} \times 0.0243 = 0.1215 \text{ kg/m}^3$$

The energy equation is

$$hA(T_s - T_\infty) + h_D A h_{fg}\left[C_{(H_2O)_s} - C_{(H_2O)_\infty}\right] = 0$$

$$hA(T_s - T_\infty) + \frac{h}{\rho C_p} A h_{fg}\left[C_{(H_2O)_s} - C_{(H_2O)_\infty}\right] = 0$$

$$(T_s - T_\infty) = \frac{-h_{fg}}{\rho C_p}\left[C_{(H_2O)_s} - C_{(H_2O)_\infty}\right]$$

$$T_s = T_\infty - \frac{h_{fg}}{\rho C_p}\left[C_{(H_2O)_s} - C_{(H_2O)_\infty}\right]$$

All the values are known except T_s. Hence, substituting the values and calculating,

$$T_s = 25 - \frac{2442.5}{1.24 \times 1.005}(0.0243 - 0.01215)$$

$$T_s = 25 - 23.8 = 1.2^0\text{C}$$

The value of T_s obtained is very less compared to the temperature ($T = 25^0$C) at which the parameters are calculated. Therefore an iterative approach should be adopted to obtain a more correct temperature T_s.

• PROBLEM 18-15

A non-Newtonian power-law fluid is flowing in a tube which is heated by steam condensing outside the tube. Calculate the outlet bulk fluid temperature for laminar flow, given the following data.

Rate of flow of fluid = 650 lbm/hr

Entering temperature of the fluid = 100^0F

Inside wall temperature = 200^0F

Density of fluid = ρ = 65 lbm/ft^3

Specific heat of fluid = C_p = 0.5 Btu/lbm^{0}F

Thermal conductivity of fluid = K = 0.7 Btu/hr^{0}F ft

Flow property constants: n' = 0.4

$k = 80$ lbm s^{n-2} ft^{-1} at 117.5^{0}F

$k = 40$ lbm s^{n-2} ft^{-1} at $T_w = 200^0$F

Internal diameter of tube = 1/12 ft.

Length of tube = 7.4 ft.

Solution: Guess a value for outlet fluid temperature (T_{bo}), then calculate h heat transfer coefficient from the relation

$$\frac{hD}{K} = 1.75\delta^{1/3}(N_{Gz})^{1/3}\left(\frac{\gamma_b}{\gamma_w}\right)^{0.14}$$

Again calculate T_{bo} from the relation

$$q = mC_p(T_{bo} - T_{bi}) = h(\pi DL)\Delta T$$

and check if this calculated value is the same as the guessed value. If this value is not the same then make a new guess and repeat the process until the required value is obtained.

Let T_{bo} = 135^{0}F for the first iteration.

$$\text{Mean bulk temperature} = \frac{T_{bo} + T_{bi}}{2} = \frac{135 + 100}{2} = 117.5^0\text{F}$$

K_b = 80 lbm s^{n-2}ft^{-1} at T = 117.5^{0}F

K_w = 40 lbm s^{n-2}ft^{-1} at T = 200^{0}F

$$\delta = \frac{3n' + 1}{4n'} = \frac{3 \times 0.4 + 1}{4 \times 0.4} = 1.375$$

$$N_{Gz} = \frac{mC_p}{KL}$$

where N_{Gz} is the Graetz number

m = mass flow rate of fluid

C_p = specific heat of fluid

K = thermal conductivity of fluid

L = length of tube

Substituting the values

$$N_{Gz} = \frac{650 \times 0.5}{0.7 \times 7.4} = 62.74$$

$$\frac{hD}{K} = 1.75\delta^{1/3}(N_{Gz})^{1/3}\left(\frac{\gamma_b}{\gamma_w}\right)^{0.14}$$

$$\frac{\gamma_b}{\gamma_w} = \frac{K_b}{K_w} = \frac{80}{40} = 2$$

All the values except h are known. Substituting and calculating

$$h = 1.75 \times (1.375)^{1/3} \times (62.74)^{1/3} \times (2)^{0.14} \quad \frac{0.7}{1} \times 12$$

$$= 1.75 \times 1.112 \times 3.974 \times 1.101 \times 0.7 \times 12$$

$$h = 71.59 \text{ Btu/hr} \cdot \text{ft}^2 \cdot {}^0\text{F}$$

The total heat flow is given by

$$q = mC_p(T_{bo} - T_{bi})$$

which is also equal to $q = h(\pi DL)\Delta T$. Therefore,

$$mC_p(T_{bo} - T_{bi}) = h(\pi DL)\Delta T$$

where ΔT is the arithmatic mean temperature difference which is given by

$$\Delta T = \left[(T_w - T_{bi}) + (T_w - T_{bo})\right]/2$$

T_w = Inside wall temperature = 200^0F

T_{bi} = Inlet bulk fluid temperature = 100^0F

T_{bo} = Outlet bulk fluid temperature

$$\Delta T = \left[(200 - 100) + (200 - T_{bo})\right]/2$$

$$= 150 - 0.5\ T_{bo}$$

Substituting the known values in this equation and solving for T_{bo}

$$mC_p(T_{bo} - T_{bi}) = h(\pi DL)\Delta T$$

$$650 \times 0.5 \times (T_{bo} - 100) = 71.59 \times \pi \times \frac{1}{12} \times 5.5\ (150 - 0.5\ T_{bo})$$

$$325(T_{bo} - 100) = 138.69(150 - 0.5T_{bo})$$

$$325T_{bo} + 69.345T_{bo} = 20803.5 + 32500$$

$$394.345T_{bo} = 53303.5$$

$$T_{bo} = \frac{53303.5}{394.345}$$

$$T_{bo} = 135.17^0 F$$

This value is close enough to the guessed value of 135°F. Hence, no further iteration is required. Therefore

$$T_{bo} = \text{outlet fluid bulk temperature} = 135^0 F$$

• PROBLEM 18-16

Air is leaking into a heating pipe 35 in. long and 0.70 in. diameter carrying water. The condenser temperature is 201°F for a heat load of 110 watts and an evaporator temperature of 212°F. Estimate the amount of air that leaked into the pipe.

Solution: First consider the case when no air is present.

The heat load is given by

$$\dot{Q} = \rho V \left(\frac{\pi}{4}\right) D^2 h_{fg} \tag{1}$$

Then, the vapor velocity is

$$V = \frac{\dot{Q}}{\rho \left(\frac{\pi}{4}\right) D^2 h_{fg}}$$

From steam tables, at 212°F

$$\rho_v = 0.0373 \text{ lb/ft}^3 \qquad h_{fg} = 970.3 \text{ Btu/lb}$$

$$\nu = 23.4 \times 10^{-5} \text{ft}^2/\text{sec}$$

Therefore,

$$V = \frac{(110)(3.41)/3600}{(0.0373)(\pi/4)\left(\frac{0.70}{12}\right)^2 (970.3)}$$

$$= 1.08 \text{ ft/sec}$$

The Reynolds number is given by

$$Re_D = \frac{VD}{\nu}$$

$$= \frac{(1.08)\left(\frac{0.70}{12}\right)}{(23.4 \times 10^{-5})} = 268.5$$

This implies the flow is laminar. Then, friction is given by

$$f = \frac{64}{Re_D}$$

$$= \frac{64}{268.5} = 0.238$$

The pressure drop can be calculated using the equation below.

$$\Delta P = f \frac{L}{D}\left(\frac{1}{2}\rho V^2\right)$$

$$= (0.238)\left(\frac{35}{0.7}\right)\left(\frac{1}{2}\right)\frac{(0.0373)(1.08)^2}{(32.2)}$$

$$= 0.00804 \text{ lb/ft}^2$$

$$= 5.58 \times 10^{-5} \text{ lb/in}^2$$

From steam tables it can be seen that the corresponding temperature drop is negligible.

Now, consider the case when air is present. Assume the concentration of air at the evaporator is very small. The variation in total pressure (14.7 psia) along the pipe is negligible. From steam tables, the saturation pressure corresponding to 201^0F is 11.8 psia, the mole fraction of air is

$$x_{2,e} = \frac{P_{2,e}}{P_{total}}$$

$$= \frac{14.7 - 11.8}{14.7} = 0.198$$

Then $x_{2,s}$ is given by

$$\ln\left(\frac{x_{2,e}}{x_{2,s}}\right) = \frac{\dot{Q}L}{M_1 C D_{12} h_{fg}(\pi/4)D^2} \qquad (2)$$

where

D_{12} = binary diffusion coefficient.

C = molar concentration

M_1 = molecular weight

For air-water vapor mixtures the diffusion coefficient is given by

$$D_{12} = 0.765 \frac{P_0}{P}\left(\frac{T}{T_0}\right)^{1.685}$$

$$= 0.765\left(\frac{14.7}{14.7}\right)\left(\frac{672}{460}\right)^{1.685}$$

$$= 1.45 \ \text{ft}^2/\text{hr}$$

The total molar concentration C is given by

$$C = \frac{P}{RT}$$

$$= \frac{(14.7)(144)}{(1545)(672)}$$

$$= 2.04 \times 10^{-3} \ \text{mole/ft}^3$$

Substituting known quantities in eq.(2) gives

$$r = \text{Ln}\left(\frac{x_{2,e}}{x_{2,s}}\right) = \frac{(110)(3.41)(2.917)}{(18)(2.04\times10^{-3})(1.45)(970)(\pi/4)(0.7/12)^2}$$

$$= 7.93 \times 10^3$$

This is very large, hence the assumption of $x_{2,s}$ very small is justified.

The total amount of air that leaked into the pipe is given by

$$W = \frac{\pi}{4} D^2 \int_0^L x_2 c\,dz$$

but,

$$\left(\frac{x_2}{x_{2,s}}\right) = \left(\frac{x_{2,e}}{x_{2,s}}\right)^{Z/L} = (r)^{Z/L}$$

Then,

$$W = \left(\frac{\pi}{4}\right) D^2 c x_{2,s} L \int_0^1 r^{Z/L} d(Z/L)$$

$$= \left(\frac{\pi}{4}\right) D^2 c x_{2,s} L \frac{r-1}{\text{Ln}\,r}$$

$$= \left(\frac{\pi}{4}\right) D^2 c x_{2,e} \frac{L}{r} \frac{r-1}{\text{Ln}\,r}$$

r is large, therefore

$$W = \left(\frac{\pi}{4}\right) D^2 c x_{2,e} \frac{L}{\text{Lnr}}$$

Substituting the known quantities gives

$$W = \frac{(\pi/4)(0.7/12)^2(2.04\times10^{-3})(0.198)(2.917)}{7.93 \times 10^3}$$

$$= 3.97 \times 10^{-10} \text{ lb·moles}$$

The mass of air in the pipe is

$$w = WM_2$$

$$= (3.97 \times 10^{-10})(29)$$

$$= 1.15 \times 10^{-8} \text{lbs.}$$

$$= 5.22 \times 10^{-6} \text{ grams}$$

Though the mass of air is only 5.22 micrograms the temperature drop is 11^0F because of the geometrical arrangement chosen.

• PROBLEM 18-17

Consider an isothermal process at $50\,^0$C to dry a gas saturated with water vapor, in a plate column, using 95% (by mass) sulfuric acid. If the sulfuric acid with a final concentration of 80% (by mass) can absorb 110 kg/hr water vapor, estimate the amount of heat to be removed by the cooling water, flowing through pipes in the plates.

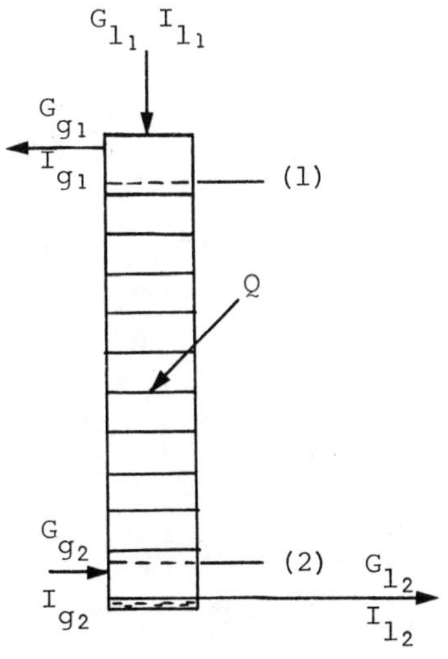

Fig. 1

Solution: In this system the water vapor in the gas is first condensed to water by the cooling water flowing through the pipes, then the liquid water is absorbed by the sulfuric acid.

Let H_2O be denoted by A and H_2SO_4 by B.

Applying mass balance on the system gives:

$$G_{g_2} - G_{g_1} = G_{\ell_2} - G_{\ell_1} = G_A = 110 \text{ kg/hr}$$

There is no change in the mass of H_2SO_4 along the flow path. Therefore

$$G_{\ell_1} u_{B_1} = G_{\ell_2} u_{B_2}$$

$$G_{\ell_1} = G_{\ell_2} \frac{u_{B2}}{u_{B_1}}$$

where u_B is the mass fraction of H_2SO_4.

Given $u_{B_2} = 0.80$ and $u_{B_1} = 0.98$, then

$$G_{\ell_1} = G_{\ell_2} \frac{0.80}{0.98}$$

but

$$G_{\ell_2} - G_{\ell_1} = 110$$

$$G_{\ell_2}\left(1 - \frac{0.80}{0.98}\right) = 110$$

$$G_{\ell_2} = 588.9 \text{ kg/hr}$$

$$G_{\ell_1} = G_{\ell_2} - 110$$

$$= 598.9 - 110$$

$$= 488.9 \text{ kg/hr}$$

Applying heat balance on the system gives

$$Q + I_{g_2} + I_{\ell_1} = I_{g_1} + I_{\ell_2}$$

where I is the enthalpy.

Then

$$Q = I_{g_1} - I_{g_2} + I_{\ell_2} - I_{\ell_1} \tag{1}$$

By visual inspection of the system, the following relations can be written,

(a) $I_{g_2} - I_{g_1} = 110 i_A^*$

where i_A^* = enthalpy of vapor in the gaseous phase

(b) $I_{\ell 2} = G_{\ell 2}(u_{A2} i_A + u_{B2} i_B + q_{r2})$

(c) $I_{\ell 1} = G_{\ell 1}(u_{A1} i_A + u_{B1} i_B + q_{r1})$

(d) $G_{\ell 1} u_{B1} = G_{\ell 2} u_{B2}$

where q_{r1} and q_{r2} are the total heats of solution of water in the solution.

Using relations (a), (b), (c) and (d) eq.(1) can be rewritten as

$$Q = -110 i_A^* + G_{\ell 2}(u_{A2} i_A + q_{r2}) - G_{\ell 1}(u_{A1} i_A + q_{r1})$$

$$Q = -110 i_A^* + i_A(G_{\ell 2} u_{A2} - G_{\ell 1} u_{A1}) + G_{\ell 2} q_{r2} - G_{\ell 1} q_{r1}$$

$$Q = -110 i_A^* + 110 i_A + G_{\ell 2} q_{r2} - G_{\ell 1} q_{r1} \tag{2}$$

Applying the approximation $i_A^* - i_A \approx r_A$

Then eq.(2) becomes

$$Q \approx G_{\ell 2} q_{r2} - G_{\ell 1} q_{r1} - 110 r_A \tag{3}$$

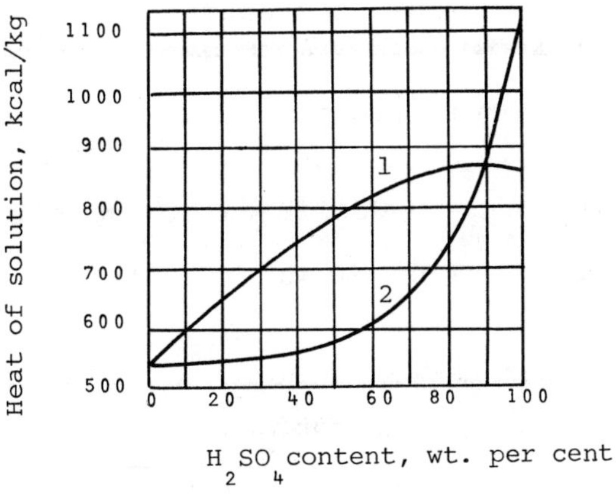

Fig. 2 Heat of solution of water vapour in sulfuric acid:
1- integral (per 1 kg of solution)
2- differential (per 1 kg of water vapour)

The figure above gives the heat of solution of the vapor in the solution for the given concentration of H_2SO_4. Let us denote it by q_{r1}^* and q_{r2}^*.

But $q_r^* = q_r - u_A r_A$

Then eq.(3) reduces to

$$Q = G_{\ell 2} q^*_{r_2} + G_{\ell 2} u_{A_2} r_A - G_{\ell 1} u_{A_1} r_A - G_{\ell 1} q^*_{r_1} - 110 r_A$$

but $$(G_{\ell 2} u_{A_2} - G_{\ell 1} u_{A_1}) r_A = 110 r_A$$

Then,

$$Q = G_{\ell 2} q^*_{r_2} - G_{\ell 1} q^*_{r_1}$$

From the graph in the figure

at 98% H_2SO_4 $\quad q^*_{r_1} = 865$ kcal/kg of solution

at 80% H_2SO_4 $\quad q^*_{r_2} = -858$ kcal/kg of solution

$$Q = 598.9(-858) - 488.9(-865)$$

$$= -90957.7 \text{ kcal/hr}$$

The negative sign indicates that heat has to be removed. Therefore, the amount of heat to be removed by the cooling water is 90957.7 kcal/hr.

• PROBLEM 18-18

Determine the humidity of the air if the wet-bulb temperature is 70°F and dry-bulb temperature is 90°F.

Solution: From psychrometric chart, at a dry-bulb temperature of 90°F.

Humidity ratio Y_s = 0.031 lb water vapor/lb dry air

Latent heat of vaporization of water is λ = 1042.7 Btu/lbm.

TABLE. Values of $h_G/k_G M_G P$ for various vapors in air.

Vapor	$h_G/k_G M_G P$
Water	0.26
Benzene	0.41
Carbon tetrachloride	0.44
Methyl alcohol	0.35

From the above table, for water

$$h_G/k_G M_G P = 0.26$$

$$Y_{Wb} - Y_G = \frac{1}{\lambda} \frac{h_G}{k_G M_G P} (T_G - T_{Wb}) \qquad (1)$$

where Y = absolute humidity of the air

λ = latent heat of vaporization

M_G = molecular weight of the gas phase

P = total pressure

Using eq.(1) the humidity of air is given by

$$Y_G = Y_{Wb} - \frac{1}{\lambda}\frac{h_G}{k_G M_G P}(T_G - T_{Wb}) \tag{2}$$

Substituting the known quantities in eq.(2) gives:

$$Y_G = 0.031 - \frac{1(0.26)(90-70)}{1042.7}$$

$$= 0.026 \text{ lb water vapor/lb dry air}$$

The humidity of the air is also given by:

$$Y_G = \frac{Y_{as} - C_a(T_G - T_{as})/\lambda}{1 + C_w(T_G - T_{as})/\lambda} \tag{3}$$

From tables $C_a = 0.24$ Btu/lbm°F

$C_W = 0.40$ Btu/lbm°F

Substituting known quantities in eq.(3) gives:

$$Y_G = \frac{0.031 - 0.24(90-70)/1042.7}{1 + 0.40(90-70)/1042.7}$$

$$= 0.026 \text{ lb water vapor/lb dry air}$$

The values of Y_G obtained with two different methods are identical, therefore $T_{as} = T_{Wb}$ for water. This makes it easier to deal with air-water system. Note that the adiabatic saturation temperature and the wet-bulb temperature are not equal for other systems.

• PROBLEM 18-19

A hot condensable vapor A diffuses through a stationary film of a non-condensable gas B towards a cold surface at $z = 0$ where it condenses. Develop the concentration and temperature profile for the gas A.

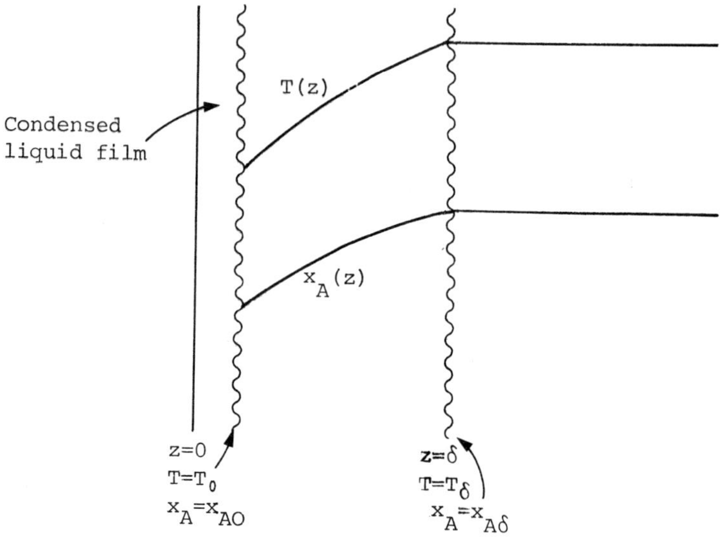

Solution: We assume

(i) The gas A behaves as an ideal gas

(ii) The pressure and physical properties of the mixture are constant.

The continuity equation for this situation reduces to

$$\frac{dN_{AZ}}{dz} = 0 \qquad \therefore\ N_{AZ} = \text{constant}$$

The energy balance equation reduces to

$$\frac{dE_Z}{dz} = 0 \qquad \therefore\ E_Z = \text{constant}$$

The mass flux of A by diffision through a stagnant film B is

$$N_{AZ} = \frac{-cD_{AB}}{1 - x_A}\frac{dx_A}{dz}$$

$$\therefore \qquad \frac{cD_{AB}}{1-x_A}\frac{d^2x_A}{dz^2} = 0$$

Integrating and using the boundary conditions, we get

$$\left(\frac{1 - x_A}{1 - x_{A0}}\right) = \left(\frac{1 - x_{AS}}{1 - x_{A0}}\right)^{z/\delta}$$

$$N_{AZ} = \frac{-cD_{AB}}{1-x_{A\delta}}\left.\frac{dx_A}{dz}\right|_{z=\delta}$$

$$= \frac{cD_{AB}}{\delta} \ln\left(\frac{1 - x_{A\delta}}{1 - x_{A0}}\right)$$

Temperature profile

For an ideal gas, energy flux

$$E_Z = -k \frac{dT}{dz} + (\tilde{H}_A N_{AZ} + \tilde{H}_B N_{BZ})$$

$$= -k \frac{dT}{dz} + N_{AZ}\tilde{C}p_A(T - T_0)$$

where T_0 is the reference temperature for the enthalpy. Using the above expression and the energy balance equation and integrating using the boundary conditions, we get

$$\frac{T - T_0}{T_\delta - T_0} = \frac{1 - \exp[(N_{AZ}\tilde{C}p_A/k)Z]}{1 - \exp[(N_{AZ}\tilde{C}p_A/k)\delta]}$$

• PROBLEM 18-20

An air-water mixture, flowing vertically inside a vertical copper tube, 5 in. in ID with $\frac{1}{4}$ in. thick wall, is immersed in a tank of cold water. At a point on the tube, the gas has an average velocity of 15 ft/sec and a temperature of 65 °C. While the total pressure is 1 atm, the partial pressure of water vapor is 0.25 atm. The film heat transfer coefficient is 2000 Btu/hr·ft^2 °R. The cold water temperature is 25 °C and has a heat transfer coefficient is 100 Btu/hr·ft^2 °R. What is the local condensation rate of water from the gas stream?

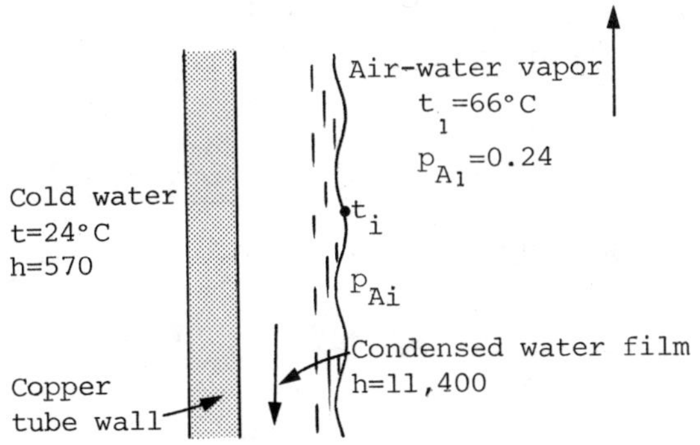

Solution: Let A be water
B be air

As the water vapor condenses, it flows as a liquid down along the inside of the tube.

Inner diameter of the tube = d_i = 5 in.

Outer diameter of the tube = d_o = 5 + 2 × 0.25 = 5.5 in.

Average diameter = $d' = \frac{5 + 5.5}{2} = 5.25$ in.

Wall thickness = w = 0.25 in.

Since A is diffusing through non-diffusing B, $\frac{N_A}{N_A + N_B} = 1$

Let $y_{A1} = \frac{p_{A1}}{p_T} = \frac{0.25}{1} = 0.25$

Let y_{Ai} and p_{Ai} be the mole fraction and the partial pressure of water at the interface temperature t_i.

Average molecular weight of the gas

$$= (M)_{AV1} = 0.25 \times 18.016 + 0.75 \times 28.86$$

$$= 26.147$$

$$\text{Density} = \rho_1 = \frac{(M)_{AV} \times P}{RT} = \frac{26.147 \times 1}{0.08205(273+65)} = 0.9428 \frac{kg}{m^3}$$

$$= 0.0588 \text{ lbm/ft}^3$$

At 65°C, $\mu = 1.75 \times 10^{-5}$ kg/m·sec = 0.04232 lbm/ft·hr

sp. heat of A = Cp_A = 1880 J/kg·°K

$$= 1880 \left(\frac{J}{kg \cdot {}^0K}\right)\left(\frac{1}{2.204}\frac{kg}{lb}\right)\left(9.478 \times 10^{-4}\frac{Btu}{J}\right)\left(\frac{1}{1.8}\frac{{}^0K}{{}^0R}\right)$$

$$= 0.4492 \text{ Btu/lb}^0\text{R}$$

sp. heat of B = Cp_B = 912 J/kg·°K $= \frac{912 \times 9.47831 \times 10^{-4}}{1.8 \times 2.204}$

$$= 0.21789 \text{ Btu/lb} \cdot {}^0\text{R}$$

Mole fraction of A in the gas = $y_A = \frac{p_A}{p_T} = 0.25$

sp. heat of the gas mixture = $y_A Cp_A + y_B Cp_B$

$$= 0.25(0.4492) + 0.75(0.21789) = 0.2757 \text{ Btu/lb}^0\text{R}$$

Sc = 0.6; Pr = 0.75

Mass velocity of the gas stream = $G' = u_1\rho_1 = 15\times0.0588\times3600$

$= 3177.436 \text{ lb/ft}^2\cdot\text{hr}$

$$\text{Molar gas velocity} = G = \frac{G'}{(M)_{AV}} = \frac{3177.436}{26.147} = 121.522 \frac{\text{lb mol}}{\text{ft}^2\cdot\text{hr}}$$

$$\text{Reynolds no.} = Re = \frac{dG'}{\mu} = \left(\frac{5}{12}\right)(3177.436)\frac{1}{0.04232} = 31283$$

From the table below, picks selecting the appropriate equation,

$$j_D = 0.0149Re^{-0.12} = (0.0149)(31283)^{-0.12} = 4.3028\ 10^{-3}$$

Fluid Motion	Range of conditions	Equation
1. Inside circular pipes	$Re = 4{,}000\text{-}60{,}000$ $Sc = 0.6\text{-}3{,}000$	$j_D = 0.023\ Re^{-0.17}$ $Sh = 0.023\ Re^{0.83}Sc^{1/3}$
	$Re = 10{,}000\text{-}400{,}000$ $Sc > 100$	$j_D = 0.0149\ Re^{-0.12}$ $Sh = 0.0149\ Re^{0.88}Sc^{1/3}$

Since

$$j_D = j_H = \frac{h}{CpG'}(Pr)^{2/3}$$

$$h = j_D\frac{CpG'}{(Pr)^{2/3}} = \frac{4.3028\times10^{-3}\times0.2757\times3177.436}{(0.75)^{2/3}}$$

$$= 4.5662 \text{ Btu/hr}\cdot\text{ft}^2\cdot{}^0\text{R}$$

where h = heat transfer coefficient in the absence of mass transfer. Also,

$$j_D = St_D Sc^{2/3} = \frac{F}{G}Sc^{2/3}$$

$$F = \frac{j_D G}{(Sc)^{2/3}} = \frac{4.3028\times10^{-3}\times121.522}{(0.6)^{2/3}} = 0.73503 \frac{\text{lb}\cdot\text{mol}}{\text{ft}^2\cdot\text{hr}}$$

The total sensible heat flux transferred to the gas-liquid interface

$$= Q = \frac{N_A Cp_A M_A}{1 - \exp\left(\frac{-N_A M_A Cp_A}{h}\right)}(t_1 - t_i) + \lambda_{Ai}N_A$$

where $t_1 = 65^0C = 149^0F$

λ_{Ai} = molar latent heat of vaporization at temperature t_i

$= 1035.98$ Btu/lb

$$\therefore Q = \frac{N_A \times 0.4492 \times 18.016}{1 - \exp\left(- \frac{N_A \times 18.016 \times 0.4492}{4.5662}\right)}(149 - t_i) + 1035.98 N_A$$

$$= \frac{8.09279 N_A (149 - t_i)}{1 - \exp(-1.772324 N_A)} + 1035.98 N_A$$

Since there is no heat build-up at the interface, heat transferred to the water = heat arriving at the interface.

$$\therefore u_o(t_i - 77) = Q = N_A \left[\frac{8.09279(149 - t_i)}{1 - \exp(-1.772324 N_A)} + 1035.98\right] \quad (1)$$

where u_0 = overall heat transfer coefficient

$$= \frac{1}{h_c} + \frac{w}{k_c}\frac{d_i}{d'} + \frac{1}{h_w}\frac{d_i}{d_0}$$

h_c = condensate-side heat transfer coefficient

$= 2000 \text{ Btu/ft}^2 \cdot \text{hr} \cdot {}^0\text{F}$

Equation (3) and (4) are solved simultaneously by trial and error to get t_i.

Thus $t_i = 82.25^0\text{F}$

The local rate of condensation

$= N_A = 0.1837 \text{ lb mol/hr} \cdot \text{ft}^2$

$= 3.3089 \text{ lb } H_2O/\text{ft}^2 \cdot \text{hr}$

• PROBLEM 18-21

Saturated steam at 1.5 std. atm. flows through a porous flat plate over which air at 700 °C and 1 std. atm. is flowing. The air-side heat transfer coefficient is 200 Btu/hr·ft²·°F when there is no steam flowing.

(a) Compute the flow rate of steam required to keep the temperature at the surface at 300 °C.

(b) What would be the flow rate if water at 30 °C is used instead?

Solution: Let N_A be the rate of steam flow in lbmole/hr·ft².

Heat given out by the steam

$$Q = M_A N_A (H_{As} - H_{Ai})$$

where i denoted steam-air interface and H denotes enthalpy.

Since there is no build-up at the interface,

Q = heat transferred to the air stream

$$= \frac{N_A M_A Cp(t_1 - t_i)}{1 - \exp(-N_A M_A Cp_A/h)}$$

$$\therefore\ N_A M_A (H_{As} - H_{Ai}) = \frac{N_A M_A Cp(t_1 - t_i)}{1 - \exp(-N_A M_A Cp_A/h)}$$

Solving for N_A,

$$N_A = \frac{-h}{M_A Cp_A} \ln\left[1 - \frac{Cp_A(t_1 - t_i)}{H_{As} - H_{Ai}}\right]$$

From steam tables, at 1.5 atm.

$$H_{As} = 2693 \text{ kJ/kg} = 1158.1 \text{ Btu/lb}$$

At 1 std. atm., and 300°C, the enthalpy of steam,

$$H_{Ai} = 3075 \text{ kJ/kg} = 1322.36 \text{ Btu/lb}$$

$$M_A = \text{molecular weight of water} = 18.016$$

$$h = 200 \text{ Btu/ft}^2\cdot\text{hr}\cdot{}^0\text{F}$$

$$Cp_A = \text{sp. heat of water} = 0.5 \text{ Btu/lb}^0\text{R}$$

$$\therefore\ N_A = \frac{-200}{18.016\times 0.5} \ln\left[1 - \frac{0.5(700 - 300)}{1158.1 - 1322.36}\right]$$

$$= -17.682 \text{ lbmole/ft}^2\cdot\text{hr}$$

$$= -318.6 \text{ lb/ft}^2\cdot\text{hr}$$

Since the flux is toward the gas, hence the negative sign.

(b) The enthalpy of liquid water at 30°C = 54.03 Btu/lb

Substituting this value for H_{As}, and solving, we get

$$N_A = -3.251 \text{ lbmol/ft}^2\text{hr} = -58.57 \text{ lb/ft}^2\cdot\text{hr}$$

APPENDIX

EQUATIONS OF CONTINUITY

Rectangular coordinates (x, y, z):

$$\frac{\partial \rho}{\partial t} + \frac{\partial}{\partial x}(\rho v_x) + \frac{\partial}{\partial y}(\rho v_y) + \frac{\partial}{\partial z}(\rho v_z) = 0 \qquad (A)$$

Cylindrical coordinates (r, θ, z):

$$\frac{\partial \rho}{\partial t} + \frac{1}{r}\frac{\partial}{\partial r}(\rho r v_r) + \frac{1}{r}\frac{\partial}{\partial \theta}(\rho v_\theta) + \frac{\partial}{\partial z}(\rho v_z) = 0 \qquad (B)$$

Spherical coordinates (r, θ, φ):

$$\frac{\partial \rho}{\partial t} + \frac{1}{r^2}\frac{\partial}{\partial r}(\rho r^2 v_r) + \frac{1}{r \sin\theta}\frac{\partial}{\partial \theta}(\rho v_\theta \sin\theta) + \frac{1}{r \sin\theta}\frac{\partial}{\partial \phi}(\rho v_\phi) = 0 \qquad (C)$$

EQUATIONS OF MOTION-RECTANGULAR COORDINATES (x,y,z)

In terms of $\boldsymbol{\tau}$:

x-component
$$\rho\left(\frac{\partial v_x}{\partial t} + v_x\frac{\partial v_x}{\partial x} + v_y\frac{\partial v_x}{\partial y} + v_z\frac{\partial v_x}{\partial z}\right) = -\frac{\partial p}{\partial x} - \left(\frac{\partial \tau_{xx}}{\partial x} + \frac{\partial \tau_{yx}}{\partial y} + \frac{\partial \tau_{zx}}{\partial z}\right) + \rho g_x \quad (A)$$

y-component
$$\rho\left(\frac{\partial v_y}{\partial t} + v_x\frac{\partial v_y}{\partial x} + v_y\frac{\partial v_y}{\partial y} + v_z\frac{\partial v_y}{\partial z}\right) = -\frac{\partial p}{\partial y} - \left(\frac{\partial \tau_{xy}}{\partial x} + \frac{\partial \tau_{yy}}{\partial y} + \frac{\partial \tau_{zy}}{\partial z}\right) + \rho g_y \quad (B)$$

z-component
$$\rho\left(\frac{\partial v_z}{\partial t} + v_x\frac{\partial v_z}{\partial x} + v_y\frac{\partial v_z}{\partial y} + v_z\frac{\partial v_z}{\partial z}\right) = -\frac{\partial p}{\partial z} - \left(\frac{\partial \tau_{xz}}{\partial x} + \frac{\partial \tau_{yz}}{\partial y} + \frac{\partial \tau_{zz}}{\partial z}\right) + \rho g_z \quad (C)$$

Velocity gradients for a Newtonian fluid with constant ρ and μ:

x-component
$$\rho\left(\frac{\partial v_x}{\partial t} + v_x\frac{\partial v_x}{\partial x} + v_y\frac{\partial v_x}{\partial y} + v_z\frac{\partial v_x}{\partial z}\right) = -\frac{\partial p}{\partial x} + \mu\left(\frac{\partial^2 v_x}{\partial x^2} + \frac{\partial^2 v_x}{\partial y^2} + \frac{\partial^2 v_x}{\partial z^2}\right) + \rho g_x \quad (D)$$

y-component
$$\rho\left(\frac{\partial v_y}{\partial t} + v_x\frac{\partial v_y}{\partial x} + v_y\frac{\partial v_y}{\partial y} + v_z\frac{\partial v_y}{\partial z}\right) = -\frac{\partial p}{\partial y} + \mu\left(\frac{\partial^2 v_y}{\partial x^2} + \frac{\partial^2 v_y}{\partial y^2} + \frac{\partial^2 v_y}{\partial z^2}\right) + \rho g_y \quad (E)$$

z-component
$$\rho\left(\frac{\partial v_z}{\partial t} + v_x\frac{\partial v_z}{\partial x} + v_y\frac{\partial v_z}{\partial y} + v_z\frac{\partial v_z}{\partial z}\right) = -\frac{\partial p}{\partial z} + \mu\left(\frac{\partial^2 v_z}{\partial x^2} + \frac{\partial^2 v_z}{\partial y^2} + \frac{\partial^2 v_z}{\partial z^2}\right) + \rho g_z \quad (F)$$

EQUATIONS OF MOTION-CYLINDRICAL COORDINATES (r, θ, z)

In terms of $\boldsymbol{\tau}$:

r-component[a]
$$\rho\left(\frac{\partial v_r}{\partial t} + v_r\frac{\partial v_r}{\partial r} + \frac{v_\theta}{r}\frac{\partial v_r}{\partial \theta} - \frac{v_\theta^2}{r} + v_z\frac{\partial v_r}{\partial z}\right) = -\frac{\partial p}{\partial r} - \left(\frac{1}{r}\frac{\partial}{\partial r}(r\tau_{rr}) + \frac{1}{r}\frac{\partial \tau_{r\theta}}{\partial \theta} - \frac{\tau_{\theta\theta}}{r} + \frac{\partial \tau_{rz}}{\partial z}\right) + \rho g_r \qquad (A)$$

θ-component[b]
$$\rho\left(\frac{\partial v_\theta}{\partial t} + v_r\frac{\partial v_\theta}{\partial r} + \frac{v_\theta}{r}\frac{\partial v_\theta}{\partial \theta} + \frac{v_r v_\theta}{r} + v_z\frac{\partial v_\theta}{\partial z}\right) = -\frac{1}{r}\frac{\partial p}{\partial \theta} - \left(\frac{1}{r^2}\frac{\partial}{\partial r}(r^2\tau_{r\theta}) + \frac{1}{r}\frac{\partial \tau_{\theta\theta}}{\partial \theta} + \frac{\partial \tau_{\theta z}}{\partial z}\right) + \rho g_\theta \qquad (B)$$

z-component
$$\rho\left(\frac{\partial v_z}{\partial t} + v_r\frac{\partial v_z}{\partial r} + \frac{v_\theta}{r}\frac{\partial v_z}{\partial \theta} + v_z\frac{\partial v_z}{\partial z}\right) = -\frac{\partial p}{\partial z} - \left(\frac{1}{r}\frac{\partial}{\partial r}(r\tau_{rz}) + \frac{1}{r}\frac{\partial \tau_{\theta z}}{\partial \theta} + \frac{\partial \tau_{zz}}{\partial z}\right) + \rho g_z \qquad (C)$$

Velocity gradients for a Newtonian fluid with constant ρ and μ:

r-component[a]
$$\rho\left(\frac{\partial v_r}{\partial t} + v_r\frac{\partial v_r}{\partial r} + \frac{v_\theta}{r}\frac{\partial v_r}{\partial \theta} - \frac{v_\theta^2}{r} + v_z\frac{\partial v_r}{\partial z}\right) = -\frac{\partial p}{\partial r} + \mu\left[\frac{\partial}{\partial r}\left(\frac{1}{r}\frac{\partial}{\partial r}(r v_r)\right) + \frac{1}{r^2}\frac{\partial^2 v_r}{\partial \theta^2} - \frac{2}{r^2}\frac{\partial v_\theta}{\partial \theta} + \frac{\partial^2 v_r}{\partial z^2}\right] + \rho g_r \qquad (D)$$

θ-component[b]
$$\rho\left(\frac{\partial v_\theta}{\partial t} + v_r\frac{\partial v_\theta}{\partial r} + \frac{v_\theta}{r}\frac{\partial v_\theta}{\partial \theta} + \frac{v_r v_\theta}{r} + v_z\frac{\partial v_\theta}{\partial z}\right) = -\frac{1}{r}\frac{\partial p}{\partial \theta} + \mu\left[\frac{\partial}{\partial r}\left(\frac{1}{r}\frac{\partial}{\partial r}(r v_\theta)\right) + \frac{1}{r^2}\frac{\partial^2 v_\theta}{\partial \theta^2} + \frac{2}{r^2}\frac{\partial v_r}{\partial \theta} + \frac{\partial^2 v_\theta}{\partial z^2}\right] + \rho g_\theta \qquad (E)$$

z-component
$$\rho\left(\frac{\partial v_z}{\partial t} + v_r\frac{\partial v_z}{\partial r} + \frac{v_\theta}{r}\frac{\partial v_z}{\partial \theta} + v_z\frac{\partial v_z}{\partial z}\right) = -\frac{\partial p}{\partial z} + \mu\left[\frac{1}{r}\frac{\partial}{\partial r}\left(r\frac{\partial v_z}{\partial r}\right) + \frac{1}{r^2}\frac{\partial^2 v_z}{\partial \theta^2} + \frac{\partial^2 v_z}{\partial z^2}\right] + \rho g_z \qquad (F)$$

EQUATIONS OF MOTION-SPHERICAL COORDINATES (r, θ, ϕ)

In terms of $\boldsymbol{\tau}$:

r-component

$$\rho\left(\frac{\partial v_r}{\partial t} + v_r \frac{\partial v_r}{\partial r} + \frac{v_\theta}{r}\frac{\partial v_r}{\partial \theta} + \frac{v_\phi}{r \sin\theta}\frac{\partial v_r}{\partial \phi} - \frac{v_\theta^2 + v_\phi^2}{r}\right)$$

$$= -\frac{\partial p}{\partial r} - \left(\frac{1}{r^2}\frac{\partial}{\partial r}(r^2 \tau_{rr}) + \frac{1}{r\sin\theta}\frac{\partial}{\partial \theta}(\tau_{r\theta}\sin\theta) + \frac{1}{r\sin\theta}\frac{\partial \tau_{r\phi}}{\partial \phi} - \frac{\tau_{\theta\theta} + \tau_{\phi\phi}}{r}\right) + \rho g_r \qquad (A)$$

θ-component

$$\rho\left(\frac{\partial v_\theta}{\partial t} + v_r \frac{\partial v_\theta}{\partial r} + \frac{v_\theta}{r}\frac{\partial v_\theta}{\partial \theta} + \frac{v_\phi}{r \sin\theta}\frac{\partial v_\theta}{\partial \phi} + \frac{v_r v_\theta}{r} - \frac{v_\phi^2 \cot\theta}{r}\right)$$

$$= -\frac{1}{r}\frac{\partial p}{\partial \theta} - \left(\frac{1}{r^2}\frac{\partial}{\partial r}(r^2 \tau_{r\theta}) + \frac{1}{r\sin\theta}\frac{\partial}{\partial \theta}(\tau_{\theta\theta}\sin\theta) + \frac{1}{r\sin\theta}\frac{\partial \tau_{\theta\phi}}{\partial \phi} + \frac{\tau_{r\theta}}{r} - \frac{\cot\theta}{r}\tau_{\phi\phi}\right) + \rho g_\theta \qquad (B)$$

φ-component

$$\rho\left(\frac{\partial v_\phi}{\partial t} + v_r \frac{\partial v_\phi}{\partial r} + \frac{v_\theta}{r}\frac{\partial v_\phi}{\partial \theta} + \frac{v_\phi}{r \sin\theta}\frac{\partial v_\phi}{\partial \phi} + \frac{v_\phi v_r}{r} + \frac{v_\theta v_\phi}{r}\cot\theta\right)$$

$$= -\frac{1}{r\sin\theta}\frac{\partial p}{\partial \phi} - \left(\frac{1}{r^2}\frac{\partial}{\partial r}(r^2 \tau_{r\phi}) + \frac{1}{r}\frac{\partial \tau_{\theta\phi}}{\partial \theta} + \frac{1}{r\sin\theta}\frac{\partial \tau_{\phi\phi}}{\partial \phi} + \frac{\tau_{r\phi}}{r} + \frac{2\cot\theta}{r}\tau_{\theta\phi}\right) + \rho g_\phi \qquad (C)$$

Velocity gradients for a Newtonian fluid with constant ρ and μ:*

r-component

$$\rho\left(\frac{\partial v_r}{\partial t} + v_r \frac{\partial v_r}{\partial r} + \frac{v_\theta}{r}\frac{\partial v_r}{\partial \theta} + \frac{v_\phi}{r \sin\theta}\frac{\partial v_r}{\partial \phi} - \frac{v_\theta^2 + v_\phi^2}{r}\right)$$

$$= -\frac{\partial p}{\partial r} + \mu\left(\nabla^2 v_r - \frac{2}{r^2}v_r - \frac{2}{r^2}\frac{\partial v_\theta}{\partial \theta} - \frac{2}{r^2}v_\theta\cot\theta - \frac{2}{r^2\sin\theta}\frac{\partial v_\phi}{\partial \phi}\right) + \rho g_r \qquad (D)$$

θ-component

$$\rho\left(\frac{\partial v_\theta}{\partial t} + v_r \frac{\partial v_\theta}{\partial r} + \frac{v_\theta}{r}\frac{\partial v_\theta}{\partial \theta} + \frac{v_\phi}{r \sin\theta}\frac{\partial v_\theta}{\partial \phi} + \frac{v_r v_\theta}{r} - \frac{v_\phi^2 \cot\theta}{r}\right)$$

$$= -\frac{1}{r}\frac{\partial p}{\partial \theta} + \mu\left(\nabla^2 v_\theta + \frac{2}{r^2}\frac{\partial v_r}{\partial \theta} - \frac{v_\theta}{r^2\sin^2\theta} - \frac{2\cos\theta}{r^2\sin^2\theta}\frac{\partial v_\phi}{\partial \phi}\right) + \rho g_\theta \qquad (E)$$

φ-component

$$\rho\left(\frac{\partial v_\phi}{\partial t} + v_r \frac{\partial v_\phi}{\partial r} + \frac{v_\theta}{r}\frac{\partial v_\phi}{\partial \theta} + \frac{v_\phi}{r \sin\theta}\frac{\partial v_\phi}{\partial \phi} + \frac{v_\phi v_r}{r} + \frac{v_\theta v_\phi}{r}\cot\theta\right)$$

$$= -\frac{1}{r\sin\theta}\frac{\partial p}{\partial \phi} + \mu\left(\nabla^2 v_\phi - \frac{v_\phi}{r^2\sin^2\theta} + \frac{2}{r^2\sin\theta}\frac{\partial v_r}{\partial \phi} + \frac{2\cos\theta}{r^2\sin^2\theta}\frac{\partial v_\theta}{\partial \phi}\right) + \rho g_\phi \qquad (F)$$

* In these equations

$$\nabla^2 = \frac{1}{r^2}\frac{\partial}{\partial r}\left(r^2\frac{\partial}{\partial r}\right) + \frac{1}{r^2\sin\theta}\frac{\partial}{\partial \theta}\left(\sin\theta\frac{\partial}{\partial \theta}\right) + \frac{1}{r^2\sin^2\theta}\left(\frac{\partial^2}{\partial \phi^2}\right)$$

STRESS TENSOR COMPONENTS FOR NEWTONIAN FLUIDS
RECTANGULAR COORDINATES (x,y,z)

$$\tau_{xx} = -\mu\left[2\frac{\partial v_x}{\partial x} - \tfrac{2}{3}(\nabla \cdot v)\right] \qquad (A)$$

$$\tau_{yy} = -\mu\left[2\frac{\partial v_y}{\partial y} - \tfrac{2}{3}(\nabla \cdot v)\right] \qquad (B)$$

$$\tau_{zz} = -\mu\left[2\frac{\partial v_z}{\partial z} - \tfrac{2}{3}(\nabla \cdot v)\right] \qquad (C)$$

$$\tau_{xy} = \tau_{yx} = -\mu\left[\frac{\partial v_x}{\partial y} + \frac{\partial v_y}{\partial x}\right] \qquad (D)$$

$$\tau_{yz} = \tau_{zy} = -\mu\left[\frac{\partial v_y}{\partial z} + \frac{\partial v_z}{\partial y}\right] \qquad (E)$$

$$\tau_{zx} = \tau_{xz} = -\mu\left[\frac{\partial v_z}{\partial x} + \frac{\partial v_x}{\partial z}\right] \qquad (F)$$

$$(\nabla \cdot v) = \frac{\partial v_x}{\partial x} + \frac{\partial v_y}{\partial y} + \frac{\partial v_z}{\partial z} \qquad (G)$$

STRESS TENSOR COMPONENTS FOR NEWTONIAN FLUIDS
CYLINDRICAL COORDINATES (r,θ,z)

$$\tau_{rr} = -\mu\left[2\frac{\partial v_r}{\partial r} - \tfrac{2}{3}(\nabla \cdot v)\right] \qquad (A)$$

$$\tau_{\theta\theta} = -\mu\left[2\left(\frac{1}{r}\frac{\partial v_\theta}{\partial \theta} + \frac{v_r}{r}\right) - \tfrac{2}{3}(\nabla \cdot v)\right] \qquad (B)$$

$$\tau_{zz} = -\mu\left[2\frac{\partial v_z}{\partial z} - \tfrac{2}{3}(\nabla \cdot v)\right] \qquad (C)$$

$$\tau_{r\theta} = \tau_{\theta r} = -\mu\left[r\frac{\partial}{\partial r}\left(\frac{v_\theta}{r}\right) + \frac{1}{r}\frac{\partial v_r}{\partial \theta}\right] \qquad (D)$$

$$\tau_{\theta z} = \tau_{z\theta} = -\mu\left[\frac{\partial v_\theta}{\partial z} + \frac{1}{r}\frac{\partial v_z}{\partial \theta}\right] \qquad (E)$$

$$\tau_{zr} = \tau_{rz} = -\mu\left[\frac{\partial v_z}{\partial r} + \frac{\partial v_r}{\partial z}\right] \qquad (F)$$

$$(\nabla \cdot v) = \frac{1}{r}\frac{\partial}{\partial r}(rv_r) + \frac{1}{r}\frac{\partial v_\theta}{\partial \theta} + \frac{\partial v_z}{\partial z} \qquad (G)$$

STRESS TENSOR COMPONENTS FOR NEWTONIAN FLUIDS S
IN SPHERICAL COORDINATES (r, θ, ϕ)

$$\tau_{rr} = -\mu\left[2\frac{\partial v_r}{\partial r} - \frac{2}{3}(\nabla \cdot v)\right] \tag{A}$$

$$\tau_{\theta\theta} = -\mu\left[2\left(\frac{1}{r}\frac{\partial v_\theta}{\partial \theta} + \frac{v_r}{r}\right) - \frac{2}{3}(\nabla \cdot v)\right] \tag{B}$$

$$\tau_{\phi\phi} = -\mu\left[2\left(\frac{1}{r\sin\theta}\frac{\partial v_\phi}{\partial \phi} + \frac{v_r}{r} + \frac{v_\theta \cot\theta}{r}\right) - \frac{2}{3}(\nabla \cdot v)\right] \tag{C}$$

$$\tau_{r\theta} = \tau_{\theta r} = -\mu\left[r\frac{\partial}{\partial r}\left(\frac{v_\theta}{r}\right) + \frac{1}{r}\frac{\partial v_r}{\partial \theta}\right] \tag{D}$$

$$\tau_{\theta\phi} = \tau_{\phi\theta} = -\mu\left[\frac{\sin\theta}{r}\frac{\partial}{\partial \theta}\left(\frac{v_\phi}{\sin\theta}\right) + \frac{1}{r\sin\theta}\frac{\partial v_\theta}{\partial \phi}\right] \tag{E}$$

$$\tau_{\phi r} = \tau_{r\phi} = -\mu\left[\frac{1}{r\sin\theta}\frac{\partial v_r}{\partial \phi} + r\frac{\partial}{\partial r}\left(\frac{v_\phi}{r}\right)\right] \tag{F}$$

$$(\nabla \cdot v) = \frac{1}{r^2}\frac{\partial}{\partial r}(r^2 v_r) + \frac{1}{r\sin\theta}\frac{\partial}{\partial \theta}(v_\theta \sin\theta) + \frac{1}{r\sin\theta}\frac{\partial v_\phi}{\partial \phi} \tag{G}$$

Conduction shape factor S for different systems: $q = k\,S(T_1 - T_2)$.

<table>
<tr><th>Physical system</th><th>Sketch</th><th>Shape factor S</th><th>Limitations</th></tr>
<tr><td>(a) Infinitely long cylinder of outside diameter D buried a distance z from an isothermal surface of a semi-infinite medium of thermal conductivity k.</td><td>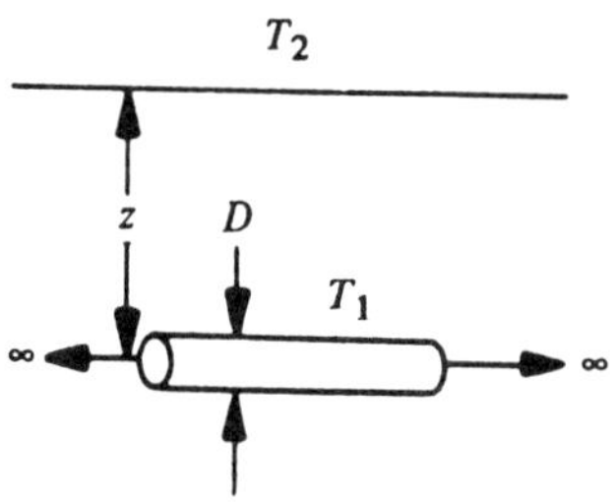
</td><td>$\dfrac{2\pi}{\cosh^{-1}(2z/D)}$
(per foot of length)</td><td></td></tr>
<tr><td>(b) Isothermal sphere of diameter D buried a distance z from the isothermal surface of a semi-infinite medium of thermal conductivity k.</td><td>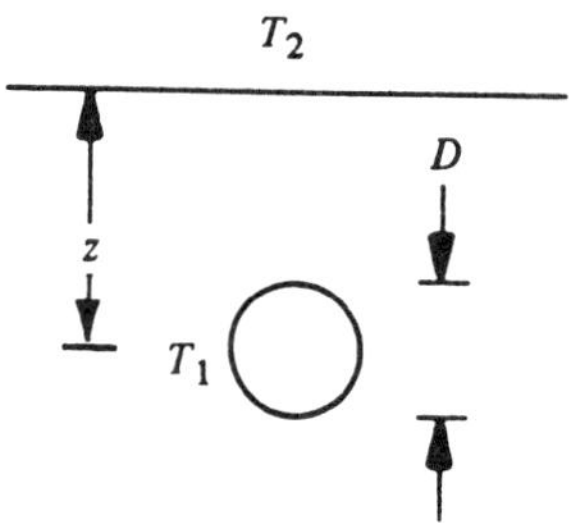
</td><td>$\dfrac{2\pi D}{1 - D/4z}$</td><td></td></tr>
<tr><td>(c) Conduction heat transfer between two parallel isothermal cylinders buried in an infinite medium of thermal conductivity k.</td><td>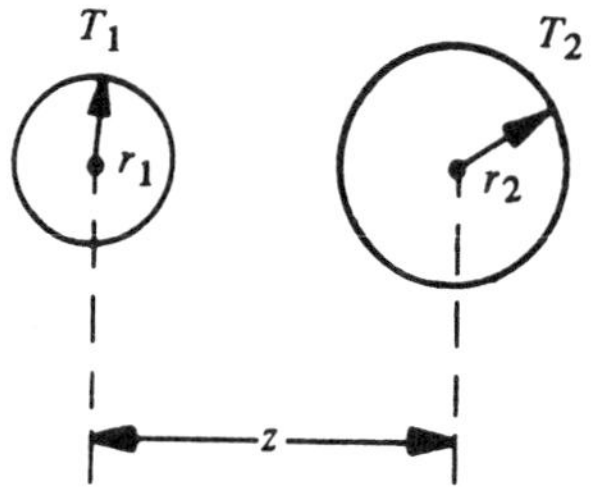
</td><td>$\dfrac{2\pi}{\cosh^{-1}\left(\dfrac{z^2 - r_1^2 - r_2^2}{2r_1r_2}\right)}$
(per foot of length)</td><td></td></tr>
<tr><td>(d) Conduction through two plane walls of equal thickness Δx and the edge along which they meet at right angles.</td><td>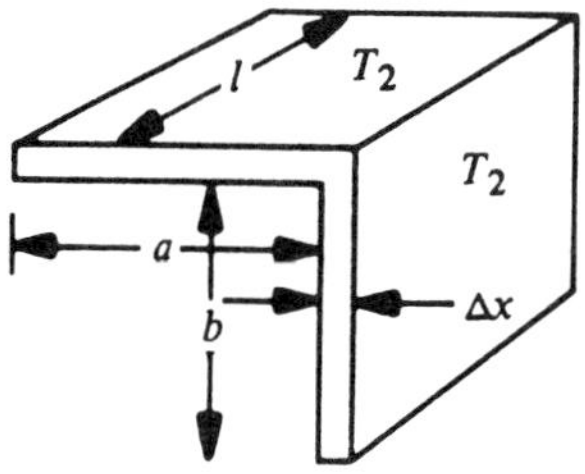
</td><td>$\dfrac{al}{\Delta x} + \dfrac{bl}{\Delta x} + 0.54\,l$
($0.54\,l$ is the shape factor for the edge alone)</td><td>$b > \dfrac{\Delta x}{5}$
$a > \dfrac{\Delta x}{5}$</td></tr>
<tr><td>(e) Conduction through a three dimensional corner consisting of three plane walls of thickness Δx and thermal conductivity k meeting in a mutually perpendicular fashion.</td><td>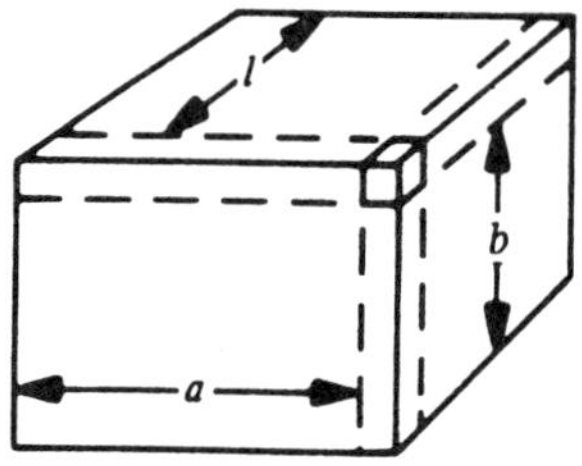
</td><td>$0.15\,\Delta x$
(for the corner shown when one side of the three walls is at T_1 and the other side of the walls is at T_2.)</td><td>$a > \dfrac{\Delta x}{5}$
$b > \dfrac{\Delta x}{5}$
$l > \dfrac{\Delta x}{5}$</td></tr>
</table>

Fluid	U	
	Btu/hr-ft²-°F	W/m²-K
Oil to oil	30–55	170–312
Organics to organics	10–60	57–340
Steam to:		
Aqueous solutions	100–600	567–3400
Fuel oil, heavy	10–30	57–170
Light	30–60	170–340
Gases	5–50	28–284
Water	175–600	993–3400
Water to:		
Alcohol	50–150	284–850
Brine	100–200	567–1135
Compressed air	10–30	57–170
Condensing alcohol	45–120	255–680
Condensing ammonia	150–250	850–1420
Condensing Freon-12	80–150	454–850
Condensing oil	40–100	227–567
Gasoline	60–90	340–510
Lubricating oil	20–60	113–340
Organic solvents	50–150	284–850
Water	150–300	850–1700

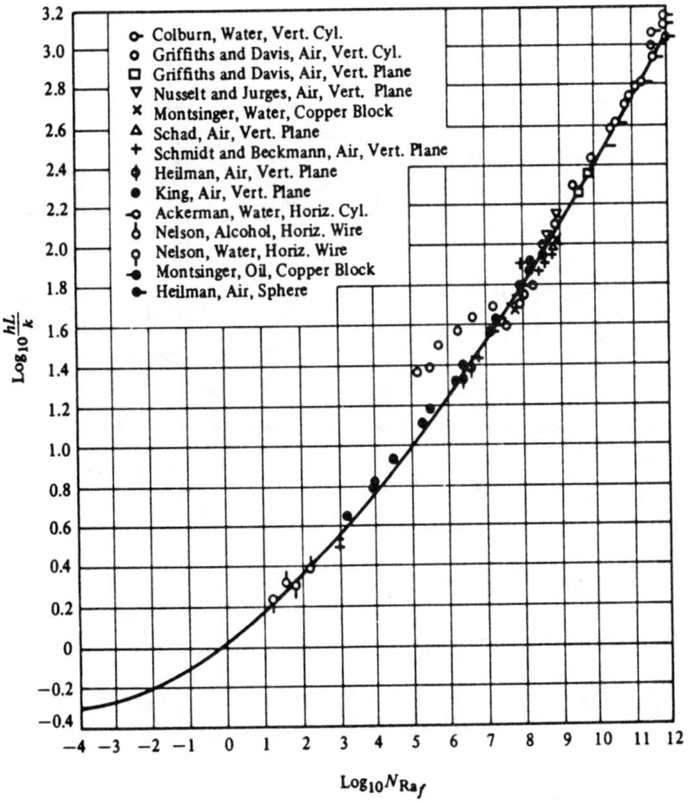

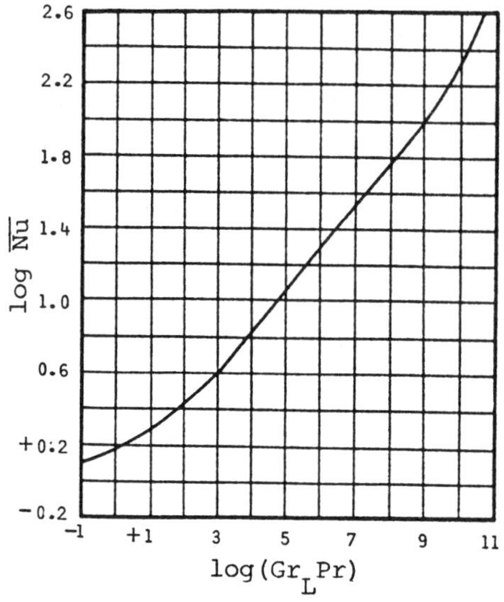

Correlation for heated vertical plates.

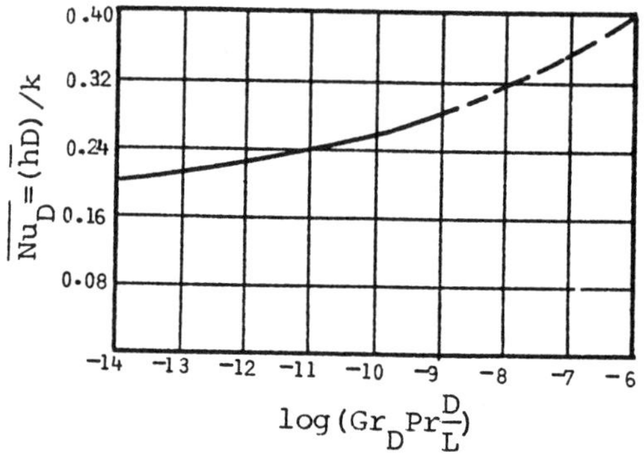

Correlation for small vertical cylinders.

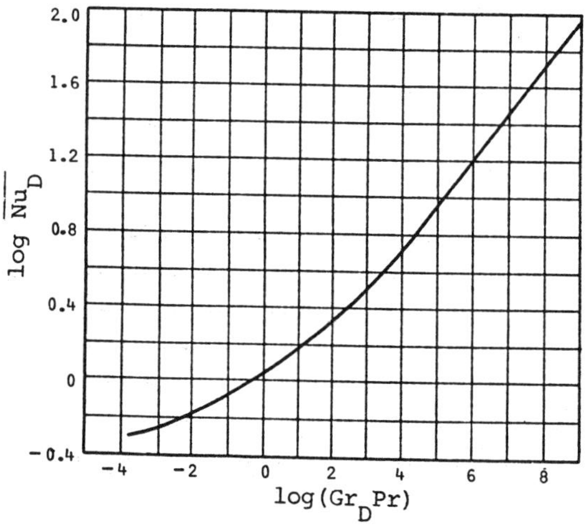

Correlation for horizontal cylinders.

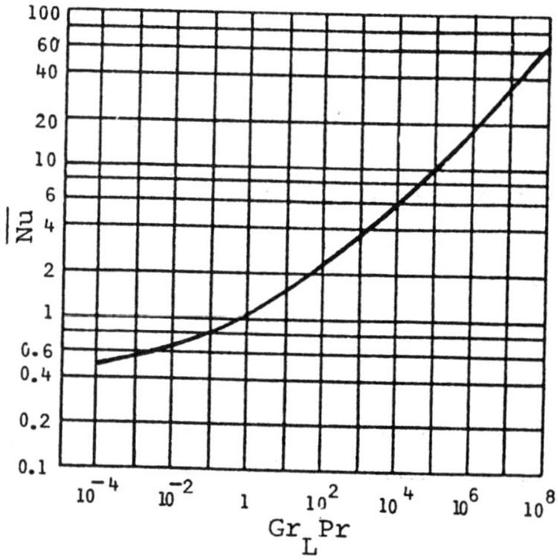

Correlation for miscellaneous solid shapes.

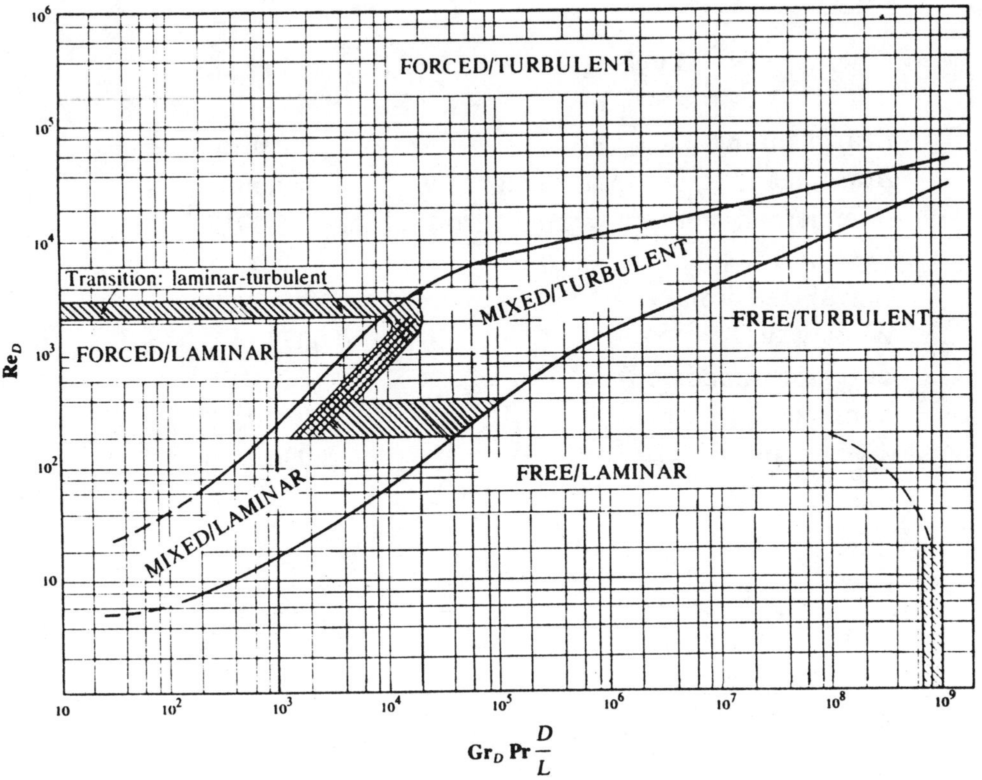

Regimes of flow in vertical tubes.

$$\overline{Nu}_D = (0.116)\left[1 + \left(\frac{D}{L}\right)^{2/3}\right](\mathbf{Re}_D^{2/3} - 125)\mathbf{Pr}^{1/3}\left[\frac{\mu_b D}{\mu_s L}\right]^{0.14}$$

Hausen

$$\overline{Nu}_D = (4.69)\mathbf{Re}_D^{0.27}\,\mathbf{Pr}^{0.21}\,\mathbf{Gr}_D^{0.07}\left(\frac{D}{L}\right)^{0.36}$$

Metais

$$\overline{Nu}_D = (1.86)\mathbf{Gz}^{1/3}\left(\frac{\mu_b}{\mu_s}\right)^{0.14}$$

Sieder and Tate

$$\overline{Nu}_D = (1.75)\left(\frac{\mu_b}{\mu_s}\right)^{0.14}[\mathbf{Gz} + (0.0083)(\mathbf{Gr}_D\,\mathbf{Pr})^{0.75}]^{1/3}$$

Oliver

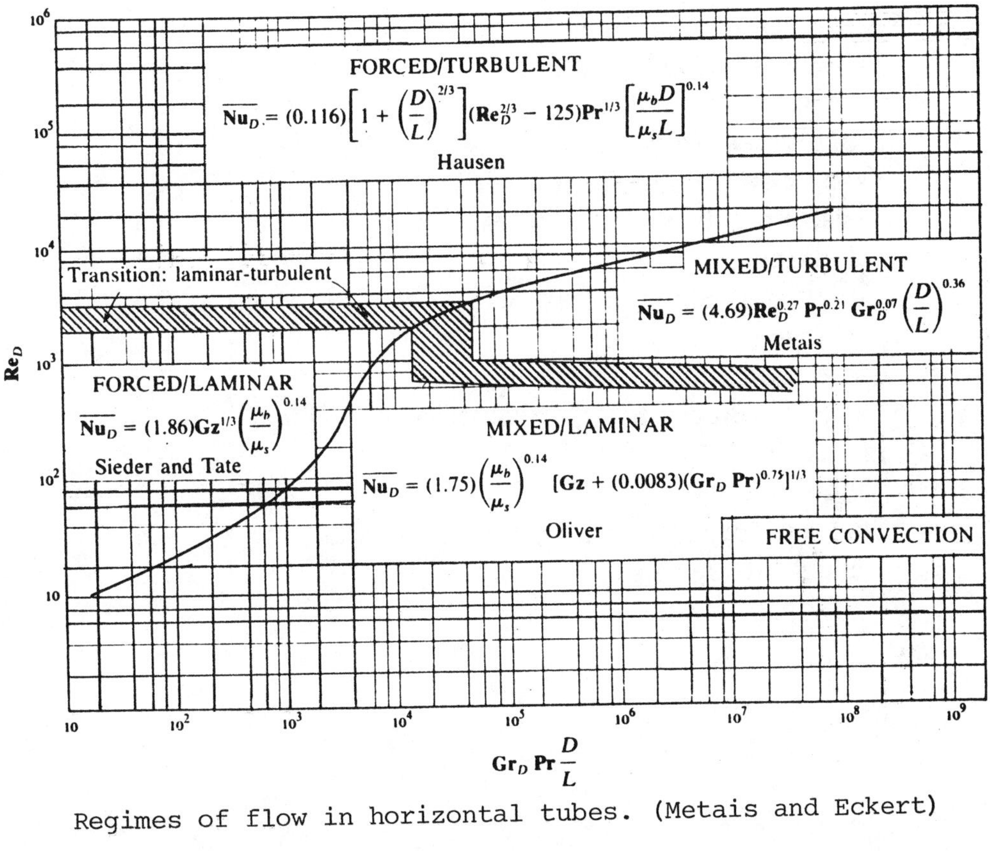

Regimes of flow in horizontal tubes. (Metais and Eckert)

Type	e, in.
Drawn tubing	0.00006
Brass, lead, glass, spun cement	≈0.0003
Commercial steel or wrought iron	0.0018
Cast iron (asphalt dipped)	0.0048
Galvanized iron	0.0060
Wool stave	0.0072 to 0.036
Cast iron (uncoated)	0.0102
Concrete	0.012 to 0.12
Riveted steel	0.036 to 0.36

Item	k_L
Angle valve, fully open	3.1 to 5.0
Ball check valve, fully open	4.5 to 7.0
Gate valve, fully open	0.19
Globe valve, fully open	10
Swing check valve, fully open	2.3 to 3.5
Regular-radius elbow, screwed	0.9
Flanged	0.3
Long-radius elbow, screwed	0.6
Flanged	0.23
Close return bend, screwed	2.2
Flanged return bend, two elbows, regular radius	0.38
Long radius	0.25
Standard tee, screwed, flow through run	0.6
Flow through side	1.8

Configuration	L/D	$\mathrm{Re}_D = V_\infty D/\nu$	C_D
Circular cylinder, axis perpendicular to the flow 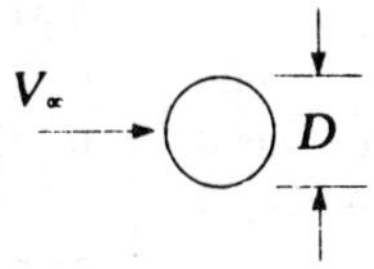	1	10^5	0.63
	5		0.74
	20		0.90
	∞		1.20
	5	$>5 \times 10^5$	0.35
	∞		0.33
Circular cylinder, axis parallel to the flow 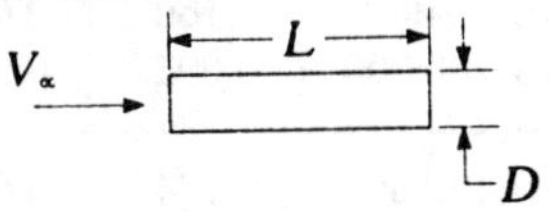	0	$>10^3$	1.12
	1		0.91
	2		0.85
	4		0.87
	7		0.99
Elliptical cylinder 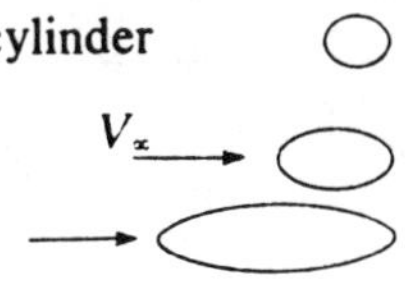 (2 : 1)*		4×10^4	0.6
		10^5	0.46
(4 : 1)*		2.5×10^4 to 10^5	0.32
(8 : 1)*		2.5×10^4	0.29
		2×10^5	0.20
Airfoil (1 : 3)†	∞	4×10^4	0.07
Rectangular plate, normal to the flow; L = length, D = width	1	$>10^3$	1.16
	5		1.20
	20		1.50
	∞		1.90
Square cylinder 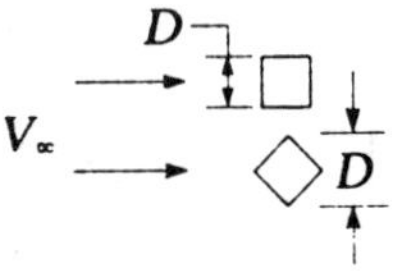		3.5×10^4	2.0
		10^4 to 10^5	1.6
Triangular cylinder 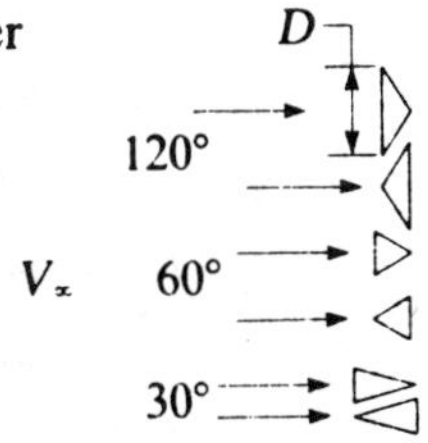		$>10^4$	2.0
			1.72
			2.20
			1.39
		$>10^5$	1.80
			1.0
Hemispherical shell 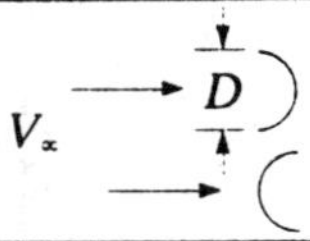		$>10^3$	1.33
		10^3 to 10^5	0.4
Circular disk, normal to the flow 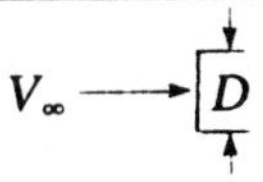		$>10^3$	1.12

*Ratio of major axis to minor axis
†Ratio of chord to span at zero angle of attack

Configuration	$\mathbf{Re}_{Df}$	C	n
	0.4 to 4	0.989	0.330
	4 to 40	0.911	0.385
	40 to 4,000	0.683	0.466
	4,000 to 40,000	0.193	0.618
	40,000 to 400,000	0.0266	0.805
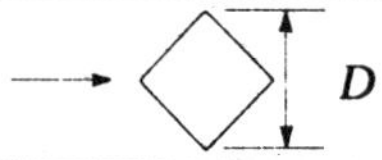	2,500 to 7,500	0.261	0.624
	5,000 to 100,000	0.222	0.588
	2,500 to 8,000	0.160	0.699
	5,000 to 100,000	0.092	0.675
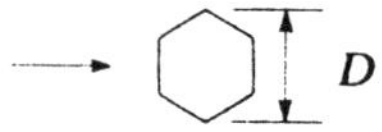	5,000 to 19,500	0.144	0.638
	19,500 to 100,000	0.035	0.782
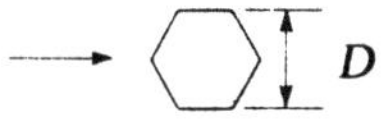	5,000 to 100,000	0.138	0.638
	4,000 to 15,000	0.205	0.731
	2,500 to 15,000	0.224	0.612
	3,000 to 15,000	0.085	0.804

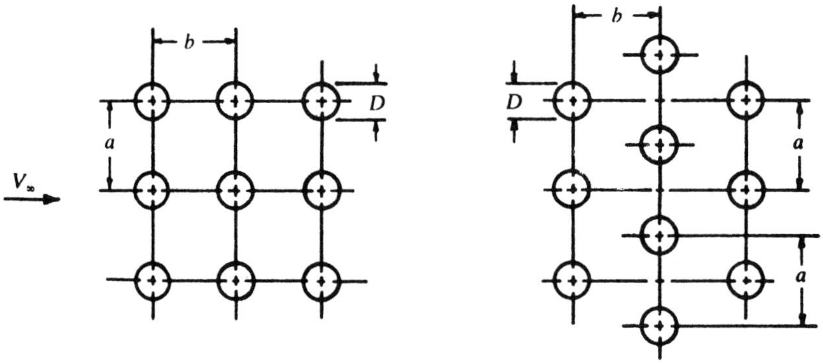

(*a*) In-Line

(*b*) Staggered

Thermal Conductivity of Gases at High Pressures.

E.W. Comings and M.F. Nathan

k_1 = thermal conductivity at 1 atm and same temperature
p_c = critical pressure.

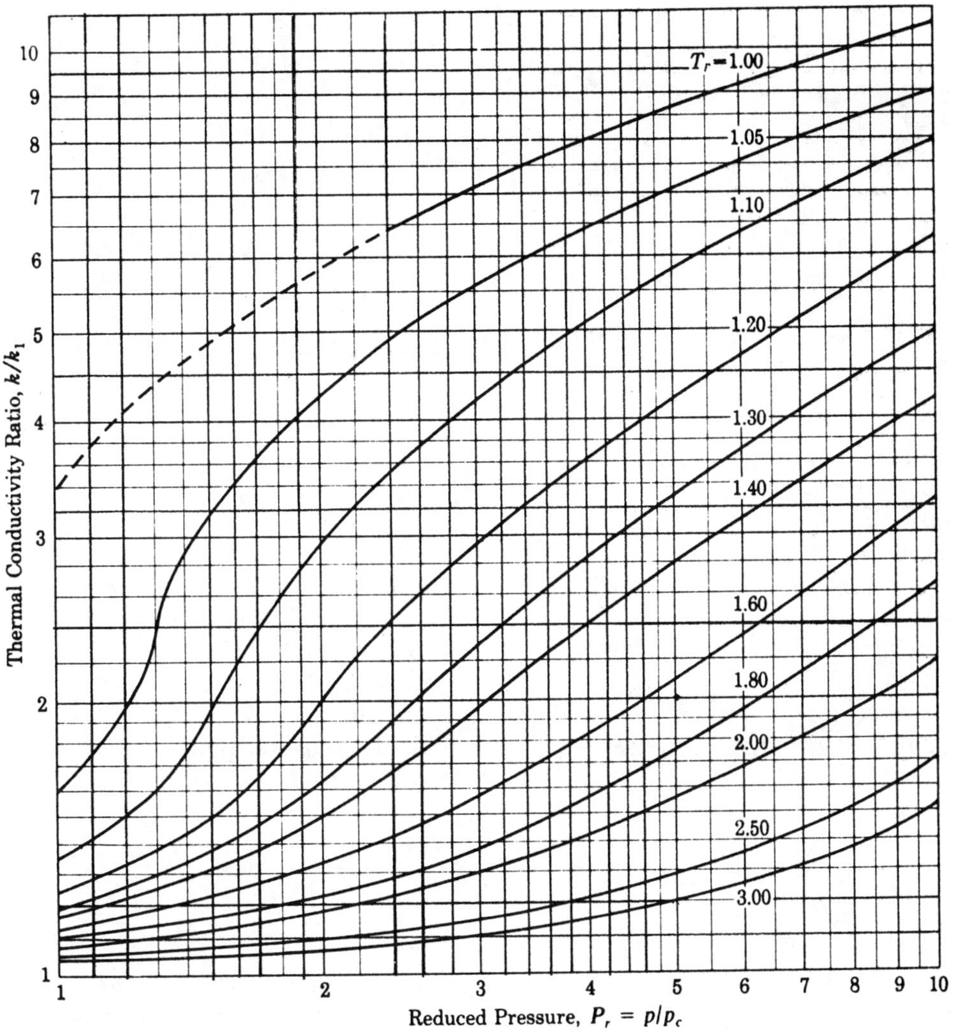

INDEX

Numbers on this page refer to PROBLEM NUMBERS, not page numbers

Numbers on this page refer to PROBLEM NUMBERS, not page numbers

Numbers on this page refer to PROBLEM NUMBERS, not page numbers

Numbers on this page refer to PROBLEM NUMBERS, not page numbers

Numbers on this page refer to **PROBLEM NUMBERS**, not page numbers

Numbers on this page refer to PROBLEM NUMBERS, not page numbers

Numbers on this page refer to **PROBLEM NUMBERS**, not page numbers

Numbers on this page refer to <u>PROBLEM NUMBERS</u>, not page numbers